Religion in America

RELIGION IN AMERICA

Winthrop S. Hudson

CHARLES SCRIBNER'S SONS

New York

To
CHARLES M. NIELSEN
friend and colleague

Preface

Three hundred years ago Thomas Fuller, an English divine and church historian, commented: "History maketh a man old, without either wrinkles or gray hairs; privileging him with the experience of age, without either the infirmities or inconveniences thereof." In terms of the long history that Fuller surveyed to give his readers the wisdom that may be derived from the past, American experience has been brief. Still knowledge is to be gained and lessons are to be learned from the American past.

The purpose of the present volume is to recount the story of American religious life in an attempt to make some sense of it for the benefit of the reader. This has necessitated interpretative judgments. It is the author's hope that these judgments have been judicious, and that they will serve to stimulate constructive reflection and response rather than to alienate and divert.

Several features of the book should be called to the reader's attention that he may be forewarned of what to expect and thus forearmed against misunderstanding.

First, the author's major concern was not to chronicle the life of individual religious groups. While the separate denominations have not been ignored, the central purpose has been to depict the religious life of the American people in interaction with other dimensions of their experience, and to depict the unity American religious life exhibits as well as its particularities.

Second, an attempt has been made to maintain proper balance in the attention devoted to the several epochs in the story of religion in America. Unlike previous volumes which have been heavily weighted in the direction of the colonial and early national periods, the present volume allots "equal time" to post-Civil War developments and to the twentieth century. Related to the question of balance is the treatment of "late-blooming" religious groups. Judaism, for example, has had a long history in America, but it did not emerge as a major community until the twentieth century. Rather than scattering snippets of information throughout the book, it seemed wise to postpone most references to Judaism to the modern period so that a more unified account could be given. For the same reason, discussions of the Holiness movement, Fundamentalism, Eastern Orthodoxy, and to a more limited degree Roman Catholicism, have been deferred to the period when they began to loom large on the American scene.

Third, an effort to keep the volume to a reasonable length was high on the list of priorities. For things omitted the only apology is an acknowledgment that choices had to be made. In some instances perhaps others would have chosen differently. Few would contend, however, that a more encyclopedic coverage would have been preferable, if it was effected by the inclusion of scattered cryptic sentences which served to oversimplify and distort.

Fourth, bibliographical references and suggestions have been placed in notes adjacent to the text where it is believed they will be most useful rather than being half-hidden in a formal bibliography. Through the index they can easily be located either by author or subject matter. The function of many of the bibliographical references in the notes is to direct attention to collections of source readings in which specific documents are readily available. Many other citations are to books that have been issued in paperback editions.

A minor point which should be noted is that colleges and universities are referred to by their modern names, and in a few instances both early and present-day names are given. Most readers may know that Princeton was once the College of New Jersey, but few would be aware that Iowa College is now Grinnell. Some institutions have had as many as five names. In order to avoid confusion, it has been thought wise to refer to these institutions by the name by which they now are known.

An incidental pleasure in writing a book is that it calls to mind the names of many friends from whom one has learned much and to whom one is deeply indebted. To Robert T. Handy, C. C. Goen, J. H. Smylie, Samuel Perlman, LeRoy Moore, and Eldon Ernst, I am more specifically indebted for reading all or parts of the manuscript. Each of them has made an important contribution to the book through helpful criticisms and suggestions.

WINTHROP S. HUDSON

Colgate Rochester Divinity School

Contents

Part I

The Formative Years, 1607–1789

   I.   The American Context   *3*
  II.   Denominational Beginnings   *23*
 III.   The Great Awakening   *59*
 IV.   The Birth of the Republic   *83*

Part II

The New Nation, 1789–1860

    V.   The Reordering of Denominational Life   *109*
  VI.   Protestant Resurgence and Expansion   *131*
 VII.   Divergent Trends and Movements   *158*
VIII.   Religious Ferment   *181*

Part III

Years of Midpassage, 1860–1914

  IX.   Post-Civil War America   *207*
   X.   The New Americans   *237*
  XI.   The New Intellectual Climate   *263*
 XII.   New Frontiers for the Churches   *291*

Part IV
Modern America, 1914–

XIII. The Shifting Religious Configuration   *327*
XIV. Protestant Reassessment and Recovery   *357*
 XV. The Maturing of Roman Catholicism   *392*
XVI. Unity and Diversity in American Religious Life   *409*

   Index   *427*

Religion in America

PART I

THE FORMATIVE YEARS

1607–1789

I

The American Context

After a long period in which historians have emphasized the uniqueness of almost everything American, it is becoming increasingly clear that the United States can properly be understood only as an integral part of a larger European society.[1]

Our roots as a nation go back to the remarkable burst of colonizing activity which transformed the Atlantic Ocean into the *Mare Nostrum* of western Europe. There is little that we, as Americans, can claim as exclusively our own. Our language is not our own, nor are our tables of weights and measures. Our most characteristic proverbs and our most familiar nursery rhymes have been inherited from others. Our concept of trial by jury came to us from abroad. Indeed, the whole structure of our legal system, with its guarantees of liberty and provisions for constitutional government, is the product of a longer history than ours. Even after

[1] See C. J. H. Hayes, "The American Frontier—Frontier of What?" *American Historical Review*, LI (1946), 199–216; reprinted in *The Turner Thesis*, ed. G. R. Taylor, "Problems in American Civilization: Readings Selected by the Department of American Studies, Amherst College" (Boston, 1949).

our declaration of political independence, we remained part of this larger society—reading the works of European poets, studying the writings of European philosophers, listening to the music of European composers, utilizing the discoveries of European scientists, reaping the benefits of European capital invested in our railroads and mines, recruiting European "hands" for our mills and factories. In almost every respect, we have been and are part of Europe; and this is as true in religion as it is in literature, law, philosophy, art, or science.

The religious heritage which links us to Europe is immediately apparent to any visitor to the British Isles. When an American walks down the street of an English city, he will be reminded of home as he passes Anglican (Protestant Episcopal), Presbyterian, Congregational, Baptist, Methodist, and Roman Catholic churches. He may be handed a Plymouth Brethren tract, encounter a Salvation Army lassie, or find a Quaker meetinghouse or Jewish synagogue half hidden in a side street. Traveling north of the Tweed, he will discover that many of the Presbyterian divisions at home had their origin in divisions which took place in Scotland.

But it is not from the British Isles only that our churches have come, for there are German, Swedish, Danish, Norwegian, and Finnish Lutheran churches; German, Dutch, and Hungarian Reformed churches; Mennonite, Moravian, Dunker, and Schwenkfelder communities. And more recent immigration from central and eastern Europe has swelled the Roman Catholic and Jewish population in the United States and has introduced the numerous national churches of Eastern Orthodoxy into the American scene.

With only a few exceptions, the varied religious groups of America have their rootage abroad; and throughout the years their relationship to the lands from which their fathers came has been intimate and continuous. The continuing European religious influence is no more than barely suggested by the names of Kant, Schleiermacher, and Ritschl; Pascal, Kierkegaard, and Von Hügel; Newman, Maurice, and Temple; Barth, Buber, and Bultmann. In religion, as in other areas of our common life, we have been and we have continued to be part of a larger European society.

The recognition that the United States, in all the fundamental features of its life save geographic location, is a part of Europe must not obscure the parallel fact that we are Americans as well as Europeans. European society has never been a monolithic whole. Within the common culture, there have always been diverse local and national traditions; and this is as true in America as it is in England and France and Germany. America has drawn most heavily, as the mere fact of language so eloquently testifies, from the English-speaking segment of European society. But it is far from an exact transcript, even of this segment, that has been reproduced on American soil. There have been modifications and adaptations of the European inheritance from the very beginning.

In part the changes that have occurred in America have been due to the differing circumstances of life in a new land; in part they have been the product of the intermingling in varying proportion of several European traditions; in part they have been the consequence of the constitutional arrangements which were effected to bring thirteen newly independent and somewhat recalcitrant colonies together under one government; and in part they have been the result of the growing and evolving life that is characteristic of any intimately related segment of a larger community. Thus while we have been and continue to be debtors to Europe, we have also developed within the larger context a distinctive life of our own and we have made contributions of our own to the European society of which we are a part.

Although it is the European heritage that has given American religious life its basic shape and substance, the purpose of this initial chapter is to focus attention upon the distinctive ethos and character of religion in America.

England as the "Bridge" from the Old World to the New

As early as 1622 John Donne was asserting with remarkable prescience that England, which hitherto as an island had been "but as the suburbs" of Europe, was destined to occupy a much more central position in the future as the "bridge" between the Old World and the New.[2] His words were prophetic so far as the Atlantic coast of North America was concerned, and the most obvious conditioning factor in American religious life has been its English beginnings. The thirteen colonies were English colonies, the vast proportion of the population was of English stock, and

[2] Louis B. Wright, *Religion and Empire* (Chapel Hill, N.C., 1943), 111.

the American Revolution was fought—so the colonists asserted—to defend and preserve their rights as Englishmen.

PROTESTANT PREDOMINANCE. The fact that the American colonies were English colonies meant, first of all, that the colonists in background if not always in active affiliation would be predominantly Protestant. Even the non-English minorities—the Scots, the Scotch-Irish, the Germans, the Dutch, the French, and the Swedes—were almost wholly Protestant in background. Only in Maryland was there a significant number of Roman Catholics and even in Maryland they were a minority. Judaism was limited to a handful of tiny congregations. Thus, to the extent that the mind of colonial America was shaped by a religious faith, it was shaped perforce by Protestantism.

This overwhelmingly Protestant religious orientation was equally true of the new nation as its borders pushed westward. In the Northwest Territory, the French trading posts on the Great Lakes were not deeply enough rooted as permanent settlements to become centers of a continuing cultural or religious tradition. Nor did the Louisiana Purchase of 1803 change the picture to any marked degree. The permanent non-Protestant area of settlement was confined to a relatively small enclave at the southern tip of the vast area embraced in the Purchase. It was not until the nineteenth century was well advanced, when their numbers began to be augmented by large-scale immigration, that Roman Catholics became sufficiently numerous to constitute a significant minority in American life; and it was not until the end of the nineteenth century that major Jewish and Eastern Orthodox communities came into existence.

As a consequence of Protestant predominance, even non-Protestant groups tended to take on a somewhat Protestant coloration in the American environment. The earnest "moralism" of American Roman Catholicism has often been attributed to the influence of a Protestant culture; and on occasion American Roman Catholics have had to defend themselves against charges of undue "Americanism," a term which usually implied the adoption of Protestant presuppositions. A more complete adjustment was represented by Reform Judaism which initially adopted even the forms of Protestant Sunday worship. Nor has Eastern Orthodoxy remained unaffected. A spokesman for the Greek church, after stanchly defending at an ecumenical gathering the unchanging integrity of the Orthodox witness, commented privately that the Orthodox in America

6

scarcely dare admit even to themselves the extent to which their life has been modified by an encounter with Protestantism.

After World War I, to be sure, the older Protestant predominance had been so greatly reduced by the shifting tide of immigration that influences which once moved only in one direction tended to become reciprocal. Not the least of the influences, for example, reshaping the Protestant understanding of the pastoral office and Protestant liturgical practice has been the influence exerted by Roman Catholicism.

THE PURITAN HERITAGE. While the United States by virtue of its English antecedents and character was predominantly Protestant throughout its early history, it was an English Protestantism with a difference. At home the great majority of the people were Anglicans, members of the Church of England; and the "Dissenting" interest composed of Presbyterians, Congregationalists, Baptists, and Quakers was relatively small. In the colonies this situation was reversed. By the end of the colonial period the Congregationalists and the Presbyterians were the two largest American denominations. The Baptists and the Anglicans were roughly equal in size, and the Quakers—widely dispersed throughout all the colonies—ranked fifth in number of adherents. It was this difference in the religious make-up of the population that Edmund Burke had in mind when he noted in his speech *On Conciliation with the American Colonies* (1775) that "the people [of the colonies] are Protestants, and of that kind which is the most adverse to all implicit subjection of mind and opinion."

What was the character of this early American Protestantism? It was diverse in its outward ecclesiastical form, but this diversity found expression for the most part within the limits of the common faith of English Puritanism.[3] The tendency in popular mythology to emphasize the priority of Plymouth and Boston at the expense of Jamestown is not historically accurate, but in a deeper sense it is a true recognition that the American people over a considerable portion of their history have had their fundamental rootage in a Puritanism which they have found most easy to identify in terms of New England.

André Siegfried, a French observer of twentieth-century America, confirmed the estimate that is implicit in the prominence given to the story

---

[3] See Alan Simpson's book *Puritanism in Old and New England* (Chicago, 1955); William Haller's *The Rise of Puritanism* (N.Y., 1938); and the several works of Perry Miller. For a brief summary of the history and emphases of Puritanism, see article in *Encyclopedia Britannica* (Chicago, 1962).

7

of the landing of the Pilgrims when he asserted: "If we wish to understand the real sources of American inspiration we must go back to the English Puritanism of the seventeenth century." James Bryce also emphasized this feature of American life in 1888 as he sought to describe the American commonwealth to his fellow countrymen at home. "There is a hearty Puritanism in the view of human nature which pervades the instrument of 1787," he wrote. "It is the work of men who believed in original sin, and were resolved to leave open for transgressors no door which they could possibly shut. Compare this spirit with the enthusiastic optimism of the Frenchmen of 1789. It is not merely a difference of race and temperaments; it is a difference of fundamental ideas." [4]

The same verdict had been expressed by Philip Schaff (1819–93) in 1844 when, shortly after his arrival from Germany, he sought to analyze the main features of American religious life. "Puritan Protestantism forms properly the main trunk of our North American church," he declared in his inaugural address as professor of church history in the Mercersburg Theological Seminary. "Viewed as a whole," the American church "owes her general characteristic features, her distinctive image, neither to the German or Continental Reformed, nor to the English Episcopal communion," but to the Puritans of New England. "To this New England influence must be added indeed the no less important weight of Presbyterianism, as derived subsequently from Scotland and Ireland. But this may be regarded as in all essential respects the same life. The reigning theology of the country . . . is the theology of the Westminster Confession." A few years later he asserted that "the six northeastern states included under the name of New England . . . are . . . in regard to culture and Christianity, the garden of America"; and from this seedbed has come "the leading religious influence in the Union," exerting "a powerful influence upon the religious, social, and political life of the whole nation." [5]

Philip Schaff's only error was to identify this Puritanism so exclusively with New England. Puritanism was far from monolithic. In England it was a many-faceted movement that embraced Presbyterians, Congrega-

[4] André Siegfried, *America Comes of Age* (N.Y., 1927), 33. James Bryce, *The American Commonwealth* (N.Y., 1910), I, 306.

[5] Philip Schaff, *The Principle of Protestantism as Related to the Present State of the Church* (Chambersburg, 1845), 114; quoted by J. H. Nichols, *Romanticism in American Theology* (Chicago, 1961), 2. Philip Schaff, *America: A Sketch of Its Political, Social, and Religious Character*, ed. Perry Miller (Cambridge, Mass., 1961), 54, 89, 107; see also 116–17.

tionalists, Baptists, large numbers of Episcopalians, and even the Quakers. It is a mistake, therefore, to limit Puritan influence in America to New England Congregationalism, for in other forms of English dissent it was strongly represented in all the colonies. As Philip Schaff noted, the Presbyterians—including those from Scotland and Ireland—stood shoulder-to-shoulder with the Congregationalists at every important point. This was equally true of the Baptists who also had adopted a modified form of the Westminster Confession[6] as their statement of faith. Nor was colonial Anglicanism for the most part "the high-flying Anglicanism" of the Restoration divines; it was "the Calvinistic Low Church Anglicanism of the period before Laud."[7] Whether in Virginia or in New England, the same books of religious edification were read, the same doctrines were taught from the pulpits, and the same laws were passed to enforce religious duties. When the Quakers, who represented the left-wing of the Puritan movement, are brought into the picture, it is evident that the Puritan influence in early America was overwhelmingly dominant. So pervasive was its influence that, as Schaff reports, even many of the Lutheran churches were remade in the Puritan image.[8]

One further word of caution that needs to be spoken is an acknowledgment that what was labeled as Puritan by Schaff, Bryce, and Siegfried was not a static theological point of view. As the Calvinism of the early Puritans was not precisely the same as the Calvinism of Geneva, so the Puritanism of nineteenth-century America was not that of seventeenth-century England and it might more properly be described as Evangelicalism. There was constant modification and change and development. But there were also large elements of continuity; and even when theological foundations were altered or eroded, habitual ways of thinking and feeling

[6] The Westminster Confession of Faith, with the modifications made by the Congregationalists, is reproduced in Williston Walker, *The Creeds and Platforms of Congregationalism* (N.Y., 1893). The Baptist recension is in W. L. Lumpkin, *Baptist Confessions of Faith* (Philadelphia, 1959). John Witherspoon, president of Princeton, noted the basic unity of the denominations in this tradition when he described the religious situation in New Jersey at the close of the Revolution. "The Baptists," he said, "are Presbyterians in all other respects, only differing in the point of infant baptism; their political weight goes the same way as the Presbyterians." *Essays on Important Subjects* (Edinburgh, 1805), IV, 203.

[7] The comment is that of William Haller in *The Constitution Reconsidered*, ed. Conyers Read (N.Y., 1938), 136. This "Calvinistic Anglicanism" was perhaps more heavily indebted to the influence of Henry Bullinger, Zwingli's successor at Zurich, than to Calvin himself. Calvinism frequently is a shorthand term for the Reformed tradition as a whole.

[8] Schaff, *America*, 93, 150–54.

9

persisted and continued to give form and structure to the common life.

RELIGIOUS DIVERSITY. The fact that the American colonies were English colonies also explains in large measure the multiplicity of religious bodies which was so prominent a feature of the English colonial scene in contrast to the religious uniformity which prevailed in the French and Spanish domains, for a deliberate policy of religious toleration was adopted by the English colonial authorities.

At the outset, to be sure, it was assumed that there would be and should be uniformity of religion in the new settlements; but in keeping with the whole system—or lack of system—of English colonial administration, the instructions at this point were not always observed. The Separatists who landed at Plymouth in 1620, for example, had set sail with the permission of the Virginia Company to establish a settlement within its territory, even though the second Virginia charter stated that no one, such as the Separatists, who refused to take the Oath of Supremacy should be allowed to embark for Virginia. Within a relatively brief time this administrative laxity was transformed into an explicit policy of toleration, and in no colony other than Virginia did the English authorities even attempt to impose a pattern of religious uniformity. When such attempts were made in the colonies, as in Massachusetts Bay, it was by the colonists themselves, and it was in spite of rather than because of English policy.

One important factor determining the tolerant attitude of the English government was the economic advantage to be gained by a policy of toleration. From the point of view of the English government, the colonies were commercial ventures designed to contribute to the wealth and prosperity of the mother country. The great need if they were to be profitable was to attract settlers who would provide the manpower to exploit the untapped resources of field and forest. Jails were emptied to provide colonists, the impoverished were sent out, adventurers were enlisted. But it soon became obvious that those who suffered from disabilities at home because of their religious profession would be prime recruits if they could be induced to leave the homeland by the prospect of greater freedom abroad.

The Dutch had early discovered the economic folly of adopting rigorous measures to suppress religious dissent, and Peter Stuyvesant was rebuked for attempting to institute such a policy in New Amsterdam. The Dutch authorities informed him that his "vigorous proceedings" should be discontinued lest he "check and destroy" the population. The secret of the prosperity of old Amsterdam, he was reminded, was the moderation displayed by the magistrates in dealing with religious minorities, with the result that "people have flocked" from every land "to this asylum." He was informed that a similar policy should be pursued in New Amsterdam. "It is our opinion that some connivance would be useful; that the consciences of men, at least, ought ever to remain free and unshackled." [9]

English policy was of a piece with the Dutch. This is self-evident in the grants that were made to Lord Baltimore and William Penn, but the clearest statement of the motivation which lay behind the policy is to be found in a communication from the Lords of Trade in London to the Council of Virginia: "A free exercise of religion . . . is essential to enriching and improving a trading nation; it should be ever held sacred in His Majesty's colonies. We must, therefore, recommend it to your care that nothing be done which can in the least affect that great point." [10] Non-English settlers were welcomed and some were even recruited with the promise of freedom to establish their own religious institutions. Most of these non-English groups arrived relatively late in the colonial period [11] and constituted, proportionately, a small segment of the total population, but they did serve to give added variety to the religious spectrum.

Economic advantage alone, however, does not explain the relative equanimity with which dissent was viewed by both the Dutch and the English. A major contributing factor was the fact that the "maxims of moderation" were already being practiced at home. The English were more halting in their progress in this direction, but throughout the colonial period England was moving steadily toward an ever broadening toleration of religious dissent. At times the toleration at home was within narrow limits. At other times, as during the two decades following the meeting of the Long Parliament in 1640, it was very broad. For brief periods under Charles I and Charles II there were efforts to impose a rigid conformity, but these efforts were never wholly successful and were not long pursued. With the adoption of the Act of Toleration in 1689, the acceptance of

[9] The text of the letter is printed in W. W. Sweet, *Religion in Colonial America* (N.Y., 1942), 151–52.

[10] *Historical Collections Relating to the American Colonial Church*, ed. William S. Perry (Hartford, 1871–78), I, 379–81.

[11] The great influx of the Germans and Scotch-Irish, the major non-English elements in the population, occurred during the last third of the colonial period.

religious diversity within the limits of trinitarian Protestantism became the settled domestic policy of the English government. Thus its religious policy in the colonies was in many ways merely a reflection of a policy that was being developed at home, and in the end England did little more than export her own religious diversity.

A new beginning in a new land

While the English inheritance was the most important single influence determining the form and substance of religious life in the colonies, both the necessities and the opportunities of life in the New World introduced changes of emphasis and modifications of practice. Faced with the task of beginning anew, the leaders of the churches found themselves far more dependent upon the laity than had hitherto been true, and they were forced to concede to the laity far greater powers than the laity had previously enjoyed. Furthermore, the long sea journey had removed many of the inhibitions and restraints to which most of the churches had been subject, leaving them free to experiment in reshaping their life to conform more closely to long-cherished convictions than had been possible at home. Finally, given the view of history that prevailed, the mere fact that a new beginning could be made cultivated an eager expectancy that this was "the Lord's doing" and was but a foretaste of the near-approaching time when all things would be made new.

THE IMPORTANCE OF THE LAITY. The Protestant Reformation with its emphasis upon the priesthood of believers and its appeal to the plain testimony of Scripture had tended to elevate the laity in the life of the church. This tendency was arrested, however, by the establishment of national churches, sanctioned and maintained by the state. The clergy, being appointed by and responsible to the state, took charge and left to the people a purely passive role. Thus, within the limits of state control, the church tended to become a clerically dominated institution. In England, to be sure, the post-Reformation struggle for dominance between contending parties within the church necessitated appeals for lay support and thus gave added influence to the laity,[12] but this influence was always limited by ordered structures of church life. In the colonies, on the other hand, the

[12] See James F. Maclear, "The Making of the Lay Tradition," *Journal of Religion,* XXXIII (1953), 113–36.

restraint provided by an established church order was reduced to a minimum.

One of the facts of life in the New World was that a new beginning had to be made, and for most of the churches this new beginning had to be made by individual clergymen recruiting their own congregations out of a population that was largely unchurched. The ready-made congregations of early New England and the parishes created by legislative fiat in Virginia were not typical. Elsewhere there were neither closely knit bodies of believers already in existence nor parishes established by law. Nor was there any ecclesiastical body close at hand to supervise and regulate the life of the churches. Furthermore, because of the diversity that prevailed, the clergy often had to compete for the allegiance of the people. Far removed from the status-giving context of an ordered church life and dependent upon what support they could enlist among the laity both for the formation and the maintenance of the congregations they served, the only real authority the clergy possessed was the authority they could command by their powers of persuasion and the force of their example. Given these circumstances, it is scarcely surprising that the laity soon began to exercise a decisive voice in church affairs, with "everything," as Henry M. Muhlenberg (1711–87) was to explain, dependent "on the vote of the majority." [13]

Even in New England, where churches had been constituted at the outset with ministers as a "speaking aristocracy" and congregations reduced to a "silent democracy," this state of affairs did not long persist. Men who had gained independent status as property holders by clearing their own land with flintlocks close at hand were not the type to be unduly submissive, and their self-assertiveness soon stripped the New England clergy of much of their independence. The same process was at work in Virginia where lay vestries gained effective control by neglecting to present the clergy to the governor for permanent induction into office, thus retaining, as the Archbishop of Canterbury complained, the right to hire and fire them like "domestic servants." [14]

[13] *The Journals of Henry Melchior Muhlenberg* (Philadelphia, 1942), I, 67. For a perceptive discussion of this point, see Sidney E. Mead, "The Rise of the Evangelical Conception of the Ministry," in *The Ministry in Historical Perspectives*, ed. H. Richard Niebuhr and D. D. Williams (N.Y., 1956), 212–18.

[14] Elizabeth Davidson, *The Establishment of the English Church in Continental American Colonies* (Durham, N.C., 1936), 19.

A further consequence of this lay predominance in the affairs of the churches was the strong support that was given to what was later described as "local autonomy." With single congregations beginning of necessity as independent self-governing units, resistance developed when attempts were made to regularize their status by subordinating them to larger units of ecclesiastical control. The laity were fearful of losing the prerogatives they possessed in the local church. Thus in Virginia and other southern colonies, where the Anglican laity had gained decisive powers in local "vestries," there was vigorous opposition to the attempt to establish an episcopate in America. A similar apprehension among the Congregational laity in Massachusetts thwarted the proposal to complete the Congregational structure there with a yearly consultative synod, while the Presbyterians in 1758 were forced to come to terms with this sentiment by conceding extensive powers to local presbyteries at the expense of synodical authority.

Thus, whatever the denomination and whatever the polity that was ostensibly professed, all the colonial churches tended to be characterized by a strong emphasis upon local autonomy and lay control. This emphasis persisted and it was only partially curtailed in the nineteenth and twentieth centuries through strenuous efforts of Presbyterian, Methodist, and Roman Catholic clergy alike to have all church property transferred to and vested in presbytery, conference, or bishop. The objective was to place a limitation upon local lay power by gaining control of the church property.

THE BREAKDOWN OF THE PARISH SYSTEM. A further consequence of the conditions that prevailed in the New World was the shattering of the parish system of ecclesiastical organization and the transformation of all the churches into what are usually described as "gathered" churches.

For almost a thousand years in western Europe, it had been generally assumed that every member of society was automatically a member of the church. Richard Hooker (1554?–1600), speaking of the situation in England, had voiced this common assumption in these words: "There is not any member of the Church of England but the same man is also a member of the commonwealth; nor any member of the commonwealth which is not also [a member] of the Church of England." [15] For purposes of worship, instruction, and discipline, people were divided geographically

[15] *Hooker's Ecclesiastical Polity: Book VIII*, ed. R. A. Houk (N.Y., 1931), 156.

into parishes. This was the basic unit of church life, and it was in marked contrast to a church whose membership was defined in terms of voluntary affiliation rather than place of residence.

Only in Virginia and in New England did a parish system, designed to embrace a total community, function with any real degree of success, and in Virginia the success was limited. The pattern of settlement in Virginia was the major problem. With the population thinly distributed on large plantations bordering the navigable rivers, a single parish could be from thirty to one hundred miles in length. In such a situation, it was difficult for the parish incumbent even to keep in touch with his parishioners, to say nothing of maintaining regular services of worship and a systematic program of instruction for them. In New England the pattern of settlement on small landholdings gathered about a village center was more conducive to an effective parish system and it was maintained largely unimpaired until the inroads of dissent destroyed the religious homogeneity of the population.

Elsewhere in the colonies, the religious diversity which was present from the beginning compromised any attempt to establish a system which presupposed that the whole community would belong to a single church. A thin façade of parish structure was maintained by legislative action in Maryland, the Carolinas, and Georgia, but in none of these colonies could the parish churches claim more than a minority of the population. Indeed, in the latter three colonies most of the parishes existed only on paper, never having been supplied with clergymen. The only thing that made possible even the pretense of maintaining a parish system was governmental authority, and the moment it was withdrawn the whole flimsy structure toppled. By this time the Anglicans had become a minority even in Virginia, and the adoption of Thomas Jefferson's "Bill for Establishing Religious Freedom" (1785) was equally effective in exposing as fiction the notion that the Anglican parishes there were anything more than "gathered" churches composed of voluntary adherents.

The New England story was somewhat more complex, for in New England the attempt was made to preserve "gathered" churches within a parish structure. This posed no great problem during the early years when the total population was largely a "sifted" people. But when the children of believers were unable to exhibit the minimum qualifications for church membership, the problem became acute. In an effort to preserve the parish concept, a form of "birthright" membership was adopted and by this means the collapse of the parish system in New England was deferred until the increase of dissent made its defense a hopeless cause. A full century before disestablishment stripped away the lingering traces of the parish structure in New England, Jonathan Edwards (1703–58) had recognized that its days were numbered and had called upon his fellow Congregationalists to return to their initial emphasis upon the church as a covenanted community of convinced believers. While certain privileges were retained until the first decades of the nineteenth century, the defenders of the attenuated establishment that survived during these final years found it necessary to adopt all the techniques of the "gathered" churches in order to carry on a rear guard defense of its few remaining prerogatives.

The "techniques of the 'gathered' churches" is a key phrase, for it calls attention to the necessity that was laid upon the churches to win support and gain recruits by voluntary means. No longer could they depend upon people being automatically members of the church and subject to its discipline. The churches had to utilize all their powers of persuasion if they were to maintain and perpetuate themselves. The techniques they devised to this end were many and varied: the fostering of revivals, the organization of mission societies, the establishment of Sunday schools, the development of programs of visitation, the publication of tracts, and more recently the utilization of advertisements in periodicals. This vigorous evangelistic and instructional activity, imposed upon the churches by their status as "gathered" groups of convinced believers, was to become one of the most distinctive features of American church life. And in the end, in order to maintain themselves on this basis, some of the churches—most notably the Roman Catholic Church—felt compelled to embark on the even more ambitious venture of establishing weekday schools for the complete education of their children.

THE POSSIBILITY OF THOROUGHGOING REFORM. The prominence of religious radicals and left-wing groups in America has frequently been noted, and it is not surprising that they should have come to the New World in disproportionate numbers. Members of the established churches in Europe could only view the situation in America with some dismay, for the necessity to make a new beginning forced them to improvise and served to shatter many of their previously cherished patterns of ecclesiastical life. In New Amsterdam, for example, Jonas Michaelius (b. 1584) was acutely conscious of the coercions imposed by the conditions of life in a new land, and he felt compelled to explain the irregularities which attended the formation of his church. "One cannot," he wrote to the authorities at home, "observe strictly all the usual formalities in making a beginning under such circumstances." [16] The nonestablished churches of Europe, however, were in a reverse situation. They welcomed the opportunity to make a new beginning free from the restraints to which they were subjected at home. This was the great attraction which enticed the Mennonites and the Moravians to risk the hazards of beginning life anew in the American wilderness. It was this prospect also which exerted so strong an appeal to that hardy band of Pilgrims who settled at Plymouth in 1620 and encouraged the founders of Massachusetts Bay Colony in 1629 to undertake their "great migration."

The necessity to make a new beginning was seen by these minority groups as something more than a mere negative release. It was an opportunity to undertake a positive work of construction. William Penn (1644–1718) could never have launched his "holy experiment" in England where the existing patterns and institutions of a settled community would have dictated compromises from the start. He needed an opportunity to begin anew where there would be "room," as he put it, for "such an experiment," and it was this opportunity that was given him in America.

The significance of the opportunity to make a new beginning can be seen most clearly through the eyes of those who sailed with the Winthrop fleet to Massachusetts Bay. Michaelius had to "make do" in New Amsterdam, but the early New Englanders had had to "make do" at home. In England they had been compelled to adjust to the irregularities imposed upon them by the requirements of the established church, and the shift to the New World was viewed by them as a release from this bondage. "It is one thing," explained John Cotton (1564–1652), "for . . . members of the church loyally to submit unto any form of [church] government when it is above their calling to reform it"; it is quite another matter for them to "choose a form of government and governors discrepant from the rule." The Great Migration had been organized with the specific purpose of providing them with this freedom to "choose," and John Winthrop

[16] His letter is printed in *American Christianity: An Historical Interpretation with Representative Documents*, ed. H. Shelton Smith, Robert T. Handy, and Lefferts A. Loetscher (N.Y., 1960–63), I, 56–59.

(1588–1649) standing on the deck of the *Arbella* made explicit the duty that was thus laid upon them. It was to "bring into familiar and constant practice" that which they previously had been able to "maintain as truth in profession only." Their purpose was clear. "We go," said Francis Higginson (1586–1630), "to practice the positive part of church reformation." [17]

America was for them, as it was to become for others, a land of opportunity, a land where a "wide door" of "liberty" had been set open before them. No longer were they to be compelled to resort to devious expedients, as they had been at home, in order to avoid "corruptions." This necessity had been lifted. But more important was the freedom they possessed to undertake a radical reconstruction of church life to conform to what they regarded as the plain prescriptions of God's "most holy Word." The goal was a full and complete restoration of the primitive church in all its pristine glory. This was their opportunity, and they were determined to take advantage of it. Looking back in 1677 to the early days of settlement, Increase Mather (1639–1723) declared: "There never was a generation that did so perfectly shake off the dust of Babylon . . . as the first generation of Christians that came to this land for the Gospel's sake." [18]

The early New Englanders were seeking freedom for themselves alone, but others found in America an equal freedom to "shake off the dust of Babylon." There was and there continued to be space enough for everyone.[19] It was this sense of being freed from the necessity to give heed to compromising restraints in making a new beginning that was to give a perfectionist cast to much of American religious life and to foster the uninhibited experimentation by smaller fringe groups that was to be the dismay of European churchmen.

THE SENSE OF EXPECTANCY. A new beginning is always a heady experience that breeds an eager expectancy among those who participate in it. Hopes are kindled and, as imagination takes over, the future becomes

[17] See Perry Miller, *Orthodoxy in Massachusetts* (Cambridge, Mass., 1933), 137, 146. Winthrop's address, "A Model of Christian Charity," is printed in *The Puritans*, ed. Perry Miller and T. H. Johnson (N.Y., 1963), I, 195–99, and in Smith, Handy, Loetscher, *American Christianity*, I, 97–102.

[18] Quoted by W. W. Sweet, *Religion in Colonial America* (N.Y., 1950), 2.

[19] For a discussion of the significance of geographic space, see S. E. Mead, "The American People: Their Space, Time, and Religion," *Journal of Religion*, XXXIV (1954), 244–55; reprinted in S. E. Mead, *The Lively Experiment* (N.Y., 1963).

pregnant with possibility. This was doubly true of the new beginning that was made in America, for European peoples had always lived with the hope—sometimes faint but never absent—that the Lord's promise in Isaiah and Revelation to "make all things new" would some day be fulfilled. And the very term "New World," which was used to describe the setting in which they were making their new beginning, was calculated to remind them of the Lord's promise.

Since every Englishman had been taught from childhood to view the course of history as predetermined by God's overruling providence, no one could regard the colonizing activity in America as an ordinary venture. As early as 1613, William Strachey was insisting that God had kept America hidden for a purpose and that those who had established the small settlement in Virginia were but pursuing a course of action which God had foreseen and willed and was now carrying to its foreordained completion.[20] This purpose of necessity was related to God's final act of redemption, for this was the end toward which all history was directed.

The specific understanding of the past which illumined God's activity in the present was that which had been made the common possession of all Englishmen by John Foxe's "Book of Martyrs"—a volume that in 1571 had been placed by official decree in every cathedral church for all to read and was later to have a place of honor beside the Bible in every Protestant home.[21] Through the eyes of Foxe the shifting course of past events was seen to be a movement within a set pattern which God had adopted as a means of instructing mankind in the ways of righteousness. Throughout the centuries there had been alternating periods of impiety and faithfulness, corruption and reform, decline and renewal. After a long period of decline in which darkness had been demonstrated to be the only result of the folly of unrighteousness, Foxe pointed out that by 1300 God had begun to summon his servants to a renewed witness to him and thus to serve as

---

[20] Perry Miller, *Errand into the Wilderness* (Cambridge, Mass., 1956), 111, 117.

[21] The first edition of 1554 was a small octavo volume which recounted the martyrdoms of the precursors of the Protestant Reformation, and to these the accounts of martyrdoms under Mary Tudor were soon added. By the time it reached its final form in 1583, it was a folio of almost 2,500 pages and its full title had become *Acts and Monuments of Matters Most Special and Memorable, Happening in the Church, with an Universal History of the Same*. See William Haller, "John Foxe and the Puritan Revolution," in *The Seventeenth Century: Studies in the History of English Thought and Literature from Bacon to Pope*, by Richard F. Jones and others (Palo Alto, Calif., 1951); and also Haller's *The Elect Nation* (N.Y., 1963).

19

harbingers of the new dispensation which was to be inaugurated with the Protestant Reformation.

When a full century had passed after the posting of the "Ninety-five Theses" by Martin Luther, it had become clear to scattered groups in England that Foxe had been overoptimistic in his estimate of the immediate outcome of the Reformation. The godly forces in Europe had proved to be unequal to the task to which God had summoned them. Why this should be so, they could only speculate; it was evident that God intended to pursue a new tactic to effect the final thrust into the new age.

The early New Englanders shared this sense of disappointment and as they reflected upon the significance of their venture in the New World they felt certain that it was to implement God's over-all design that they had been sent, as Samuel Danforth (1626–74) put it, on an "errand into the wilderness." When old England "began to decline in religion," declared Edward Johnson (1598–1672), Christ raised "an army out of our English nation, for freeing his people from their long servitude" and created "a new England to muster up the first of his forces in." This new England, he continued, "is the place where the Lord will create a new heaven and a new earth in, new churches and a new commonwealth together." [22]

God had "sifted a whole nation" in order to plant his "choice grain" in the American wilderness, but his purpose was more far-ranging than merely to enable them to escape the inhibitions they had suffered at home. They were not fleeing from persecution; they were executing a flank attack upon the forces of unrighteousness everywhere. Their role, John Winthrop had reminded them, was to be "a city set on a hill" to demonstrate before "the eyes of the world" what the result would be when a whole people was brought into open covenant with God. As part of God's program of instruction, they were to provide the nations with a working model of a godly society and by the contagion of their example were to be God's instruments in effecting the release from bondage of all mankind. [23]

The New Englanders, however, were not alone in the conviction that

[22] *Johnson's Wonder-working Providence, 1628–1651*, ed. J. F. Jameson (N.Y., 1910), 23, 25. A portion of Johnson's narrative is in *The Puritans*, ed. Perry Miller and T. H. Johnson (N.Y., 1938), I, 143–62.

[23] Smith, Handy, and Loetscher, *American Christianity*, I, 102; *The Puritans*, ed. Miller and Johnson, I, 199. Perry Miller discusses this "errand" in *Errand into the Wilderness*, 11 f.

America had a decisive role to play in God's plan of redemption. William Penn was equally convinced that God intended his "holy experiment" to be "an example . . . to the nations" and a means of forwarding the remodeling of life everywhere. And Samuel Purchas' history of Virginia, written in 1625, began its account of that colony's varied experiences with Adam and Eve in order to "show how God had so managed the past that English colonization in the present was the fulfillment of his plan." [24] Even Roger Williams (1604?-84), "the New England firebrand" who dissented at several crucial points from his neighbors in the Bay Colony, lived in daily expectation of a new dispensation.

This understanding of the decisive role that America was to have in the divine economy was appropriated and popularized in the eighteenth century by leaders of the Great Awakening. (For the Great Awakening, see Chap. III.) Jonathan Edwards, reflecting upon the outbreak of the revival, was convinced that "this work of God's Spirit, so extraordinary and wonderful, is the dawning or at least a prelude of that glorious work of God so often foretold in Scripture, which in the progress and issue of it shall renew the world of mankind." He saw the Awakening as the vindication, after so many successive disappointments, of the earlier expectation that the final act of God's work of redemption would begin in America. And if "in any part of America," he continued, "I think if we consider the circumstances of the settlement of New England, it must needs appear the most likely of all American colonies to be the place whence this work shall principally take its rise." [25] Whatever other leaders of the revival may have thought of Edwards' speculation as to the precise point at which the new age would first manifest itself, they shared his belief that God's Spirit was making itself felt in an unusual way and that God had a special destiny in store for America.

This mood of eager expectancy was to continue to be characteristic of American religious life. Having escaped in so many ways the limitations of a bounded existence, men and women were easily persuaded of the reality of unlimited possibilities. The hope of all things being made new, in the course of time, was often subtly secularized and frequently restated in political terms. But the conviction remained that somehow this was God's

[24] Miller, *Errand into the Wilderness*, 115. See also Wright, *Religion and Empire*, 115-33.

[25] *Work of Redemption, The Works of Jonathan Edwards* (Worcester, Mass., 1808-09), II, 153, 158.

country with a mission to perform. For the churches this sense of mission was the source of much of their restless energy as they sought to keep abreast of the westward tide of migration and to make sure that the United States would fulfill its calling as a godly nation.

22

II

Denominational Beginnings

Where to begin an account of the various religious groups in colonial America is a puzzling question. There was no single dominant group to provide a logical point of departure and to serve as a foil for the discussion of the others. The Congregationalists were the largest of the denominations but they were a regional group. The Anglicans were the first to establish themselves on the American scene but they were to be neither the largest nor the most influential of the colonial religious bodies. The Presbyterians and the Baptists were to be both numerous and widely dispersed by the end of the colonial period but their growth was relatively late and presupposed in part the founding of Pennsylvania by the Quakers. A purely chronological approach would be awkward and confusing, for it would introduce the Dutch Reformed and the Swedish Lutherans much too early in a story whose dominant motif was almost wholly English. Even the attempt to deal with the various groups on a regional basis would involve distortion, for few of them were confined to a single area. The most satisfactory solution would seem to be to provide a brief review of the founding and the religious complexion of each of the colonies, and then to deal with each of the English-speaking denominations in roughly chronological order before giving attention to the highly significant but much less numerous groups of Continental origin.

Religious characteristics of the different colonies

The thirteen colonies came into being as a result of two great waves of English colonizing activity separated by the twenty distracting years (1640–60) of the English civil wars and the regime of Oliver Cromwell. Virginia, Maryland, the several New England colonies, and the island possessions (Bermuda, Barbados, St. Kitts, Nevis, and Antigua) were products of the early years. Following the restoration of the Stuarts to the English throne in 1660, the gap between Maryland and New England on the Atlantic coast was closed by the capture of New Netherlands from the Dutch in 1664 and by the founding of New Jersey in 1674 and of Pennsylvania and Delaware in 1681 and 1682. The southern frontier was extended by the settlement of Charleston in 1670 in accordance with a proprietary patent to the territory which was later divided into the royal colonies of South and North Carolina. Georgia, the last of the thirteen colonies, was founded in 1733.

THE SOUTHERN COLONIES. Virginia, the earliest of the colonies, was unique in several other respects. In Virginia alone did the Anglicans command a clear majority of the religious population; in Virginia alone was Anglicanism the established religion from the beginning; and in Virginia alone of all the colonies was provision made to enforce conformity to the Church of England. The instructions of James I in the first charter of Virginia were explicit. "The true word and service of God" was to be "preached, planted, and used" in the new colony "according to the doctrine, rights [rites?], and religion now professed and established within our realm of England." [1] To this end, chaplains were appointed by the Company, and repeated legislation required everyone to attend the services of the church. It is true that these laws were seldom rigorously enforced, but the intention was that there should be no toleration of dissent.

[1] Peter G. Mode, *Source Book . . . for American Church History* (Menasha, Wisc., 1920), 10.

The first major break in the pattern of religious uniformity in Virginia came after 1660 when Quaker missionaries were successful in establishing scattered communities of adherents, but it was not until the later decades of the colonial period that the Anglican predominance was to be sharply reduced and then surpassed as new population flowed into the area which lay beyond the tidewater region. The surge of non-Anglican strength was partially the result of Anglican neglect to form parishes and to provide a ministry for the new arrivals, but it was more largely due to other factors. Many of the new settlers who spread out in the territory adjacent to the Shenandoah were Scots from northern Ireland, some were Germans, others were from New England. The potential Presbyterian strength represented by the Scotch-Irish was marshaled with great effectiveness by Samuel Davies (1723–61) who had been sent to Virginia by the Synod of New York in 1748 and who continued to spearhead the Presbyterian advance until 1759 when he became president of the College of New Jersey (now Princeton). The moderate growth of the Baptists was transformed into a phenomenal expansion by the exciting preaching of a transplanted New Englander, Shubal Stearns (1706–71), who began his activity in Virginia in 1754. The success of these dissenting groups was facilitated by the tension that existed between the older and newer areas of settlement. Anglicanism suffered because of its identification with the early planters of the tidewater region, whose descendants had become a ruling aristocracy which controlled the Assembly, denied full representation to the upcountry districts, and refused to heed their grievances. Furthermore, the attempts to suppress dissent by this time could be countered by an appeal to rights guaranteed by the English Act of Toleration of 1689.

From the standpoint of religion, North Carolina, South Carolina, and Georgia had little in common with Virginia beyond a nominal establishment of Anglicanism as the official faith of the three colonies. Religious toleration had been granted at the outset and there was little religious homogeneity to the population. The settlement of North Carolina was haphazard, with runaway servants from Virginia as the earliest inhabitants, and for many years the Quakers were the largest single religious group. Later the Scotch-Irish tide which swept down the Shenandoah valley into all three colonies gave major strength to the Presbyterians, and the Baptists were active and growing rapidly at the close of the colonial period. Strong German communities—mostly Lutherans and Moravians—were found in both North Carolina and Georgia. Only in South Carolina was there any significant Anglican strength south of Virginia. In 1704 "by dint of political trickery" an act was passed by the South Carolina Assembly providing for an Anglican establishment, and after some modifications it was put into effect in 1706. Its provisions, however, were never fully carried out because of lack of clergymen, and at best it was a highly precarious establishment depending upon shifting majorities in an Assembly controlled at intervals by the dissenting groups. A similar establishment was secured in North Carolina in 1715 and in Georgia in 1758, but in neither colony did the establishment become operative in more than a handful of parishes.

Maryland, founded in 1634 by the second Lord Baltimore, had many affinities with the middle colonies, both geographic and otherwise. Its proprietor was Roman Catholic; and like the Quaker William Penn, he was as interested in providing a place where his co-religionists could settle as he was in making his colony a profitable financial investment. And for both these reasons, like Penn, he pursued a forthright policy of religious toleration from the beginning. In actuality, of course, for the first decade or two, Roman Catholics were the only persons in Maryland who received any benefit from this toleration, for there were no other dissenting groups. The non-Catholic Christians there were Anglicans, and one can scarcely speak of tolerating in English territory a church whose "supreme governor" was the English monarch himself. Indeed, the charter presupposed that churches would be "dedicated and consecrated according to the ecclesiastical laws of our kingdom of England."

The Roman Catholics who participated in the colonization of Maryland were a minority of even the first contingent that sailed for the new colony; and in order not to jeopardize the charter they were instructed by the proprietor that "no scandal nor offense" was "to be given any of the Protestants." On shipboard they were "to cause all acts of the Roman Catholic religion to be done as privately as may be" and were "to be silent upon all occasion of discourse concerning matters of religion." [2]

The wise precautions by which the proprietor sought to secure the toleration of his co-religionists were not entirely successful, for Roman

[2] "The Calvert Papers," No. 1, *Maryland Historical Society Proceedings*, XXVIII (Baltimore, 1889), 132.

Catholics were disfranchised for a brief period in the 1650's after their leaders had proclaimed allegiance to Charles II in opposition to the authority of the English Parliament. And after the expulsion of James II from the English throne because of his efforts to subvert the Protestant faith, Roman Catholics in Maryland were again subjected to various disabilities. Nevertheless, they remained one of the most important and influential segments of Maryland society.

By 1677 both Roman Catholics and Anglicans had been reduced to the status of minority groups if credence is to be given Lord Baltimore's report to the Privy Council concerning the shifts that had occurred in the religious affiliations of the Maryland populace. "The greatest part of the inhabitants of that province (three of four at least) do consist of Presbyterians, Independents, Anabaptists, and Quakers; those of the Church of England, as well as those of the Romish, being the fewest." [3] In spite of this numerical inferiority, the overthrow of James II in 1688 marked the beginning of a vigorous campaign to secure an Anglican establishment in Maryland, an objective which was achieved in 1702 when the Board of Trade and Plantations in London was finally satisfied that the rights of other minorities would be adequately safeguarded. By this time Presbyterians, Baptists, and Quakers were becoming more numerous, and German Protestants were soon to spill over the border from Pennsylvania.

THE NEW ENGLAND COLONIES. Plymouth, the first of the New England colonies, was almost immediately overshadowed by and in 1691 was absorbed into Massachusetts Bay Colony, and its religious history differed in no significant way from its larger neighbor. Both colonies were established by Congregationalists: Plymouth by Separatist Congregationalists and Massachusetts Bay by Nonseparatist Congregationalists (see below, pp. 36–37), but in the New World this difference was not of great moment.

A degree of intrigue and perhaps deception lay behind the establishment of Massachusetts Bay. In 1629, when the repressive ecclesiastical measures of the Laudian regime had begun to make life in England difficult for them, a group of Nonseparatist Congregationalists obtained from Charles I a royal charter for the Massachusetts Bay Company. For some reason the usual clause which required the headquarters of such a

[3] L. J. Trinterud, *The Forming of an American Tradition* (Philadelphia, 1949), 26.

company to be in England and thus subject to the immediate control of the crown was omitted from the charter. This could scarcely have been an oversight, for when the great Winthrop fleet sailed in the summer of 1630 it carried with it all the officers and stockholders of the company together with the charter itself. With charter and company in America, the colony was in effect an independent republic. The stockholders were called "freemen" and they became the electorate; the directors or "deputies" became legislators; and the governor of the company became the chief executive of the colony. When it became inconvenient for the whole body of freemen to attend the annual meeting or "general court" of the company, a representative system was devised whereby their "assistants" became a second house of the legislative assembly. When the English authorities finally discovered what had occurred, efforts were made to have the charter returned and the status of the colony regularized. Tactics of delay, however, were adopted; the turmoil of the two decades from 1640 to 1660 intervened; and it was not until 1684 that the charter was finally revoked and a royal governor appointed.

With freedom to pursue an independent course, the early settlers of Massachusetts Bay were in no mood to permit dissent from the "due form" of ecclesiastical government which they established. Having forsaken their homes to found a new Zion in the American wilderness, they saw no reason why their endeavor should be compromised by dissidence. Others, they contended, had full liberty to stay away; and they noted that there was ample room elsewhere in America for them to establish settlements of their own. As early as 1635 the first of a long succession of heresy trials imposing banishment as the most common penalty was held.[4]

The attempt to suppress dissent in Massachusetts Bay was never wholly successful for several reasons. The mere fact of space, even in Massachusetts itself, made policing difficult. And the policy of banishment created centers just across its borders from which the contagion of dissent filtered back to the older settlements. Furthermore, their fellow Congregationalists in England were embarrassed by their proceedings and exerted constant pressure upon them to adopt a more liberal policy. But the major reason was the fact that within the heart of New England Puritanism there was a steady and persistent acknowledgment that "the Lord hath more

[4] Among those banished were Roger Williams in 1635, Samuel Gorton in 1637, and Anne Hutchinson and John Wheelwright in 1638.

light yet to break forth out of his Holy Word" and that therefore they must ever be ready "to receive whatever truth shall be made known . . . from the written Word of God."[5] These were the words of John Robinson (1576?–1625), pastor of those who came to Plymouth in 1620 when they were exiles at Leyden, but they represent the basic assumption upon which the whole Congregationalist enterprise was founded. In the light of this fundamental principle, it is not surprising that Congregationalism was forever spawning its own dissidents—men and even women who defended themselves by appealing to the truth that had been made known to them from "the written Word of God."

While these three factors mitigated the effectiveness of the attempt by the Massachusetts Bay authorities to enforce conformity, they persisted in their endeavor until 1684 when the loss of the charter made it impossible for them to proceed independently of English authority. Three years later the end of the Congregational monopoly in the colony was dramatically signalized in Boston when the governor forced the Congregationalists to permit the Old South meetinghouse to be utilized for Anglican worship.

New Hampshire, in its basic pattern of church life, was little more than an extension of Massachusetts Bay. This was also largely true of Connecticut, founded by Thomas Hooker (1586?–1647) in 1635 and later incorporating the smaller colony of New Haven. Connecticut in several respects was more conservative than Massachusetts, and the *Saybrook Platform* of 1708 provided a more centralized control over the churches.

Rhode Island was a different story. The territory around Narragansett Bay had become the refuge for many of those expelled for reasons of religious dissent from Massachusetts Bay. Roger Williams, who was to be briefly a Baptist and then a Seeker, made his way there in 1636.[6] Anne Hutchinson (1591–1643), the "antinomian" prophetess whose trial shook the whole ruling hierarchy of the Bay colony, arrived with a number of her adherents in 1637. John Coggeshall and William Aspinwell came in 1638,

---

[5] Cotton Mather, *Magnalia Christi Americana* (Hartford, 1855), I, 64.

[6] For Williams, see Ola E. Winslow, *Master Roger Williams* (N.Y., 1957); Perry Miller, *Roger Williams: His Contribution to the American Tradition* (Indianapolis, 1953); and Mauro Calamandrei, "Neglected Aspects of Roger Williams' Thought," *Church History*, XXI (1952), 239–58. For a brief account of his characteristic emphases, see Introduction to his *Experiments of Spiritual Life and Health*, ed. W. S. Hudson (Philadelphia, 1951).

and a little later were joined by John Clarke (1609–76) and William Coddington. Samuel Gorton (1592?–1677), a contentious mystic who was always as ready to stir up a fight over politics and property rights as over religion, arrived in 1640. Williams, fearful lest the leading of God's Spirit and one's faithfulness to Christ be impaired by the sinful corruption of men, was a firm advocate of complete religious freedom. On this basis he succeeded in bringing together the disparate religious elements represented in the communities at Providence, Portsmouth, Newport, and Warwick to form the colony of Rhode Island and Providence Plantations, traveling to England in 1643 to secure the necessary patent from the English Parliament. Although the Baptists initially were the largest group in Rhode Island, they were soon rivaled and then surpassed by the Quakers who utilized the freedom the colony afforded as a base from which to attempt the evangelization of other parts of New England.

THE MIDDLE COLONIES. When the English took over control of New Netherlands in 1664, the new colony was the most religiously heterogeneous area in America. The Dutch Reformed church quite understandably was the largest single religious group, and throughout the seventeenth century it was to continue to have more adherents than all other groups combined. But, as Governor Dongan reported in 1687, there were also French Calvinists, German Lutherans, Congregationalists from New England, several varieties of Quakers, Mennonites, Baptists, some Roman Catholics, and a few Jews. "In short," he explained, "of all sorts of opinion there are some, and of the most part none at all."

The terms of capitulation to England provided that the Dutch should have freedom of conscience, worship, and church discipline. This was interpreted to mean that the Dutch Reformed church retained a measure of its established character, and the early English governors considered that the Dutch Reformed ministers were entitled to support from public funds. The Duke of York, to whom the colony had been granted by royal patent, also issued instructions that no one who professed the Christian faith was to be in any way disturbed for differing judgment in religious matters. Thus the policy of religious toleration which hitherto had prevailed was continued, with only the status of the Jews left in doubt.

After the Glorious Revolution of 1688 which brought William and Mary to the English throne, the governor of New York was instructed to secure an Anglican establishment in the colony. After repeated rebuffs, the

Assembly was finally induced in 1693 to adopt a measure which stipulated only that a "sufficient Protestant minister" should be supported by an annual tax in each of six parishes to be set up in New York City and three adjoining counties. Although the governor protested the vagueness of the wording and sought without success to have the act amended, he interpreted it (contrary to the intention of the Assembly) as a legal establishment of the Church of England. It was a small victory, for there were too few Anglicans in the colony to give it much substance. As the chaplain of the English garrison reported two years later, there were only ninety Anglican families in the entire colony in contrast to the 1,754 Dutch Reformed families and the 1,355 families of various types of English dissent.

The colony of New Jersey had a checkered development. Initially it was part of the grant to the Duke of York in 1664, but almost immediately he gave it to two friends. A few hundred Dutch and New England emigrés were already there and in order to attract more settlers laws were promulgated which provided for freedom of conscience and an Assembly. In 1674 West New Jersey was sold to two Quakers who let William Penn become one of the proprietors, and it was not until 1702, when New Jersey became a royal colony, that the two sections were reunited. Delaware was purchased by Penn from the Duke of York in 1682 and was administered jointly with Pennsylvania until it was given a separate Assembly in 1704.

The founder of Pennsylvania was the son of Admiral Sir William Penn. In 1667 at the age of twenty-three, after a grand tour of the Continent and a term of residence at the gay court in Dublin, he was converted to Quakerism. He was eager to secure a colony where, free from the pressure of bad example and worldly corruption, he could carry out a "holy experiment" in establishing a society fashioned in accordance with Quaker ideals. His share of West (New) Jersey did not satisfy his ambitions and a tactful reminder to the Duke of York of a debt to his father that had not been repaid led to his becoming the proprietor of the vast slice of territory which was given the name Pennsylvania.

The settlement of the new colony began without delay. A few Swedes, Finns, and Dutch were already there, and large-scale Quaker immigration set in at once. Other English-speaking inhabitants were enticed by the easy terms for the purchase of land described in Penn's promotional brochure,

Some Account of the Province of Pennsylvania (1681). The prospect of full religious freedom was a major factor in the successful effort to induce several German minority religious groups—Mennonites, Dunkers, Moravians, and Schwenkfelders (see below, pp. 51–55)—to come as settlers, while the lure of economic advantage drew many other Germans from the economically depressed Palatinate. The population was further swelled by the arrival of large numbers of Scotch-Irish Presbyterians who had encountered economic hardship at home as the result of the Woolens Act of 1699 and who were suffering from religious disabilities imposed in 1704 at the beginning of Queen Anne's reign. The Quakers, however, continued to set the tone of the colony and, due to unbalanced representation in the Assembly, they continued to be able to outvote any opposition until near the end of the colonial period.

The English-speaking denominations

THE ANGLICANS. The Church of England had been drastically reformed at the time of the Protestant Reformation. The ties with Rome were severed, monasteries were suppressed, prayers for the dead were abolished, altars were transformed into tables, the liturgy was reshaped and rewritten, the service was conducted in English, and the monarch was acknowledged as the "supreme governor" of the church. But the outward structure of the church, with its parishes and dioceses and with its threefold order of the ministry (deacons, priests, and bishops), remained unchanged. Although the English church was heavily indebted to the major Reformed theologians—to Zwingli, Calvin, Bucer, and Bullinger—for its basic theological orientation, the impact of the variant form of Calvinism known as Arminianism [7] was beginning to be felt by the time Jamestown was settled. From the outset there was a "High Church" movement that emphasized continuity with the pre-Reformation church. With only brief exceptions, however, "Low Church" sentiment—whether Puritan, Latitudinarian, or Evangelical—was to be dominant both in England and in America until the middle of the nineteenth century. While these shifting

[7] Jacob Arminius (1560–1609) was a Dutch Calvinist who opposed the developing hyper-Calvinism of the late sixteenth century. Later the term "Arminian" was used to designate any tendency to stress the human role in redemption. For the moderate Wesleyan version, see John Wesley, "What Is an Arminian?" a portion of which is printed in *Great Voices of the Reformation*, ed. Harry Emerson Fosdick (N.Y., 1952), 514–17.

32

theological currents were important, it was the Book of Common Prayer more than anything else that served as the focal point of the church's life.

Virginia was the great center of Anglican strength in colonial America.[8] The first ministers were chaplains sent out by the Virginia Company, but between 1619 and 1622 the rudiments of a parish system with glebe lands and assessments for parochial support were put into operation. Lay vestries which assumed responsibility for ordering the life of the parishes probably came into existence at this time, although they were not given statutory authority until 1641 when the Assembly ordered that the vestrymen should be chosen by the voters of each parish. After the Restoration the vestries were transformed into self-perpetuating bodies and became the preserves of the socially and economically privileged.

There was a perennial shortage of ministers throughout the colonial years. This was partly due to the fact that the establishment of a college to train a native ministry, though earnestly sought, was long delayed. Although Harvard College was founded as early as 1636, it was not until 1693 that Virginia was able to secure a similar institution for the training of its clergy. Even after William and Mary College opened its doors, the problem was not wholly solved. Since a bishop alone could ordain, young Anglicans who desired to enter the ministry of the church were compelled to undertake the long and hazardous journey to England to secure ordination.

Various expedients were devised to entice ministers to come to Virginia, including the payment of a bounty of twenty pounds to anyone who would transport a "sufficient minister" to the colony. Later the bounty was paid directly to the minister himself. It is not surprising that clergymen secured by such means were of uneven quality. While several of the ministers were men of unusual ability, many were not. Some had been unable to secure a "living" at home, but even competent and faithful men had a difficult time. Their parishes were too large, the population was too scattered, and a legal technicality frequently deprived them of both security and authority. An act of 1629 provided that the governor should "induct the said minister into any parish that shall make presentation of him." The vestries early discovered that by neglecting to present their

---

[8] For an account of Anglicanism in colonial Virginia, see G. MacLaren Brydon, *Virginia's Mother Church*, 2 vols. (Richmond, 1947–52).

minister for induction, the parish remained technically vacant and they could keep him under their control by hiring him on a temporary basis. If the faithful and competent had a difficult time as a result of being subjected to the whims of the vestry, those whose zeal and devotion left something to be desired found the absence of episcopal supervision a distinct advantage. Charges of indolence, drunkenness, and even immorality among the clergy were not uncommon. While immorality was not as widespread as has sometimes been suggested, the significant fact is that there were few means by which it could be restrained.

Conditions were much the same elsewhere in the colonies—in Maryland and South Carolina, for example—where the parish system had been instituted. What supervision of the Anglican clergy there was in these areas was exercised by the Bishop of London. Apart from certain formalities, his jurisdiction was not given any practical implementation until after the Revolution of 1688 when Bishop Compton began to delegate his disciplinary authority to resident "Commissaries," the most notable of whom were James Blair (1655–1743) in Virginia and Thomas Bray (1656–1730) in Maryland.[9] Although they did much to improve the condition of both church and clergy, they lacked the full episcopal powers which were indispensable to a fully developed church life. Bray was one of the first men to make an earnest plea for an American episcopate, but despite continuing agitation this was to remain an unrealized hope throughout the whole colonial period. Much of the opposition to the appointment of a bishop came from the laity who felt that he would jeopardize their own prerogatives in the church. William White (1748–1836), who became one of the first bishops of the newly formed Protestant Episcopal Church after the American Revolution, declared in 1782 that "there cannot be produced an instance of laymen in America, unless in the very infancy of the settlements, soliciting the introduction of a bishop." Even the clergy in the southern parishes were opposed to the establishment of an American episcopate, Samuel Auchmuty reported, since without a bishop they were "their own pastors."[10]

The missionaries sent out by the Society for the Propagation of the Gospel (S.P.G.) presented a brighter picture than did the general run of

[9] For Bray, see Henry P. Thompson, *Thomas Bray* (London, 1954).
[10] William White, *The Case of the Episcopal Churches in the United States Considered*, ed. R. G. Salomon (Philadelphia, 1954), 29. Carl Bridenbaugh, *Mitre and Sceptre* (N.Y., 1962), 249.

the parish clergy. The primary objective of the Society, which was organized in 1701 at the insistence of Thomas Bray and with the full support of the Archbishop of Canterbury, was to provide for "the administration of God's Word and the sacraments" in those areas where there were no settled Anglican clergy. From the time of its inception until 1783 when it officially ceased operations in the newly independent colonies, eighty-four of its missionaries labored in New England, fifty-eight in New York, fifty-four in South Carolina, forty-seven in Pennsylvania, forty-four in New Jersey, thirty-three in North Carolina, thirteen in Georgia, five in Maryland, and only two in Virginia. In all, three hundred and nine missionaries were recruited to serve in these colonies and well over one million dollars (£227,454) was raised in England for their support.[11]

The S.P.G. missionaries constituted a superior caste among the Anglican clergy. A measure of idealism and devotion was required of those whose only prospect of financial remuneration was the relatively small stipend provided by the Society. A life of ease and modest comfort might be envisioned by those who sought appointment to established parishes but this was never the lot of the missionaries. Furthermore, the absence of episcopal authority and discipline was in a measure remedied by the Society. The Society, to be sure, could not unfrock an erring minister, but it could and did dismiss the indolent, the disobedient, and the immoral from its service. Everywhere, even in New England and Pennsylvania, the missionaries had the advantage of varying degrees of official support, an advantage which they were not slow to exploit. The advantage, of course, became a liability with the coming of the American Revolution. The missionaries almost to a man identified themselves completely with the English cause and in the end few of them remained to carry on the ministry of the Protestant Episcopal Church in the United States.

Since the S.P.G. missionaries were to disappear with the coming of independence, a development of greater long-range significance was the emergence of an indigenous Anglicanism in New England. The break came on the day after commencement in September, 1722, when Timothy Cutler (1684–1765), president of Yale College, announced to the astonished trustees that he and one of the tutors and three neighboring ministers had been persuaded that their Congregational ordinations were invalid.

---

[11] C. S. Pascoe, *An Historical Account of the Society for the Propagation of the Gospel* (London, 1901), 86–87.

This change of view went back in part to a gift of books to the library, some of which detailed the Anglican claim to be the lineal descendant of the apostolic church. A more decisive factor perhaps was the influence exerted by an S.P.G. missionary stationed at Stratford, for Cutler and his friends did not reveal their new sentiments until they had been assured of support by the Society. Four of the converts went abroad to seek episcopal ordination. One of them died there of the smallpox but the others returned to serve as missionaries of the Society—Cutler becoming the first rector of Christ Church in Boston, James Whetmore serving the mission station at Rye, and Samuel Johnson (1696–1772) ultimately becoming the first president of King's College (Columbia University) in New York.

The apostasy of the president of Yale was a traumatic shock to New England Congregationalism, and as a result of his influence and example there were to be continuing conversions among the students at New Haven. These conversions gave the Church of England in the colonies a nucleus of native-born and native-trained ministers who were "convinced" rather than "birthright" Anglicans, and they brought to their pastoral endeavors all the zeal and ardor that is commonly found among converts.

THE CONGREGATIONALISTS. The "congregationalism" of the early New Englanders was the product of the peculiar history of the English Reformation which in several respects was an "arrested" reformation. Some of the early advocates of a more thoroughgoing reform, especially liturgical reform, broke from the parish churches and established independent churches of their own. These were the Separatists.[12] They restricted church membership to convinced believers and insisted that, since all members were equally priests, all should share in the determination of church affairs. Others who were dissatisfied with the slow pace of official reform found a considerable measure of freedom to carry out their desired reforms within the established parishes. So long as they engaged in no concerted organizational activity, both Elizabeth and James I were content for the most part to leave them to their own devices. When pressure was applied they found patrons to aid them, and they became adept at defending their rights in the common-law courts. They did not reject the Church of England as a false church, although they acknowledged that in many ways it was deformed and tainted with corruptions. This point of

---

[12] Robert Browne (1550?–1633?), author of *Reformation without Tarrying for Any[one]* (1582), was the early leader.

view was made explicit in the words Francis Higginson is reported to have said on shipboard as the shores of England faded from view:

> We will not say as the Separatists are wont to say at their leaving England, "Farewell Babylon, Farewell Rome"; but we will say, "Farewell dear England, Farewell the Church of God in England and all the Christian friends there." We do not go to New England as Separatists from the Church of England, though we cannot but separate from the corruptions in it.[13]

Prior to Higginson's departure in 1629, these Nonseparatist Congregationalists had elaborated the theory that in the hidden essence of its constitution the Church of England was basically congregational in structure. They differed from the Presbyterians at two points. Since they had had unworthy and unwanted ministers thrust upon them in their parish churches, they were unwilling to concede the power of ordination even to a presbytery, reserving it to the local congregation alone. Furthermore, since they had been pressured on occasion by the threat of excommunication wielded by a bishop, they were insistent that this power also must be reserved to the local congregation so that an individual might be tried by those who knew him best and not by any higher judicatory.

The Separatists provided the nucleus of the settlement at Plymouth, while those who came to Massachusetts Bay were Congregationalists of the Nonseparatist variety. The difference between the two groups was not great, and two factors served to obliterate it. First, shortly before their departure from their refuge in the Netherlands, the leader of this particular group of Separatists, John Robinson, had been persuaded of the validity of most of the Nonseparatist contentions. Second, in the New World the old issue that had divided them, whether or not the parish churches of England could in some way be viewed as true churches, was not of great significance, for they had to establish new churches of their own. Thus they became joint representatives of what was to be a single denomination. There were a few isolated individuals like Roger Williams, of course, who insisted that they should repudiate the Church of England in profession as well as in practice, but this counsel was rejected as politically inexpedient.

---

[13] Cotton Mather, *Magnalia*, I, 362. For an elaboration of the Separatist–Nonseparatist distinction, see Perry Miller, *Orthodoxy in Massachusetts*, 53–101.

Unlike other religious groups the Congregationalists in America were well supplied with ministers from the beginning, with no less than one hundred and thirty graduates of Cambridge and Oxford having come out to serve the churches prior to 1647. "Such a concentration of educated men in a new settlement in proportion to the population," it has been stated, "has never occurred before or since," and one of the first concerns of the early settlers was to make provision for the future supply of educated ministers. *New England's First Fruits* (1643) emphasized this point in its account of the founding of Harvard in 1636.

> After God had carried us safe to New England and we had builded our houses, provided necessaries for our livelihood, reared convenient places for God's worship, and settled the civil government; one of the next things we longed for and looked after was to advance learning and perpetuate it to posterity, dreading to leave an illiterate ministry to the churches when our present ministers shall lie in the dust.[14]

So successful were they in this endeavor that of the 1,586 ministers who served the Congregational churches of New England during the colonial period, only 79 were not college graduates.

Elementary education was of equal concern, it being "one chief project of that old deluder Satan to keep men from the knowledge of the Scriptures." [15] To counter this "project," a grammar school was established in every town. The consequence of this systematic effort, as Andrew Eliot informed Thomas Hollis in 1761, was that "scarce any are to be found among us, even in the obscurest parts, who are not able to read and write with tolerable propriety."

"The convenient places for God's worship" that were erected were called "meetinghouses" so that people would not be confused and make the mistake of thinking that the church was a building. These houses in which the church met were plain structures, often beautiful in their simplicity, with the people gathered about the table which stood at the center and with a high pulpit on one side for the reading and preaching of God's Word. The worship was equally plain, with the singing of psalms, a

---

[14] A portion of *New England's First Fruits* is printed in Smith, Handy, Loetscher, *American Christianity*, I, 123–26; and in *The Puritans*, ed. Miller and Johnson, II, 701–7.

[15] S. E. Morison, *The Puritan Pronaos: Studies in the Intellectual Life of New England in the Seventeenth Century* (N.Y., 1936), 65.

long prayer, the reading of Scripture, and a sermon being the principal features. The government of these churches was given its classic definition in the *Cambridge Platform* of 1648,[16] a document drafted and adopted in response to a "Remonstrance" which challenged the Congregational way of proceeding and threatened an appeal to the English Parliament if the restrictions upon church membership and voting were not liberalized. The same synod which framed the *Platform* also adopted as a statement of the Congregationalist doctrinal position the Confession of Faith which had just been issued in England by the Westminster Assembly of Divines, thus emphasizing their doctrinal solidarity with both the English and Scottish Presbyterians.

The *Cambridge Platform* had sidestepped one issue with regard to church membership which had begun to trouble the churches, and it proved to be an issue which could not long be ignored. According to Congregational theory both the believing adult and his infant child belonged to the church, the latter being "federally holy" and entitled to receive baptism. On reaching the age of discretion, however, the child was required to give an account of his own repentance and faith in order to qualify for full communicant standing, including the right to partake of the Lord's Supper and to vote at church meetings. It was understood that true faith, even among the weakest Christians, would be confirmed by some specific experience of God's redeeming grace, and that in the absence of such an experience a person was not to be admitted to full membership. This practice posed no problem until grandchildren began to be born whose parents were but "half-way" embraced within the covenant community and the question was raised as to whether their children were "federally" related to the church and qualified to receive baptism.

The controversy that ensued was heated, for whatever the decision, one of two equally cherished "goods" would be sacrificed. If baptism were denied to children of unregenerate parents, the integrity of the churches as gathered communities of convinced believers would be preserved but an increasing proportion of the population would be removed from the discipline of the church, and the endeavor to fashion a holy commonwealth in the American wilderness would be brought to naught. If baptism were granted, the churches would be in danger of becoming "mixed multitudes"

[16] A portion is reprinted in Smith, Handy, Loetscher, *American Christianity*, I, 128–40. The full text is in Walker, *Creeds and Platforms of Congregationalism*.

of the regenerate and unregenerate. Seventeen ministers from Massachusetts and Connecticut met in Boston in 1657 and announced that they were persuaded that the children of half-way convenanters should be baptized. Their action served only to inflame the opposition which was led by Charles Chauncy (1589–1672), president of Harvard. Finally the General Court of Massachusetts Bay intervened in 1662 and sought to end the controversy by summoning a synod of the churches to reach an authoritative decision. When the vote was taken after long debate, the earlier judgment of the seventeen ministers was sustained.

The decision of the synod opened the door to further laxity. Within little more than a decade, the restriction which kept unregenerate church members from partaking of the Lord's Supper began to break down. Solomon Stoddard (1643–1729), pastor of the church at Northampton, became the chief advocate of lowering the bar at this point. He insisted that the germ of grace is latent in all the children of the covenant and that it should be nourished by partaking of the Lord's Supper as soon as possible. To him it seemed contradictory that those who were in need of grace should be denied this means of grace because of their weakness in grace. His arguments were persuasive to many and his practice was widely adopted.

A further breach was effected in Boston toward the close of the century. The instigators were two Harvard tutors, William Brattle (1662–1717) and William Leverett (1662–1724), who insisted that all distinctions among church members should be discarded and that even those who could not testify to an experience of grace should be allowed to participate in the government of the church, including the right to vote in the selection of the minister. Without the consent of the other churches, they proceeded to organize a new church upon this basis.

The formation of the Brattle Street Church in 1699, which was followed by Increase Mather's ejection from the presidency of Harvard in 1701, stirred the conservatives to action. Their plan, embodied in the *Massachusetts Proposals* of 1705, was to bring the churches under a form of synodical control so that further innovation could be held in check. This proposal of the ministers received no support from the governor and council appointed under the new charter of 1691, for they were far from friendly to strict Congregationalism and were primarily responsible for Mather's discomfiture at Harvard. It received equally short shrift from many church members whose fear that their rights and privileges might thereby be lost was articulated by John Wise (1652–1725) of Ipswich in two tracts which later became part of the ideological arsenal of the American Revolution.[17]

Though defeated in Massachusetts, the conservative party was more successful in Connecticut where Yale College had been founded in 1701 with the aid of the Mathers as a counter to the lax influences emanating from Harvard. The *Saybrook Platform* of 1708 embodied all the essential features of the *Massachusetts Proposals*. It provided that the churches of each county were to be formed into a Consociation which was to have disciplinary oversight over them and from whose decision there was to be no appeal. These churches were further bound together by a General Association made up of delegates from each of the local Associations. The approval of the colonial authorities was secured by including the proviso that no church should be compelled to join the "united churches" or hindered, if allowed by the general laws of Connecticut, from exercising discipline in its own way.

As a result of the stabilizing influence exerted by Yale and the achievement of a measure of disciplinary oversight of the churches, Connecticut became the citadel of Congregational orthodoxy. Over the course of time, many of the Connecticut Congregationalists came to feel a greater sense of kinship with the Presbyterians than they did with their fellow Congregationalists of Massachusetts, who had been unable to complete their system with any connectional body, and thus pursued a more independent development.

THE PRESBYTERIANS.   The classic form of Presbyterianism, with its presbyteries, synods, and general assembly, took shape in Scotland where the Reformation had been carried forward under the leadership of John Knox, after his return from John Calvin's Geneva, and it did not differ greatly from the structures devised by the other Reformed churches on the Continent. Incipient presbyterian tendencies had long been present in English Puritanism, and they came to the fore when the Long Parliament met in 1640. One reason for the strength of the Presbyterian party that emerged at that time was the influence of the Scottish Commissioners. The

[17] *The Churches Quarrel Espoused* (1713) and *A Vindication of the Government of New England Churches* (1717). An excerpt from the latter tract is printed in Smith, Handy, Loetscher, *American Christianity*, I, 384–92; and in *The Puritans*, ed. Miller and Johnson, I, 257–69.

meeting of Parliament had been precipitated by a Scottish invasion which in turn had been occasioned by an attempt to impose "Laud's liturgy" upon the Scottish churches. The Scots supported Parliament in its controversy with the King but they insisted, as a condition of their support, that the Church of England be brought into conformity with the Church of Scotland so that the occasion for future strife might be avoided.

Presbyterian sentiment was constantly cropping out in early New England and gained strength from the course of events at home. Hingham and Newbury were two notable centers, and several Presbyterian churches were established by migrating New Englanders, first on Long Island, and then in New Jersey, Pennsylvania, Maryland, and South Carolina. Several of these churches were brought together to form the Presbytery of Philadelphia in 1706. Ten years later three additional presbyteries were organized and the Synod of Philadelphia was established with representatives from each of the four subsidiary presbyteries. Although there were scattered groups of Scotch-Irish in the colonies as early as the 1680's, the great influx of population from northern Ireland which contributed so greatly to Presbyterian strength did not begin until 1720. Those who settled in the backcountry of New England tended to be absorbed into the Congregational churches, but the major flow of Scotch-Irish was into the middle colonies and up the Shenandoah valley into the Piedmont region of the South, and these areas became the great centers of Presbyterian strength and influence.

Francis Makemie (1658?–1708), a Scotch-Irishman with strong ties to both England and New England, was the key figure in the early growth of American Presbyterianism. He was in effect a missionary-at-large, itinerating widely to gather churches and to supervise their work. He had been sent to the colonies in 1683 by the Presbytery of Laggan in Ireland, but after 1691 he served as the agent of the newly formed United Brethren (Congregationalists and Presbyterians) in London, receiving support from their General Fund. Although he was the leading spirit in the formation of the Presbytery of Philadelphia in 1706, he did not think in terms of denominational aggrandizement and he insisted that it was the height of folly to magnify the small differences that existed among Protestants.

In 1707 Makemie became one of the heroes of the struggle for religious freedom. He had been arrested by the governor of New York for unlicensed preaching, and he responded that "to give bond not to preach" was one thing he did not dare do. He appealed to the Boston ministers for help; they enlisted the aid of the United Brethren in London, and the case became a *cause célèbre*.[18] Makemie was acquitted after a brilliant defense but the governor forced him to pay the costs of his own prosecution, the rather considerable sum of £83/7s/6d. This injustice so incensed the colonial legislature that an act was passed prohibiting the assessment of such costs in the future. Charges were also brought against the governor, which led to his being recalled to London in disgrace.

Makemie died in 1708 and the subsequent history of the Presbyterians in colonial America was to be inextricably entangled in the story of the Great Awakening. This was true even of the Adopting Act of 1729 [19] by which the Synod of Philadelphia established the Westminster Confession of Faith as the doctrinal standard of American Presbyterianism, since freedom was given the presbyteries to distinguish between the essential and nonessential doctrines contained therein.

THE BAPTISTS.   The English Baptists were another offshoot of the Puritan movement. The Baptists were Congregationalists who had become convinced that if churches were to be composed of believers only, then baptism should be restricted to those who were able to give some account of their own faith. Prior to 1640 the Baptists in England were few in number. It was during the decade that followed that they became a significant and influential group, with their most notable strength being gained among the officers and men of Cromwell's army. Some of the Baptists—the General Baptists—were Arminian in theology, deriving their name from their adherence to the doctrine of a general atonement. What was destined to be the major Baptist body, however, was firmly rooted in the Calvinistic tradition which found its classic expression in the Westminster Confession of Faith.[20]

Baptist beginnings in America closely paralleled those of the Presbyterians. It was not the intention of the founders of New England to foster

---

[18] An account of Makemie's apprehension and examination is printed in *The Presbyterian Enterprise: Sources of American Presbyterian History*, ed. M. W. Armstrong, L. A. Loetscher and C. A. Anderson (Philadelphia, 1956), 13–18. For an account of colonial Presbyterianism, see L. J. Trinterud, *The Forming of an American Tradition*.

[19] Printed in *The Presbyterian Enterprise*, 30–32. See also Jonathan Dickinson's *Remarks* in Smith, Handy, Loetscher, *American Christianity*, I, 262–68.

[20] The several strands of Baptist life are discussed in *Baptist Concepts of the Church*, ed. W. S. Hudson (Philadelphia, 1959), 11–29.

dissent, but dissent there was from the start, and the considerations which had led some of the English Congregationalists to become Baptists were equally persuasive to some New Englanders. Henry Dunster (1609–59?), for example, rejected infant baptism in 1654 and was forced to resign as president of Harvard. The key figure initially, however, was Roger Williams who was instrumental in forming a Baptist church at Providence in 1639, three years after his ejection from Massachusetts. Williams soon abdicated his Baptist leadership, for he became convinced that all existing churches, including the newly established Providence church, lacked a proper foundation, a defect which could be remedied only by a new apostolic dispensation in which new apostles, authoritatively commissioned and divinely authenticated, would appear to re-establish the true church. A more important person in early Baptist history was John Clarke who had gathered a church at Newport, Rhode Island, in 1641. It was Clarke's *Ill News from New England* (1652) which gave notoriety to the case of Obadiah Holmes who was publicly whipped by the Massachusetts authorities for conducting unauthorized worship in Lynn.

While Rhode Island remained a center of Baptist activity and a Baptist church was organized in Boston as early as 1665, the major Baptist growth prior to the Great Awakening stemmed from the formation of the Philadelphia Baptist Association in 1707. This Association was founded almost simultaneously with the Presbytery of Philadelphia and was similar in character to the presbytery although it lacked the latter's "authoritative" judicial power. Initially the Association was composed of churches in New Jersey, Pennsylvania, and Delaware; later it also included churches in Connecticut, New York, Maryland, and Virginia; ultimately subsidiary Associations were formed in Massachusetts and Virginia, and a relationship was established with the Charleston Association in the Carolinas. The Association carried on vigorous missionary activity from Nova Scotia to Georgia, and established the College of Rhode Island (Brown University) as a training center for its ministers. The Philadelphia Confession of Faith of these American Baptists was a slightly emended version of the Westminster Confession of Faith, following the changes introduced by the Savoy Declaration (1658) of the English Congregationalists with an additional modification at the point of baptism.[21]

[21] The "Platform of Government" which the English Congregationalists had appended to the Savoy Declaration was incorporated in the body of the Confession by the Baptists.

While the growth of the Baptists was substantial during the first half of the eighteenth century, the large-scale accessions which made them one of the major religious groups in America occurred just prior to and during the American Revolution.

THE QUAKERS. The Society of Friends, as the Quakers are more properly termed, emerged in England around 1650 out of the turmoil and confusion of the religious controversies which had accompanied the English civil wars.[22] During these years many people had pursued what was in effect a spiritual pilgrimage from one group to another. In the end there were many who became completely disenchanted by the welter of competing claims and, like Roger Williams, became Seekers waiting for a new apostolic dispensation when the true Church would be restored. Others, whom Oliver Cromwell was to describe as "happy finders," believed that the new dispensation, in the form of a new age of the Spirit, had already arrived. It was from among these "happy finders" that George Fox gathered the people known as Quakers. They were a plain people—plain in dress, plain in speech, and plain in behavior. They gathered in silence for worship until one of their number was led by the Spirit to speak. Many of them became itinerant "publishers of truth," moving from place to place to declare that Christ had already returned to reign, that he was rising up as the "Christ within" in innumerable sons and daughters, and that the terrible day of the Lord was at hand when the whole creation would be purged of dross and corruption.

Few groups have exhibited the intense missionary zeal that characterized the early Quakers. In many ways they were a most attractive people of simple honesty and integrity, but in terms of their missionary activity they were frequently the most troublesome of people. It became customary for them to invade churches and to interrupt the sermon with denunciations of false worship and the folly of seeking God through empty forms and human inventions. A few felt themselves called by the Spirit to even more bizarre behavior, such as going naked through the streets of a town as a "sign." By 1700, however, the early excesses had disappeared and

---

[22] For the Puritan antecedents, see G. F. Nuttall, *The Holy Spirit in Puritan Faith and Experience* (Oxford, Eng., 1946). Two standard accounts of the Quakers are Howard Brinton, *Friends for 300 Years: The History and Beliefs of the Society of Friends* (N.Y., 1952), and Rufus M. Jones, *The Quakers in the American Colonies* (London, 1911). See also S. V. James, *A People among Peoples: Quaker Benevolence in Eighteenth Century America* (Cambridge, Mass., 1963), and F. B. Tolles, *Quakers and the Atlantic Culture* (N.Y., 1960).

45

Quakerism entered a period of "quietism." Henceforth they were to be the most restrained of people in their behavior and were to become increasingly esteemed for their humanitarian sympathies and concerns. John Woolman (1720–72) is the most famous representative of this latter tendency and the journal in which he tells of his itinerant ministry in bearing testimony against the slave trade is a moving testament of devotion.[23]

The first Quaker missionaries to reach the New World were two women, Mary Fisher and Ann Austin, who arrived in Boston in 1656 and were followed a few weeks later by eight additional publishers of truth. The following year Quaker missionaries made their appearance in New Amsterdam and Virginia. Everywhere, except in Rhode Island, they were harried with fines, imprisonment, and deportation. The most savage persecution occurred in Massachusetts where a law was enacted subjecting Quaker missionaries who returned to the colony, after once having been banished, to the death penalty. Four suffered martyrdom before Charles II intervened in 1661 and put an end to the executions.

Rhode Island and Long Island, where the followers of Anne Hutchinson had been embryonic Quakers for twenty years, quickly became centers of Quaker strength. By the time George Fox and his twelve companions arrived for a missionary tour in 1672 persecution had practically ceased and Quaker "meetings" were to be found in every colony from New Hampshire to South Carolina. Two years later, when West (New) Jersey came under the control of Quaker proprietors, the flow of Quaker settlers to the New World set in, and the number of Quaker immigrants swelled to a great tide after Pennsylvania was established as a Quaker domain in 1681. As a result of the earlier missionary activity and the later migration, the Quakers ranked fifth numerically among the various religious bodies at the close of the colonial period and were one of the most widely dispersed of all the denominations.

As the number of Quakers increased, zeal tended to diminish. The passage of time and growing prosperity took their inevitable toll. In 1764 an aged Quaker minister summarized the decline that had taken place over the past sixty years. He well remembered, he declared, that in the early days

[23] *The Journal of John Woolman* (Chicago, 1950).

Friends were a plain lowly minded people and that there was much tenderness and contrition in their meetings; and that at the end of twenty years from that time, the Society increasing in wealth and in some degree conforming to the fashions of the world, true humility decreased and their meetings in general were not so lively and edifying; that at the end of forty years many of the Society were grown rich, that wearing of fine costly garments and with fashionable furniture, silver watches became customary with many and with their sons and daughters, and as these things prevailed in the Society and appeared in our meetings of ministers and elders so the powerful overshadowings of the Holy Spirit were less manifested amongst us . . . and that the weakness amongst us in not living up to our principles and supporting the testimony of truth in faithfulness was matter of much sorrow.[24]

With the passing of the first generation, there were many who were Quakers by birth rather than conviction. This tendency was both accelerated and sanctioned by the action of the London Yearly Meeting in 1737 which permitted "the wife and children to be deemed members of the Monthly Meeting of which the husband or father is a member, not only during his life but after his decease." Thus the Quakers with their "birthright membership" were pursuing much the same path as the New England Congregationalists with their progressive lowering of the bars to church membership after the adoption of the Half-way Covenant.

THE ROMAN CATHOLICS. Of all the churches which took definitive shape at the time of the Reformation, the Roman Catholic Church was by far the largest. As certain elements in the pre-Reformation church had been made normative for Lutherans by the Augsburg Confession and the Formula of Concord, so other elements were made normative for Roman Catholics by the decrees of the Council of Trent (1545–63). In spite of their predominance in many parts of Europe, the Roman Catholics were a small minority in England. Although their faith was proscribed by law, few Roman Catholics found the hard conditions of life in America an attractive prospect. In England they were mostly landed gentry and they had friends at Court to offer them protection. Consequently, enjoying at least modest comfort and relative security, these English Roman Catholics did not bulk large in the colonizing activity of their compatriots. Since there was to be

[24] F. B. Tolles, *Meeting House and Counting House* (Chapel Hill, N.C., 1948), 123–24.

no significant Roman Catholic immigration from the Continent until after the American Revolution, the Roman Catholic population in the colonies was largely limited to Maryland where the proprietor had granted large manors to his Catholic friends. There were a few Roman Catholics in New York and a larger number in Pennsylvania, but elsewhere only isolated individuals were to be found.[25]

When the *Ark* sailed from England late in 1633 with the first contingent of settlers for Maryland, it stopped briefly at the Isle of Wight to pick up two Jesuit priests, Fathers Andrew White (1579–1656) and John Altham (1589–1640), who were to distinguish themselves in the new colony by their earnest pastoral care and by their missionary activity among the Indians. Later they became involved in controversy with the proprietor because of their zeal in attempting to proselyte among non-Catholics and because of their purchase of land directly from the Indians. In different ways both of these proceedings appeared to threaten Lord Baltimore's authority, and when he carried the issue to Rome they were ordered to yield to his demands. The resolution of the controversy was hastened by the arrival of two secular priests in 1642 to replace the dissident Jesuits. In 1669 the proprietor complained that only two priests remained in the colony, and as a result two Franciscans were sent out in 1673 and were joined four years later by three additional Franciscans and three more Jesuits. Within a few years Catholic families were moving northward into Pennsylvania, and in 1706 the Jesuits opened a mission near the border of Pennsylvania and for a brief period conducted a school there. This school was apparently the only Catholic educational venture until the founding of Georgetown Academy in 1791.

Denominations of Continental origin

With the exception of a half-million Negro slaves who had little opportunity to develop any independent religious life, there were only three nationality groups of measurable size at the end of the colonial period that were of non-British stock. These were the Germans, representing roughly 8.7 per cent of the white population; the Dutch, 3.3 per cent; and the French, 1.7 per cent.[26] Of these, the Dutch and the French were the earliest arrivals, with most of the latter initially being French-speaking

[25] For a brief account of Roman Catholicism in colonial America, see John Tracy Ellis, *American Catholicism* (Chicago, 1956), 1–39.

[26] W. L. Sperry, *Religion in America* (N.Y., 1946), 266–70.

Walloons. Practically all these people, whether Dutch, French, or German, were of Protestant background.

THE DUTCH AND FRENCH REFORMED. Reformed Protestantism had no single outstanding early leader. It had its origin as a distinct movement within the pre-Reformation church in the reforming activity of such men as Huldreich Zwingli, Henry Bullinger, Martin Bucer, and William Farel. Later John Calvin emerged as the most influential of the Reformed theologians, and his *Institutes of the Christian Religion* became the most representative statement of the Reformed understanding of the Christian faith. Almost everywhere the Reformed churches had to struggle for existence, and in the face of unrelenting persecution they stressed the sovereignty of God and man's duty to glorify him by full and unyielding obedience.

The efforts to suppress the Reformed church in France led to a series of inconclusive Wars of Religion between 1562 and 1593. A resolution of the conflict was effected when Henry of Navarre, the Protestant, or Huguenot, leader, succeeded to the throne, declared himself a Catholic, and in 1598 issued the Edict of Nantes guaranteeing freedom of worship to the Protestants. During the same period, the Dutch were struggling to free themselves from the rule of Spain, a struggle that was intensified by the religious issue as a result of the Spanish attempt to stamp out Dutch Protestantism. The armed revolt which broke out in 1566 culminated in a declaration of independence by the five northern provinces at Utrecht in 1581, and by 1609 the Dutch had made good their claim to independence.

With the energies released by their struggle for independence, the Dutch became the great trading power of Europe with the largest and most efficient merchant marine in the world. Dutch traders were everywhere, reaching Java as early as 1595. Within the next few decades they had driven the Portuguese out of most of their trading posts in the Far East, had conquered Brazil, and had occupied several islands in the West Indies. Their attention had been called to the possibilities of the fur trade in North America by the pioneering voyages of Henry Hudson, and in the same year that they gained control of Brazil they established a trading-post at the present site of Albany on the Hudson River. Two years later, in 1626, another trading-post—New Amsterdam—was established on the tip of Manhattan Island.

Peter Minuit, the first Director of New Netherlands, had been a ruling elder of the French Reformed church at Wesel, and he brought with him in 1626 two "comforters of the sick" to minister to the religious needs of the infant settlement. In 1628 the first minister, Jonas Michaelius, arrived and immediately organized a church. Michaelius reported that there were "fifty communicants, Walloons and Dutch," at the first administration of the Lord's Supper, it being observed with "great joy and comfort to many." Since few of the Walloons and others from French-speaking areas could not understand Dutch, Michaelius thought it unnecessary to have weekly services for them in their own tongue. Every four months, however, he did administer the Lord's Supper "in the French language and according to the French mode." On these occasions he read his sermon because, as he explained, he was not sufficiently fluent in French to speak extemporaneously. When Michaelius returned to Holland in 1632 he brought charges of incompetence and irregularity against the Director with the result that both men were replaced.

New Amsterdam was a typical sailors' town. Many of the inhabitants were rough and boisterous, and the lot of the early ministers was far from easy. It was not until Peter Stuyvesant became the Director of the colony in 1647 that they received any real support from the governing authority. Stuyvesant, the son and son-in-law of Dutch Reformed ministers, was a zealous churchman and a strict disciplinarian. He restricted the sale of liquor, ordered strict observance of the Sabbath, decreed that there should be preaching in the afternoon as well as in the morning on the Sabbath, and required all persons to attend the services of the church. Stuyvesant's zeal included an attempt to impose a rigid religious uniformity upon the colony, but his treatment of Lutherans, Quakers, and Jews earned him a stern rebuke and he was ordered to leave any dissenter "unmolested as long as he is modest, moderate, [and] his political conduct irreproachable."

By the time the colony was surrendered to the English in 1664, there were eleven Dutch Reformed churches in the colony which included settlements in what was to be New Jersey. Although the shift to English control involved problems of readjustment, the Dutch Reformed churches continued to grow with the natural increase in the Dutch population; and it has been estimated that there were one hundred and twenty Dutch Reformed congregations at the time of the Declaration of Independence.

For at least two decades prior to the revocation of the Edict of Nantes in 1685, the increasing pressures which were brought to bear upon them led many Huguenots to leave France and seek refuge in other European countries. Some of them made their way to America, with the largest number settling in New York and South Carolina. Several of the Dutch Reformed ministers had made it a practice to preach in French, and the French Reformed in New York had generally become members of the Dutch churches. In 1683, however, the French Reformed in New York secured a pastor of their own, and congregations also were formed at New Rochelle and New Paltz. By the end of the century there were five or six French Reformed churches in the vicinity of New York City. Another church had been formed in Boston, at least one in Virginia, and several in South Carolina. The tendency everywhere was for the Huguenots to disperse and to become denationalized, due partly perhaps to an eagerness to forget the language and customs of the native land that had subjected them to such relentless persecution. In the South they tended to become Anglicans. In New York they were absorbed by the Dutch Reformed; the "French church" at New Paltz, for example, kept its records in Dutch after the first fifty years of its existence.

MENNONITES, DUNKERS, AND MORAVIANS. Pennsylvania was the great center of German immigration to the colonies, for William Penn's efforts to recruit settlers found an eager response among the inhabitants of the Palatinate (an area between the upper Rhine and France) which had been repeatedly ravaged and devastated by the armies of Louis XIV. This eager response was movingly expressed in a letter, dated February 6, 1681, from a father in Heilbron to his son who had been among the first to arrive in the new colony.

> Dear Son:—Your letter from far away America . . . gave us great joy. . . . America, according to your writing, must be a beautiful land. . . .
>
> Dear Henry, since you have been away from us conditions in South Germany have become very much worse. The French have wrought much devastation . . . , and besides we now suffer from the plague of high taxes. Thousands would gladly leave the Fatherland if they had the means to do so.
>
> A merchant from Frankfort was with us last week and informed us how along the Rhine a number of families have banded together to

accept the invitation of an Englishman named William Penn, who had recently visited that community, to settle in that beautiful land and there establish new homes.

After I had received this information I went at once to our minister, whose parents live at Worms on the Rhine, and begged him earnestly to learn what truth there was in these reports and to find out, if possible, if there would be any opportunity for us to join them. . . . He then informed me that these reports were all true. . . .

It is the good providence of God that has shown these burdened people so glorious a land. We . . . are only waiting for a good opportunity when the dear Lord will bring us to you. Your brother Peter is learning shoemaking and will soon be free. America is the only dream of Elizabeth. Catharine, only six years old, asks us daily, "Will we soon be going to our brother in America?" [27]

While a half dozen different religious groups were to be represented in the German migration to Pennsylvania, the family at Heilbron were Mennonites, an Anabaptist group which took its name from Menno Simons (1492–1559).[28]

Of all the Reformation groups none had been subjected to more bitter persecution than the Anabaptists. They were earnest people, deeply devout, who rejected infant baptism and sought to practice full obedience to the commands of Christ, refusing among other things to take oaths, hold public office, or bear arms. They had managed to survive in small scattered communities throughout the Rhineland from Rotterdam to the valleys of Switzerland. The earliest Mennonite group to arrive in Pennsylvania came from Krefeld in 1683. Most of this initial contingent had been won to Quaker views prior to their departure, and separate Mennonite worship was not established until 1690. The Swiss Mennonites who began arriving around 1710 settled in what is now Lancaster County and this became the principal Mennonite center. Each Mennonite congregation conducted its own affairs, frequently choosing its officers—a bishop, elders, and deacons—by lot. Consequently they were seldom troubled by lack of ministerial leadership and they never needed to await the arrival of a minister in order to organize their church life

The Dunkers (Church of the Brethren) in many ways were not

[27] Smith, Handy, Loetscher, *American Christianity*, I, 183.
[28] See C. Henry Smith, *The Mennonites of America*, 4th ed., rev. by Cornelius Krahn (Newton, Kan., 1957); George H. Williams, *The Radical Reformation* (Philadelphia, 1962); and Franklin H. Littell, *The Anabaptist View of the Church* (Boston, 1958).

unlike the Mennonites. They also were a "plain" people who sought to live in strict obedience to New Testament precepts. Their founder was Alexander Mack, a man of some means who had come under Pietistic influences after reacting against the spiritual lethargy of the German Reformed church in which he had been reared. At Schwarzenau in Hesse-Kassel in 1708 he formed into a church the little group he had gathered for Bible study, and other congregations were soon formed in neighboring provinces. Unlike the Mennonites, many of whose practices they adopted, the Dunkers baptized by a threefold immersion rather than by pouring. It was this practice that gave them their popular name. Their worship centered in the Lord's Supper, which was preceded by a "love feast" and the washing of feet, and was concluded with the "holy kiss of charity" and the "right hand of fellowship." The Dunker migration to America was initiated in 1719 by the congregation at Krefeld, and four years later their first church in America was formed at Germantown.

The Schwenkfelders were a much smaller group than either the Mennonites or the Dunkers, and they differed from the larger groups in that they looked to the Holy Spirit rather than to the "letter" of Scripture for guidance. They stemmed from one of Martin Luther's fellow reformers, Caspar Schwenkfeld, who anticipated George Fox's emphasis upon the authority of the "Christ within." Condemned as a heretic, Schwenkfeld managed to gather a small following and for almost a century these hunted people were able to maintain a precarious existence in southern Germany. When the Emperor Charles VI undertook their final extermination in 1720, some of them found refuge on the estates of a Saxon nobleman, Nicholas Ludwig, Count von Zinzendorf (1700–60). From there they made their way in 1734 to Pennsylvania.

Zinzendorf was the key figure in the story of the Moravians. He was a Lutheran who early in life had come under the influence of Pietism, a movement which, in reaction to the seeming lifelessness of Lutheran and Reformed orthodoxy, stressed the importance of religious experience and the practical aspects of the devotional life.[29] Its most characteristic feature

[29] Pietism stemmed from the activities of Philipp J. Spener (1635–1705) and August H. Francke (1663–1727). The former gathered small groups for Bible study, prayer, and discussion of the Sunday sermon in his home at Frankfort. The latter developed a similar ministry among students at the University of Leipzig. The founding of the University of Halle in 1691 by the Elector of Brandenburg provided them with a center for the dissemination of their views.

was the gathering of earnest Christians in small groups to study the Bible, sing hymns, and engage in prayer. The Pietists were not hostile to the churches and they were far from heterodox, but they found theological discussion distasteful and regarded it as a source of division and strife among Christians. Christianity was a life, they insisted, not a creed. Thus the Pietists tended to sit rather loosely to their confessional traditions, to emphasize the common experience of Christ which bound all Christians together, and to be characterized by a strong missionary fervor. It was this spirit that Zinzendorf imbibed and it led him to welcome to his estates any refugees among whom he espied any signs of true piety.

The Moravians, or the Unitas Fratrum, had their origin in the evangelical movement which sprang from the preaching of John Hus of Prague in the fifteenth century.[30] They had been buffeted by persecution for more than two centuries when Zinzendorf offered them asylum in 1722. Zinzendorf, together with other Lutheran Pietists whom he had gathered about him, soon became deeply involved in the activities of the Moravian community. He gradually emerged as their leader and was consecrated Bishop in 1737. Under his leadership the Moravians launched a far-flung missionary campaign which had several objectives—the conversion of the heathen, the renewal of spiritual life among nominal Christians, and the reuniting of all Christian groups in a single spiritual communion. An early project had been the establishment of a Moravian settlement in Georgia in 1735 where some missionary work was carried on among the Indians and Negroes. Their refusal to bear arms, however, aroused the opposition of the colonial authorities and in 1740 the Moravians shifted their settlement to Pennsylvania where they established the towns of Nazareth and Bethlehem.

In the meantime Zinzendorf, having been charged with harboring religious fanatics and promoting views contrary to accepted Lutheran standards, had been banished in 1738 from his estates. He utilized his banishment as an opportunity to embark on a missionary tour which brought him to Pennsylvania in 1741. His immediate objective was to draw together the various German Protestant denominations in Pennsylvania to form what he called "the Church of God in the Spirit." His intention was to create spiritual ties among them by an acknowledgment of

[30] See Edward Langton, *History of the Moravian Church* (London, 1956), and J. R. Weinlick, *Count Zinzendorf* (N.Y., 1956).

agreement in "essentials," but this intention was misunderstood and the project interpreted as a scheme to subordinate all the churches to Moravian control and direction. As a result the seven consultations which were held with representatives of the different denominations ended in failure. During the remaining months of his stay, Zinzendorf busied himself in establishing contact with the Indians and in organizing churches and schools at scattered points in Pennsylvania and New York. For a brief time he served as pastor of the Lutheran congregation in Philadelphia. Before his departure in 1743 he made arrangements for the orderly supervision of both the itinerant preachers and the rapidly expanding missionary activity among the Indians. In 1753 a tract of land was secured in North Carolina and this became another major Moravian center.

THE GERMAN LUTHERANS AND THE GERMAN REFORMED. The economic havoc wrought by Louis XIV's repeated spoliation of the Palatinate which had spurred the emigration of the small religious minorities was equally effective in prompting other inhabitants of the region to respond to William Penn's promotional efforts to recruit settlers for his new colony. There had been Germans of Reformed background in New Netherlands and a Dutch Lutheran congregation had been formed there. There were also Swedish Lutherans who remained in America after the short-lived Swedish colony on the Delaware was taken over by the Dutch. The Lutherans and the German Reformed, however, derived their major strength from the flow of Palatine Germans into Pennsylvania.

Organized church life among the German Lutherans and German Reformed was not effected immediately for several reasons. For one thing, they migrated as individuals and not as religious communities. They generally had no financial resources of their own and they had no group to help provide the expense of travel. Many of them came as "redemptioners," given free passage by shipowners who recouped themselves financially by selling their passengers for a term of service as indentured servants. Others were assisted by the English government which recognized the need for settlers but had placed restrictions upon the emigration of English subjects lest the homeland should be impoverished. Most of these Germans had no strong religious interest, and neither the Reformed nor the Lutherans had a tradition of lay initiative in church affairs. Consequently their adherents tended to be dependent upon outside help for leadership in the formation of churches.

55

Although a Swedish Lutheran church had been formed in 1639 and the Dutch Lutheran church in New Amsterdam had secured a minister as early as 1658, the first German Lutheran church was not organized until 1703. This was the church at New Hanover, Pennsylvania, and it was established under the leadership of Daniel Falckner (1666–1741?). In the same year his brother, Justus Falckner (1672–1723), became pastor of the Dutch Lutheran church in New York where the growing German population became the primary concern of his pastoral labors. These were small beginnings and further work among the Germans who were swarming into Pennsylvania was long delayed. Another minister, Anthony Jacob Henke, arrived in 1717 and John Casper Stover and his son in 1728. The latter worked mostly as an itinerant missionary following the German population into Maryland and Virginia. There were a few other early ministers but a decisive change did not occur until the arrival of Henry Melchior Muhlenberg in 1742.

Muhlenberg was sent to America by the Pietists at Halle in response to a plea for help which had been made much earlier by the Lutherans of Philadelphia. The failure to respond immediately had been occasioned by the unwillingness of the American congregations to commit themselves to a definite salary, but when news of Zinzendorf's activities reached Halle the debate as to salary ceased and Muhlenberg set out without further delay. When he arrived he found the people badly divided. Some had been drawn away by Zinzendorf, while others had come under the influence of a minister of dubious character, Johann Valentin Kraft. Within six weeks Muhlenberg had mastered the situation and was installed as pastor of the Philadelphia Lutherans. He soon took additional churches under his care, and ultimately seven churches looked to him for pastoral leadership. Whenever possible he responded to calls for help from more distant places and frequently was asked to arbitrate church quarrels. The regular reports which he sent to Halle stimulated further interest in his work and brought reinforcements in both men and money. Muhlenberg's most important achievement was the forming of the Ministerium of Pennsylvania in 1748. This was the first permanent Lutheran Synod in America, and its influence became decisive in the developing life of the churches.

While most of the Lutheran population in the colonies stemmed from the influx of Germans into Pennsylvania, being largely a dispersion from this center, the Salzburg Lutherans in Georgia were the product of an independent odyssey. They had been driven from their homes in Austria in

1731 by the Roman Catholic archbishop of Salzburg. Fourteen thousand of them in the dead of winter made the long trek to Prussia where they had been promised refuge. Accounts of their sufferings aroused interest in England and provision was made to send some of them to Georgia, where they arrived in four contingents between 1734 and 1741. The first group was accompanied by two ministers who had been trained at Halle, and they had a vigorous church life from the beginning.

The plight of the German Reformed in America was much the same as that of the Lutherans. They also came without pastors and with meager economic resources. The first churches to be formed among them were an exception to the general rule of waiting until a minister appeared on the scene. John Philip Boehm (1683–1749) had settled in Pennsylvania in 1720 as a farmer. He was the son of a Reformed minister at Frankfort-on-the-Main and he had taught school for a period of twelve years. Almost immediately after his arrival his neighbors persuaded him to conduct religious services for them. Five years later the three informal congregations he had gathered pressed him to assume the pastoral office. With some reluctance he agreed to do so, although he was not ordained. When a German Reformed minister, George Michael Weiss, arrived two years later, he was scandalized by Boehm's action, challenged his right to assume ministerial prerogatives, and attempted to take over his congregations. The people rallied to Boehm's support, appealed to the Dutch Reformed ministers in New York for advice, and were referred by them to the Classis of Amsterdam for a decision. In due time an answer was received which approved Boehm's emergency assumption of pastoral duties but advised him to seek ordination. As a result he was ordained by the Dutch Reformed ministers of New York on November 23, 1729. Weiss was present at the ordination and afterward the two worked together in complete harmony.

Although several German Reformed ministers came to America in the next two decades, most of the people of German Reformed background were without either ministers or churches. Their numbers were rapidly increasing, being augmented by an influx of settlers from Switzerland, and they were becoming widely dispersed in the backcountry of most of the colonies. The appeal to the Classis of Amsterdam had enlisted the interest of the Synods of Holland in the plight of the German immigrants, and a committee of the Synods was appointed to send aid—money, Bibles, and medicines—to the German Reformed congregations in America. In 1746

Michael Schlatter (1716–90), a Swiss who had been educated and ordained in the Netherlands, was sent to Pennsylvania as the representative of the Dutch Synods with instructions to visit the existing congregations, to form new ones where needed, and to bring them together as soon as possible in a presbytery, or "coetus," subject to the Synods of Holland. He immediately made a tour of the churches and discovered that in Pennsylvania there were four ordained men to care for an estimated German Reformed population of fifteen thousand. Within a year he had organized the "coetus," and in 1751 he returned to Europe to plead the cause of the German Reformed churches. When he returned the following year, he brought with him six young ministers, seven hundred Bibles, and the promise of an annual subsidy of two thousand gulden from the states of Holland and West Friesland.

THE JEWS. With the exception of such transient groups as the Sandemanians, Rogerenes, and the Ephrata community, the Jews were the smallest of the religious minorities in colonial America.[31] Twenty-three Jews, fleeing from Brazil when the Portuguese regained control from the Dutch, arrived in New Amsterdam in 1654. Most of them failed to remain but those who did were not permitted to maintain public worship until after the end of Dutch control. Their number gradually increased and by 1695 they were worshiping in a rented room. Thirty-five years later, in 1730, a synagogue was built and dedicated. There were isolated Jews in New England as early as 1649 and a community was gathered in Newport, Rhode Island, about 1658. This early congregation had disappeared by 1690 and was not revived until about 1750. The beautiful synagogue which still survives in Newport was erected in 1763. Apart from these two centers, the only other congregations in America prior to the American Revolution were at Savannah (1733), Philadelphia (1747), and Charleston, South Carolina (1749).

This account of denominational beginnings in America can be misleading. While there was a profusion of religious groups, most of the people belonged to no church at all. It was not until the Great Awakening, when America experienced its "national conversion,"[32] that this situation began to change.

[31] See Jacob R. Marcus, *Early American Jewry*, 2 vols (Philadelphia, 1951–53).
[32] The term is supplied and explicated by H. Richard Niebuhr, *The Kingdom of God in America* (N.Y., 1959), 126.

III

The Great Awakening

The Great Awakening, which was to exert a decisive and far-reaching influence upon the development of American religious life, was but one manifestation of a general spiritual quickening during the eighteenth century. There were scattered "awakenings" of new religious life in England, Scotland, and Wales, as well as in America, and the Pietist movement on the Continent was a parallel phenomenon. These several awakenings quickly reinforced each other and initiated the great tide of evangelical religion which swept through the English-speaking world, reaching a crest of influence in the latter half of the nineteenth century before it began to ebb away. Churches of all denominations were caught up in the surge of religious fervor and were profoundly affected by its impact. A new type of preaching dominated the pulpits, the structure of public worship was altered, and the "revival" became the most widely accepted means of introducing people to the Christian life.

Although the immediate effect of the Awakening was to arouse opposition, split congregations, set minister against minister, and divide most of the denominations, the opposition in the end was almost every-where overwhelmed and the ultimate consequence was to mold the various denominations to a common pattern, to subordinate differences, and to make possible wide-ranging cooperative endeavors. Above all, this surging tide of evangelical religion supplied the dynamic which emboldened the Protestant churches of America to undertake the enormous task of Christianizing a continent, nerved those of the British Isles to assume a similar responsibility for an expanding population at home and overseas, and led both the British and the American churches to join forces in a vast mission to the entire non-Christian world.

Why the spark provided by any one of the local quickenings should suddenly have ignited a general conflagration is something of a mystery. The earlier drive and enthusiasm of the Puritan movement, which sprang from a transforming experience of God's grace and a consequent dedica-tion to warfare against sin, had long since lost much of its force.[1] For some the consciousness of entering the Christian life through a "new birth" had been replaced by an insistence upon mere assent to orthodox beliefs as the foundation of the Christian life. Others stressed the reasonable character of the "grand essentials" of all religion and emphasized moral behavior as the distinguishing mark of the Christian. At best the successors of the Puritans tended to appeal to the head without captivating the heart; at worst they promoted a spirit of rationalism (an attempt to validate the Christian faith by human reason) that frequently ended in indifference. There were, of course, exceptions to this general characterization. When Jonathan Edwards spoke of "the time of extraordinary dullness in reli-gion" which preceded the outbreak of the revival in Northampton, Massachusetts, he was but echoing the lament that had been voiced by many of the New England clergy for the better part of a century. And from time to time there had been local awakenings—even in Northampton under the preaching of Solomon Stoddard—when consciences would be touched, faith awakened, and people brought into the churches in unusual numbers. But no general revival had occurred.

Nor is the suggestion that the revivals were the product of the unsettled conditions of frontier life an adequate explanation of a phenome-non that was equally widespread in both Britain and America. Further-

---

[1] For the definition of Puritanism as a "revival" and its relationship to Evangeli-calism, see Alan Simpson, *Puritanism in Old and New England*, 103–10.

more, the communities along the Connecticut River and between New York and Philadelphia, where the revivals first appeared, were centers of an established agrarian economy rather than frontier settlements. Even after revivalism became an accepted feature of American religious life, revivals seldom occurred in an area until the frontier period was over; and they manifested themselves with equal power in many of the oldest communities.[2]

It is true that the revivals were initially welcomed and later eagerly promoted as an answer to the problem posed by the fact that a large part of the population, in both England and America, stood outside the churches altogether. In England the parish system, which through custom and tradition provided the possibility of long-term nurture and instruction in the Christian faith, had broken down.[3] And in America, with the possible exception of New England, the parish system had never been successfully established. Even in New England the loss of the charter in Massachusetts had made it clear that little confidence could be placed in external guarantees that were designed to ensure that at least the outward formalities of religion would continue to be observed. Thus the churches were confronted by a clear-cut summons to missionary endeavor. Given the circumstances that prevailed, the time was ripe for a type of preaching that would prick the conscience, convict men of sin, and lead them through the agony of repentance into a personally apprehended experience of the new life that was to be found in Christ. The mystery nonetheless remains, for such preaching had never completely disappeared. The novelty of the Awakening was the widespread response it suddenly elicited, a response so unexpected that it surprised even those who sought it.

The first stirrings of revival

The Great Awakening in America had its antecedents in local revivals which developed among the Dutch Reformed churches of northern New Jersey under the leadership of Theodore J. Frelinghuysen (1691–1748?); among the Presbyterian churches of the same general

[2] The appearance of revivals in postfrontier areas is documented in the illuminating study of Whitney R. Cross, *The Burned-over District: the Social and Intellectual History of Enthusiastic Religion in Western New York, 1800–1850* (Ithaca, N.Y., 1950), 75–76.

[3] For the significance of unaltered parish boundaries in relationship to England's shifting population, see Winthrop S. Hudson, *The Great Tradition of the American Churches* (N.Y., 1963), 99–100.

area under the leadership of the Tennents, father and sons; and in Northampton and other communities of the Connecticut valley under the leadership of Jonathan Edwards. Although these local revivals were not to be consolidated into one great movement until George Whitefield (1714–70) arrived on the scene, they provided a foretaste of what was to come and did much to shape the subsequent outburst of religious fervor and activity.

THEODORE J. FRELINGHUYSEN. The "beginner of the great work" [4] in America was a German born near the Dutch border, educated under Dutch auspices, ordained to the ministry of the Dutch Reformed church, and sent to America in 1719 to become the pastor of four Dutch Reformed churches in the Raritan valley of New Jersey. Although he has sometimes been described as a German Pietist, his real affinities and affiliation were with a group of Dutch Calvinists who had been deeply influenced by the experiential piety of the English Puritans.[5]

When Frelinghuysen assumed his new responsibilities, he discovered, much to his dismay, that most of his parishioners were content with a perfunctory orthodoxy which had become for them more a symbol of their Dutch nationality than an expression of any deep-seated Christian conviction. He immediately embarked on a program of reform, seeking to rouse them from their lethargy by a strict enforcement of the provisions of the Reformed discipline with regard to admission to the Lord's Supper, by personal conferences in their homes, and above all by pointed evangelistic preaching which sought to induce the members of his congregations to take seriously the understanding of the Christian faith they ostensibly professed.[6] Perhaps the emotional response he evoked was partially due to the vigor of the opposition he aroused. Many were scandalized by his bluntness, and his congregations were disrupted and thrown into turmoil. The cause of the disaffected was championed by the Dutch ministers of New York, one of whom visited them in their homes to encourage their opposition. Frelinghuysen, however, refused to be daunted and conversions became so frequent in the heated atmosphere that opposition within

[4] The phrase is Whitefield's; quoted by L. J. Trinterud, *The Forming of an American Tradition*, 34.

[5] The absence of any trace of Pietist influence is discussed by Trinterud, *op. cit.* 54–57.

[6] His program of reform is illustrated in a sermon, a portion of which is printed in Smith, Handy, Loetscher, *American Christianity*, I, 316–21.

his own congregations was silenced. By 1726 the revival was at its height, had begun to spread to other Dutch communities, and within the next few years Frelinghuysen was to gain the support of the majority of the Dutch ministers. Nevertheless the rift between the two parties persisted and was not healed for several decades.

THE TENNENTS. William Tennent (1673–1746) and his sons were the key figures in the outbreak of the revival among the Presbyterians. A graduate of the University of Edinburgh and an unusually able teacher and scholar, the father followed Irish precedent in giving his sons their theological training in his own home while he was a pastor at Bedford, New York, from 1720 to 1727. Gilbert Tennent (1703–64), his eldest son, received a Master's degree from Yale in 1725, perhaps in partial compensation for his father's disappointment in not being named to succeed Timothy Cutler as president of that institution. Two years later, the father moved to Neshaminy, Pennsylvania, where he established an embryo college of his own. Deeply indebted to the Puritan devotional classics for his own understanding of the Christian faith, the elder Tennent succeeded in transmitting his earnest concern for a vital inward faith both to his sons and to the graduates of his "log college" at Neshaminy.

The chronology of the awakening among the Presbyterians is somewhat obscure, for Gilbert Tennent reports that his brother John had the first actual revival.[7] This must have been sometime in 1727 or 1728 when he was serving as a licentiate in the Presbytery of New Castle. Later, when John Tennent was pastor at Freehold, New Jersey (1730–32), another revival occurred which was carried forward after John's death by his brother William, Jr. Gilbert Tennent, however, was the most important of the brothers. He was the outstanding preacher and the natural leader of the men his father had trained.

In 1726 Gilbert Tennent had been called to the Presbyterian church at New Brunswick, New Jersey, where the revival among the Dutch Reformed was at its height. He and Frelinghuysen immediately recognized each other as kindred spirits, for the views of both men had been shaped by the characteristic emphases of evangelical Puritanism. Tennent's ministry, by his own account, was not conspicuously successful at first, but Frelinghuysen encouraged him and Frelinghuysen's success served both as

---

[7] Trinterud, op. cit., 58–59. This account of the Tennents is largely based on the careful and thorough research of Trinterud.

a rebuke and as an inspiration. After a period of sickness, during which he was "exceedingly grieved" that he had "done so little for God" and had vowed to "promote his kingdom" with all his might if God would be pleased to spare him for this purpose, Tennent began to secure the response his father had taught him to seek.

The nub of the problem, as Tennent defined it, was what he called the "presumptuous security" of those who professed to be Christians. They had been baptized, catechized, and inducted into full membership in the church. They affirmed orthodox doctrines and were fully persuaded that one is saved by faith and not by works. But faith was interpreted as merely assent to orthodox ideas and was quite unrelated to most of the Christian graces. There was little of the inwardness and transforming power of the Christian faith to be found among them. To counter this smugness and complacency Tennent adopted the old Puritan technique of preaching for "conviction"—an acknowledgment or conviction of one's own sinful estate. He insisted that no one ever became a Christian without first being subjected to the terrifying realization that he is not a Christian. He must first know himself as a sinful creature, estranged from God, and rightfully subject to condemnation, before he can apprehend and receive God's forgiveness and acceptance.

Tennent's preaching had the desired effect and by 1729 scattered Presbyterian congregations from New Brunswick to Staten Island had begun to throb with new life under his leadership. Other products of his father's tuition, notably Samuel Blair (1712–51), were equally active. The participation of Presbyterian ministers of New England background, such as Jonathan Dickinson (1688–1747) at Elizabeth and Aaron Burr (1716–57) at Newark, was also enlisted. By the end of the 1730's there had been eight or ten local revivals of some degree of intensity. In the meantime Gilbert Tennent was gaining a wider hearing through the publication in 1735 of three of his sermons in New York and one in Boston. Earlier in the same year two sermons by John Tennent with an account of the revival at Freehold had also been published in Boston.

JONATHAN EDWARDS. The third manifestation of religious excitement occurred in the Connecticut valley with Jonathan Edwards playing the central role. Edwards, one of the most brilliant and original minds America has produced, scarcely conforms to the popular image of the revivalist. His interests seem to have been wholly academic, and he spent long hours each day in his study. His sermons were tightly knit and closely reasoned expositions of theological doctrine which he read rather than speaking extemporaneously. But, however one may explain it, a revival of extraordinary power did spring from his preaching.

Edwards had been educated at Yale, graduating in 1720 at the age of seventeen. For some years he served there as a tutor, leaving in 1727 to assist his grandfather, Solomon Stoddard, who was pastor of the church at Northampton, Massachusetts, and succeeding him two years later when he died. Edwards was greatly distressed by the "licentiousness" which so generally prevailed among the youth of the town.

> Many of them [were] very much addicted to night walking, and frequenting the tavern, and lewd practices. . . . It was their manner very frequently to get together in conventions of both sexes for mirth and jollity, which they called frollics, and they would often spend the greater part of the night in them.

Furthermore, many of them were "indecent in their carriage at meeting." Edwards began to meet with the young people in their homes; they in turn responded to his pastoral concern; reformation in behavior set in; and by 1733 Edwards was able to report that they had grown "observably more decent in their attendance on public worship." [8]

In the meantime he had been becoming increasingly alarmed by the complacency that was being engendered by the spread of "Arminian" principles. The doctrine of human ability, he was convinced, destroyed the very foundation of the Christian faith. To counter this threat, he preached a series of five sermons in 1734 on justification by faith alone. This, Edwards reported, proved to be "a word spoken in season" and was attended by "a very remarkable blessing of heaven to the souls of the people in this town." A young woman of questionable morals was converted, other young people were stirred by her example, the tempo of religious interest increased, and conversions multiplied.

> This work of God . . . made a glorious alteration in the town, so that in the spring and summer following (anno 1735) the town seemed to be full of the presence of God. It never was so full of love, nor so full of joy, and yet so full of distress, as it was then. There

[8] *A Faithful Narrative of the Surprising Work of God*, reprinted in *The Works of President Edwards* (Worcester, Mass., 1808), III, 11–12. A portion of the *Narrative* is in Peter G. Mode, *Source Book . . . for American Church History* (Menasha, Wisc., 1920), 214–17.

were remarkable tokens of God's presence in almost every house. It was a time of joy in families on the account of salvation being brought unto them; parents rejoicing over their children as new born, and husbands over their wives, and wives over their husbands.

There had been other revivals from time to time in the valley, most notably those which occurred under the ministry of Edwards' grandfather, Solomon Stoddard. None of them, however, had proved to be contagious. With the quickening of 1734 it was otherwise. News was carried to other communities, visitors came to Northampton, Edwards was invited to preach in neighboring churches, and by 1736 the revival had spread throughout the Connecticut valley. But by 1737 the revival in Northampton had come to a halt, ceasing almost as abruptly as it had begun. Even this, Edwards interpreted as further evidence of God's mercy, for by withdrawing his Spirit to other places he was but demonstrating "how entirely and immediately the great work lately wrought was his" and "how little we can do and how little effect great things have without him." [9]

Edwards' fame as a revivalist was the product in part of his *Faithful Narrative of the Surprising Work of God in the Conversion of Many Hundred Souls in Northampton* which was published in London in 1737 and reprinted in Boston in 1738. John Wesley read it as he walked from London to Oxford, George Whitefield read it during his first brief visit to Georgia in 1738, and it had a decisive effect upon both men. Much more important than the stimulation and inspiration the book provided was the way in which it shaped subsequent revival efforts by the precise and detailed account it gave of how the revival at Northampton actually developed. The duplication of this pattern, of course, became a major objective of those who followed him. Even the conversion process itself tended to become stereotyped. Less influential but of greater inherent significance was the series of writings—*The Distinguishing Marks of a Work of the Spirit of God* (1741), *Some Thoughts concerning the Present Revival of Religion* (1742), and *A Treatise concerning Religious Affections* (1746)—in which he analyzed with amazing psychological insight and scientific detachment the twin phenomena of conversion and revival. [10]

[9] Quoted by Edwin S. Gaustad, *The Great Awakening in New England* (N.Y., 1957), 22.
[10] For Edwards' life, see Ola E. Winslow, *Jonathan Edwards, 1703–1758* (N.Y., 1940). For his thought, see Perry Miller, *Jonathan Edwards* (N.Y., 1949); and C. H. Faust and T. H. Johnson, *Jonathan Edwards: Representative Selections* (N.Y., 1935).

The Great Awakening

It was not until 1740 that the local manifestations of intense religious interest and concern were transformed into a Great Awakening which was to spread throughout every colony from Nova Scotia to Georgia and to touch every area—urban and rural, tidewater and backcountry—and every class—rich and poor, educated and uneducated—before its power was finally dissipated. There had been interconnections, to be sure, between the revival movements led by Frelinghuysen, the Tennents, and Edwards. Frelinghuysen and Gilbert Tennent actively supported one another. Edwards was at Yale when William Tennent was sufficiently well known there to think of himself as a possible choice for the presidency and when Gilbert Tennent received a degree. In his *Faithful Narrative* Edwards mentions an earlier revival "under the ministry of a very pious young gentleman, a Dutch minister, whose name as I remember was Frelinghuysen." But these were mostly tenuous connections and the revivals remained local in character until they were consolidated into a single movement by the itinerant activity of George Whitefield.

"THE GRAND ITINERANT." A recent graduate of Oxford University, where he had been an intimate friend of the Wesleys and a member of the "Holy Club," Whitefield had spent a few months in Georgia in 1738. Upon his return to England he had adopted, much to the dismay of John Wesley, the expedient of preaching in the open air. Since both men had come to look upon "all the world" as their "parish" to the extent that they were convinced that wherever they chanced to be it was their "bounden duty to declare unto all that are willing to hear the glad tidings of salvation," Whitefield's expedient had the distinct advantage of making it unnecessary to secure an invitation from a local church in order to have an opportunity to preach. Moreover Whitefield's preaching in the open air met with such success that by the time he returned to America late in 1739 he had persuaded Wesley to "become more vile" and to preach in his stead to the great throngs he had assembled in the vicinity of Bristol.

Whitefield arrived in Philadelphia on November 2, 1739. He was a "slim slender youth," twenty-four years of age, with a strong but mellow voice, perfect enunciation, a keen sense of the dramatic, and an ability by subtle inflection to clothe almost any word with emotion. Later it was said that by merely pronouncing the word "Mesopotamia" he could bring tears to the eyes of his listeners. Although his intention had been to proceed immediately to Georgia to look after the affairs of his projected orphanage, Whitefield was prevailed upon to preach first in the Anglican church, then in other churches, and finally he spoke to great crowds each evening from the steps of the courthouse. The response was astonishing. Even Benjamin Franklin was impressed, both with the young man himself and with the good moral effect of his preaching. William Tennent visited him and persuaded him to make a rapid evangelistic tour of the area between Philadelphia and New York, which had already been stirred by revivals. Conscious of the new opportunity that had opened before him, Whitefield determined to preach his way to Georgia, traveling by land instead of going by ship. After a brief period in Savannah, he was back in the Philadelphia area from the middle of April to the middle of May to collect funds for the building of his orphanage, announcing his intention to visit New England in the autumn on a similar mission.

Whitefield arrived at Newport, Rhode Island, on September 14, 1740, having sailed from Charleston three weeks before. His arrival had been well publicized, and the Boston newspapers carried advertisements of numerous books and tracts by and about Whitefield and even called attention to other writings which he approved. During the next seventy-three days he was to travel eight hundred miles and to preach one hundred and thirty sermons. He was met everywhere by great throngs. The ministers of Boston were enthusiastic in the welcome they extended (Charles Chauncy may have had some reservations), Harvard and Yale threw open their doors, the visit to Jonathan Edwards at Northampton was a triumphant pilgrimage, and by the time Whitefield had made his way through New York and New Jersey to Philadelphia he was convinced that America was to be his "chief scene of action." [11] While this was not to be true, he did make three other tours of the colonies and had just embarked upon a fourth when he died at Newburyport, Massachusetts, on September 30, 1770.

If America was not the chief scene of his labors, Whitefield nonetheless did as much to shape the future of American religious life as anyone else. Previous to his coming the "quickening" sermons had been preached in churches and at stated hours of public worship. And when sermons were delivered to congregations other than one's own it was at the invitation of

---

[11] Joseph Tracy, *The Great Awakening* (Boston, 1842), 112. For Whitefield's life, see Stuart C. Henry, *George Whitefield: Wayfaring Witness* (N.Y., 1957).

the pastor. But Whitefield knew no such restrictions. He preached whenever and wherever he could find anyone to listen; and in this, as well as in his extemporaneous preaching, he had many imitators. Through him also, with his incessant traveling and a catholicity of spirit that welcomed an opportunity to preach from any pulpit that was opened to him, the revival impulse permeated every denomination. America in turn did much to shape Whitefield. He was early indebted to Edwards, and Gilbert Tennent helped win him to a type of Calvinism that later cost him the friendship of the Wesleys.[12] Henceforth he was to be firmly convinced that the doctrine of election was the only sure guard against the notion that one is saved by one's own choice and decision.

THE MOUNTING OPPOSITION.   Although the early revivals among the Dutch Reformed and Presbyterians had provoked discord and strife and although Whitefield had encountered vigorous opposition among his fellow Anglican ministers, the Edwardsean revival and the subsequent visit of Whitefield to New England had been viewed with remarkable equanimity and approval. In 1741, however, the storm broke.

Among the Presbyterians the occasion for the violent rupture was Gilbert Tennent's sermon on *The Danger of an Unconverted Ministry*, delivered at Nottingham, Pennsylvania, on March 8, 1740, and published at Philadelphia before the end of the year. It was an intemperate discourse. Even though he had been goaded into a denunciation of "pharisee-teachers" by the persistent efforts of men who gave little evidence of any serious Christian concern to sabotage his father's "log college," Gilbert Tennent's response only served further to inflame them. "Is a blind man," he asked,

> fit to be a guide in a very dangerous way? Is a dead man fit to bring others to life? . . . Is an ignorant rustic that has never been at sea in his life fit to be a pilot? . . . Isn't an unconverted minister like a man who would learn others to swim before he has learned it himself, and so is drowned in the act and dies like a fool?

And the sermon ended with an open invitation for people to forsake the ministry of "natural" men and to seek out instead a congregation where they would receive profitable instruction.[13]

[12] Trinterud, *Forming of an American Tradition*, 88.

[13] A major portion of the sermon is reprinted in Smith, Handy, and Loetscher, *American Christianity*, I, 321–28; and a smaller portion in Armstrong, Loetscher, Anderson, *The Presbyterian Enterprise*, 40–44.

The result could have been predicted. The opposition was both consolidated and angered. At the meeting of the Synod of Philadelphia in 1741 the revivalist group was expelled, and later formed the rival Synod of New York.[14] At the time of the expulsion the antirevivalist group was slightly stronger with twenty-seven ministers as against the twenty-two members of the Tennent party. Seventeen years later, in 1758, when the schism was finally healed with the formation of the Synod of New York and Philadelphia, the antirevivalist ministers in the old Synod of Philadelphia had dwindled in number to twenty-three while the ministers of the newer Synod of New York had more than tripled in number to seventy-three. The initial defeat was turned into an ultimate triumph by the withering of the antirevivalist party and by the subsequent conciliatory spirit displayed by Gilbert Tennent.

When Whitefield left New England on his way to Philadelphia he had met Gilbert Tennent and had insisted that Tennent must go to New England in order to carry forward the work Whitefield had begun. Tennent's tour, from December 13, 1740, to March 3, 1741, was marked by the same large crowds that had greeted Whitefield, and at New Haven many of the students were converted. There was, however, an undercurrent of opposition among some of the clergy. Charles Chauncy (1705–87) in particular had had second thoughts which caused him to regard Tennent's preaching as unlearned, confused, ill-prepared, and ill-delivered. Rumors had begun to circulate concerning Tennent's Nottingham sermon which, if the rumors were true, was clearly calculated to undermine and foster disrespect for ministerial authority.

After Tennent's departure a sizable portion of the New England clergy exploded in indignation. Not only were the rumors concerning Tennent's sermon confirmed, but printed copies of Whitefield's journal of his New England tour were found to contain disparaging comments concerning the caliber of many of the New England ministers. Whitefield, to be sure, had paid tribute to the general level of religious life in New England which he regarded as exceeding that of any other part of the world, but many of those who preached, he felt, did not "experimentally know Christ."

---

[14] Technically the revivalists withdrew, but it was under duress. Furthermore, it is clear that the powers reserved to the presbyteries by the Adopting Act of 1729 had been usurped by the Synod.

70

> The ministers' preaching almost universally by note is a certain
> mark they have in a great measure lost the old spirit of preaching. . . .
> It is a sad symptom of decay of vital religion when reading sermons
> becomes fashionable where extempore preaching did once almost uni-
> versally prevail.

Whitefield even echoed Tennent's denunciation of unconverted ministers.
The reason that congregations have been dead, he wrote, is that "dead men
preach to them," and "how can dead men beget living children?" God
may, if he chooses, "convert people by the Devil," and he may also "by
unconverted ministers," but "he seldom or never makes use of either of
them for this purpose." Nor could one look to the New England colleges,
Harvard and Yale, to supply ministers of different caliber, said Whitefield,
for "their light is become darkness, darkness that may be felt and is
complained of by the most godly ministers." [15]

Opposition was further aroused by the fanatical spirit and emotional
extravagance of James Davenport (1716–57) who projected himself on
the scene at this particular juncture. The revival preaching, to be sure, was
highly emotional and on occasion people were known to cry out, to weep
and sob, and even to faint and swoon. But the leaders of the revival were
careful to restrain such public displays and to cast doubt upon them as
evidence of conversion. Thomas Prince (1687–1758) reported that he did
not "remember any crying out or falling down or fainting, either under
Mr. Whitefield's or Mr. Tennent's ministry all the while they were here [in
Boston]." [16] It was otherwise with James Davenport who did so much to
bring the revival into disrepute by encouraging all manner of excess.

The grandson of the founder of New Haven and a graduate of Yale,
Davenport had been called to a pastorate on Long Island in 1738. Stirred
by the revival excitement, he crossed to Connecticut in the summer of 1741
to follow the itinerant path blazed by Whitefield and Tennent. His sermons
were marked by invective, incoherent ejaculations, and indiscriminate
denunciations of ministers. He sang as he made his way through the streets
to the place of worship. He claimed to be able to distinguish infallibly the
elect from the damned, publicly greeting the former as "brethren" and the
latter as "neighbors." He was obviously unbalanced mentally, and the

---

[15] Gaustad, *The Great Awakening in New England*, 30; C. C. Goen, *Revivalism and
Separatism in New England, 1740–1800* (New Haven, 1962), 49.

[16] Goen, *Revivalism and Separatism in New England*, 18.

leaders of the revival immediately sought to dissociate themselves from him. But the damage was done, and the revival cause was brought into further disrepute when Davenport invaded Massachusetts the following summer. He had been arrested in Connecticut and transported under guard out of the colony. In Massachusetts he was jailed, again adjudged insane, and sent back to Long Island. In the end his sanity seems to have been restored, and through the friendly counsel of Eleazar Wheelock and Solomon Williams he came to see the error of his ways. In 1744 he published his *Confessions and Retractions,* expressing the hope that this would remove the prejudices which his extravagant behavior had evoked. It was a vain hope, for those who had been affronted by Whitefield's ill-considered observations were only too happy to utilize Davenport's excesses as a weapon to discredit the revivalists as a whole.

Charles Chauncy led the attack and blasted the revival from the pulpit of the First Church of Boston in a sermon entitled *Enthusiasm Described and Cautioned Against.* This was followed in 1743 by a more extended denunciation, *Seasonable Thoughts on the State of Religion in New England.* The Harvard faculty was also incensed. When Whitefield had first visited Boston he had been entertained and commended by the president of the college, and the Overseers had set aside a day of thanksgiving for the beneficent effects of his labors. When he returned in 1744 the doors of the college were closed to him and the faculty issued a statement, later endorsed by the Yale faculty, blistering his message, his methods, and his character.

The situation was quite confused and the ministers were badly divided. The "Old Lights," under the leadership of Chauncy, embraced perhaps a third of the ministers of New England. They tended to move in the direction of "rationalism" in theology and constituted the group out of which Unitarianism was later to emerge. As many as another third were "New Lights" who favored the revival and participated wholeheartedly in it, while deploring the unfortunate excesses which the "Old Lights" so vigorously denounced. Only a handful were ready to insist upon emotional manifestations as evidence of conversion and to defend itinerancy and lay preaching. The others were uncommitted. This basic division among the Congregational ministers of New England between "Old Lights" and "New Lights," with certain subsequent refinements and shifts in alignments, was to persist until it was finally obliterated in the first quarter of the nineteenth century by the coming of the "Second Great Awakening" and by the withdrawal of the Unitarians from the Congregationalist fold (see below, pp. 159–62).

In the meantime a further split began to develop within the revivalist camp. Some of those who had been persuaded of the necessity of a work of grace as the indispensable door to the Christian life became disturbed by the continued reception and retention of unconverted members by the churches. For all its emphasis upon conversion, the revival had not led to the abrogation of the lax membership practices which had been introduced by the adoption of the Half-way Covenant. Even when ministers wished to tighten disciplinary procedures, few congregations were willing to accept the rigorous standards implicit in the preaching of their pastors. The most shocking evidence of this fact was the callous ejection of Jonathan Edwards from his Northampton church in 1750 when he insisted upon some evidence of a personal religious experience as a prerequisite to church membership. The unhappiness of the more "experienced" Christians with this lax state of affairs led a considerable number of them to withdraw and to form separate churches of their own.

While the movement was fairly general throughout New England, the real stronghold of the "Separate" or "Strict" Congregationalists was in eastern Connecticut. It has been suggested that this was a lower-class revolt but a careful examination of the Separate churches has revealed that they were composed of a representative cross-section of the population and included prominent and even wealthy members of their respective communities.[17] The constant factor was the earnestness of their religious concern. In all, no fewer than ninety-eight Separate churches were formed, and there were at least thirty-two temporary separations. But this scarcely indicates their full strength, for the strong and ultimately overwhelming tendency was for the Separates to become Baptists. The doctrine of believer's baptism, of course, was a fitting expression of the Separates' conception of the church as a community of "experienced" Christians. At least nineteen of the Separate Congregational churches became Baptist, but a better indication of the Separates' strength is the additional one hundred and thirty Baptist churches that were formed by disaffected Congregationalists. Although not participating directly in the earliest New

[17] This is the conclusion reached by C. C. Goen as a result of his thorough and careful research, *Revivalism and Separatism*, 188–91.

England revivals, the Baptists reaped the largest harvest, siphoning off the strength of the remaining Separate churches to such an extent that they tended to dwindle and die.

THE SOUTHERN PHASE OF THE AWAKENING.   In the South the Awakening developed more slowly. Although Whitefield preached to large numbers in the South, the way had not been prepared for him by earlier revivals and there was little leadership to conserve the results he obtained. The old established areas of Virginia were Anglican territory and the Anglican clergy were unsympathetic and even hostile. The other areas were more recently settled and, without a modicum of leisure and existing centers of church life, there had been scant opportunity for revivals to develop. Thus throughout the South it was Whitefield who blazed the way for the spread of the Awakening instead of consolidating existing interest into a single movement as he had done elsewhere.

The earliest indication of a spiritual quickening in Virginia occurred east of the mountains in Hanover county. As a result of Whitefield's influence as he made his way overland to Georgia in December, 1739, a few lay people had begun to meet in private homes to read some of Whitefield's sermons and other devotional literature. A spontaneous revival broke out. As religious concern spread, the homes of the leaders became too small to hold the gatherings and "reading houses" were erected. This was the situation when William Robinson (d. 1746), a graduate of William Tennent's "log college," was sent by the New Brunswick Presbytery on a missionary tour of Virginia during the winter of 1742–43. Those who had erected the "reading houses" invited him to preach and were persuaded by him to become Presbyterians. Robinson was followed by a succession of revivalist itinerants sent out by the Synod of New York and its subsidiary presbyteries, the most important of whom was to be Samuel Davies who succeeded Robinson at Hanover in 1747.[18] Under his leadership the revival spread rapidly, numerous churches were organized, which were brought together in 1755 to form a new presbytery. After Davies' departure in 1759 to become president of Princeton, the Presbyterian activity became less pronounced.

In the meantime the revival had broken out in another quarter. Two brothers-in-law, Shubal Stearns and Daniel Marshall (1706–84), had come to Virginia from New England in 1754. They had been converted by

[18] See George H. Bost, *Samuel Davies* (Chicago, 1944).

Whitefield, had become Separate Congregationalist itinerants, and then had been ordained as Baptist preachers. Within a year of their arrival in Virginia they were told of a large tract across the border in North Carolina where there was no preaching of any kind and the people "so eager to hear that they would come forty miles each way when they could have opportunity to hear a sermon." Here at Sandy Creek a church was gathered. In three years two additional churches had been formed, and in seventeen years there were forty-two churches. Daniel Marshall went on to Georgia where he labored with almost equal success, and throughout the whole Piedmont region, but especially in Virginia, Separate Baptist churches multiplied at an astonishing rate. At first considerable tension existed between the hyperenthusiastic Separates and the old "regular" Baptist churches which had been formed or reorganized by itinerant evangelists of the Philadelphia Baptist Association. By 1787, however, this breach had been healed and both groups resolved that henceforth they should be known as "the United Baptist Churches."

As Hanover was the center of Presbyterian expansion, and Sandy Creek the center from which radiated Baptist evangelistic activity, so Dinwiddie County was to be the center of the revival impulse among the Anglicans. It was a delayed response, for no leader appeared until Devereux Jarratt (1733–1801) was installed in 1763 as rector at Bath. He had been influenced in his early years by Whitefield, and when he went to England for ordination he had come into contact with both Whitefield and John Wesley. Under Jarratt's zealous preaching his three churches became so crowded that he was compelled to hold services in adjacent groves, and he followed the precedent of Whitefield and Wesley in meeting with the more earnest Christians in small groups.

As early as 1765 two of John Wesley's lay preachers had come to America as immigrants—Robert Strawbridge (d. 1781) to Maryland and Philip Embury (1728–73) to New York. They were followed by two others who arrived in 1769, and in the same year Wesley commissioned the first two of eight officially appointed lay missionaries to serve in America. In 1772 Robert Williams, one of Wesley's lay preachers, appeared in Dinwiddie County and enlisted Jarratt's participation in a more widespread endeavor. Jarratt began to itinerate beyond the bounds of his own parish and the great assemblies gathered in the open air to hear him preach were impressive. Jesse Lee, one of his young converts, reported:

I have been at meetings where the whole congregation would be bathed in tears, and sometimes their cries would be so loud that the preacher's voice could not be heard. Some would be seized with trembling and in a few moments drop on the floor as if they were dead, while others were embracing each other with streaming eyes and all were lost in wonder, love, and praise. [19]

With the assistance of several lay preachers, Jarratt was busily forming converts into "methodist" societies, and as a result of his activity the great strength of the revival movement among the Anglicans was to be found in Virginia and the adjoining counties of North Carolina. By 1777 there were 4,379 members of the societies in this area, while the total for all the colonies was only 6,968. After the Revolution when the societies broke with Anglicanism and formed the Methodist Episcopal Church in 1784, Jarratt expressed resentment at the separation. He felt that he had been deceived by the assurances of loyalty that he had received from the lay preachers. Within a few years his bitterness was gone, but he remained within the Anglican fold where his influence contributed greatly to the strength of the evangelical movement within the newly formed Protestant Episcopal Church.

The impact of the Awakening

The Awakening was much more than the activity of a few conspicuous leaders. It was "Great" because it was general. People everywhere were caught up in the movement, and its influence was spread by innumerable local pastors, passing itinerants, and lay exhorters. No one could escape the excitement or avoid the necessity to declare himself as friend or foe.

And because the Awakening was general, it played an important role in forming a national consciousness among people of different colonies whose primary ties were with Europe rather than with one another. As a spontaneous movement which swept across all colonial boundaries, generated a common interest and a common loyalty, bound people together in a common cause, and reinforced the conviction that God had a special destiny in store for America, the Awakening contributed greatly to the development of a sense of cohesiveness among the American people. It was

[19] W. W. Sweet, *Methodism in American History* (N.Y., 1954), 76.

more influential in this respect than all the colonial wars the colonists were called upon to fight, more influential in fact than many of the political squabbles they had had with the mother country since the latter as often served to separate as to unite them. Whitefield, Tennent, and Edwards were rallying names for Americans a full three decades before Washington, Jefferson, Franklin, and Samuel Adams became familiar household names. Perhaps it is significant that the Awakening did not reach Nova Scotia until 1776, too late to create the intangible ties which bound the other colonies together.

INSTITUTIONAL CONSEQUENCES. No exact estimate can be made of members added to the churches by the Awakening, but the number in all denominations was large. Interest in Indian missions was revived. A wide variety of charitable projects, including schools for Indians, Negroes, and the children of indentured servants, were initiated. The role of the laity in the churches was enhanced. The setting of minister against minister undermined ministerial authority at a time when a stress upon a self-authenticating religious experience was freeing the individual from dependence upon clerical opinion. On the other hand, quite paradoxically, the ministerial office was also given added luster by the fame of the revivalists, and the number of young men drawn into the ranks of the ministry rapidly mounted.

Apart from the multiplication of churches, the major institutional survivals of the Awakening came from the impulse that was given to higher education by the necessity to provide educational opportunities for the swelling number of ministerial recruits. The Presbyterians were especially active in this endeavor and many of their ministers established classical academies, similar in character to William Tennent's "Log College" and patterned after the small private Presbyterian academies of Ireland and the Dissenting academies of England which at this time enjoyed an educational reputation that was greater than that of the ancient universities. Several colleges—Washington and Lee, Washington and Jefferson, and Dickinson—trace their ancestry back to these early academies. In 1746 the Synod of New York secured a charter for the College of New Jersey (Princeton) which was designed as the capstone of the Presbyterian educational structure, and in 1776 the Hanover Presbytery in Virginia established Hampden-Sydney College. The Baptists also organized several academies and in 1764 founded the College of Rhode Island (Brown University) as their major center for the training of the ministry. In 1766 the prorevivalists among the Dutch Reformed obtained a charter for Queen's College (Rutgers University). Dartmouth, an outgrowth of an Indian charity school, was incorporated in 1769. Columbia University (originally King's College), of course, had no connection with the Awakening, nor did the University of Pennsylvania which became a degree-granting college in 1755. The latter, it is true, had its origin in the tabernacle which had been constructed in 1740 for George Whitefield to use when inclement weather made it impossible for him to speak in the open air.

Although the clergy of the English settlements along the seaboard did not have the opportunity to duplicate the work of the priests who accompanied the French traders and trappers on their far-ranging travels through the interior of the continent, the evangelization of those tribes with whom the English came into contact did not suffer neglect.[20] The effect of the Awakening was to pour new enthusiasm into this task. Eleazar Wheelock, Samuel Kirkland, David Brainerd, and for a time Jonathan Edwards were among those who devoted themselves to Indian missions. The diary of David Brainerd, edited by Jonathan Edwards, is a moving testament of devotion which tells the story of his experiences among the Indians, and it inspired many others to give themselves to mission work.

THE THEOLOGICAL TEMPER GENERATED BY THE AWAKENING. Evangelicalism, to use the term by which the new surge of spiritual life is usually described, has often been interpreted as a revolt against Calvinism. While this may have been its ultimate consequence, it was far from that in the beginning. The understanding of the Christian faith as set forth in the great Reformed Confessions was taken for granted. John Wesley was an important exception but, in many respects, even Wesley stood firmly within the Genevan tradition. Evangelicalism, however, was much more a mood and an emphasis than a theological system. Its stress was upon the importance of personal religious experience. If it was a revolt against anything, it was a revolt against the notion that the Christian life involved little more than observing the outward formalities of religion.

Only in New England was significant theological discussion pro-

---

[20] If the Indians were not neglected, the story of mission work among them has been. It is true that Anglicans lost heart for Indian missions after the massacre of three hundred of the colonists in 1622, but the Congregationalists carried on work among the Indians with notable success. This was also true of the Moravians. Presbyterians, Baptists, and Quakers were also active in Indian evangelization.

voked by the Awakening and only in New England did clearly defined theological alignments appear. From a theological standpoint the "Consistent Calvinists" or Edwardseans made the most impressive contribution to the debate. This "New England Theology" was fashioned by Jonathan Edwards and his two most influential disciples, Joseph Bellamy (1719–90) and Samuel Hopkins (1721–1803), in an effort to buttress the revival by a bold and intellectually rigorous restatement of those doctrines which they were convinced had been verified by the revival.[21] The truth that man's redemption was effected by God's sovereign grace alone was to be defended at whatever cost to human pride, and all attempts to substitute man's moral attainments for the righteousness that comes only as a gift were to be resolutely opposed. Those, especially in the vicinity of Boston, who had become impressed with the powers of natural reason through the influence of Isaac Newton, John Locke, and John Taylor, on the other hand, regarded the Edwardsean doctrines as an affront to common sense which tended to undermine all morality. The doctrine of original sin, pictured in terms of innocent infants burning in hell, was denounced as inhuman, unreasonable, and indefensible; while the doctrine of predestination was condemned as destructive of all moral effort. Between these two extremes were the middle-of-the-road travelers who for some unaccountable reason were called the "Old Calvinists." The latter were a varied group. But whether more traditionally oriented or more rationalistically inclined, they tended to be distressed by theological wrangling, viewing it as the consequence of an overly fussy concern for "theological niceties", and advocating in its stead a "large measure of charity." Ezra Stiles (1727–95) was typical of their point of view when he announced that the reigning theological debate was only a verbal dispute.

> Interrogating so-called Arminians, he found they believed in the redemptive grace of Christ; inquiring of so-called Calvinists, he learned that they did not deny the importance of good works. On the whole, "I cannot perceive any very essential real difference in their opinions respecting the fundamental principles of religion."[22]

[21] For a discussion of the Edwardseans, see Joseph Haroutunian, *Piety versus Moralism: The Passing of the New England Theology* (N.Y., 1932).

[22] Gaustad, *The Great Awakening*, 130. Stiles was a representative figure through whom many of the tendencies of the age are to be seen. A graduate of Yale, he was pastor at Newport, R.I., and Portsmouth, N.H., before returning to Yale in 1778 as president of the college. See Edmund S. Morgan, *A Gentle Puritan: A Life of Ezra Stiles, 1727–1795* (New Haven, 1962).

In this lack of concern for careful theological distinctions and in the emphasis upon "the fundamental principles of religion," the Old Calvinists were more closely akin to the general spirit of Evangelicalism than were the Edwardseans. Evangelicalism as a whole tended to prize a "warm heart" and to be impatient with theological controversy. What distinguished the Edwardseans from other Evangelicals was their firm conviction that a warm heart was not enough. In keeping with the earlier Puritan heritage they insisted that both heart and head—faith and reason—must be brought together in the service of God. Thus the Edwardseans were to provide the major portion of whatever intellectual content Evangelicalism was to have. Without the influence of this theological structure which Evangelicalism took largely for granted, Evangelicalism would have had small staying power. Reduced to little more than sentiment, its thrust would quickly have evaporated.

Although the Awakening was productive of controversy and strife, it was, paradoxically, at the same time a great unifying force which gave to "four-fifths" of the Christians in America "a common understanding of the Christian life and the Christian faith." [23] Since the revival had penetrated many denominations quite indiscriminately, this common understanding tended to minimize the importance of denominational distinctions and to provide a basis for mutual respect, appreciation, and cooperation. Typical of the new spirit was John Wesley's emphatic declaration that he renounced and detested all distinctions among Christians, and refused to be distinguished from other men by anything but "the common principles of Christianity." From "real Christians" he had no desire to be distinguished at all. "Dost thou love and fear God? It is enough! I give thee the right hand of fellowship." [24] This catholicity of spirit was even more conspicuously exhibited in George Whitefield. Whitefield spoke with equal readiness from Anglican, Presbyterian, Congregational, Baptist, and Dutch Reformed pulpits, and he counted men of all denominations among his converts. Preaching from the courthouse balcony in Philadelphia, he raised his eyes to the heavens and cried out:

Father Abraham, whom have you in heaven? Any Episcopalians? No! Any Presbyterians? No! Any Independents or Methodists? No, no,

[23] Trinterud, *Forming of an American Tradition*, 197.
[24] From *The Character of a Methodist*, reprinted in *The Works of John Wesley*, 4th ed. (London, 1841), VIII, 332–33.

no! Whom have you there? We don't know those names here. All who are here are Christians. . . . Oh, is this the case? Then God help us to forget party names and to become Christians in deed and truth.

His attitude was echoed by Samuel Davies in Virginia.

My brethren, I would now warn you against this wretched, mischievous spirit of party. . . . A Christian! a Christian! Let that be your highest distinction; let that be the name which you labor to deserve. God forbid that my ministry should be the occasion of diverting your attention to anything else. . . . It has . . . been the great object of my zeal to inculcate upon you the grand essentials of our holy religion, and make you sincere practical Christians. Alas! . . . unless I succeed in this, I labor to very little purpose though I should presbyterianize the whole colony.[25]

In addition to a common understanding of the Christian faith, a particular understanding of the nature of the Church underlay this broad-minded spirit. It was what has been called the "denominational" concept of the Church, and it had been elaborated a century earlier by the Dissenting Brethren in the Westminster Assembly of Divines.[26]

This concept of the Church was to be of decisive future importance in American religious life. Denominationalism, as these men used the term, was the opposite of sectarianism. A "sect" regards itself alone as the true Church. By definition a "sect" is exclusive. "Denomination," on the other hand, was adopted as a neutral and inclusive term. It implied that the group referred to is but one member, called or denominated by a particular name, of a larger group—the Church—to which other denominations belong. Gilbert Tennent stated the concept with clarity and incisiveness when he declared: "All societies who profess Christianity and retain the foundational principles thereof, notwithstanding their different denominations and diversity of sentiments in smaller things, are in reality

[25] A. L. Drummond, *The Story of American Protestantism* (Boston, 1950), 115. Samuel Davies, *Sermons on Important Subjects* (N.Y., 1842), I, 217–18.

[26] The Westminster Assembly had been summoned by the Long Parliament in 1643 to advise the Parliament in its task of effecting a religious settlement for the nation. Presbyterian sentiment was dominant among the assembled clergymen. The Congregational minority, led by Thomas Goodwin, Philip Nye, and Jeremiah Burroughes, was known as the Dissenting Brethren. The case for "denominationalism" as developed by the Dissenting Brethren is discussed by W. S. Hudson in "Denominationalism as a Basis for Ecumenicity," *Church History*, XXIV (1955), 37–47, and in *American Protestantism* (Chicago, 1961), 33–48.

but one Church of Christ, but several branches (more or less pure in minuter points) of one visible kingdom of the Messiah." [27]

On the basis of this understanding of the Church which acknowledged the unity that existed within the diversity of outward ecclesiastical forms, the Protestant churches were able to develop a functional catholicity which was to find expression in the creation of a whole system of cooperative societies for the promotion of a host of worthy causes, including both home and foreign missionary activity. These were to be the instruments into which much of the evangelical fervor released by the Awakening was to be channeled when the Protestant churches subsequently addressed themselves to the overwhelming task of attempting to Christianize a whole continent.

[27] Trinterud, *Forming of an American Tradition,* 132.

IV

The Birth of the Republic

When Edmund Burke in 1775 sought to help his fellow members of Parliament understand the "love of freedom" and "fierce spirit of liberty" which had occasioned the uproar in the colonies over sugar and stamps and tea and taxes, he reminded them that "the people of the colonies are descendants of Englishmen." And then he added:

> England, Sir, is a nation which still I hope respects, and formerly adored, her freedom. The colonists emigrated from you when this part of your character was most predominant; and they took this bias and direction the moment they parted from your hands. They are therefore not only devoted to liberty, but to liberty according to English ideals, and on English principles.

Representative institutions in harmony with English practice had indeed developed very early in all the colonies. Some of the colonial charters were explicit in guaranteeing that the settlers would have "the rights of Englishmen," and the colonists had become accustomed through long practice to the idea that they could not be taxed except by their own consent as expressed in the colonial assemblies.

Religion and politics

While the "love of freedom" had deep and ancient roots in English society, it had been nurtured and transformed into a "fierce spirit of liberty" during the first half of the seventeenth century when the religious issue had come to the fore and had become inextricably intermingled with the liberties of Englishmen. During the course of the constitutional struggle in England it became evident to the participants that certain theological convictions had definite political implications, and these implications were rather fully explored and explicated by both royalists and parliamentarians before the nation finally regained its equilibrium. It was the emotion and spirit generated in the struggle between King and Parliament that Burke had in mind when he noted that the colonists were not only Englishmen but "Protestants, and of that kind which is the most adverse to all implicit subjection of mind and opinion."

THE PURITAN POLITICAL HERITAGE. These Protestants whom Burke described as "the most adverse to all subjection of mind and opinion" had their rootage in Reformed or Calvinist Christianity. It has been said of the early Calvinists that they feared God so much that they could not fear any man, be he king or emperor. And they had much to fear from men, for almost everywhere the Reformed churches were "churches under the cross"—suffering persecution and struggling to survive. But they remained undaunted, sustained in part by a firm confidence in God's overruling providence and impelled by a strong conviction that the chief end of man is to glorify God and insisting that God is glorified by full and complete obedience. When John Knox informed Queen Mary that "right religion takes neither origin nor authority from worldly princes but from the eternal God alone" and then told her that subjects therefore must not "frame their religion according to the appetite of their princes," he was speaking in an accent that was familiar to all sons of Geneva.[1]

[1] See John T. McNeill, "The Democratic Element in Calvin's Thought," *Church History* (1949), 153–71, and W. S. Hudson, "Theological Convictions and Democratic Government," *Theology Today*, X (1953), 230–39. There is no satisfactory treatment of the whole Calvinist political tradition, but G. P. Gooch, *English Democratic Ideas in the Seventeenth Century* (Cambridge, Eng., 1927) and A. S. P. Woodhouse, *Puritanism and Liberty* (London, 1938) are useful.

The Reformed churches remembered the apostle Paul's admonition that Christians must be subject to "the powers that be," and this served as a prod to political theorizing for they were not of a temper patiently to endure bloody repression if a plausible excuse for active resistance could be found. Goaded by the burnings in England under Mary Tudor, the persecution in Scotland under Mary Stuart, the wars of religion in France, and the massacre of the Dutch by the Spanish troops of the Duke of Alva, the Reformed leaders explored every possible concept that could be utilized to justify resistance and rebellion. Rights derived from natural law and from the origin of government in a compact between the ruler and the ruled were explicated, and the role of lesser magistrates as guardians of the liberties of the people was carefully defined. Even tyrannicide, in exceptional circumstances, was defended.[2]

Doctrines of resistance and rebellion were purely negative features of Reformed political thought. From a positive point of view, a distinct preference was exhibited for the checks and balances of a "mixed state." Noting with characteristic irony that "it very rarely happens that kings regulate themselves so that their will is never at variance with justice and rectitude," Calvin himself had suggested the importance of broadening the franchise so that the self-interest of the one may be checked by the self-interest of the many. "It is safer and more tolerable for the government to be in the hands of the many that they may afford each other mutual assistance and admonition, and that if any one arrogate to himself more than is right, the many may act as censors and masters to restrain his ambition." "No kind of government is more happy than this, . . . and I consider those most happy people who are permitted to enjoy such a condition" in which they have the right and the duty to "exert their strenuous and constant efforts" to preserve their liberties.[3]

This was the seedbed of the Puritan political thought which reshaped the English constitution through the ordeal of civil war and became so deeply rooted in the consciousness of Englishmen that the ejection of

---

[2] See, e.g., *A Defense of Liberty against Tyrants: A Translation of the Vindiciae contra Tyrannos*, ed. H. J. Laski (London, 1924) and John Ponet, *A Shorte Treatise of Politike Power*, facsimile reproduction in W. S. Hudson, *John Ponet: Advocate of Limited Monarchy* (Chicago, 1942).

[3] John Calvin, *Institutes of the Christian Religion*, IV, xx, 8; and *Commentary on Micah*, 5:5. For a later explication of the necessity for checks and balances, see the preface to John Cotton's *The Keys of the Kingdom of Heaven* (1644) by Thomas Goodwin and Philip Nye; reprinted in A. S. P. Woodhouse, *Puritanism and Liberty*, 293–98.

James II from the throne in 1688 was effected by a "bloodless" revolution. Defenders of the royal prerogative had few doubts as to the source of the rebellious and seditious notions of the time. Richard Bancroft, chaplain to Elizabeth's Archbishop of Canterbury and soon to be archbishop himself, pointed an accusing finger at Geneva and documented the charge in his book *Dangerous Positions and Proceedings* (1593). James I echoed the accusation at the Hampton Court Conference in 1604. And in 1663 Robert South repeated the charge, saying: "In our account of the sons of Geneva, we will begin with the father of the faithful (faithful, I mean, to their old antimonarchical doctrines and assertions), this is, the great mufti of Geneva"—John Calvin.

The fact that this "fierce spirit of liberty" was part of the intellectual baggage carried to the New World by the Puritans has often been obscured by two much-quoted statements of John Winthrop and John Cotton. "A democracy," said Winthrop, "is among most civil nations accounted the meanest and worst of all forms of government." "Democracy?" Cotton asked rhetorically. "I do not conceive that ever God did ordain it as a fit government either for church or commonwealth." [4] Winthrop and Cotton, of course, were using the word in terms of its classical meaning which had no connotation of representation and delegation of authority. The democracy they were repudiating was not the "mixed" government which the nineteenth century became accustomed to calling democracy. Cotton's inclusion of the "church" in his rejection of democracy should make it immediately apparent that some definition of terms is required, for Cotton was a major architect of the "congregational" form of church government. Thomas Jefferson was one of the few of the Founding Fathers who had a good word to say for democracy and he did not believe that it "would be practicable beyond the extent of a New England township." [5] What Winthrop and Cotton were advocating, and what the Founding Fathers sought to establish, was a "mixed government" with a separation of powers that would provide "guards for their future security."

No one was more aware than John Cotton that all men and especially men in power are prone to corruption. "Let all the world," he declared, "learn to give mortal man no greater power than they are content they

---

[4] From Winthrop's "Reply on the Negative Vote" in R. C. Winthrop, *Life and Letters of John Winthrop* (Boston, 1869), II, 430; and from Cotton's "Letter to Lord Say and Seal" in *The Puritans*, ed. Miller and Johnson, I, 209.

[5] *The Constitution Reconsidered*, ed. Conyers Read (N.Y., 1938), 106.

shall use, for use it they will. . . . It is necessary that all power that is on earth be limited. . . . It is counted a matter of danger to the state to limit prerogatives, but it is a further danger not to have them limited." John Winthrop told the men of Hingham that in signing the covenant they had agreed to submit to the rulers which were thus set over them for their own good, but this admonition had the important qualification—unless they could prove that their rulers were violating the good they had been appointed to serve.[6] This was the common conviction. Thus, while minority rights were not cherished with equal ardor by all Protestant churches in America, most of them through tradition, conviction, and experience had developed an ingrained antipathy to arbitrary rule and had been taught that upon just occasion people had the right and even the duty to rebel.

FEARS GENERATED BY ANGLICAN AGGRESSIVENESS. In the colonies the Puritan political heritage had not been allowed to fade into the past as mere ancient history, nor had the memory of distant events which surrounded that heritage with deep emotion been permitted to grow dim. Provoked by an Anglican aggressiveness which aroused old fears of ecclesiastical tyranny, both pulpit and press rehearsed past history to counter what was considered a present threat. And because the royal power and the episcopal pretensions were so closely linked, the controversy generated a widespread spirit of disaffection which in the course of time was transformed into a deeply rooted rebellious temper. Since the most prominent of the immediate grievances which led to the American Declaration of Independence were economic and political, the importance of the ecclesiastical issue as a major factor in precipitating the American Revolution has been frequently neglected.[7]

The Glorious Revolution of 1688 which brought William and Mary to the English and Scottish thrones had a marked effect upon Anglican fortunes in the New World. Under James II the Church of England had

[6] John Cotton, *An Exposition of the Thirteenth Chapter of Revelation* (London, 1656), 72, as reprinted in *The Puritans*, ed. Miller and Johnson, I, 213. For Winthrop, see Perry Miller, "From the Covenant to the Revival," in *The Shaping of American Religion*, ed. J. W. Smith and A. L. Jamison (Princeton, 1961), 334–35. It is made clear by Edmund Morgan, *The Puritan Dilemma: the Story of John Winthrop* (Boston, 1958), that Winthrop's emphasis was usually upon the duty of obedience.

[7] Arthur L. Cross, *The Anglican Episcopate and the American Colonies* (N.Y., 1902), explored this aspect of the Revolutionary background. His book has now been supplemented by the further research and analysis presented in Carl Bridenbaugh, *Mitre and Sceptre: Transatlantic Faiths, Ideas, Personalities, and Politics, 1689–1775* (N.Y., 1962).

been given scant support in the colonies, had numbered few adherents, and had been officially established only in Virginia. This situation was altered by the Revolution. Dissenting "dissidence" at home was temporarily quieted by the Act of Toleration, while the Anglican bishops were freed from their almost complete preoccupation with the domestic problems created by a Roman Catholic king. Thus the way was cleared for a more aggressive Anglican policy in the colonies. With the support of a sympathetic Court it now became possible to marshal sufficient pressure to secure Anglican establishments in Maryland, South Carolina, and the city of New York, with North Carolina and Georgia later being brought into line.

The Society for the Propagation of the Gospel was designed to spearhead and implement the new Anglican thrust. It had been organized in 1701, with royal and archiepiscopal blessing, to send "orthodox clergymen" to the colonies to instruct such as lacked "the administration of God's Word and Sacraments" in the "principles of true religion." If the clause in the charter which defined the purpose of the Society had been interpreted to mean providing a ministry for the numerous communities in the middle and southern colonies that lacked any ministry whatsoever, the Society would have aroused little opposition. The Society, however, was determined that Anglicanism should shed its regional character and this meant expansion into the older settled areas north of Maryland. Consequently the charter was interpreted as a directive to proselyte members of other communions. In 1750, for example, one-third of the S.P.G. missionaries were stationed in New England where already there was at least one "orthodox minister" in every town and where the converts to Anglicanism were drawn almost exclusively from the ranks of professing Christians. Elsewhere in the colonies S.P.G. activity was similarly restricted to a very great degree to older communities which already had a settled ministry, and the zeal of its missionaries was primarily engaged in making Anglicans out of Quakers, Presbyterians, Baptists, Lutherans, and Reformed.

Under such circumstances it is scarcely surprising that friction developed—a friction that was augmented, as Jonathan Edwards and the "Associated Ministers of Hampshire" explained, by the "uncharitable and unchristian spirit" of the missionaries in "intimating that our ministry is no ministry, not having had episcopal ordination," and thereby inferring with self-evident satisfaction that all other "churches are no churches of Christ, and that our people are to be looked upon as strangers to the commonwealth of Israel—a tenet or principle which came from Rome and which in years past has been disclaimed in England and is still by all the other reformed churches in Europe." The "grand business" of the missionaries, a correspondent of the *Boston Evening Post* declared, "seems to be not to convert men from paganism to Christianity but to proselyte Protestant Dissenters to the Church of England, as if they imagine there can be no salvation out of that church." [8]

Other irritations and grievances, some of them profoundly disturbing, stemmed from what William Smith, Jr. (1728–93), of New York called the Anglican "lust for dominion." Anglican clergy in the middle and northern colonies sought to impress the local populace by convening their conventions in the presence of the governor and by having them preceded by a public procession of the clergy in gowns and cassocks. This ostentation was a minor annoyance but it was not calculated to reduce friction. More serious were deliberate harassments, such as the arrest of Francis Makemie for preaching in New York; the ejection of the Presbyterian minister at Jamaica and the installation of an S.P.G. missionary in his pulpit; the repeated intervention of the S.P.G. to prevent non-Anglican churches in New York from being incorporated so that title to their property might be made secure; the order of the Board of Trade that no schoolmasters from England were to be permitted to teach in New Hampshire without a license from the Bishop of London; the attempt of the missionaries to thwart the founding of the College of New Jersey by the Presbyterians, their efforts to subvert the interdenominational character of King's College and the College of Philadelphia, their constant scheming to gain control of Harvard and Yale, their effective role in frustrating the establishment of a Presbyterian college in North Carolina; and the successful intimidation of printers so that for a time there was no freedom of the press for non-Anglicans in New York. Even the granting of a charter to enable Congregationalists to carry on mission work among the Indians was denied. Ill-feeling was further intensified when news was received that the plight of the Dissenters in England had worsened after Queen Anne had come to the throne, with the disabilities imposed by the Occasional Conformity Act and the Schism Act being added to those of the Test and

[8] Bridenbaugh, *Mitre and Sceptre*, 79–80, 90.

Corporation Acts.[9] Nor were reports of the burning of Dissenting meeting-houses by English mobs reassuring.

It was, however, the persistent efforts of S.P.G. missionaries to persuade the British government to establish an Anglican episcopate in America that did more than anything else to awaken old fears and to spread a spirit of disaffection. The proposal to send bishops to regularize the status of colonial Anglicanism seems innocuous enough if one fails to take into account the close link that existed between Anglican ecclesiastical authority and British political authority. To many of the colonists, bishops were a symbol of incipient tyranny; and Anglican activity in America had done little to disabuse them of the notion that powers, once granted to bishops, would be extended and abused. Jonathan Mayhew (1720–66) put the point succinctly when he stated: "People have no security against being unmercifully priest-ridden but by keeping all imperious bishops and other clergymen who love to lord it over God's heritage from getting their feet into the stirrup at all." [10] Even so, the traditional fear of bishops might not have evoked such a concerted and long-sustained campaign of opposition had the proposal not been promoted from time to time as part and parcel of a plan to secure a tax-supported Anglican establishment in all the colonies and had it not, in order to facilitate this goal, involved a scheme for regrouping the colonies in more efficient administrative units which would necessitate the withdrawal of the existing colonial charters. The struggle against bishops thus came to be regarded by many as a struggle to defend both the civil and the religious liberties of the colonists.

A further alienation occurred when the S.P.G. missionaries sought to advance their cause by suggesting that an American episcopate would bind the colonists more closely to England. No argument could have been better calculated to antagonize the other churches, for its plain implication was that their members were an alien and disloyal people. Nor did the missionaries hesitate to spell out this implication. In seeking to counter the antibishop attack, they accused "dissenting" churchmen of being "avowed

[9] The Test and Corporation Acts excluded non-Anglicans from governmental positions. The Occasional Conformity Act tightened this restriction and the Schism Act required all teachers to be licensed by a bishop and to teach nothing but the Anglican catechism. Had the latter act been enforced, it would have suppressed all schools run by Dissenters and would have taken from Dissenters the education of their children.

[10] A. L. Cross, *Anglican Episcopate*, 145.

republicans," "enemies to monarchy," and constituting a "restless and turbulent faction"; whereas if the Church of England were properly established the populace would quickly be reduced to "passive obedience" since the Anglican clergy "inculcate the great principles of loyalty and submission to government." An article in the *Boston News-Letter* in 1750 reached back to the Hampton Court Conference of 1604 to find the proper slogan to state the case for episcopacy as the indispensable support of monarchy: "The good old saying, 'No Bishop, no King,' however grating it may be to some people, ought to be the standing maxim of the English government." [11]

Although the tactical skill and political connections of the Dissenting Deputies [12] in London thwarted the successive schemes to secure an American episcopate, the fears and apprehensions that were aroused created a smouldering fire of discontent and provided repeated occasion for preachers to utilize their sermons for purposes of political instruction. The campaign for bishops had been launched by the first S.P.G. missionaries and had been pushed with intermittent vigor in succeeding decades, but in the 1760's the agitation was stepped up and a mounting militancy of political activity reached its peak in 1770. This coincided with the new economic and political policies of the government which were to result in a general conflagration. Within this context, according to the *St. James's Chronicle*, "stamping and episcopizing" were commonly regarded as "only different branches of the same plan of power"; and Ezra Stiles indicated that much of the opposition to the Stamp Act was based on a recognition that if "a Parliamentary revenue had been established independent of the [colonial] Assemblies," the door would have been opened to the appropriation of funds "for half a dozen bishops on this continent." John Adams put it more bluntly: "If Parliament could tax us, they could establish the Church of England with all its creeds, articles, tests, ceremonies, and tithes; and prohibit all other churches as conventicles and schism shops." [13]

In the seventeenth century the Church of England had reaped a

---

[11] Bridenbaugh, *Mitre and Sceptre*, 102, 181, 262.

[12] A committee of lay representatives of "the Three Denominations" (Congregationalists, Presbyterians, and Baptists) which was formed in 1732 to direct the political agitation of English Dissenters in their struggle to secure the repeal of restrictive legislation. See B. L. Manning, *The Protestant Dissenting Deputies* (N.Y., 1952).

[13] Bridenbaugh, *Mitre and Sceptre*, 239, 259. Anson Phelps Stokes, *Church and State in the United States* (N.Y., 1950), I, 234.

whirlwind of disaster when Archbishop Laud identified it so completely with the ill-considered economic and political policies of Charles I that the church became an equal victim with the crown in the Revolution that followed. In the eighteenth century the role was reversed. The colonial structure came tumbling down at least partly because the Church of England identified the crown so intimately with its own "lust for dominion" in the New World that it became an albatross about the neck of the government. The precise weight to be given ecclesiastical grievances as a contributing cause of the American Revolution is impossible to determine, but John Adams, the most reflective and perceptive participant in the events which led to war, always insisted that "the apprehensions of episcopacy contributed . . . as much as any other cause to arouse the attention not only of the inquiring mind but the common people and urge them to close thinking on the constitutional authority of parliament over the colonies." [14]

THE PROPONENTS OF NATURAL RELIGION. While a pervasive Puritanism as recast by Evangelicalism was the dominant religious emphasis in colonial America, a theological revolt was brewing during the decades immediately preceding the War of Independence. A "rationalizing" tendency in religion had become fashionable among the more sophisticated, and much of the leadership of the American Revolution was provided by men who were far from orthodox in their religious views. Some (Thomas Jefferson and Benjamin Franklin were notable examples) were Deists.

Deism had a double rootage. First of all, it may be traced back to seventeenth-century men of "latitude" in England who sought to overcome the divisions among Christians by suggesting that only those affirmations on which all reasonable men can agree are essential articles of faith. The tendency of Deism was to reduce these "essentials" to a simple fivefold affirmation that God exists, that he is to be worshiped, that the practice of virtue is the true worship of God, that man must repent of wrong-doing, and that there are future rewards and punishments. The most noteworthy feature of this Deist "creed" was its omissions. There was nothing distinctively Christian about it—no mention of any special work of Christ, of man's sinful nature and consequent need of redemption, or of any necessary dependence upon biblical revelation. This was "natural religion," a term which points to the other source of Deism.

[14] *The Works of John Adams,* ed. C. F. Adams (Boston, 1850–56), X, 185.

If Deism was partly the product of latitudinarian sentiment, it was even more deeply rooted in the rationalism which is associated with "the Age of Reason" or the era of the "Enlightenment." [15] The period from the Peace of Westphalia (1648) to the French Revolution (1789) was a time of rapid scientific advance, an advance that is best epitomized in the work of Sir Isaac Newton (1642–1727). To his contemporaries Newton seemed to have solved all the chief problems of astronomy, optics, physics, and mathematics. Alexander Pope gave the popular estimate when he wrote:

> Nature and Nature's Laws lay hid in night.
> God said 'Let Newton be!' and all was light.

As a result of his studies, Newton was thought to have discovered "a universal law of nature" which banished mystery from the world. The universe was simply a vast mechanism—intelligible, harmonious, and thoroughly rational—the product of God the Great Mathematician. It was within this context that such men as John Toland in *Christianity Not Mysterious* (1696) and Matthew Tindal in *Christianity as Old as Creation* (1730) affirmed that the "essentials" of true religion are those truths which can be known by human reason without the aid of any special revelation.

John Locke (1632–1704) provided a connection, in his person, between the rationalist type of religious thought and the political ideas which found expression in the American Revolution. His *Essay concerning Human Understanding* (1690) had exalted man's rational powers by asserting that knowledge comes from the senses as a result of experience and reflection, and his *Reasonableness of Christianity* (1695) argued that the essence of Christianity is to be found in its ethics (the practice of virtue) and that its excellence consists in the fact that it is fully in accord with the dictates of human reason. More moderate than the Deists, Locke did not suggest that revelation was superfluous, nor did he doubt the inspiration of the Bible or the messiahship of Jesus. These were means by which essential truths beyond the grasp of common people were made known to the mass of mankind, and they were equally useful in confirming the deductions of the intellectually elite. In his *Treatises on Government* (1690) Locke had come to the defense of the Revolution of 1688 with the

[15] See Gerald R. Cragg, *The Church and the Age of Reason, 1648–1789* (N.Y., 1961).

93

assertion that all peaceful governments were established by the consent of the governed in order to protect their natural rights to life, liberty, and property, and that whenever this trust is betrayed the people have the right to resist.

The writings of Locke were widely read in America and many of the leaders of the struggle for independence were deeply influenced by both his religious and his political views. It was for this reason, we may assume, that G. A. Koch defined Deism as "Republican Religion." [16] Actually there was no necessary connection between Locke's religious views and his political thought. His political views were little more than a distillation of concepts that had long been current in Calvinist political theory—a fact which John Adams acknowledged [17]—and had become fundamental postulates of a large portion of the English people in the earlier conflict between King and Parliament. Although Thomas Jefferson wrote the Declaration of Independence, the key paragraph which justified the resort to arms could quite easily have been written by a Puritan divine. When it came to writing a constitution for the new nation, the happier view of human nature implicit in John Adams' assertion that unaided reason is "a revelation from its Maker which can never be disputed or doubted" gave way to a more pessimistic estimate.[18] Even those who thought men good enough to win heaven by their own efforts were skeptical about statesmen making the grade and insisted that the exercise of power must be checked by adequate safeguards.

The winning of independence

During the years prior to the Revolution "rational religion" exerted little influence in America except among some of the "intellectuals" of the coastal ports and among some of the plantation owners of the South. Few

[16] *Republican Religion: The American Revolution and the Cult of Reason* (N.Y., 1933).

[17] *Works*, VI, 4. For an explication of this point, see W. S. Hudson, "John Locke—Preparing the Way for the Revolution," *Journal of Presbyterian History*, XLII (1964), 19–38; reprinted in J. T. McNeill and G. L. Hunt, *Calvinism and the Political Order* (Philadelphia, 1965).

[18] For an analysis of the basic Puritan-Calvinist assumptions reflected in the United States Constitution, see H. Richard Niebuhr, *The Kingdom of God in America*, 45–87. The specific application of these assumptions in the drafting of the Constitution is discussed in W. S. Hudson, "Theological Convictions and Democratic Government," *Theology Today*, X (1953), 230–39.

of those who regarded themselves as emancipated from traditional Christian doctrine had any desire to promote their views among the populace at large. Believing as they did that orthodox religion served to inculcate the necessary principles of private and public morality among the common people, the rationalists tended to maintain at least a nominal connection with the existing churches and to contribute to their support. Thus to the extent that religious concerns played a decisive part in enlisting mass support for the colonial cause, this support of necessity was marshaled by the orthodox churches.

THE ATTITUDE OF THE VARIOUS DENOMINATIONS. Not all the churches, of course, supported the war with Great Britain, nor did any single denomination present an unbroken front. There were both Tories and Patriots in every religious group, as well as many who were apathetic. Nevertheless the general attitude which was to characterize each of them would not have been difficult to predict.

The Church of England had a long tradition of intimate identification with the English government and in the colonies this governmental relationship constituted its major source of strength. It is not surprising therefore that the Anglican clergy, with a few notable exceptions, were zealous Tories who condemned the conflict as an unjustified rebellion against constituted authority. The Anglican laity in the South, on the other hand, gave strong support to the struggle for independence. The pacifist groups—Quakers, Mennonites, Moravians, and Dunkers—held themselves aloof as a matter of principle. The Dutch and German Reformed and the Lutheran churches had no real stake in the perpetuation of British rule. While many sought to avoid taking sides in the conflict, the majority ranged themselves on the side of the colonists. This was also true of Roman Catholics and Jews, with Charles Carroll among the former contributing notable service to the colonial cause. These latter groups, however, were relatively small. The more significant support came from the Congregational, Presbyterian, and Baptist churches.

The Congregationalists had early nurtured a tradition of independence in the colonies which they had founded, and later British rule came to be associated in their minds both with Anglican proselyting activity and with pressure to give increased recognition to the status of the Church of England as the official church of the governing authority. But above all, Congregationalists had been fed a steady diet of "election sermons" which emphasized concepts of fundamental law, constitutional rights, limited government, and the duty to resist abuses of power—all of which were notions calculated to create a climate of opinion opposed to any infringement of the people's liberties.

These latter concepts which were so important in generating a revolutionary temper were not, of course, the exclusive possession of the Congregationalists. Having been formulated by early Calvinist political theorists and further refined by English Puritan and Scottish Presbyterian divines, they were shared in America by Presbyterians, Baptists, and others who stood within the Reformed tradition. Indeed, as we have seen, they had been popularized in the "political Calvinism" of John Locke, and in this form they had been appropriated by many who regarded themselves as otherwise quite emancipated from key doctrines of the Reformed understanding of the Christian faith.

The Presbyterians and the Baptists embraced these ideas the more zealously because of the disabilities to which they had been subjected in several of the colonies. Even in New England where Congregationalists often made life difficult for Baptists, the Baptists responded by accusing the Congregationalists of being disloyal to their own tradition and by asserting that the Baptists were the true heirs of the founders of New England.[19] In Virginia both Presbyterians and Baptists were thrown into a perpetual state of disaffection by irritations arising from Anglican tactics of oppression. The attitude of the Scotch-Irish among the Presbyterians was further colored by bitter memories of the ill-treatment their fathers had received at the hands of the English in northern Ireland.

THE ROLE OF THE CLERGY. In 1781 when arch-Tory Peter Oliver (1713–91) reviewed the course of the Revolution in his *Origin and Progress of the American Rebellion,* he suggested that if one wished to understand the inflamed public opinion which swept the colonies into war one must look to "Mr. Otis's black regiment, the dissenting clergy."[20] They certainly were key figures, for their influence penetrated remote communities that were seldom reached by newspapers and books. And if it is true, as a British official reported of the people of rural Connecticut, that "they are all politicians and Scripture learnt," this was the result of the

[19] This was the whole thrust of the argument of Isaac Backus in his *History of New England, with Particular Reference to . . . the Baptists* (Boston, 1777–96).

[20] James Otis (1725–83), a Boston lawyer, was one of the most conspicuous and effective leaders in arousing anti-British sentiment.

work of the preachers. Practical politics may have been learned at the town meeting but the undergirding political theory was picked up from the Sunday sermon and the weekly lecture as well as from the annual election sermon. So well rehearsed were these common folk in political thought that they knew all the arguments, delighted in the subtleties of debate, and were familiar with the facts of past crises which pointed up the present moral. Ezra Stiles could refer to "half a dozen bishops on this continent and a long string of &c. &c. &c.," in perfect confidence that the reader would recognize the allusion to be to the "Et cetera Oath" which had troubled the consciences of Englishmen more than a century before. Thus a few cliché-studded sentences were often sufficient to evoke a broad context of meaning. Perhaps the general run of the populace was best informed in New England, but elsewhere less widespread literacy and less ample access to the press made people even more dependent upon the preachers for information concerning issues of the day.[21]

The role of the clergy was not restricted to fostering and perpetuating notions of fundamental and "inalienable" rights. What Peter Oliver had in mind when he spoke of the importance of "Mr. Otis's black regiment" was the indispensable aid they provided in enlisting active support by "preaching up" the Revolution in innumerable "fast day" and recruiting sermons. This they did in a curiously roundabout fashion. While American rights were defended, there was little stress upon American righteousness and few direct and forthright attempts to enlist divine aid against the British. Their understanding of God's relationship to his people in terms of a covenant that involved more responsibilities than privileges left scant room for such unabashed presumption, and they knew that a simple invocation of the powers of heaven was no way to secure the assistance of a Supreme Governor whose favor was far from capricious.[22]

The preachers and those who had been taught by them knew that under the providential government of God the occasion for troubles and disasters must be sought within rather than without. Thus they viewed the present affliction that had been visited upon the colonies as less the result of the iniquity of the British than the consequence of the infidelity of the Americans. The remedy therefore was to confess their sins and to mend

---

[21] Bridenbaugh, *Mitre and Sceptre*, 189, 259.

[22] For an analysis of this type of approach, see Perry Miller, "From the Covenant to Revival," in *The Shaping of American Religion*, ed. J. W. Smith and A. L. Jamison, 322–68.

their ways. Only then could they reasonably expect that God would impart the necessary wisdom, energy, and will to push the war to a successful completion.

The successive "recommendations" of the Continental Congress that days of "public humiliation, fasting, and prayer" be observed played upon this theme as a repetitive refrain, expressing the hope that "we may with united hearts and voices unfeignedly confess and deplore our many sins, and offer up our joint supplications to the all-wise, omnipotent, and merciful Disposer of all events; humbly beseeching him to forgive our iniquities, to remove our present calamities, to avert those desolating judgments with which we are threatened" (1775); summoning the colonists to "implore the mercy and forgiveness of God, and beseech him that vice, prophaneness, and extortion, and every evil may be done away and that we may be a reformed and happy people" (1777); lamenting the fact that "too few have been sufficiently awakened to a sense of their guilt, or warmed with gratitude, or taught to amend their lives and turn from their sins, so he might turn from his wrath" (1779); and asking God's gracious intervention "to make us sincerely penitent for our transgressions; to prepare us for deliverance, and to remove the evil with which he hath been pleased to visit us; to banish vice and irreligion among us, and to establish virtue and piety by his divine grace" (1780).

This call to repentance, revival, and reform was a familiar theme to all who had been nurtured in the piety of the early Puritans and their revivalist successors. And it had always elicited not a failure of nerve but a vigorous response, for a program of action in terms of obedience to the ordinances of God was always implicit in their summons to repentance. It may seem strange to a later generation that this theme of abnegation would have been coupled with another theme from their past which demanded immediate and concerted action against any magistrate who violated the fundamental rights of the people. But to the great mass of the religiously oriented in the Revolutionary generation there was no contradiction. These rights, if variously derived, were divinely ordained, and to defend them—even when their abrogation was viewed as punishment for their sins—was part of their Christian obedience. The outcome was always in the hands of God, but since he uses men as instruments to serve the purposes of his providential government, the call to repentance and humiliation was at the same time a summons to battle.

RELIGIOUS FREEDOM. The securing of religious freedom in America is sometimes viewed as a sequel to the winning of independence, but this is a mistake. Philip Schaff was right when he asserted that the whole question of religious freedom had been settled prior to the formation of the national government by the previous history of the American colonies.[23] Of the original thirteen colonies, four—Rhode Island, New Jersey, Pennsylvania, and Delaware—had long been fully committed to a policy of religious liberty, and the Anglican establishments in five of the remaining colonies—in New York, Maryland, North Carolina, South Carolina, and Georgia—quickly toppled after the outbreak of hostilities when the supporting prop of English authority was withdrawn. The speedy action of New York in repealing all laws or acts which "may be construed to establish or maintain any particular denomination of Christians" was typical. Indeed, the North Carolina Assembly anticipated the repudiation of British authority when it refused in 1773 to renew the Vestry Act, an action which had the practical effect of bringing the establishment there to an end. Only in Virginia, and in Massachusetts, Connecticut, and New Hampshire, was there any delay; and even in these four areas the struggle for religious liberty was carried on during the war years as part of the revolutionary struggle itself. In Virginia, as early as June 12, 1776, an effort was made to forestall the popular tide and to preserve some remnant of the establishment by adopting a "Declaration of Rights" which asserted that "all men are equally entitled to the free exercise of religion." [24]

Obviously the urgent necessity which the war imposed to find a basis of unity among people who were religiously diverse was a compelling consideration in this rapid shift of many of the former colonies to a policy of full religious freedom. But the story is much more complex than simple necessity would suggest. For one thing, the shift was facilitated by a growing spirit of harmony and good will among many of the denominations. The Great Awakening had done much to promote this irenic ecclesiastical temper, bridging religious barriers in much the same way as

[23] Schaff, *Church and State in the United States* (N.Y., 1888), 23. The literature dealing with the church-state issue in America is voluminous. Much of the relevant source material has been assembled in Stokes, *Church and State in the United States*. Sidney E. Mead, *The Lively Experiment* (N.Y., 1963) is a perceptive and discerning commentary on the consequences that have flowed from the policy of religious freedom.

[24] The motion for its adoption was made by a conservative, Edmund Pendleton, who viewed the *Declaration* as a means of relieving the pressure for the more radical action of disestablishment. Stokes, *Church and State in the United States*, I, 380.

it had tended to dissolve colonial boundaries by the sweeping tide of new religious life and activity. At the same time the major non-Anglican religious groups also were being drawn together to resist Anglican encroachments, and both a catholic spirit and a developing national consciousness were fostered by the interdenominational and intercolonial committees of correspondence that were set up to coordinate this resistance. But an even more important factor in the movement toward full and complete religious freedom was a developing awareness among the colonists of the meaning of the American experience.

While all non-Anglican churchmen cherished the security and safety they had found in the vast expanse of the New World, the classic interpretation of their common experience which gave meaning to the American adventure was fashioned by the New Englanders. As clear a statement as any of this meaning was supplied by Cotton Mather (1663–1728) in an election sermon before the General Court of Massachusetts early in the 1690's. "What went ye into the wilderness to see?" the forefathers were asked rhetorically.

> And the answer to it is not only too excellent but also too notorious to be dissembled. Let all mankind know that we came into the wilderness because we would worship God without that Episcopacy, that Common Prayer, and those unwarranted ceremonies with which the "land of our forefathers' sepulchures" had been defiled. We came hither because we would have our posterity settled under pure and full dispensation of the gospel, defended by rulers that should be ourselves.

It is true that these early settlers were seeking freedom for themselves and not for others, but they were being constantly needled by their fellow Congregationalists in England to adopt a more liberal policy than that of reminding those who differed from them that they had equal freedom to establish settlements of their own in the American wilderness. By the early decades of the eighteenth century this more liberal policy had been forced upon them by the concessions they had been compelled to grant Anglicans, Baptists, and Quakers. Thus the tables were turned when the Anglicans launched their drive for ecclesiastical power in New England. Formerly the Congregationalists had squirmed under charges of intolerance, but now they could pin the label of bigotry upon the Anglicans and could

29467

remind them that the New England Congregationalists conceded more freedom to Anglicans than the Anglicans in England were willing to concede to Congregationalists.

Under this Anglican pressure, the New Englanders turned increasingly in their sermons, lectures, and writings to recasting the story of their past to bring it into accord with the necessities of the present. The Founding Fathers were pictured as apostles of liberty, and the need to maintain intact the liberties that had been bequeathed to them was constantly reiterated. Typical was the pointed application that was given by Thomas Prince in the dedication of his *Chronological History of New England* (1736) in which he spoke of

> the worthy Fathers of these plantations, whom yourselves and posterity cannot but have in everlasting honor, not only for their eminent self-denial and piety wherein they set examples for future ages to admire and imitate, but also for their great concern that the same vital and pure Christianity and LIBERTY, both *civil and ecclesiastical,* might be continued to their successors, for which they left their own and their fathers' houses in the most pleasant places then on earth with many of their dearest relatives, and came over the ocean into this then hideous wilderness.

By 1760 Ezra Stiles was declaring:

> The right of conscience and private judgment is unalienable; and it is truly the interest of all mankind to unite themselves into one body for the liberty, free exercise, and unmolested enjoyment of this right. . . . And being possessed of the precious jewel of religious liberty, a jewel of inestimable worth, let us prize it highly and esteem it too dear to be parted with on any terms lest we be again entangled with that yoke of bondage which our fathers could not, would not, and God grant that we may never, submit to bear. . . . Let the grand errand into America never be forgotten.[25]

And five years later, in an essay on canon law, John Adams rehearsed once again the history of New England and issued a peremptory summons. "Let the pulpit resound with the doctrines and sentiments of religious liberty," for there is "a direct and formal design on foot to enslave America."

So effective a propaganda device was not neglected in the other

[25] Bridenbaugh, *Mitre and Sceptre,* 3.

colonies. In New York, William Livingston (1723–90) shrewdly included the Dutch forefathers with the English when he reminded the governor in 1755 that

> the greatest number of our inhabitants are descended from those who with a brave and invincible spirit repelled the Spanish tyranny in the *Netherlands,* or from those who for their ever-memorable opposition to the arbitrary measures of King Charles I were constrained to seek a refuge from the relentless sword of persecution in the then inhospitable wilds of AMERICA. From such ancestors we inherit the highest relish for civil and religious LIBERTY.

The following year the Anglican William Smith (1727–1803) of Philadelphia sent word to London that "the impartial Presbyterian historian," William Smith, Jr., of New York, had explained the prevailing discontent of the people as the product of their desire "for an equal universal toleration of Protestants" and their aversion to "any kind of an ecclesiastical establishment." Twelve years later Livingston asserted that all good and loyal Protestants affirm "the natural right of every man to choose his own religion." Everywhere the religious issue was inextricably entangled with the revolutionary struggle. From South Carolina the Anglican Commissary, Charles Martyn, reported to the Bishop of London that the principles of most of the colonists "are independent in matters of religion as well as republican in those of government" and that "it would be as unsafe for an American bishop . . . to come hither as it is at present for a distributor of stamps." The watchword which united them all was "liberty, both civil and religious." Little wonder then that, with the cry of religious liberty having been constantly upon their lips, the Assemblies in those areas where Anglicanism had been established took immediate steps at the outbreak of war to give substance to one of the major slogans under which the colonists were being called upon to do battle.[26]

All the details of what was involved in a policy of religious freedom, to be sure, had not been worked out. In most of the newly independent colonies, for example, voting was restricted to Christians, Trinitarian Christians, or Protestants. In Massachusetts, Connecticut, and New Hampshire, those in control were confident that a policy of religious liberty had long since been put into practice. To be sure, their policy had differed

[26] *Ibid.,* 167, 176, 249, 304.

102

from that of other colonies where no faith enjoyed any privileges. As Ezra Stiles explained it, "the happy policy of establishing one sect without infringing on the essential rights of others is peculiar to the three New England provinces where Congregationalism is the establishment." Basic to this "happy" state of affairs was the polity of the dominant Congregationalism. This polity, on the one hand, provided a sure guarantee against ecclesiastical despotism, for churches can only be said "to be perfectly free when each congregation has an unlimited, absolute, and self-determining power in the choice of their officers." On the other hand, this polity provided a sure guarantee of "universal liberty" because by it, said Stiles, every congregation enjoys sole power in the regulation of its own affairs. Beyond these established congregations other churches were permitted to exist, and while all the inhabitants were taxed for the support of religion, they were allowed to assign their taxes to the church of their choice. This latitude, Stiles concluded, made possible "the friendly cohabitation of all." [27] Obviously, this was a somewhat idealized portrait, but it need not detain us, for this was a pattern which belonged to the past and the crucial struggle was to be fought not in New England but in Virginia.

Although the penalties imposed on religious dissent in Virginia were progressively eliminated during the war years as a result of Baptist and Presbyterian pressure, the Anglicans who dominated the "unreapportioned" Assembly had continued to fight a rear-guard action in defense of the establishment. Their last endeavor was the attempt in 1784, after the coercion imposed by the necessity to maintain united support for the war effort had been removed, to regain some measure of tax support for the Anglican church by levying a "general assessment" to be distributed impartially among all Christian churches. It was this "general assessment," again as a result of Baptist and Presbyterian pressure, that was defeated as inconsistent with the principles of liberty. Since the proposed benefits would be restricted to Christian churches, the point was made that the state would be required to determine what constitutes Christianity and thus would be compelled to set up its own standard of orthodoxy. Furthermore, "the same authority which can establish Christianity in exclusion of all other religions may establish with the same ease any particular sect of Christians in exclusion of all other sects" and "the same authority which can force a citizen to contribute threepence only of his

[27] *A Discourse on the Christian Union* (Boston, 1761), 37, 43, 97-99.

property for the support of any one establishment may force him to conform to any other establishment." [28] The following year the issue was settled with the adoption of the "Bill for Establishing Religious Freedom" which rejected the whole idea of any multiple establishment as well as any religious test for public office.

When the delegates assembled to draft the United States Constitution, the controversy in Virginia had been brought to an end and for most Americans the issue of religious liberty was no longer a subject for debate. If the Constitution in its primary form failed to deal with the issue beyond providing that "no religious test shall ever be required as a qualification to any office or public trust under the United States," it was not because there was any question at this point but because the instrument of 1787 gave the federal government no powers to deal with religious matters and it was assumed that no other guarantee was needed. As soon as it became apparent that an affirmative statement was necessary to win ratification by reluctant states, the necessary affirmation was promptly made by amendment—an amendment carefully devised to establish religious freedom, defined in terms worked out in Virginia, as binding national policy. The restrictions of the federal Bill of Rights did not apply to acts of the individual states, but only Massachusetts, Connecticut, and New Hampshire, with their emasculated Congregational establishments, remained out of step with the rest of the country. And long before the courts by invoking the Fourteenth Amendment imposed federal policy at this point upon the states, Massachusetts, Connecticut, and New Hampshire had fallen into line with guarantees in their own constitutions which gave to all religious groups a purely voluntary status.

Partisans of differing camps have quarreled as to who should receive primary credit or blame for the government surrendering all control over the religious life of its citizens. In many respects this is a fruitless debate. Beyond the decisive necessity imposed by the simple fact of religious diversity, claims and counterclaims can easily be made. The Virginia Bill for Establishing Religious Freedom was drafted by Thomas Jefferson, and Jefferson was both a "rationalist" and an ardent advocate of full and complete religious liberty. But other "rationalists" were not as clear as was

[28] The arguments were presented in the "Memorial and Remonstrance" of 1784 drafted by James Madison. See Stokes, *Church and State*, I, 341–42, 344. The "Bill for Establishing Religious Freedom" is reprinted in Smith, Handy, Loetscher, *American Christianity*, I, 445–48.

Jefferson at this point. Washington favored the "general assessment" in Virginia; Franklin had favored an American episcopate and was not unduly disturbed by the Congregational establishment in New England; and John Adams was vigorous in his defense of the New England pattern. The low-pressure religion of the pre-Revolutionary "rationalists," on the whole, did not lend itself to a crusading spirit, and an establishment that did not interfere with private reflection was frequently viewed as a good thing for the masses.

Few of the more orthodox religious groups, on the other hand, presented an entirely unbroken front in support of full and complete religious freedom. The Congregationalists developed an intricate defense of their own distinctive solution to the problem. At least a majority of the Presbyterian clergy in Virginia were ready to settle for a "general assessment" in contrast to the lay elders who were adamant in rejecting it. Even some Baptist churches in New Hampshire accepted the status and legal privileges of establishment in their respective towns. What seems clear is this. In several of the crucial struggles, leadership was supplied by "rationalists" while the ardor and indispensable political pressures were supplied by troops in the field who represented more conventional religious ideas. The latter created the problem, popularized the orthodox Protestant conviction expressed by Jefferson that all "legislators and rulers, civil as well as ecclesiastical," are "but fallible and uninspired men" (a conviction which struck at the heart of any rationalization of enforced conformity), and committed the war effort to the slogan of "liberty, both civil and ecclesiastical."

For good or ill—whether as a result of mere necessity, the influence of "rational" religion, or the principles of liberty that had been resounding from orthodox pulpits for more than a generation—the revolutionary struggle had committed the new nation at its birth to a policy of complete voluntaryism in religion. Freed from the threat of governmental interference, the churches were also denied the possibility of governmental support. They were thrust upon their own resources, and were henceforth (as most of them had been heretofore) to be dependent upon purely persuasive powers to marshal the necessary support to maintain themselves and to make their influence felt.

PART II

THE NEW NATION

1789–1860

V

The Reordering of Denominational Life

The winning of independence presented to the American people a prospect that was at first exhilarating and then sobering. The initial exuberant optimism was voiced by Ezra Stiles in the Connecticut election sermon of 1783, entitled *The United States Elevated to Glory and Honor.*

> This will be a great, a very great nation, nearly equal to half Europe. . . . Before the millennium the English settlements in America may become more numerous millions than that greatest domain on earth, the Chinese Empire. Should this prove to be a future fact, how applicable would be . . . [our] text [Deut. 26:19] when the Lord shall have made his American Israel high above all nations which he has made—in numbers, and in praise, and in name, and in honor.
>
> I am sensible some will consider these as visionary utopian ideas; and so they would have judged had they been told . . . at the battle of Lexington that in less than eight years the independence and sovereignty of the United States should be acknowledged by four European sovereignties, one of which should be Britain herself. How wonderful the revolutions, the events, of Providence! We live in an age of

wonders; we have lived an age in a few years; we have seen more wonders accomplished in eight years than are usually unfolded in a century.

Nor was the prospect dismaying to Stiles that the churches were to be dependent solely upon their powers of persuasion, for he was confident that in a free market truth would prevail. "Here Deism will have its full chance; nor need libertines [any] more to complain of being overcome by any weapons but the gentle, the powerful ones of argument and truth. Revelation will be found to stand the test to the ten thousandth examination." [1]

But when the exhilaration of the moment was past, there were second thoughts. The war had left the former colonies exhausted, impoverished, and disorganized. Soon the government of the Confederation was mired in confusion, and the very grounds of promise—vast expanse of territory, multiplying population, and diversity of interest—came to be seen as dangers which threatened the nation. Hopefulness gave way to anxiety, and several decades were to elapse before it became evident that the multiple experiment in independence, republicanism, federal union, and religious liberty would be crowned with success.

After the initial intoxication of independence, churchmen were further sobered when they considered the present plight and the future prospect of the churches. Church life had been disrupted by the war. Pastors had marched off with the troops, congregations had been scattered, meetinghouses had been requisitioned as barracks, colleges established for the training of ministerial recruits had been forced to close, synods and associations had been unable to meet, and the close of hostilities witnessed that ebb tide of religious life which often characterizes every postwar era. Furthermore a broader responsibility for the common life had been thrust upon the churches by the mere fact that they now existed within the context of a self-governing nation.

The churches had always been conscious of their role in fostering a godly society but their participation in the shaping of the future had been limited by the dependent colonial status of the American people. Many of the decisions affecting life in the colonies had been made in England, but when the war was won responsibility for the destiny of America—to the

---

[1] The sermon is reprinted in John W. Thornton, *The Pulpit of the American Revolution* (Boston, 1860). See pp. 440–41, 471.

extent that God by his favor or disfavor would permit them to determine it—was placed squarely in American hands. President Witherspoon (1723–94) of Princeton joined President Stiles of Yale in acknowledging that God had indeed blessed the American people beyond all expectation in the winning of independence, but he pointed out that the work of reformation which had elicited divine favor must be continued. If the new nation was to be a godly nation, it was more crucial than ever for the American people to be won to Christian obedience. But before the churches could give themselves wholeheartedly to this task, they had institutional problems of their own to put in order.

While no denomination escaped the effects of the general impoverishment and disruption of the war years, they survived the conflict with varying fortunes. Anglicans, Quakers, Mennonites, and Moravians suffered most; and Congregationalists, Presbyterians, and Baptists suffered least. But all of them had institutional housekeeping chores to perform. Some had been linked to ecclesiastical bodies abroad and needed to fashion ecclesiastical structures of their own. Some needed to re-establish connectional bodies whose functioning had been disrupted by war. And some, having been organized along colonial lines or in regional areas, were confronted by the need to effect a national organization.

Presbyterians, Congregationalists, and Baptists

During the latter decades of the colonial period, an increasing number of Presbyterians and Congregationalists had come to think of themselves as a single denomination. Scotch-Irish Presbyterians moving into the backcountry areas of New England were absorbed into Congregational churches, while New England Congregationalists moving into the middle colonies became Presbyterians. Ministers also moved freely between the pulpits of the two denominations, and the first three presidents of the Presbyterian college at Princeton were New England Congregationalists. Congregationalists had sprung to the defense of Presbyterian interests in New York and New Jersey; Presbyterians had turned to New England for counsel and advice; and joint committees had been formed to carry on the fight to prevent the establishment of an Anglican episcopate in America. In the years immediately preceding the Revolution, this intimate fraternal relationship had been formalized by the exchange of delegates between the Synod of New York and Philadelphia and the General Association of Connecticut, and this tie was reinforced by the tendency of Congregationalists to refer to themselves as Presbyterians.

No religious body was so well equipped for independence as the Presbyterians. Next to the Congregationalists, they were the largest of the American denominations. They had wealth, learning, able leadership, and numerical strength on what was to be the growing edge of the country—a fact which led Theodore Roosevelt to call the Scotch-Irish Presbyterians America's first frontiersmen. They also were a united denomination, the breach between the Old Side and the New Side having been healed in 1758. Furthermore, the Presbyterians enjoyed the prestige of being so strongly identified with the winning side of a war which some had labeled a Presbyterian rebellion. "When the war is over," an agent of Lord Dartmouth had declared, it will become apparent that "Presbyterianism is really at the bottom of this whole conspiracy." [2] And organizationally the Presbyterian house had been put in order. Since the healing of the breach between the Old Side and New Side parties, the Presbyterian churches had been united in the Synod of New York and Philadelphia, and shortly after the close of hostilities a committee of the synod proposed the reorganization of the church into sixteen presbyteries, four synods, and an annual General Assembly. This it was felt would provide a more effective structure for an expanding nation. A "book of discipline and government," embodying this scheme and preserving the right of local presbyteries to control the examination of candidates for the ministry, was approved by the synod in 1787, referred to the presbyteries for consideration, and then formally adopted in 1788. The new General Assembly met for the first time in 1789.

Following the Revolution, steps had been taken by the Presbyterians and the Congregationalists to renew and strengthen the bonds which previously had united them. The practice of exchanging delegates—with full right "to vote in all questions"—was revived, and this "union" was given further implementation when westward migration brought about an intermingling of Presbyterians and Congregationalists in the new settlements. Instead of dividing "the sparse population holding the same faith," as John Blair Smith (1756–99) put it, into "two distinct ecclesiastical

[2] Trinterud, *Forming of an American Tradition*, 250, "Presbyterian," of course, was used in the broad sense which also included Congregationalists.

organizations" and thus preventing "each from achieving those means of grace which both might sooner enjoy but for such division," it was proposed that Presbyterians and Congregationalists be encouraged to form union churches in the frontier areas.[3] In 1801 this "Plan of Union" was put into effect, and seven years later it was supplemented by an "Accommodation Plan" which provided for more complete unity between the two denominations in a "uniform system of church government." For the next three decades Presbyterians and Congregationalists were to all intents and purposes a single denomination in New York, Ohio, Indiana, Illinois, Michigan, and Wisconsin.

Outwardly the Congregationalists were as well prepared as the Presbyterians for independence. They also had prestige, education, and able leaders; and they had larger numbers and greater wealth. In 1760 Ezra Stiles had calculated that a century hence the Congregationalists would have a "population" or "constituency" of seven million, and in 1783 he still was confident that the Congregationalists and Presbyterians would far outdistance all other denominations in number of adherents. The promise was there but, in the event, his calculations proved to be hopelessly wrong. Despite outward signs of strength, Congregationalists were troubled by internal weaknesses and their energies were largely diverted to the task of waging a rear-guard defense of the special privileges they possessed in New England.

The end of the war posed no immediate organizational problem for the Congregationalists. At least two factors forced them to be content with the minimum relationships they had been able to develop prior to the war. For one thing, their status as the state churches of Massachusetts, Connecticut, and New Hampshire inhibited them from fashioning any official structure that would have bound them together across state lines. Moreover, a strong emphasis upon local autonomy had developed which fostered a rigid resistance to any surrender of local prerogatives. This jealous defense of local rights was most pronounced among those who were not church members but who, as inhabitants of the towns, controlled much of the outward affairs of the state-established churches. Later when old fears

[3] W. W. Sweet, *Religion on the American Frontier*, Vol. II, *The Presbyterians, 1783–1840* (N.Y., 1936), 41. The Plan of Union is printed in M. W. Armstrong *et al.*, *The Presbyterian Enterprise*, 102–4, and in Smith, Handy, Loetscher, *American Christianity*, I, 545–47. For a discussion of the "Accommodation Plan," see R. H. and J. H. Nichols, *Presbyterianism in New York State* (Philadelphia, 1963), 83–87.

of ecclesiastical tyranny had been accentuated by the ejection of New School synods from the Presbyterian Church, this spirit of extreme localism was to make it difficult for the Congregationalists to effect a national organization even after they had been disestablished in the three New England states.

The lack of a central organization, however, was not necessarily a liability, as the experience of the Baptists and later of the Disciples was to demonstrate. Nor was it an insuperable obstacle to cooperative endeavors, for the Congregationalists appropriated the English technique of forming voluntary societies of individuals to forward their corporate concerns—a technique which permitted quick response to immediate needs and flexibility in the marshaling of support. Furthermore, it had the great advantage of facilitating joint effort by Congregationalists and Presbyterians without raising too many ecclesiastical complications.

The major weakness of Congregationalism was not ecclesiastical but doctrinal, for the Congregationalists were torn by dissension. There were at least three contending parties within Congregationalism—the "consistent Calvinists" who were the heirs of Jonathan Edwards as he was reinterpreted by Joseph Bellamy and Samuel Hopkins; the "old Calvinists" who were moderate antirevivalists; and the even more rationalistically inclined "liberals" centering in Harvard College and eastern Massachusetts. The warfare among them was increasingly intense and was ultimately to result in the founding of three new centers for ministerial training—at Andover in 1808, at Bangor in 1814, and at Hartford in 1834. Not only was there this continuing controversy within the Congregational churches, but it led to actual schisms with large numbers of the revivalist faction being siphoned off into "Separate Congregational" and Baptist churches, while the "liberal" wing, after the explosion of 1815, found its spiritual home in an independent Unitarianism. As early as 1760 Ezra Stiles reported that there were already 22,000 Baptists in New England in comparison to 60,000 to 70,000 Congregational church members, and during the next fifty years this gap was to be steadily narrowed. In Connecticut there had been an upper-class defection to Anglicanism, and before the end of the century Methodists had begun to make significant inroads.

The growing religious diversity in New England was accompanied by an unrelenting attack upon the remnants of the Congregationalist establishments and Congregationalists became preoccupied with defending what remained of the "Standing Order." This proved to be a fruitless endeavor, for the battle was lost almost before it was begun. At best it was a delaying action, and successive acts of disestablishment brought it to an end in Connecticut in 1818, in New Hampshire in 1819, and in Massachusetts in 1833. When the issue was finally resolved and the Congregationalists had found "in their new insecurity and nakedness a kind of self-respect and self-reliance that made for good health," [4] a degree of doctrinal unity had also been restored to Congregationalism by the conversion of the "old Calvinists" to a revivalist point of view and by the defection of the Unitarians. By this time, however, the opportunity which had been theirs was lost. Although southern New England alone had exported some 800,000 of its population to the West between 1790 and 1830, much of the Congregational blood in the newer regions was flowing through other denominational veins. To the extent that those veins were Presbyterian this was partly by design, for it was not until after 1837 that the tie with the Presbyterians was severed.

The Baptists were the popular wing of the Puritan-Reformed phalanx, and they were growing rapidly during the years immediately preceding and following the Revolution. So marked was their growth that by 1800 the Baptists had become the largest of the American denominations. In spite of the striking gains that they were to make in the West, the Baptists were far from a frontier phenomenon. The greatest gains were made in the East, and throughout the nineteenth century most of the centers of Baptist strength were along the seaboard—in Maine, New Hampshire, Massachusetts, Rhode Island, New York, Pennsylvania, Virginia, and the Carolinas. In New York State alone from 1784 to 1812 the Baptists grew in number of churches from eight to two hundred and thirty-nine, while in New England the increase was from two hundred and sixty-six churches to four hundred and thirty.

Noah Worcester, a Congregational minister in New England, was puzzled by this surge of Baptist growth, and in 1794 he sought to account for it in his *Impartial Inquiries concerning the Progress of the Baptist Denomination*. He could not attribute it to "the rectitude of their peculiar sentiments," but he found other reasons to explain their success—the coldness of ministers and members of other denominations, the sympathy

[4] Edwin S. Gaustad, *Historical Atlas of Religion in America* (N.Y., 1962), 42.

and respect Baptists had gained from persecution, the advantage they had been able to take of revivals and subsequent divisions in other churches, the confident manner in which they made use of "irrelevant" Scripture, and finally "the want of qualifications in some Baptist teachers." An emphasis upon the necessity for a "conversion" experience of the Christian life did give added weight to the Baptist insistence upon believer's baptism, and the appeal to Scripture was persuasive to those who had been taught to accept Scripture as their final authority. But Worcester's explanation of the influence exerted by "some Baptist teachers" who lacked "qualifications" probably missed the point. "Many people," he said, "are so ignorant as to be [more] charmed with sound than sense."

> To them the want of knowledge in a teacher . . . may easily be made up and overbalanced by great zeal, and affecting tone of voice, and a perpetual motion of the tongue. If a speaker can keep his tongue running in an unremitting manner . . . and can quote memoriter a large number of texts from within the covers of the Bible, it matters not to many of his hearers whether he speaks sense or nonsense.

Except in the backcountry of the South, not many of the Baptist preachers were unusually emotional in their preaching, nor did they prize an unlearned ministry. As Baptists got under motion in the closing decades of the eighteenth century, they were busy with projects for establishing academies and a college, and after the turn of the century they became increasingly active in promoting ministerial education. But, overwhelmed by the rapidity of their growth, Baptists had little opportunity to enforce educational standards. Mature men who exhibited gifts of leadership were called into service, and this readiness to utilize what leadership was available was one of the secrets of their growth. As was to be true of the Methodists, the Baptists helped to fill the vacuum that was left by the shortage of ministers among those denominations which adhered more rigidly to formal educational requirements.

The major current of Baptist life prior to the Revolution had had a central ecclesiastical body in the Philadelphia Baptist Association and its subsidiary associations in New England and the South. But this orderly development had been interrupted by the dislocations of war, and by the time peaceful conditions had been fully re-established the denomination had proliferated to such an extent that it was difficult to draw it together again in a national organization. Between 1776 and 1799 more than forty local associations of churches had been formed, and both churches and associations continued to multiply. While these associations maintained correspondence with one another, they had become so deeply infected with a hyperindividualistic spirit that they resisted the formation of any structure which might be utilized to impose any overhead control. Thus the Baptists, like the Congregationalists, resorted to the technique of voluntary societies to implement their common concerns. For a long time, apart from local associations of churches, these voluntary societies were to be the only links which bound Baptists together.[5] This solution to the problem of national organization was to create problems in the future, but at the moment it had the advantage of combining concerted action with a high degree of local initiative.

Anglicans and Methodists

The Church of England was the greatest casualty of the American Revolution. Disestablishment stripped it of the privileges, prestige, and support it had hitherto enjoyed. As the church of the royal officials it had become both disliked and distrusted, and its unpopularity was augmented by the ardent Toryism of many of its clergy, most of whom "to the utmost of their power opposed the spirit of disaffection and rebellion." This was a stance scarcely calculated either to retain or to win the adherence of republicans. Its ranks were also depleted by the Methodist defection in the South and by the emigration to Canada of the "United Empire Loyalists" in the North. In the end only a remnant survived the war. And in many areas, where "latitudinarian" sentiment (see above, p. 92) had stripped them of a sense of mission, this remnant continued to diminish in size. An 1817 report of the diocese of Maryland stated:

> Of the fifty parishes which the diocese contains, the greater part are vacant. The forty clergymen who, about fifteen years ago, labored in the ministry are reduced to twenty-seven. . . . We claim more than eighty places of worship, but of these some do not exhibit one stone or one brick lying upon another, . . . and many for years past, except

[5] A General Convention of the Baptist Denomination was formed in 1814 to enlist support for the work of Adoniram Judson in Burma. For a little more than a decade, this gave promise of developing into a general ecclesiastical body. But after 1826 it reverted to the status of a voluntary foreign-mission society.

when accidentally visited by traveling preachers, have been occupied by the fowls of the air and the beasts of the field.

Within the next two or three years the situation had begun to improve both in Maryland and elsewhere, but the gains were small. In 1820 it was reported that in the former Anglican colony of North Carolina there were 350 Anglican communicants, whereas "a few years ago the number of communicants did not exceed fifty." The total in New Jersey had risen to 800, in Pennsylvania to 1,600, and in New York to 4,000.[6]

The Anglicans were subjected to a triple coercion by the signing of the peace treaty in 1783. First of all, if they were to be at all indigenous to the American scene, it was necessary for them to make an explicit break with a church that acknowledged the King of England as its "supreme governor." Second, since the limited supervision of the clergy and the coordination of their activities by the Commissaries of the Bishop of London had been brought to an end, some other connectional structure had to be devised if the American Anglicans were not to flounder in utter confusion. Third, and most urgent of all, was the major readjustment demanded by a desperate shortage of clergymen, for most of them had fled and had not been replaced. At this point the Anglicans were plagued by their dependence upon England for their ministry. Not only was it impossible to secure ordination in America, but a large portion of the Anglican ministers had been missionaries who drew their support from the Society for the Propagation of the Gospel in London. Independence cut off both this source of supply and this source of support, for the charter of the Society restricted its activity to colonial territory. Moreover, English ordination was no longer available to those who were unable to take an oath of allegiance to the British crown. Nothing less than the forming of an American church would provide the needed independence and supply the needed means of ordination, supervision, and coordination.

Unless the episcopal character of the church were to be abandoned, ordination required an American bishop. An abortive attempt to meet this need was initiated in 1783 by Samuel Seabury (1729–96) with the endorsement of the ten Anglican clergymen of Connecticut. Seabury's

---

[6] F. E. Hawks, *Contributions to the Ecclesiastical History of the United States* (N.Y., 1836–39), II, 428, and *Journal of the Proceedings . . . of the Protestant Episcopal Church . . . A.D. 1820* (Philadelphia, 1820), 37; cited by Gaustad, *Historical Atlas*, 66. W. S. Perry, *The History of the American Episcopal Church* (Boston, 1885), I, 458.

intention was to secure episcopal consecration in England, but after his arrival in London he found this to be impossible since he was not free as an American to take the necessary oath of allegiance to a foreign monarch. As an alternative he was able to secure in Scotland consecration at the hands of the nonjuring bishops, the successors to those bishops who had refused in 1688 to take an oath of allegiance to William and Mary. Seabury, however, was scarcely a man around whom other Anglicans in America could rally. He was held in ill-repute by many for his unyielding Toryism during the war; he was criticized for his rashness in proceeding independently to secure consecration at the hands of schismatic bishops; and his temper was rigid and far from conciliatory. In brief, he constituted more of a problem than a help in the immediate task of fashioning an American church, although his subsequent influence in shaping the life of the church was considerable.

Much of the constructive leadership in the organization of the Protestant Episcopal Church was supplied by William White (1748–1836), of Christ Church in Philadelphia and former chaplain to the Continental Congress. It was he who laid the groundwork for the General Convention which met in Philadelphia in 1785 to frame a constitution, revise the liturgy, and arrange for the consecration of bishops. After the necessary legal adjustments had been made by the British Parliament, White and Samuel Provoost (1742–1815) of New York were sent abroad where they were elevated to episcopal rank in Lambeth chapel on February 4, 1787. White's tactful efforts effected a reconciliation with Seabury and it was a united and fully equipped church which met in the General Convention of 1789. The constitution of the church, in keeping with the temper of the times, carefully safeguarded the rights of local vestries and of lay representation at all levels in the life of the church.

The new Protestant Episcopal Church, however well constituted, looked forward to no very hopeful future. Bishop Provoost relinquished his episcopal duties in 1801, being convinced that the church would "die out with the old colonial families." And others were equally certain that no more than a languishing life of brief duration could be expected.[7] It was not until a new generation of men, most notably Bishops Griswold, Moore, Chase, and Hobart, infused new vigor into its leadership that the Protestant Episcopal Church began to make a significant recovery.

[7] See L. W. Bacon, *A History of American Christianity* (N.Y., 1907), 213, 232.

Prior to 1784 the Methodists were not a church but only "a religious society" which maintained a nominal relationship to the Church of England.[8] Local Methodist societies had been formed in America during the last decade prior to the Declaration of Independence, and they were mostly concentrated in the Chesapeake Bay region and southward through Virginia to North Carolina. One would have supposed that the Revolution would have had the same disastrous effect upon the Methodists as it had upon other Anglicans, for John Wesley was as vocal as the S.P.G. missionaries in his opposition to American independence. Furthermore, almost all the lay preachers which Wesley had sent out to the colonies returned to England after the outbreak of hostilities. Francis Asbury (1745–1816) was the significant exception. The common estimate of Methodist prospects was voiced by an observer when Barrett's Chapel was being built in Delaware during the war years: "It's no use putting up so large a dwelling for Methodists, for after the war a corncrib will hold them all." [9] This may have been the popular opinion, but it was wrong. The eager and contagious enthusiasm of the Methodist societies thrust forward native lay preachers to replace the departed English itinerants, and Asbury spent much of his time in the saddle in order to supervise them. As a result of their activity, the membership of the societies roughly doubled during the period of the Revolution, increasing from approximately five thousand at the beginning of the war to more than ten thousand in 1781. Perhaps the Methodists benefited in part from the suspicion with which they were viewed by most of the Tory Anglican clergy, but their growth was basically little more than additional documentation of the truism that for the next three-quarters of a century the future in America—numerically speaking—belonged to those groups which could provide an ample supply of ministerial leadership, even if much of that leadership was restricted to lay preachers.

The winning of independence was seized upon by American Methodists as an opportunity to form themselves into a separate church. With the ranks of the Anglican clergy largely depleted, John Wesley was prevailed upon in 1784 to ordain ministers for his American brethren so that they would not be denied the consolation of the sacraments. Although he was

[8] John Wesley's two tracts describing the Methodists—*A Plain Account of the People called Methodists* and *The Character of a Methodist*—are reprinted in *Great Voices of the Reformation*, ed., Harry Emerson Fosdick (N.Y., 1952), 499–513.

[9] J. M. Buckley, *A History of Methodists in the United States* (N.Y., 1896), 186.

violating the laws of the Church of England, Wesley was convinced that ordination by presbyters was valid when dictated by necessity, and he found justification for his act in the practice of the ancient church at Alexandria where presbyters had even ordained bishops. Thomas Vasey (1742–1826) and Richard Whatcoat (1736–1806) were the two men ordained, and when they sailed for America they were accompanied by the Rev. Thomas Coke (1747–1814) whom Wesley had appointed to be "joint superintendent" with Francis Asbury "over our brethren in North America." After their arrival, the "Christmas Conference" of 1784 was convened at Baltimore. There the new Methodist Episcopal Church was constituted with the adoption of a form of government and discipline. On Christmas Day Asbury was ordained a deacon; the following day, Sunday, a presbyter; and on Monday Wesley's appointment of Coke and Asbury as "joint superintendents" was confirmed. Before the Conference ended twelve others had been ordained to the ministry of the new church.

"The Revolutionary War now being closed and a general peace established," wrote Jesse Lee (1758–1816), the first official historian of Methodism, "we could go into all parts of the country without fear; and we soon began to enlarge our borders and to preach in many places where we had not been before." [10] The borders were enlarged, and numbers also. New York had been an early center of Methodist activity, and western Pennsylvania and the Ohio valley had been penetrated in 1781. In 1785 the Methodists moved into the seaboard areas of the deep South; in 1786 Kentucky was entered; and in 1789 a rapid extension into New England was initiated. In 1784, at the time of the Christmas Conference, the Methodists had numbered almost 15,000. Six years later, in 1790, there were 57,631 members. By 1820 they had overtaken the Baptists and had become the largest of the American denominations. Coke spent little time in the United States, and it was Asbury who spearheaded the advance, averaging some five thousand miles annually on horseback during these years.

While the importance of Asbury's leadership should not be minimized, a major reason for the astonishingly rapid spread and growth of Methodism is to be found in the adoption by American Methodists of the "circuit system" which Wesley had devised for his English societies. Thus the new church from the beginning was equipped with a highly mobile

[10] *Short History of the Methodists* (Baltimore, 1810), 84.

ministry of traveling preachers who covered a vast territory instead of being rooted in a single locality. The more intimate nurture of the flocks they gathered was provided by local lay preachers and class leaders. No system could have been more admirably designed for moving quickly into new territory, whether that new territory was in the older settled regions of the seaboard or over the mountains in the new communities of the frontier. In both areas Methodists were to meet with equal success, and had they not put down deep roots in the East they would never had had the strength to move so boldly with the initial tide of migration into the West.

The "Christian" movement

John Wesley was partly responsible for another denominational grouping which began to take shape in the early years of the new republic. This grouping was the product of a widespread movement that sought to achieve unity among Christians on the basis of the use of Bible names, the rejection of "human" creeds, and a strict adherence to New Testament precedents in worship and church government. Although the Methodist societies were nominally related to the Church of England, Wesley had taught his followers to be impatient with the theological points which had served to divide "experienced" Christians from one another. Of those seeking admission to his societies, Wesley wrote:

> Methodists do not impose in order to their admission any opinions whatever. Let them hold particular or general redemption, absolute or conditional decrees; let them be churchmen or dissenters, Presbyterians or Independents, it is no obstacle. Let them choose one mode of baptism or another, it is no bar to their admission. . . . [Methodists] think and let think. One condition, and only one, is required—a real desire to save the soul. Where this is, it is enough; they desire no more; they lay stress upon nothing else; they only ask: "Is thy heart herein as my heart? If it be, give me thy hand." [11]

George Whitefield, Samuel Davies, and other leaders of the Great Awakening in America had exhibited a similar spirit, and had urged their converts to "forget party names" and to labor instead to deserve the name

[11] Quoted by W. W. Sweet, *The American Churches: An Interpretation* (N.Y., 1948), 46–47. Wesley assumed, of course, that members of his societies belonged to churches formed on a confessional basis.

"Christian" as their "highest distinction." These men were thinking primarily of the unity of spirit which bound together members of different denominations, permitted them to recognize one another as Christians, and impelled them to work together harmoniously in common tasks without seeking partisan advantage. But there were to be others who thought that the full implication of this type of thinking should be more forthrightly pursued and all denominational divisions abandoned. Believing that a return to the practices of the primitive church would provide a basis upon which all Christians could unite, their program of action was expressed in Thomas Campbell's slogan: "Where the Scriptures speak, we speak; where the Scriptures are silent, we are silent." [12]

This latter sentiment first appeared among a group of Methodists in Virginia led by James O'Kelly (1735?–1826). They had been impressed by the stress of the revivalists upon the name "Christian" as the bond which unites, and in 1784 these Virginia Methodists resolved to be known by no other name and to adopt the Bible as their sole guide to faith and practice. In 1801 a similar movement was initiated in New England when Abner Jones (1772–1841), a Vermont Baptist, became convinced that "sectarian names and human creeds should be abandoned and that true piety alone . . . should be made the test of Christian fellowship and communion." Three years later in Kentucky several Presbyterian ministers, including Barton W. Stone (1772–1844), became persuaded by their happy relationship with the Methodists in the great camp meeting revivals that Christians could and should live together in love. When two of the Presbyterian leaders were charged by the Synod of Kentucky in 1803 with teaching Wesleyan doctrines, they were joined by others in withdrawing from the Synod and forming their own independent Springfield Presbytery. Within months, however, they repudiated this latter action in *The Last Will and Testament of the Springfield Presbytery* and announced that henceforth they were resolved to be known by no name but "Christian." A fourth point of origin was in western Pennsylvania where Thomas Campbell (1763–1854) had settled after his arrival from Ireland in 1807. He had been deeply influenced, as a student at Glasgow, by Scottish Evangelicalism, and he was dismayed that in America he was not permitted to invite all Christians to participate in the communion service whatever their denominational affiliation might be. In 1809 he organized the "Christian

---

[12] This was the motto of the "Christian Association of Washington County, Pa."

Association of Washington County, Pa.," and issued a *Declaration and Address* to summon Christians of every denomination to abandon all unscriptural doctrines and usages and to restore the original unity and purity of New Testament Christianity. A month later he was joined by his son Alexander (1788–1866), who was destined to become the best-known leader of the western "Christians," or "Disciples of Christ." [13]

There was little communication between the eastern and western "Christians." In the East the "Christians" were gradually brought together in the General Convention of the Christian Church, and this was the branch of the movement which a little more than a century later was to unite with the Congregationalists. In the West the Campbellite wing spread rapidly throughout western Pennsylvania, western Virginia, and into Ohio. For a little more than a decade the Campbellites were affiliated with the Baptists, but when Alexander Campbell began publishing the *Christian Baptist* in 1823 his proposed reforms aroused a storm of Baptist opposition and his followers began to withdraw from the Baptist associations. Nine years later a union was effected with the followers of Barton W. Stone in Kentucky and Tennessee. This was to be the larger "Christian" group (the Campbellites tended to prefer the name "Disciples of Christ"), and by 1850 Alexander Campbell claimed that they numbered no fewer than 225,000 adherents. While the "Christian movement" failed in its objective to unite all Christians, it did succeed in becoming one of the larger Protestant denominations.

The smaller denominations

The American Revolution was a time of troubles for the peace churches—Quakers, Mennonites, Moravians, and Dunkers. Often their members were subjected to fines, abuse, and public opprobrium. Conflicting loyalties led to defections which sharply reduced their membership. The consequence was a withdrawal into further isolation as small enclaves within the larger society. This was least true of the Quakers who lacked the defensive rampart of another language and who on occasion moved into the world to exercise an influence far greater than their numbers war-

[13] *The Last Will and Testament* and the major portion of the *Declaration and Address* are printed in Smith, Handy, Loetscher, *American Christianity*, I, 576–86. For the full text, see *Historical Documents Advocating Christian Union*, ed., Charles A. Young (Chicago, 1904).

ranted. Although the Quakers survived the war in greater numbers than the Anglicans, they were soon to be torn by internal divisions and entered what Howard Brinton has called their period of "conflict and decline." [14] Never again were they to be one of the major religious denominations in America.

The Dutch Reformed, as was true also of the German Reformed and Lutherans, were primarily preoccupied in the postwar years with problems of reorganization. The area in the vicinity of New York City which was the center of Dutch Reformed strength had borne the brunt of British occupation. Congregations had been scattered and at the end of the war more than thirty of the seventy-five Dutch congregations were without pastors—a situation which led them in 1784 to set up a professorship of theology in New York City and to focus their attention upon the need to strengthen their fledgling college at New Brunswick. Independence also impressed the Dutch Reformed leaders with the need to organize a General Synod (1792) that would be independent of the ecclesiastical judicatories of the Netherlands. The German Reformed followed the Dutch example, seizing upon independence as an opportune time to break their relationship to the Classis in Holland, which had provided them with support and supervision, by establishing an independent Synod of the German Reformed Church in 1793. The Lutherans were less successful in forming a single ecclesiastical body, but regional synods were organized and four of them were brought together in 1820 to form a General Synod. Later both Reformed groups and the Lutherans were to be strengthened by a growing tide of immigration from their homelands.

The German-speaking churches were also affected by Methodist influence and activity. Jacob Albright (1759–1808) was converted and became a Methodist in 1790, and in 1796 he felt a call to preach among the Germans in eastern Pennsylvania, Maryland, and Virginia. By 1800 several "classes" had been organized, and three years later he was ordained to the ministry by his followers. The first General Conference of what was later to be called the Evangelical Association was held in 1807 and Albright was elected bishop. During the same years Philip William Otterbein (1726–1813), a German Reformed minister in Baltimore, had become a close friend of Francis Asbury. Otterbein began to appropriate Methodist techniques—organizing "classes" and appointing lay leaders to

[14] *Friends for 300 Years*, 175.

assist him. He was joined by Martin Boehm, a former Mennonite, and in 1800 the United Brethren in Christ Church was launched, with Otterbein and Boehm as its bishops.[15] Later the spirit represented by "the Christian movement" came to the fore among the Germans. John Winebrenner (1797–1860), a German Reformed minister in Harrisburg, Pennsylvania, was censured for his revivalist preaching and in 1825 withdrew from the German Reformed Church. In 1830 he formed the General Eldership of the Church of God, announcing his opposition to nonbiblical names, creeds, and forms, and asserting that the only cure for sectarianism was a restoration of the primitive purity of the apostolic church.

Roman Catholics

Excluding slaves and children under twelve, Roman Catholics numbered few more than 16,000 at the close of the Revolution, and they were concentrated almost exclusively in Maryland and Pennsylvania. Just prior to the outbreak of hostilities, ill-feeling had been aroused by the Quebec Act of 1774 which placed the triangular territory south of the Great Lakes and between the Ohio and Mississippi rivers within the boundaries of the province of Quebec. The Act was interpreted by some ardent patriots as evidence that the British government was ready to surrender this vast inland empire to Roman Catholicism, and it was exploited by them as a religious issue to whip up anti-British feeling. By the end of the war, however, the fears and apprehensions thus generated had been largely forgotten. Charles Carroll (1737–1832) had rallied many of his coreligionists in Maryland to the colonial cause, and Irish Catholics in Pennsylvania had demonstrated their unwillingness to dishonor the memory of their fathers by any hesitancy to fight the English. This display of loyalty plus military support by the French allayed former suspicions, and when the guarantee of religious liberty was formulated in the First Amendment there was no thought of denying such liberty to Roman Catholics.

The Roman Catholic Church in the colonies had been under the jurisdiction of the Vicar Apostolic in London but independence made this arrangement inappropriate. In 1784 John Carroll (1735–1815), a cousin

[15] A century and a half later, in 1946, these two groups united to form the Evangelical United Brethren Church. A further merger with the Methodist Church is planned to be consummated in 1972.

of Charles Carroll, was appointed "superior of the missions" with full responsibility to direct the affairs of the church in the United States, and six years later he was elevated to episcopal rank. In 1808 the diocese of Baltimore was given metropolitan status with Carroll as archbishop, and four suffragan sees were created with headquarters in Boston, New York, Philadelphia, and Bardstown, Kentucky. Eighteen years later four additional sees—Richmond, Charleston, St. Louis, and New Orleans—had been established.

In the new republic the Roman Catholic Church was to experience many growing pains. The number of adherents rapidly mounted, partly as the result of the acquisition of the older French settlements along the Mississippi but more largely as a consequence of mass immigration from Ireland and southern Germany. Tension between the various nationality groups often was acute and this complicated the task of maintaining an orderly development of church life. The installation of refugee priests from France as pastors of Irish congregations, for example, aroused resentment.

One of the more serious problems was posed by "lay trustees." All churches in America had been vexed by the self-assertiveness of the laity and the Roman Catholic Church was no exception. In the immediate postwar years, Americans in general were especially conscious of their "rights" and "liberties" and were determined not to be pushed around. The effect of this pervasive spirit upon Roman Catholics was explained by Archbishop Ambrose Maréchal of Baltimore in 1818.

> The American people pursue with a most ardent love the civil liberty which they enjoy. For the principle of civil liberty is paramount with them, so that absolutely all the magistrates from the highest to the lowest are elected by popular vote. . . . Likewise all the Protestant sects . . . are governed by these same principles, and as a result they elect and dismiss their pastors at will. Catholics in turn, living in their midst, are evidently exposed to the danger of admitting the same principles of ecclesiastical government.[16]

They were not only exposed to the danger; many succumbed to it. As early as 1786 the trustees of St. Peter's Church in New York City asserted their right to choose and dismiss their pastor, and three years later the congregation of Holy Trinity Church in Philadelphia followed the example

[16] *Documents of American Catholic History*, ed. John Tracy Ellis (Milwaukee, 1955), 219.

of St. Peter's in choosing their own pastor. Similar acts of disobedience occurred in Charleston and New Orleans; and a congregation at Norfolk went so far as to assert that the bishop, according to the "civil rights and religious liberties" guaranteed by the laws of Virginia, had no authority to interfere in the affairs of any congregation or in "any of their religious matters whatever." As late as 1847 Bishop Timon of Buffalo was shut out of his own cathedral by rebellious trustees, and a decade earlier the cathedral trustees in New York City withheld the salary of Bishop Dubois. Even where overt defiance was absent, there was frequently chronic friction. It was not until the custody of property was transferred from lay trustees to the bishops that the situation was finally regularized.

The flood of Roman Catholic immigrants constituted the greatest problem of the church during these years. No fewer than one million immigrants of Roman Catholic background arrived in the United States between 1790 and 1850.[17] Had it not been for extensive assistance from abroad in the form of both funds and personnel, the task of ministering to these new Americans would have been completely impossible. As early as 1791 the French Sulpicians had founded St. Mary's Seminary in Baltimore to provide training for a native priesthood, but throughout the nineteenth century major reliance had to be placed upon men sent from various European countries. The religious orders rendered notable service, especially in the field of education. Colleges, academies, and parochial schools were established. By 1840 there were at least two hundred parochial schools, staffed in part by native sisterhoods—the Sisters of Charity, the Friends of Mary, the Sisters of Nazareth, the Visitandines, and the Society of St. Catherine of Siena—which had come into being during the first three decades of the century. The "school controversy," which was to agitate the life of the nation, was initiated in 1840 when Bishop John Hughes (1797–1864) of New York petitioned for Roman Catholics to be given a proportionate share of public education funds for their parochial schools.

By 1852, when the First Plenary Council of American bishops was held, the Roman Catholic Church had become the largest single ecclesiastical body in the nation, and a number of noteworthy converts testified to its growing indigenous character. Among these converts were Elizabeth

17 Gerald Shaughnessy, *Has the Immigrant Kept the Faith?* (N.Y., 1925), 73, 117, 125, 134.

Bayley Seton (1774–1821) who founded the Sisters of Charity in 1809; Orestes A. Brownson (1803–1876) whose pilgrimage led him from Presbyterianism into the Universalist and then the Unitarian ministry before he became a Roman Catholic in 1844; and Isaac Thomas Hecker (1819–88), a colleague of Brownson at Brook Farm (see below, pp. 188–89), who became the founder of the Paulist Fathers. Compared with total membership, however, there were relatively few converts, and throughout the rest of the century Roman Catholicism was to continue to gain its greatest strength from immigration.

Estimating the influence of the churches

Subsequent chapters will detail the response of the churches to the larger problems bequeathed to them by independence. Their goal was a Christian nation. While there is room for debate as to the adequacy of their understanding of what this implied and as to the propriety of the means they employed in pursuing this goal, one should not be misled in estimating their influence by interpreting early nineteenth-century statistics of church membership as if they were comparable to twentieth-century membership figures. Such statistics are always uncertain and ambiguous, but it is probable that the estimated increase in church membership from one out of every fifteen persons in the total population in 1800 to one out of eight in 1835 is reasonably accurate. The doubling of membership is significant. The point at which misunderstanding occurs is when these figures are compared to post-Civil War and twentieth-century membership figures. Even before the Civil War membership requirements had begun to be relaxed, and after the war there was a progressive decline in church discipline. There is remarkable uniformity of evidence which indicates that during the early decades of the nineteenth century the number attending a Sabbath service was usually three times as large as the membership.[18] Furthermore, churches computed their church "popula-

---

[18] For the 1837–38 conference year Allen Wiley, a pioneer Indiana presiding elder, gave roughly 3,000 as the membership of the Crawfordsville Methodist District and 12,000 as the total of those present at services, Allen Wiley, "Methodism in Southeastern Indiana," *Indiana Magazine of History* (1927). Andrew Reed, an English Congregationalist, reported in 1835 that two Presbyterian churches in Lexington, Kentucky, had 300 members and 1,200 at services; two Baptist churches had 200 members and about 1,000 attendants; two Methodist societies had 400 members and 1,100 attendants. Andrew Reed and James Matheson, *A Narrative of the Visit to the American Churches* (N.Y., 1835), I, 132. See also Edwin S. Gaustad, *Historical Atlas of Religion in America*, 158; *Minutes of the Philadelphia Baptist Association, 1707–1807*, ed. A. D. Gillette (Philadelphia, 1851), 458–59; and Robert Baird, *Religion in America* (N.Y., 1856), 378.

tion" or "constituency" (those nominally related to the church) as approximately twice the number of attendants. In terms of twentieth century definitions of church membership (when what was once the "constituency" has become the "membership"), the increase in church membership would have been from approximately 40 per cent of the population in 1800 to something in the neighborhood of 75 per cent in 1835. One suspects that the estimate of church "population" may have been overoptimistic, but the translation of the statistics into twentieth-century terms is sufficiently arresting to confirm the reports of contemporary observers that by 1835 the churches had succeeded in dominating much of the life of the new nation.

But this is to anticipate the story. The initial outlook for the churches was far from auspicious. They had little reason to expect that by the 1830's, when Alexis de Toqueville visited the United States, he would report that "there is no country in the world in which the Christian religion retains a greater influence over the souls of men than in America." [19]

[19] *Democracy in America,* ed. Phillips Bradley (N.Y., 1945), I, 303.

VI

Protestant Resurgence and Expansion

It took the major Protestant churches until about 1800 to regroup and reorder their forces. By this time the churches had become acutely aware that the nation which had prospered in war had become, from the point of view of religious observance, slovenly in peace. The Presbyterian General Assembly in 1798 echoed the common lament when it bewailed the "general dereliction of religious principle and practice among our fellow citizens" and the "visible and prevailing impiety and contempt for the laws and institutions of religion." This conventional irreligion was sufficiently disturbing to those who believed that the health of any society was dependent upon the moral principles and virtuous habits inculcated by true religion, but even more alarming was the aggressive Deism of Thomas Paine (1737–1809), Ethan Allen (1738–89), and Elihu Palmer (1764–1806), for they had launched a frontal attack upon the whole concept of revealed religion.[1]

Deist sentiment was not new in America, but hitherto it had been confined to an aristocratic elite who frowned upon any widespread

[1] See G. A. Koch, *Republican Religion.*

dissemination of their views because they believed that the "superstitions" of revealed religion did little harm and actually had the beneficial effect of promoting morality among the common people and thus helped to preserve good order in society. In the first flush of enthusiasm evoked by the French Revolution, however, Deism was transformed into a popular movement, and pamphleteers began to attack the churches as the great enemies of progress. Although Robert Baird (1798–1863) was later to speak of the French Revolution as that "volcano" which for a time "threatened to sweep the United States into its fiery stream," the danger was more apparent than real.[2] It is true that "deistical societies" were formed and that students in most of the colleges took delight in shocking their elders by calling each other Voltaire and Rousseau, but in retrospect it is clear that this type of rationalism had no deep rootage. The depraved "state of nature" which engulfed France in the years following 1793 dismayed Americans generally and was utilized to discredit and overwhelm the whole Deist movement. At the time, however, the danger posed by French "infidelity" seemed real and threatening, and for a decade or two it provided churchmen with an effective hortatory device to rouse the churches from their lethargy and to summon them to action.

By 1800 the churches had also become aware of another problem that was to be of serious and continuing concern. This was the problem presented by the flow of population into the fertile valleys beyond the mountains. Even prior to independence small pockets of settlement had been expanding south of the Ohio River, and after 1790 this westward migration became a stampede. Population spread quickly to the Mississippi River. Kentucky was admitted as a state in 1792, Tennessee in 1796, Ohio in 1803, Louisiana in 1812, Indiana in 1816, Alabama in 1817, Illinois in 1818, Mississippi in 1819. By 1821 the barrier of the Mississippi River had been sufficiently breached for Missouri to become a state. Then within two decades, without waiting for the intervening territory to be fully occupied, the rush to the Pacific began.

As early as 1760 Ezra Stiles had called attention to the importance of the West, and a sense of alarm was created as soon as it became apparent that within a short time the balance of political power in the new nation

---

[2] *Religion in America* (N.Y., 1844), 102. Baird's work is one of the classic accounts of the American religious scene. Philip Schaff drew heavily upon its insights when he wrote his account in *America: A Sketch of Its Political, Social, and Religious Character.*

would be in the hands of those who were migrating in such numbers to the newer settlements. The great fear was that the people of the West, being far removed from the civilizing and Christianizing influence of the settled communities of the East, would revert to "barbarism" and thus subvert the moral order of society. Throughout the first half of the nineteenth century, an insistence upon the urgent necessity to find some means of countering a possible lapse of the West into barbarism was to be a repetitive refrain on the lips of earnest churchmen.[3] John England (1786–1842), Roman Catholic bishop of Charleston, South Carolina, recognized the crucial importance of what was to become the heartland of the nation when he declared: "Give us the West, and we shall take care of the East." [4]

Establishing churches and providing a ministry in the newer settlements was to be a task of overwhelming magnitude, but it would be a mistake to draw too sharp a distinction between the East and the West, between the conditions of life in the older setlements and on the frontier. The frontier rapidly receded and the new settlements quickly assumed the characteristics of those areas from which the settlers had come. Life in the Kentucky and Tennessee hills, for example, did not differ greatly from life in the backcountry regions of Virginia and the Carolinas. The plantations of the southern seaboard were quickly duplicated in Alabama and Mississippi, and replicas of the mansions of Charleston dotted the banks of the Ohio River. Farther north, along the trail of westward-migrating Yankees through western New York, Ohio, Michigan, Illinois, Wisconsin, and Iowa, farmhouses and villages indistinguishable from those of New England were to be found almost within a decade of the first penetration.

Nor did the manner of life differ greatly after the first adventurers and speculators had pushed on to a newer frontier. It was a rural society both East and West, and in both East and West there was relative isolation for those who desired it. A European traveler in the East was apt to be more impressed with unbroken stretches of woodland than with any vast expanse of open fields. In 1790, in the entire country, there were only six communities with as many as eight thousand inhabitants—Philadelphia, New York, Boston, Charleston, Baltimore, and Salem—and these as

---

[3] The most eloquent statement of the threat was Horace Bushnell's *Barbarism, the First Danger* (N.Y., 1847). See also Lyman Beecher's *A Plea for the West* (Cincinnati 1835), a portion of which is reprinted in M. W. Armstrong *et al.*, *The Presbyterian Enterprise*, 140–43. John Mason Peck was also a key figure in publicizing the danger.

[4] Schaff, *America*, 187.

seaports were far from typical. And the West almost immediately began to produce port cities of its own. By 1820 Cincinnati and New Orleans were cities of consequence. By 1830 Pittsburgh, Rochester, Buffalo, Louisville, and St. Louis had become thriving centers with a population that ranked them among the top cities of the country. A decade later Cleveland, Detroit, Chicago, and Milwaukee had become boomtowns of importance. And, as in the East, there were lesser urban centers that were growing in size.

There were differences, to be sure. The population in the West was much younger and more uninhibited. Migration itself was a selective process. As a rule only the more adventuresome and sturdy-spirited were willing to undertake the long trek to the unsettled areas. But, on the whole, the population mirrored its own background. Where there were many who tended to be crude, turbulent, and illiterate, as was true along the tributaries of the lower Ohio, they did not differ greatly in these respects from their fathers and mothers in the regions from whence they had come. In religion, the strands linking the West to the East are equally evident. The Methodists tended to be exuberant wherever they were. The Kentucky revivalists were mostly products of Virginia and they moved with equal freedom into North Carolina. The revivalists preceding and following Charles G. Finney (see below, pp. 141–44) in western New York made repeated tours of New England. Lyman Beecher on one occasion, it is true, said that if Finney ever came to New England, he would meet him at the border and fight him all the way to Boston. But later it was Beecher himself who invited Finney to come to Boston. Edwin S. Gaustad has rightly called attention to the fact that during the first half of the nineteenth century the churches were engaged not only in a "conquest of the West" but also in a "reconquest of the East," and both these conquests were closely interrelated and can be understood only as part of a single surge of new religious life and activity.[5]

The second awakening

As was to be expected in the light of their past experience, an initial reaction of the Protestant churches to the need for action was a renewed emphasis upon the tried and proved expedient of revivalistic preaching.

[5] *Historical Atlas of Religion in America*, 37, 42.

And this preaching, in turn, was to provoke the great wave of revivals—known as "the Second Great Awakening"—which was to sweep back and forth across the country for almost two generations after 1800.[6]

The onset of this Second Awakening is difficult to chart, for it appeared in many localities almost simultaneously. The earlier colonial Awakening, of course, had been perpetuated to some degree among both Baptists and Methodists. And during the 1790's scattered revivals had begun to occur among the Congregationalists in the more remote sections of New England. In Virginia the most significant event was a revival among the students at Hampden-Sydney and Washington colleges in 1787, which sent some thirty to forty men into the Presbyterian ministry. Joined by James McGready (1758?-1817), a graduate of John McMillan's "log college" at Washington, Pennsylvania, these young men fanned out into the Carolinas and into Kentucky and Tennessee, and were responsible for the quickening religious interest which culminated in 1800 in the great camp-meeting revival that was held in Logan County, Kentucky. The excitement generated by the camp meeting spread rapidly throughout Kentucky and Tennessee; back into the Carolinas, Virginia, and western Pennsylvania; and then northward into the new settlements beyond the Ohio River. In central and western New York there were revivals of sufficient number and scope in 1800 for local annalists to refer to that year as the year of "the great revival." And in 1802 there was a revival at Yale where, as the result of a notable series of chapel sermons by Timothy Dwight (1752-1817), one-third of the student body professed conversion.[7] President Dwight had stumbled into the revival quite inadvertently. Distressed by the "freethinking" views being espoused by the students, he had boldly launched an attack in which he sought to demonstrate that the only alternative to godliness was first anarchy and then despotism. The intensity of the student response was surprising. It convinced Dwight that revivals could be exploited as an effective antidote to "infidelity," and this he proceeded to do.

The revival at Yale was significant for several reasons. Dwight commanded wide respect among the "old Calvinists" and under his

---

[6] For a general account, see B. A. Weisberger, *They Gathered at the River* (Boston, 1958), 3-158.

[7] For Dwight, see C. E. Cuningham's biography, *Timothy Dwight* (N.Y., 1942).

leadership these heirs of the moderate antirevivalist party among the Congregationalists were brought into the revivalist camp. It was also significant in terms of the students it sent out to become leaders of the revival campaign, most notably Lyman Beecher (1775–1863) and Nathaniel W. Taylor (1786–1858). Beecher was to be the great organizer and promoter of the New England Awakening, while Taylor was the theologian who worked out the appeal and provided the intellectual defense.[8] Finally, through the contagion of Yale's example the revival spread to other colleges and soon became an established institution on most American campuses with the number of "hopeful converts" being regularly reported. In this way additional leadership was recruited to carry on the campaign.

The new revivalism was markedly different from the revivalism of the first Awakening under Jonathan Edwards when the outpouring of God's spirit was regarded as a by-product of the faithful preaching of God's Word. Christians "waited" for these earlier revivals, Calvin Colton remarked, "as men are wont to wait for showers of rain, without even imagining that any duty was incumbent upon them as instruments."[9] In the Second Awakening, however, a change began to be introduced. More and more preachers sought to provoke a revival by utilizing "means" that were calculated to cause the hearers to make a decision and to make it right. Thus the revival became a technique—a technique, to be sure, that had been earlier somewhat self-consciously developed by George Whitefield, but never had it been quite so instrumental in character. Heretofore the revival had always been in a sense an end in itself; now it became an adjunct to other ends, and discourses could be written on "The Necessity of Revivals of Religion to the Perpetuity of our Civil and Religious Institutions."[10]

The early revivals in the West were not greatly dissimilar in character to those in the East, being no less deliberately sought and provoked. What distinguished them was a more undisciplined emotionalism. The western revivalists in the early years were dealing with a moving, floating, migrating population, and they were operating in a situation where

[8] See S. E. Mead, *Nathaniel W. Taylor* (Chicago, 1942), and C. R. Keller, *The Second Great Awakening in Connecticut* (New Haven, 1942).

[9] *History and Character of American Revivals of Religion* (London, 1832), 2–6.

[10] It was published as an article in *The Spirit of the Pilgrims of* 1831. See *The Shaping of American Religion*, ed. J. W. Smith and A. L. Jamison, 362.

opportunities for Christian nurture were few and often nonexistent. Consequently they had to push for a much quicker decision than their eastern contemporaries. Subjected to this coercion, the revivalists in the West tended to turn on all the heat they could and to appeal to the emotions much more than to the intellect. This was especially true in Kentucky and Tennessee where much of the early population was unusually rough, turbulent, and unlettered. In the upland regions of the South, from whence they had come, opportunities for schooling had been scant, and uninhibited displays of religious emotion had been a frequent occurrence. Many of them were like Augustus Longstreet's "honest Georgian" who "preferred his whiskey straight and his politics and religion red hot."

THE CAMP MEETINGS. A distinctive feature of frontier religious life was the camp meeting—a technique developed by the fiery Presbyterian minister James McGready.[11] McGready had stormed into Kentucky in 1796 and had become the pastor of three small congregations on the Red, Gasper, and Muddy rivers. They were all in Logan County on the Tennessee border—a section that Peter Cartwright (1785–1872) described as "Rogue's Harbor" because of the reputed horse thieves, runaway servants, and desperadoes who sought to lose their identity in this remote region. Cartwright further reported that "there was not a newspaper printed south of the Green River, no mill short of forty miles, and no schools worth the name. We killed our meat out of the woods, wild; and beat our meal. . . . As for coffee, I am not sure that I ever smelled it for ten years." [12] Among these backwoodsmen, McGready's impassioned preaching began to elicit a growing response and many, he reported, were struck with "an awful sense of their lost estate." But it was not until 1800 that their pent-up emotions burst loose.

A four-day sacramental meeting was held at Red River in June. Two Presbyterian ministers, William Hodges and John Rankin, were there to assist McGready, and the two McGee brothers—William, a Presbyterian minister, and John, a Methodist minister—were also present. During the first three days McGready, Hodges, and Rankin spoke, and several times

[11] Charles A. Johnson, *The Frontier Camp Meeting* (Dallas, 1955) is by far the ablest treatment of this subject.

[12] Cartwright was a Methodist circuit-rider and his *Autobiography* is a vivid and fascinating account of frontier life. A voluminous collection of essays and source materials dealing with religious life in the West is contained in W. W. Sweet's four volumes, *Religion on the American Frontier, The Baptists* (N.Y., 1931), *The Presbyterians* (N.Y., 1936), *The Congregationalists* (Chicago, 1939), *The Methodists* (Chicago, 1946).

the audience was reduced to tears. On the final day, John McGee—the Methodist brother—could restrain himself no longer. He rose and began to exhort the people "to let the Lord Omnipotent reign in their hearts." When a woman "shouted" for mercy, he moved to her side.

> Several spoke to me: "You know these people. Presbyterians are much for order. They will not bear this confusion. Go back and be quiet." I turned to go back and was near falling, [but] the power of God was strong upon me. I turned again, and losing sight of fear of man, I went through the house shouting and exhorting with all possible ecstasy and energy.

Soon the floor was "covered by the slain" and "their screams for mercy pierced the heavens." According to McGready, the most notorious "prophane swearers and Sabbath-breakers" were "pricked to the heart" and many were "crying out 'what shall we do to be saved?' " [13]

News of the excitement at Red River spread rapidly and, flushed with success, McGready decided to capitalize upon this interest by circulating word throughout the scattered settlements that the Gasper River sacramental service would be held the last week in July. Stirred possibly by curiosity as much as anything else, great numbers came to Gasper River from distances of fifty and even one hundred miles. Makeshift tents of sheets, quilts, or branches were erected, and the underbrush near the church was cleared away so that the services could be held out of doors to accommodate the throng that had assembled. Events at Gasper River were even more exciting than those of the previous month at Red River, and its success quickly led to the staging of other camp meetings which drew larger and larger crowds. The most famous of them all was at Cane Ridge in Bourbon County the following summer, when the number attending was variously estimated from ten to twenty-five thousand. Even ten thousand was a fantastic total at a time when Lexington, the largest settlement in the state, had only 1,795 inhabitants.

Whatever the actual numbers may have been at the camp meetings, there was abundant confusion. Preachers of every denomination attended and were encouraged to exhort the throng simultaneously from preaching stands erected at suitable distances. People would drift from one stand to

---

[13] Johnson, *The Frontier Camp Meeting*, 34–35. Weisberger, *They Gathered at the River*, 24–25.

another. They would gather in smaller groups to hear recent converts relate their experience, and then would burst into hymns of praise. And the conversions that were effected released tidal waves of feeling. With "the traditionally slow cycle of guilt, despair, hope, and assurance" being compressed into a few days or even hours, the emotional stress was agonizingly intensified and it cut deep into normal restraint. Not only were there outbursts of weeping and shouts of joy, but frequently in the frenzied excitement of the moment men and women were suddenly swept into physical "exercises"—falling, running, jumping, jerking—which were attributed to the smiting power of the Holy Spirit. The accounts of these physical manifestations were undoubtedly exaggerated by both friendly and hostile witnesses, but they were sufficiently numerous to arouse misgivings in the minds of many.

There were many reasons why the camp meetings should have caused the faithful to rejoice. There is no way to prove that they elevated the moral tone of the communities along the tributaries of the Ohio, but George A. Baxter, president of Washington College in Virginia, who visited Kentucky in 1801 had no doubts on this score.

> I found Kentucky . . . the most moral place I had ever been. A profane expression was hardly ever heard. A religious awe seemed to pervade the country. Upon the whole, I think the revival in Kentucky the most extraordinary that has ever visited the church of Christ; and all things considered, it was peculiarly adapted to the circumstances of that country. . . . Something of an extraordinary nature seemed necessary to arrest the attention of a giddy people who were ready to conclude that Christianity was a fable and futurity a dream. This revival has done it. It has confounded infidelity, awed vice into silence, and brought numbers beyond calculation under serious impressions.[14]

More tangible evidence of the beneficent effect of the camp meetings was the swelling membership of the churches. In Kentucky alone between 1800 and 1803 the Baptists gained more than ten thousand members and the Methodists had an equal number of accessions. The Presbyterian growth may have been as large but it was obscured and then reduced by a triple secession.

Many Presbyterians were disturbed by the camp-meeting extrava-

[14] Quoted from the *Methodist Magazine* (London), XXVI (1803), 93, by L. W. Bacon, *A History of American Christianity* (N.Y., 1907), 237.

gances they had helped to foster, and in 1805 the General Assembly expressed a stern note of disapproval when it announced that "God is a God of order and not of confusion, and whatever tends to destroy the comely order of his worship is not from him." The disenchantment of the General Assembly had been hastened by the tendency of the Presbyterian camp-meeting revivalists to accept "the doctrine of grace as held by the Methodists" and by their undue laxity in enforcing adequate educational standards for ordination. Both issues had led or were leading to schism. The first, centering in the doctrinal issue, was the "New Light" schism of 1803 which, under the leadership of Barton W. Stone, was quickly transmuted into the Kentucky wing of the "Christian movement." The second schism had its beginnings in 1805 when the Cumberland Presbytery was dissolved by the Synod of Kentucky for ordaining "illiterate" exhorters. The problem of the presbytery, of course, had been to find ministers for the mushrooming churches. When repeated appeals to the General Assembly proved to be unavailing, the revivalist members of the presbytery formed what was to become the Cumberland Presbyterian Church. A third secession also took place in 1805 when Shaker emissaries from New York appeared on the scene and won a considerable number of Presbyterians in southern Ohio and Kentucky, including three ministers, to the peculiar tenets of Ann Lee (see below, pp. 183–85).

If the Presbyterians had trouble handling the energies generated by the camp meetings, the Methodists did not. They had long been accustomed to noise and excitement and they were equally accustomed to "on-the-job" training for their preachers. Furthermore, the theology of the camp-meeting exhorters with its implicit rejection of predestination and its explicit emphasis upon salvation as potentially available to all, which proved to be so divisive among Presbyterians, posed no problem for the Methodists. This was the gospel they had preached from the beginning. At Gasper River it had been a Methodist preacher, John McGee, who had set the theological tone for the subsequent camp meetings by demonstrating that even the hardest sinners would respond if it was made clear to them by a blunt approach that in winning one's way to heaven the help of the Holy Spirit would not be denied the truly penitent.

Within little more than a decade the camp meeting had become almost exclusively the property of the Methodists. By 1811 Methodists were holding their own camp meetings—at least four hundred of them scattered throughout the country. As the camp meetings were domesticated by the Methodists and were adapted to the conditions of life in other sections of the nation, much of the frenzied excitement of the first few years disappeared. Grounds were policed, admittance was restricted, crowds were carefully controlled, and the meetings became much more sober, dignified, and orderly. By the 1830's, even among the Methodists, the camp meetings had become an occasion when the faithful gathered to combine an annual outing with an opportunity to listen to inspirational addresses. Ultimately the camp grounds—at Chautauqua, New York; Ocean Grove, New Jersey; Junaluska, North Carolina; Oak Bluffs, Massachusetts; Bayview, Michigan; and at a hundred other locations—were transformed into conference centers or summer resorts.

The camp meeting as such did not play a great part in the development of American religious life because it was the product of a particular frontier, and the frontier period in any given locality was of brief duration. As soon as the scattered population and isolated life that characterized the earliest penetration of the Ohio valley was replaced by settled communities with churches and schools and a social life of their own, the death knell of the camp meeting as an effective evangelistic device had been sounded. A new technique—the protracted meeting—was developed to marshal the group pressure that the camp meetings had demonstrated to be so successful in inducing conversions.

NEW MEASURES. The final thrust of the Second Awakening took shape in central and western New York under the aegis of Charles G. Finney (1792-1875).[15] Until Finney's appearance on the scene, the northern phase of the Awakening had been kept firmly in the hands of settled ministers and only the ordinary "means of grace" had been used. Even when the "gifts" of a traveling evangelist such as Asahel Nettleton (1783-1844) were utilized, the evangelist stayed with the local pastor, preached the Sunday sermons, delivered an extra lecture or two, participated in the prayer meeting, and visited the homes. Disorder and confusion were discouraged. If an audience began to show signs of undue emotion, the people were apt to be dismissed and the distraught would be

[15] Whitney R. Cross, *The Burnt-over District: The Social and Intellectual History of Enthusiastic Religion in Western New York, 1800-1850,* which treats western New York as a case study of westward transit of New England culture, gives major attention to Finney. This is also true of B. A. Weisberger, *They Gathered at the River,* and William G. McLoughlin, Jr., *Modern Revivalism* (N.Y., 1959).

counseled in private. Finney was much too impatient to put up with such restraint. Before his conversion in 1821, Finney had said that he did not believe that Christians were really sincere. How could they believe that people "were on the verge of hell and yet be so indifferent in regard to this terrific fact"? If he were ever converted, he said, he would be a Christian in earnest and "pull men out of the fire."

At the age of twenty-nine, Finney was a lawyer in Adams, New York, and by his own confession a sinful, worldly man. He attended the Presbyterian church, led the choir, and debated theological points with the pastor. But the dazzling insight which led to his conversion was the product of his own reflections. On an October day as he was walking to his office, it dawned upon him that salvation was a much simpler matter than he had supposed. All that was needed to receive it was "my own consent to give up my sins and accept Christ." As he remembered it, he stopped dead in the middle of the street and said to himself: "I will accept it today or I will die in the attempt." He recalled the word of Scripture: "Then shall ye go and pray unto me, and I will hearken unto you" (Jer. 29:12). To Finney this was a contract, and that night his prayers were answered with a "mighty baptism" that overwhelmed him. "The Holy Spirit descended upon me in a manner that seemed to go through me body and soul. . . . I wept aloud with joy and love; and I do not know but I should say, I literally bellowed out the unutterable gushings of my heart." The next morning when a deacon of the church called to remind him of a case in court that was set for ten o'clock, Finney's response was immediate and decisive: "Deacon B——, I have a retainer from the Lord Jesus Christ to plead his cause, and I cannot plead yours." [16]

Finney pursued his theological studies under George W. Gale (1789–1861), the Presbyterian pastor at Adams, and began to make preaching expeditions into neighboring communities. In 1824 a Female Missionary Society sent him on a missionary tour of Jefferson County. He began at Evans Mills and Antwerp where he converted "the great mass of the population." His success was equally great in other communities. Six feet two inches in height, with great piercing eyes that had an uncanny hypnotic effect, he was a commanding figure in the pulpit. He had few mannerisms, and spoke the simple language of everyday life. He said that

[16] Finney's account of his conversion is printed in Smith, Handy, Loetscher, *American Christianity*, II, 19–24.

he merely talked about the things the preachers preached about, but he did it with a bluntness that few could evade. In 1825 he moved into the Mohawk valley. The village of Western was the first to catch fire. Then Rome exploded; Utica, Boonville, and Verona were swept by the conflagration. By this time Finney was attracting national attention and he was wanted everywhere at once. In 1827 he went to Wilmington, then spent the winter in Philadelphia, and in 1828 made a brief foray into New York City.

It has been said that Finney arrived in New York City with "his backwoods invasion of civilization" at about the time Andrew Jackson entered the White House, but the analogy is not too accurate. Finney was no backcountry rustic. Nor, for that matter, was Jackson. Finney had been trained as a lawyer, had mastered the points of theology with sufficient thoroughness to be able later to write a book on systematic theology, and was to end his career as a professor at, and for a time president of, Oberlin College. His great talent was to make the complicated doctrines of Nathaniel W. Taylor's "New Divinity" as clear and sensible as the multiplication table. He boasted, with good reason, that his success was greatest with the business and professional classes. Rochester, the scene of his greatest single triumph, was typical in this respect. "The exceptional feature," Whitney R. Cross observed, "was the phenomenal dignity of this awakening. No agonizing souls fell in the aisles, no raptured ones shouted hallelujahs. . . . The great evangelist, 'in an unclerical suit of gray,' acted 'like a lawyer arguing . . . before a court and jury,' talking precisely, logically, with wit, verve, and informality. Lawyers, real-estate magnates, millers, manufacturers, and commercial tycoons led the parade of the regenerated." [17]

The controversial feature of Finney's revivals was what were called his "new measures." [18] He was "bred a lawyer," he said, and he refused to be inhibited from winning his case by being restricted to conventional practices. His were the tactics of a trial lawyer. He said "you" instead of "they" when speaking of the wicked, and on occasion he did not hesitate to mention a notorious sinner by name. The "convicted" were brought forward to the "anxious bench"—a front pew roughly analogous to the

[17] *The Burned-over District*, 155.
[18] See his *Lectures on Revivals of Religion*, ed. W. G. McLoughlin (Cambridge, Mass., 1960).

witness stand—where attention was centered upon them and where they served to dramatize the struggle for heaven in the soul of every man. Women, to the scandal of many, were encouraged to testify and to pray in public. But the great "innovation" was Finney's adaption of the revival to an urban environment. The entire community was mobilized by bands of workers visiting the homes. Prayer meetings were held at "unseasonable hours"—unseasonable, that is, for farmers. And the conventional routine of stated services—the Sunday sermons and the weekday lecture—was displaced by special services held each night and often prolonged for hours in inquiry sessions. This was the "protracted meeting"—a communitywide revival campaign of several weeks' duration—which was designed to marshal the group pressure in settled areas that the camp meetings had been so effective in fostering on the frontier by intensifying the conviction of sin and the hope for assurance. In a very real sense, the protracted meeting was the camp meeting brought to town.

While the last phase of the Second Awakening can be seen most clearly in the person and activity of Charles G. Finney, it must not be supposed that it was the work of a single man.[19] There were others who were already proceeding along the path he was to take, and Finney gathered about him many of the zestful young graduates of the revival-infected colleges and established training institutes for other young converts. In more remote sections his methods were widely copied—among Lutherans and Dutch Reformed as well as among Presbyterians, Congregationalists, Baptists, and Methodists. Even Quakers under the leadership of a visiting Englishman, Joseph John Gurney (1788–1847), conformed to the general pattern.[20] In 1832 Albert Barnes (1798–1870) of the First Presbyterian Church in Philadelphia reported that there was scarcely "a city or town or peaceful hamlet" in the country that had not been "hallowed" by a revival. And a decade later Robert Baird noted that revivals had become "a constituent part of the religious system" to such an extent that "he who should oppose himself to revivals, as such, would be regarded by most of our evangelical Christians as, *ipso facto*, an enemy to spiritual religion itself." [21]

[19] Daniel Nash, Jedediah Burchard, James Boyle, Luther Myrick, Jabez Swan, and Jacob Knapp were a few of the better-known men who actively promoted the revival.

[20] See D. E. Swift, *Joseph John Gurney* (Middletown, Conn., 1962).

[21] Quoted by S. E. Mead in *The Ministry in Historical Perspectives*, ed. H. Richard Niebuhr and D. D. Williams, 226, 227.

Missionary and benevolent activity

While revivals added numbers to the churches and generated enthusiasm and energy, Protestant expansion in America was primarily the product of missionary activity. This was almost exclusively true in the frontier areas of Maine, Vermont, central and western New York, western Pennsylvania, and the vast area surrounding the Great Lakes; and it was to continue to be the principal means employed as the frontier marched westward to the Pacific. It was also true to a very large degree in the camp meeting territory bounded by the watershed of the Ohio, for here the groundwork for Protestant expansion had been laid by men sent out to gather congregations and to establish churches. Even among the Methodists who utilized the camp meetings most widely, the meetings did no more than supplement the regular work of the churches which was carried on from day to day by circuit-riders and class leaders.

Prior to the Second Awakening, the typical form of missionary activity was for presbyteries, associations, synods, conventions, and general assemblies to secure the release of settled pastors for brief periods of time so that they could go on missionary tours of the newer settlements. On these tours the missionaries would seek out professing Christians, attempt to win new converts, and where possible establish churches. The major burden was carried by those bodies which were located nearest the frontier. Among Presbyterians, for example, the Synod of Virginia was the most active in this respect during the last decade of the eighteenth century. Among the Baptists it was the Shaftsbury Association in western Massachusetts and southern Vermont that was most active, and among the Congregationalists the General Association of Connecticut took the lead. Other synods and associations also sent men on missionary tours, but most of these bodies were less advantageously located to participate in this informal type of missionary endeavor.

By 1800 it had become apparent that a more systematic approach to missionary activity was necessary. With the stampede of people to the West that had begun in 1790, the distances were becoming too great and the new settlements too numerous to be left to the haphazard and intermittent efforts of pastors on leave as short-term missionaries. Furthermore, for so large a task the full resources of the churches had to be marshaled. The recognition of this need occurred at the very moment that the spreading revivals which marked the onset of the Second Awakening were quickening missionary interest and concern, and the energies released by the revivals were channeled almost immediately into a new missionary thrust.

THE EARLY MISSIONARY SOCIETIES. It has often been noted that whenever an Englishman is confronted by an urgent need, his almost instinctive reaction is to form a committee or "voluntary society" of likeminded friends in order to do what needs to be done. In England this had been the technique of securing quick and concerted action throughout the seventeenth century, and at the beginning of the eighteenth century a host of societies had been formed for a wide variety of ends, including the reformation of manners, the promotion of Christian knowledge, and the propagation of the gospel. And when new evangelical zeal appeared at the close of the eighteenth century, this folk-pattern of response found expression in the formation of foreign mission, Bible, and tract societies. The colonists had not been oblivious to the advantages of the voluntary society technique. They had used it to promote missionary activity among the Indians, to forestall the introduction of an American episcopate, to coordinate resistance to the Stamp Act, and—through committees of public safety—to carry on the Revolutionary struggle itself.

With this heritage, it was almost inevitable that voluntary societies should have been formed to enable the churches to match the increasingly rapid pace of settlement with a more systematic and widely supported missionary endeavor.[22] The beginning of the new era in mission activity is usually dated from the formation of the New York Missionary Society in 1796 by Presbyterians, Baptists, and Dutch Reformed. The primary object of this society, however, was to promote Indian missions. The Missionary Society of Connecticut, organized by Congregationalists in 1798, was the first society to undertake the task of establishing churches in the frontier areas. This was followed by the formation of the Massachusetts Missionary Society in 1799, the New Hampshire Missionary Society in 1801, and by numerous county and local societies. The Baptists quickly fell into line with the formation of the Massachusetts Baptist Domestic Missionary

---

[22] The two standard accounts of this development are O. W. Elsbree, *The Rise of the Missionary Spirit in America, 1790–1815* (Williamsport, Pa., 1928), and C. B. Goodykoontz, *Home Missions on the the American Frontier* (Caldwell, Idaho, 1939). Both, however, have been largely superseded by the information assembled in Sweet's four-volume *Religion on the American Frontier.*

Society in 1802, a society in Pennsylvania in 1803, in Maine in 1804, and in New York in 1806. The Presbyterians were more ambivalent. For more than a generation they were unable to make up their minds whether to channel their efforts through voluntary societies or through the official structure of the General Assembly. Actually they did both. They formed the Western Missionary Society of New Jersey in 1800 and participated in a congeries of societies in New York, while at the same time the General Assembly in 1802 established a Standing Committee of Missions. The Episcopalians were too preoccupied with internal problems to give much thought to the frontier, and it was not until 1821 that the Domestic and Foreign Missionary Society of the Protestant Episcopal Church was organized. The Methodists were almost equally tardy in forming their first missionary society (1819), but they had little need of this type of organization since every conference was in effect a missionary society and every itinerant a missionary. As soon as a traveling elder could be recruited, a circuit would be laid out that would take him through the newest settlements no matter how remote. A Presbyterian missionary in Kentucky paid tribute to the effectiveness of the Methodist system when he reported that wherever he went a circuit-rider had preceded him.

> I at length became ambitious to find a family whose cabin had not been entered by a Methodist preacher. In several days I traveled from settlement to settlement on my errand of good, but into every hovel I entered I learned that the Methodist missionary had been there before me.[23]

The circuit-riders were indeed almost everywhere, and nothing daunted them. This was made clear by the common remark, when people wished to describe the severity of a blizzard or cloudburst, that "nobody was out but crows and Methodist preachers."

The societies published magazines to enlist support. Local societies, including female and children's "mite" or "cent" societies, were organized to stimulate interest and to solicit and forward contributions to the "sending" societies. Men were sent out on longer tours than heretofore, sometimes for more than a year, and some were given indeterminate appointments. For the latter appointments, the Congregationalists and

[23] A. H. Redford, *The History of Methodism in Kentucky* (Nashville, 1868–76), 530.

Presbyterians, and to a limited extent the Baptists, looked increasingly to the colleges where Societies of Inquiry concerning Missions had been formed. On occasion, as at Williams in 1806 and later at Andover and Yale, groups of students would "band" themselves together and pledge themselves to a "group ministry" in the West.

The touring missionaries, whether they were Presbyterians, Congregationalists, or Baptists, functioned in much the same manner as did the circuit-riders.[24] They preached wherever they could gain a hearing, and they took with them an ample supply of books and pamphlets to distribute. Instead of forming "classes," their practice was to gather any small cluster of hopeful Christians they encountered into a "conference." Since these conferences were temporary expedients without any ecclesiastical status, the missionaries were under greater pressure than the Methodist itinerants with their classes to transform the conferences as soon as possible into churches. The goal of the missionaries who were given an indeterminate appointment was to win sufficient support in a given locality for them to become settled pastors and thus allow the sending society to utilize its funds to send out additional missionaries. From the center he established in this way, the former traveling missionary would provide what supervision he could to neighboring conferences and would labor to nurture them into full-fledged churches.

It was not always easy to effect the transition from conference to church, for this implied assuming responsibility for paying the preacher, and money was scarce. But if money was scarce, land was not. Life was simple and anyone could readily become self-supporting. In many instances ministers supplemented their meager stipend by tilling a few acres, and in some instances they supported themselves until a church was strong enough to maintain them. The latter practice was most common among Baptists, particularly on the southern frontier. Typical in this respect was Joab Powell (1799–1873) of Tennessee who experienced a call to preach as a Baptist minister and, not waiting for an association or missionary society to send him, went to Missouri where he spent twenty years farming and preaching, before moving on to Oregon where he gained fame as an itinerant preacher of revivals. As early as 1757 the Synod of Philadelphia had noted that Presbyterians in the newer settlements "were highly

[24] See M. W. Armstrong, *et al.*, *The Presbyterian Enterprise*, 106–08, for an extract from the journal of a Presbyterian "circuit-rider."

pleased with the prevailing principles that gospel ministers should work for their livings and preach for charity" with the result that many of the most pious ministers have "struggled and earned their bread in a great measure with the sweat of their brows." [25] Three-quarters of a century later in Illinois, a Baptist missionary encountered the same spirit. He had preached sixty-nine sermons and baptized twenty-two persons, and the people had said to him: "We love to hear you preach. Come as often as you can." But when he reminded them that "the laborer is worthy of his hire," they began to grumble about "missionary-beggars" and "money-hunters." [26]

The difficulty was aggravated by a clash of cultures along the Ohio River. Farther north the eastern-educated missionaries were readily accepted. In western New York, for example, Aaron Kinne reported in 1793 that "the principal part of the inhabitants are directly or indirectly from New England and retain the spirit and manners of their native states." They are "exemplary in their reverence for the Sabbath, zeal for religious worship, and the decent manner in which they attend." There were exceptions, to be sure, as at Tioga on the Pennsylvania border where the people were "intemperate" and "contentious," and were delighted to be "without law, without order, without Sabbaths, and without God in the world." [27] On the southern frontier, the preachers had learned to address themselves to the analogues of the people of Tioga, and ill-feeling flared when the two streams of migration met. The people from south of the Ohio River had become accustomed to a stronger brew than the missionaries were prepared to provide. The missionaries reminded Peter Cartwright, a rough-hewn Methodist circuit-rider, of "pale lettuce growing under the shade of a peach tree," and he told one of them that he should "quit reading his old manuscript sermons and learn to speak extemporaneously" or "the Methodists would set the whole western world on fire before he could light his match." [28] Glasgow-educated Alexander Campbell was equally contemptuous of the products of the "priest factories" who had not learned to speak the idiom of the people. The missionaries who came into the area with the northern stream of migration, on the other hand, often

[25] M. W. Armstrong, et al., The Presbyterian Enterprise, 69.
[26] Goodykoontz, Home Missions on the American Frontier, 205.
[27] Ibid., 113.
[28] Sweet, Religion on the American Frontier, Vol. III, The Congregationalists, 257-58.

sent back disparaging reports of the preachers who had been schooled by the necessities of the southern frontier. John Mason Peck (1789–1838), pioneer Baptist missionary in southern Illinois and Missouri, reflected this attitude when he declared that at least one-third of the preachers in this region were "doing positive injury to religion" while another third were capable of rendering no more than "minor service."[29] Given these conflicting points of view, it is understandable that antimission sentiment should have arisen; but fortunately it was localized and, apart from small isolated enclaves among the Baptists, did not long endure.

A NATIONAL STRATEGY. The initial decades of the nineteenth century witnessed, first, the proliferation of the voluntary societies, and then their consolidation and coordination in the interest of a unified strategy for the nation as a whole.[30]

The earliest societies had been local and regional missionary societies devoted to the establishment of churches. A second group of societies was formed to service the mission enterprise—Bible and tract societies to furnish the necessary literature, Sunday school societies to provide religious instruction for children, and education societies to maintain the supply of trained missionary personnel and pastors by establishing colleges and seminaries and by providing funds to aid needy theological students. A third group of societies was organized to promote a wide variety of humanitarian causes and projects for moral and social reform. Before many years had passed the societies had become so numerous and so varied that Orestes Brownson was led to complain that "matters have come to such a pass that a peaceable man can hardly venture to eat or drink, to go to bed or get up, to correct his children or kiss his wife" without the guidance and sanction of some society.[31]

The picture of confusion, chaos, and anarchy that one might gain from the multiplicity of societies that had been formed would be misleading, for there was purpose in the apparent disorder. To understand this it is

[29] Goodykoontz, *Home Missions on the American Frontier*, 33.

[30] The development and implementation of a unified strategy, both in England and America, has been described by Charles I. Foster, *An Errand of Mercy: the Evangelical United Front* (Chapel Hill, N.C., 1954). For various facets of Protestant concern, see Charles C. Cole, Jr., *The Social Ideas of the Northern Evangelists, 1826–1860* (N.Y., 1954); John R. Bodo, *The Protestant Clergy and Public Issues, 1812–1845* (Princeton, 1954); Timothy L. Smith, *Revivalism and Social Reform in Mid-Nineteenth Century America* (N.Y., 1957); and C. S. Griffin, *Their Brothers' Keepers: Moral Stewardship in the United States, 1800–1865* (New Brunswick, N.J., 1960).

[31] Stow Persons, *American Minds* (N.Y., 1958), 160.

necessary to appreciate what was regarded as the peculiar genius of the voluntary society. The voluntary society, first of all, was an instrument for quick and concerted action by groups of concerned individuals. There was no need to wait until a majority of some official body could be persuaded to act. A few friends could take the initiative and then, through the society they had created, could proceed to enlist further support for their cause. The voluntary society, in the second place, was a device to enlist the broadest possible support for the attainment of a single objective. Members of a society might be divided on other issues but on this single issue they could unite. Furthermore, by limiting a society to a single objective, the possibility of its energies being diverted and diluted by other concerns would be avoided. "Concentrated action is powerful action" was the way the manifesto of the American Bible Society put it.[32] Finally, the voluntary societies which united "the best hearts, the most willing hands, and the most vigorous and untiring enterprise"[33] in common tasks were regarded as the heaven-sent means by which the divided denominations could pool their efforts to meet particular needs.

Three factors had coverged to give the voluntary societies their distinctive character, direction, and force. First, the major Protestant denominations had become increasingly conscious of the ties that bound them together. Samuel S. Schmucker (1799-1873), president of the Lutheran seminary at Gettysburg, was to declare that while each evangelical (the qualifying word is important) "denomination must naturally prefer its own peculiarities," it would be a "dangerous error" to regard "these peculiarities as equal in importance with the great fundamentals of our holy religion held in common by all." In similar vein Samuel Miller (1769-1850) of the Presbyterian seminary at Princeton affirmed that "it would never occur to us to place the peculiarities of our creed among the fundamentals of our common Christianity." Albert Barnes was even more explicit when he asserted that "the church of Christ is not under the Episcopal form, or the Baptist, the Methodist, the Presbyterian or the Congregational form exclusively; all are, to all intents and purposes, to be recognized as parts of the one holy catholic church."[34]

[32] Smith, Handy, Loetscher, *American Christianity*, I, 555.
[33] Lyman Beecher, "Propriety and Importance of Efforts to Evangelize the Nation," *The National Preacher*, III (1829), 154.
[34] Schmucker, Miller, and Barnes are quoted by S. E. Mead in *The Ministry in Historical Perspectives*, ed. H. Richard Niebuhr and D. D. Williams, 222-24.

Second, the concern of the churches was not simply to evangelize individuals but also to remake society. They were the heirs of the millennial tradition voiced by Mark Hopkins (1802–87), president of Williams College, when he declared that the time was coming when "wars, and intemperance, and licentiousness, and fraud, and slavery, and all oppression" shall be brought to an end "through the transforming influence of Christianity." [35] While this was to be "the Lord's doing," Christians could help to speed the coming of the perfect society by promoting revivals, establishing churches, and participating in the host of societies designed specifically to counter the evils Hopkins had listed as well as to promote humanitarian enterprises which he neglected to mention.

Third, the revival campaigns of the Second Awakening stressed a doctrine of "disinterested benevolence" that had been elaborated by Samuel Hopkins and Nathaniel W. Taylor as the key to Christian social responsibility.[36] Sin was defined as including "selfishness," and the effect of conversion was to shift "the controlling preference of the mind" from a "preference for self-interest" to a "preference for disinterested benevolence." If one's conversion was genuine, it was insisted, this shift in the preference of the mind would express itself in action. The conversion experience, therefore, was not the end of the Christian life but only its beginning. Working was quite as necessary as believing, and working meant participating fully in every good cause.

The societies always had local beginnings but within a decade or two they had been pulled together into national organizations so that their work might be consolidated throughout the nation. This was particularly true after 1818 when the fight to save the establishment in Connecticut was lost, thus permitting Lyman Beecher—the real architect of the voluntary system in America—to devote his full attention to transforming the societies into "a gigantic religious power," thoroughly "systematized" and "compact" in organization.[37]

There was little difficulty in combining most of the local reform and

<hr>

[35] Ralph H. Gabriel, *The Course of American Democratic Thought* (N.Y., 1940), 36.
[36] A selection from Hopkins' *System of Doctrines* which illustrates his concept of "disinterested benevolence" is printed in Smith, Handy, Loetscher, *American Christianity*, I, 539–45. See also the portion of Taylor's *Concio ad Clerum*, *ibid.*, II, 28–36.
[37] Gilbert H. Barnes, *The Anti-Slavery Impulse, 1830–1844* (N.Y., 1933), 17.

service societies into national organizations on an interdenominational basis. The American Bible Society and the American Education Society were the earliest, being formed in 1816; the American Colonization Society was next in 1817; then the American Sunday School Union was formed in 1824, the American Tract Society in 1825, the American Temperance Society in 1826, the American Peace Society in 1828, the American Seamen's Friend Society in 1828, and the American Antislavery Society in 1833. Extra precautions, of course, had to be taken to preserve the interdenominational character of the Sunday school and tract societies. The publishing committee of the American Tract Society, for example, was composed of an equal number of Baptists, Congregationalists, Dutch Reformed, Episcopalians, and Presbyterians who were charged with protecting their denominational "peculiarities," it being believed that there was sufficient common ground to load each tract with an ample measure of "divine truth." The missionary and education societies were of a different character. Their task was to establish churches and train ministers, and this made it necessary for them to be organized on a denominational basis. The Presbyterian United Domestic Missionary Society of New York was reorganized in 1826 as the American Home Missionary Society and it became the arm of the Presbyterian-Congregational coalition. Similar national societies were formed for the other denominations.

The whole cluster of national societies has sometimes been referred to as the "benevolent empire," and it is true that their activities were closely coordinated through a series of "interlocking directorates." Most of the leadership at the national level was concentrated in a relatively small group; and the annual meetings, which were held in New York in May, were so scheduled that one could participate in most of them. They did not act alone, an auxiliary society assured its members in 1826. They moved together "harmoniously" and thus formed "so many parts of the grand whole" in seeking to fulfill "that last command of our ascended Lord, 'Go and spread the influence of the gospel over every creature.'"[38]

The growing cities and the West were major concerns of those who participated in the formation of the national societies. Impelled by the conviction that the cities were citadels which must be captured at all costs, Lyman Beecher had gone to Boston in 1826, Albert Barnes accepted a call

[38] Foster, *Errand of Mercy*, 143, 154.

to Philadelphia in 1830, and Charles G. Finney was persuaded to become a pastor in New York City in 1832. The cities were strategic for two reasons. They were centers of an influence which radiated to the remotest hamlet, and they were the repositories of concentrated wealth. While the Bible, tract, Sunday school, and missionary societies devoted great attention to the religious life of the cities, the leaders of the national societies were equally concerned with mastering the wealth of the urban centers. "The purposes of Christianity," declared Barnes, "require that that wealth should be consecrated to the Redeemer," and consecrating it to the Redeemer meant primarily devoting it to the work of the benevolent societies.[39] So successful was this enlistment of wealth that by 1834 the total annual receipts of the societies were in excess of nine million dollars.

The West became of even more urgent concern than it had been hitherto when the election of Andrew Jackson to the Presidency in 1828 dramatized the shift of political power that had been taking place. "The strength of the nation," a report to the American Home Missionary Society in 1829 declared, "lies beyond the Alleghany. The center of dominion is fast moving in that direction. The ruler of this country is growing up in the Great Valley. Leave him without the gospel and he will be a ruffian giant." [40] With this fact in mind the whole voluntary society apparatus launched a great "saturation" campaign to save the Mississippi valley and thus to save the nation. The goal was a Bible for every family, a Sunday school in every neighborhood, a pastor in every locality, and tracts in abundance. Each of the societies—Bible, tract, Sunday school, missionary—were assigned their allotted tasks and a multiple-agency system was devised to facilitate their work. The statistics tell an incredible story of Bibles shipped, tracts distributed, Sunday schools organized, and churches established. So successful was the operation that by 1833, the societies were beginning to turn their major attention to those sections of the South where the population was scattered and ignorance seemed widespread.

CONTRIBUTIONS TO EDUCATION. For those who feared that "barba-

[39] Albert Barnes, *Sermons on Revivals* (N.Y., 1841), 96; see also 109–10.
[40] W. B. Posey, *The Presbyterian Church in the Old Southwest, 1778–1838* (Richmond, 1952), 111. For the valley campaign of 1829–31, see Foster, *Errand of Mercy*, 190–205, and Hudson, *American Protestantism*, 84–90.

154

rism" would overtake the nation, the provision of adequate educational opportunities became a primary concern. Both the political order of America and the ecclesiastical order of Protestantism presupposed a literate laity and, with only minor dissent, an educated leadership. Along the seaboard the churches had long been active in fostering education at all levels, and in the West the Ordinance of 1785 had set aside land in every township for the maintenance of publicly supported elementary schools. Even so, some time usually elapsed in newly opened territory before these schools could be brought into operation, and during this period ministers often filled the breach by serving as schoolmasters.

It was in the area of secondary and higher education, however, that the churches made their greatest contribution. Presbyterians and Congregationalists were the most active in the founding of academies and colleges; but the Baptists did not lag far behind, and other denominations made their own contribution.[41]

Some of the academies were adjuncts of colleges, some developed into colleges, but the great majority were local institutions, the product of an individual minister's zeal for learning. Most of those that survived ultimately became village high schools, but for a considerable period of time secondary education was largely carried on under denominational auspices. The same situation prevailed at the college level. Of the five hundred

[41] Among the early Presbyterian colleges were Transylvania (1783), University of Tennessee (1784), Washington and Jefferson (1802), Centre (1823), Lafayette (1826), Hanover (1833), Wabash (1834), Davidson (1837).

Congregationalists founded Williams (1793), Middlebury (1800), Amherst (1821), and Oberlin (1833). Some were founded jointly by Congregationalists and Presbyterians, such as: Hamilton (1812), Western Reserve (1826), Illinois College (1829), and Knox (1837).

Baptist colleges that survived the century included Colgate (1817), Colby (1818), George Washington (1821), Furman (1826), Mississippi College (1826), Shurtleff (1827), Georgetown College (1829), Denison (1832), Richmond (1832), Kalamazoo (1833), Mercer (1833), Wake Forest (1834), Franklin (1834).

The Episcopalians had only a brief flurry of college founding, with Hobart (1822), Trinity (1823), and Kenyon (1824).

Methodist participation was somewhat delayed, with Randolph-Macon (1830), Wesleyan (1831), McKendree (1834), Albion (1835), Emory (1836), and DePauw (1837) being their earliest colleges. On the Pacific coast, however, the Methodists took the lead with Willamette (1842) and the College of the Pacific (1851).

The Disciples of Christ, of course, did not emerge as a denomination until the 1830's, but they quickly captured control of Transylvania, and established Bethany (1841) and Hiram (1850).

Gettysburg (1832) was the first Lutheran college, and Franklin and Marshall (1836) the earliest German Reformed.

155

and sixteen colleges and universities that were founded before the Civil War, only a few had no religious affiliation.[42] The dominant motive in the founding of colleges was to provide an educated ministry for the churches, but the classical education they offered was also designed to prepare men for other professions. The mortality rate among these infant enterprises was high. Many were inadequately staffed, some were left isolated by the developing pattern of settlement, and others were the victims of mismanagement. In the end, less than half survived the nineteenth century.

The founding of theological seminaries was another feature of Protestant educational activity during the first half of the nineteenth century. Prior to this time specifically theological education, as distinguished from the classical education given aspiring ministers in the colleges, was commonly acquired under the direction of older clergymen. Such supervised training combined advanced study with practical experience in the ministry. After 1800, however, it became increasingly evident that more adequate training could be given in a graduate professional school. New Brunswick Theological Seminary, which traces its beginnings back to 1784 when theological instruction was initiated in New York City, antedated the general movement which is usually considered to have begun with the founding of Andover Theological Seminary in 1808. In the next few years the movement rapidly gained momentum in most denominations, with only the Methodists and the Disciples being laggard in their participation.

OVERSEAS MISSIONS. Thus far attention has been centered on the new nation, but the religious enthusiasm of the Second Awakening could not be contained within the national boundaries. News of the Orient had been seeping back into New England during the early years of the Awakening. This was the era of the clipper ships and the Pacific trade, and every ship that returned to Salem or Boston brought tales of distant lands and strange people. Furthermore, exciting reports of William Carey's pioneering missionary venture in India were being published in the religious press. In 1810 the "banding" of a number of students at Andover Theological Seminary—not far from Salem—to offer themselves for foreign-mission service led to the founding of the American Board of

[42] The chief authority in this area is Donald G. Tewksbury, *The Founding of American Colleges and Universities before the Civil War* (N.Y., 1932). See also Albea Godbold, *The Church College of the Old South* (Durham, N.C., 1944).

Commissioners for Foreign Missions.[43] Two years later five of the students—Samuel Newell, Adoniram Judson, Luther Rice, Samuel Nott, Jr., and Gordon Hall—set sail for India. Judson became persuaded of the validity of Baptist contentions while on shipboard, and when he arrived in India he discovered that Rice shared his views.[44] When Judson went on to Burma, Rice returned to America to enlist Baptist support for foreign mission work. By 1850 the foreign mission work of all denominations called for an annual expenditure of about $650,000.

The Protestant resurgence in America during the decades that followed the formation of the new nation was part of a much larger movement whose achievements led Kenneth Scott Latourette to describe the nineteenth century as "the great century" in the history of Christianity.[45] In Britain and on the continent of Europe, as well as in America, a sweeping tide of evangelical religion brought new life to the Protestant churches at a time when the Roman Catholic Church was waging a defensive struggle against the forces of nationalism and "liberalism" in Roman Catholic lands. It was not until the end of the century that the Roman Catholic Church, either in America or elsewhere, was to be able to abandon its defensive posture. In the meantime, the Protestant churches in America were not without pressing problems of their own.

[43] See W. E. Strong, *The Story of the American Board* (Boston, 1910).

[44] See Courtney Anderson, *To the Golden Shore: the Life of Adoniram Judson* (Boston, 1956).

[45] Latourette's primary focus was upon the achievements of the far-flung missionary enterprise. Only by a repetitive refrain of superlatives could he describe what had taken place. "Never before in a period of equal length had Christianity or any other religion penetrated for the first time as large an area as it had in the nineteenth century." "Never before had any religion been planted over so large a portion of the earth's surface." "Never before had Christianity, or any other religion, been introduced to so many different peoples and cultures." "Never before had so many hundreds of thousands contributed voluntarily of their means to assist the spread of Christianity or any other religion." "Never before . . . had Christians come so near the goal of reaching all men with their message." "Never had it exerted so wide an influence upon the human race." "Measured by geographic extent and the effect upon mankind as a whole, the nineteenth century was the greatest thus far in the history of Christianity." *A History of the Expansion of Christianity* (N.Y., 1937–45), IV, 1, 4; V, 469; VI, 442, 443, 450; VII, 450.

VII

Divergent Trends and Movements

The evangelical religion of the first third of the nineteenth century bred a spirit of unity which was expressed both in the revivals of the period and in the activities of the voluntary societies. The societies were explicitly designed to secure the broadest possible cooperation in common tasks. And indispensable to the success of a revival in any community was the participation of a major portion of the churches, for without this broad participation the necessary psychological climate and group pressure could not be created. "The spirit of sectarianism," therefore, was the great "hindrance" and "quencher" of revivals; and Finney constantly warned his helpers not "to dwell upon sectarian distinctions or to be sticklish about sectarian points." [1] With Christians working side by side in the revivals and in the societies, further impetus was given to the development of cordial relations among the major denominations.

There were discordant notes, however, in the midst of the harmony.

[1] Calvin Colton, *History and Character of American Revivals*, 116–17. Finney, *Lectures on Revivals of Religion* (2nd. ed., N.Y., 1835), 369.

The Great Awakening of the colonial period, with its "New Lights" and "Old Lights," and "New Sides" and "Old Sides," had demonstrated that revivals could divide as well as unify. And the Second Awakening was equally productive of controversy and division. The reactions surprisingly were quite diverse. The doctrinal harshness of revivalist preaching, on the one hand, contributed to the Unitarian and Universalist defections; while its doctrinal laxity, on the other hand, helped to produce a reaction which led to a revived confessionalism. Still others found the lax churchmanship of the evangelicals disturbing, and this led to J. W. Nevin's stress upon the importance of the priestly office and the sacramental life and to John Henry Hobart's zealous defense of what he considered to be the primitive church order. All the dissenters, whatever form their protest might take, reacted strongly against what Horace Bushnell called the "artificial fireworks" and the "jump and stir" of the revivals.

Unitarians and Universalists

While Unitarianism (i.e., antitrinitarianism) in Boston was the product of many influences, its roots went back to the "liberal" tendencies which developed in reaction to the first Great Awakening, and during the succeeding years there had been a steady but barely perceptible drift toward greater emphasis upon the human role in redemption.[2] By the time Ashbel Green (1762–1848), a young Presbyterian minister from Philadelphia who was later to be president of Princeton University, made a tour of New England in 1791, he found many of the Boston ministers to be unsound in the faith. Among them, he reported, were Arminians, Universalists, Arians, and one professed Socinian. Ten years later Archibald Alexander (1772–1851), then president of Hampden-Sydney College in Virginia, found the situation in Boston even more dismaying. Heretical notions of all types abounded, and the only agreement he could discover was a rejection of the doctrine of the Trinity.[3]

The reports of Green and Alexander are somewhat misleading, for heretical doctrines were not being openly proclaimed. The only overt

[2] The background is described in detail by Conrad Wright, *The Beginnings of Unitarianism in America* (Boston, 1955). See also E. M. Wilbur, *A History of Unitarianism in Transylvania, England, and America* (Cambridge, Mass., 1952). Several key documents are printed in W. E. Channing, *Unitarian Christianity and Other Essays*, ed. Irving H. Bartlett (Indianapolis, 1957).

[3] Wilbur, *History of Unitarianism*, 399.

break occasioned by the theological ferment had occurred not among the Congregationalists but at King's Chapel, the former church of the royal governor. In 1782 the Episcopalian proprietors of the Chapel, being unable to obtain a minister, had invited James Freeman (1759–1835), a recent graduate of Harvard, to serve as reader. In deference to his scruples, the liturgy was revised to eliminate certain trinitarian references, the Athanasian and Nicene Creeds were omitted, and in 1787 the congregation proceeded to ordain him as its pastor. The Congregational clergy were much more cautious. Without the problem posed by a set of liturgy, most of them were content to let "sleeping dogmas lie." Orthodox doctrines were not openly opposed and rejected; they were quietly ignored. A clearcut party alignment began to appear only when Henry Ware (1764–1845), a known liberal, was elected to the Hollis professorship of divinity at Harvard in 1805, one consequence being the founding of Andover Seminary in 1808.

It was not until after 1815, however, that a definite separation took place. The event which brought the uneasy truce to an end was the publication in Boston of a chapter from the *Memoirs* of Theophilus Lindsey (1723–1808), which reproduced letters that had been written to the English Unitarian leader by several of the New England "liberals." One of the letters noted that, while most of the Boston clergy were Unitarian in sentiment, "the controversy is seldom or never introduced into the pulpit." But now names had been named and sentiments had been exposed, and there was little hope of preventing an open breach. A pamphlet war ensued with Jedediah Morse (1761–1826) writing a tract entitled *Are You of the Christian or the Boston Religion?* and John Lowell (1769–1840) replying in kind with one entitled *Are You a Christian or a Calvinist?*

The classic exposition of Unitarian doctrine was William Ellery Channing's (1780–1842) Baltimore sermon on "Unitarian Christianity" which he delivered in 1819 at the ordination of Jared Sparks.[4] The foundation was the inspired Word of God made manifest in the Scriptures; but, being "written for men" and "in the language of men," the meaning of Scripture must be sought "in the same manner as that of other books." The special divine office of Christ as Savior was not questioned. Though

---

[4] The sermon has been reprinted many times. A portion of it is in Smith, Handy, Loetscher, *American Christianity*, I, 493–502.

Jesus was not God, he was sent by the Father to effect the "moral and spiritual deliverance of mankind; that is, to rescue men from sin and its consequences, and to bring them to a state of everlasting purity and happiness." It is evident from other writings that if the early Unitarians were allowed to define their terms, they could have affirmed the Trinity. The basic issue which set them apart was their optimistic view of human nature. There is an "essential sameness" between God and man, declared Channing, and "all virtue has its foundation in the moral nature of man." The great significance of Jesus is that he leads and entices men to divine perfection. Having been made for "union" with the Creator, the "infinite perfection" of the Creator is "the only sufficient object and true resting place for the insatiable desires and unlimited capacities of the human mind." Later the Unitarian position was to be summarized in James Freeman Clarke's (1810–88) Affirmation of Faith: "The fatherhood of God, the brotherhood of man, the leadership of Jesus, salvation by character, and the progress of mankind onward and upward forever."

The publication of the extract from Lindsey's *Memoirs* precipitated a struggle for the possession of church property. Often the Trinitarians constituted a majority of church members, but the courts ruled in 1820 that church property was vested in the "parish" which embraced both church members and nonmembers. In many instances, with all the eligible voters of the parish or town participating in the decision, even a minority Unitarian faction among the church members was able to gain possession of the property. Oliver Wendell Holmes's "One-Hoss Shay" was supposed to be a symbol of the sudden crumbling of "Calvinism," but it collapsed only in eastern Massachusetts; and even there only momentarily, for within a very brief time orthodox Congregational churches were re-established in almost every parish. When the American Unitarian Association was formed in 1825 it numbered one hundred and twenty-five churches, one hundred of them in Massachusetts and most of them within forty miles of Boston, a fact which led the irreverent to quip that the Unitarians believed in the fatherhood of God, the brotherhood of man, and the neighborhood of Boston.

Unitarianism, on the whole, was the faith of well-to-do, urban New Englanders who rejected the notion of human depravity. Universalism was its counterpart among less urbane rural folk who were repelled by the idea of eternal damnation and thus led to affirm the doctrine of universal salvation.[5] Their mood in part was reflected in the reaction of a seventeen-year-old New Hampshire girl to uninhibited revivalist preaching: "We went this evening to hear Lorenzo Dow, a famous Methodist preacher, his appearance was enough to frighten one and his preaching disgusted all—the meeting house was crowded full. Think we should have been as wise if we had staid home." [6]

Although Universalism had been brought to America by John Murray (1741–1850) in 1770, it did not gain much headway until after Elhanan Winchester (1751–97), a Baptist minister, was converted in 1781. Later under the leadership of Hosea Ballou (1771–1852), whose *Treatise on Atonement* was published in 1805, the Universalists adopted an antitrinitarian position and, except for social status, became indistinguishable from the Unitarians. As a lower-class denomination, the Universalists competed with the Methodists and Wesleyan-oriented Free-Will Baptists for the allegiance of the common people. While the Universalists were concentrated initially in New England, they moved into the newer settlements of the West with such success that by 1850 they had more than twice as many churches as the Unitarians.

The resurgence of Old School "confessionalism"

The protest against revivalism was not limited to the "liberal" wing of the churches. Orthodox Calvinists also were alarmed by what they considered to be the dangerous narrowing of the distinction between Calvinism and Arminianism that was being effected by Nathaniel W. Taylor and Lyman Beecher in the interest of getting results, and the "new measures" employed by Finney in New York state seemed to them to be a clear confirmation of the unhappy practical consequences. Nathaniel Emmons (1745–1840), one of the most distinguished heirs of Jonathan Edwards, grumbled in his old age about the "undue excitements" of "modern" awakenings; and Asahel Nettleton, who had been one of the earliest leaders of the Second Awakening, was worried about the harm that was being done by "the imprudence of a few zealous individuals." Others were complaining that the revivals were becoming the work of "revival-makers" rather than a work of God. Even at Andover, which had been a

[5] See Richard Eddy's "History of Universalism" in Joseph Allen and Richard Eddy, *A History of the Unitarians and Universalists in the United States* (N.Y., 1894).
[6] Alice Felt Tyler, *Freedom's Ferment* (Minneapolis, 1944), 29.

seedbed of revival preachers, anxiety was beginning to be expressed.

Although strict Calvinists among the New England Congregation-alists had fretted and chafed over the concessions that were being made, their dissent was muted by the necessity to maintain a united front to fight disestablishment and then to counter the Unitarian threat. Open conflict did not break out until 1828 when one of Taylor's more disturbing sermons, *Concio ad Clerum* ("Advice to the Clergy"), was published. The sermon dealt with the crucial issue of man's natural depravity and insisted that sin "is man's own act, consisting in a free choice of some object rather than God as his chief good." The "circumstances" of man's nature makes it certain that he will sin, but he has "power to the contrary." [7] The sermon made it abundantly clear to the conservatives that the New Haven Theology (or the "New Divinity" of Yale) had departed from orthodox Calvinism at one of its most essential points. The Yale group, on the other hand, argued that they were only offering a more acceptable and convinc-ing explanation of the doctrine. The conservatives, finding the explanation neither convincing nor acceptable, raised the cry: "Shall we sustain our Calvinism or see it run down to the standard of Methodists and laxer men?" [8]

The pattern of response had been set at Andover where Jedediah Morse had persuaded the founders of the seminary to "guard against the insidious encroachments of innovation" by shackling the institution to two creeds: the *Westminster Shorter Catechism* and the so-called Andover Creed, which was based upon Samuel Hopkins' restatement of the views of Jonathan Edwards. The center of the controversy was in Connecticut, where a Pastoral Union was formed in 1833 and steps were taken to found a new seminary to combat the influence of Yale. The following year the (Hartford) Seminary was established at East Windsor and Bennet Tyler (1783–1858) was summoned from Portland, Maine, to assume the presi-dency. The integrity of both the Pastoral Union and the seminary was carefully guarded by Articles of Agreement which defined Calvinism in terms that would exclude any New Haven sentiments. The rift which was to continue for many years amounted to an open schism among the loosely organized Congregational churches.

A similar alarm among Presbyterian conservatives had precipitated

[7] A major portion of the sermon is reprinted in Smith, Handy, Loetscher, *American Christianity*, II, 28–36.

[8] S. E. Mead, *Nathaniel W. Taylor*, 221.

the formation of what came to be known as the Old School party in opposition to the New School or New Divinity men. The Presbyterian conservatives worked in close alliance with the strict Calvinists of New England, and as early as 1827 the Presbyterian *Christian Advocate,* published in Philadelphia and edited by Ashbel Green, was accusing the professors at Yale of promulgating doctrines which subverted the principles of orthodoxy. The ensuing controversy was marked by a whole series of heresy trials, beginning in 1831 when charges were brought against Albert Barnes in Philadelphia and ending in 1835 with the arraignment of Lyman Beecher before the Presbytery of Cincinnati. In each instance, after appeal to higher judicatories, the charges were dismissed, but the trials contributed greatly to the inflamed climate of opinion which led in 1837 to the exclusion of four New School synods in New York and Ohio from the Presbyterian church.[9]

While the theological issue was the most obvious factor in the division of 1837, the division was partly the product of a geographically based power struggle within the Presbyterian denomination, and lurking in the background was the disruptive issue of slavery. From the beginning Pennsylvania had been the center of power and prestige within the Presbyterian fold, but by 1828 its position of dominance had been badly eroded. In that year Ashbel Green noted that, whereas there were one hundred and ninety-six licentiates and ministers in Pennsylvania, New York had four hundred and twenty-six. And the damaging aspect of this imbalance was the fact that the New York ministers were within the New England rather than the Pennsylvania orbit of influence. Beecher, who had gone west to become president of the newly established Lane Theological Seminary, was certain that his trial for heresy was triggered by men of the Philadelphia-Pittsburgh axis who were alarmed at the prospect of a New England man rising to leadership in Cincinnati.

Within the Old School party, theological and political concerns intermingled and reinforced each other. The growing strength of the New School party heightened the apprehensions that had been aroused by the shifting emphasis of the New England Theology. In order to strengthen its position, the Old School group began to raise the issue of church

---

[9] The Old School–New School controversy is illuminated by documents reproduced in M. W. Armstrong, *et. al., The Presbyterian Enterprise,* 146–71. There is no entirely satisfactory history of the Presbyterians for the period from 1789 to the Civil War, but the story of the controversy is given in Robert E. Thompson, *A History of the Presbyterian Church* (N.Y., 1895), 102–49.

government. The "union" with the Congregationalists had been welcomed initially by all parties within the church. Ashbel Green, for example, had been one of the leading proponents of the Plan of Union. But now the whole arrangement was brought under attack. Since the rival political power and the New School strength were both chiefly concentrated in the churches, presbyteries, and synods which had been formed under the provisions of the articles of "accommodation," these bodies were now denounced as being faulty in their constitutional foundation. Furthermore, since the great instrument of the New York–New School advance had been the independently controlled American Home Missionary Society and American Education Society, the Old School men demanded that these societies be repudiated and that all denominational funds be channeled through denominational boards that would be fully committed to the church's confessional position.

With the exception of a single year, the Old School party had not been able to gain control of the General Assembly prior to 1837. The balance of power was represented by Princeton Theological Seminary, and the faculty there hesitated to commit its influence to any program that would divide the church. Princeton regarded itself as the theological center of Presbyterian life, and it had looked with misgiving upon the establishment of Auburn Seminary in 1818 and Lane in 1829. But it was the founding of Union Theological Seminary in New York by New School men in 1836 that threw Princeton, though not without some reservations, behind the political program of the Old School Party. The new seminary in New York City could only be regarded as a direct challenge to Princeton's central role in the life of the church.

During the months preceding the General Assembly of 1837 the Old School faction had organized carefully to obtain a maximum representation, and when the Assembly met it proceeded with dispatch to carry out the Old School program. The "union" with the Congregationalists was abrogated, the relationship with the American Home Missionary Society and the American Education Society was severed, and three synods in New York and one in Ohio were expelled from the church. The following year, after attempting unsuccessfully to gain readmittance, the New School Presbyterians organized as a separate body which, with the adherence of scattered presbyteries and churches in other parts of the country, was roughly equal in size to the Old School body.

Although he took no great part in the division of 1837, Charles

Hodge (1797–1878) was destined to be the great theologian of Old School Presbyterianism. He had been appointed to a professorship at Princeton Seminary in 1822 and he remained there for fifty years, sharing in the training of over three thousand ministers and contributing more than any other single person to the shaping of American Presbyterianism. He had been deeply influenced by Swiss orthodoxy, and a strong confessionalism became the hallmark of his theology. Hodge was convinced that "no such thing exists on the face of the earth as Christianity in the abstract. . . . Every man you see is either an Episcopalian or a Methodist, a Presbyterian or an Independent, an Arminian or a Calvinist. No one is a Christian in general." [10] His theological system was based solidly on the Westminster Standards and other Reformed confessions which he sought faithfully to expound and defend. It was with this in mind that he boasted that "a new idea never originated" at Princeton Seminary while he was there. His great monument and the source of much of his later influence was his three-volume *Systematic Theology* which was explicitly designed as a defensive rampart against all doctrinal aberrations.[11] While Hodge attempted to keep Presbyterianism in a theological strait jacket, it has been justly pointed out that his learning, doctrinal rigor, respect for confessional tradition, and insistence upon intelligible discussion did much in succeeding years to prevent anti-intellectual tendencies, sentimentality, and emotional partisanship from overwhelming theological concern.

During the 1830's the Baptists also were torn by an Old School–New School division which was in part a reaction to the growing influence in their ranks of the New England Theology.[12] The Baptist Old School party, however, failed to capture the denominational machinery which, above the

---

[10] *Biblical Repertory and Theological Review*, VIII (1836), 430.

[11] It is necessary to speak of "later" influence, for Hodge's *Systematic Theology* (N.Y., 1872–75) was not published until the last years of his life. Prior to this time his influence was mediated primarily through the classroom and his articles in the *Biblical Repertory and Theological Review* (later known as the *Princeton Review*).

[12] The theological issue was clearly delineated by Thomas Smiley (1759–1832), who was to become an Old School leader, in a letter to John Davis, April 27, 1811, and in his manuscript "History of the Chemung Association," 88–102, both of which are in the Samuel Colgate Baptist Historical Collection. Smiley, a pastor on the New York–Pennsylvania border, was shocked and dismayed by "the high Hopkinsian or all but fully Arminian sentiments" of the "Eastern missionaries" sent out by the Baptist board in Boston. For the missionaries' account of their tours through the Chemung River area, see the *Massachusetts Baptist Missionary Magazine*, II (1808–10), 302–7; and the *American Baptist Magazine*, I (1817–18), 269–71.

associational level, existed solely in the form of voluntary societies. A defection thereupon occurred both in the East and the West, but the defensive posture that these "Primitive Baptists" adopted became so permeated by an anti-mission spirit that the defecting churches and associations were left to eke out no more than a dwindling existence.

A revived confessionalism among the Reformed and the Lutherans came from another quarter. Both groups had been heavily infiltrated, first by Wesleyan doctrines, then by the more moderate evangelicalism of early Princeton, and finally by Taylorism and its associated Finneyite "new measures." In 1822 five ministers withdrew on doctrinal grounds from the Dutch Reformed Church, but their adherents were able to maintain only a meager church life until 1857 when the Christian Reformed Church was established on a strong confessional base by Dutch immigrants in Michigan. Not only did the new church prosper; its influence had the effect of drawing the older Dutch church back to a more conservative position.

A theological shift among the German Lutherans followed much the same pattern. S. S. Schmucker, graduate of Princeton and president of the Lutheran seminary at Gettysburg, was the great symbol of the Lutheran adjustment to the American theological climate.[13] It was Schmucker who issued in 1838 a *Fraternal Appeal* summoning all branches of evangelical Protestantism in America to unite in a single Apostolic Protestant Church, and who with other "liberal" leaders exerted strong influence on behalf of "new-measures" revivalism. The defeat of the Americanizing Lutherans, however, was foreshadowed by the arrival in Missouri of a group of immigrant Germans from Saxony the following year. They had left Germany because they could "see no possibility of retaining in their present home" the "pure and undefiled" faith of the historic Lutheran confessions and thus had felt "duty bound to emigrate and to look for a country where this Lutheran faith is not endangered."[14]

With their numbers augmented by continuing immigration, the Missouri group at a meeting in Chicago formed the Evangelical Lutheran Synod of Missouri in 1847. Other equally conservative synods were formed by immigrants from other parts of Germany—the Buffalo Synod in 1845, the Wisconsin Synod in 1850, and the Iowa Synod in 1854. While

[13] See Vergilius Ferm, *The Crisis in American Lutheran Theology: A Study of the Issue between American Lutheranism and Old Lutheranism* (N.Y., 1927), and J. A. Brown, *The New Theology: Its Abettors and Defenders* (Philadelphia, 1857).

[14] A. R. Wentz, *A Basic History of Lutheranism* (Philadelphia, 1955), 116.

these synods engaged in doctrinal controversy among themselves, the conspicuous leader who influenced them all and who played a large part in the reshaping of American Lutheranism as a whole was Carl F. W. Walther (1811–87). As his biographer reports, he was "easily the most command-ing figure in the Lutheran church in America during the nineteenth century," and another scholar has noted that Walther "stood almost alone in the nineteenth century American theological scene as one fully aware of the crucial importance of the problems of Law and Gospel to the Christian faith." In this latter respect he anticipated "the emphasis of Karl Barth and the 'Luther renaissance' of the next century, but by the same fact he doomed himself to attack and misunderstanding in his own time." [15]

The great wave of German immigration did not leave Lutheranism in the eastern part of the United States unscathed. Not only was pressure exerted by the newer synods in the West, but immigration also altered the theological complexion of the older synods in the East. By the 1850's, even at Gettysburg, Schmucker had been displaced in influence by Charles Philip Krauth (1797–1867) who was urging the churches to maintain their fidelity to the traditional Lutheran standards. Later his son, Charles Porterfield Krauth (1823–83), was to devote his attention to inaugurating a liturgical and sacramental renaissance among American Lutherans, and at this point his interests closely paralleled those of John W. Nevin. As a third-generation American, Krauth was an especially effective advocate of a revived confessionalism in the English-speaking Lutheran churches.[16]

"High Church" sentiment:
John W. Nevin and John Henry Hobart

While others were fighting defensive battles against New School doctrines and assuming a rigid stance behind their confessional ramparts, John W. Nevin (1803–86)—the chief spokesman for what came to be known as "the Mercersburg theology" or "evangelical catholicism"—was undertaking the more positive task of restoring the sacramental life of the churches which, in his view, had been wrecked by rampant revivalism.[17]

---

[15] D. H. Steffens, *Carl F. W. Walther* (Philadelphia, 1917), 10. Sydney E. Ahlstrom, "Theology in America," in *The Shaping of American Religion*, ed. J. W. Smith and A. Leland Jamison, 275.

[16] See Charles Porterfield Krauth, *The Conservative Reformation and Its Theology* (Philadelphia, 1871), and Adolph Spaeth, *Charles Porterfield Krauth* (N.Y., 1898).

[17] See James H. Nichols, *Romanticism in American Theology: Nevin and Schaff at Mercersburg* (Chicago, 1961).

Born of Scotch-Irish parents in 1803, Nevin attended Union College and Princeton Seminary, and in 1829 became a professor of the Western Theological Seminary, a Princeton outpost at Allegheny, Pennsylvania. There his antislavery views involved him in constant controversy and, although theologically he was fully in accord with Old School views, he was violently attacked because he regarded the expulsion of the New School synods in 1837 as an unconstitutional act. Convinced that his future usefulness at Western had been impaired, he accepted a call in 1840 to the struggling German Reformed theological seminary at Mercersburg, a move which was interpreted to him as merely a shift from the "Scotch Reformed" branch of the church to the "German Presbyterian" branch. In the isolation of Mercersburg, Nevin underwent the radical theological reorientation that caused him to break with Princeton orthodoxy at three crucial points: its lack of any sense of historical development, its individualistic view of the church, and its Zwinglian view of the sacraments.

Many influences, some of long standing, combined to produce Nevin's change of front. Not the least of these was the influence of Coleridge, but Nevin reported that it was the writings of J. A. W. Neander (1789-1850), the German church historian, which had actually awakened him from his "dogmatic slumber." Neander taught him that Christianity was a life, an experience, a communion with invisible realities, rather than a dogmatic system. This enabled him to appreciate diverse doctrinal conceptions and to find in all the diversities a movement toward a divinely ordained purpose. Finally, at Mercersburg, Nevin was introduced to a psychology, based upon Hegel, which he discovered had direct bearing on doctrines of the Incarnation, the mystical union of Christ and the believer, and the presence of Christ in the Eucharist.

Nevin's shift to a new theological position was signalized in 1843 by the publication of *The Anxious Bench,* a forthright attack upon the "new-measures" revivalism which had invaded the German Reformed churches and which Nevin regarded as "unfavorable to deep, thorough, and intelligent piety," "fatal to the true idea of devotion," and "injurious to the worship of God." [18] His major work, *The Mystical Presence: A Vindication of the Reformed or Calvinistic Doctrine of the Holy Eucharist,*[19] was

[18] *The Anxious Bench* (Chambersburg, Pa., 1843), 56.
[19] A selection is printed in Smith, Handy, Loetscher, *American Christianity,* II, 92-100.

published three years later, and it brought him into a head-on clash with Hodge—a clash that ended with Nevin demolishing Hodge's attempt to marshal support from the Reformed confessions.

In contrast to those who understood Christianity as a relationship of individuals to Christ who are only subsequently brought together to form the church, Nevin held that individuals do not constitute the church. The church is not something added to the gospel; it is an essential part of the gospel. It is the context within which men have access to Christ's saving presence, the means by which the living Christ gives himself to his people. It was constituted and continues to be constituted as a "whole" through communion with Christ rather than being simply the sum total of predestined individuals—past, present, and future. Central to Nevin's understanding of communion with Christ was his conception of the Eucharist. "The question of the Eucharist," he declared, "is one of the most important belonging to the history of religion. It may be regarded indeed as in some sense central to the whole Christian system. For Christianity is grounded in the living union of the believer with the person of Christ; and this great fact is emphatically concentrated in the mystery of the Lord's Supper." [20] Thus it is in the mystical participation of the faithful in the life of Christ through the sacrament of the Lord's Supper that the church is most truly the Church.

Liturgical reform, ecumenical concern, and questions of ministerial order were other subjects to which Nevin devoted his attention, and his thought was enriched and in some instances explicated by his colleague Philip Schaff who arrived in Mercersburg from Germany in 1844. Nevin's views aroused much opposition from defenders of New School doctrines and practices, and after the Civil War the German Reformed Church was bitterly divided between the Nevinists and the anti-Nevinists. Competing educational insitutions were established and the denomination barely escaped actual schism.

Of Nevin it was said: "He is always instructive, even when he is in error." [21] Unfortunately, few were instructed, for he moved in a restricted circle. He belonged to a small denomination and taught in a remote seminary. But the main reason for his failure to be heard was the fact that

[20] *The Mystical Presence* (Philadelphia, 1846), 51.
[21] J. H. Nichols, "John Williamson Nevin," in *Sons of the Prophets*, ed. H. T. Kerr (Princeton, 1963), 81.

he addressed himself to issues which were not to be keenly felt until the twentieth century.

In some respects John H. Hobart (1775–1830), Episcopal bishop of New York, was a kindred spirit to Nevin. His emphases were much the same as those of the Mercersburg theologian, but he really lived in another world. Hobart's interest was practical rather than theological. Unlike Nevin he was stirred by no ecumenical vision and he had little appreciation of historical development. Hobart was a strict "denominationalist," a "sectarian" in the eyes of Evangelicals.

Consecrated bishop in 1811, Hobart spent the remaining nineteen years of his life in an amazing burst of activity directed to reviving the flagging fortunes of the Protestant Episcopal Church in the State of New York. He was constantly on the move visiting the churches of his diocese and establishing missions. He wrote and compiled handbooks as practical aids to the laity: *Companion for the Altar, Companion for the Festivals and Fasts, The Pocket Almanac, The Church Catechism, The Christian's Manual on Faith and Devotion*. He rebuked those who participated in the interdenominational voluntary societies, and to counter the influence of those societies he organized the Protestant Episcopal Tract Society, the Protestant Episcopal Sunday School Society, and the New York Bible and Common Prayer Book Society. In a church that was predominantly "Low Church" or "Evangelical" in sentiment, Hobart was proud to acknowledge the name "High Churchman," and the explication of what it meant to be a High Churchman was the constant theme of his annual "charges" as well as of his other writings.

A "Low Churchman" to Hobart was one "who deprecates the distinguishing characteristics of the Church or who is lukewarm or indifferent in advancing them," whereas the "High Churchman" exhibits "an eminent degree of attachment to the essential characteristics of the Church and zeal for their advancement." The essential characteristics were "those of the first and purest ages of Christianity, of the age of the apostles, of martyrs and confessors," and Hobart dedicated himself to arresting "the progress of an indifference and laxity of opinion" which threatened the destruction of the Church as "it was constituted by its divine head." [22]

[22] E. C. Chorley, *Men and Movements in the American Episcopal Church* (N.Y., 1946), 143, 146.

171

Hobart rejected what he called the "invidious distinction" that so many made "between the doctrine and the institutions of the gospel." Both, he insisted, "have a divine origin" and "are inseparably connected." Indispensable to the being of the Church are the "essential elements of doctrine, ministry, sacraments, and worship." In developing this fourfold form of the Church, Hobart displayed little creative thought. His liturgical interest was limited to defending the existing Episcopal liturgy as embodying evangelical truth in the "purest" language of devotion. While he regarded the sacraments as central and indispensable and thought that "he hazarded his salvation if he refused or neglected to receive these means and pledges of divine favor," he considered the bread and wine to be no more than "symbols and memorials of the body and blood of Christ." His interest in doctrine was equally commonplace. The point of his central concern was the ministry, as he made clear when he declared that the true High Churchman adheres "in all essential points to the faith, ministry, and worship which distinguished the apostolic and primitive Church, and particularly to the constitution of the Christian ministry under its three orders of bishops, priests, and deacons." [23]

Lawful ministers, Hobart maintained, are "those who derive their authority from Christ himself by regular succession from the apostles." Consequently, there cannot be "a lawful bishop, priest, or deacon who hath not had episcopal consecration or ordination." Episcopacy is the essential point and it is "unchangeable because it is the originally constituted mode of conveying that commission without which there can be no visible ministry, no visible sacraments, no visible Church." Thus "we continue in the fellowship of the apostles when we adhere to the ministry of bishops, priests, and deacons who have been from the apostles' times." Nor did Hobart hesitate to draw the harsh conclusion which offended so many of his fellow Episcopalians: "I could not maintain the divine authority of the Episcopal ministry without denying the validity of a nonepiscopal ministry." [24]

Scholars have often speculated as to the source of Hobart's uncompromising churchmanship which ran so counter to the spirit of his age. One clue perhaps is to be found in his family tradition, for his grandfather was a displaced New Englander who had become an Episcopalian. Another

[23] *Ibid.*, 143–44, 147.
[24] *Ibid.*, 142, 184, 186–87.

influence may have been a feeling of defensiveness that developed during his college days in the Presbyterian atmosphere of Princeton. More decisive undoubtedly was the influence of his father-in-law, Thomas Bradbury Chandler, who had led the fight for a colonial episcopate and who had taken care to make sure that his daughter was "well instructed in the doctrines of primitive episcopacy." But whatever their source Hobart's views, which represented only a minority opinion in his own time, were destined to become, after having been enriched and deepened by insights derived from the Oxford Movement in England, one of the dominant currents in the life of the Protestant Episcopal Church in the twentieth century.[25]

By the mid-nineteenth century, views analogous to those of Hobart had also begun to develop within Baptist ranks. This "High Church" sentiment, which emphasized apostolic succession through an unbroken line of New Testament churches, was the distinctive characteristic of a group of Baptists who called themselves "Landmarkists." The name was derived from a tract *An Old Landmark Reset* (1854) by James M. Pendleton (1811–91),[26] but the basic tenets, which included a refusal to recognize other "societies" as true churches and a rejection of "alien immersion" and "pulpit affiliation" with non-Baptists, had been set forth by James R. Graves (1820–93) three years earlier at a meeting in Cotton Grove, Tennessee. While the major Baptist bodies repeatedly repudiated the Landmarkists, their "High Church" views had gained wide currency in the South by the end of the century.

Transcendentalism

Little more than a decade after the founding of the American Unitarian Association, the Boston churches were torn again by a new reformation led by rebellious young preachers, members of the "Transcen-

[25] The Oxford Movement was initiated in 1833 by John Keble (1792–1866) with a sermon on "National Apostasy," and was carried forward through a series of *Tracts for the Times,* the first of which was published by J. H. Newman (1801–90) in the same year. The aim of the movement was to win support within the Church of England for the "High Church" views that had been explicated by seventeenth-century divines. A dominant motif of the movement was its renewed interest in primitive and medieval Christianity.

[26] See selection reprinted in Smith, Handy, Loetscher, *American Christianity,* II, 108–12. See also R. G. Torbet, "Landmarkism," in *Baptist Concepts of the Church,* ed. W. S. Hudson (Philadelphia, 1959), and J. E. Steely, "The Landmark Movement in the Southern Baptist Convention," in *What Is the Church?* ed. D. K. McCall (Nashville, 1958).

dental Club" which first met in the home of George Ripley (1802–80).[27]
Among the more prominent of the rebel clergymen, in addition to Ripley,
were Ralph Waldo Emerson (1803–82), Theodore Parker (1810–60),
James Freeman Clarke (1810–88), Frederic Henry Hedge (1805–90),
William Henry Channing (1810–84), and Orestes Brownson (1803–76).
And they were ably abetted by several influential lay recruits, such as
Bronson Alcott (1799–1888), Henry David Thoreau (1817–62), Margaret Fuller (1810–50), and Elizabeth Peabody (1804–94). Repelled by
what they regarded as the cold logic of their Unitarian elders and deeply
influenced by Coleridge's *Aids to Reflection,* the Transcendentalists sought
to reconcile the rationalism of their tradition with the romanticism of their
age by introducing a strong note of mysticism into Unitarian formulations.

Since they were basically eclectic in their approach to truth, it is
difficult to characterize the Transcendentalists. No two of them agreed at
every point; and while some exhibited an intense individualism, others
displayed a passionate zeal for communal life. James Freeman Clarke on
one occasion suggested that their group might be called "the Club of the
Like-Minded" because "no two of us thought alike." They were, nonetheless, bound together by what they called "the spiritual principle"—a
principle which was articulated in three major agreements: an insistence
upon divine immanence, a dependence upon intuitive perception of truth,
and a rejection of all external authority. Every created thing had deep
religious meaning, and they found "sermons not just in stones but in bean
rows at Walden Pond and mud puddles on Boston Common." They were
called Transcendentalists, said Ripley, because they believed "in an order
of truths which transcends the sphere of the external senses." And since
"the truth of religion does not depend on tradition, nor historical facts, but
has an unerring witness in the soul," they refused to acknowledge any
authority beyond themselves. The Transcendentalist, Emerson declared,
"believes in miracles, in the perpetual openness of the human mind to the
new influx of light and power; he believes in inspiration and ecstasy." The
individual soul is linked to God and through the gift of intuition—instinct,

[27] See William R. Hutchison, *The Transcendentalist Ministers* (New Haven, 1959).
For basic documents, see *The Transcendentalists: An Anthology,* ed. Perry Miller,
(Cambridge, Mass., 1950). There are several paperbacks containing Emerson's "Divinity
School Address" and Theodore Parker's sermon on "The Transient and Permanent in
Christianity," both key Transcendentalist documents. These also are reprinted in part in
Smith, Handy, Loetscher, *American Christianity,* II, 130–52.

imagination, insight—the soul can penetrate beyond the outer shell of life and consummate the union with God by participating in the life of the "oversoul." [28]

Andrews Norton (1786–1853) and other old-line Unitarians were horrified by this "latest form of infidelity" and were restrained from ejecting the Transcendentalists from the Unitarian fellowship only by an awareness of the scandal that a heresy trial among the Unitarians would create. Consequently the members of the Club were permitted to proceed in their churches with their program of reformation. Unlike Nevin who had been spurred by Coleridge to move in a more churchly direction, the Transcendentalists were led by their romantic vision to a quite contrary emphasis. They sought to turn their churches into free religious associations in which the distinction between clergy and laity would disappear and worship would be so ordered that leadership might be rotated. Furthermore, their goal was a comprehension which would embrace the best elements of all former religious systems and within which radical movements would not be looked upon as heresies but as "providential" clues to some need which God wished the churches to fulfill.

The mediating theology of Horace Bushnell

After several false vocational starts, which included teaching, journalism, and law, a quiet conversion experience in the solitude of his own room sent Horace Bushnell (1802–76) to Yale Divinity School and from there to the pastorate of the North Congregational Church in Hartford, Connecticut, where he was to spend the rest of his active pastoral life. [29] Bushnell was to be both "conservative" and "liberal" in his emphases, finding much of Christian truth in the older tradition of New England and yet appropriating and incorporating into his thinking insights derived from the Unitarian critique. He could speak of "free," "self-governed" individuals, and yet emphasize the way in which individuals are bound, either for good or for evil, by the organic character of the communities—family, church, neighborhood, and nation—in which they

[28] Hutchison, *Transcendentalist Ministers*, vii, 29. Tyler, *Freedom's Ferment*, 48. O. B. Frothingham, *George Ripley* (Boston, 1882), 84–85. Key selections from Ripley, Emerson, Parker, and William Henry Channing are reprinted in Smith, Handy, Loetscher, *American Christianity*, II, 130–52.

[29] See Barbara M. Cross, *Horace Bushnell* (Chicago, 1958).

exist. His endeavor was to be a mediator, seeking to reconcile the intimations of Christian truth that were to be found in diverse theological camps. While Bushnell's views won little acceptance prior to the Civil War, they later became of major importance in preparing the way for the New Theology of the 1870's and 1880's.

Bushnell, Nevin, and the Transcendentalists all acknowledged the decisive influence that had been exerted upon them by the "mysticism" of Coleridge and Schleiermacher, but each domesticated this dual influence in different ways. The Transcendentalists were led to reject the past and to reduce the church to a pragmatically justified religious association. Nevin, on the other hand, experienced no such compulsion, for he had been freed from any notion of static orthodoxy by a sense of historical development which he derived from reading Neander. Thus his appreciation both of the past and of the Church as an embodiment of Christ had been enhanced by the stress on mystic communion. Bushnell's escape from orthodoxy was not dissimilar to that of Nevin, but for Bushnell it was made possible by a theory of language. To him language was an imprecise instrument. Words are but "faded metaphors" which cannot be transferred from mind to mind with their meaning clear and transparent. Each word is organically related to its own history, to the history of the one who uses it and of the one who hears it, and to the situation in which it is used. With these variables, all creedal statements and even the words of Scripture must be understood in a "spirit of accommodation," for they are but linguistic and hence poetic attempts to speak the unspeakable. Christian truth was something which lay behind doctrinal propositions, but Bushnell did not sympathize with the Unitarian rejection of creeds. They were testimonies to that which lay beyond them and he was ready to accept them all, for "when they are subjected to the deepest chemistry of thought . . . they become so elastic and run so freely into each other that one seldom need have any difficulty in accepting as many as are offered him." [30]

Horace Bushnell is best remembered as the author of *Christian Nurture* (1847) which, while not his most important work, was one of the most influential books ever to be published in America. It was a criticism of revivalism and a plea for what in its broadest sense could be called

---

[30] "Preliminary Dissertaion on Language," in *God and Christ* (Hartford, 1849), 81–83. See also his discussion of "Language and Doctrine" in *Christ and Theology* (Hartford, 1851).

Christian education. With his understanding of language as a social phenomenon, Bushnell was driven to recognize the formative influence of the community of faith. No person exists in isolation. He lives within a social context which shapes and determines his character. There is no reason to suppose that a child of believing parents cannot "grow up in the Lord." Take any scheme of human nature you please, Bushnell declared, and you will find nothing in it "to forbid the possibility that a child should be led, in his first moral act, to cleave unto what is good and right." Instead of assuming that "the child is to grow up in sin, to be converted after he comes to mature age," the "aim, effort, and expectation" should be that he may "grow up a Christian and never know himself as being otherwise." The great trouble with revivalism, as Bushnell saw it, is that as a result of its "jump and stir" the ordinary operations of God's grace tend to be "swallowed up and lost in the extraordinary" and people are led to believe that the only entrance into the Christian life is through a convulsive conversion experience in a revival meeting.[31]

Bushnell was not opposed to revivals. He believed that they rendered a great and necessary service to those who have been caught in the web of the kingdom of evil. Sin no less than virtue can be transmitted by the social context.

> Evil, once beginning to exist, inevitably becomes organic and constructs a kind of principate or kingdom opposite to God. . . . Pride organizes caste and dominates in the sphere of fashion. Corrupt opinions, false judgments, bad manners, and a general body of conventionalisms that represent the motherhood of sin, come into vogue and reign. And so, doubtless, everywhere and in all worlds, sin has in its nature to organize, mount into the ascendant above God and truth, and reign in a kingdom opposite God.[32]

With God's help and the Christian nurture provided by family and church, no one need sink into the slough of sin; but if he has, then a drastic rebirth to change his "reigning love" is necessary. As early as 1838 Bushnell had published an article in the *Quarterly Christian Spectator* "to establish a higher and more solid confidence in revivals," an article in which he insisted that "nothing was ever achieved in the way of great and radical

---

[31] *Christian Nurture* (N.Y., 1923), 4, 10; "Spiritual Economy of Revivals of Religion," *Quarterly Christian Spectator*, X (1838), 143–45.

[32] *Nature and the Supernatural* (N.Y., 1858), 135.

change in men without some degree of excitement; and if any one expects to carry on the cause of salvation by a steady rolling on the same dead level and fears continually lest the axles wax hot and kindle into a flame, he is too timorous to hold the reins of the Lord's chariot." While religion need not be for everyone "a fireball shot from the moon," [33] for some it must be.

As Bushnell reconciled revivalism to the ordered life of home and congregation, so he reconciled the major contentions of the Unitarians with an evangelical understanding of the Christian faith. He refashioned his conception of God, of man, of Christ, and of the Atonement to take the force from the Unitarian critique, and in the process reached back to Jonathan Edwards for some of the themes that helped him to make his case. He reaffirmed the Trinity by acknowledging that it applied only to God as revealed and not as ultimate being, as descriptive not of his person but of the modes of self-disclosure by which he makes himself known as Father, Son, and Spirit. In similar fashion, Bushnell bridged the gap between the natural and the supernatural without allowing them to become completely indistinguishable.

The fate which befalls most mediators was not withheld from Bushnell. He was appreciated at one point and criticized at another. No one seemed completely happy with his solutions. He was saved from being subjected to a heresy trial only by the withdrawal of his church from the local Congregational association which was dominated by Bennet Tyler, president of Hartford Seminary and leader of the Old School forces in Connecticut. But Leonard Bacon (1802–81), pastor of the Center Church in New Haven who had stood astride the Taylor-Tyler controversy, pronounced what was to be the growing conviction when he said that "brother Bushnell is essentially sound." [34] During the second half of the century, Bushnell's "progressive orthodoxy" was to sweep through many of the seminaries, and men who had been deeply influenced by him were to be among the most distinguished preachers in the land.

The triumph of Methodism

Whatever the future verdict was to be, the men discussed in this chapter represented lost causes in their own generation. They were

[33] *An Argument for "Discourses on Christian Nurture"* (Hartford, 1847), 16.
[34] Roland H. Bainton, *Yale and the Ministry* (N.Y., 1957), 124.

minority voices in a time of evangelistic urgency. The tide was running in another direction, and the decades immediately preceding the Civil War witnessed the triumph of the distinctive emphases of Methodism in practically all the denominations.[35]

Earlier defections to Methodist views and techniques had produced a cluster of new ecclesiastical bodies such as the United Brethren, the Evangelical Association, the Winebrennerians, the Free-Will Baptists, the Cumberland Presbyterians, and the Disciples of Christ or "Christians"— the latter combining a Presbyterian heritage with Methodist doctrines and Baptist polity and practice. But more significant than these defections was the fact that the Calvinism of the other denominations was becoming so diluted as to be unrecognizable. Taking their lead from Nathaniel W. Taylor, the revivalists had placed such stress upon the ability of the sinner to acquire conversion as in effect to transform Calvinism into an operational Arminianism. Finney illustrated the progression that was taking place. He was first a Presbyterian and then a Congregationalist, but his theology became more and more that of the Methodists until he finally embraced the Wesleyan doctrine of Christian perfection. By mid-century Robert Baird was testifying that it was necessary in all progressive churches "to preach to sinners as if they believed them to be possessed of all the powers of moral agency, capable of turning to God, and on this account, and no other, inexcusable for not doing so."[36]

Curiously enough, Baird's comment appeared in—of all places—the *Princeton Review*. Old School Presbyterians had been greatly distressed by the infiltration of Arminian views and Finneyite techniques into their denominational life, but after the break of 1837 they exhibited astonishing alacrity in climbing on the bandwagon and turning again to revivalism as "the only effective weapon in the church's arsenal for turning back the tide of uncouthness, materialism, and moral disintegration."[37] Ultimately Barnes, Beecher, and even Finney were defended in the pages of the *Princeton Review*; and James W. Alexander (1804–59) could refer with equal approval to the Calvinist and Arminian revivals of the past, saying: "Accidents may vary but the essence is the same."[38] It was Charles Hodge

---

[35] See W. S. Hudson, *American Protestantism*, 71–74, 99–104.

[36] *Princeton Review*, XXII (1850), 204.

[37] Elwyn A. Smith, *The Presbyterian Ministry in American Culture* (Philadelphia, 1962), 214.

[38] *Ibid.*, 215.

himself who was the architect of the theory that permitted the Old School Presbyterians to reverse their basic commitment. He did this by adopting Jonathan Edwards' distinction between natural ability and moral inability and then glossing over the distinction to such an extent that his position was not dissimilar to that of the New School revivalists.[39]

The "prayer meeting" or "businessmen's" revival of 1857–59 serves as a symbol of how thoroughly the oversimplified piety of the revivalists had become domesticated in the American scene. This was a laymen's revival, growing out of noonday prayer meetings sponsored by the New York Y.M.C.A. and being carried forward by Y.M.C.A.'s in other major cities. The emphasis upon "holiness" and "the higher Christian life" which characterized the revival was a reflection of the influence of Finney's doctrine of Christian perfection, but the revival itself was in the hands of the laity and revealed little theological sophistication. Its major feature was its thorough respectability. Unlike earlier revivals, it seems to have evoked no opposition. A contemporary report noted that "there was remarkable unanimity of approval among religious and secular observers alike, with scarcely a critical voice heard anywhere." [40]

While there was much that was superficial in this "Methodist" or "evangelical" piety, its achievements were not inconsiderable. Philip Schaff, when reporting the American scene in 1854 to his former colleagues in Berlin, felt compelled to confess despite his reservations that "the United States are by far the most religious and Christian country in the world." "Table prayer," he noted, is "almost universal," "daily family worship" is the rule "in religious circles," and church attendance is "inseparable from moral and social respectability." In contrast to Berlin where there were only forty churches for a population of 450,000 with an attendance at public worship of no more than 30,000, New York with a population of 600,000 had "over 250 well-attended churches, some of them quite costly and splendid." In Brooklyn the proportion of churches to the population was even larger, and a similar state of affairs prevailed throughout the country.[41]

[39] For a discussion of the Old School "capitulation," see Elwyn A. Smith, *op. cit.*, 220–24.

[40] J. E. Orr, *The Second Evangelical Awakening* (London, 1949), 21.

[41] Schaff, *America*, 11, 35, 56, 78.

VIII

Religious Ferment

The first half of the nineteenth century in the United States was a time of eager expectancy, unbridled enthusiasm, and restless ferment. A new nation and a new world were being born, and to many anything and everything seemed possible. It was a period when the comet's tail was said to have swept America and everyone went a little mad. "We are all a little wild here with numberless projects of social reform," Emerson wrote to Carlyle in the autumn of 1840. "Not a reading man but has a draft of a new community in his waistcoat pocket." The hyperbole is obvious.

Not everyone went mad and many were sufficiently prosaic to think that nothing more than a watch belonged in a waistcoat pocket. Still there were many who were not of the mind or spirit to keep their expectations under control. While European visitors were impressed by the popularity and vigor of conventional religion, they were also struck by the many new ways to heaven that were being fashioned in the American environment and by the strenuous efforts of others to give the heavenly existence earthly embodiment.

Two factors combined to produce the unusual religious ferment of these years. One was the social context. The other was the religious climate. In the American environment there was an absence of tradition and a sense of pregnant possibility which encouraged a spirit of experimentation. Nor was this experimentation inhibited by law. Unlimited freedom had been granted religious expression, no matter how eccentric it might be. And an abundance of cheap land and open space provided an unequaled opportunity to implement and institutionalize religious ideas. If the context was hospitable to innovation, the actual impetus that gave rise to most of the novel cults, sects, and movements was the climate of opinion generated by successive waves of revivalism.

Noah Worcester had pointed out in 1794 that the "sects" had profited from revivals, and this continued to be true. Successive harvests were to be reaped by the Shakers, the Mormons, the Oneida community, the Millerites, the Spiritualists, and a host of smaller and more transient groups. The revivals left many individuals distraught and torn by anxiety; and, having tried without success to gain a sense of assurance in their own churches, they were in a receptive mood to listen to new prophets who offered definite guarantees of spiritual security. While the emotional disturbance which revivalism left in its wake explains why even the most bizarre groups, once established, could garner adherents, it does not account for their origin. Here it was the spirit—ideas, attitudes, hopes—fostered by the revivals which played the creative role.

Three emphases stimulated by revivalistic preaching would seem to have been of decisive importance in creating the climate of enthusiasm out of which the new cults, sects, and communities emerged. For one thing, the revivalists demanded an immediate confrontation with God. This often took the form of an ecstatic vision or mystical illumination which could easily be interpreted as a new revelation. Second, the revivalists placed increasing stress upon the possibility of perfect sanctification, thus arousing a hunger for holiness and a life free from sin. Finally, they tended to dwell upon the ancient millennial expectation of a golden age to come, whether inaugurated by the personal return of Christ or established through the preaching of the gospel. All the groups which deviated from the norm of conventional religion during these years stemmed from at least one of these emphases, and most of them represented a blending of all three.[1]

---

[1] See A. L. Jamison, "Religions on the Christian Perimeter," in *The Shaping of American Religion*, ed. J. W. Smith and A. L. Jamison, 197–202.

The utopian vision

A prominent feature of the first half of the nineteenth century in America was the rise and decline of a variety of communal societies. All of them were impelled by a vision of an ideal or perfect life which they sought to actualize. These societies were never numerous, nor was the total number of adherents great. Most of them quickly appeared and as quickly disappeared. Only a few maintained themselves for any considerable period of time. Some were nonreligious in origin and orientation, and these exhibited the least staying power. Some were imported from abroad—the Rappites at "Harmony" in western Pennsylvania and later at "Harmony" in Indiana; the Separatists of "Zoar" in Ohio; the followers of William Keil at "Bethel" in Missouri and "Aurora" in Oregon; the Amana Society (The Community of True Inspiration) at "Ebenezer" near Buffalo and then in Iowa; the community of Swedish immigrants established by Eric Janson at Bishop Hill in Illinois. With the partial exception of William Keil's Rappite seceders, all these immigrant groups remained isolated from American life. But there were also indigenous communal societies. Of the indigenous communities where men and women sought sanctification in a perfect society, the Shaker settlements of Ann Lee and the Oneida community of John Humphrey Noyes were the most important. The Transcendentalist ventures at Fruitlands, Brook Farm, and Hopedale, on the other hand, were more typical in that they illustrated the pathos of shattered hopes which was the lot of most of the communal enterprises.

THE SHAKERS.   The followers of Ann Lee (1736–84) provide an outstanding example of the blending of new revelation with perfectionist and millenarian ideas in the formation of a communal society.[2] Although "Mother Ann" had come to America with eight followers in 1774, the United Society of Believers in Christ's Second Appearing was not organized until 1787, three years after her death, when a former Free-Will Baptist preacher took charge and gave the Society its definitive shape.

Ann was the wife of a blacksmith in Manchester, England, and the mother of four children, all of whom died in infancy. She had become a member of a small group of Shaking Quakers who were crying out warnings of Christ's approaching second advent and predicting that

[2] The two best accounts of Shakerism are Marguerite F. Melcher, *The Shaker Adventure* (Princeton, 1941), and Edward D. Andrews, *The People Called Shakers: A Search for the Perfect Society* (N.Y., 1953).

famine and pestilence were about to descend upon the wicked. The distinguishing feature of their worship, which gave them their name, was the frequency with which they would be "seized with a mighty trembling, with violent agitations of the body, running and walking on the floor, with singing, shouting, and leaping for joy." [3] In 1770 Ann became the vehicle of a revelation that the root and foundation of human depravity and the source of all evils afflicting mankind was the sex act. This was the original sin of Adam and Eve. This was the forbidden fruit. In the words of a later Shaker hymn:

> As lust conceived by the Fall
> Hath more or less infected all;
> So we believe 'tis only this
> That keepeth souls from perfect bliss.

The basic summons was to a celibate life, and it was about this emphasis that Ann gathered her first little company of disciples.

After leaving England and settling in Watervliet, New York, Ann gained no new adherents until 1779 when a revival at New Lebanon proved so disturbing that it brought Joseph Meacham (1742–96) and several members of his congregation into the fold. Other recruits were won as scattered revivals began to appear in western Massachusetts and Connecticut. During the final four years of her life, Ann was reported to have performed miracles which convinced her followers that she was Christ in his "second appearing," making manifest the female element in the Godhead and inaugurating the beginning of the millennium by gathering a faithful remnant out of the churches of Antichrist.

In 1787, three years after the death of Mother Ann, Joseph Meacham assumed leadership of the group, gathered the members into several "families" for communal living, drafted the constitution of the United Society, and elaborated and systematized Shaker doctrine. Everything was carefully regulated, and the violence of the earlier physical manifestations was subdued and reduced to a ritualistic dance in which worship was expressed by the body as well as by speech and song. In the new order that was at hand, all that had been "earthly, sensual, devilish" would become "spiritual, divine, and heavenly," and the whole endeavor of the Shakers

---

[3] See Benjamin Silliman's account of the Shakers in Smith, Handy, Loetscher, *American Christianity*, I, 586–96.

was to live a life of perfection as preparation for the perfect state promised to them. Since there would be no further need for the propagation of the human race in the new age, the inclusion of celibacy among the twelve virtues which must be pursued and practiced did not seem unreasonable.

Under Meacham's leadership the Society experienced a surge of growth with the onset of the Second Awakening. Within five years ten communities with more than two thousand members had been formed in Maine, New Hampshire, Massachusetts, Connecticut, and New York. A second period of growth began in 1805 when emissaries were sent West to reap a harvest in the wake of the great Kentucky revival, including two of the prominent leaders of the revival—Richard McNemar and John Dunlavy. By 1825 there were at least twenty communities scattered throughout Ohio, Indiana, and Kentucky, as well as in New England and New York, and within a few years the Society had about six thousand members.

Economically the Shakers prospered from the beginning. Farming was the basis of their economy but they quickly developed successful commercial and handicraft enterprises. For five or six years after 1837 the various communities were troubled by a wild burst of spirit-inspired communications which had the result of creating a deep fear of any further enthusiasm. After this loss of fervor and with the waning of rural revivalism, the Shakers attracted fewer and fewer new members. Although the communities remained prosperous, a steady decline in numbers had set in by 1850. A century later only a handful of elderly men and women remained.

THE ONEIDA COMMUNITY. While the Shakers were seeking perfection in celibacy, others were going to the opposite extreme, moving in an antinomian direction with their claims to holiness and even lapsing into sexual promiscuity. While opposed to the "spiritual wifery" which swept through certain perfectionist circles, John Humphrey Noyes (1811–86) was the most conspicuous perfectionist leader who placed the stamp of approval upon a departure from the accepted code of sexual relationships.[4]

Noyes was a product of the Finney revivals. A graduate of Dartmouth and the son of a successful Vermont businessman who was prominent in state politics, Noyes had begun the study of law when Finney

[4] See Robert A. Parker, *A Yankee Saint: John Humphrey Noyes and the Oneida Community* (N.Y., 1935).

captured him for the ministry and sent him off for a year at Andover Seminary and two years at Yale Divinity School. When he asserted that conversion brought complete release from sin, he was refused ordination. This, however, did not keep him from preaching wherever he could find groups of like-minded perfectionists and from giving further study to what he called "the Sin system, the Marriage system, the Work system, and the Death system." After much pondering, he concluded that it was necessary to create a society in which conditions would be favorable to the practice of perfection. He was later to declare that, as "the revivalists had for their great idea the regeneration of the soul," he had as his great idea "the regeneration of society, which is the soul's environment." [5]

The system which Noyes worked out was based on three fundamental doctrines. The first was total security from sin, but this security was so defined that it did not eliminate the need of discipline and improvement. The second was the conviction that the millennium had been introduced in A.D. 70, but had been obscured by spurious post-millennial growths of the second and third centuries. The third and most distinctive principle was the insistence that, since the saints were equally yoked in dedication to faith, the practice of primitive Christian communism—a communism which included the marriage relationship—was the only logical arrangement.

Noyes gathered a small group in Putney, Vermont, and in the early 1840's instituted a communism of property. When this communism was extended in 1846 by putting into operation his theory of "complex marriage," the local citizens were aroused and to avoid the possibility of being mobbed the community was re-established at Oneida, New York, two years later. A major stroke of luck was the conversion of Samuel Newhouse, the inventor of a highly effective small-animal trap. Trap manufacturing placed the community on a sound financial basis, until it was replaced as the chief industry by silver plate ("Community Plate") production. But economic considerations were incidental. The philosophy of the community was stated by Noyes in these words:

> Our warfare is an assertion of human rights; first the right of man to be governed by God and to live in the social state of heaven; second the right of woman to dispose of her sexual nature by at-

[5] J. H. Noyes, *History of American Socialism* (Philadelphia, 1870), 24. See also Tyler, *Freedom's Ferment*, 186.

traction instead of by law and routine and to bear children only when she chooses; third the right of all to diminish the labors and increase the advantages of life by association.

These principles, he insisted, must find expression in "one living organization before the Kingdom of Heaven can come." Thus personal sanctification and social regeneration went hand-in-hand.[6]

While Noyes fashioned a detailed and closely supervised pattern of life for the community, including procedures for "mutual criticism" and innovations in the education of children, it was the theory and practice of "complex marriage" which gained for the community its notoriety. This theory, which regarded each woman in the group as the wife of every man and every man as the husband of every woman, was instituted on religious grounds. Noyes's followers thought of themselves as saints purified by religious experience and disciplined to the practice of absolute fellowship among themselves by a total love of God. As a consequence, they believed that there was a basic incompatibility between absolute good will among the regenerate and the exclusive legal and physical bonds of conventional marriage. "Sexual communion," Noyes insisted, "differs only in its superior intensity and beauty from other acts of love" and it contributes to true mutality. But when sexual communion is restricted to acts of "special love" it becomes unsocial and dangerous to communal interests. The Oneida perfectionists resented the charge that they were practicing "free love," for sexual intercourse among them was "organized" rather than promiscuous, and they believed that it was inspired by true spirituality.

For thirty years the community remained true to its original ideals, but pressure from the outside world persuaded Noyes in 1879 to abandon the practice of "complex marriage." This in turn led to the abandonment of communal ownership of property the following year. A joint-stock company was formed, the shares were distributed among the former communitarians, and silver-plated tableware became the chief reminder of their former effort to institutionalize a sinless life and thus provide a foretaste of the kingdom of God.

TRANSCENDENTALISM'S "WILD OATS." When Emerson spoke of the draft of utopia to be found in almost every reading man's waistcoat pocket, he was thinking pre-eminently of some of his fellow Transcendentalists, for

[6] Cross, *The Burned-over District*, 335, 337.

in a curiously romantic way they also had appropriated the perfectionist and millenarian tendencies of the time. Emerson himself remained skeptical, but others were driven by an overpowering desire to anticipate the millennium by perfecting human institutions. Three small communal societies—Fruitlands, Brook Farm, and Hopedale—were the product of what in retrospect can be seen as their moment of aberration.[7]

Louisa May Alcott's *The Transcendental Wild Oats* is a fictionalized account of Bronson Alcott's venture in communal living at Fruitlands which began with high hopes in the spring of 1843 and collapsed before winter set in. Believing that "our freer, but yet far from freed, land is the asylum . . . for the hope of man," Bronson Alcott was convinced that only in America could "the second Eden . . . be planted in which the divine seed is to bruise the head of Evil and restore Man to his rightful communion with God in the Paradise of Good." This was his vision of Fruitlands. Unfortunately, what might have been at least a summer's idyl was spoiled by the domineering spirit of Charles Lane, a dour ascetic Englishman, who was determined that every natural human desire should be denied. One by one the members slipped away, the crops were left unharvested, and Lane finally departed to join the Shakers.

Brook Farm was a happier experiment. George Ripley, Unitarian minister and leading member of the "Transcendental Club," was its founder and director. In 1840, before resigning from the pulpit of his Purchase Street congregation in Boston, Ripley had told his parishioners that it was the business of Christianity to overthrow every social evil, and Brook Farm was designed to be, "if not the sunrise," at least "the morning star" of the new day in which the thinker and the manual laborer would be united in a noncompetitive society.

Most of the literary lights of the time participated at Brook Farm either as members, visitors, or supporters. The intellectual life at the Farm was exciting, and the social life, which included plays, dances, picnics, and boating parties, was gay. Since the members were better dreamers than farmers, the community was dependent upon outside support except for the income derived from its school, which was recommended by the Harvard faculty as an excellent place to send young boys who aspired to

[7] See Clara Endicott Sears, *Bronson Alcott's Fruitlands, with Transcendental Wild Oats by Louisa M. Alcott* (Boston, 1915); Lindsay Swift, *Brook Farm: Its Members, Scholars, and Visitors* (N.Y., 1900); Zoltan Haraszti, *The Idyll of Brook Farm* (Boston, 1937); Adin Ballou, *History of the Hopedale Community* (Lowell, Mass., 1897).

become college students. In 1844, however, the members became entranced by the ideas of the French socialist, Charles Fourier (1772–1837), and decided to turn Brook Farm into a Fourierist phalanx. This necessitated conforming to a rigid theory of social organization and involved establishing industries and forming specialized labor groups. Money was borrowed, the school was neglected, and in 1846 a fire left the community insolvent. By this time many of the sponsors had lost interest, having been diverted by newer fads, and in 1847 the community wound up its affairs. Later Nathaniel Hawthorne looked back with nostalgia to "our beautiful scheme of a noble and unselfish life" at the Farm. "How fair in that first summer appeared the prospect that it might endure for generations, and be perfected as the ages rolled by into the system of a people and a world. Were my former associates now there—were there only three or four of those true-hearted men still laboring in the sun—I sometimes fancy that I should direct my world-weary footsteps thitherward and entreat them to receive me for old friendship's sake."

The community at Hopedale was a less dilettante effort. Established near Milford, Massachusetts, in 1841, it managed to maintain itself for fifteen years. Adin Ballou (1803–90), a Universalist minister, was the founder and guiding spirit. He was not a member of the "Club," but was a Transcendentalist nonetheless and a friend of Channing and Parker. Since "it was one of the declared objects of Christ's labors to inaugurate the kingdom of heaven on earth," Ballou was convinced that "the imperative duty" of Christ's disciples is "to pray and to work for that sublime end." Working meant "actualizing" New Testament teachings in order to initiate a world movement toward the perfect life. Some thirty persons responded to Ballou's summons to subject themselves to "all the moral obligations" of the religion of Jesus and to take the lead in banishing from the world "all things known to be sinful against God or human nature." Ten years later the community had grown to nearly two hundred members and was a moderate financial success. But when Ballou retired from active leadership, it was decided that the common fund would be more productive if diverted to private enterprise, and in 1856 the whole project was liquidated. The failure, Ballou remarked with sadness, was not financial but "moral and spiritual"—"a deficiency among its members of those graces and powers of character which are requisite to the realization of the Christian ideal of human society."

Other variant religious groups

Utopian communities which sought to reproduce the heavenly existence in earthly institutions were but one manifestation of the religious ferment of the first half of the nineteenth century. Other variant groups came to the fore in which the perfectionist motif was more subdued. Such groups as the Mormons, the Millerites, and the Spiritualists were no less symptomatic of the energies released by the prevailing religious climate, but they found their primary orientation in some other point of emphasis—in a new and supplementary revelation, in the reduction of the millennial expectation to a definite timetable of events, in the sudden bursting of the barriers to the spirit world.

THE MORMONS.   The Church of Jesus Christ of Latter-day Saints which was to create for itself a great intramountain empire in the West had its origin in the remarkable story of Joseph Smith (1805–44), who in 1816 at the age of ten had come with his parents from Vermont to the vicinity of Palmyra, New York.[8] Here he absorbed much from the religious excitement of what came to be called "the burned-over district." Smith later reported that he was greatly disturbed by the religious controversies that swirled about him. "In the midst of this war of words and tumult of opinions, I often said to myself, what is to be done? Who of all these parties be right? Or are they all wrong together?" Troubled by these anxieties, he "retired to the woods" to seek wisdom of God. His prayer was answered by the appearance of two heavenly personages—the Father and the Son—who told him to hold himself apart from the contending denominations for a special task was to be given him. After a period of testing in which he received a series of further revelations, he was guided by the angel Moroni to discover long-buried golden plates which told the story of the Nephites and Lamanites, descendants of a lost tribe of Israel, who had inhabited the American continent centuries before. Among them Christ had appeared after his resurrection and had established the proper church order. The Lamanites, progenitors of the Indians, had apostatized

---

[8] The best biography of Smith is Fawn Brodie, *No Man Knows My History: the Life of Joseph Smith* (N.Y., 1946), and the best account of the movement is Thomas F. O'Dea, *The Mormons* (Chicago, 1957).

and had defeated the faithful Nephites in a battle in which all the Nephites except Mormon and his son Moroni were slain. The records of this ancient people were buried by Moroni in the hill Cumorah, and it was there that Smith discovered them together with the translating spectacles which enabled him to decipher what he later described as the Reformed Egyptian hieroglyphics of the text. In 1830 Smith's translation of the *Book of Mormon* was published at Palmyra.

This new scripture provided a basis for resolving the sectarian jangling which Smith had found so disturbing throughout his adolescent years, for it gave an authoritative judgment upon almost every issue that was in dispute. This fact was quickly recognized by Alexander Campbell who pointed out in his *Delusions: An Analysis of the Book of Mormon* (1832) that the golden plates had anticipated and given a definitive answer to "every error and almost every truth discussed in New York for the last ten years," including "infant baptism, ordination, the trinity, regeneration, repentance, justification, the fall of man, the atonement, transubstantiation, fasting, penance, church government, religious experience, the call to the ministry, the general resurrection, eternal punishment, who may baptize, and even the question of freemasonry, republican government, and the rights of man." And the *Book of Mormon* both buttressed its own judgments and provided for the future adjudication of controversy by insisting that anyone who denies "the revelations of God" and says "that they are done away, that there are no revelations, nor prophecies, nor gifts, nor speaking with tongues and interpretation of tongues" betrays his ignorance and denies "the gospel of Christ."

It is scarcely surprising that one of the first converts to embrace the new revelation should have been Sidney Rigdon (1793–1876), an ex-Disciple minister who had once contested Campbell's leadership, for the *Book of Mormon* stressed many of the basic themes of Campbellite preaching—free grace, free will, repentance, restoration, plainness of doctrine, democratic church government, opposition to "priestcraft," rejection of infant baptism, and even the distinctive Campbellite doctrine of baptism "unto the remission of sins." Nor in view of this heritage is it surprising that when young Joseph Smith on October 30, 1830, met with five friends in Fayette, New York, to restore "the Church of Christ in these last days," he should have chosen the typically Campbellite designation of

"Church of Christ" for his reincarnation of the ancient order of church life. Four years later, at the instigation of Rigdon, the name was changed to the Church of the Latter-day Saints, and in 1838 it was given its present expanded form.

A further theme running throughout the *Book of Mormon*, which had wide appeal to people who were stirred by the romantic nationalism of the time, was the portrayal of America as the promised land—"a land which is choice above all other lands," a land to which none shall come "save they shall be brought by the hand of the Lord." Indeed, the whole biblical setting of the drama of salvation was transferred to an American setting. To the successive declarations of political, economic, diplomatic, and intellectual independence penned by Jefferson, Clay, Monroe, and Emerson was now added a declaration of religious independence. The Old World heritage was declared to be both obsolete and irrelevant, for the restoration of the true church was dependent upon the recovery of an independent American tradition which extended back to the time of the Babylonian Exile and had been validated by the postresurrection appearance of Christ on American shores.

Prior to the formation of the new church, Smith had had a revelation in which John the Baptist had appeared and had ordained him and Oliver Cowdery [9] to the "Priesthood of Aaron, which holds the keys of the ministering of angels, and of the gospel of repentance, and of baptism by immersion for the remission of sins." Thus equipped, he was directed to form the church by a revelation which designated "Joseph Smith, Jun., who was called of God and ordained an apostle of Jesus Christ, to be the first elder of this church," and "Oliver Cowdery, who was also called of God, an apostle of Jesus Christ, to be the second elder of this church." Then at the first meeting of the church, Smith's full office was made clear by a further revelation which stated that he should "be called a seer, a translator, a prophet, an apostle of Jesus Christ, an elder of the church through the will of God the Father and the grace of your Lord Jesus Christ," with the added admonition that the church should "give heed unto all his words and commandments . . . for his word shall ye receive as if from mine own mouth."

---

[9] Cowdery was Smith's clerical assistant. While in Vermont prior to moving to Palmyra, Cowdery had embraced some "extraordinary doctrines, apparently involving millennial expectations and direct revelation as well as some mysterious treasure hunting." Cross, *Burned-over District*, 38–39.

By 1830 the new scripture had been published, the new church formed, and the new prophet designated with powers of immediate revelation to deal with troublesome problems as they arose. In the course of time more distinctive doctrines were elaborated—a plurality of gods, for example, as well as of wives—which set the Mormons further and further apart from the generality of Christians. Adaptations of Masonic ritual were introduced, marriage for time and eternity was adopted, baptism for the dead was instituted, and the priesthood of Melchizedek was restored by the miraculous intervention of Peter, James, and John. Mormon millennialism, on the other hand, remained moderate and never became the focal point of enthusiasm. Its perfectionism was restrained, and the communitarianism introduced by Rigdon at Kirtland, Ohio, probably owed more to the Campbellite stress on the authoritative example of the New Testament Church (see Acts 2:44–45; 4:34–35) than to any perfectionist drive. The communal tendencies were not central, being a peripheral feature sustained of the exigencies of their hegira, and the United Order of Enoch—a form of co-operative economic activity—was never transformed into a full communism. Still it was abundantly clear that the Mormons were not a part of conventional society, and their separateness created antagonism. This hostility, in turn, increased their sense of separateness, and the sense of separateness encouraged further innovation.

The impact of Joseph Smith's new church in the area of its origin was scant, for it was removed almost immediately to Kirtland, Ohio, where Sidney Rigdon's congregation provided a larger nucleus of adherents. The growth of the church was astonishing, and new recruits were won in Missouri to which missionaries had been dispatched in a fruitless endeavor to convert the Indians. Trouble at Kirtland, stemming in part from the failure of Smith's "Anti-Banking Company" (so named to circumvent the legislature's refusal to grant a bank charter) in the Panic of 1837, led to shifting the base of operations to Independence and then Far West, Missouri. Pitched battles there brought about another removal, this time to Nauvoo, Illinois, where Smith attempted to establish a semi-independent domain. The tragic murder of Smith by an angry mob in 1844 while he was confined in the jail at Carthage precipitated one of the epic stories of American history—the heroic trek of the majority of the Mormons under the leadership of Brigham Young (1801–77) to a new "Zion in the

Wilderness." Sheltered by the mountains surrounding the basin of the Great Salt Lake, they at last found a measure of peace and security. By 1870 the number of Mormons in the intramountain region exceeded 140,000, many of them converts that had been won abroad.

THE MILLERITES. The movement which created the greatest flurry of excitement during the years of religious ferment had as its single point of emphasis a specific date for the literal fulfillment of the ancient expectation that Christ would return in glory to rule upon the earth. In various forms the millennial hope had been a consistent theme of revivalistic preaching, and the increasing number and magnitude of revivals heightened the interest of many in the Second Coming. By 1825 references to the belief that the return of Christ was approaching began to become more numerous, and the phenomenal awakening of 1831 convinced many that it must be quite near. This millennial expectation was in part a reflection of the overpowering optimism and perfectionist temper of the American people, but the Panic of 1837 gave it another turn. With their buoyant optimism having been dissipated by the distress and disaster attendant upon an economic depression, many found in millennialism a compensatory substitute for their shattered hopes. An immediate judgment day became the simplest solution to all earthly problems, the shortest possible cut to millennial perfection, a panacea which would set all things right at a single stroke.

William Miller (1782–1849), a farmer at Low Hampton, New York, was the key figure in the Adventist excitement of the late 1830's and early 1840's.[10] After his conversion in 1816, he had become a member of the Baptist church and had begun an avid study of the Bible with particular attention to prophecies of the last times. His interest was in calculating the date of Christ's return and he probably found the clue which pointed to 1843 in the publications of the British Continental Society. By nimble arithmetic (years of 360 days—twelve 30-day months—instead of 365), he ultimately was able to prove to his satisfaction that "God in his wisdom has so interwoven the several prophecies that . . . they tell us the same things." In 1828 he felt a "call" to tell the world of his discovery that Christ would come "about 1843." "I tried to excuse myself," he later

---

[10] See Francis D. Nichol, *The Midnight Cry* (Washington, 1944); Clara E. Sears, *Days of Delusion* (Boston, 1924); Sylvester Bliss, *Memoirs of William Miller* (Boston, 1853).

explained. "I told the Lord that I was not used to speaking . . . that I was slow of speech and slow of tongue. But I could get no relief." By 1831 he had developed sufficient courage to begin to issue local warnings by sharing his discovery with neighbors and friends. Then he was asked to discuss his views in a nearby church, and he suddenly found that on this one subject at least he was eloquent. Invitations multiplied and he began to gain a measure of local notoriety. Although he was never ordained, Miller's ministerial status was somewhat regularized in 1833 with a license to preach.

While revivalism had bred a mentality which predisposed many to become ready converts to Miller's dating of the end of time, three events combined to give him a more than local reputation. The first was the publication in 1838 of his computations in book form under the title *Evidence from Scripture and History of the Second Coming of Christ, About the Year 1843.* The second was the Panic of 1837 which created for the book at the moment of its publication an unusually receptive audience. The third was the chance discovery of Miller by Joshua V. Himes (1805–95) at Exeter, New Hampshire, in 1839 while Miller was on a speaking tour of New England. Minister of a Christian Connection church in Boston and an indefatigable promoter, Himes had all the gifts that a century later would be associated with Madison Avenue. He immediately sensed the potency of the message of the plain-spoken farmer, and attached himself to Miller as his manager and publicity agent. He equipped Miller with a great chart displaying Miller's calculations in graphic form, purchased the biggest tent in the country for Miller's meetings, edited two journals—the *Midnight Cry* in New York and *Signs of the Times* in Boston—and helped to found others in Philadelphia, Cincinnati, Cleveland, Rochester, and Montreal. Other evangelists were recruited and sent on speaking tours; camp meetings were organized; children's books, catechisms, tracts, pamphlets, and even a hymnbook—*The Millennial Harp*—were published.

Despite vigorous condemnation of the movement by the majority of the ministers and ridicule by neighbors and friends, thousands were convinced by Miller's detailed calculations. Members of all denominations were enlisted, for the Adventist cause was nonsectarian and noncreedal, but Baptists, Free-Will Baptists, and "Christians" seem to have been the most susceptible. At the height of the Millerite fever there were probably more than 50,000 convinced believers and there may have been as many as a million others who were skeptically expectant.

Miller had been hesitant to be more specific than to say that Christ would return "about 1843," but in January, 1843, he announced that *this* year (from March 21, 1843, to March 21, 1844, taking into account the change in the calendar year) must see the end of time. The tension mounted as the year progressed, and was heightened by the appearance of a comet in the heavens. Meetings grew larger and converts more numerous, but March 21, 1844, came—and time still continued. On May 2, Miller confessed his error and acknowledged his disappointment, but one of his followers called attention to Habakkuk 2:3 and Leviticus 25:9 and announced that there obviously was to be a "tarrying time" of seven months and ten days. October 22, 1844, was to be the day of Christ's triumphant return and people were rallied once again with the slogan: "The Tenth Day of the Seventh Month." Miller was finally converted to the new date: "I see a glory in the seventh month which I never saw before. Thank the Lord, O my soul! . . . I am almost home. Glory! Glory! Glory! I see that the time is correct." The excitement revived, and the number living each moment as if it were their last exceeded that of the preceding summer.

With the second disappointment, most of those who had been caught up in the movement were completely disillusioned and the reaction of others was often bitter. Miller, for example, was excommunicated by the Baptist church at Low Hampton, and in 1849 he died, discredited and almost forgotten. A few became Shakers, giving that group its last important influx of new members. Some of those who remained steadfast in their hope, believing that only a minor error in calculation had been made, met in Albany in 1845 to form a conference which later splintered into three groups, the largest of which was the Advent Christian Church. Others were persuaded by Ellen Gould White (1827–1915) that Christ's failure to appear was due to a neglect of proper Sabbath observance and they formed the nucleus of what was to become the Seventh-day Adventist Church.

THE SPIRITUALISTS. Before the Millerites had fully recovered from their disenchantment, "the Rochester rappings" of the Fox sisters in 1848 created a new sensation which led to the development of modern Spiritualism.[11] The way had been prepared by the teachings of Emanuel Swedenborg (1688–1772) whose views had become something of a vogue among religious liberals and whose works had just been republished in a new English edition. Swedenborg claimed to have received communications from the spirit world by which knowledge of all things in the heavens and below the heavens had been given him. Interest in his teachings was reinforced by the spread of Mesmerism which utilized the strange power of "animal magnetism" to produce a hypnotic trance which was thought to point to the basic laws of the spirit world and to give promise of unlocking the mysteries of the life beyond. All that was needed to transform these embryonic ideas into Spiritualism was a mechanism for communicating with the dead, and it was such a device that was supplied unwittingly by two young girls, Maggie and Katie Fox.

The "rappings" began at Hydesville, New York, as a childish prank which some adults took seriously and was exploited by an older sister who lived in nearby Rochester. Soon the Fox sisters were holding public seances and notable converts were being won, including Horace Greeley, editor of the *New York Tribune*. By 1851 seven Spiritualist periodicals were being published, and six years later the number had increased to sixty-seven. The Universalists provided the most recruits, and their denomination never really recovered from its encounter with the spirit world. While interest had begun to subside prior to the Civil War, the movement found institutional expression in a number of Spiritualist "associations" which were to enjoy several flurries of renewed enthusiasm. In 1888 the Fox sisters acknowledged their hoax and demonstrated how they had produced the "rappings" by cracking their toe joints, but this exposure had little effect upon convinced believers.

The humanitarian impulse

Utopian communities and novel sectarian emphases were not the only expressions of religious ferment. Most of the enthusiasm generated by the Second Awakening was devoted to more conventional enterprises in which the concerns of the evangelically awakened often paralleled those of

[11] See J. A. Hill, *Spiritualism, Its History, Phenomena, and Doctrine* (Garden City, N.Y., 1919) ; Joseph McCabe, *Spiritualism: A Popular History* (London, 1920) ; W. G. L. Taylor, *Katie Fox: Epoch Making Medium* (N.Y., 1933).

the heirs of Channing. The revivalists were generally postmillennialists who assumed that an era of peace, justice, and goodness would precede the return of Christ. Consequently where there were revivals, there must be reform. Every aspect of society began to be subjected to eager scrutiny in order to scour and purify the earth in preparation for God's final act of redemption. Scarcely any phase of American life was left untouched. Temperance, Sabbath observance, world peace, profanity, vice, women's rights, slavery, the condition of penal institutions, educational innovations—all became objects of concern. The whole impulse was carefully articulated in a series of related societies and closely integrated with revivalistic efforts, as was made clear in 1835 by Theodore Dwight Weld (1803–95) in a letter to Lewis Tappan.

> God has called some prophets, some apostles, and some teachers. All the members of the body of Christ have not the same office. Let Delevan drive temperance, McDowell moral reform, Finney revivals, Tappan antislavery, etc. Each of these is bound to make his own peculiar department his main business, and to promote collaterally as much as he can the other objects. I have no doubt but Finney has erred in not giving as much collateral attention to antislavery as the present emergent crisis demands. And I am equally certain that I have not done as much collaterally to promote temperance and revivals while I have been lecturing on slavery as I ought.[12]

The revivals provided the impetus, summoning men and women to battle against sin; and the reform movements were the implementation of the thrust toward the coming kingdom of righteousness. The task of those who enlisted in the struggle was put succinctly by Finney: "Every member must work or quit. No honorary members."

THE EXPANDING CONCERN. While initially the reforms were mainly limited to rectifying individual vices—such as infidelity, drunkenness, Sabbath-breaking, dueling, gambling, and profanity—by methods of persuasion, the concern quickly expanded to include larger social issues. The masthead of the *New York Evangelist* illustrated the broadening of the reform impulse. In 1831, when it was insisting that "the emancipation of the world must engross the desires . . . and the enterprise of the world," the masthead announced that the paper was "Devoted to Revivals, Doc-

---

[12] *Letters of Theodore Dwight Weld,* ed. G. H. Barnes and D. L. Dumond (N.Y., 1934), I, 243.

trinal Discussion, and Religious Intelligence." In 1835 it added "Practical Godliness," and in 1837 "Human Rights." The establishment of world peace was one of the early preoccupations, and colonizing projects in Africa were advocated as a solution to the problem of slavery. Later antislavery sentiment was channeled into a demand for "immediate emancipation." Prison reform captured the interest of some, and women's rights the interest of others. The latter movement culminated in the Seneca Falls Convention of 1848, held in the heart of Finneyite territory and convened by women who had received their initial impetus in evangelical reform activity.

Economic problems did not bulk large in the thinking of the evangelical reformers. This was partly because they tended to think that individual conversions would remedy the ills of poverty, but primarily it was because an abundance of unsettled land in an economy that remained largely agrarian served as an escape valve for economic discontent. The antislavery agitation, of course, had deep economic implications, and there were some who dabbled with peripheral problems of the city and of labor when they established havens for out-of-work sailors and experimented with societies to reclaim prostitutes from their shame. After the Panic of 1837 further hesitant steps in the direction of a social gospel began to be taken. In 1842 revivalist Edward Norris Kirk (1802–74) emphasized the importance of ferreting out the causes of poverty and applying a remedy. In 1851 an influential Presbyterian layman, Stephen Colwell (1800–71), published his *New Themes for the Protestant Clergy* in which he advocated legislative enactments to better the condition of workingmen. Two or three years later the *Independent* turned its attention from revivals to urge a program of "urban renewal" that would have as its aim low rents, clean buildings, and healthy surroundings.

Although the reform activity in the beginning was a balanced thrust with each reform being seen as part of a larger strategy, there was a tendency among many to move in the direction of what was called "ultraism" or "one-ideaism." This was a passionate concentration upon one particular reforming cause as the panacea for all human ills. Temperance, for example, tended to be thought of by many as the remedy for poverty, vice, corruption, brawling, ill health, premature death, and marital discord. The benefits to be derived from securing the rights of women were sometimes viewed from a similar universal perspective.

Reforms of diet, dress, and education also became the objectives of specific crusades. Ultimately, the growth of antislavery sentiment terminated the "ultraist" dispersal of the reform movement by the simple expedient of focusing attention on the sin of slavery and absorbing the reformist energies and personnel into this one great cause.

THE SLAVERY CONTROVERSY. Of all the reform crusades, the one that disrupted the churches and shook the nation to its foundations was the antislavery movement.[13] Other reform movements had taken an individualistic turn which enabled the existing denominations for the most part to contain them. They had developed within the context of revivalism and most of them were no more than urgent summons to individuals to free themselves from the entanglement of sin. The antislavery crusade, as conducted by the evangelicals, had begun with the same emphasis. Although the adoption of the British motto—"immediate emancipation" —seemed to imply a drastic abolitionism, it was interpreted to mean "immediate emancipation gradually accomplished" or "gradual emancipation immediately begun." The emphasis was upon persuasion and a personal renunciation of slavery as sin. The campaign of Theodore Dwight Weld and his band of rebels recruited at Lane Theological Seminary and later expanded to a biblical "Seventy" exhibited all the characteristics and methods of revival meetings. The immediatism they preached was an immediate repentance of the sin of any personal involvement in and support of the slave system. However gradual the emancipation was to be, there was a point at which persuasion would end and abolition would be required, and as antislavery sentiment was intensified it became increasingly difficult to keep the movement from going beyond the scope of revivalism to a demand that its moral standard be imposed and enforced by legislative action.

The disruptive effect of the antislavery agitation was accentuated because it appeared at a time when an equally aggressive proslavery movement was developing. During the first third of the century, there were many in the South who were quite as critical of slavery as anyone in the North, but by the 1830's this sentiment had declined and highly vocal

---

[13] See G. H. Barnes, *The Antislavery Impulse, 1830–1844* (N.Y., 1933); D. L. Dumond, *Antislavery: The Crusade for Freedom* (Ann Arbor, Mich., 1961); Louis Filler, *The Crusade against Slavery, 1830–1860* (N.Y., 1960). For representative documentary materials illustrating both proslavery and antislavery views, see Smith, Handy, Loetscher, *American Christianity*, II, 167–210.

champions of the South's "peculiar institution" were beginning to dominate southern opinion. The most influential factor in this shift was the
increasing importance of cotton in the South's economy and the accom-
panying conviction that profitable cotton production was dependent upon
slave labor. The bitter attacks of northern and western abolitionists also
contributed to the consolidation of proslavery sentiment in the South, as
did the anxiety aroused by the growing minority status of the slaveholding
states in a rapidly expanding nation.

Thomas R. Dew (1802–46), professor of political economy at the
College of William and Mary, laid down the basic lines of the slavery
defense in 1832 when he argued that slavery not only had been from
earliest times the chief means of advancing civilization but that it had been
established by divine authority.[14] Southern clergymen picked up this final
point and began to respond to the antislavery arguments by appealing to
the sanction of Scripture and by depicting the abolitionists as anti-
Christian atheists who reject the Word of God. "We defend the cause of
God," Benjamin Morgan Palmer, minister of the First Presbyterian
Church of New Orleans, was to declare.

THE DISRUPTION OF THE CHURCHES. The disruptive effect of the
slavery issue upon the churches was foreshadowed by its role in the hidden
agenda of the Presbyterian Old School–New School division in 1837, and
it was more clearly evident in the formation of perfectionist "union"
churches and in perfectionist defections among Methodists, Baptists, and
Lutherans. Perfectionist tendencies, of course, always threatened to get
out of hand. The revivals had multiplied conversions so rapidly that it
became increasingly easy to overlook the great obstacle which man's sinful
nature placed in the path to perfection and to believe that it was only an
individual's willful perversity which caused him to temporize with sin.
Thus many were moving into a perfectionist phase, which emphasized the
abolition of sin almost to the exclusion of any preoccupation with creed,
just at the moment that slavery was coming to be regarded by many as the
one great sin. Since the established denominations tended to play down
slavery in the interest of maintaining denominational unity, they appeared
increasingly to be condoning sin.

---

[14] See *The Pro-Slavery Argument as Maintained by the Most Distinguished Writers
of the Southern States* (Charleston, S.C., 1852), and W. S. Jenkins, *Pro-Slavery Thought
in the Old South* (Chapel Hill, N.C., 1935).

Although this perfectionist antislavery sentiment was to become widespread, its early focal point was in upper New York State. As early as 1835, the reorganized Central (formerly Oneida) Evangelical Association, with fifteen ministers, eight licentiates, and seven churches, was proposing that it be considered as the nucleus of a network of true churches free from all sin to which all right-minded congregations could repair as they found their old denominations entangled in unrighteousness. "Union of feeling and sentiment," ran the resolution, can never be obtained until the churches "abandon their exclusive creeds and incorporate nothing in their articles that will shut off their fellowship with any child of God." The one thing demanded by these "union" churches was an unequivocal stand against slavery, since "proslavery or apparently neutral churches are anti-Christian." By 1855 there were no fewer than eighty-three of these "union" churches in New York State alone and others were scattered through New England and the Middle West. In addition the entire Genesee Association was read out of the Congregational fold in 1844 for its perfectionist tendencies.[15]

New York State was also the center of antislavery agitation among the Methodists. In spite of the attempt of the national General Conference in 1836 to stifle discussion of the issue, hundreds of petitions demanding disciplinary rules against slavery continued to flood in from New York, especially from the Genesee conference. The bishops resorted to expulsions and discriminatory appointments in an endeavor to silence the antislavery forces, and at the 1840 General Conference they maintained their ironclad control in the face of petitions signed by ten thousand laymen and five hundred preachers. Between 1839 and 1842 isolated groups in New England, New York, and Ohio began to withdraw from the church, and finally in 1843 at a meeting in Utica the Wesleyan Methodist Church was formed on a typically perfectionist platform which included abolitionism as one of its tests for membership.

The Baptists suffered a similar defection which extended from Maine through New York to Michigan. It took shape in the formation of a competing Baptist Free Mission Society in 1843 and in the establishment of New York Central College at McGraw, New York. Among the Lutherans an antislavery faction of twenty-one perfectionist congregations in

15 Cross, *Burned-over District*, 261, 278–81.

central New York in 1837 formed the Franckean Synod which denied membership to anyone who sanctioned the principle of slavery.

These were minor schisms, and their growth was nipped by a shift in the policy of the major bodies. Responding to the increasing pressure of antislavery sentiment, the Methodist General Conference of 1844 adopted a strengthened antislavery rule which preserved the unity of the northern section of the church at the expense of the southern portion which departed the following year to form the Methodist Episcopal Church, South. The Baptist foreign and home mission societies also were forced to take a firmer stand, which resulted in the formation of the Southern Baptist Convention in 1845. The Congregationalists, as a regional denomination, were able to move into the abolitionist camp without suffering disruption, while the Disciple or "Christian" churches were too loosely affiliated to suffer schism. The Old School and the New School Presbyterian churches, having divided in 1837, sought to muffle the controversy in order to avoid further division. The New School group succeeded in doing so for a time but it finally split in 1857, while the Old School churches forestalled any break until after the Civil War began. Lutherans were torn by controversy but the General Synod was able to steer a neutral course. The Episcopalians and the Roman Catholics tended to remain aloof from the controversy. Remaining aloof, of course, often meant that the proponents of a slave-based social order were free to speak while their opponents were urged to avoid creating dissension by remaining silent.

The division of the churches was prophetic of the political division that was to follow. By 1860 the crisis was at hand. As soon as the outcome of the presidential election was certain, the South Carolina legislature summoned a state convention which met on December 20, 1860, and unanimously declared "that the Union now subsisting between South Carolina and other states under the name of 'The United States of America' is hereby dissolved." Four months later Fort Sumter was shelled and the Civil War had begun. It was a war that was to bruise almost every family in the land, to change the face of the nation, and to create new problems for the churches.

PART III

YEARS OF MIDPASSAGE

1860–1914

IX

Post-Civil War America

The Civil War was a watershed between an old and a new America. The American people became much more heterogeneous in background. The advent of modern science drastically altered the intellectual climate. And the quickening pace of industrialization created new centers of power in national life.

The changing composition of the population was one of the conspicuous contrasts between the old and the new America. After 1840 a sharply increasing percentage of the population was of foreign birth. From 1850 to 1860 the number of foreign born had increased 84.4 per cent. From 1860 to 1870, in spite of the dislocation of war, there was a further increase of 34.5 per cent. The first great influx had come from Ireland and Germany, but before the end of the century many nations were contributing to the growing number of new Americans. In contrast to the overwhelming predominance of British elements in the population at the beginning of the century, only a small percentage of the new arrivals were from England, Scotland, and Wales. By 1900, out of a population of 75 million, one-third were either of foreign birth or children of foreign-born parents. Of these 25 million new Americans, 8 million were German in background; 5 million were Irish; 2½ million had come from Austria, Hungary, Poland, and Italy; another 2½ million had come from the Scandinavian countries; 850,000 were French Canadians; and 774,000 had come from Russia. In addition to these totals, there were several million grandchildren of the immigrants who had arrived in the 1840's, 1850's, and 1860's.

A second contrast between the old and the new America was the radical shift in the intellectual climate. Geology, in the person of Charles Lyell (1797–1875), had been busy rewriting the Genesis account of the origin and early history of the earth. But it was the new biology, as set forth by Charles Darwin (1809–82) in his *Origin of the Species* (1859), that was to become the chief symbol of the intellectual revolution. The idea of evolution, of course, was not new. It had been championed by Hegel (1770–1831) and Comte (1798–1857), and the writings of Herbert Spencer (1820–1903) were to be more important than those of Darwin in pointing up the full implications of evolutionary thinking. Spencer adopted the doctrine of evolution as a unifying philosophical principle and sought to apply it to all phenomena. *Progress, Its Law and Cause* (1857) set forth the basic thesis that was elaborated in his subsequent writings: *First Principles* (1862), *Principles of Biology* (1864–67), *Principles of Psychology* (rev. ed., 1870–72), *Principles of Sociology* (1876–96), and *Principles of Ethics* (1892–93). With this evolutionism penetrating every realm of thought, a "new history" began to be written which was based on the application of evolutionary theories to the understanding of the past. And this "new history" quickly led to the "higher criticism" of the Bible—first in Germany and then in Britain and America—which many were to find so disturbing.

A third feature of post-Civil War America was a marked shift in the center of power. Before the war the agrarian democracy envisaged by Jefferson still reigned supreme, although the lure of the city had begun to replace the lure of the West among young men of spirit and ambition. The census statistics for the decade 1840 to 1850, which revealed that the population of the cities had increased 90 per cent while the population of the country as a whole had increased only 36 per cent, gave a foretaste of what was to come. Ten years later, in 1860, the capital invested in industry, railroads, commerce, and urban property was greater than the value of all the farms from the Atlantic to the Pacific. The Civil War had "the effect of a hothouse" on this industrial growth. Military needs and currency inflation caused the mills to roar louder and the blast furnaces to flame higher. By the time Ulysses S. Grant took the oath of office as President of the United States, there was no longer any doubt that the dominant influence in American life had shifted from the rural countryside to the burgeoning urban communities. The successive efforts of Grangers, Greenbackers, and Populists to dislodge the commercial and industrial interests from the centers of power simply confirmed the fact that they were fighting a lost cause, for they never were able to win more than regional victories.

Each of these facets of post-Civil War society was to pose critical problems for the churches, but their full significance did not become clear for a decade or two. In the meantime, there were pressing problems which demanded immediate attention.

Reconstituting the nation

When Abraham Lincoln stood on the windswept fields of Gettysburg and spoke of those who "four score and seven years" before had "brought forth on this continent a new nation, conceived in liberty, and dedicated to the proposition that all men are created equal," he was recalling the theme which had given meaning and significance to the sense of American nationhood. But now this venture had been brought into question. Although Lincoln looked forward to the time when "this nation, under God, shall have a new birth of freedom," there was no blinking the stark, stubborn, present fact that the American people were engaged "in a great civil war, testing whether that nation, or any nation so conceived and so dedicated, can long endure."

THE BOND OF RELIGION. From the beginning of national life, religion had served as a bond of unity which helped to overcome the divisive effects of competing local interests and regional concerns. The Great Awakening had done much to make the several colonies emotionally one by binding them together in a common cause, generating a common loyalty, fostering common sentiments, and thrusting forward a common leadership. But it was a theological interpretation of the American past, present, and future that had contributed most to making them one nation.

What had welded the diverse people of the colonies—Englishman, Scots, and Germans; Georgians, Virginians, and New Yorkers—together was the consciousness of being summoned to a God-given mission. God had "designed this continent . . . to be the asylum of liberty" and had selected America to be an example to the nations. There was scarcely anyone who had not believed with Lyman Beecher that the establishment of the United States "in the full enjoyment of civil and religious liberty" had been a "design of Heaven" to demonstrate to the world "by one great successful experiment of what man is capable" and thereby to awaken among peoples everywhere the "desire and hope and effort" that would produce "revolutions and overturnings" until the whole world was free.[1] It was this conviction that had given Americans whatever sense of a common nationality they had, and it was this conviction that gave such moving power to the few brief words spoken by Lincoln at Gettysburg.

As tension had mounted between the North and the South, there had been agonized efforts to preserve the unity of the nation by reminding people of their God-given vocation. But the slavery question proved so disruptive that not even the churches could be kept from separating, and their divisions were prophetic of the tragedy that was to follow. Few had believed that the war could come. The notion that the nation could descend to fratricidal strife was unthinkable to most Americans. "There must be no war," had been a repetitive refrain. But the war had come, and its effect was shattering. The great "experiment" had gone wrong. The protective hand of divine Providence seemingly had been removed. No longer could Americans picture themselves as an example to the nations. Nor could they ease their tortured spirits by placing the blame for the disaster upon extraneous circumstance. The responsibility could not be sought beyond the American people themselves. No outside nation was involved. No foreign influence played any part in precipitating the tragedy. The machinery of peace was at hand in the orderly procedures of national life, but it had not been utilized.

The traumatic effect of the war was doubly compounded when what had been the bond of union was twisted to serve the cause of division. It was both natural and appropriate for the churches, North and South, to provide chaplains for the combatants and to organize agencies to minister to the temporal as well as the spiritual needs of the soldiers. It was no less

[1] Quoted by Tyler, *Freedom's Ferment*, 1.

natural for them to seek God's blessing and to claim divine sanction for their opposing armies, but it was profoundly disconcerting and disturbing. Those on both sides of the Mason-Dixon line in theology and piety were brothers, yet they offered contradictory prayers. In both North and South, the God who had made them a nation was being reduced to the partisan of a section.[2] When the bond which had united them was being utilized by apologists in both camps to justify the resort to arms, it was clear that the war itself must somehow be brought within the scope of a larger design of God if the nation were to be reunited.

Although not many gave themselves to this latter task, Lincoln was struggling throughout the war years to find a larger meaning to the conflict than that suggested by any simple alliance of Providence with either the North or the South.[3] Displaying a deeper theological perception than many preachers, he wrote to John Hay in 1862 that "it is quite possible that God's purpose is something different from the purpose of either party; and yet the human instrumentalities, working just as they do, are of the best adaptation to effect his purpose. I am almost ready to say that this is probably true; that God wills this contest, and wills that it shall not end yet." Later in the same year he told a Congressional delegation that he believed that God "will compel us to do right in order that he may do these things, not so much because we desire them as that they accord with his plans for dealing with this nation." And then he continued: "Sometimes it seems necessary that we should be confronted with perils which threaten us with disaster in order that we may not get puffed up and forget him who has much work for us yet to do." In his Second Inaugural Address, he reverted once again to this theme.

> On the occasion corresponding to this four years ago, all thoughts were anxiously directed to an impending civil war. . . . Neither party expected for the war the magnitude or the duration

[2] Two Presbyterian theologians, J. H. Thornwell and R. L. Dabney, were the most effective apologists in linking the position of the South with the cause of God and religion. Thornwell declared that "the Scriptures not only fail to condemn slavery, they as distinctly sanction it as any other social condition of man." To call slavery sinful, therefore, is to reject the Bible. "Our policy," wrote Dabney, must be "to push the Bible argument continually" and force the enemies of slavery to reveal their true infidel colors. Presbyterians, of course, were not alone in this enterprise. Episcopalians, Baptists, and Methodists played their part. Even John England, Roman Catholic bishop of Charleston, wrote a sturdy defense of slavery on biblical grounds. For representative statements, see Smith, Handy, Loetscher, *American Christianity*, II, 177–78, 182–86, 201–10.

[3] See W. J. Wolf, *The Almost Chosen People: A Study of the Religion of Abraham Lincoln* (N.Y., 1959).

which it has already attained. . . . Each looked for an easier triumph, and a result less fundamental and astounding. Both read the same Bible, and pray to the same God; and each invokes his aid against the other. It may seem strange that any men should dare to ask a just God's assistance in wringing their bread from the sweat of other men's faces; but let us judge not, that we be not judged. The prayers of both could not be answered—that of neither has been answered fully.

The Almighty has his own purposes. . . . If we shall suppose that American slavery is one of those offenses which, in the providence of God, must needs come, but which, having continued through his appointed time, he now wills to remove, and that he gives to both North and South this terrible war, as the woe due to those by whom the offense came, shall we discern therein any departure from divine attributes which the believers in a living God always ascribe to him?

Fondly do we hope—fervently do we pray—that this mighty scourge of war may speedily pass away. Yet, if God wills that it continue until all the wealth piled by the bondman's two hundred and fifty years of unrequited toil shall be sunk, and until every drop of blood drawn with the lash shall be paid by another drawn with the sword, as was said three thousand years ago, so still it must be said, "The judgments of the Lord are true and righteous altogether."

Lincoln, of course, was not alone in exploring the theme of God's hand in the conflict. Of the theologians who picked it up and elaborated it, Horace Bushnell and Philip Schaff were most prominent.[4] Like Lincoln, they both saw the war as the product of the guilt of the whole nation, the humiliation of an arrogant and boastful people, a supreme hour of trial designed to aid the nation to fulfill rather than to forfeit its destiny. Slavery had been the Achilles' heel of a nation called to exemplify what it meant for all men to be created free and equal, but slavery was not the sin of the South alone. The evil was inherited by the whole nation. Nor was slavery the real cause of the war. The real issue was whether or not the American people were to be a true people—a true nation—and thus

[4] See W. A. Clebsch, "Christian Interpretations of the Civil War," *Church History,* XXX (1961), 212–22. This is a summary of his unpublished dissertation, "Baptism of Blood: Christian Contributions to the Interpretation of the Civil War" (Union Theological Seminary, N.Y., 1957).

capable of fulfilling their destiny. Hitherto—"half-loyally and half-lawlessly"—Americans had claimed a self-made and thus a false nationality. Too many had thought of the nation as their own creation and they had never given themselves fully to it. The several states had "simply kenneled under the Constitution" and had not been merged and compacted into a true nation.

As the product of the collective guilt of the American people, the war was an act of divine judgment. But to Bushnell and Schaff it was more than that, for it presented the possibility of redemption and renewal. Believing as they did that without the shedding of blood there is no atonement, they viewed the war as a sacrificial and cleansing tragedy that contained within it the possibility not only of preserving but also of regenerating the nation. The "baptism of blood" was thus to be seen as an act of divine mercy through which the nation could be reborn, purged of its sin, and recalled to its proper vocation. Upon the anvil of suffering and under the hammer of a providential God, it was to be hoped that what had been only a federation made up by a temporary surrender of power would be forged into a true nationhood. It seemed clear to them that nothing less than a common tragedy was sufficient to effect the necessary reconciliation that would unify a heterogeneous population into the free and responsible society which from the beginning had been God's intention for the American people.

What Lincoln, Bushnell, and Schaff were seeking to do was to restore to the American people their former bond of union by helping them to understand that even in the war itself God's will was being worked out in the life of the nation. The verdict of the war could then be accepted with grace both by those who gained the triumph and by those who suffered defeat, for by this reappropriation and reinterpretation of the American experience the conflict could be transmuted into something more than an occasion for future bitter memories. It was with this thought in mind that Lincoln looked forward to the future task as he brought his Second Inaugural Address to a close with words that have never been forgotten: "With malice toward none; with charity for all; with firmness in the right, as God gives us to see the right, let us strive on to finish the work we are in; to bind up the nation's wounds; to care for him who shall have borne the battle and for his widow and orphan—to do all which may achieve and cherish a just and lasting peace among ourselves, and with all nations."

THE FAILURE OF RECONSTRUCTION. Having compressed into four years a bloody slaughter that was comparable in magnitude only to the losses inflicted over a decade and a half by the Napoleonic wars, it was to be expected that festering sores would be left which would complicate and long delay the task of binding up the nation's wounds. Still there were many factors that could be counted upon to facilitate the healing process, not the least of which was the general weariness of the people with the war. The generous spirit exhibited by Grant in victory and the dignified acceptance of defeat by Lee had the immediate effect of tending to minimize recrimination. Reconciliation was further eased by "mystic chords of memory" which stretched back beyond the strife to the common history that previously had been shared. And having been schooled in the providential view of history, there were many who were prepared to accept the outcome of the war as a clear manifestation of God's will for the nation. Reduced to its simplest form, the plain implication of the providential understanding of defeat was stated by a young South Carolinian: "I think it was in the decrees of Almighty God that slavery was to be abolished in this way, and I don't murmur." [5] Other Southerners found it possible to take the more positive view articulated by Bushnell and Schaff. Stephen Elliott (1806–66) of Georgia and Richard H. Wilmer (1816–1900) of Alabama were conspicuous examples of theologians who were able to find in the war grounds for gratitude to God for settling "the meaning of the Constitution," restoring to the American people "one undivided country," and making clear the true mission of the nation. [6] Within this perspective, both Lee and Lincoln had served as instruments in the hands of God to effect his purposes; and it was this understanding which made it possible for both men to be lifted from the status of partisan leaders to that of national heroes.

Unfortunately the universal esteem in which Lincoln and Lee came to be held was deceptive, for the reconciliation was destined to be incomplete and a unified national life was never fully re-established. However decisive the war had been, the peace proved to be inconclusive. In the absence of strong leadership, the national government could not agree on what to make of its victory. Efforts at reconstruction were delayed, confused,

[5] Quoted by S. E. Mead, *Lively Experiment*, 143.
[6] Clebsch, *Church History*, XXX (1961), 221.

indecisive, and of short duration.[7] There was little evidence of that "firmness" to "strive on to finish the work we are in" of which Lincoln had spoken. Some, to be sure, sought to gain political advantage by "waving the bloody shirt," but this did not conceal the increasing disposition in the North to leave the South to its own devices and to get on with the business of tapping the national till and reaping the profits of a booming economy. Seldom in history has a nation been so heedless of the fruits of victory. The issues which had stood at the center of the conflict were subordinated to partisan politics and the task of restoring the Union by protecting the fundamental rights of all its people was neglected.

As soon as it became apparent that little support was to be given the law-abiding elements in the South, unrepentent extremists became convinced that their cause was not wholly lost. Bands of hoodlums—Jayhawkers, Red Shirts, Knights of the White Camellia, and Klansmen—were recruited to intimidate law-abiding citizens by night-riding forays of pillage and torture. With amazing rapidity unreconstructed malcontents gained control of the former seccessionist states, silenced the dissent of other white Southerners, and put the Negroes "in their place"—a place that sometimes afforded them less protection than their previous status as slaves. While Lee continued to be revered, it was General Nathan Bedford Forrest—Grand Wizard of the Ku Klux Klan—who was to become the romantic hero that young white Southerners of spirit were encouraged to admire and emulate.

Although the outward ties of national life had been restored by the war, the resulting unity was far removed from that true nationhood which some had dared hope would be the consequence of the baptism of blood through which the American people had passed. In 1880, to be sure, Atticus G. Haygood (1839–96), Methodist president of Emory University, preached a Thanksgiving sermon on "The New South"[8] in which he repeated the theme that had been articulated by Elliott and Wilmer. But many of his fellow Southerners did not heed his appeal to recognize that the abolition of slavery had been a blessing and that their duty now was to

---

[7] See J. H. Franklin, *Reconstruction after the Civil War* (Chicago, 1961); C. Vann Woodward, *Reunion and Reaction: The Compromise of 1877 and the End of Reconstruction* (Boston, 1951); and Lawanda and J. H. Cox, *Politics, Principle, and Prejudice, 1865–1866* (N.Y., 1963).

[8] Reprinted in Smith, Handy, Loetscher, *American Christianity*, II, 372–77.

rejoin the Union in spirit as well as in fact. As early as 1865 another Methodist preacher in Mississippi had exhorted the South: "If we cannot gain our *political*, then let us establish our *mental* independence." [9] Actually, in the vacuum created by the withdrawal of national leadership, a very large degree of political independence was achieved, and this fostered a growing mental independence. The successful defiance of the brief effort at Reconstruction along the lines of a national policy made it possible for many Southerners to ignore the verdict of the war and to cling to an understanding of the American Constitution that had few points of contact with either the realities of the past or the necessities of the future. This essentially romantic interpretation of the American experience left the South intellectually and emotionally isolated from the rest of the nation. There was no conversion to an understanding that the nation was anything more than a mere aggregation of sovereign states. What unity there was had been achieved by leaving the major issues—so far as the South was concerned—unresolved, and from these unresolved issues a later generation was destined to reap a bitter harvest.

THE SOUTHERN CHURCHES. The independent regional course of development that the South was permitted to pursue following the Civil War fostered a growing sectional self-consciousness that was to manifest itself in the religious as well as in the political and intellectual life of the southern states. There were, of course, some ecclesiastical links with the rest of the nation. Those denominations which had not divided over the issue of slavery prior to the Civil War experienced no great difficulty in resuming their former unified denominational life. For them there was no prewar heritage of bitterness to overcome, and they had had scant time and opportunity to develop the vested interests of an independent institutional life.

The ease with which the latter denominations effected the reunion of their severed branches is illustrated by the Protestant Episcopal Church. Although a separate Episcopal church had been formed in the South following Secession, the fact that a schism had occurred was never recognized nor accepted by northern Episcopalians. At the General Convention of 1862, the roll call included the southern dioceses—an action which implied that the missing bishops and deputies were only temporarily

[9] K. K. Bailey, "Southern White Protestantism at the Turn of the Century," *American Historical Review*, LXVIII (1963), 618.

absent. The next convention was held in October, 1865, six months after Lee had surrendered. Prior to the convention, the Presiding Bishop wrote to all the southern bishops inviting them to attend and assuring them of a cordial welcome. The response to the invitation was varied. Those who attended, however, were received with such friendly warmth that a month later the General Council of the southern Episcopal church voted that, since the circumstances which had brought it into existence had ceased, the southern dioceses were free to renew their former affiliation.

The denominations which were able to reunite, however, represented only a minority of southern church members. The three major denominations were the Methodists, Baptists, and Presbyterians. The Methodists and Baptists had gone their separate ways since 1845. While there was much initial sentiment for reunion in both communions, the Methodist Episcopal Church, South, and the Southern Baptist Convention had become too firmly established to be quickly dismantled. Time was needed to untangle the existing institutional structures, but each year of delay made the prospect of success less promising as a result of the steadily increasing southern regional self-consciousness. By 1869 the Methodist *Richmond Christian Advocate* was declaring: "We consider reunion neither possible nor desirable." [10]

The Presbyterian division was more recent but it was complicated by an earlier schism. Since 1837 the Presbyterians had been divided into Old School and New School bodies. In 1857 the New School Presbyterians divided over the issue of slavery, and in 1861 the southern Old School Presbyterians formed a separate church. In 1864 the New School and Old School Presbyterians in the South united. Thus at the close of hostilities the major body of Presbyterians was confronted by a three-way split. The first task seemed to be the healing of the breach in the North as a preparatory step to ending the schism between North and South. This occasioned delay, for negotiations initiated in 1866 were not brought to a successful conclusion until 1870. By this time an intense sectional spirit had reasserted itself in the South, and Presbyterians were to be no more successful than Methodists or Baptists in bridging the institutional barriers that had been erected.

The three large southern denominations justified their separate existence by constantly reminding themselves that Southerners were "a

[10] Sweet, *Virginia Methodism* (Richmond, 1955), 285.

different people," [11] and over the years their ecclesiastical isolation helped to give substance to their assertion. Several factors combined to produce this result. The most obvious, of course, was the mere fact of institutional separation which left most of the southern churches out of touch with the developing religious life of the rest of the nation. Equally important in giving the religious and ecclesiastical ethos of the South its own distinctive cast was the nostalgia which caused Southerners to idealize the past and to look askance at any innovation in either thought or practice. And further heightening the insularity of the southern churches was their role as the only available vehicle for the institutional expression of sectional feeling. Politically the South was divided into several states. Economically the South was not homogeneous and its new commercial and industrial ventures were tied to northern financial centers. Thus the southern Methodist church, the southern Presbyterian church, and the Southern Baptist Convention were the only institutional links which bound the South together. While the regional character of these denominations contributed to the popular esteem in which they were held throughout the South, this culturally grounded popularity tended to insulate them further from the larger Christian community.

The folk-religion of the southern churches was further heightened by an adherence to the doctrine of "the spirituality of the church." This concept had been first formulated by a Presbyterian, John Holt Rice

[11] The *New Orleans Christian Advocate* was to declare in 1880 that the "civilization of the two sections, and the customs and character of the people are in many things diverse. . . . One broad distinction is that the Southerner, as a matter of honor and principle, minds his own business, while the inborn nature of the North is to meddle. The South is tolerant, courteous, and refined in its contact with people in the ordinary associations of life. The North has a prying, inquisitive disposition, and is bent on bringing every one to its way of thinking and doing." There are also differences in religion. "There is a south side to churches and religion, not so much in regard to their creeds, articles of religion, and church polity, as in the type of piety that prevails. Methodists and Presbyterians in the South profess the same faith as Methodists and Presbyterians in the North, and yet they are not the same people. The political meddling of the Northern churches is, of course, one difference. . . . There is a secularity about them, and a style that brings them into near fellowship with worldly enterprises and organizations. They *run* things up there—churches as well as factories and railroads. The style of their preaching is in contrast with ours, and is largely of the politico-sensational order. The North has been over-run with professional evangelists, whose methods and teachings have in many instances done harm. People raised in these churches, and imbued with their spirit, if converted, are apt to be essentially defective in the higher traits of Christian character. With many excellent people and exemplary Christians among them, and with much that is good and worthy of imitation in their church work, there is a spirit and practice, and a type of religion, that we should regret to see in our southern churches." Quoted by H. D. Farris, *The Circuit Rider Dismounts* (Richmond, 1938), 148–49.

(1777–1831). When it became apparent in 1827 that the slavery issue was apt to disrupt church life, Rice suggested that the church should "confine itself to making good Christians" and not concern itself with matters beyond its competence, such as the civil arrangements of society. By this means a bifurcation was introduced which permitted the churches to condone slavery while condemning card-playing and dancing, and which was reflected in the subsequent attitude of southern Methodist bishops who rejoiced that their church held aloof from political questions and was "satisfied to perform her own legitimate duties." [12]

Basically, however, the southern churches preserved and perpetuated the popular evangelicalism of the immediate prewar period, stressing sentimental preaching, periodic revivals, and heartfelt religion. While outsiders could point to many defects, including a rigid biblicism which sometimes tended to become obscurantist, there were also manifestations of an impressive vitality that on occasion broke the bonds of established custom. This southern evangelicalism was not distinctive in itself. Parallel expressions were to be found in other sections of the country. What made it distinctive was its almost complete predominance throughout the South and its success in withstanding any fundamental change in either thought or practice over a long period of time.

The churches and the freedmen

When he assumed the Presidency in 1861, Abraham Lincoln had noted the obligation imposed upon him by the Constitution to see that "the laws of the Union be faithfully executed in all the States." A month later he issued a call for seventy-five thousand volunteers in order to fulfill this constitutional duty. Combinations "too powerful to be suppressed by the ordinary course of judicial proceedings" had arisen, and this left him with no alternative but to utilize the armed forces of the United States "to cause the laws to be duly executed." The integrity of the nation was at stake, and the fundamental issue of the conflict that followed was the preservation of the nation. The precipitating cause of the war, however, had been the issue of human bondage, and before the strife was over the system of human slavery had been brought to an end by executive proclamation. As a

[12] E. T. Thompson, *The Spirituality of the Church* (Richmond, 1961), 21. Sweet, *Virginia Methodism*, 298.

consequence of the presidential action and the later constitutional amendment, American Negroes—for the first time in any significant numbers—were given an opportunity to determine their own destiny. Legal and extralegal restrictions were to limit this freedom, and its exercise was to prove hazardous in many localities. Nonetheless the Emancipation Proclamation marked the beginning of a new era.

EDUCATIONAL WORK AMONG THE NEGROES. Almost immediately after the outbreak of the war, the need of the Negro "contrabands" who were soon to become freedmen was self-evident—a need for food, clothing, shelter, work, and protection. But perhaps the greatest need was education, for throughout much of the South it had been illegal to teach a slave to read. While some slaveowners found it to their advantage to evade the law, the great mass of the Negroes were illiterate. It was at this point that the northern churches felt that they could best help, and a whole cluster of agencies—Julius H. Parmalee listed seventy-nine [13]—were organized for this purpose. The early interdenominational Freedmen's Aid Commissions quickly gave way to more firmly established denominational societies and boards, and their work was strongly supplemented for a five-year period after 1865 by the Freedmen's Bureau of the federal government.

As early as September, 1861, a representative of the American Missionary Association reported that among the "contrabands" at Fortress Monroe in Virginia there were many, both parents and children, who were delighted by the prospect of learning to read, and before the end of the month classes had been organized to provide them with the necessary instruction.[14] Shortly thereafter a representative of the American Baptist Home Mission Society was at Fortress Monroe to investigate conditions among the Negro refugees, and later another representative gave a dismaying account of the plight of the 15,000 "contrabands" in Washington, D.C., and Alexandria, Virginia. "What are we to do for the freedmen which are being thrown in increasing numbers upon our hands?" he asked. "One thing is certain, they must not be neglected." The response of the Society was an appeal for funds to send missionaries "to engage in such instruction of the colored people as will enable them to read the Bible and to become self-supporting." [15]

[13] "Freedmen's Aid Societies," U.S. Department of Interior, Office of Education, *Bulletin No. 38* (1916), 268–95.
[14] A. F. Beard, *A Crusade of Brotherhood* (Boston, 1909), 121.
[15] *Baptist Home Missions in North America* (N.Y., 1883), 398–99.

At the end of the war there were 3,500,000 freedmen and most of the denominations participated in the attempt to rectify the consequences of two centuries of neglect. The most extensive work was that of the American Missionary Association, a society primarily Congregational in support and personnel. By the end of 1863 it had eighty-three teachers in the field, and by 1867 the number had increased to 528. Among the surviving institutions which the Association fathered are Fisk, Atlanta, and Tougaloo universities, Talladega College, and Hampton Institute. Northern Methodists and Baptists also carried on broadscale programs among the freedmen, while more modest contributions were made by northern Presbyterians, Disciples, Episcopalians, Quakers, and Roman Catholics. The southern white churches exhibited a brief flurry of interest in Negro education at the end of the war, but hostile sentiment in the South soon put an end to almost all official activity. Isolated individuals continued to provide help, and by 1880 there were signs of a renewed interest in Negro education among southern Methodists, Baptists, and Presbyterians. The editor of the *Alabama Christian Advocate,* however, still spoke for many southern Christians in 1883 when he sought to squelch the emerging concern for Negro education in his denomination by calling it a "form of negrophilism" which smacks of "Yankee fanaticism." [16]

The men who went South to aid the Negroes were frequently distinguished persons. The Baptist missionary-teachers were typical in this respect. J. G. Binney had been president of Columbian College (now George Washington University) and a missionary to Burma; Nathaniel Colver was professor of biblical theology at Morgan Park Theological Seminary (later the Divinity School of the University of Chicago); Marsena Stone was a professor at Denison University; Joseph T. Robert had taught modern languages at Iowa State University and was president of Burlington University when he accepted a call to go to Augusta, Georgia; J. W. Parker had gained distinction during a twenty-year pastorate in Cambridge, Massachusetts; and Henry M. Tupper and Charles H. Corey were recent graduates of Newton Theological Seminary, one having served as an army chaplain and the other as an agent of the United States Christian Commission during the war. The young women who volunteered for service in the South were equally able and devoted.

The beginnings were crude and meager. Most of the pupils could

[16] Farish, *The Circuit Rider Dismounts,* 196-97.

neither read nor write, and those who could had little further training. Housing was a major problem. Few whites dared sell or lease a building to the missionaries. In Richmond they had to make-do with an old slave pen known as "Lumpkin's Jail." In Raleigh two old log cabins and a delapidated cotton shed served to house the fledgling institution that was established. In Nashville an abandoned government building was purchased. And the missionaries were subjected to all manner of harassment by rougher elements among the whites. They were ostracized, threatened, and on occasion the school buildings were burned. Even the church press of the South invited the "white cravatted gentlemen from Andover" and the "pretty Yankee girls" to go home.[17]

The opposition to the missionary-teachers was based on a determination to keep the Negro "in his place." "He is and must continue to be," declared the *New Orleans Christian Advocate* in 1867, "the laboring man of the South, because he is not fitted . . . for anything higher." [18] Particular scorn was directed at the idea of providing the Negro with a classical education. The Rev. Samuel A. Steele of Mississippi declared: "*Hic, haec, hoc* will be the ruin of the African." Actually, of course, little classical education was provided. In addition to instruction in the most rudimentary subjects, most of the curriculum was pre-empted by industrial arts, agriculture, and homemaking, with due attention being given to Bible study. Prior to the twentieth century only a handful of institutions attained anything that even resembled a collegiate status. But the contribution that was made by those who gave themselves in sacrificial service to the education of the Negroes was great. Two-thirds of them were women, and an eloquent tribute was paid them by one who had been lifted from ignorance to enlightenment by their endeavors.

> These noble women left homes, their friends, their social ties, and all that they held dear . . . to labor among the recently emancipated slaves. Their courage, their self-sacrificing devotion, sincerity of purpose, purity of motive, and their unshaken faith in God were their pass keys to the hearts of those for whom they came to labor. . . . Their monument is builded in the hopes of a race

[17] Franklin, *Reconstruction*, 52.
[18] R. M. Cameron, *Methodism and Society in Historical Perspective* (N.Y., 1961), 209.

struggling upward from ignorance. . . . As long as the human heart beats in grateful response to benefits received, these women shall not want a monument of living ebony and bronze.[19]

THE NEGRO DENOMINATIONS. Scattered Negro churches were to be found throughout the North for several decades prior to the Civil War.[20] While Negroes belonged to existing churches and a few served as pastors, there was a tendency to organize separate congregations whenever a sizable Negro community began to develop. Among the Methodists two independent denominational structures appeared at an early date. The African Methodist Episcopal Church, organized in 1816, grew out of a separation from other Methodists which occurred in Philadelphia in 1794; and the African Methodist Episcopal Zion Church, organized in 1820, stemmed from a similar separation in New York in 1796. Among Baptists local African congregations were formed in Boston in 1805, in New York in 1807, and in Philadelphia in 1809. There was a similar movement in the West where churches in Ohio and in Pittsburgh, Buffalo, and Detroit were brought together in 1836 to form the Providence Baptist Association; and in Illinois where the Wood River Association was organized in 1838. Fifteen years later, in 1853, the Western Colored Baptist Convention was established. Although a Negro Congregational church was organized in New Haven in 1829, few Negroes outside the South seemed to have belonged to denominations other than the Baptist and the Methodist.

In the South, Negro membership also was concentrated in Baptist and Methodist churches, and the Negro members of these churches sometimes far outnumbered the white members. In Richmond, Virginia, for example, there were 387 white members of the First Baptist Church in 1841 and 1,708 colored members. In 1846 the First Baptist Church of Charleston, South Carolina had 261 white members and 1,382 Negro members; at Georgetown, South Carolina, there were 33 and 798; at Natchez, Mississippi, there were 62 white and 380 colored. These figures were not exceptional and a similar situation prevailed among the Methodists. In isolated instances separate Negro churches were organized but few,

[19] Beard, *Crusade of Brotherhood*, 234.
[20] See E. Franklin Frazier, *The Negro Church in America* (N.Y., 1963), for a perceptive interpretation of the development of the church among Negroes. Although dealing with a specialized concern, J. R. Washington, Jr., *Black Religion: the Negro and Christianity in the United States* (Boston, 1964), contains several helpful insights.

if any, of them were permitted to be fully independent. The property was held by white trustees and the congregations were subject to the supervision of neighboring white-controlled churches. The single attempt of the African Methodist Episcopal Church to penetrate the South prior to the Civil War was quickly stamped out.

It is scarcely surprising that the defeat of the South should have been accompanied by the withdrawal of most Negroes from the churches of their former masters. For one thing, the mere act of leaving was a symbolic expression of their new freedom. Furthermore, few congregations were prepared to give the Negro any different status than he had had as a slave. He was still expected to sit in the back seats or the gallery, was given no voice in church affairs, and had little chance of attaining even the humblest office. Even had the churches pressed for some tangible integration, it is unlikely that the mass of Negroes would have gone along. As slaves they had had enough of white churches. Much of the preaching addressed specifically to them had not been particularly inspiring if Molly Finlay's report was at all typical. "He just say, 'Serve your masters; don't steal your master's turkey; don't steal your master's chicken; don't steal your master's hog; don't steal your master's meat; do whatsomever your master tell you to do." [21] Nor, even with the best of intentions, could white ministers have spoken pointedly and effectively to their needs, for the white ministers had not experienced what it meant to be a slave.

Negro Episcopalians and Presbyterians defected in large numbers. The Episcopalians made no effort to form them into a separate church, while the Presbyterians waited until 1898 to transfer its Negro remnant in a new Afro-American Presbyterian Church. The smaller Cumberland Presbyterians acted more expeditiously, organizing the Colored Cumberland Presbyterian Church as a separate body in 1874. Two other small withdrawals occurred when Negro members of Primitive (Old School) Baptist churches in the South established a separate organization in 1865 called the Colored Primitive Baptists in America, and when Negro members of the Methodist Protestant Church in 1866 formed the African Union Colored Methodist Protestant Church. The Roman Catholic Church also suffered defections, with the greatest number being lost in Louisiana, the center of Roman Catholic strength in the South.

The Methodist Episcopal Church, South, which had had a Negro

[21] Hodding Carter, *The Angry Scar: The Story of Reconstruction* (N.Y., 1959).

224

membership of 207,766 in 1860, had become an all-white body by 1870. A considerable number of the Negroes who had belonged to the southern Methodist church were formed into new congregations by missionaries of the northern Methodist church. But the greatest harvest of Negro Methodists in the South was reaped by the African Methodist Episcopal Church and the African Methodist Episcopal Zion Church. The former body grew from 20,000 members in 1864 to almost 400,000 twenty years later, while the latter group increased from 6,000 to approximately 300,000 during the same period. In 1866 the remaining 49,000 Negro members of the Methodist Episcopal Church, South, were placed in a separate conference, and four years later they were set adrift to pursue an independent existence as the Colored Methodist Episcopal Church.

The largest number of Negroes were Baptists, and they rapidly outdistanced their only rival—the Methodists. This surge of growth was due perhaps to the ease with which Baptist congregations could be formed. Negro Baptist state conventions were organized in North Carolina in 1866, and in Virginia and Alabama in 1867. Within a few years every southern state had its own Negro Baptist convention. After several abortive attempts to establish a national organization, the majority of Negro Baptists were brought together in 1886 as constituent members of the National Baptist Convention.

The Negro churches made striking gains in membership which far surpassed the growth of other churches. Prior to the Civil War the percentage of Negroes who were church members was less than half that of the white population. By 1916 it was slightly larger, having increased from about 11 per cent to approximately 43 per cent. The popularity of the church among Negroes stemmed at least in part from the fact that it was one of the few institutions that was exclusively their own. Cut off from most areas of social and political life, the Negroes found in the church an opportunity for self-expression, recognition, and leadership. It was hardly a coincidence that until well into the twentieth century most of the outstanding Negro leaders had been ministers, for the ministry provided one of the few opportunities for leadership open to a Negro. Furthermore, the church was the primary agency of self-help in the Negro community, and it played an important role in maintaining group cohesion under difficult circumstances and in fostering the self-respect which is gained only through the exercise of independent responsibilities.

Renewal of home missionary concern

Apart from the South, where the white churches shared the impoverishment of their region, the post-Civil War years witnessed a marked resurgence of missionary activity. For more than two decades after 1840, the evangelistic thrust of the churches had been blunted by a variety of circumstances. The theological disputes spawned by Finneyite "new-measures" revivalism had proved to be divisive and distracting, and the available energy had been further sapped by the task of countering the disaffection created by the Mormons, Millerites, and Spiritualists. The attention of the churches was also diverted by the increasing demands of the slavery controversy, and finally the war itself had thrust to one side all other preoccupations. By the time the smoke had cleared from the battlefields, however, the earlier theological controversies had been forgotten and the churches in the North were ready to redirect to other pressing tasks the energy which had been devoted to ministering to the soldiers. Part of this energy was pre-empted by needs in the South, but the needs of the West and of the multiplying cities were not forgotten.

CHURCH EXTENSION IN THE WEST. The endeavor of the churches to match the pace of the westward migration was a continuation of their missionary activity on the earlier frontier, but "church extension" now became a more popular term than "home missions" to describe this activity. While a fairly substantial society had been established along the Pacific coast prior to the Civil War, the population was vastly augmented in the postwar years, and large numbers of people began to pour into the intervening territory. There was a steady succession of new states admitted to the Union, with four being added in 1889 alone.

The three enticements which drew people to the newer West were mining, cattle, and wheat. The initial discoveries of gold and silver in California, Nevada, and Colorado were followed by similar discoveries—including copper—in Arizona, Idaho, and Montana. Then the discovery that cattle could live on the prairie grass that stretched from the Missouri to the mountains and could survive the winter without shelter led to the creation of a great cattle empire. And when it became clear that it was feasible to raise winter wheat on the plains, there was a swelling influx of homesteaders. The whole development was spurred by the rapid extension of railroads throughout the area, with the first transcontinental track being completed in 1869.

Establishing churches in the new West was an unusually difficult enterprise, for the early population was scattered and transient. In the mining camps, the inhabitants—mostly men—had been stirred by a lust for gold and they had come not to establish homes but to make a "killing." Few men could have cared less than the miners about the desirability of establishing churches. When G. A. Reeder, a Methodist missionary at Yuma, attempted to hold meetings in the schoolhouse, he found himself preaching to empty seats. It was not until he took up a "position on the chief corner of the town, having the wholesale liquor establishment for my 'backing,' all the leading saloons near by, and a score of liquor dealers and drinkers within hearing," that he was able to make any impression on the community.[22] Effective missionary endeavor was equally difficult in the cow country, for it also had a floating population of men who were not greatly addicted to the practice of religion. And unlike the miners, the cowhands were not even gathered into temporary communities. The homesteaders provided a more stable population, but even among them a drought or a disastrous grasshopper infestation might provoke a further migration that would suddenly deplete the membership of a newly established church. With few exceptions, it was not until trading centers began to develop along the railroads that the churches were able to establish themselves on a permanent basis.

Methodists led the westward march of the churches, with Presbyterians, Congregationalists, and Baptists only a step behind.[23] The Methodist Church Extension Society was founded in 1864, and the Presbyterian and Baptist boards also allocated funds for the evangelization of the West. After the long period in which it had merged its interests with the Presbyterians, Congregationalism had developed a resurgent denominational consciousness and it was determined not to allow itself to be eclipsed on the new frontier. The Congregational General Council, which met in Boston in 1865, authorized the raising of a rather astonishingly large sum to be used in the West, and thereafter the Congregationalists engaged in a surge of church-building activity. By 1882 there was not a western state or territory in which Congregationalism was unrepresented. The Baptists

[22] W. C. Barclay, *History of Methodist Missions*, Vol. III, *Widening Horizons* (N.Y., 1957), 242.

[23] In addition to Barclay's *History of Methodist Missions*, see C. M. Drury, *Presbyterian Panorama* (Philadelphia, 1952); C. B. Goodykoontz, *Home Missions on the American Frontier* (Caldwell, Idaho, 1939); *Baptist Home Missions in North America* (N.Y., 1883); and C. L. White, *A Century of Faith* (Philadelphia, 1932).

pioneered in the use of "chapel cars" which were shunted onto railroad sidings and used as places of worship until church buildings could be constructed. The Baptists also persuaded the Union Pacific and Central Pacific railroads to give them a site for a church and parsonage in every village along their rights-of-way. C. C. McCabe of the Methodist Church Extension Society rode up and down the western lines establishing churches, and boasted that the Methodists were building more than one Methodist church for every day in the year and proposed to make it two a day.

Other religious bodies were also represented in the West. The Disciples expanded into the new territory mostly through individual initiative until the church extension board was formed in 1884. The Episcopalians organized the whole area into missionary dioceses but they were hampered by the problem of recruiting a sufficient number of ministers to implement their ambitious plans. The Unitarians established a few churches, and the Lutherans exhibited real strength among German and Scandinavian immigrants who took up land in the West. Roman Catholics were to be found in increasing numbers in the mining centers, and their ranks were swelled by the acquisition of those territories in the Southwest which had a Spanish-speaking population. Furthermore, largely through the instrumentality of Bishop John Ireland (1838–1918) of St. Paul, Minnesota, colonies of Roman Catholics from Ireland were established in the northern tier of states.

URBAN REVIVALISM. While the churches were busy evangelizing the West, they continued to be concerned with the population flowing into the cities. The rural area of the nation was being enormously expanded as the frontier receded before the plows of the homesteaders, but even this expansion did not counterbalance the denuding of the older rural areas as young people left marginal farms to man the mills and the stores in the new communities that were springing up at every important railroad junction. And an even greater attraction was being exerted by the major metropolitan centers that were developing at key points throughout the country. In the 1830's Finney, Beecher, and Barnes had experimented with conducting revivals among urban people; and the "prayer meeting" revival of 1857–59 was an urban phenomenon. A fully systematized urban revivalism was to be the major contribution of Dwight L. Moody (1837–99) to American church life. Whereas Finney's great successes were won in communities where the population rarely exceeded ten thousand,[24] Moody was to achieve fame by galvanizing into action the religious forces of cities with a million or more inhabitants. Finney's triumphs in Western, Utica, Rome, and Rochester were duplicated by Moody in London, New York, Philadelphia, Boston, and Chicago.

If the new revivalism was shaped and systematized by Moody, it was fathered and promoted by the Y.M.C.A.[25] Contemporary observers noted that the move to the cities tended to relax the ties of habit, social pressure, and emotional association which had bound the new arrivals to the church in their former places of residence. The Young Men's Christian Association was a British import designed to counter this tendency among teen-age boys who were striking out on their own for the first time. The Boston Y.M.C.A., organized on the British model in 1851, was the earliest American association, and its prospectus expressed its hope of becoming "a social organization of those in whom the love of Christ has produced love to men; who shall meet the young stranger as he enters our city, take him to the church and Sabbath school, bring him to the Rooms of the Association, and in every way throw around him good influences, so that he may feel that he is not a stranger, but that noble and Christian spirits care for his soul."

Initially established as "a mission of the evangelical churches to young men," the eager members of the "Y" soon turned the tables and transformed the Y.M.C.A. into a mission to the whole community. They collected funds to aid the destitute and cared for the sick in hotels and lodging houses, but their principal activity was evangelistic—working in rescue missions, organizing groups for Bible study, distributing tracts, and going out to preach on street corners or wherever they could gather an audience. Soon they were to become the chief agency of the churches in promoting communitywide revival campaigns. It was through participation in such activities of the Chicago Y.M.C.A. that Dwight L. Moody was introduced to organized evangelistic work and induced to forsake his commercial pursuits in order to devote himself wholly to the business of conducting revivals.[26]

[24] Rochester, with a population of 14,404 in 1835, was the single exception.
[25] For the Y.M.C.A., see C. H. Hopkins, *History of the Y.M.C.A. in North America* (N.Y., 1951).
[26] For Moody, in addition to Hopkins, *History of the Y.M.C.A.*, see McLoughlin, *Modern Revivalism*, and Weisberger, *They Gathered at the River*.

The "business" of conducting revivals is the appropriate term for Moody. He not only was a businessman, he looked like a businessman, talked like a businessman, took things in hand like a businessman. By utilizing every technique of efficient business promotion—"planning, organization, publicity, vast sums of money, a host of workers, skillful executive direction"—Moody was able to demonstrate that citywide revivals could be produced almost at will, and in the process he became the first and foremost representative of a new breed of professional evangelists. Whitefield, Wesley, Nettleton, and Finney had made revivalism a full-time profession, but the "new breed" was distinguished by their strong emphasis upon the results to be gained by efficient business methods. Had Moody not been deflected from his business career, it is likely that with his ebullient energy and talent for organization he would have carved out a financial empire for himself analogous to those of such friends and supporters as Cyrus McCormick, Marshall Field, and John Wanamaker. As it was, he made a fortune in religious work, but gave it all away so that at his death his only estate was $500 which he did not know he had.

Moody had been born in Northfield, Massachusetts. He had gone to Boston at the age of seventeen to enter his uncle's shoe business, and two years later, in 1856, had shifted to Chicago in order to take advantage of the greater opportunities offered by that lustily growing city. "I can make more money here in a week than I could in Boston in a month," he wrote to his brother. Within five years he had an upper-bracket income and a comfortable nest egg in the bank. Having professed conversion in Boston, he displayed equal vigor in church work. In Chicago he participated in the activities of three different churches, organized a mission Sunday school, dragooned passers-by into the noonday prayer services of the Y.M.C.A., and served as chairman of its visitation committee. In 1861, finding Y.M.C.A. work—where every person was a potential customer—much more challenging than the shoe trade, he abandoned his business career in order to give full time to the "Y." The war years were spent commuting to army camps as an agent of the United States Christian Commission (the Civil War analogue of the United Service Organization of World War II), while at the same time continuing to look after his mission Sunday school. In the final year of the war, he organized the Illinois Street Church for those graduates of his mission who felt ill-at-ease in the other churches of the city.

After the war, Moody became something of a civic institution in Chicago. "Every man has his own gifts," he said. "Some start things; others can organize and carry them on. My gift is to get things in motion." Operating on the basis that "it is better to get ten men to work than to do ten men's work," he soon had a host of projects under way, most of them connected with the Y.M.C.A. of which he had now become "librarian and agent." By a clever scheme of financing he was instrumental in erecting a spacious building—including an auditorium that would seat three thousand persons—for the work of the association. At the dedication in 1867 he gave unabashed expression to his aggressive spirit: "When we stop trying to enlarge our work for the Lord and raise money for it, we shall become stale and stupid. . . . We must ask for money, *money*, MORE MONEY at every meeting; not for the support of the Association—as it now is—but to enlarge its operations." Shortly after its completion the building burned down, and before the embers were cool Moody is reported to have solicited sufficient new subscriptions to replace it.

In the meantime, through informal talks at meetings of one type and another and by shrewdly observing the successes and failures of the preachers who conducted services at his Illinois Street Church, Moody was gaining skill as an evangelist—a skill that he perfected in addresses at Y.M.C.A. and Sunday school conventions. It was a triumphal two-year tour of the British Isles from 1873 to 1875, however, which was to make him a public figure with a national reputation. A chance encounter with two philanthropic laymen on a visit to England in 1872 in connection with his Y.M.C.A. work had led to an invitation to come back the following year to conduct a series of evangelistic meetings. Taking Ira D. Sankey (1840–1908) with him as his song leader, the tour had begun inauspiciously at York. Minor triumphs in the north of England were followed by major victories at Edinburgh and Glasgow, and when London was invaded for a four-month period the total attendance at the meetings was more than two and one-half million.

With the unbroken series of successes of the British campaign having being reported in sensational terms by the press, Moody was greeted on his return to the United States by the query as to what he would do in America. If there was a question in the minds of others, there was no question in his. He had found his vocation. As a New England country boy, he knew that "water runs down hill," and he was convinced that in the life of the nation "the highest hills are the great cities." If we can stir the cities, he contended, "we shall stir the whole nation." In the next five years he duplicated his British triumphs in America. Beginning in Brooklyn, where a skating rink was remodeled to hold the crowds; he moved on to Philadelphia for the winter, with John Wanamaker purchasing a freight warehouse to serve as an auditorium. In New York, P. T. Barnum's Hippodrome was rented; and in Chicago and Boston, where no buildings of sufficient size could be found, tabernacles were constructed. From Boston, after a period spent in the smaller New England cities, he went on to Baltimore, St. Louis, Cleveland, and San Francisco.

An editorial in the *Nation* (March 9, 1876) commented that "the Moody and Sankey services are an old-fashioned revival with modern improvements." The improvements were mostly highly efficient methods of organization. Everything was carefully planned in advance. Nothing was left to chance. There were committees for finance, prayer, publicity, home visitation, Bible study, music, tickets, and ushering. An executive committee was appointed to make sure that all the other committees functioned properly. No advertising device was neglected, and considerable sums were spent on posters and newspaper notices. When someone complained that it was undignified to advertise religious services, Moody replied that he thought it more undignified to preach to empty pews. Cities were divided into districts, and squads of workers were trained and sent out to visit each home. Notables were recruited to grace the platform. Sankey's music was a great attraction, as was that of the massed choirs. And the singing of gospel songs by the congregation was a stirring experience. But it was Moody's warmhearted, slap-dash, no-nonsense, colloquial style of preaching that established complete rapport with those who attended and persuaded vast numbers to proceed to the inquiry rooms, where they were given "decision cards" to sign for the use of local pastors in following up the conversions that were professed.

Moody never pretended to be anything more than a layman. Such theology as he had was rudimentary at best. Finney had written a book of almost one thousand pages to explain the points at which he differed from orthodox Calvinist doctrine. Even had he had the necessary training, Moody would never have thought of embarking upon such an enterprise. Once when Moody was confronted by a woman who said that she did not believe in his theology, he answered: "My theology! I didn't know I had any." [27] He insisted that instead of troubling his hearers with the disconcerting intricacies of theology, he simply stuck to the "three R's" of the gospel: "Ruin by sin, Redemption by Christ, and Regeneration by the Holy Ghost." God loves everyone, and all that you need to do to be saved is to believe that Christ died for you. To the man who said, "I am so constituted I can't believe," Moody said, "Men can believe if they will. It is not because men cannot believe; it is because they will not believe." The central fact, so far as Moody was concerned, was that any man can obtain salvation. He called attention to Acts 17:30, God "commandeth all men to repent," and insisted that this left no room for questions of innate depravity, predestined election, and human inability. "When God commands anything, he gives you the power to obey," said Moody. "We are free agents. God allows us to choose." And it was a very simple choice, a "fair, square, practical" choice, that permitted no neutrality: "We are either for God or against him."

To those who criticized either his methods or his message, Moody had a stock reply: "It doesn't matter how you get a man to God provided you get him there." And to most of the churchmen of the time this was a persuasive answer. Endorsements of his campaigns cut across almost all denominational lines and embraced almost all shades of theological opinion, for he had developed what seemed to be a quick and easy system to reach the unchurched masses of the cities. After a few years, however, it became clear that Moody was not reaching "the masses." His audiences, as was repeatedly pointed out, were made up of "the better class of people." Nor was there much evidence, in spite of claims to the contrary, that the campaigns boosted the rate of growth of the churches.[28] Moody's greatest contribution was to lift the morale of the churchgoing segment of the population, to infuse it with new enthusiasm, and to stimulate giving to a wide variety of Christian enterprises.

Moody exerted his most lasting influence on the college campuses where the students were greatly impressed by his openhearted spirit of devotion. A surprising feature of his student conferences at Northfield was

[27] For a discussion of the theology of Moody's sermons and of the inquiry room, see McLoughlin, *Modern Revivalism*, 246–62.

[28] McLoughlin made a careful statistical analysis which indicates that the Moody campaigns had little effect, either in Britain or in America, in increasing church membership. *Modern Revivalism*, 200–2, 262–67.

their distinctly liberalizing effect. Moody found it helpful to invite as featured speakers some of the ablest theological scholars who were competent, as Moody was not, to deal with the acute threats to their faith that the students were experiencing as a result of the new scientific inquiries and the new biblical studies. In spite of feeling himself singularly ill-equipped to speak to students, Moody was successful in deeply influencing many of the "first minds" of the college campuses, including Henry Drummond, George Adam Smith, John R. Mott, Robert E. Speer, Sherwood Eddy, and Charles Foster Kent.

THE SUNDAY SCHOOL MOVEMENT. The other great evangelistic enterprise of the Protestant churches following the Civil War was the Sunday school movement.[29] Since early in the century missionaries of the American Sunday School Union had been busy establishing Sunday schools for the children of the nation, and they had been given powerful support when Horace Bushnell, in *Christian Nurture* (1847), argued the need to supplement revivals with "more natural" and "more constant means of grace." Though the Sunday School Union continued to exist, the dynamic new agency was to be the International Sunday School Association. This was a popular lay enterprise which carried forward the whole endeavor in a burst of new enthusiasm and devotion.

As was true of so many religious movements in the latter part of the nineteenth century, Dwight L. Moody was the chief instigator, having conceived the idea of breathing new life into Sunday school work and having recruited B. F. Jacobs (1834–1902), a Chicago wholesale grocer and real estate man, to forward the project. Described by his friends as "a steam engine of a man," Jacobs quickly became the key figure. He captured control of the informal conventions assembled at the time of the Sunday School Union meetings, and turned them into an independent organization which promoted city, county, state, and national conventions of Sunday school workers. The movement was frankly interdenominational, and its goal was to multiply through united effort the number of communities throughout the land where the influence of the Christian religion reigned supreme. This was to be done by enlisting, training, and inspiring a corps of dedicated teachers in every community to revitalize

[29] See E. M. Fergusson, *Historic Chapters in Christian Education in America* (N.Y., 1935); M. C. Brown, *Sunday School Movements in America* (N.Y., 1901); and *Encyclopedia of Sunday Schools and Religious Education*, ed., J. T. McFarland and B. S. Winchester, (N.Y., 1915).

234

the Sunday school and to supplement its traditional instructional purpose with a definite evangelistic objective. The heart of the project was a highly efficient county-convention system which utilized mass rallies to kindle ardor and zeal while at the same time introducing the workers to new methods and providing them with a modicum of training. So great was the enthusiasm awakened at the rallies that a convention often became the occasion for a revival in the city in which it was held.

One of the major innovations, which had been adopted at the insistence of Jacobs by the national convention of 1872, was the Uniform Lesson Plan. This was a plan proposed by John H. Vincent (1832–1920), a member of the Rock River Methodist Conference in Illinois who had become editor of Methodist Sunday school publications in 1868. The idea was to have each class within a Sunday school, and Sunday schools of all denominations, studying the same lesson each week. The plan had at least two distinct advantages. For one thing, "next Sunday's lesson" became a bond of union between members of different denominations and thus contributed to a growing sense of Protestant solidarity. But an equally great advantage was that it facilitated lesson preparation. Teachers of all age groups and of all Protestant denominations could be gathered on Saturday afternoon to study the lesson they were to teach the following day.

Vincent also was responsible for spearheading the development of teacher-training institutes. These institutes were designed primarily for prospective teachers and sought to equip them with tested methods of Bible teaching before they assumed any instructional responsibilities. The institute idea caught on quickly and swept across the country. In Chicago it ultimately found more elaborate institutional expression in the establishment of the Moody Bible Institute in 1886. At Chautauqua Lake in western New York, the summer training institute founded by Vincent in 1874 developed into the elaborate summer program of the Chautauqua Institution.

Within a very brief time, the Sunday school—benefiting from its surge of popularity—had begun to replace revivalism as the primary recruiting device of the churches. No longer was it merely a children's school. Adult classes were formed which frequently rivaled the stated services of the church in attendance. Slogans, such as "Each one win one," were adopted, and the whole program of instruction marched forward inexorably each year to "Decision Day." So great was the enthusiasm that by the end of the century annual Bible school parades had become a fixture in many communities, with the mayor and other civic notables ensconced in the reviewing stand. In 1910, when the Adult Bible Class Federation held its national convention in Washington, Congress adjourned to witness the parade. The following year at San Francisco the parade was headed by a platoon of mounted police, and there were ten thousand men in the line of march, each with a Bible, carrying banners, and singing hymns and official delegation songs. A more sober but scarcely less ecstatic expression of this enthusiasm was reflected in the 1888 Beecher lectures at Yale in which H. Clay Trumbull rehearsed the beneficent influence that was being exerted by the Sunday school. As a result of "God's blessing on the revival and expansion of the Bible school as his chosen agency for Christian evangelization and Christian training," Trumbull declared, "Bible study and Bible teaching have a prominence never before known in the world's history" and "vital godliness is shown and felt in unprecedented potency in the life and progress of mankind." [30]

The eager optimism of the Sunday school workers was not shared by everyone. The more thoughtful were aware of the serious problems being posed for the churches by the new intellectual climate and the new industrial growth. Furthermore, it was now becoming evident how drastically the shape of American religious life was being altered by immigration. Hitherto the population of the United States had been relatively homogeneous. After the Civil War, as immigration steadily mounted, it became much more heterogeneous. And this shift in the make-up of the population was immediately reflected in the proportionate strength of the various religious groups. By the end of the century the Lutherans had outdistanced the Presbyterians and were exceeded in number of adherents among Protestants only by the Methodists and the Baptists. Judaism had become a sizable community, Eastern Orthodoxy had been launched on its American career, and even Buddhism had made its appearance on the Pacific coast. But the most spectacular feature of the post-Civil War years was the growth of the Roman Catholic Church.

[30] *The Sunday School: the Lyman Beecher Lectures* (Philadelphia, 1888), 142.

X

The New Americans

The influx of millions of Europeans into the United States during the fifty years from Appomattox to the assassination of Archduke Franz Ferdinand at Sarajevo was a phenomenon comparable in magnitude only to the migrations which overwhelmed the Roman Empire in the fifth and sixth centuries. The invasion was spurred by the spreading ganglia of the iron horse which had begun to bind the nation into a single economic unit on the eve of the Civil War. And even in the midst of the fighting, Congress had sped with lavish grants the advance of the railroads to the Pacific coast, thereby opening the whole continent to rapid settlement and creating a market, national in scope, that served as a powerful stimulus to commercial and industrial growth. With free farms awaiting the enterprising, employers bidding for cheap labor, and steamship companies drumming up passengers, the surge of immigrants broke all precedents. From 1865 to 1900 no fewer than 13½ million foreigners entered the United States. The pace at which they arrived was even greater after the turn of the century when almost 9 million immigrants passed through the ports of entry from 1900 through 1910. What this influx meant to the life of the nation can be fully understood only when it is remembered that the total population of the United States at the close of the Civil War was little more than 30 million.

The Irish and German invasions had begun prior to the war, with the incoming tide of Irish attaining major proportions during the "hungry forties" and the influx of Germans gaining momentum after the abortive Revolution of 1848. By the 1870's, when German immigration had reached floodtide and outstripped the Irish, the wave from Scandinavia had begun. Finally, from southern and eastern Europe came waves of Italians, Poles, Croats, Czechs, Slovaks, Hungarians, Greeks, Russians, and Romanians to work the mines, man the factories, and ply the needle in the garment trades.

Many of the Germans and most of the Scandinavians pushed on to the farmlands northwest of Chicago, but the other nationality groups tended to cluster in the cities. The ethnic composition of the cities changed in startling ways. Boston ceased to be the citadel of the Cabots and the Lodges and became the stronghold of the Kellys and the O'Briens. Other cities received a strong German, Polish, or Italian coloration. New York, as the chief port of entry, became a polyglot center of many nationalities. So rapid was the change that the number of foreign born in Chicago, for example, in 1890 nearly equaled the entire population of the city in 1880. The concentration of new Americans was even greater in some of the small industrial cities where almost all the inhabitants had been recruited abroad to staff the mills. Charles A. Beard, in describing the impact upon American society of the incoming tide of cheap labor, commented that "not since the patricians and capitalists of Rome scoured the known world for slaves—Celts, Iberians, Angles, Gauls, Saxons, Greeks, Jews, Egyptians, and Assyrians—to serve them," had the world witnessed such a drastic alteration in the composition of a social order as occurred in America during these years.[1]

The response of the older Americans

It is not surprising that so great a flood of immigrants should have created alarm among many of the older Americans. Peaceful coexistence

[1] *The Rise of American Civilization* (N.Y., 1927), II, 247.

seldom comes naturally. Tension usually develops whenever differing social groups first come into contact.

NATIVIST CONCERNS. The reasons for the sense of alarm that fostered a resurgence of nativist sentiment during the 1880's and 1890's were mixed. Apprehension built up at almost every level. There was a *cultural* concern at the introduction of differing folkways, customs, mores, and patterns of behavior. *Social* apprehensions were aroused by the poverty, illiteracy, and unsanitary habits of many of the immigrants. Whether the immigrants were herded into slums or created slums, there was widespread agreement that they constituted a social hazard. Even at best they had had a bad start. They were fleeing a life of poverty; and long, unsanitary voyages across the Atlantic meant that many of them went from the ship to the hospital to be cared for at public expense. Francis J. Lally has reported that a New York almshouse commissioner sadly exclaimed: "Many of them had far better been cast into the deep sea, than linger in the pangs of hunger, sickness, and pain, to draw their last agonizing breath in the streets of New York." [2] Not only did these new Americans tax the public dole, they committed crimes far out of proportion to their number. The *political* impact of the new arrivals was expressed in the saying that the immigrants "landed on Monday and voted on Tuesday," being met at the dock by the "bosses," quickly registered, and then shepherded to the polls. While this overstated the situation, the shifting of control in the cities from the native born to the foreign born was bound to produce unhappy reactions even without the suspicion that the immigrant vote was being manipulated. From an *economic* point of view, the new Americans also were not an unmixed blessing. They did provide cheap labor for an expanding America, but not too many of the native born appreciated this fact. Much more evident to them was the way in which the immigrants tended to depress wages and lower the standard of living by competing with the existing labor force.

All these factors were heightened by the sense of an alien intrusion into American life. The various nationality groups tended to cling together in "ghettos" of their own, separating themselves from the rest of the community. Many spoke no English. They were suspected of exalting foreign ties and cherishing foreign ideals. To many native Americans it

[2] *The Catholic Church in a Changing America* (Boston, 1962), 29–30.

seemed that the America they had known was doomed unless the immigrant invasion could somehow be checked.

In the post-Civil War period the labor leaders were the first to voice alarm at the threat posed by the incoming tide from Europe. At a later date even so uncompromising a "social liberal" as John A. Ryan (1869–1945) of Catholic University was to advocate restricting the flow of immigration. Only small victories, however, were won. The first general immigration law, adopted in 1882, excluded only convicts, lunatics, idiots, and those likely to become public charges. Nine years later polygamists and those suffering from dangerous diseases were banned. It was not until 1917 that a literacy test was imposed, and the highly restrictive "quota" system was not adopted until 1924.[3]

PROTESTANT-CATHOLIC TENSIONS. Nativist sentiment frequently had religious overtones, with Roman Catholicism being depicted as part of an international conspiracy to subvert the free institutions of America. This had been the theme of Samuel F. B. Morse (1791–1872), inventor of the telegraph, in a series of letters entitled "A Foreign Conspiracy against the Liberties of the United States" which he wrote to the *New York Observer* in 1834. During this early period, such prominent Protestant leaders as Lyman Beecher, Horace Bushnell, and Albert Barnes believed that there was a deliberate design by Roman Catholics to capture middle America, which was thus to be the great battlefield where the destinies of the world were to be decided. The Order of United Americans (the "Know-Nothing" party of the 1850's) both fed upon and generated this fear, but it subsided with the onset of the conflict between North and South. The conspiracy theme was revived, however, in 1887 with the formation of the American Protective Association (A.P.A.) at Clinton, Iowa, whose members were pledged to endeavor "to strike the shackles and chains of blind obedience to the Roman Catholic church from the hampered and bound consciences of a priest-ridden and church-oppressed people." The A.P.A. was a fringe group which flourished most in areas where Roman Catholics were least numerous, as in Iowa, Nebraska, and

[3] The renewed immigration after World War I coincided with a period of economic recession and brought renewed agitation for restrictive legislation. A temporary measure was adopted in 1921 limiting the number of immigrants annually to 3 per cent of the foreign born of each nationality resident in the United States in 1910. Three years later the Johnson-Reed Act restricted total annual immigration to 150,000 and assigned quotas to each nationality on the basis of its present representation in the population. A complete prohibition of Japanese immigration made the exclusion of Orientals almost complete.

Kansas. While the A.P.A. was an active political force which won local victories, it was bluntly rebuffed in its attempt to influence national politics, and it withered away within a few years. Anti-Catholic feeling, nevertheless, continued to persist among many segments of the American population.[4]

Although Joseph H. Fichter has suggested that anti-Catholicism in the United States was more largely rooted in ethnic rather than religious antagonisms,[5] the religious element should not be minimized. It is true that much of the hostility to Roman Catholicism was generated by its "foreignness." And it is likely that native-born Catholics would have continued to be accepted, like other Americans, had Catholic immigrants not arrived in such overwhelming numbers. Moreover, nativist sentiment was not absent among Roman Catholics. Native-born Roman Catholics were often dismayed by the Irish immigrants, criticizing their lack of cleanliness, their boisterous conduct, their raucous laughter, their disgraceful fights. The Irish in turn frequently denounced the Germans with as much vigor as other nativists. In 1854 the Boston diocesan paper, the *Pilot*, welcomed a decline in immigration, urged the tightening of the naturalization laws, and was of the opinion that if the Know-Nothings succeeded in obstructing the Germans, posterity would overlook their crimes of bigotry. A few decades later, Archbishop John Ireland (1838–1918) alerted the Associated Press to the "general un-American character" of the American German Catholic Assembly. German Catholics exhibited similar hostility to still newer immigrant groups. And when Roman Catholics in the southern states were urged to welcome coreligionists from Ireland and Germany, they insisted that only those who would be friendly to southern interests be sent. "We must not," they declared, "warm vipers into life that may sting us when they grow warm."[6] While all this is true, religious concerns were present in the tension between Protestants and Roman Catholics.

[4] The excesses of the earlier anti-Catholic movement have been described in detail by R. A. Billington, *The Protestant Crusade, 1800–1860* (N.Y., 1938). For the later movement, see D. L. Kinzer, *An Episode in Anti-Catholicism: The American Protective Association* (Seattle, 1964).

[5] "The Americanization of Catholicism," in McAvoy, *Roman Catholicism and the American Way of Life*, 116–17.

[6] W. E. Wright, "The Native American Catholic, the Immigrant, and Immigration," in McAvoy, *Roman Catholicism and the American Way of Life*, 213–14, 216. See also C. J. Barry, "The German Catholic Immigrant," *ibid.*, 199. And Robert D. Cross, *The Emergence of Liberal Catholicism in America* (Cambridge, Mass., 1958), 92.

Protestants, of course, did not constitute a single homogeneous anti-Catholic bloc, a fact which Archbishop Ireland acknowledged and Robert D. Cross has documented.[7] Expressions of friendship and good will were not uncommon, and such organizations as the A.P.A. seldom reflected responsible Protestant opinion. There were nonetheless serious fears and apprehensions, stimulated in part by the harsh anti-Protestantism of some Roman Catholics. Michael Muller (1825–99), a Redemptorist Father, did little to foster good feeling when he published *The Catholic Dogma: Out of the Church There Is No Salvation* (1886). His purpose in writing the book, he said, was to refute "those soft, weak, timid, liberalizing Catholics, who labor to explain away all the points of Catholic faith offensive to non-Catholics, and to make it appear there is no question of life and death, of heaven and hell, involved in the difference between us and Protestants." There were other Catholics who felt no hesitancy in denouncing Protestants as infidels, and even the suggestion by a bishop in 1870 that non-Catholics could be persons of good faith and good character was sufficient to cause him to be called "a Luther or a Lucifer." Ten years later, Augustine Thébaud (1807–85), a Jesuit who had been in America since 1838, insisted that Protestants who "profess to be friendly to Catholics" are not sincere. And Archbishop John Hughes of New York denounced as "Protestant priests" those Catholic clergymen who enjoyed good relations with Protestants.[8]

Further antagonism was aroused by the generally negative attitude of some Catholics toward American life as a whole. The influential *Church Progress* of St. Louis was not particularly tactful when it made unfavorable comparisons between the United States and the Catholic nations of Europe, and the statement of Condé Pallen (1858–1929) that American culture "exhales an atmosphere filled with germs fatal to Catholic life" was hardly calculated to win friends. This negativism was most conspicuous among German-speaking Catholics. Anton Walburg, (1840–1910), a leading priest in Cincinnati, was emphatic in his criticism of the United States. In 1889 he depicted American culture as a "hotbed of fanaticism, intolerance, and radical ultra views on matters of politics and religion." Even the language, he insisted, was so permeated with Protestant ideas that an English-speaking Catholicism could never prosper. In contrast to

[7] Cross, *The Emergence of Liberal Catholicism in America*, 30, 32–37, 44, 48, 52, 65.
[8] *Ibid.*, 51–52, 56.

the United States, Father Walburg pointed to Germany as standing "foremost in the ranks of civilized nations," and he advised Americans to stop worrying about getting involved in European quarrels since the United States was too weak to defeat Ecuador, let alone a European power.[9]

While mutual animosities fostered mutual estrangement, Protestant uneasiness had its basic rootage in apprehensions concerning the changes that a continuing massive Roman Catholic immigration might introduce into American society. The existing social order, which embodied in so many ways the ideals and moralities of evangelical Protestantism, seemed to many thoughtful people to be in danger of being completely subverted. The most obvious, if perhaps the most superficial, threat was the challenge to two of the most conspicuous folk moralities of American Protestantism—Sabbath observance and temperance. The "Continental Sunday" of the immigrant groups both scandalized and spread consternation in the Protestant camp. And Protestants, long schooled in the evils of strong drink, noted with dismay that these new Americans were bringing "their grog shops like the frogs of Egypt upon us."[10]

Of more serious concern were the attacks leveled by Catholics against the public schools. Universal public education had been fostered as a counter to the project of that "old deluder Satan" to keep people from a knowledge of the Scriptures, and the "little red schoolhouse" was regarded, along with motherhood and the home, as one of the most cherished institutions of American life. While it was understandable that Catholics might wish schools of their own, nothing could have been better calculated to raise Protestant hackles than the attempt to drum up support for parochial education by attacking public education. The public schools were described as "godless," and those who defended them were charged with being "fanatics." Bishop Bernard McQuaid (1823–1909) called the public school system "a huge conspiracy against religion, individual liberty, and enterprise," while Michael Muller regarded it as a disease which would "break up and destroy the Christian family" and described the public schools as "hotbeds of immorality" where "courtesans have disguised themselves as school-girls in order the more surely to ply their foul vocation." Zachariah Montgomery was convinced that free love would

[9] *Ibid.*, 26, 28, 72, 90.
[10] Lally, *The Catholic Church in a Changing America*, 29.

243

be the ultimate consequence of free public education. "Free teaching draws after it free books, free clothes, free food, free time," he contended. "All this is going very far with the communists. . . . If we admit a right . . . to take the child out of the family, they will ask next for the wife." Other Catholics were convinced that not everyone should be taught to read, for this would serve to unfit them for the station in life into which they had been born. Still others argued that godly innocence was more often associated with childlike ignorance than with worldly knowledge. A few, appalled by the thought of a system that mixed innocents with the "crime-steeped progeny of the low and vile," went so far as to urge that all free (i.e., public) education be abandoned.[11]

Perhaps the greatest apprehension was aroused by the fear that Roman Catholicism might serve to undermine American democracy. While no more than a small minority of the American people may have shared the conviction of the radical nativist fringe that massive Catholic immigration was a deliberate plot to overthrow the free institutions of America, there were many who feared that the tenets and spirit of Roman Catholicism were antithetical to religious and political liberty. The memory of events in Europe after the defeat of Napoleon in 1814 and after the abortive revolutions of 1848–49 did little to reassure them, and they were equally disturbed by the condemnations contained in the *Syllabus of Errors* of 1864 and by the decrees of the Vatican Council in 1870. Moreover, in the encyclical letter *Immortale Dei* (The Christian Constitution of States) of 1885, Leo XIII had explicitly affirmed the right of the papacy to judge when the affairs of the civil order must yield to the superior authority of the Roman Church.[12] And somewhat later the Vatican newspaper *Osservatore Romano* pointed out that "as the Pope is the sovereign of the Church . . . , he is also the sovereign of every other society and of every other kingdom." [13] Some comments by American Catholics were no more reassuring. An article in the *American Catholic Quarterly Review* in 1877 dismissed the Declaration of Independence as a flock of vague clichés, and five years later a pastoral letter of the bishops of

[11] Cross, *The Emergence of Liberal Catholicism in America*, 95, 96, 98, 131–32, 135–36.

[12] For the *Syllabus of Errors*, see Smith, Handy, Loetscher, *American Christianity*, II, 112–15. The constitution promulgated at the Vatican Council in 1870 and the encyclical *Immortale Dei* are reprinted in W. S. Hudson, *Understanding Roman Catholicism* (Philadelphia, 1959), 37–45, 66–90.

[13] Cited in Cross, *Emergence of Liberal Catholicism*, 60.

244

the province of Cincinnati took a dim view of the notion that a people should rule themselves.[14]

Other Catholics, most notably Cardinal James Gibbons (1834–1921), Archbishop John Ireland, and Bishop John J. Keane (1839–1918), were as disturbed as most Protestants by the reactionary stance of the conservative wing of the Roman Catholic Church in America. They resented both the aspersions cast upon the public schools and the innuendoes which suggested that the American form of government was less desirable than the nondemocratic regimes of Europe. They repeatedly voiced their own approbation of American democratic principles, and were forthright in condemning the antidemocratic views of some of their fellow Catholics. In contrast to the conservative Catholics, the liberals were widely acclaimed and publicly honored by Protestants. Gibbons was invited to preach in Protestant pulpits, Keane gave the Dudleian lecture at Harvard, and a Baptist minister affectionately addressed Ireland as "my archbishop." The result of the Catholic ambivalence was a degree of ambivalence in the Protestant mind, with varying opinions being held as to the future course that the Roman Church would pursue in America.

PROTESTANT MINISTRIES TO THE IMMIGRANTS. The Protestant approach to the newcomers to the American scene was motivated by a varying mixture of religious concern, humanitarian sentiment, patriotic fervor, and anti-Catholic feeling. Not many after the turn of the century viewed the Catholic portion of the incoming tide as part and parcel of a carefully laid plot to capture the United States for the Pope. Many were convinced, however, that the "safety and welfare and Christian civilization of our country depends in no small degree upon transforming" the immigrant "into a true American," and that "nothing but Christianity, as incarnated in American Protestantism," can accomplish this end. The new arrivals, declared mission executive Charles A. Brooks (1871–1931), must be "born again of the American spirit." [15] In spite of attempts to enlist support for mission work among the immigrants by equating Protestantism with patriotism, the literature of the time makes it clear that much of the motivation was rooted in a truly humanitarian and religious solicitude for the friendless and poverty-stricken. Methodists, for example,

---

[14] *Ibid.*, 99.
[15] H. B. Grose, *Aliens or Americans?* (N.Y., 1906), 237, 255. C. A. Brooks, *Immigration: Its Extent, Its Effect on America, Its Call to the Churches* (N.Y., 1915), 8.

were as assiduous in their work among Lutherans from Sweden and Calvinists from Hungary as they were among Roman Catholics from any land.

Apart from informal "welfare" or "relief" programs, the major response of the Protestant churches to the presence of the new Americans in their midst was a strenuous effort to provide them with a religious ministry in their own language. Later, as a phase of their expanding humanitarian activity, the churches developed a systematized program of "Christian Americanization" or "Christian Friendliness" to assist the immigrant families in making a successful adjustment to American life. Women were enlisted to go into the homes to show mothers how to cook the food available in American stores, to teach them English, to help them prepare for naturalization examinations, and generally to befriend them.

Almost every Protestant denomination developed foreign-language ministries. Mission work was established among the Germans, Scandinavians, French Canadians, Italians, Poles, Hungarians, Czechs, Romanians, and Portuguese. Baptists, for example, maintained a ministry to twenty-one different nationality groups in as many different languages. The recruiting of a "native ministry" to labor among their fellow immigrants was haphazard at first, but as soon as any specific group began to arrive in significant numbers training institutes were organized to train converts for mission work. Within a relatively short time foreign-language "departments" were established in theological seminaries to provide more adequate ministerial training. The Baptists were typical in this respect, establishing a German department at Rochester Theological Seminary in 1858, a department for Swedish, Danish, and Norwegian students at the seminary in Chicago in 1871, a French-Canadian department at Newton in 1889, and an Italian department at Colgate Theological Seminary in 1907. "So ample were these facilities," Aaron I. Abell reported in his study of urban Protestantism, "that by 1900 a body of clergymen ready to meet all calls for independent or assistant pastorates had come into existence." As early as 1895 the problem of the Congregationalists had become one of sufficient financial support rather than of available personnel, for their home missionary society reported that the once "greatest desideratum —trained Congregational pastors—to supply these churches of foreign tongues, is now supplied in a degree almost beyond our power to use, through Oberlin and Chicago theological seminaries, whose well-equipped graduates stand ready to enlarge the field of our missionary service wherever the means are at the command of this society to employ them." [16]

While by no means negligible, the number of non-English-speaking immigrants added to the membership of churches of British background accounted for only a small fraction of the new Americans. As was to be expected, it was the churches of their homelands which experienced the great surge of growth.

Adjustments and tensions within Roman Catholicism

The most spectacular development in American religious life during the latter half of the nineteenth century was the growth of the Roman Catholic Church. In spite of repeated alarm that vast losses were being suffered among those who came to America, the Roman Catholic Church was remarkably successful in retaining the allegiance of Catholic immigrants. [17] Although the number of Roman Catholics had rapidly mounted during the pre-Civil War years, giant strides in membership took place in the decades that followed. The four million Catholics of 1870 increased to six million in 1880. Ten years later the total was nine million, and in 1900 it was twelve million. By 1920 every sixth person and every third church member was a Roman Catholic. [18]

INSTITUTIONAL DEVELOPMENT. The challenge presented to the Roman Catholic Church by the immigrant flood was prodigious. The immigrants were poor. They came from different countries, spoke different languages, and—within the limits of their common faith—had different

[16] A. I. Abell, *The Urban Impact upon American Protestantism* (Cambridge, Mass., 1943), 182, 183.

[17] A careful study which exploded the myth of vast losses was made by Gerald Shaughnessy, *Has the Immigrant Kept the Faith?* (N.Y., 1925).

[18] The older standard accounts of the Roman Catholic Church in America are John G. Shea, *History of the Catholic Church in the United States*, 4 vols. (N.Y., 1886–92), and Thomas O'Gorman, *A History of the Roman Catholic Church in the United States* (N.Y., 1895). These were supplemented by the popular and impressionistic account of Theodore Maynard, *The Story of American Catholicism* (N.Y., 1941), and the more pedestrian presentation of institutional data by Theodore Roemer, *The Catholic Church in the United States* (St. Louis, 1950). John Tracy Ellis, *American Catholicism* (Chicago, 1956) is a briefer chronological treatment which stresses the relationship of Catholics to the larger society. The key documents in the history of American Catholicism are reprinted in John Tracy Ellis, *Documents of American Catholic History*, rev. ed. (Milwaukee, 1962).

traditions and customs and loyalties. Even had they not been poverty-stricken, they came in such numbers that the task of recruiting priests, erecting parishes, and building churches must have seemed almost insurmountable. Financial help did come from Europe. From France the Society for the Propagation of Faith had sent more than six million dollars by 1914. Additional help came from similar societies in Germany, Austria, and Switzerland. But the major financial burden was carried in America. In terms of personnel the assistance from abroad was much more important and substantial. Religious orders and congregations sent over priests, lay brothers, and nuns, with Ireland, Germany, France, and Belgium contributing the greatest number. Secular priests also were dispatched. Although the bishops constantly stressed the importance of encouraging vocations to the priesthood and founded seminaries to provide the necessary training, it was the recruits from abroad who made it possible for the ranks of the clergy to swell from slightly more than two thousand in 1860 to six thousand in 1880, to twelve thousand in 1900, and to seventeen thousand in 1910. Nor was it an easy task to maintain effective oversight of the multiplying parishes. New dioceses were constantly being formed. The seventeen dioceses in 1840 had increased to forty-four by 1860. From 1868 to 1900 forty more had been established, and by 1914 the total exceeded one hundred, grouped in fourteen provinces.

Prior to the period from 1846 to 1850 when five new provinces were constituted, there had been but a single province—that of Baltimore—in the United States. Beginning in 1829 the bishops had met approximately every three years in a provincial council to deal with their common problems. When other provinces were established, this procedure had to be altered. In place of the provincial gatherings, plenary councils of the whole American episcopate were summoned to coordinate the work of the church on a national basis with appropriate legislation. The first plenary council met in 1852, the second in 1866, and the third in 1884.[19] Thereafter such national councils were either suppressed or suspended, presumably to avoid the dangers implicit in the idea of a national church. A similar concern had dictated the refusal of Rome to accede to the petition of the bishops that the archbishop of Baltimore be granted the place of primacy among the bishops in the United States. In place of these alternatives, both

[19] For these councils, see Peter Guilday, *A History of the Councils of Baltimore, 1791–1884* (N.Y., 1932).

248

containing the potential hazard of undue independence, an Apostolic Delegate (papal representative) was appointed in 1893 to provide the necessary coordination and direction for the American church. With the structure of government having been completed in this fashion and with the arrangement functioning effectively, Pius X on June 29, 1908, removed the church in the United States from the jurisdiction of the Congregatio de Propaganda Fide. The effect was to place the Roman Catholic Church in America on a basis of full equality with the older branches of the church in Europe and to bring to an end its missionary status.

The resources of manpower, money, and ingenuity were further taxed by the policy of developing a whole system of Catholic education. The first provincial council of Baltimore in 1829 declared it to be "absolutely necessary that schools should be established in which the young may be taught the principles of faith and morality while being instructed in letters." In 1852 the first plenary council re-emphasized the need for parochial schools, and in 1884 the third plenary council decreed that schools should be established in every parish within the next two years unless the bishop permitted a postponement because of serious difficulties. Support for the program of parochial education, however, was not as uniform as these decrees suggest. German Catholics were among the most ardent proponents of parochial schools, viewing them as a means of preserving their German language and culture. Liberal prelates, such as Gibbons, Ireland, and Keane, preferred to work out an accommodation with public education as a means of integrating Catholics more fully into the main stream of American life. A hard-fought struggle ensued, with Irish conservatives, such as Archbishop Michael A. Corrigan (1839-1902) of New York City and Bishop McQuaid of Rochester, giving the Germans stanch support. Ultimately the issue was settled by papal intervention in favor of a complete system of parochial education, with deviations being tolerated if judged necessary by a bishop in the light of local conditions.

Progress in fulfilling the ideal of a school in every parish was slow. Had the Roman Catholic population not been concentrated in the major cities and in a few largely self-contained rural enclaves, the whole project would have been doomed from the start. And even with this concentration, parochial education was made possible only by the sacrificial devotion of the members of numerous sisterhoods who were recruited to staff the schools. In spite of the fact that the council of 1884 had decreed that within two years every parish must have its own school, the parishes so equipped had increased only from 40 per cent to 44 per cent by 1892. Thereafter, with dissidence having been quelled, progress was somewhat more rapid. In 1914 the parochial schools enrolled over one million pupils, had over twenty thousand teachers, and were maintained at a cost of over $15,000,000 per year. But even an achievement of this magnitude was not enough, for a very large proportion of Catholic children were still being educated in the public schools.

Interest in secondary education lagged, with the total enrollment in 1915 being less than seventy-five thousand. Colleges and universities, on the other hand, were beginning to receive vigorous support after a long period of precarious existence.[20] Georgetown, St. Louis, Fordham, Notre Dame, and Holy Cross, among others, had become strong institutions, and in 1884 the third plenary council took the necessary decisive action to effect the establishment in 1889 of the Catholic University of America as a full-fledged graduate institution to serve as the capstone of the Catholic educational structure.

"AMERICANISM." In addition to their other problems, Roman Catholics had the difficult task of adjusting people of diverse nationality both to one another and to the American environment. To weld Irishmen, Germans, Italians, Czechs, French Canadians, and many others into a single church was a taxing effort. Tension often was acute. The earlier trustee controversy had been in part a rebellion of the Irish against the imported French priests who had been displaced from their homeland by the Revolution of 1789. After the Civil War the German-Irish tension came to the fore, and in the 1890's Polish dissatisfaction produced a schismatic movement which was to result in the formation of the Polish National Catholic Church.[21] In 1914 a parallel Lithuanian National Catholic Church was organized.

[20] Of thirty-eight colleges established between 1791 and 1850 only seven survived, and of fifty-five established between 1850 and 1865 only eighteen survived. Maynard, *The Story of American Catholicism*, 474.

[21] In 1916 the Polish group reported a membership of 28,245. Consecration of its bishops had been obtained from the Old Catholic Church in Europe, a small Dutch group which had refused to accept the decrees of the Council of Trent. Old Catholics in Germany and Switzerland had been alienated by the dogmatic pronouncements of the first Vatican Council in 1870.

The German-Irish issue, which had long smoldered and had been reflected in the school controversy, was brought to a head in 1891 when the St. Raphael Society of Switzerland, with Peter Paul Cahensly as its secretary, in a petition to Rome declared that in the United States the Roman Catholic Church had lost ten million souls through failure to make proper provision for them in their own language. As was true of other nationality groups, provision had been made for the establishment of German congregations under the leadership of German-speaking priests. And of the sixty-nine bishops in 1886, fifteen were of Germanic extraction. But this was not enough for the St. Raphael Society, which had been founded to aid German-speaking immigrants. In its petition to the papacy the Society proposed that each of the nationality groups in America be organized into separate dioceses. This attempt to fragment the church in America by institutionalizing Old World divisions was rejected by the papacy, but it serves to illustrate a difference in point of view as to the proper strategy to be pursued in the United States.

Most of the German leadership was convinced that the way to hold the immigrants was to keep them isolated from American life. German culture, customs, and language were defended with the slogan "Language Saves the Faith," and it was insisted that only priests proud of being German, and schools in which German was the language of instruction, could save German Catholics and their children from being de-Catholicized. To those who contended that "we are apostles to bring the people to Christ . . . , not to maintain or implant a nationality or to spread a language," the *Herald des Glaubens* responded that priests who voiced such sentiments "would rather see several million Germans go to hell than forego the opportunity to convert a few hundred Yankees." [22]

The Germans, of course, were not alone in believing that the only way to prevent defections was to insulate the faithful and to resist all accommodation to the American environment. Some of the most influential of the Irish bishops, while not concerned with the language problem, were equally uncompromising in their determination that no concessions should be made to American culture. There were others, however, who believed that resistance to Americanization not only created unnecessary antagonism and impeded the winning of converts, but actually was a policy

[22] *Roman Catholicism and the American Way of Life*, ed. McAvoy, 192-94; Cross, *Emergence of Liberal Catholicism*, 25-26, 91-92.

calculated to speed the defection of those who had been Catholics in their homelands. If being an American meant ceasing to be a Catholic, they had little doubt of the choice that many of them, especially their children, would make. While Isaac Hecker and the Paulist Fathers, the order of missionary priests which he had founded in 1859, were the most conspicuous advocates of this point of view, it found strong support among members of the hierarchy, most notably from the triumvirate of Gibbons, Ireland, and Keane.

Gibbons' *The Faith of Our Fathers* (1876) was one of the most successful Catholic apologetics ever written in English, and the response it elicited seemed a clear demonstration of the effectiveness of the Americanizing tactic. At the centenary in 1889 of Baltimore's establishment as a diocese, Gibbons re-emphasized the Americanist theme, saying that Carroll's aim had been "that the clergy and people—no matter from what country they sprung—should be thoroughly identified with the land in which their lot was cast; that they should study its laws and political constitution and be in harmony with its spirit; in a word, that they should become, as soon as possible, assimilated to the social body in all things pertaining to the common domain of civil life." And then, turning to the present, Gibbons called upon his contemporaries to emulate Carroll. Ireland was even more emphatic, believing that people unwilling to be assimilated did not deserve to be admitted to the country and that anyone who did not rejoice in the blessings of America "should in simple consistency betake his foreign soul to foreign shores, and crouch in misery and subjection beneath tyranny's sceptre."

> We should live in our age, know it, be in touch with it. . . . We should be in it and of it, if we would have its ear. . . . For the same reason, there is needed a thorough sympathy with the country. The Church of America must be, of course, as Catholic as even in Jerusalem or Rome; but as far as her garments assume color from the local atmosphere, she must be American. Let no one dare to paint her brow with a foreign taint or pin to her mantle foreign linings.[23]

But it was not simply a tactic that the liberal coterie had adopted. They were fully committed to American democracy, glorying in it,

---

[23] Roemer, *Catholic Church in the United States,* 303–04; Maynard, *Story of American Catholicism,* 511; Cross, *Emergence of Liberal Catholicism,* 89.

believing in it, and willing to defend it. "If I had the privilege of modifying the Constitution of the United States," declared Gibbons, "I would not expunge or alter a single paragraph, a single line, or a single word of that important instrument."

> The Constitution is admirably adapted to the growth and expansion of the Catholic religion, and the Catholic religion is admirably adapted to the genius of the Constitution. They fit together like two links of the same chain.

Furthermore, these Americanizers believed that America had a mission to the world. God intended America to be more than a "motherland," asserted Keane. "She was meant to be a teacher through whose lips and in whose life he was to solve the social problems of the Old World." [24]

The leaders of the liberal contingent also were certain that America could teach lessons in religion as well as in politics. The role of the laity was emphasized and lay congresses were organized. Close clerical supervision and direction were minimized by a stress upon the necessity for individual initiative in the apostolate of the church. The contemplative life exalted by most of the religious orders tended to be disparaged. "An honest ballot and social decorum," Ireland contended, "will do more for God's glory and the salvation of souls than midnight flagellations or Compestellan pilgrimages." Protestants were not to be regarded as implacable enemies but as "brothers to be brought back to the fold." Love and persuasion should replace harsh polemic. The technique of seeking to exert religious influence through the formation of a Catholic political party, a practice widely adopted in Europe, was likewise decried. Even the almost automatic identification of American Catholics with the Democratic party ("Have you heard the news? John Danaher has become a Republican!" "It can't be true. I saw him at mass just last Sunday.") was deplored on the ground that it deprived Catholics of influence because the Democrats took them for granted while the Republicans felt no obligation to them. [25]

The 1880's and 1890's were heady years for the liberals, but they were also years when the issue of "Americanism" was being sharply

[24] J. T. Ellis, *Perspectives in American Catholicism* (Baltimore, 1963), 124; Cross, *Emergence of Liberal Catholicism,* 184.

[25] Maynard, *Story of American Catholicism,* 514; Cross, *Emergence of Liberal Catholicism,* 187.

drawn.[26] The peak of the liberal ascendancy was reached in 1893 at the seventeen-day Parliament of Religions held in conjunction with the Chicago Columbian Exposition. The American archbishops, presumably influenced by Ireland, had decided that the Parliament presented a signal opportunity to present Catholic truth to those outside the fold. At the opening session, Archbishop Patrick A. Feehan (1829–1902) gave an address of welcome, and Cardinal Gibbons (he had received the red hat in 1886) led the assembly in the Protestant version of the Lord's Prayer. Bishop Keane presented two papers, read an address prepared by Gibbons, and presided on the day assigned for a specifically Catholic program. While those who participated felt that a real service had been rendered the Catholic Church, others were scandalized by the appearance given by Catholic participation of waiving the Roman claim to unique and final truth. By sharing the platform with every religious sect "from Mohammedanism and Buddhism down to the lowest form of evangelicalism and infidelity," the participating bishops were accused of having taken a dangerous first step toward "indifferentism." Even prior to this, in an article in the *American Catholic Quarterly Review*, the vicar general of Archbishop Corrigan had charged Ireland, Gibbons, and Keane of being guilty of the "liberalism" condemned by the *Syllabus of Errors*.[27]

Many issues, in addition to those strictly related to "Americanism," contributed to the coalescing of two parties in the church, each striving for ascendancy. There were differences of opinion over parochial schools and the language question, tensions between nationality groups, differing attitudes toward "temperance," and debates as to the position the church should take with regard to the Knights of Labor and the "single-tax" proposal of Henry George. The establishment of Catholic University in 1889 had been displeasing to many. Some feared it as a rival to their own institutions. Some were opposed to its location in Washington where students would be exposed to the corrupting influences of the nation's capital. Others were dismayed that an undergraduate college for women would be adjacent to a campus where priests and members of religious orders would be pursuing graduate studies. Still others were alienated by

[26] The two indispensable books dealing with the "Americanism" controversy are Cross, *Emergence of Liberal Catholicism*, and T. T. McAvoy, *The Great Crisis in American Catholic History, 1895–1900* (Chicago, 1957). The latter volume makes full use of archival material. It has been reprinted under a new title, *The Americanist Heresy in Roman Catholicism* (Notre Dame, Ind., 1963).

[27] McAvoy, *The Great Crisis in American Catholic History*, 76–77.

the "progressive" auspices under which the university had been established and by the pretension of its board of trustees to serve as a standing council of the church. The latter pretension was related to a centralizing tendency which also aroused antagonism. Gibbons was being encouraged to assume the role of spokesman and unofficial primate of the church by exploiting the precedence he derived from being the archbishop of Baltimore and the only American cardinal, and the archbishops had begun to function as a committee in a way that seemed to abridge episcopal liberties. Perhaps as important as any of these issues in the process of polarization was the personal rivalry of Archbishops Ireland and Corrigan, each of whom aspired to be the next American to possess a cardinal's hat. Thus ties of friendship, common convictions and ideals, and mutual antipathies were involved in the struggle that was to take place.

When Archbishop Francesco Satolli was sent to represent the papacy at the Chicago World's Fair in 1892, he was privately instructed to adjudicate the controversies among American Catholics and to make known at an appropriate time that Leo XIII wanted him to remain in America as a resident apostolic delegate to ensure that the desired unity would be maintained. For a variety of reasons, nearly all the bishops were opposed to the appointment of any such permanent papal representative in the United States. Ireland was the major exception to this opposition. He had sensed the hopelessness of resistance and had decided to seek advantage by being the first to welcome the establishment of an apostolic delegation in Washington. He was confident that Satolli could be won to the liberal cause. Ireland's confidence was buttressed by the favor he had enjoyed at Rome during a visit of the preceding year, and by Leo XIII's apparent sympathy with progressive views. Furthermore, Denis J. O'Connell (1849–1927), rector of the American College in Rome and a close collaborator of the liberal triumvirate, had been assured that Satolli would restore unity by driving Corrigan "to the wall." [28] Ireland therefore was far from dismayed when Satolli announced on January 14, 1893, that he had received a papal commission appointing him as apostolic delegate in the United States.

For a time Ireland's hopes seemed to be confirmed. Satolli's early

[28] Cross, *Emergence of Liberal Catholicism,* 180. But McAvoy presents evidence that Leo did not really favor either faction. See *Great Crisis in American Catholic History,* 89–90.

decisions were generally in harmony with the views of the liberals. The first indication that their fortunes were to suffer reverse came in 1895 when Leo XIII issued the encyclical letter *Longinqua Oceani* to the American church. After praising the notable accomplishments of American Catholics and noting the absence of any hostile legislation in the United States, Leo added the disturbing comment that it "would be very erroneous to draw the conclusion that in America is to be sought the type of the most desirable status of the Church." Indeed, the church in America "would bring forth more abundant fruits if, in addition to liberty, she enjoyed the favor of the laws and the patronage of the public authority." Ireland was so upset by this reprimand that he canceled a previous agreement to write an explanatory article on the anticipated encyclical for the *North American Review*. The encyclical was followed by a series of further blows. A papal warning later in 1895 against taking part in "promiscuous assemblies" was obviously directed against the liberals' enthusiasm for parliaments of religion. But the most shocking rebukes were the forced resignation in 1895 of Denis O'Connell as rector of the American College in Rome and the equally involuntary resignation in 1896 of Keane as rector of Catholic University. When news of Keane's dismissal reached Bishop McQuaid of Rochester, he wrote jubilantly to Corrigan:

> The failure of the University is known at last. . . . What collapses on every side! Gibbons, Ireland, and Keane!!! They were the cock of the walk for a while, and dictated to the country, and thought to run our dioceses for us.[29]

Several things had combined to change the attitude of Rome toward the liberal triumvirate. First, the appointment of Satolli had given the papal court its own independent source of information concerning American affairs, and his recommendations increasingly favored the conservatives. After initially relying on the advice of the liberal prelates, Satolli had been won to the views of their opponents through the influence of Joseph Schroeder, one of the few stanchly conservative professors at Catholic University. Second, Leo XIII himself had taken a conservative turn, having become disappointed by the failure of his liberal tactic to win support for the restoration of the temporal power of the papacy. Third, the

[29] Maynard, *Story of American Catholicism,* 518–19.

central issues of the dispute in America had been carried to Europe where they accentuated existing unrest and dissension. Ireland had toured France in 1892 calling upon the French to emulate the Americans, Keane had spoken in similar vein at Brussels in 1894, Gibbons had been equally eloquent at Rome some years earlier, and many of the speeches and writings of the Americanizers had been translated and circulated in Europe. The conservatives were no less active, with William Tappert reporting in Cologne that the American liberals had surrendered to rationalism, and Joseph Schroeder telling another German audience that they were attacking the universality of the church and undermining the authority of the papacy. The net result of this dual incursion was to win some support for the liberals but also to arouse an even more powerful opposition. Fourth, a papal rebuke of McQuaid for an intemperate attack upon Ireland had given McQuaid an opportunity to make a detailed reply and to state fully the conservative concern. He warned the Pope of a "false liberalism" in America "that, if not checked in time, will bring disaster on the Church," and it may have been this communication that tipped the scales against the progressive prelates.[30]

The liberal triumvirate refused to be daunted by its several defeats and immediately launched a counteroffensive. This in turn provoked a detailed indictment of their views in an article in the February, 1897, issue of the *American Ecclesiastical Review*. The liberals were accused of "an excessive 'flaunting' of American patriotism at the expense of Catholic loyalties; an undue reliance upon scholarship as a source of truth, coupled with a disregard for doctrinal uniformity; extreme libertarianism within the Church to the detriment of sound hierarchical principles; and a muting of Catholic truths in order to attract converts from Protestantism."[31] The article went on to declare that the church could be saved from this dangerous "American religious liberalism" only by the direct and forthright intervention of Rome. The sole liberal victory was Schroeder's forced departure from Catholic University at the beginning of 1898, but the price of this small triumph was to strengthen the demand for a formal condemnation of "Americanism." Meanwhile the "jingoism" of the American press in the months preceding the declaration of war against Spain heightened and consolidated European opposition. It gave substance to the

[30] McAvoy, *The Great Crisis in American Catholic History*, 124-25.
[31] Cross, *Emergence of Liberal Catholicism*, 198.

insistence of the Catholic conservatives that all forms of expansionism by the barbarous Americans were aimed at the destruction of the civilization of Christian Europe.

On January 22, 1899, Leo XIII issued a condemnation of what had become known as "Americanism" in the letter *Testem Benevolentiae* which he addressed to Cardinal Gibbons.[32] Although the purpose of the condemnation was "to put an end to certain contentions" which had "arisen lately" among American Catholics, the pretext for the letter was the controversy aroused by the publication in 1897 of an abridged French translation of Walter Elliott's *Life of Father Hecker* (1891).[33] Ireland was informed by Cardinal Rampolla, the papal secretary of state, that centering attention on the Hecker biography was designed to ease the embarrassment and humiliation of submitting to the papal directive. "The words of the letter," Ireland was told, would "allow us to say that the things condemned were never said or written in America" but "were set afloat in France" as a result of the translation and interpretation of the Hecker biography in a foreign language. He was further told that he should do his best "to spread this view." This was "small comfort," wrote Ireland, "but we must make the most of it." And then he added: "In my letter to the Pope, I accepted the letter, swore against all the opinions condemned in it, which I said had never been heard of in America, and declared it an insult to America to have covered such extravagances with the name of Americanism."[34]

Ireland was joined by Gibbons and Keane in coupling submission with a declaration that "Americanism" was a "phantom heresy"[35] which could only have flourished abroad. The conservatives, however, knew better. The bishops of the province of Milwaukee, incensed at the suggestion that the Pope had been "deceived by false reports" and "had beaten the air and chased after a shadow," affirmed that the condemned opinions

[32] The encyclical is reprinted in Smith, Handy, Loetscher, *American Christianity*, II, 336–40.

[33] Ireland had written a glowing introduction for the French translation, Keane had presented a copy to Leo XIII, O'Connell had rushed to the defense of Hecker in a speech at Fribourg during the summer of 1897, and Gibbons defended Hecker in a letter published in France, as "a providential agent for the spread of the Catholic faith" and rejoiced that through the biography Europeans had an opportunity to learn more about him. McAvoy, *The Great Crisis in American Catholic History*, 173–76, 180, 182–83, 200.

[34] For Ireland's letter from Rome, dated February 24, 1899, see *ibid.*, 281.

[35] The term was coined by Felix Klein, the leader of the Americanizing party in France. The fourth volume of his autobiography, *Americanism: A Phantom Heresy*, was published in an English translation in 1951.

had "most assuredly and evidently been proclaimed among us orally and in writing." McQuaid publicly denounced those who said the heresy did not exist, and Corrigan rejoiced that "the monster" had been "struck down dead" by the timely intervention of the Holy See.[36] It was obvious, of course, that Leo XIII had the United States in mind as the seat of the infection. He addressed the letter of condemnation to Gibbons and not to the primate of France, and directed that it be sent to other members of the American hierarchy. Furthermore, Keane was privately but specifically instructed, when appointed archbishop of Dubuque, to heed the warnings contained in the letter to Gibbons. And Ireland was placed under leash and died without his coveted cardinal's hat.

Roman Catholics in America, of necessity, had little time for creative theological reflection. Most of the priests and bishops were forced to be "brick and mortar" men rather than theologians. Their major preoccupation was building new churches and institutions to minister to the tremendous influx of Catholics from abroad. Thus the effect of the condemnation of "Americanism" was only to accentuate the generally conservative temper of American Catholicism. Whatever bold experimentation there had been now gave way to timidity. Discussion and debate within the church largely ceased, and any innovation tended to be viewed with suspicion. The papal condemnation of "Modernism"[37] in 1907 caused scarcely a ripple among American Catholics, although it did contribute further to the theological silence which was to characterize the Catholic Church in the United States for the next few decades.

Other immigrant faiths and accessions

While Roman Catholicism accounted for the largest number of the religiously affiliated among the new Americans, there were significant accessions to other churches and several additional faiths were introduced for the first time. Buddhism, for example, made its appearance among the Chinese and Japanese immigrants on the West coast, and a Young Men's Buddhist Association was founded in 1898. The annexation of Hawaii, also in 1898, gave added strength to the Buddhist community in the United States.

[36] McAvoy, *The Great Crisis in American Catholic History*, 293, 296, 329.
[37] Reprinted in Smith, Handy, Loetscher, *American Christianity*, II, 340–45.

LUTHERAN ACCESSIONS. Of the Protestant groups, the Lutherans benefited most from the growing immigrant tide. By 1910 the Lutherans had become the third largest Protestant denominational grouping, being exceeded in number only by the Methodists and the Baptists. From fewer than 500,000 confirmed members in 1870, they had increased to more than 2,225,000 communicants in 1910. During this period three million Germans had entered the country, with perhaps nearly two-thirds of them being of Protestant background; and during these same years one and three-quarters million Scandinavians had arrived, almost all of whom were Lutheran by heritage and tradition. While many of these new Americans were intensely anticlerical and served to swell the ranks of the unchurched, others among them were deeply pious and zealously orthodox.

So far as influence in the general religious life of the nation was concerned, the Lutheran segment of American church life remained something of a sleeping giant until after World War I. There were several obvious reasons for this. First, apart from some of the cities of the Middle West, the overwhelming proportion of Lutherans were located in largely self-contained and self-sufficient rural communities. Second, most of them were further isolated by language barriers. Third, their energies were almost wholly absorbed by the taxing demands of the attempt to keep abreast of the multiplying population from their homelands. Fourth, they had no organizational unity, being badly divided by national origin, place and time of settlement, and doctrinal differences. And throughout the period prior to World War I, they kept splintering apart, regrouping, and then splintering again. Among the German Lutherans, the major bodies were the General Synod, the General Council, the United Synod in the South, the Missouri Synod, and the Joint Synod of Ohio. The Scandinavians were represented by the Swedish Augustana Synod, the United Norwegian Lutheran Church, the Norwegian and Hauge synods, the Danish Lutheran Church, the United Danish Lutheran Church, and both Finnish and Icelandic churches. By 1900 there were twenty-four different Lutheran groups, with the family tree of most of them so complicated by constant reshuffling that it was difficult to chart even their individual histories.

OTHER PROTESTANT ACCESSIONS. The older German Reformed (Reformed Church in the United States) and Dutch Reformed (Reformed Church in America) churches both profited by the arrival of recruits from abroad. The Christian Reformed Church, though small, gained what strength it had from renewed Dutch immigration, and in 1904 Hungarian Reformed immigrants formed a church of their own. More significant statistically was the growth of the Evangelical Synod,[38] the American counterpart of the Prussian Union of 1817 (the Evangelical United Church of Prussia) which had brought both Lutherans and Reformed together in a single church. Although the Evangelical Synod had roots which antedated the Civil War, the scattered groups of "unionizing" Germans, whose major centers of strength were in the Midwest, were not fully organized as a united body until 1877. The number of Mennonites also multiplied as a result of successive infusions from Switzerland, Prussia, and Russia. But they remained small and divided, with a membership of 54,000 in 1910 distributed among eleven different Mennonite groups.

JUDAISM AND EASTERN ORTHODOXY. Immigration from eastern Europe, which mounted to a peak during the two decades that bridged the turn of the century, introduced the ancient churches of the East to the American scene and brought to Judaism the large-scale accessions which made it a major religious community in the United States.

Between 1880 and 1900 more than a half million Jews entered the country, fleeing the anti-Semitic pressures being directed against them in Russia, Poland, Austria-Hungary, and Romania. During the next decade and a half more than a million arrived. These were added to an estimated Jewish community of 250,000 in 1880. The figures, however, are somewhat deceptive, for only a small proportion initially became affiliated with a synagogue. And those who did become affiliated were sharply divided, some adhering to orthodox rabbis and others embracing the tenets of Reform Judaism.

The Eastern Orthodox Christians had a long history, antedating the gradual separation within the Roman Empire of the East from the West, the Greek from the Latin, the Byzantine from the Roman. The estrangement of eastern from western Christianity began in the sixth century, and the final breach occurred in 1054 when Rome and the ancient patriarchates of the East found it no longer possible to gloss over the divisive

---

[38] The Evangelical Synod should not be confused with the Methodist-oriented Evangelical Association which later became the Evangelical Church and then joined with the United Brethren in 1946 to form the Evangelical United Brethren Church. The Evangelical Synod united with the Reformed Church in the United States in 1934 to form the Evangelical and Reformed Church, which in turn united with the Congregational-Christian churches in 1957.

issue of Roman primacy. Of the Eastern Christians, the Russian Orthodox have chronological priority in the United States by virtue of the purchase of Alaska in 1867. Apart from this former Russian territory, the Eastern Orthodox churches became statistically significant in America only in the twentieth century. By 1916 the Russian Orthodox and the Greek Orthodox churches each had a constituency of about 100,000 people. Although the Albanian, Bulgarian, Romanian, Serbian, Syrian, and Ukrainian Orthodox churches all had their beginnings in the United States prior to World War I, all of them were subordinated to the jurisdiction of the Russian church at that time.

Since Judaism and Eastern Orthodoxy both reached their full maturity in America after 1920 and since the course of their later development is intimately related to the problems raised and the issues faced in earlier years, a subsequent chapter provides a more meaningful context for a discussion of their initial growth (Chap. XIII).

Difficult as were the growing pains experienced by the churches of the new Americans, the churches of the older Americans had problems of their own during these years. It was a time, as Arthur M. Schlesinger, Sr., pointed out, when the path of these churches was "beset with pitfalls and perils," being confronted simultaneously with "two great challenges"—the one to their "system of thought," the other to their "social program." [39] The first focuses attention on the new intellectual climate of the post-Civil War period, and the second on the new urban and industrial environment. The response to this dual challenge is the concern of the next two chapters.

[39] Schlesinger's essay, "A Critical Period in American Protestantism, 1875–1900," is printed in the *Massachussetts Historical Society Proceedings*, LXIV (1930–32), 523–48.

XI

The New Intellectual Climate

During the post-Appomattox years when most of the Protestant churches were preoccupied with problems related to Reconstruction in the South and missionary expansion in the West and were devoting their energies to revival campaigns and Sunday school work, crucial theological issues were being raised by radical changes in the intellectual climate —issues that could not long be ignored.

Within a decade after the Civil War practically every important American scientist had been converted to Darwin's theory of biological evolution, and Herbert Spencer's "social Darwinism" was equally influential.[1] Indeed, as early as 1872, the *Atlantic Monthly* was able to report that within the scientific community "natural selection" had "quite won the day in Germany and England, and very nearly won it in America." This new intellectual current penetrated the public consciousness with astonishing rapidity. "Ten or fifteen years ago," Whitelaw Reid declared in an address at Dartmouth in 1873, "the staple subject here for reading

[1] See Richard Hofstadter, *Social Darwinism in American Thought* (N.Y., 1959).

and talk, outside study hours, was English poetry and fiction. Now it is English science. Herbert Spencer, John Stuart Mill, Huxley, Darwin, Tyndall, have usurped the places of Tennyson and Browning, and Matthew Arnold and Dickens." And the discussion was not limited to college students. Equally avid interest in the new scientific theories was displayed by the general public, if the amount of space devoted by the popular periodicals and newspapers to academic lectures and debates is an accurate index of what was being read and discussed.

The new biblical studies were another feature of the postwar intellectual climate. These studies, stemming mainly from the German universities but partly the work of British textual critics, utilized the techniques of "scientific history" to exhibit the Bible as a varied compilation of poetry, prophecy, history, and folklore that had been assembled over a period of a thousand years. The extent of the popular interest that was awakened by these studies is indicated by the reception that was given in 1881 to the English Revised Version of the New Testament which incorporated the results of scholarly analysis of the text. The *Chicago Times* and the *Chicago Tribune* both printed the entire text, while 200,000 copies of the revised New Testament were sold in New York within less than a week.

Furthermore, the study of comparative religion was coming to the fore as an academic discipline, and it soon became apparent that the non-Christian religions also were of fascinating interest to the reading public. James Freeman Clarke's sympathetic appraisal of *Ten Great Religions* went through twenty-one editions after it was published in 1871.[2] Toward the end of the century when a World's Parliament of Religions was held in connection with the Columbian Exposition of 1892–93 more than 150,000 people attended its sessions.

Finally, before the century was out the burgeoning "sciences" of psychology and sociology had made their appearance as forces to be reckoned with in the intellectual life of the nation. Almost immediately attention was centered on subjecting religious phenomena to psychological and sociological analysis. E. D. Starbuck (1866–1947) was one of the pioneers, and his *Psychology of Religion* (1899) was something of an overnight sensation. When William James (1842–1910) published his Gifford Lectures, *The Varieties of Religious Experience* (1902), the

[2] Clarke's views were initially expressed in an article published in 1857, a portion of which is reprinted in Smith, Handy, Loetscher, *American Christianity*, II, 160–64.

interest was so great that within a dozen years it had been reprinted twenty-one times. Ten years later J. H. Leuba (1868–1946) pointed up in provocative fashion the disturbing implications of the psychological approach in his *Psychological Study of Religion* (1912). In the meantime, William Graham Sumner (1840–1910) had published *Folkways* (1906), a sociological study of human behavior which stressed the socially conditioned character of religion and rejected any notion of absolute or eternal truth.

Each of these several currents of thought constituted a threat to accepted understandings of the Christian faith. The psychological and sociological studies tended to reduce religion to a social phenomenon. The accounts of other religions raised questions with regard to the uniqueness of the Christian faith. Both Darwinian biology and the new biblical studies seemed to undermine the authority of the Bible. How could one reconcile Darwinism with the Genesis accounts of creation? And how could one adjust the doctrine of biblical inspiration to take account of the errors and contradictions in the biblical text that were being noted by the scholars? What was one to make of a composite authorship of the books of Moses, with fragments of the text being assigned to different sources in widely separated times? What happened to the prophetic character of the book of Isaiah if parts of it were written by a later "second Isaiah" who was reporting events rather than predicting them? These were unsettling questions and their disturbing implications were made plain to the thousands who listened to Robert G. Ingersoll (1833–99), "the notorious infidel," as he ranged back and forth across the land questioning the basic tenets of Christian belief.[3] Other thousands read his lectures—*The Gods* (1872), *Some Mistakes of Moses* (1879), *Why I Am an Agnostic* (1896)—in printed form. On a less popular level, J. W. Draper sought to demonstrate the incompatibility of science and religion in his *History of the Conflict between Religion and Science* (1874), a task which was also undertaken by Andrew D. White in his *History of the Warfare of Science with Theology* (1896).

The pattern of response among Protestants, Roman Catholics, and Jews to the challenge of scientific modes of thought was remarkably

---

[3] Ingersoll, the son of a Congregational minister, was a great orator who had electrified the Republican convention of 1876 with his famous "plumed knight" speech nominating James G. Blaine for the presidency.

similar. There were some who resisted the new intellectual currents and rejected any modification of inherited theological formulations. There were others who came to believe that the traditional forms of faith were no longer relevant and must be discarded and replaced with idioms and practices that were forthright expressions of a scientific world-view. A third group occupied an intermediate position between the two extremes, seeking to effect adjustments that would do justice both to the essential elements of the inherited faith and to the newer scientific patterns of thought. The radical tendency never loomed large on the American scene, and the moderate "liberal" tendencies in Roman Catholicism were arrested by papal intervention. But both Reformed Judaism (see chap. XIII) and liberal Protestant evangelicalism were destined to flourish.

Protestant liberalism

The mood of most Protestant churchmen at the close of the Civil War was reflected in the proceedings of the Congregational National Council which met in Boston on July 14, 1865. The assembly listened "with profound attention for two full hours" to an opening sermon on the text: "Ask for old paths" (Jer. 6:16), and then proceeded to adopt a Declaration of Faith to serve as a bulwark "for the defense of the Word of God now assailed by multiform and dangerous errors." This was not an entirely ritualistic performance, for the Council was aware of new and urgent problems. But many of the errors it had in mind were those of an earlier generation which the "old paths" had been designed to skirt, and it soon became obvious that signposts pointing to "old paths" were to have only limited utility in helping Christians avoid the perils and pitfalls of the theologically unmapped terrain of the postwar years.

Henry Ward Beecher (1813–87), pastor of Plymouth Congregational Church in Brooklyn from 1847 to 1887 and easily the most prominent preacher of his time, was one of the earliest to recognize that the mere repetition of ancient doctrines would no longer do. In 1872, as the first Lyman Beecher lecturer at Yale, he warned the students of the Divinity School of the danger they faced of being left behind by "the intelligent part of society."

> There is being now applied among scientists a greater amount of real, searching, discriminating thought . . . than ever has been expended . . . in the whole history of the world put together. . . .

> If ministers do not make their theological systems conform to the facts as they are; if they do not recognize what men are studying, the time will not be far distant when the pulpit will be like a voice crying in the wilderness. And it will not be "Prepare the way of the Lord," either. . . .
>
> The providence of God is rolling forward in a spirit of investigation that Christian ministers must meet and join.

The one thing ministers cannot afford, insisted Beecher, is to become "apostles of the dead past" by letting "the development of truth run ahead of them." [4]

THE FUNDAMENTAL ISSUE OF BIBLICAL AUTHORITY. The most heated initial debate centered on the notion of biological evolution, for it was a dramatic issue and, by its apparent contradiction of the Bible, Darwin's theory seemed to strike at the very root of a biblically grounded faith. Charles Hodge, the towering theological oracle of Princeton Theological Seminary, declared in 1874 that "a more absolutely incredible theory was never propounded for acceptance among men," and Mark Hopkins, the equally distinguished president of Williams College, denounced the whole concept as "essentially atheistic." A different verdict, however, had been pronounced three years earlier by Hodge's neighbor James McCosh (1811–94), president of Princeton University. "I am inclined to think," he said, "that the theory contains a large body of important truths." If one distinguished the "major assumptions" of the biblical accounts of creation from their literary form, McCosh saw no reason why creation as described in Genesis should be regarded as inconsistent with developmental theories. Holding fast to the traditional doctrine of design in nature, he interpreted "natural selection" as the product of "supernatural design." [5]

A similar resolution of the problem was proposed by John Fiske (1842–1901). In his *Outline of Cosmic Philosophy* (1874) and subsequent volumes, he transmuted the struggle for survival into a struggle for the lives of others. Infusing the whole process with divine purpose, Fiske coined the sentence—"Evolution is God's way of doing things"—which was later popularized as a slogan by Lyman Abbott (1835–1922). In the meantime, Henry Ward Beecher had given further impetus to this type of

---

[4] *Yale Lectures on Preaching*, 3 vols. (N.Y., 1872–74), I, 87–89.
[5] See Charles Hodge, *What Is Darwinism?* (N.Y., 1874), and James McCosh, *Christianity and Positivism* (N.Y., 1871).

adjustment by announcing in the *Christian Union* (Aug. 2, 1883) that he was "a cordial Christian evolutionist." [6] But perhaps the most reassuring evidence to many faithful Christians that evolutionary views could be assimilated without harm to the Christian faith was provided by Henry Drummond (1851–97), the author of *Natural Law in the Spiritual World* (1883). This gifted young Scottish theologian was an intimate friend of Dwight L. Moody, and when Drummond visited the United States in 1887 Moody enlisted his aid both at Northfield and in his revival meetings.

The theory of biological evolution was actually the least serious of the intellectual problems which the churches were being compelled to face. While it could be handled by construing the first chapter of Genesis allegorically or by contending that the Bible was never intended to be a scientific encyclopedia, other problems could not be side-stepped so easily. This was notably true of the issues that were being raised by the "scientific" study of the Bible, for the new biblical studies were making it increasingly evident that any attempt to justify even the "major assumptions" of the Christian faith by an appeal to the authority of Scripture was fraught with difficulty. Biblical scholars were demonstrating that at many points of Christian doctrine conflicting evidence could be adduced from within the biblical text itself.

In 1867 these difficulties were pointed out by Thomas F. Curtis (1816–72) of Bucknell University in *The Human Element in the Inspiration of the Sacred Scriptures,* and the measure of the confusion he evoked is indicated by the reaction to his book of a fellow Baptist, Henry G. Weston (1820–1909), who was soon to become president of Crozer Theological Seminary. "I am all at sea," wrote Weston, "except so far as a dogged belief in inspiration goes, without being able to define what 'inspiration' is or what its metes and bounds are." Small wonder that Weston was determined to hold fast to a belief in inspiration, for this had been the major line of defense of the whole dogmatic structure.[7]

The central issue was the authority of the Bible. Few great religions have been so dependent as Christianity upon a sacred book. Preaching

---

[6] For Beecher and Abbott, see Beecher's *Evolution and Religion* (N.Y., 1885), and Abbott's *The Theology of an Evolutionist* (N.Y., 1897).

[7] There is no satisfactory study of the impact in America of the new biblical studies analogous to Willis B. Glover's study of the parallel situation in England, *Evangelical Nonconformity and Higher Criticism in the Nineteenth Century* (London, 1955). N. H. Maring, "Baptists and Changing Views of the Bible, 1865–1918," *Foundations,* I (July, 1958), 52–78, (Oct., 1958), 30–61, helps remedy this deficiency to some extent.

elucidated its texts. Prayer claimed its promises. And theology and conduct alike were grounded on its teachings. While both Protestants and Roman Catholics had long regarded the Bible as the inspired and inerrant Word of God, the Roman Catholic Church had found it necessary at the Council of Trent (1545–63) to supplement biblical teaching with that of "tradition," and at the first Vatican Council (1870) to affirm papal infallibility in the interpretation of Scripture and tradition. Protestants, on the other hand, had clung to the sole authority of Scripture, which in the first half of the nineteenth century was almost universally understood in terms of an inspired and infallible text. Since they had no recourse to any supplementary authority, the questioning of biblical inspiration was peculiarly threatening to Protestants. Once this point was surrendered, a thoroughgoing reconsideration of the whole basis of the Christian faith was required. Ultimately Protestants were to work out different ways of understanding biblical authority, but first many of them were to seek in "evangelical liberalism" and in "scientific modernism" other sources of authority.

EVANGELICAL LIBERALISM. The striking feature of the liberal movement in Protestantism which began to take shape during the 1870's was its conservative intent. The leaders of the movement were evangelicals, standing firmly within the church, cherishing their Christian experience, and uncompromising in their loyalty to Christ. They had little in common with the earlier rationalistic liberalism which had become dominant in Unitarianism. The central concern of the evangelical liberals was quite explicitly apologetic. They wished to preserve the truth of the gospel as it spoke to the hearts of men. In the face of what many feared might be fatal assaults on the Christian faith, they sought to restate the essential doctrines of evangelical Christianity in terms that would be both intelligible and convincing and thus to establish them on a more secure foundation.

Henry Ward Beecher was the most conspicuous of the early liberal leaders and it would be easy to overestimate his importance.[8] The influence he exerted was great, but he was no theologian. At most he was a

[8] F. H. Foster made this mistake in *The Modern Movement in American Theology* (N.Y., 1939), devoting a whole chapter to "The School of Henry Ward Beecher," J. W. Buckham also asserted that, next to Horace Bushnell, Beecher was "the greatest liberator of American theological thought." *Progressive Religious Thought in America* (N.Y., 1919), 32.

popularizer—a "weather cock" some called him. The real theological task of adjusting the inherited formulations of the faith to the new "scientific" climate of opinion was the work of other men.

While isolated individuals in various parts of the country helped to fashion what came to be called the "New Theology" and "Progressive Orthodoxy," the most important contribution was made by a notable group of pastors in prominent New England pulpits, all of whom had been deeply influenced by Horace Bushnell. In neighboring churches on the New Haven green, Theodore T. Munger (1830–1910) and Newman Smyth (1843–1925) gave new luster to a tradition of distinguished theological preaching that had been exemplified in these same pulpits by Jonathan Edwards, Jr., and Nathaniel W. Taylor. Munger, at the United (Congregational) Church was the author of *The Freedom of Faith* (1883) which the *New York Times* called the "most forcible and positive expression" of the new theology to appear in this country; [9] while Newman Smyth, at the Center (Congregational) Church, had argued the same case in three pioneering volumes: *The Religious Feeling* (1877), *Old Faiths in New Light* (1878), and *The Orthodox Theology of Today* (1881). In Boston, Phillips Brooks (1835–93) at Trinity (Episcopal) Church and George A. Gordon (1853–1929) at Old South (Congregational) Church were making Copley Square a center of the new theological outlook. Washington Gladden (1836–1918) was less philosophically inclined than Munger, Smyth, and Gordon, but he was equally creative in his own way and was the most effective propagandist of the new point of view. As early as 1873 he had written for the *Independent* (July 3, 1873) an editorial entitled "Immoral Theology," which exhibited the journalistic flair that won such a widespread circulation for his subsequent books dealing with current theological issues: *Burning Questions* (1886), *Who Wrote the Bible?* (1891), *Ruling Ideas of the Present Age* (1895), *Seven Puzzling Bible Books* (1897), and *How Much Is Left of the Old Doctrines?* (1899). By the time these books were published, Gladden had left New England, having resigned his Springfield pulpit in 1882 to accept a call to the First Congregational Church of Columbus, Ohio. All these young men were responding in the immediate post-Civil War years to the practical necessity of relating the Christian faith from week to week to questions that were uppermost in the minds of alert and inquiring congregations.

[9] C. H. Hopkins, *The Rise of the Social Gospel in American Protestantism* (New Haven, 1940), 61.

Meanwhile in the theological seminaries a less conspicuous intellectual ferment was beginning to take place, the consequence in part of the stimulus provided by an increasing number of the younger members of the faculties who had spent a period of study abroad where they had imbibed the relatively advanced theological thinking of the German universities. The most dramatic shift occurred at Andover Theological Seminary, which had been established in 1808 as a counter to the Unitarian tendencies of Harvard and had been shackled with a creed designed to prevent any deviation from the orthodoxy of its founders. A new type of thinking began to be introduced at Andover in the 1860's, but no open break occurred until 1880 when William J. Tucker (1839–1926) qualified his subscription to the creed with the comment:

> The creed which I am about to read and to which I subscribe, I fully accept as setting forth the truth against the errors which it was designed to meet. No confession so elaborate and with such intent may assume to be the final expression of the truth or an expression equally fitted in language or tone to all times.[10]

When Edwards A. Park (1808–1900), the last great champion of New England orthodoxy, retired the following year, the liberals were left in complete control. Three years later the faculty began the publication of the *Andover Review* to elucidate the principles of their "progressive orthodoxy."

While this developing liberal sentiment was indebted to insights supplied from abroad by Friedrich Schleiermacher (1768–1834) and Albrecht Ritschl (1822–89), it was an indigenous movement which owed much more to categories and understandings provided by Horace Bushnell. In many ways Bushnell was the key figure who eased the transition for evangelical Christians from the old to the new theology. As early as 1844 Bushnell had provided the basis for an adjustment to evolutionary views when he asserted that "growth not conquest" was "the true method of Christian progress." [11] Through his analysis of the use and limitations of language, he also offered a way of escape from bondage to the verbal form in which doctrinal statements had been cast. But the real key to the

[10] See D. D. Williams, *The Andover Liberals* (N.Y., 1941), 28.
[11] See Buckham, *Progressive Religious Thought*, 11. Bushnell, of course, had found much in Schleiermacher, and even more in F. D. Maurice (1805–72), that was suggestive. For some of the points at which he diverged from the German theologian, see Fred Kirshenmann, "Horace Bushnell: Orthodox or Sabellian?" *Church History*, XXXIII (1964), 49–59.

influence Bushnell exerted upon his younger contemporaries was his success in fashioning a definitely Christocentric theology that was based upon Christian experience rather than upon any external dogmatic authority. Thus the believer was no longer under compulsion to find his security in biblical proof texts. He could accept the conclusions of the biblical scholars with relative equanimity and appropriate the results of other scientific investigations without great difficulty because his faith was validated by the inward testimony of the heart. Bushnell had discovered this path of escape from his "arrant doubts" at the very beginning of his ministry. What shall I do with the doctrine of the Trinity, he had asked, when "logic shatters it all to pieces and I am all at the four winds"?

> I am glad that I have a heart as well as a head. My heart wants the Father; my heart wants the Son; my heart wants the Holy Ghost—the one just as much as the other. My heart says the Bible has a Trinity for me, and I mean to hold by my heart.[12]

Secure in the conviction that "the heart has its reasons, which reason does not know," Bushnell found a freedom denied to those who felt compelled to meet a rationalistic assault with a purely rationalistic defense.

In keeping with their apologetic concern, the starting point of all theology for the heirs of Bushnell in pulpit and classroom was to be found in Christ. Christ stood at the heart of the religious experience they were seeking to defend. Christ alone, declared Egbert C. Smyth of Andover Theological Seminary, "fulfills the aspirations and harmonizes the discords in man's religious history."

> The history of religion leads on and up to him, and he possesses all the resources requisite for its greatest possible future growth. He is the Alpha and Omega; the Absolute, revealed; the Infinite, personally disclosed; the eternal Power that makes for righteousness, realized in the Righteous One. . . . A theology which is not Christocentric is like a Ptolomaic astronomy; it is out of true relation to the earth and heavens, to God and the universe.[13]

Thus, while there was much that earlier generations had affirmed that could be surrendered as nonessential and much that had to be adjusted

---

[12] *Life and Letters of Horace Bushnell*, ed. M. B. Cheney (N.Y., 1880), 56; quoted by Mead, *Lively Experiment*, 136.

[13] *Progressive Orthodoxy*, by the Editors of the *Andover Review* (Boston, 1886), 35–36.

and accommodated to new knowledge, the person and work of Christ as the clue to the nature of God, the worth of human personality, and the meaning of life was indispensable. His life and teachings constituted "the final principle" of "interpretation," the standard by which all else must be judged. The goal of the New Theology, as William Adams Brown (1865–1943) was to point out in 1898 in his inaugural address as professor of systematic theology in Union Theological Seminary, was no more than "the old cry, 'Back to Christ.' Let no theology call itself Christian which has not its center and source in him."

Although these evangelical liberals clung tenaciously to the Bible and repaired to it for consolation and inspiration, they viewed it as a document which recorded the historical experience out of which the Christian faith had emerged, a vivid personal record of suffering and travail which culminated in the disclosure in Christ of true and perfect communion with God. It was a record not of dogma but of experience, an experience that was to be reproduced "in our own times and in our own souls." While it told them what they knew of Christ, there was no need to seek "scientific arguments for Christian truth," for their own experience of Christ was self-authenticating. "The foundation of spiritual faith is neither in the church nor in the Bible, but in the spiritual consciousness of man." [14] The doctrines which "form the subject matter of theology," declared Brown in his inaugural address, are not "dogmas to be received on authority"; they are "living convictions, born of experience, and maintaining themselves in spite of all opposition because of the response which they wake in the hearts and consciences of men."

Few of these men exhibited any great metaphysical interest, but those who did found in idealistic philosophy a way of theologizing that did not depend upon complicated processes of biblical criticism. Some, like George A. Gordon, appropriated the "monistic" form of idealism of which Josiah Royce (1855–1916) was the most conspicuous American representative. Others, mostly fellow Methodists, adopted the "personalism" of Borden P. Bowne (1847–1910) of Boston University. The greater number, however, were content to give only passing attention to philosophical issues and to structure their theological thinking within more familiar biblical categories. Typical in this respect was William Newton Clarke (1840–1912), the Baptist theologian at Colgate Theological Semi-

[14] See Lyman Abbott, *Reminiscences* (Boston, 1915), 451, 461–62.

nary, whose *Outline of Christian Theology* (1898) was so widely used that it has been called "virtually the Dogmatik" of evangelical liberalism.[15]

The great advantage of this New Theology of evangelical liberalism was that it enabled its proponents both to maintain what to them was the heart of their inherited faith and at the same time to come to terms with the whole intellectual temper of the modern world. The stress upon self-authenticating religious experience permitted them to bridge the gap between the natural and the supernatural, and enabled them to give due recognition to the claims of science and of the scientific method. The acceptance of the idea of development made it possible to view the Bible in a way that was congenial to both their religious and their cultural orientation, allowed them to share to varying degrees the growing confidence in man and his future, and fostered an openminded attitude toward differing opinions and new modes of thought.

SCIENTIFIC MODERNISM. While evangelical liberalism continued to be the dominant liberal current in American Protestantism, a more radical approach to the issue of the relation of science to religion began to emerge in the first years of the twentieth century. Those who in retrospect have been called "scientific modernists"[16] stood in marked contrast to the conservative intent of the evangelical liberals, for they viewed as a lost cause the endeavor of the evangelical liberals to maintain continuity with the inherited faith by abstracting religion from the realm of scientific verification. These men recognized that the sanctuary of the heart which the evangelical liberals sought to preserve inviolate had been invaded by the scientists. "Science," E. D. Starbuck had proclaimed in 1899, "has conquered one field after another, until now it is entering the most

[15] The phrase is that of Sydney E. Ahlstrom, "Theology in America," *The Shaping of American Religion*, ed. Smith and Jamison, 292. G. B. Smith described it as "perhaps the most influential book of its kind in American religious thinking." *Current Christian Thinking* (Chicago, 1928), 83. W. A. Brown's *Christian Theology in Outline* (1906) was largely based upon Clarke's text. Kenneth Cauthen, *The Impact of American Religious Liberalism* (N.Y., 1962), 42–43. Insight into the changing attitude toward the Bible can best be gained from William Newton Clarke's *Sixty Years with the Bible* (N.Y., 1909), a moving autobiographical account of the development of his own views through six decades.

[16] The term was coined by Sidney E. Mead. While exact lines of demarcation between the evangelical liberals and the scientific modernists are difficult to draw, there was a clear difference of intention and emphasis. The liberals were committed first and foremost to the Christian tradition and from that vantage point attempted to effect any necessary adjustments. The scientific modernists took their stand with the presuppositions of science, and then sought to reclaim what they could of the traditional faith. For them the scientific method was accepted as the starting point for all human investigation. Complicating the picture is the fact that evangelical liberals frequently called themselves "modernists."

274

complex, the most inaccessible, and of all the most sacred domain—that of religion." The scientific modernists were impressed by the way in which psychological and sociological analysis was able to explain not only religious experience, but also doctrinal concepts and ecclesiastical practice, in terms of inner personal drives and conditioning social forces. Thus they were ready to grant "to the data of religious experience the same scientific status as the data of the physical sciences," and then to fashion a religious faith "out of the materials furnished by the several sciences." [17] They did not seek a complete break with the Christian past, as is made clear in Shailer Mathews' classic definition of modernism—"the use of the methods of modern science to find, state, and use the permanent and central values of inherited orthodoxy in meeting the needs of a modern world." [18] The values of orthodoxy were not to be ignored, but "science" was the arbiter in determining what they were and how they were to be stated and used.[19] It is safe to assume, Mathews was to assert, that "scientists know more about nature and man than did the theologians who drew up the Creeds and Confessions." The whole tendency, therefore, was to become less and less concerned with a distinctively Christian witness and more and more interested in general religious affirmations based on a "scientific world-view."

Unlike liberal evangelicalism which initially was the product of the reflections of men who were pastors of churches, scientific modernism was indigenous to the theological seminaries. The great center was in Chicago where William Rainey Harper (1856-1906) and John D. Rockefeller had established their Baptist super-university in 1892, assembling for that purpose a faculty of many of the most noted scholars in America. While many pastors found comfort and reassurance and themes for sermons in the reports that filtered down to them from the psychologists and sociologists that religious beliefs integrated personality, fostered mental health, and served socially useful ends; the theological professors at Chicago, with John Dewey, Albion W. Small, and George Herbert Mead numbered among their university colleagues, were compelled to face the fundamental

[17] E. E. Aubrey, "Religious Bearings of the Modern Scientific Movement," in *Environmental Factors in Christian History*, ed. J. T. McNeill *et al.* (Chicago, 1939), 368.
[18] See the portion of Mathews' *The Faith of Modernism* which is reprinted in Smith, Handy, Loetscher, *American Christianity*, II, 238-45.
[19] A typical monograph was that of George A. Coe, "What Does Modern Psychology Permit Us to Believe in Respect to Regeneration?" *American Journal of Theology*, XII (1908), 353-68.

theological issue that was raised by the empiricism upon which these new disciplines were based.

The Chicago approach to theology (they hesitated to call it more than a theological method) was not fully elaborated until after World War I, but its basic character was clearly evident much earlier. The key figures of the Divinity School faculty, in addition to a distinguished corps of biblical scholars headed by Harper himself, were Shailer Mathews (1863–1941), George Burman Foster (1858–1918), and Gerald Birney Smith (1868–1929); while Edward Scribner Ames (1870–1958)—simultaneously professor of philosophy in the university, pastor of the University Church of the Disciples of Christ, and dean of the Disciples Divinity House—also provided strong leadership in the task of theological reconstruction. The dominant emphasis, exemplified pre-eminently by Mathews, was upon a socio-historical approach to theology which viewed all doctrinal statements as reflections of historic cultural patterns, and consequently were functional and not normative, changeable and not permanent. They were to be tested and applied "in the same way that chemists and historians reach and apply their conclusions," and they must be stated in terms that would make sense to intelligent men and women within the contemporary cultural context. "The God of the scientifically minded will assume the patterns of science." [20]

In spite of the fact that some members of the Chicago group moved to a nontheist position and others found it difficult to find anything either unique or normative in the Christian faith, the influence they exerted in the life of the churches was far from insignificant. This was partly due to the fact that for a period of thirty or forty years a very large proportion of professors in other theological seminaries received their graduate training at Chicago. Scarcely less important was the fact that most of the key figures remained stanch churchmen and played a leading role in ecclesiastical affairs. Shailer Mathews, for example, was president of the Federal Council of Churches from 1912 to 1916 and of the American (Northern) Baptist Convention in 1915. Finally, the men at Chicago exhibited at intensely practical propagandist zeal. William Rainey Harper set the pattern when he became superintendent of the Hyde Park Baptist Sunday School in order to put his theories into practice, and with the stimulus of

---

[20] *The Faith of Modernism*, as reprinted in Smith, Handy, Loetscher, *American Christianity*, II, 240–41; and Shailer Mathews, *The Growth of the Idea of God* (N.Y., 1931), 184.

Harper's interest the University of Chicago pioneered in the new "scientific" approach to religious education. One of the most effective means of penetration was a scheme of adult education known as the American Institute of Sacred Literature, through which books, pamphlets, and study courses in a steady stream were made available and were widely used in Protestant churches throughout the Middle West.

Protestant conservatism

The mounting accommodation within Protestantism to the new intellectual climate did not go unchallenged. From the beginning resistance was both vocal and widespread, but the opposition seldom grappled profoundly or creatively with the issues involved. The response was mainly limited to strong dogmatic denials grounded in a pietistic indifference to the new "scientific" studies. Charles Hodge, in an earlier debate, had set the tone of the unyielding defensive posture of the conservative elements when he declared: "We can even afford to acknowledge our incompetence to meet them in argument, or to answer their objections; and yet our faith remains unshaken and rational." [21] There was no prominent theologian to play a constructive role comparable to that of a P. T. Forsyth (1848–1921) in Britain or a Martin Kähler (1835–1912) in Germany, unless the attempt of Augustus H. Strong (1836–1921) to find a mediating position qualifies him to be ranked with his European contemporaries. Nevertheless, when the defenders of the inherited formulations of the faith chose to fight the battle on the basis of biblical inerrancy, they were astute enough to recognize that the central issue was the authority of the Scriptures even if they failed to recognize that there may have been a more tenable position than a doctrine of "inspiration" upon which to base their defense.

THE HERESY TRIALS. The Congregationalists and Baptists, with their loose form of organization, offered the freest field for the growth of liberal sentiment.[22] Neither denomination had any ready means of taking

---

[21] *Princeton Review*, XXIX (1857), 662.

[22] The Disciples offered an equally free field but among them the issue assumed a somewhat different form. The division was between those who placed primary emphasis upon the Disciples' traditional theme of the "restoration" of the primitive church and those who gave major stress to the equally traditional theme of Christian unity. Such men as Peter Ainslee and Charles Clayton Morrison gained their chief distinction as advocates of Christian unity. Herbert L. Willett, of course, made a major contribution to the field of biblical study, and Edward Scribner Ames was one of the most prominent of the "scientific modernists." By 1906 the rigidly biblistic wing of the Disciples—the "Churches of Christ" of the middle South—had gone its separate way.

action to enforce conformity to doctrinal standards. Once installed in a church, a pastor was secure as long as he retained the support of his own congregation, and most of their theological seminaries were independently organized and not subject to denominational control. Although Ezra P. Gould (1841–1900) was dismissed from Newton Theological Seminary in 1882 and Nathaniel Schmidt (1862–1939) from Colgate in 1896, all the northern Baptist seminaries were firmly in the liberal camp by the end of the century. This was also true of the Congregational seminaries, with Andover's status having been clarified in 1892 when the Supreme Court of Massachusetts sustained the trustees and voided the action of the Board of Visitors in dismissing Egbert C. Smyth from the faculty.

The Methodists had the means of closing ranks to prevent doctrinal innovation, but in the North at least they exhibited little inclination to do so. In spite of the fact that such men as Nathan Bangs (1778–1862), Daniel D. Whedon (1808–85), and Miner Raymond (1811–97) had whetted their theological scalpels and used them with great effectiveness in running debates with Calvinists, the Methodists as a result of their continuing emphasis upon the centrality of heart religion had developed no sharply defined theological position. To the extent that they held to any external tests of fellowship, their stress was upon morality rather than dogma. When charges of denying the inerrancy of Scripture were leveled in 1904 against Hinkley G. Mitchell (1846–1920) of the Boston University School of Theology and then against Borden P. Bowne, the General Conference of 1908 put a stop to any further proceedings of this type by relieving the bishops of responsibility for investigating charges of erroneous teaching in Methodist schools. While there were to be subsequent flurries of controversy among northern Methodists, the official policy of the denomination hewed closely to the line represented by John Wesley's oft-repeated dictum: "Is thy heart as my heart? Then give me thy hand." The Protestant Episcopal Church followed a similar policy of comprehension, with the trial of Algernon S. Crapsey (1847–1927) in 1906 being the only conspicuous exception. And even Crapsey probably would not have been summoned to defend his heterodox theological views had he not embarrassed his bishop by combining his doctrinal errors with radical attacks upon the existing economic order.

The Lutherans, in contrast to these other denominations, maintained an almost solidly unbroken orthodox front. The most liberal of the major Lutheran bodies—the General Synod of the Lutheran Church in the United States—tightened its discipline in 1895 and affirmed that its doctrinal basis was "the Word of God as the infallible rule of faith and practice, and the unaltered Augsburg Confession as throughout in perfect consistence with it—nothing more, nothing less." Thus the heresy trials which gained so much attention in the public press were largely confined to the reunited Presbyterian church in the North.

Among northern Presbyterians the issue was raised as early as 1874 when Francis L. Patton (1843–1932) of McCormick Theological Seminary lodged charges of heresy against David Swing (1830–94), pastor of the Fourth Presbyterian Church in Chicago. The local presbytery acquitted him, but when Patton filed notice of his intention to appeal the verdict, Swing resigned his pastorate and established an independent congregation. During the following decade several other men, including William C. McCune of Cincinnati, W. W. McLane of Steubenville, Ohio, and J. W. White of Huntington, Pennsylvania, were dismissed from the ministry on doctrinal grounds. The most celebrated trials, however, were those of Charles A. Briggs (1841–1913) and Henry Preserved Smith (1847–1927).[23]

The Briggs case was precipitated in 1891 by his inaugural address as the first occupant of the newly created chair of biblical theology in Union Theological Seminary (New York), an address in which he vigorously condemned "the dogma of verbal inspiration."[24] There were two immediate consequences. First, the Presbyterian General Assembly withheld its approval of his appointment. Second, charges of heresy were filed with the presbytery of New York. Briggs was acquitted by the presbytery, but the General Assembly set aside the verdict and suspended Briggs from the ministry. The veto of his appointment by the General Assembly was brushed aside by the Seminary as irrelevant. Two decades earlier the Seminary had granted the General Assembly the right to confirm appointments to its faculty. In this instance, however, Briggs had been a member of the faculty since 1874 and the Seminary contended that the authority it had conferred upon the General Assembly did not extend to a transfer

[23] For the context of these trials, see L. A. Loetscher, *The Broadening Church: A Study of Theological Issues in the Presbyterian Church since 1869* (Philadelphia, 1954).

[24] A portion of the address is in Smith, Handy, Loetscher, *American Christianity*, II, 275–79.

within the faculty from one chair to another. In the end, the Seminary revoked its earlier grant of authority, severed this somewhat tenuous official connection with the Presbyterian church, and retained Briggs who solved the problem of his ministerial standing by becoming an Episcopalian.

At the same time the Briggs affair was before the General Assembly, the case of Henry Preserved Smith, a professor in Lane Theological Seminary, was also being adjudicated. Smith had come to the defense of Briggs and was convicted of heresy on similar grounds in 1892 by the presbytery of Cincinnati, a verdict which was sustained by the General Assembly. This meant the end of his relationship to Lane Seminary, but Union Seminary provided him with a haven as librarian and Smith transferred his denominational affiliation to the Congregationalists. A few years later another member of the Union faculty, Arthur Cushman McGiffert (1861–1933) had charges preferred against him, and to avoid another heresy trial he quietly withdrew from the Presbyterian church and became a Congregationalist.

The heresy trials failed to halt the growing theological cleavage even among the Presbyterians. Not only did the trials bring the issues to the fore and publicize them, they awakened popular sympathy for the "persecuted." And this sympathy in turn was exploited and heightened by widely read novels such as Margaret Deland's *John Ward, Preacher,* and Mrs. Humphrey Ward's *Robert Elsmere.* Henry Van Dyke (1852–1933), minister of Brick Presbyterian Church in New York City, spoke for many laymen when he declared: "This great city wants the bread of life. Don't give it the stone of controversy instead." A church that had cast out a warmly devout Professor Briggs was reminded by Van Dyke that it had

> Something to learn and something to forget:
> Hold fast to the good, and seek the better yet:
> Press on, and prove the pilgrim-hope of youth—
> That creeds are milestones on the path to truth.

If orthodoxy was to flourish, Van Dyke insisted, it must breathe the air of freedom. "The best way to defend the Bible is in the open air and in the light of the facts." [25] His admonitions were not without effect, and after the turn of the century at least two of the Presbyterian seminaries—Auburn in

[25] Tertius Van Dyke, *Henry Van Dyke A Biography* (N.Y., 1935), 129.

upstate New York and McCormick in Chicago—were exhibiting definite liberal tendencies.

CENTERS OF CONSERVATIVE STRENGTH. The theological climate of the country varied from section to section. By the time of World War I, New England had long been the great stronghold of Protestant liberalism. New York State, with its Yankee heritage and "New School" tradition, was scarcely less liberal in its dominant theological mood. The Middle West was generally moderate, with radicals of both the "right" and the "left" exerting influence within the churches. The Pacific coast was beginning to manifest its distinctive sense of freedom in a variety of new sects and cults, but otherwise its tone was conservative. The South had witnessed a few attempts to break with orthodoxy. Alexander Winchell (1824–91) at Vanderbilt had contradicted the Genesis account of creation in 1878, thereby provoking a pointed censure by the General Conference of the southern Methodist church of those who bend "all the energies of their most exalted genius to the inculcation of theories which are calculated, if not designed, to destroy the credibility of the Holy Scriptures." [26] When Winchell refused to resign, the university abolished his position. The following year Crawford H. Toy (1836–1919) was forced to resign from the faculty of the Southern Baptist Theological Seminary at Louisville, Kentucky, for teachings which allegedly undercut the absolute authority of Scripture. And in 1886 James Woodrow (1828–1907), uncle of Woodrow Wilson and professor at Columbia Theological Seminary, was condemned and dismissed from his post by the General Assembly of the southern Presbyterian church for suggesting that the theory of evolution could be reconciled with a "not unreasonable interpretation of the Bible." [27] Such incidents were significant only as an occasion for the closing of ranks by the southern churches against any departure from the inherited theological formulations. A placid and undisturbed orthodoxy continued to prevail throughout the South as a whole.

Pennsylvania and New Jersey stood in marked contrast to their neighboring states to the north, for they were dominated by a vigorous, articulate, and strongly intrenched conservatism. This was the Presbyterian citadel, and it was a Presbyterianism that was shaped by the

[26] K. K. Bailey, *Southern White Protestantism in the Twentieth Century* (N.Y., 1964), 10.
[27] *Ibid.*

unyielding orthodoxy of Princeton, Western, and Pittsburgh (United Presbyterian) theological seminaries. Also contributing to the conservative cast of the Middle Atlantic states was the strength of the denominations of German origin in this area. The rallying center of the conservative forces was Princeton Theological Seminary, where the mantle of Charles Hodge had been bequeathed first to his son Archibald Alexander Hodge (1823–86) and then to Benjamin Warfield (1851–1921), both of whom were as convinced as the elder Hodge that the truth of the gospel had been definitively set forth in the Westminster Confession of 1646. In response to the issues raised by biblical criticism, the younger Hodge and Warfield fashioned the "Princeton doctrine of Inspiration" which became a major defense of biblical inerrancy.[28]

Meanwhile, throughout the northern half of the United States, a new movement was arising that was to give added strength to the conservative forces. This was a movement which found its inspiration in the "dispensationalist" and "premillennialist" speculations of J. N. Darby (1800–82) in England. It was spearheaded in America by itinerant evangelists, popularized at "prophetic" Bible conferences which met annually after 1876, and supplied with leadership by newly established "Bible Schools." [29] Displaying little concern for denominational peculiarities, the proponents of this "prophetic" understanding of the Scriptures made inroads in practically all the Protestant denominations. This penetration was greatly facilitated by the popularity of the *Scofield Reference Bible*, an annotated edition of the Bible prepared by C. I. Scofield (1843–1921), which imposed a rigid schematization on the complex biblical materials by relating each part of Scripture to a timetable of "dispensations" which were to culminate in the return of Christ to reign in glory. Among the leaders of the movement were such men as Reuben A. Torrey (1856–1928), J. W. Chapman (1859–1918), A. C. Dixon (1854–1925), and James M. Gray (1851–1935), all of whom were related in one way or another to the Moody Bible Institute in Chicago. Associated with them in New England were A. J. Gordon (1836–95) and A. T. Pierson

[28] For their doctrine, of inspiration, see article by Hodge and Warfield reprinted in Smith, Handy, Loetscher, *American Christianity*, II, 324–32.

[29] See C. N. Kraus, *Dispensationalism in America* (Richmond, 1958) ; C. B. Bass, *Backgrounds to Dispensationalism* (Grand Rapids, 1960) ; and F. E. Gaebelein, *The Story of the Scofield Reference Bible* (N.Y., 1959). Among the more prominent survivals of the early Bible Schools, in addition to the Moody Bible Institute, are Philadelphia College of the Bible, Bible Institute of Los Angeles, and Multnomah School of the Bible.

(1837-1911), both of whom had also been influenced by the "holiness" emphasis of the Keswick conferences in England.[30] These men tended to interpret every manifestation of theological liberalism as the work of Satan, and the Niagara Bible Conference of 1895 supplied them with a statement of five "essential" points of Christian doctrine—the verbal inerrancy of Scripture, the deity and virgin birth of Christ, the substitutionary atonement, the physical resurrection of Christ, and his bodily return to earth—which could be utilized to spot any heretic by a few pointed questions.

Most Protestant conservatives hesitated to identify themselves with the "Bible School" men, for they were not willing to accept the "dispensationalist" doctrine which colored their premillennialist interpretation of the Bible. On occasion, to be sure, the old-line conservatives welcomed "dispensationalist" support when other issues were at stake. And in 1910 the northern Presbyterian General Assembly appropriated the "dispensationalist" technique when it named five "essential and necessary" doctrines which were to be used as tests of orthodoxy. Though not mentioning premillennialism, these "five points" closely resembled those of the 1895 Niagara Conference.

While party alignments did take place in every denomination during the years which bridged the turn of the century, the centering of attention on the theological debates between conservatives and liberals can be misleading. Few of the rank-and-file members of the churches were caught up in the controversy. To the extent that they were theologically self-conscious, the great body of American Protestants were undoubtedly conservative and traditional in their basic beliefs, but they were not rigidly so. They had no thought of abandoning the faith of their fathers, but, having been subjected to several solvents, their definition of that faith was somewhat vague and imprecise. What was most admired was not the rigid stance of embattled theologians, but the great-heartedness of a Dwight L. Moody who did not stickle at working with those whom he could not regard as doctrinally sound at all points. In the theologically relaxed atmosphere of late nineteenth-century evangelicalism, Daniel Dorchester (1827-1907), the eminent Methodist historian, probably pronounced the

---

[30] The Keswick conferences were held each summer for the purpose of "promoting practical holiness," and had been initiated in 1875 by men who had been influenced by Dwight L. Moody during his British tour of 1873-75. See C. F. Harford, *The Keswick Convention* (London, 1907).

verdict of the majority when he rejoiced that theology had become "less scholastic and repulsive," had been "lubricated and broadened," and was "the better for its siftings." [31]

Variant radical responses

During these same years much more radical attempts to come to terms with the new intellectual climate were taking place outside the established churches. Most of them were not numerically significant, but they are important in illustrating the ferment that had been precipitated. Some were sober attempts at a thoroughgoing reconstruction of religion without a "supernatural" dimension, others were impressed by "discoveries" in the field of comparative religion, but the most successful were those that constructed a new "science" out of evidence supplied by mesmerism and utilized it as the basic datum for a whole new system of religious belief. What bound these diverse groups together was a common revolt against any accepted understanding of the Christian faith.

THE RELIGION OF HUMANITY. On Memorial Day in 1867 the Free Religious Association was formed by a militant group of young Unitarians who had become convinced that organized Christianity, even in its Unitarian form, had become the chief enemy of freedom and progress. They were devotees of science who had been deeply influenced by the positivist philosophy of Auguste Comte (1798–1857) and were persuaded that with the tools of science man could become the master of his own destiny.[32] But to release the latent energies of men and to awaken the necessary idealism for the fashioning of a new society in which the peoples of the world would be united in a universal brotherhood, they believed that the inspiration of religion was required. The religion they had in mind betrayed many overtones of the transcendentalism of Ralph Waldo Emerson and Theodore Parker, but its major thrust was toward an empirical and scientific naturalism. Conventional theism was abandoned. This was made clear by Octavius Brooks Frothingham (1822–95), president of the Association, when he declared in *The Religion of Humanity:* "Whether there shall be peace or war, rule or misrule, purity or corrup-

---

[31] *The Problem of Religious Progress* (N.Y., 1881), 41.

[32] There were other more explicitly Comtean societies, including the Positivist Society which was formed in New York City in 1871 and two Societies of Humanity, one of which Leon Trotsky attended.

tion, justice or injustice, . . . are questions which men must answer for themselves. There is no higher tribunal before which they can be carried; there is no super-human or extra-human will by which they can be dealt with. If things go well or ill rests with those who are commissioned to make them go." [33]

The fundamental convictions of the "religion of humanity" were summarized in "Fifty Affirmations" which Francis Ellington Abbot (1836–1903) published in each issue of the *Index*, the official organ of the Association. The Affirmations begin with the assertion that "religion is the effort of man to perfect himself." This is the oft-times hidden but universal element in all historical religions, and the objective of free religion is the perfecting of man by emancipating him from outward laws and winning him to a voluntary obedience to the inward fundamental law of true humanity. Perhaps the spirit of this free religion was best expressed in the lines of Walt Whitman:

> If I build God a church it shall be a church to men and women.
> If I write hymns they shall be all to men and women.
> If I become a devotee, it shall be to men and women.[34]

Although the Free Religious Association had its origin in Boston, it had representatives elsewhere. Abbot moved to Toledo in 1870, and the Association's most prominent pulpit was in New York City where Frothingham preached each Sunday in the Lyric Hall to a congregation that included notable figures in the arts and letters. The watchwords of the movement were freedom and unity, and because its strong-minded members believed so wholeheartedly in freedom there was often little unity and frequently considerable dissension.[35] By 1890 most of the Free Religionists had been reabsorbed into Unitarianism.

The "religion of humanity" found more permanent institutional expression in the Society for Ethical Culture founded by Felix Adler (1851–1933) in 1876. Adler had been trained for the rabbinate but had revolted against his religious heritage. For a time he was president of both his own society and the Free Religious Association. The Ethical Culture movement was never large. It enjoyed, however, a slow but steady growth

[33] *The Religion of Humanity*, 3rd. ed. (N.Y., 1875), 171.
[34] *Walt Whitman's Workshop* ed. C. J. Furness, (Cambridge, Mass., 1928), 43.
[35] For the inability of the Free Religionists to act on the basis of complete freedom, see Stow Persons, *Free Religion: An American Faith* (New Haven, 1947), 93–94.

as long as Adler lived. In 1926 there were six societies in the United States with a membership of more than two thousand and perhaps an equal number of peripheral adherents.

ESOTERIC WISDOM FROM THE EAST. Theosophy was a faith which capitalized, on a more popular level, upon much the same interest which had led to the formation of the Free Religious Association. It also emphasized fundamental truths which lay behind all the great religions, assimilated in a curious way the discoveries of modern science, and stressed the godlike potentialities of men and the universal brotherhood of the human race. The founder of the movement was Madame Helena P. Blavatsky (1831–91) who came to New York in 1872 and three years later established the Theosophical Society.[36] As the wife of a Russian general, she had led a peripatetic existence in the Orient where she had busied herself accumulating occult lore. She claimed that during a visit to Tibet she had been instructed in the esoteric wisdom of the ages by a group of "adepts" or "masters"—gifted seers who stood in direct succession to Moses, Krishna, Lao-tze, Confucius, Buddha, Christ, and other great religious prophets. Her teaching combined many features of Spiritualism with a bowdlerized understanding of Buddhism, and interpreted reincarnation as an extension of the evolutionary process. Indicative of her central emphasis are titles of two of her many books: *Isis Unveiled: A Master Key to the Mysteries of Ancient and Modern Science and Theology* (1877), and *The Secret Doctrine: the Synthesis of Science, Religion, and Philosophy* (1893).

After Madame Blavatsky's death the movement was divided into two camps when Mrs. Annie Besant (1847–1933) [37] began to replace some of the characteristic Buddhist doctrines with concepts derived from Hinduism. Mrs. Besant, with a suave and cultured Hindu brahmin sleeping outside her door to guard her against intrusion, was the leading sensation at the World's Parliament of Religions in 1893. But the conference with the words of Malachi as its motto—"Have we not all one Father? Hath not one God created us?"—provided an opportunity for other representatives of Eastern religions to gain a hearing. The Vedanta Society, a Hindu cult, had its American origin here in the teaching of Swami Vivekananda. A

[36] See C. E. B. Roberts, *Mysterious Madame, Helena Petrovna Blavatsky* (N.Y., 1931), and A. B. Kuhn, *Theosophy* (N.Y., 1930).

[37] See the two-volume biography by A. H. Nethercot, *The First Five Lives of Annie Besant* (Chicago, 1960) and *The Last Four Lives of Annie Besant* (Chicago, 1963).

similar movement was the Yogoda Sat-Sanga or Self-Realization Fellowship which taught the Hindu practice of yoga. Baha'i, of Moslem origin,
received some notice in 1893 at Chicago, but its real American rootage
dates from the arrival of 'Abdu'l-Baha in 1912.[38] It had been founded in
Persia in 1853 when Mirza Husayn 'Ali (1817–92) announced that he
was the Baha'-u'llah—"the Glory of God." Operating from the premise
that God is unknowable except through a "manifestation," he claimed to
be the manifestation for this age commissioned by divine command to
unify humanity within one faith and one order. When he died in 1892 he
left a testament appointing his son 'Abdu'l-Baha—"the Servant of God"
—as his authoritative interpreter. In its stress upon human brotherhood
and the essential unity of all religion, Baha'i is scarcely distinguishable
from Theosophy, except in pressing the necessity for full and unquestioning acceptance of Baha'-u'llah as the authoritative manifestation of God.

SCIENCE, RELIGION, HEALTH. An interest in "mental healing"
had been developing in America prior to the Civil War. It was based on the
experiments with hypnosis by a German physician, Franz Anton Mesmer
(1733?–1815), who concluded that a mysterious magnetic fluid was the
explanation of the mental power that one person could exercise over
another. Phineas Parkhurst Quimby (1802–66) of Portland, Maine, was
one of the many who became intrigued by the therapeutic power of
mesmerism. Ultimately he became convinced that disease could be cured
by cultivating healthy attitudes—positive thoughts instead of negative
ones—through suggestion and without the use of hypnotism. Sickness, he
insisted, was the consequence of wrong beliefs. The remedy, therefore, was
to displace the erroneous ideas of the ill with healing truth.

One of Quimby's patients was Mary Baker Eddy (1821–1910), the
founder of Christian Science.[39] As a child she suffered from what appears
to have been nervous disorders and perhaps hysteria. Her ill health
continued to plague her through three marriages. Although she was helped
by Quimby in 1862 and 1864, she and her followers have insisted that she
was guided through her own experience to an original discovery of the

---

[38] See William M. Miller, *Baha'ism; Its Origin, History, and Teachings* (N.Y., 1931).

[39] Sibyl Wilbur, *The Life of Mary Baker Eddy* (Boston, 1907), and L. P. Powell, *Mary Baker Eddy* (N.Y., 1930), are official biographies. See also E. F. Dakin, *Mrs. Eddy: the Biography of a Virginal Mind* (N.Y., 1929), and E. S. Bates and J. V. Ditte- more, *Mary Baker Eddy* (N.Y., 1932).

divine law of life which surpassed in importance Newton's discovery of the law of gravitation when he saw the apple fall. Whether she built upon the foundation provided by Quimby or gained her insight from a unique revelation, Mrs. Eddy was soon embarked upon an independent healing career based upon the conviction that the Eternal Mind is the source of all being, that matter is nonexistent, that disease is caused by erroneous thought (compounded, to be sure, by the Malicious Animal Magnetism projected by one's enemies), and that power is released through Christian Science to overcome all the illusions that have troubled mankind. "The control mind holds over matter," she declared, "becomes no longer a question when with mathematical certainty we gain its proof and can demonstrate the facts assumed." In Christian Science this proof has been reduced to a scientific statement that "furnishes a key to the harmony of man and reveals what destroys sickness, sin, and death." [40]

In 1875 Mrs. Eddy formed a small group of adherents into a society at Lynn, Massachusetts, and published the first edition of the authoritative textbook of Christian Science doctrine, *Science and Health with Key to the Scriptures*. The movement did not prosper, however, until she shifted her base of operation to Boston and established the Massachusetts Metaphysical College to train "practitioners." In 1892 complete control of the movement was vested in the self-perpetuating board of trustees of "the Mother Church" in Boston. Membership multiplied rapidly thereafter. By the time of Mrs. Eddy's death in 1910, the Church of Christ, Scientist, with its various local units, had grown to almost one hundred thousand members.

There were other heirs of Quimby. The most important were his former patients Julius A. Dresser (1838–93) and Warren Felt Evans (1817–89).[41] The latter was a former Methodist minister who had become a Swedenborgian. Evans began to practice "mental medicine" at Claremont, New Hampshire, and set forth the principles of the new science in a series of books: *The Mental Cure* (1869), *Mental Medicine* (1872), *Soul and Body* (1876), and *The Divine Law* (1881). In Boston other disciples of Quimby who had formed the Church of the Divine Unity were joined by Dresser in 1882. The movement spread rapidly under many names—Mental Science, Higher Thought, Higher Life, and Divine Science. The term

[40] *Science and Health* (Boston, 1875), 9.
[41] See J. A. Dresser, *The True History of Mental Science* (N.Y., 1899), H. W. Dresser, *A History of the New Thought Movement* (N.Y., 1919), and C. S. Braden, *Spirits in Rebellion: the Rise and Development of New Thought* (Dallas, 1963).

"New Thought" was coined in 1889 by William Henry Holcombe (1825–93), a homeopathic physician; and in 1894 this was chosen as the title of a little magazine published in Melrose, Massachusetts. The first national convention was held in San Francisco in 1894 under the auspices of the Divine Science Association and five years later the name of the sponsoring body was changed to the New Thought Alliance. The annual conventions failed to develop any centralized organization and the movement continued to be highly individualistic, with considerable variation in doctrine, and with personal preference dictating the choice of name by local groups. One current, represented by M. J. Barnett's *Practical Metaphysics* (1889), interpreted New Thought doctrine within a theosophical context; another current was strongly influenced by Spiritualism. The most prolific of the New Thought writers were Ralph Waldo Trine (1866–1958) and Emmet Fox (1886–1951), whose books were widely read by people who had no connection at all with the movement.

A less amorphous expression of the "mind cure" idea was the Unity School of Practical Christianity founded at Kansas City, Missouri, by Charles and Myrtle Fillmore.[42] They had been attending Christian Science and New Thought lectures in 1886 when "Truth" came to Myrtle Fillmore. It was a discovery of the power of positive thinking— "the establishment of a healing consciousness through the constant repetition of an affirmation, 'I am a child of God and, therefore, I do not inherit sickness.' " With this new power, the Jesus-power, the power to release through divine affirmations the electronic forces sealed in the nerves, the Fillmores began to advertise themselves as "Healers and Teachers." Gradually a small group of adherents was formed which they named the Society of Silent Help. In 1889 a periodical, *Modern Thought*, was launched to publicize their views, and two years later the name "Unity" was seized upon as more adequately expressing their basic principle.

> Unity! . . . Unity! . . . That's the name for our work! The name I've been looking for! . . . It embodies the central principle of what we believe: unity of the soul with God, unity of all life, unity of all religions, unity of the spirit, soul, and body; unity of all men in the heart of truth.[43]

---

[42] See J. D. Freeman, *The Household of Faith: the Story of Unity* (Lee Summit, Mo., 1951), and C. S. Braden, *These Also Believe* (N.Y., 1949).

[43] Freeman, *Household of Faith*, 44, 61–62. Cf. Marcus Bach, *They Have Found a Faith* (Indianapolis, 1946), 223.

The Fillmores denied that they were starting a new sect; they were only teaching a practical philosophy to supplement the teachings of the existing churches. To make it evident that a break with one's present religious affiliation was neither intended nor required, the name of the Society of Silent Unity was changed in 1903 to the Unity School of Practical Christianity.

Unity, for all its practical down-to-earth emphasis was far from simple. It developed a highly complex metaphysical system which incorporated ideas of reincarnation and spirit-communication borrowed from Theosophy and Spiritualism. It also emphasized the power of positive thinking to guarantee economic prosperity as well as physical health. "God will pay your debts," declared Fillmore.

> Do not say money is scarce; the very statement will drive money away from you. Do not say that times are hard with you; the very words will tighten your purse strings until Omnipotence itself cannot slip a dime into it. Begin now to talk plenty, think plenty, and give thanks for plenty. . . . It actually works.
>
> Every home can be prosperous, and there should be no poverty-stricken homes, for they are caused only by inharmony, fear, negative thinking and speaking.[44]

Basically Unity became a vast publishing enterprise, producing a constant stream of literature that had an astonishingly large circulation among members of conventional churches. While the practice of holding propagandist meetings in hotels and other public halls was an early phenomenon, it was not until the middle of the twentieth century that Unity began to establish churches of its own.

Such were the disparate religious responses to the new intellectual climate. It was a difficult time for the churches, for their whole system of thought had been challenged at many points. But this was not the only problem with which the churches had to grapple. They had to come to terms at the same time with revolutionary changes in the economic and social order which were being made manifest by the rapid pace at which the country was becoming urbanized and industrialized. This challenge demanded changes in practice as well as in thought.

[44] Charles Fillmore, *Prosperity* (Kansas City, Mo., 1938), 103–4, 117.

290

XII

New Frontiers for the Churches

While the mind of America was being reshaped by the intellectual revolution of the years of midpassage from 1865 to 1914, the outward aspects of American life were undergoing swift and bewildering change as a result of rapid technological advance. "Steam and electricity have tremendously increased the pace of life," reported an observer in 1896.

> Everybody is in a hurry. . . . St. Martha is the patron saint of the women, and St. Vitus of the men. Nervous prostration is our characteristic disease. Leisure is a word for whose meaning we consult the dictionary. In the clatter of the train, in the click of the keys at the telegraph office, the spirit of the age finds speech.[1]

The click and the clatter were symbols of a surging industrial advance sped by a flood of inventions. In contrast to the fewer than 62,000 patents that had been issued prior to 1865, the number granted by the Patent Office in the following thirty-five years was in excess of 637,000. Large-scale steel production was made possible by the introduction of the Bessemer con-

[1] George Hodges, *Faith and Social Service* (N.Y., 1896), 6.

verter. The efficiency of the railroads was multiplied by automatic cou-
plings and Westinghouse air-brakes. Refrigerator cars made feasible the
centralized slaughterhouses of the meat-packers. The discovery of oil,
coupled with the use of tank cars and pipe lines, gave further impetus to
industrial development. The McCormick binder, the typewriter, the transatlantic cable, the telephone, the incandescent lamp, the electric motor,
and the gasoline engine, each fostered growing commercial enterprises.
Before the end of the century the linotype, the automobile, and the motion
picture had made their appearance. Meanwhile, through an increasing
utilization of machinery and the adoption of interchangeable parts, the
factory system had been established in almost all areas of production. By
1894 the United States had become the leading manufacturing nation of
the world, with its production of manufactured goods surpassing the
combined output of its two closest rivals—Great Britain and Germany.

Many rubrics have been used to characterize the impact upon society
of this massive industrial development. Some have viewed these years as
"the gilded age"; others have called it "the tragic era." To some these
were "fifty years of progress"; to others they were "years of unrest and
corruption." The most obvious label has been "the age of big business,"
for this was the era of the empire builders—the steel kings, the coal
barons, the railroad magnates, the merchant princes, the Napoleons of
finance, and the potentates of the stockyards, the oil wells, and the street
railways. Another rubric has been "the rise of the city," for these were the
years when cities were "springing up and growing great and splendid as it
were in a night." A further facet of this adolescent period in the emergence
of modern America has been suggested by Harold U. Faulkner's phrase
"the quest for social justice." And those who placed the period against a
larger canvas have used the term "imperial America" to convey the
expansionist spirit of an awakening industrial giant. All these aspects of
this new industrial society—the problems and opportunities posed by the
city, the economic order, and the outward thrust of imperialism—were to
replace the West as urgent new frontiers for the churches.

The challenge of the cities

Urbanization spawned a wide variety of human needs, for in its wake
came slums, poverty, vice, and political corruption. Each of these needs

was to claim the attention of the churches, but the most pressing problem was the basic task of evangelism. Even before the Civil War extensive sections of rural America had begun to experience a steady and persistent decline in population as people moved from farms and backcountry villages to growing commercial centers and newly established mill towns. After the war the process was vastly accelerated. Previously tilled acres reverted to woodland and whole villages disappeared, leaving only a few foundation stones as monuments to the past. The cities, in contrast, were lusty infants. During the three decades from 1860 to 1890, the population of Detroit and Kansas City grew fourfold, Memphis and San Francisco fivefold, Cleveland sixfold, Chicago tenfold, Los Angeles twentyfold, and Minneapolis and Omaha fiftyfold and more. Even such previously major centers as New York, Philadelphia, and Baltimore more than doubled in population. "There is a city of thirty-five thousand added to Chicago, and one of fifty thousand added to New York, every year," reported Josiah Strong in 1887. With the overwhelming proportion of the churches located in rural areas and with many of them left stranded to dwindle and die as people departed, it became more obvious than ever that the future influence of the churches in the life of the nation was to be decisively conditioned by their success or lack of success in evangelizing the cities.

At the outset most of the urban inhabitants came from the farms and villages of the hinterland where many of them had been regular in church attendance. They may not have been conspicuous for piety and they may not even have been church members, but they had been accustomed to going to church. When they pulled up their roots and moved to the city, this pattern of habit and custom was broken, the emotional ties to a particular church were severed, and the pressure exerted by the expectation of friends and neighbors was removed. In their new environment, the tendency was for these former churchgoers to drift into "indifference." Later the problem of re-evangelization was complicated by the sweeping tide of population arriving from abroad.

Conspicuous as were the effects of urban revival campaigns and Sunday school activity, the greatest successes were won in the smaller commercial and industrial centers where social relationships remained relatively intimate. In these communities, where employer and employee lived in somewhat close proximity, patronized the same stores, sent their children to the same schools, and frequently knew each other by name, the churches were able to bridge the gap between the social classes. In this respect the American experience duplicated that of the English churches. Even the Primitive Methodists of England who were famed for bringing the gospel to people who were "rude, poor, and even brutish" did not bring the gospel to more than a very small portion of the rude and poor, and what success they had was restricted to the smaller industrial settlements.[2]

In larger industrial communities, whether in America, Britain, or France (and presumably in the developing urban concentrations of Belgium, Germany, and northern Italy), the working-classes tended to be impervious to the message and ministry of the churches.[3] It was not that the churches had "lost" these people; they never had most of them. If people generally attended church from habit, most of the laboring group who were born in the city never had the habit. And it was to this habit of nonattendance that newer additions to the urban labor force conformed.

Among other portions of the urban population churchgoing was a normal, mannerly, and even a fashionable activity. Signs of the popularity of the churches abounded. The churches were well attended. Costly and imposing edifices were being built to match the increasing prosperity of their clientele, and congregations vied with one another to possess the tallest steeple as a symbol of wealth and prestige. Pipe organs were installed, paid soloists were employed, and the preachers were polished orators who ranked in status with the most substantial citizens. Some of the preachers—men like Henry Ward Beecher and T. DeWitt Talmage in Brooklyn, Phillips Brooks and George A. Gordon in Boston, David M. Swing and Frank W. Gunsaulus in Chicago, Russell Conwell in Philadelphia, and Washington Gladden in Columbus—were figures of national prominence, but every city boasted eloquent preachers who could hold their congregations spellbound and who were regarded with deference and respect. Furthermore, the most influential leaders of business and society—Jay Gould, J. Pierpont Morgan, John D. Rockefeller, Samuel Colgate, Jay Cooke, Cyrus McCormick, Marshall Field, James J. Hill,

---

[2] K. S. Inglis, *Churches and the Working Classes in Victorian England* (Toronto, 1963), 10–13, 327.

[3] For France, see H. Desroche, *Archives de Sociologie des Religions*, VI (1958), 197–98; cited by Inglis, *op. cit.*, 327. The Roman Catholic Church in the United States provided the major exception to the prevailing situation, and the strength it developed among working people was closely related to the insecurities of their immigrant status.

William H. Vanderbilt, P. D. Armour, G. A. Swift, A. J. Drexel, John Wanamaker, and many others—were prominent churchmen, active in religious enterprises, and frequently Sunday school teachers.

To many of the immigrants from abroad, the Roman Catholic Church was the one familiar landmark in a strange and alien land, and its role in easing the transition to a new life in America helped it to retain the loyalty of many of the urban workers. With this single major exception, the great evangelistic successes of the city churches were won among the white-collar workers who had come from the rural areas, not to work in a mill, but to "clerk" in a store or an office, and who aspired to win, if not a fortune, at least a comfortable competence in the city. These young men, their wives, and their children, constituted the greater portion of those who were recruited for the churches by the revival campaigns, the Sunday school, and the Y.M.C.A. Beyond this potentially middle-class group was the hard core of nonchurchgoers—the urban masses, they were sometimes called, the poor, the destitute, the day-laborers—who were to constitute a continuing challenge to the churches.

NEW TECHNIQUES FOR CITY CHURCHES. In 1865, almost before Grant had time to haul the artillery from the Virginia battlefields, James S. Yeatman (1818–1901) of St. Louis—banker, philanthropist, and head of the Western Sanitary Commission during the Civil War—had drafted a *Circular of Inquiry* calling attention to urban religious needs and proposing that the energy devoted to wartime service to combatants be redirected to peacetime service in the cities. He noted the comparative ineffectiveness of the Protestant churches in urban communities and suggested that they were handicapped by four major deficiencies—"want of knowledge" of the true "moral condition" of the cities; "lack of organization of the wealth, piety, and labor which exist there"; need of information concerning the "best agencies" for city work; and "want of trained, tried, permanent laborers in the various spheres of city labor." [4] As a result of his initiative, those who had been active in the United States Christian Commission (the agency of the churches in ministering to soldiers) met in Cleveland in the autumn of 1865 and organized the American Christian Commission to help the churches develop a systematic program of urban missionary endeavor. They viewed the task of the Commission as twofold:

[4] A. I. Abell, *The Urban Impact on American Protestantism, 1865–1900* (Cambridge, Mass., 1943), 11.

(1) to ascertain the actual conditions prevailing in the cities, and (2) to assemble information concerning the "experience already gained" as to the best methods to be employed to gain the ends desired.

Information, based on a personal investigation of thirty-five cities by the two secretaries of the Commission, was presented the following year. "Greatly as these cities differ in most respects," they declared, "certain causes are in operation to a greater or less extent in each that necessitates special missionary effort." Fortunately, while "no mission field is more necessitous," there is "none more easily accessible, none which appeals to so many interests of the Christian patriot and philanthropist as this in our very midst." In addition to authorizing the secretaries to make a survey of the cities, the Commission established a department of foreign correspondence to gather intelligence of European experience, in ministering to the unchurched masses of the cities. The purpose was to secure helpful suggestions for American churches, and the information that was compiled was given wide circulation through the Commission's monthly periodical, *The Christian at Work.*

The investigators had discovered that most American churches did little in any systematic fashion for those "who neglect the house of God." The city mission societies and the Y.M.C.A., to be sure, sponsored street-preaching and tract distribution, and occasionally there were citywide revival campaigns. While these activities were to be encouraged, the Commission believed that the great need was to recover "the simplicity and entire consecration of the early Christians," when "every disciple was a missionary and every church a missionary society," so that the church itself would reach out to people where they live. The most obvious means of doing this was by regular house-to-house visitation of working-class neighborhoods. Many of the poverty-stricken, it was contended, had been alienated "because in their affliction they were not visited," and the only remedy was "personal, living, love-convincing" contact between the churchgoer and the nonchurchgoer. This, of course, demanded lay effort. Pastors of churches in densely populated communities were urged to "seek out and employ all such talent in their congregations as they shall believe to possess qualifications for this important and pressing work." [5]

The volunteer visitation program never worked too successfully. Even when the Evangelical Alliance picked up the idea of a cooperative

[5] *Ibid.*, 12–13, 15, 33.

296

monthly citywide house-to-house visitation and, as a result of vigorous promotion, had put it into operation by 1889 in forty cities, the actual implementation was sporadic. As an alternative, the utilization of female assistants or women missionaries was strongly advocated. It was recognized that women could be especially effective in going into the homes, and considerable support developed for the establishment of sisterhoods or deaconess orders patterned after the German model. In an eloquent plea for the churches to adopt the German practice, a speaker at the 1868 convention of the Commission asserted that the "theory that woman has no place in the church deprives America of two-thirds of its Christian force." The eloquence of the proponents of the use of women workers, however, was not sufficient to quell popular hostility. In 1857 William A. Muhlenberg had aroused a storm of opposition among his fellow Episcopalians when he established a deaconess order in New York. A Lutheran attempt after the Civil War was equally abortive. The Methodists were somewhat more successful, but official recognition was withheld until 1889. By the end of the century, the Lutherans and the German Reformed were making extensive use of deaconesses, the Episcopalians had established a training school, and even the Congregationalists and Baptists had taken a few tentative steps toward the employment of deaconesses. The Methodists, however, were far in the lead, having nearly as many deaconesses as all other denominations combined. In the next few years the number of deaconesses began to decline. Perhaps their quaint hats and distinctive dress militated against any continuing popularity. But the battle over the employment of women had been won and the churches generally began to make use of women as church visitors and missionaries.

A second problem highlighted by the Commission and underscored in the actual process of house-to-house visitation was the fact that often no churches were located in the neediest neighborhoods. The city mission societies were encouraged to establish mission chapels in these areas. Most of these were conventional in character. Much more dramatic were the "rescue missions" designed to reach and reclaim the dregs of society—vagrants, alcoholics, former convicts, jobless men, and fallen women. While the Water Street Mission in New York was the most famous and the Pacific Garden Mission in Chicago the most successful of these rescue operations, by the 1880's every city boasted one or more missions of this type. The real pioneer of the movement was Jerry MacAuley (1837–84) who founded the Water Street Mission in 1872, and his own early career was typical of those to whom he sought to minister. He had arrived in New York from Ireland at the age of thirteen. Living in the streets, he soon became a petty thief and then graduated to gambling, organized burglary, and drunkenness. At the age of nineteen he was sentenced to a fifteen-year term in prison, and while confined he was converted by an ex-prizefighter. Back on the streets after having been pardoned in 1864, he resumed his criminal career until he was finally redeemed by agents of the Howard Mission. He then established his own mission outpost in his former neighborhood, ministering primarily to the homeless men who congregated there.

Among both the conventional missions and the rescue missions, there was a growing conviction that attention must be given to immediate material necessities before spiritual needs could be fully met. The managers of the North End Mission in Boston put it quite bluntly: "Till the cravings of hunger are satisfied, we cannot develop the moral nature," adding that they believed this to be "the biblical way of reaching the heart." [6] As a result of this conviction the rescue missions began to provide food, lodging, and employment services, while missions of all types launched a wide variety of enterprises which included model tenements for the poor, homes for working mothers, and hospitals for the care of sick children.

Yeatman's initial *Circular of Inquiry* had emphasized the importance of "trained" leadership for the specialized tasks of city work, and a number of institutions were established to meet this need.[7] A further step in this direction was taken when followers of Jerry MacAuley organized the Convention of Christian Workers in 1886. John C. Collins, a Yale graduate and manager of the Union Gospel Mission in New Haven, was the guiding spirit. By means of annual gatherings a type of "in-service" training was provided through the sharing of experience with new methods and techniques. Within little more than a decade it had gained more than

[6] *Ibid.*, 36.
[7] Among these schools were Stephen H. Tyng's Home of the Evangelists (1870) in New York, T. DeWitt Talmage's Tabernacle Lay College (1872) in Brooklyn, and Dwight L. Moody's Chicago Evangelization Society (1886) in Chicago. The latter institution was designed "to raise up men and women who will be willing to lay their lives alongside the laboring class and the poor and bring the gospel to bear on their lives." They were to do work that ministers could not do—"get in among the people and identify themselves with the people." W. G. McLoughlin, *Modern Revivalism*, 272–73.

2,500 members, and Graham Taylor (1851–1938), professor of Christian sociology at Chicago Theological Seminary, declared the annual Convention of Christian Workers was "a great exhibit of the work and working forces of modern Christianity" and "as nearly ecumenical a gathering of the church in America as is held on this continent." The *Christian Union*, which had been founded as Henry Ward Beecher's personal journal, was equally enthusiastic, asserting that the stenographic reports of the conventions furnished "the best literature on practical Christian work that can be secured." [8]

Meanwhile a new instrument of urban evangelization had made its appearance. This was the Salvation Army.[9] It had been founded in London in 1878 by William Booth (1829–1912), an ex-Methodist preacher. Booth had come to the conclusion that "we can't get at the masses in the chapels," and consequently he was determined to move out into the streets. Organized on the basis of strict military discipline, the Army was geared for a many-sided attack on the problems of the city. The program was spelled out in Booth's famous volume, *Darkest England and the Way Out* (1890). The familiar brass band and tambourines which were used to gather a crowd for street-preaching was only an incidental feature of a broad range of activities. Booth aimed to supply the poverty-stricken people of England with at least the three things that any dray horse enjoyed—"shelter for the night, food for its stomach, work allotted to it by which it can earn its own corn." In addition to the usual provision made by rescue missions for meals, lodging, and an employment service, the Army moved out into the community with its Slum Brigades, Sewing Battalions, and visiting nurses. Legal aid bureaus were opened, day nurseries for children set up, and rescue homes for prostitutes established. And to give men and women the benefit of a new and wholesome environment, farm colonies were founded. Although the Salvation Army was ultimately to take on the characteristics of a church, its initial intention was to serve only as a recruiting agent of the churches among the most neglected elements of the population.

The Salvation Army was introduced into America in 1880, but its

---

[8] Abell, *Urban Impact on American Protestantism*, 97–98.

[9] The English background is summarized by Inglis, *Churches and the Working Classes in Victorian England*, 175–214; and is given in detail by Robert Sandall, *The History of the Salvation Army*, Vol. I, *1865–1878* (N.Y., 1947). For its American career, see H. A. Wisbey, *Soldiers without Swords: A History of the Salvation Army in the United States* (N.Y., 1955).

major expansion took place after 1886 when Booth's son, Ballington Booth (1859–1940), was sent over to take charge. A schism occurred in 1896 when Ballington Booth refused to obey his father's order that he return to England. Instead he and his wife founded the Volunteers of America, which patterned its activities after the parent organization but was organized on a more democratic base. One of the major features of its program was "prison work"—the rehabilitation of ex-convicts. Aid to unwed mothers was also stressed.

THE INSTITUTIONAL CHURCH. The problem of the city churches was complicated by the mobility of the urban population. As commercial establishments encroached upon residential areas and the housing grew old and deteriorated, the more prosperous sought newer and more spacious accommodations on the outskirts, leaving room at the center for newer arrivals. Without endowments to sustain them, most churches seemed to face the choice either of following their congregations or of being marooned in poverty and left to eke out a dwindling existence. Rather than subject themselves to a lingering death, many churches elected to follow their congregations and to erect new edifices in the sections to which their members had moved. It was this solution to their problem, of course, that necessitated the founding of mission chapels in areas formerly occupied by churches. This whole process became deeply disturbing to sensitive Christians as they became aware of what was taking place. Instead of moving the church and then seeking to discharge its responsibility to the people of its former neighborhood by proxy through missions of various types, some proposed that the churches adapt themselves to the changing population of the inner city by adopting and utilizing the techniques that were being developed by the missions.

Edward Judson (1844–1914), the pre-eminent theoretician of an institutionalized ministry, defined an institutional church as "an organized body of Christian believers, who, finding themselves in a hard and uncongenial social environment, supplement the ordinary methods of the gospel—such as preaching, prayer meetings, Sunday school, and pastoral visitation—by *a system of organized kindness*, a congeries of institutions, which, by touching people on physical, social, and intellectual sides, will conciliate them and draw them within reach of the gospel." [10] With the

---

[10] "The Church in Its Social Aspect," *The Annals of the American Academy of Political and Social Science*, XXX (Nov., 1908), 436. For an impressionistic appraisal of the institutional church, see Gaius G. Atkins, *Religion in Our Times* (N.Y., 1932), 69–85.

slogan "open church doors every day and all the day," the institutional churches became hives of activity with athletic programs, gymnasiums, reading rooms, day nurseries, medical clinics, industrial education courses, cooking schools, sewing classes, lecture series, concerts, entertainments, employment bureaus, penny savings associations, choral societies, and drama clubs.

The honor of establishing the first institutional church probably belongs to Thomas K. Beecher (1824–1900), one of the numerous Beecher progeny, who served as pastor of the Park Congregational Church in Elmira, New York, from 1854 to 1900. In 1872 he induced his congregation to erect a block-long structure equipped for a full range of social services as well as for worship. Mark Twain, his brother-in-law, described the building with its gymnasium, lecture rooms, library, and free baths in his *Curious Dreams and Other Sketches* (1872) and commented that "we have at least one sensible but very curious church in America." Within a few years there were to be many of these "sensible" churches.[11] By 1900 one observer listed 173 churches with a full-blown institutional program and acknowledged that there were probably others which had escaped his attention. In addition, scores of churches were appropriating parts of the institutional program.

When the Open or Institutional Church League was formed in 1894 to promote "educational, reformatory, and philanthropic" activities by the churches as an evangelistic device, its leaders self-confidently proclaimed that the question "how to reach the masses" had been "practically solved." It was true that the institutional churches were experiencing phenomenal growth. By 1900 the Baptist Temple in Philadelphia, in the process of fathering what was to become Temple University, had become the largest congregation in America. St. George's Episcopal Church in New York, which with only six families left had been ready to close its doors, now numbered five thousand members. The Congregationalists reported that their institutional churches had six times as many additions as the average noninstitutional church. But there were problems. For one thing, an

---

[11] Among the more prominent institutional churches were St. George's and St. Bartholomew's Episcopal churches on Manhattan, and St. Andrew's Episcopal in Rochester; Fourth Congregational in Hartford, Plymouth Congregational in Indianapolis, Berkeley Temple in Boston, and Jersey City Tabernacle (modeled after the People's Palace in London); Baptist Temple in Philadelphia, Ruggles Street Baptist in Boston, and Judson Memorial Baptist in New York; Bethany Presbyterian in Philadelphia, and First Presbyterian in Brooklyn; Wesley Methodist Chapel in Cincinnati, and Metropolitan Methodist Tabernacle in New York.

institutional church was an incredibly costly enterprise. Not many churches could command the necessary financial support. St. George's was fortunate in having J. Pierpont Morgan as a member of its initial remnant. St. Bartholomew's, whose parish house was erected by Cornelius Vanderbilt and his mother, had an annual budget of over one million dollars.[12] Edward Judson's begging expeditions were successful in tapping the resources of John D. Rockefeller. Furthermore, as Edward Judson noted, "social problems are so difficult and so fascinating that they easily absorb all a minister's time and energy." The tendency is for him to neglect "his study and the care of his flock," to lose "his priestly character," and to become "a mere social functionary."[13] Becoming more and more absorbed in the social activities which initially were intended to serve as a bridge into the life of the church, the ideal of mere humanitarian service tended to replace the earlier evangelistic concern. As a result the congregations dwindled almost as rapidly as they had increased. In the end, far from being a means of building up a congregation to support a ministry in areas of deterioration, many of the institutional churches became social agencies which other churches had to find money and leadership to maintain and support.

The churches and the economic order

The decade preceding the great railroad strike of 1877 has been described as the "summit" of American economic complacency. This complacency was as evident among churchmen as it was among other Americans. Leaders of the churches may have disagreed about many things, but they displayed remarkable unanimity in their approbation of the existing economic order and of the "principles" or "laws" of political economy which provided its theoretical foundation. Gone was the radical criticism and ferment of the 1830's and 1840's. Henry F. May has observed that "in 1876 Protestantism presented a massive, almost unbroken front in its defense of the social status quo,"[14] and this was equally true of Roman Catholicism. Within a dozen years, however, this situation

---

[12] Abell, *The Urban Impact on American Protestantism*, 150–51.
[13] "The Church in Its Social Aspect," *op. cit.*, 437.
[14] *Protestant Churches and Industrial America* (N.Y., 1949), 91. This is an important study based on an analysis of the periodical literature of the major Protestant bodies.

began to change as a result of people being shocked from their complacency by outbreaks of violent social conflict. Roman Catholics remained cautious,[15] but by the 1890's vigorous demands for social reform were being voiced in every major Protestant denomination and a few of the leaders were calling for the complete reorganization of society. By the turn of the century the adherents of two antithetical gospels— "the gospel of wealth" and "the social gospel"—were locked in combat and were struggling for predominance.

THE GOSPEL OF WEALTH. For many Americans the years following the Civil War marked the beginning of a period of unrivaled prosperity. Rapidly as the population increased, the nation's wealth multiplied three times as fast. Those who benefited by this tremendous economic expansion were confident that they were living in the best of all possible worlds. The American economy had been tested and had not been found wanting. This smug self-satisfaction lent an aura of eminent reasonableness and even sanctity to the *laissez-faire* economic doctrines which had been fathered by Adam Smith, popularized in America by Francis Wayland (1796– 1865),[16] and given strong reinforcement by the teachings of Herbert Spencer. The most persuasive argument for allowing economic self-interest free play was the seemingly obvious fact that it worked for the economic betterment of men generally. Perhaps it worked, as the *Congregationalist* put it, because there were "thousands upon thousands of acres of magnificent soil" beyond the Mississippi that could be secured "at a merely nominal price" so that "no man who is blessed with health and willingness to work, be his family large or small, need come to the poorhouse." [17] But it worked nonetheless, at least for a time.

The classic statement of "the true gospel concerning wealth," obedience to which will "solve the problem of the rich and the poor," was

[15] Francis J. Lally has pointed out that Roman Catholics gave little evidence of being "socially progressive" prior to the New Deal years. The papal encyclical *Rerum Novarum* (1891) had little immediate impact in America, and the few occasions when Roman Catholics displayed an interest in social reform were "sporadic and mostly short-lived." This was true of the 1919 "Bishops' Program of Social Reconstruction" which did not receive strong support until the 1930's. Participation in the labor movement was the single notable exception to the generally conservative outlook. *The Catholic Church in a Changing America*, 47–48. For an account of developing social consciousness among Roman Catholics, see A. I. Abell, *American Catholicism and Social Action* (N.Y., 1960).

[16] Wayland was president of Brown University and the author of *The Elements of Political Economy* (1837). The most popular textbook on the subject, it went through many printings.

[17] March 17, 1870; quoted by May, *Protestant Churches and Industrial America*, 55.

written by Andrew Carnegie (1835–1919), the steelmaster of Pittsburgh, and was published in the June, 1889, issue of the *North American Review*.[18] Carnegie insisted that "civilization depends" upon the triple law of the "sacredness" of private property, free competition, and free accumulation of wealth. This triple law, which allows free play to economic forces, is indispensable to all progress, and nothing should be permitted to interfere with its operation. Its indispensability is one of the facts of life which cannot be changed. One can only make the "best of it." It is true that a price is exacted, since the law of competition forces the employer "into the strictest economies, among which the rates to be paid to labor figure prominently," and this often creates friction. But even if the operation of the law "may sometimes be hard for individuals," it is "best for the race, because it insures the survival of the fittest in every department" and produces "a wonderful material development" that benefits all. "The laborer has now more comforts than the farmer had a few generations ago," "the farmer has more luxuries than the landlord had," and the landlord has more than "a king could then obtain." This inequality is much better than the "universal squalor" that would otherwise prevail.

The harshness of Carnegie's views was somewhat tempered by his view of the proper use of wealth. In words reminiscent of John Wesley's slogan, "Gain all you can, save all you can, give all you can," he declared that "the man who dies . . . rich, dies disgraced." [19] Instead of leaving vast sums to one's children or even making bequests for public purposes, Carnegie insisted that one's wealth should be distributed in ways that served the common good during one's own lifetime. Indiscriminate charity, of course, could only serve "to encourage the slothful, the drunken, the

[18] Carnegie's brief dissertation on "Wealth" is reprinted, with other essays, in *Democracy and the Gospel of Wealth*, ed. Gail Kennedy, *Problems in American Civilization: Readings Selected by the Department of American Studies, Amherst College* (Boston, 1949), and in *The Gospel of Wealth and Other Essays*, ed. Edward C. Kirkland (Cambridge, Mass., 1962). The former includes Ralph Gabriel's analysis of "The Gospel of Wealth of the Guilded Age," reprinted from *The Course of American Democratic Thought*.

[19] Wesley's concern, of course, was different. "Religion," he said, "must necessarily produce both industry and frugality, and these cannot but produce riches." And "whenever riches have increased," religion "has decreased in the same proportion." "Is there no way to prevent this—this continual declension of pure religion?" What way "can we take that our money may not sink us to the nethermost hell? There is but one way, and . . . no other. . . . If those who 'gain all they can,' and 'save all they can,' will likewise 'give all they can'; then the more they gain, the more they will grow in grace." *The Works of John Wesley*, 4th ed. (London, 1840–42), XIII, 246–47.

unworthy." The race has never been improved by almsgiving, for it rewards vice rather than aids virtue. "Those worthy of assistance, except in rare cases, seldom require assistance." The objective should be to help those who will help themselves. "The best means of benefitting the community is to place within its reach the ladders upon which the aspiring can rise." Parks, museums, libraries, schools are ways of returning surplus wealth to the masses in a form "best calculated to do them lasting good."

Carnegie's gospel of wealth was closely intertwined with the doctrine of stewardship of time, money, and talent that had been staple fare in Protestant moral teaching. Consequently it was but a small step for current principles of economics to be translated into laws of God's providential ordering of society. Phillips Brooks, Henry Ward Beecher, and a host of lesser luminaries of the Protestant pulpit embraced the gospel of wealth with fervent devotion, but Russell Conwell—with his lecture on *Acres of Diamonds* (they are in one's own backyard) and his exhortation that everyone has a "duty to get rich"—was its most eloquent clerical spokesman.[20]

Roman Catholics, for the most part, represented an older conservatism which enjoined passivity and acceptance of one's lot in society, God permits poverty as "the most efficient means" of fostering "some of the most necessary Christian virtues." Charity should be directed to the relief of suffering and not to its elimination, for "a country where there are no beggars" would be "a veritable branch of hell." It was suggested that "to let well enough alone is a very wise old saw." Liberal Catholics, on the other hand, took a more positive view of the benefits derived from the free play of economic forces. Bishop Spalding assured a graduating class at Notre Dame that "the organs of the social body" had never been so healthy, and Cardinal Gibbons applauded Carnegie's essay on "Wealth." Archbishop Ireland insisted that "respect" for capital "must be supreme," and admonished Roman Catholics to stop considering money as evil and—with "will," "energy," "pluck," "push," and "ambition"—to set about acquiring some. "It is energy and enterprise that wins everywhere," he declared with the briskness of an entrepreneur; "they win in the

[20] For Brooks and Beecher, see H. F. May, *Protestant Churches in Industrial America*, 64–72. For Conwell, see W. S. Hudson, *The Great Tradition of the American Churches*, rev. ed. (N.Y., 1963), 180–86. There is no standard text of Conwell's *Acres of Diamonds*, for it underwent constant revision.

Church, they win in the state, they win in business." In 1890 the *Catholic World* published a minor classic of the gospel-of-wealth literature which pointed out that the three men Christ restored to life were all men of wealth and recommended that, after praying for faith, hope, and charity, Catholics should add the petition: "O Lord! give me good sense. Give me hard, practical, everyday gumption. If I had a little of that, I shouldn't act as foolishly as I generally do; I shouldn't waste my time nor money." The ability to make "frequent and handsome donations" to the church, it was suggested, is a "pretty" sure indication "that a man has the right sort of zeal." [21]

Many wealthy men had this "right sort of zeal," for this was a great age of philanthropy. Even without the incentive of benefit to be derived from income-tax exemption, benefactions were large and numerous. George Peabody, with gifts amounting to eight and one-half million dollars, was only one of many who, in the words of William Gladstone, demonstrated "how a man may be master of his fortune, not its slave." There were, of course, incongruities symbolized by the image of Daniel Drew as both "master fleecer of the lambs" and "founder of a theological seminary." Jay Cooke presented a curious picture as a skilled corrupter of legislatures and president of the Education Society of the Protestant Episcopal Church. Considerations of self-interest may have spurred the Armour brothers to lavish more than a million dollars on a mission in Chicago. But many took their stewardship seriously. John P. Crozer, whose many benefactions included the theological seminary which bears his name, was not exceptional when he confessed his perplexity as to "how I shall use, as I ought, the great and increasing stores of wealth which God has bestowed upon me."

> Excuses are so easily framed, and the heart of man so deceitful, that one can easily reason himself into the belief that, all things considered, he has done pretty well. I find such a process of reasoning in my own mind, but calm reflection tells me that I have not done well. I am a very unprofitable servant to so good a Master.

Troubled lest the good he designed be lost in the mere satisfaction of giving, he asked the Lord to direct him "clearly and decisively" to the "path of duty and usefulness." Commenting on Crozer's careful assessment of his responsibility, Sidney E. Mead observed that "only the sneering

[21] R. D. Cross, *Emergence of Liberal Catholicism in America*, 107–09, 111–12, 163–64.

souls of the mean in mind" could belittle such transparently "honest and consecrated devotion" to sacred duty.[22]

THE RISE OF SOCIAL DISCONTENT. The prosperity of a booming economy was not equally shared by all sections of the population, and the result was smoldering discontent among both farmers and workingmen. The woes of the farmers, apart from the natural hazards of the weather and periodic insect infestations, were due to their growing dependence upon the railroads and a system of mass marketing, both of which were susceptible to manipulation by the "moneyed interests." [23] The earlier subsistence farming had been replaced by the production of money crops—bought, shipped, and processed by others. Selling in a distant market in open world competition, the farmer purchased his machinery, supplies, and personal necessities in a market subsidized by protective tariffs. And his shifting fortunes from year to year frequently made him dependent upon credit to finance his next crop. The great enemy was the triple alliance of railroads, banks, and tariff-protected industry.

Caught in a web woven by railroad monopolists, buccaneering market speculators, tight-fisted money-lenders, and hardheaded industrialists, the farmers rose in sporadic movements of protest and revolt. The Grangers of 1867, the Greenbackers of the 1870's, the Farmers' Alliance of the 1880's, the Populists of 1891, and Bryan's "free silver" campaign of 1896—all were expressions of this agrarian discontent which sought to impose systematic government control over the economic life of the nation to mitigate the plight of the farmers. The *Congregationalist Record* of Boston represented the attitude of most eastern churchmen when it described the leaders of the agrarian protest as "dangerous characters of the inflammable and covetous West." Lyman Abbott of Plymouth Congregational Church in Brooklyn was probably equally representative when he spoke disparagingly of William Jennings Bryan as a western "medicine man" who set up his tent to hawk "one medicine which will cure all the ills to which humanity is subject." [24] The evangelical religion of the rural and village churches of the Midwest and South, however, was implicated in the farm revolt and contributed to its continuing impetus.[25] Unfortunately the relationship of evangelical religion to rural radicalism has received little

[22] *The Lively Experiment*, 149.
[23] See R. B. Nye, *Midwestern Progressive Politics: A Historical Study of Its Origins and Development, 1870–1950* (East Lansing, Mich., 1951).
[24] *Ibid.*, 5.
[25] *Ibid.*, 160. The Grange, for example, was and has continued to be closely related to the churches.

detailed study, partly because the religious press gave little attention to the agrarian problem. The religious press was urban oriented and its attention was absorbed by the much more spectacular labor uprisings.

The plight of the workers was even more serious than that of the farmers. Wages were low, hours were long, and working conditions were almost uniformly bad. Where women and children were employed, they labored from dawn to dusk for a pittance. And the situation steadily worsened, for the mounting national wealth was being concentrated in fewer and fewer hands. As early as 1867 a magazine reported that ten men owned one-tenth of the taxable property in New York City, and it listed their holdings. By 1890 it was estimated that 1 per cent of the families of the country received one-quarter of the national income, and seven years later one-tenth of the American people were said to own nine-tenths of the national wealth. Wages, to be sure, were rising. From 1860 to 1881 they increased 31 per cent, but prices rose 41 per cent and more than offset the gain.[26] The crises came, however, when workers were laid off in large numbers or had their pay cut as the result of recurring financial crashes. The crash of 1873 set off the first crisis. This was followed by the panic of 1884 and then by the disastrous depression of 1893, when Coxey's "army" marched on Washington.

Numerous workingmen's associations were being formed throughout these years, and their efforts to improve the lot of the workers led to large-scale labor warfare. Strikes were frequent and bloody. Four were particularly frightening to the nation as a whole. The first was the railroad strike of 1877 in which pitched battles were fought in many cities, arousing widespread fear of imminent revolution and anarchy. The second was the McCormick Harvester strike of 1886. On May 3 six pickets were killed in a clash with the police. The following day at a protest meeting of the workers in Haymarket Square a bomb was exploded which killed a policeman and injured many others. In the subsequent riot ten more persons died. The third was the Homestead strike of 1892 at the Carnegie Steel Plant in Pennsylvania where ten were killed and sixty wounded in a battle between the workers and three hundred "Pinkerton" men. The fourth, the Pullman strike of 1894 which affected rail transportation in twenty-seven states,

[26] See Charles B. Spahr, *An Essay on the Present Distribution of Wealth in the United States* (N.Y., 1896), 128 ff.; Robert Hunter, *Poverty* (N.Y., 1912), 61 ff.; Washington Gladden, *Applied Christianity* (Boston, 1894) 120; W. E. Garrison, *March of Faith*, 62, 120.

was accompanied by widespread burning, looting, and killing, and was finally brought to an end by President Cleveland's use of federal troops.

The reaction of the churches to the revolt of the workingmen was one first of shock and then of panic. Orthodox economic theory had taught them that labor was a "commodity," subject "like all other commodities" to "the imperishable laws of demand and supply," and that in a free country the sole responsibility of government to both capital and labor was "the simple duty of enforcing contracts" and preserving peace.[27] Thus they were more shocked by the riots of the strikers than by the conditions which caused the strikers to riot. The whole fabric of society seemed in danger of being torn apart, and many of the Protestant periodicals responded with almost incredibly brutal denunciations of the workers. The issue is between "law and anarchy," declared the *Independent* on July 26, 1877. The safety of society demands that no concessions be made to rioters. A week later its mood was near hysteria. "If the club of the policeman, knocking out the brains of the rioter, will answer, then well and good; but if it does not promptly meet the exigency, then bullets and bayonets, canister and grape . . . constitute the one remedy and the one duty of the hour." The *Christian Union* agreed. "There are times when mercy is a mistake," it asserted.[28] But there were others who were deeply troubled. Washington Gladden, for example, in the late 1860's had defended the cause of the strikers in North Adams, Massachusetts; and in 1876 he published his first book on social questions, *Workingmen and Their Employers*. By the 1880's many were to share his concern.

Roman Catholics were often equally intemperate in their denunciation of strikes. James R. Bayley, archbishop of Baltimore, took a dim view of labor unions, insisting that "no Catholic with any idea of the spirit of his religion will encourage them," and a Catholic periodical asserted that the proper solution for economic troubles was for the workers to "Pray, Pray, Pray." [29] The Knights of Labor, the first really effective mass labor union, was condemned in Quebec by papal decree in 1884, and Archbishop Corrigan of New York insisted that membership in the Knights was forbidden in the United States as well. Cardinal Gibbons, on the other

---

[27] *Watchman and Reflector*, June 4, 1874, quoted by May, *op. cit.*, 55; and the *Independent*, July 26, 1877, quoted by Garrison, *March of Faith*, 64.

[28] May, *Protestant Churches and Industrial America*, 92–93.

[29] *The American Apostolate*, ed. L. R. Ward (Westminster, Md., 1952); Cross, *Emergence of Liberal Catholicism*, 118.

hand, believed that many of the workers' grievances were just, and he was alarmed by the prospect of major defections from the church if the censure was maintained. In 1888, with the help of Ireland and Keane, Gibbons obtained a ruling from Rome which stated that the Knights could be "tolerated." Gibbons then proceeded to warn the Knights against the use of strikes and boycotts. While the liberals sympathized with the plight of the workers, they tended to oppose any proposals that would restrict free economic activity. Even the great labor encyclical, *Rerum Novarum* (1891), provided no clear guidance in America, for the workingmen's associations sanctioned by Leo XIII were to be Catholic societies and were to include employers as well as employees. Joseph Schroeder, the conservative leader at Catholic University, quickly pointed out that these approved associations were a far cry from anything to be found in the United States.[30]

THE SOCIAL GOSPEL.[31] The developing social concern among American Protestants was stimulated in part by influences from abroad. The writings of Thomas Chalmers (1780–1847), the Scottish theologian and philanthropist, were widely read and exerted the earliest influence in this direction,[32] and immediately after the Civil War interest in the distinctively English "Christian socialism" of Frederick Denison Maurice (1805–72) and Charles Kingsley (1819–75) was aroused by their books and novels.[33] Later the "Christian socialists" of Germany and Switzerland contributed a strong theological emphasis upon the centrality of the doctrine of "the kingdom of God." The chief American precursors were Henry M. Dexter (1821–90), a New England clergyman, who published

[30] *Ibid.,* 118. For Gibbons' defense of the Knights of Labor and for portions of *Rerum Novarum*, see Smith, Handy, Loetscher, *American Christianity*, II, 377–91.

[31] The term "social gospel" did not come into common use until after 1900. Prior to this the term most widely used was "social Christianity." The basic account of the movement is C. H. Hopkins, *The Rise of the Social Gospel in American Protestantism, 1865–1915* (New Haven, 1940). See also James Dombrowski, *The Early Days of Christian Socialism in America* (N.Y., 1936).

[32] Chalmers' *The Application of Christianity to the Commercial and Ordinary Affairs of Life* was reprinted at Hartford and at Boston in 1821, at Lexington, Ky., in 1822, and at New York in 1855. His *Christian and Civic Economy of Large Towns*, first published in 1821, was considered to be of such value that an abridgment was published in 1900 by Charles R. Henderson, professor of Christian sociology at the University of Chicago.

[33] Maurice's key writings were *The Gospel and the Kingdom of Heaven* (1864), *The Commandments Considered as Instruments of National Reformation* (1866), and *Social Action* (1869). *Faith and Action*, a compilation of selections from his writings, was published at Boston in 1886. Kingsley's two important novels were *Alton Locke* (1850) and *Yeast* (1851).

The Moral Influence of Manufacturing Towns in 1848, and Stephen Colwell (1800–1871), a Philadelphia iron merchant, who became preoccupied with social problems in the 1850's.[34]

The indifference and, on occasion, the hostility of the churches to the cause of the worker was due largely to ignorance. Consciences were disturbed and sympathy and support were enlisted when the clergy became personally acquainted with the workingman's plight. Typical in this respect was the sturdy defense of the workers in the great Pullman strike of 1894 by William H. Carwardine. He was no student of the labor question. He had no theory to support his opinions. But he was the minister of a Methodist church in Pullman, Illinois, and he was drawn by his immediate and firsthand experience of conditions there into a firm belief in the justice of the strikers' demands. For Washington Gladden, the conversion was not so sudden and dramatic. He was first exposed to the plight of the workers during his pastorate at North Adams, Massachusetts, and when he was called to Springfield he found the situation there much more acute. But his views did not mature until the Hocking Valley coal strike of 1884 when he was minister of the First Congregational Church of Columbus, Ohio. The officials of the coal company were members of his congregation, and Gladden was aware of the lengths to which they were prepared to go to crush the strike and break the union. This they succeeded in doing at great cost to the men and to themselves, only to have a new strike break out a year later. This time the miners won. A contract was signed, and the manager of the company admitted to Gladden that it was much better to bargain with the union over a table than to attempt to deal with a mob.

The social gospel leaders represented no unified point of view. They shared a common concern and they were agreed that the people in the churches needed to be exposed to the "facts." Most Protestants were isolated from the scenes of industrial conflict and had no personal acquaintance with the lot of the worker. To remedy this situation, socially minded clergymen organized forums and study groups to discuss industrial problems and invited representatives of labor to speak before men's brotherhoods in the churches. In addition they busied themselves with producing a voluminous literature dealing with social issues from a

---

[34] Colwell's books were *New Themes for the Protestant Clergy* (1851), *Politics for American Christians* (1852), and *The Position of Christianity in the United States* (1854). He also wrote the Preface to William Arnot's *The Race for Riches* (1853).

Christian point of view.[35] But beyond this common pattern of activity, there were deep divergences.

Washington Gladden represented a rather mild "progressivism" which recognized the rights of labor, advocated municipal ownership of public utilities, and placed strong emphasis upon the Golden Rule as the royal law of brotherhood. The latter theme was picked up and romanticized by Charles M. Sheldon (1857–1946), minister of the Central Congregational Church of Topeka, Kansas, in a parable-novel that was destined to win a place beside *Uncle Tom's Cabin* and *Ten Nights in a Bar Room* as one of the great American tracts. *In His Steps, or What Would Jesus Do?* (1897) [36] was the story of the revolution which occurred in a small city when members of a single congregation resolved to live for a year in accordance with the teachings of Jesus. At the opposite pole from Sheldon's nonprogramatic sentimentalism was the demand for a radical reconstruction of society voiced by such men as George D. Herron (1862–1925), professor of applied Christianity at Grinnell College, and W. D. P. Bliss (1856–1926), an Episcopal clergyman in Boston and guiding spirit of the Society of Christian Socialists. A "scientific" approach to social problems was represented pre-eminently by a Chicago coterie whose chief luminaries were Shailer Mathews, Graham Taylor, and Charles R. Henderson (1848–1915). Social melioration based upon careful sociological analysis was their forte, and they were strong advocates of the utility of "social settlements" in forwarding the necessary process of social adjustment.

The social settlements were patterned after Toynbee Hall, a pioneer settlement house established in London in 1884. Their purpose was to bring together a company of university-trained social workers who would live together in the slums where they could study conditions at first hand and initiate projects of social betterment. Two of the best known American "settlements" were in Chicago—Hull House, founded by Jane Addams, and Chicago Commons, with Graham Taylor as its guiding light. Others were to be found in most of the major cities, usually being established in connection with either a university or a seminary.

---

[35] Typical in this respect was Gladden's own literary output which included *Working People and Their Employers* (1876), *The Christian League of Connecticut* (1883), *Applied Christianity* (1886), *Tools and the Man* (1893), *Ruling Ideas of the Present Age* (1895), *Social Facts and Forces* (1899), *Social Salvation* (1902), *Christianity and Socialism* (1905), *The Church and Modern Life* (1908), *The Labor Question* (1911).

[36] Its circulation has been estimated to have exceeded 20 million copies. Conwell's *Acres of Diamonds* occupied much the same place in the gospel-of-wealth literature.

In terms of continuing influence, Walter Rauschenbusch (1861–1918) was the outstanding prophet of the social gospel. His social awakening took place during the ten years he spent as pastor of a small Baptist church of German immigrants in a tenement section of New York City, but it was not until after he had been appointed to the faculty of Rochester Theological Seminary in 1897 that he became a figure of national prominence. His three major works were *Christianity and the Social Crisis* (1907), *Christianizing the Social Order* (1912), and *A Theology for the Social Gospel* (1917). Equally important were many of his more incidental writings, and his *Prayers of the Social Awakening* (1910) is one of the few devotional classics America has produced.[37]

Rauschenbusch is difficult to classify in relation to other social gospel leaders. His fellow Baptists at the University of Chicago dismissed him as "rhetorical" rather than "scientific." [38] He called himself on occasion a "Christian socialist," but he was careful to distinguish his reformist position from any doctrinaire socialism. While he did not wholly escape the sanguine temper of his time, he showed few traces of the sentimental optimism that characterized so much of the social gospel literature. As early as 1892 he had rejected the "comforting" doctrine of "the inherent upward forces of nature," and in 1907 he spoke strong words of caution to those who had imbibed the heady wine of inevitable progress.[39] After a brief flirtation with uninhibited hopefulness which found expression in *Christianizing the Social Order*, he returned to a more sober view of human nature in *A Theology for the Social Gospel*. As the title of the latter volume indicates, his interest was much more theological than most of the others, and his great contribution was to clothe the social gospel with passion and a sense of destiny. He did this by relating the social gospel in dynamic fashion to the concept of the kingdom of God, placing it in juxtaposition to the inherited, massive, and stubbornly resistant structures of the kingdom of evil.[40]

Rauschenbusch's flurry of optimism just prior to World War I was rooted in the growing popular support and official recognition that was

[37] For selections from his writings, see *A Rauschenbusch Reader*, ed. B. Y. Landis (N.Y., 1957).

[38] For the distinction between Mathews and Rauschenbusch, see W. S. Hudson, "Walter Rauschenbusch and the New Evangelism," *Religion in Life*, XXX (1961), 416–20. For Rauschenbusch's instrumental use of the term "socialism," see *ibid.*, 429–30.

[39] *Ibid.*, 421–22; and W. S. Hudson, *The Great Tradition of the American Churches*, rev. ed. (N.Y., 1963), 228–30.

[40] A brief statement of Rauschenbusch's concept of the kingdom of God is reprinted in Smith, Handy, Loetscher, *American Christianity*, II, 402–07.

being won by proponents of the social gospel. The social concern had reshaped the curricula of many of the theological seminaries, induced a considerable number of them to move from isolated hamlets to urban communities ("What medical school," asked Graham Taylor, "is thus remote from the centers of suffering men, and deprived of hospital clinics?"), and prompted others to provide scholarships for a summer's exposure of theological students to urban problems.[41] In addition, almost all the major denominations had established departments or commissions with specific responsibility for implementing their social concerns. And in 1908 the Federal Council of Churches (predecessor of the National Council of Churches) was formed to enable the churches by joint endeavors to deal more effectively with the problems of an industrial society. One of the first acts of the new Council was to adopt a "Social Creed of the Churches," [42] with an address appended which declared: "To the toilers of America and to those who by organized effort are seeking to lift the crushing burdens of the poor, and to reduce the hardships and uphold the dignity of labor, this Council sends the greeting of human brotherhood and the pledge of sympathy and of help in a cause which belongs to all who follow Christ."

Apart from their manifest concern to combat injustice, the advocates of "social Christianity" had also been motivated by a desire to overcome what was described as the alienation of the workingman from the churches. A survey in Pittsburgh in 1888 had disclosed that business, professional, and salaried men constituted less than 10 per cent of the population, yet they accounted for more than 60 per cent of the Protestant church membership. Eight years earlier, Washington Gladden had noted that only one-tenth of his congregation were wage earners, whereas the census reports revealed that almost one-fourth of the population belonged to the laboring class. It is "all too evident," he declared, "that the proportion of working people who attend church is much smaller than the proportion of churchgoers to the entire population." [43] The basic assumption was that the gap which separated the churches from the workingmen would be closed if the churches would only exhibit an interest in their plight and support them in their struggle for justice. This assumption,

[41] Abell, *The Urban Impact upon American Protestantism,* 224–45.
[42] Reprinted in Smith, Handy, Loetscher, *American Christianity,* II, 396–97. It had been drafted and adopted by the Methodist Episcopal Church earlier in 1908.
[43] From "The Working People and the Churches," *The Independent,* July 23, 1885.

however, proved to be illusory, for the tactic of wooing the workers in this fashion met with little success. The workers remained largely unresponsive to the appeal of both the churches and radical political causes. Indeed, the election of 1896 witnessed a massive shift in the labor vote from its traditional Democratic affiliation to the Republican party of William McKinley and Mark Hanna.[44] Neither of the major parties in their urban strongholds (the Republicans, for example, in Philadelphia and Chicago, and the Democrats in Boston and New York) was characterized by any radical political or economic program.

THE "PROGRESSIVE" MOVEMENT. Much of the popular support of "social Christianity" was related to the "progressivism" that found expression in Theodore Roosevelt's "Square Deal" and "Bull Moose" platforms and in Woodrow Wilson's "New Freedom." Most of the social gospel leaders were deeply involved in "progressive" politics, and the 1912 campaign of the Progressive party had a strong religious flavor. The party convention had as its theme song "Onward, Christian Soldiers," and Theodore Roosevelt closed his acceptance speech with the ringing challenge, "We stand at Armageddon and we battle for the Lord." Ministers campaigned openly from the pulpit for the party, and one justified himself by maintaining that, while "it is not the province of the pulpit to say that any man ought to be elected president," it is "the province of every pulpit to say that the principles of the Progressive party should guide the nation for the next four years." [45]

Progressivism, like the social gospel, was almost exclusively a manifestation of middle-class idealism. Middle-class opinion had been deeply shocked by the muckrakers' exposure of widespread vice and corruption, of the ruthless tactics employed by the trusts, and of the special privileges accorded "vested interests" by city governments, state legislatures, and the national Congress. The progressives had no consistent philosophy and their program was a miscellaneous collection of reforms which included direct primaries, women's suffrage, the initiative, referendum, and recall; regulation of interstate commerce, revision of banking and currency laws, effective antitrust legislation, municipal ownership of public utilities, the income tax, the eight-hour day, prohibition of child

[44] Samuel P. Hays, *The Response to Industralism, 1885–1914* (Chicago, 1957), 46–47. The Democrats did not recover their former urban strength until the elections of 1928 and 1932.

[45] *Ibid.*, 93.

labor, safeguards against industrial accidents and occupational diseases, and either strict regulation of the liquor traffic or its outright prohibition.

The related issues of conspiracies in restraint of trade and the corrupting of government officials were the great objects of concern. When most of the reforms designed to curb the "vested interests," restore power to the people, and eliminate other abuses, had been adopted, attention was concentrated upon women's suffrage and the abolition of the liquor traffic as the final goals to be achieved. Each was regarded as something of a universal panacea for the ills of society. The women's vote, it was believed, would strengthen at every point the cause of virtue, morality, altruism, and humanitarian endeavor. The crusade for prohibition, which was equally integral to the progressive program, was viewed from a similar universal perspective.

The liquor industry with its increasing monopolistic tendencies was regarded by the progressives as the most dangerous and predatory of all big business. It was lavish in its expenditures both to gain desired legislation and to thwart the enforcement of bothersome regulations adopted as concessions to public opinion. Often arrogant in its control of government, the liquor industry had been exposed again and again by the muckrakers as a principal source of political corruption and a strong ally of political reaction. Its links with vice and crime were more indirect but nonetheless real. As a progressive reform, prohibition drew upon the same moral idealism as the rest of the progressive program. It was popularly believed that the abolition of the liquor traffic would eliminate at a single stroke a primary cause not only of political reaction, corruption, vice, and crime, but also of poverty, disease, economic inefficiency, marital discord, and broken homes. While some of the progressives disliked the reform, believing it to be too extreme, this loss of support was more than compensated by that received from conservative Protestants. But the leadership which pushed the adoption of the Eighteenth Amendment remained with the socially liberal progressives.[46]

The temperance cause had long been gaining ground in the United States, and it had become much more vigorous with the organization of the Woman's Christian Temperance Union in 1874.[47] The emphasis shifted

[46] See J. H. Timberlake, *Prohibition and the Progressive Movement, 1900–1920* (Cambridge, Mass., 1963).

[47] More study could profitably be devoted to the W.C.T.U. Its influence was great, and its literature reveals a wide-ranging social concern.

from temperance to total abstinence to a full-scale attack upon the saloon. By 1900 five of the forty-five states had adopted statewide prohibition laws which banned the manufacture and sale of intoxicating beverages, and others had made provision for local option. The big thrust, however, was launched with the formation of the Anti-Saloon League in 1895, an agency which was to become an instrument of sophisticated political action. It was manned by socially progressive Protestant churchmen, and also enlisted the support of liberal Catholics.[48] As was true of the progressive movement as a whole, the drive for prohibition found its greatest strength in an alliance between the old-stock middle-class element in the cities and the rural and small-town population, both groups being stanchly Protestant and united in their determination to rid the cities of vice, crime, poverty, and corruption. Unless this was accomplished, it was feared that the growing influence of the cities would subvert the character of American society and thwart all further attempts at progress and reform.

The drive to suppress the liquor traffic had the great advantage of enlisting the support of both liberal and conservative Protestants, and in the end it became a great Protestant crusade. By April, 1917, twenty-six states had gone "dry," and before the end of the year a constitutional amendment to ban the liquor traffic had been passed by Congress and submitted to the states for ratification. With the approval of forty-five of the forty-eight states, the Eighteenth Amendment came into effect on January 16, 1920. Later in the same year the Nineteenth Amendment, which established the right of women to vote, came into operation. Of the major reforms sought by the progressives, the only unfinished business was a federal ban on child labor. The national child labor statute was declared unconstitutional by the Supreme Court in 1918, and subsequent attempts to secure a child labor amendment were to be unsuccessful.

Imperialism and world missions

A third frontier of the new industrial society that was to be of urgent concern to the churches lay beyond the seas. Conscious of its growing industrial power, the United States had begun to assume a more positive and vigorous role in international affairs. Foreign trade had mounted

---

[48] Bishop John J. Keane attended the Anti-Saloon League's founding convention, Archbishop Ireland served as one of the vice-presidents, and Catholic clergymen regularly addressed subsequent conventions.

rapidly and American entrepreneurs were eager to exploit the untapped markets of Latin America and eastern Asia. James G. Blaine, as secretary of state under Presidents Garfield and Benjamin Harrison, championed vigorous action to expand American economic and political influence abroad, and negotiated reciprocal trade agreements and arbitration treaties to further American interests. As early as 1878 a United States naval base was established on the Samoan Islands and the process of reducing the Hawaiian Islands to an American possession had begun. President Cleveland's bold defiance of Great Britain in the Venezuelan crisis of 1895 was symptomatic of the new temper which led to the Spanish-American War of 1898 and to the prompt support of Panama's revolt against Colombia in 1903. As an aftermath of the war with Spain, Puerto Rico, Guam, and the Philippines were claimed as United States possessions, and "protectorates" were established in several Caribbean countries. In the meantime the United States was intervening in China to preserve an "open door" for American commerce.

DOLLAR DIPLOMACY AND RELIGION. American imperial expansion was accompanied by a mounting enthusiasm among the churches for overseas missions. In its more bellicose form this enthusiasm was utilized as an excuse for territorial aggrandizement and what came to be called "dollar diplomacy." This was the note struck by President McKinley when he sought to explain to some Methodist friends how he had come to change his mind with regard to the acquisition of the Philippine Islands.

> I am not ashamed to tell you, gentlemen, that I went down on my knees and prayed Almighty God for light and guidance more than one night. And one night late it came to me this way. . . . There was nothing left for us to do but to take them all and to educate the Filipinos and uplift and civilize and Christianize them, and by God's grace do the very best we could by them, as our fellow men for whom Christ also died.

Senator Albert J. Beveridge was not troubled by such hesitation and uncertainty, and his defense of annexation was positive and to the point.

> We will not renounce our part in the mission of the race, trustee under God of the civilization of the world. . . . He has marked the American people as his chosen nation to finally lead in the regeneration

of the world. This is the divine mission of America. . . . The judgment of the Master is upon us: "Ye have been faithful over a few things; I will make you ruler over many things."

The fact that Scripture contained the possibility of a different understanding of American policy was made clear when Senator George F. Hoar rose to his feet in response to Beveridge and quoted another biblical text: "The Devil taketh him up into an extremely high mountain and showeth him all the kingdoms of the world and the glory of them and saith unto him, 'All these things will be thine if thou wilt fall down and worship me.' " [49]

Without the results of public opinion polls there is no way to determine which of the senators represented the majority view in the churches. There were many who shared the militant spirit of Senator Beveridge,[50] but other influential churchmen rallied to the cause of peace and international justice. This anti-imperialist spirit was notably true of those who had been drawn into the progressive movement, and in this respect William Jennings Bryan rather than Theodore Roosevelt was their spokesman. Peace societies of many types multiplied in numbers and membership. Dollar diplomacy and the "big stick" (the naval construction program) were attacked. The newly organized Federal Council of Churches established a department of peace, and the Student Y.M.C.A. which enlisted hundreds of young people for foreign mission work was also inspiring them with the ideal of human brotherhood and a warless world. On February 10, 1914, twenty-nine of America's most distinguished religious leaders—Protestant, Roman Catholic, and Jewish—were brought together to form the Church Peace Union for the purpose of coordinating the activities of all religious groups into a single thrust for the peaceful settlement of international disputes. Andrew Carnegie provided an endowment to underwrite the program, and so great was his optimism that he included as a proviso of his gift that "after war is abolished" the income may be used "to relieve the deserving poor . . . , especially those who have struggled long and earnestly against misfortune

[49] Charles S. Olcott, *The Life of William McKinley* (Boston, 1916), II, 110-11. Mark Sullivan, *Our Times, the United States, 1900-1925* (N.Y., 1926-35), I, 47-48. Garrison, *March of Faith*, 174.

[50] See K. M. MacKenzie, *The Robe and the Sword: the Methodist Church and the Rise of American Imperialism* (Washington, D.C., 1961).

and have not themselves to blame for their misfortune." [51] One of the first projects of the new organization was to aid in the establishment of the World Alliance for International Friendship through the Churches. This was accomplished in August, 1914, the month which marked the beginning of World War I.

THE EVANGELIZATION OF THE WORLD. When William R. Williams (1804–85), a scholarly Baptist preacher, wrote in 1846 that "our heavenly Father has made us a national epistle to other lands," [52] he was reiterating a conviction that had long been held by most American Christians. Until late in the nineteenth century, however, Great Britain had taken the lead in the foreign-mission enterprise and the United States had served as the junior partner. At the close of the century this role was reversed.

The expansion of American commercial and political interests abroad riveted the attention of the churches upon the needy people beyond the seas. In 1885 Josiah Strong, in a little book entitled *Our Country*, summoned the churches of America to assume their full responsibility for the Christianization of the world. [53] American ideals, he insisted, rather than its national power should be the focal point of concern in America's relationship to other lands. The Anglo-Saxon race in general and the American people in particular, he contended, are the bearers of two great interrelated ideas—"civil liberty" and "spiritual Christianity." And but for the "salt" provided by the second, the first would "speedily decay." These in turn are the "two great needs" of all mankind.

> Without controversy, these are the forces which, in the past, have contributed most to the elevation of the human race, and they must continue to be, in the future, the most efficient ministers to its progress.

The obvious corollary of this fact was that "the Anglo-Saxon [in the United States all immigrants by the alchemy of the 'melting pot' quickly became Anglo-Saxons [54]], as the great representative of these two ideas,

[51] Charles S. MacFarland, *Pioneers for Peace through Religion: Based on the Records of the Church Peace Union* (N.Y., 1946), 22.

[52] John R. Bodo, *The Protestant Clergy and Public Issues, 1812–1848* (Princeton, 1954), 241.

[53] *Our Country: Its Possible Future and Its Present Crisis*, ed. Jurgen Herbst (Cambridge, Mass., 1963). The quotations that follow are taken from chaps. XIV and XV, pp. 201–3, 205, 210, 212, 215–18, 252, 256.

[54] *Ibid.*, 203.

the depository of these two great blessings, sustains peculiar relations to the world's future" and "is divinely commissioned to be, in a peculiar sense, his brother's keeper."

Strong was more eloquent than exact in his terminology. His words sound "racist," but he states that Anglo-Saxon superiority "is due in large measure to its highly mixed origin," it being "almost universally admitted by ethnologists that the mixed races of mankind are superior to the pure ones." Thus the Anglo-Saxon is not to be defined in terms of a racial strain but as the heir of a dual tradition—"civil liberty" and "spiritual Christianity"—of which he is the custodian. And the influence of these twin concepts served as a corrective to the inevitable temptation to exercise tyrannical domination over other peoples. Nor did Strong explain the energy and vigor of the Anglo-Saxon in terms of "blood" or "genes." It was largely the product of climate and diet.

As Strong reviewed past history, it seemed evident to him that, with "two hands," God had been "preparing in our Anglo-Saxon civilization the die with which to stamp the peoples of the earth" and at the same time, through the revolutionary ferment that contact of Christian with heathen nations was creating, had been "preparing mankind to receive our impress."

> The door of opportunity is open in all the earth; organizations have been completed, languages learned, the Scriptures translated, and now the triumph of the Kingdom awaits only the exercise of the power committed to the church.

Whether the perils which threaten to delay "the coming of the kingdom wherein dwelleth righteousness" will be permitted to retard its advance "is now being swiftly determined" by the men and women of this generation. Living as they do in one of the plastic moments of history, Strong declared, "it is fully in the hands of the Christians of the United States, during the next ten or fifteen years, to hasten or retard the coming of Christ's kingdom in the world by hundreds, and perhaps thousands, of years."

Strong's stirring summons elicited a remarkable response the following summer among the students gathered for a conference at Dwight L. Moody's Mt. Hermon School. The enthusiasm was sparked by Robert P. Wilder (1863–1938) who had just graduated from Princeton, and he was aided and abetted by Luther D. Wishard (1854–1925), secretary of the

321

Student Y.M.C.A. at Princeton, and John R. Mott (1865–1955), a student at Cornell. Before the conference was over an even one hundred had volunteered for foreign-mission service. The delegates carried their contagious enthusiasm back to their campuses, Wilder made a whirlwind tour of the colleges, and by the end of the succeeding year the number of volunteers had grown to more than two thousand.[55] In 1888 the growing enthusiasm was channeled into a permanent organization, the Student Volunteer Movement, which adopted as its slogan "The evangelization of the world in this generation." For the next three decades this organization was to enlist the very ablest men and women on the college campuses of the nation and to send them to the far corners of the earth.

The motivation which lay behind this surge of foreign-mission interest was varied. A. T. Pierson (1837–1911) and A. J. Gordon (1836–95), both of whom played a part in arousing Wilder's concern, were premillennialists who believed that the gospel had to be preached throughout the world as a prerequisite to the second coming of Christ. Others were distressed at the thought of millions of souls being lost forever. J. Hudson Taylor (1832–1905) at the Student Volunteer convention at Detroit in 1894 declared:

> There is a great Niagara of souls passing into the dark. . . . Every day, every week, every month, they are passing away! A million a month in China . . . are dying without God.[56]

Democratic and humanitarian sentiment, however, seems to have played the strongest role in winning support for missions. Robert E. Speer (1867–1947), who with Wilder and Mott constituted the great triumvirate of the Student Volunteer Movement, emphasized this when he asserted that the great need for the world was "to be saved from want and disease and injustice and inequality and impurity and lust and hopelessness and fear." [57]

The whole foreign mission enterprise was marked by widespread interdenominational cooperation. Not only did the mission boards recruit

---

[55] R. W. Braisted, *In This Generation: The Story of Robert P. Wilder* (N.Y., 1941).

[56] *The Student Volunteer Enterprise: Addresses and Discussions of the Second International Convention of the Student Volunteer Movement for Foreign Missions* (N.Y., 1894), 48.

[57] *Christianity and the Nations: the Duff Lectures for 1910* (N.Y., 1910), 29.

their personnel through the joint endeavors of the Student Volunteer Movement; they allocated territory on a comity basis in the mission fields and formed interdenominational councils in mission lands for purposes of consultation and sharing of experience. At home the work of the denominational boards was coordinated through the formation of the Foreign Missions Conference of North America in 1893, and later it was also coordinated through the International Missionary Council which grew out of the Edinburgh conference of 1910. In 1902 the Missionary Education Movement was launched to quicken missionary interest in all the major denominations. A continuing problem, of course, was to provide sufficient financial support for the youth who were offering themselves in increasing numbers for missionary service. A Presbyterian layman, John B. Sleman, Jr., sought to meet this need. He had been deeply moved when thousands of college students had gathered in Nashville in 1906 for a Student Volunteer convention. As a result of his prodding the Laymen's Missionary Movement was organized in the autumn of that year to challenge laymen throughout the nation to match the devotion of youth with the dedication of their dollars. Until the outbreak of World War I, the Laymen's Missionary Movement was carried forward with the same surge of enthusiasm that characterized the Student Volunteer Movement.

The years of midpassage following the Civil War had introduced many changes into American life and had presented the churches with multiple problems of adjustment. These problems had been met with varying degrees of success, but never were they tackled with more exuberance than during the first decade and a half of the new century, which Gaius Glenn Atkins described as "the age of crusades." The unusual moral idealism and superabundance of zeal which found expression in the allied enterprises of the missionary movement was channeled into a whole galaxy of causes, only a few of which have been noted in this chapter. World War I brought to an end all these peaceful crusades by diverting the idealism and zeal of the American people into the one great crusade to end war and make the world safe for democracy through military power.

World War I also marked the end of the years of transition. The era of the frontier was brought to an end in 1912 when Arizona and New Mexico were granted statehood, and the great tide of immigration was cut off in 1914 when the German armies smashed through Belgium and into France. The economic effect of the war was to hasten the process of industrial development and to bring to maturity the urban world of modern America. In most parts of the country the agrarian democracy of earlier years was to be little more than a memory as backcountry villages and smaller cities were brought within the orbit of great metropolitan centers.

PART IV

MODERN AMERICA

1914–

less emphasis a major
world empires keep & how
they affected american religion

XIII

The Shifting Religious Configuration

By 1914 when the onset of World War I brought to an end the massive influx of new Americans, the proportionate strength of the various religious groups in the United States had been sharply modified. The numerical predominance of Protestantism had been steadily reduced throughout the latter half of the nineteenth century by continuing Roman Catholic immigration. And during the two decades immediately preceding the outbreak of war the striking gains which transformed both Judaism and Eastern Orthodox Christianity into numerically significant communities further altered the religious configuration of the nation. A realignment also had been taking place within Protestantism. By 1910 a flood of recruits from abroad had made the Lutherans the third largest Protestant denominational group. Smaller but important gains from immigration had been registered by the German and Dutch Reformed, the Evangelical Synod, and the Mennonites. Meanwhile, the Negro churches, having fashioned more effective ecclesiastical structures, had made great strides in membership. Moreover, there were numerous disaffected Protestants, some of whom were swelling the ranks of existing Adventist and Holiness churches while others were participating in incipient Fundamentalist and Pentecostal defections. And finally, some of the older Protestant denominations were undergoing a change in character. Thus the American religious scene had become outwardly even more multiform and diverse than it had been previously.

The four groups which were emerging into relative prominence for the first time were Judaism, Eastern Orthodoxy, the Negro churches, and the "disaffected" Protestants of the Adventist-Fundamentalist-Holiness-Pentecostal fringe. Of these, Judaism had the longest history.

Judaism

Jewish life finds its focus in the giving of the Law to Moses some three thousand years ago and in the consciousness of being a people chosen of God to exhibit both his righteousness and mercy.[1] The Temple in Jerusalem was the center of Jewish worship. The synagogue appeared for the first time during the Babylonian exile and was given definite shape by Ezra after the return to Jerusalem where it occupied a subordinate position to the renewed Temple worship. Among Jews of the Diaspora (those living outside Palestine), except for a rare pilgrimage to Jerusalem, the synagogue provided the sole opportunity for communal worship. While its prayer services were modeled after the Temple service, the central emphasis was upon the instruction of the people rather than upon priestly acts performed in a sacred place. The Torah (the Law contained in the Pentateuch, the five books of Moses) was read and explained and applied to the needs of daily life. When the Temple was again destroyed in A.D. 70 and the Jewish nation dispersed, synagogue worship took on heightened significance as a corporate reminder of the ancient bond symbolized by the Temple and its Ark of the Covenant.

Closely related to the developing life of the synagogue were the rabbis. The rabbis, or teachers, were businessmen or workers who had devoted their leisure to studying the heritage of Israel and, as learned scholars, had been recognized as competent authorities of Jewish law.

---

[1] For an account of Jewish faith and practice, see Milton Steinberg, *Basic Judaism* (N.Y., 1947), and also Arthur Hertzberg, *Judaism* (N.Y., 1961). For an interpretative history of Jewish life by a Reform rabbi, see Bernard J. Bamberger, *The Story of Judaism* (N.Y., 1957). The best compact account of Jewish religious developments in America is Nathan Glazer, *American Judaism* (Chicago, 1957).

Although they had no official relationship to the synagogue, the rabbis had always played a prominent role in synagogue life as spokesmen and interpreters of God's claim upon his people. After the shattering events of A.D. 70, the rabbis gradually gained a more central position. Broken and forlorn, the members of the scattered Jewish communities were groping for guidance and comfort. The rabbis gave them both, for in their preaching they reinterpreted the Law to make it applicable to the new situation and at the same time combined this instruction with glowing words of encouragement and hope. Official leadership, to be sure, did not belong to the rabbis. Others conducted the services of worship, reciting the prayers and reading from the Torah. But it was the rabbi who won the full respect and esteem of the community. More than a millennium was to pass, however, before it became customary to provide the rabbi with a salary, and even as late as the fifteenth century this was far from a universal practice.

REFORM JUDAISM. Life in America introduced a significant change in Jewish life. In medieval Europe a pattern of Jewish life developed which tended to be perpetuated in some areas until the twentieth century. These European Jewish communities were tightly knit enclaves set apart from the larger community. An individual Jew had no independent civic status. But within the ghetto there was considerable self-government, with the Jewish leadership being responsible for maintaining order, levying taxes to satisfy the demands of the civil government, and imposing additional assessments to meet their own communal needs. The synagogue was but one of several communal institutions, and it both embraced and was controlled by the total Jewish community.[2] In America these self-contained Jewish enclaves disappeared. The synagogue became the primary institution of Jewish life, with membership a matter of individual choice. Instead of one synagogue there could be several within a given area. And the synagogue was controlled by its own congregation rather than by the whole Jewish community, some of whom might not be members of any synagogue. In a sense the synagogue was the community, for it exercised whatever social control there was.

The first Jews to arrive in America were "Sephardim," Jews of Spanish or Portuguese antecedents who came by way of Brazil beginning in 1654, but they never came in large numbers. Until the last decade of the nineteenth century, most American Jews were "Ashkenazim," German-

[2] See Glazer, *American Judaism*, 18–19.

speaking Jews from central Europe. Both groups were thoroughly orthodox, differing in ritual but not in doctrine. What may be called Jewish denominationalism dates from 1802 when a group of Philadelphia Jews who wished to adhere to the practices of the Ashkenazic rite formed a separate synagogue. This was a time of small beginnings, of course, for in 1825 there were only about a half-dozen active congregations in the United States and in 1848 there were not more than fifty.

Almost everywhere throughout the world Jews had been forced to regard themselves as a separate entity, living apart from the general community and governing themselves, to the extent that they were permitted to do so, by Talmudic law.[3] In the United States the legal restrictions which fostered this isolated life were absent. Jews could become full citizens. They could be Americans of Jewish faith rather than an alien people. In this situation a growing number of Jews came to regard many of the ancient laws as anachronistic. Particular sources of embarrassment were some of the ancient folk customs associated with synagogue worship, and the general lack of decorum and dignity of the religious services. An initial attempt to simplify synagogue worship and to make it more comprehensible and appealing was made at Charleston in 1824. While this was abortive, a similar effort in 1836 was more successful. The first congregations that were founded to foster Reform were Har Sinai of Baltimore in 1842 and Emanu-El of New York in 1845.

American Jews, of course, were few in number. The great impetus for Reform came from Germany where the Jews had been emancipated by constitutional changes. At Frankfort-on-the-Main in 1843 the Frankfort Society of the Friends of Reform was organized and issued the following declaration:

> First, we recognize the possibility of unlimited development in the Mosaic religion. Second, the collection of controversies, dissertations, and prescriptions commonly designated by the name Talmud possesses for us no authority from either the doctrinal or practical standpoint. Third, a Messiah who is to lead back the Israelites to the land of Palestine is neither expected nor desired by us; we know no fatherland except that to which we belong by birth or citizenship.[4]

[3] The Talmud is a distillation of the biblical interpretation and wise counsel of the ancient rabbis.
[4] David Philipson, *The Reform Movement in Judaism* (N.Y., 1931), 122.

These were to be the classic guiding principles of Reform Judaism. As a result of the storm of protest the declaration aroused among the more conservatively inclined, many German Jews sympathetic to Reform emigrated to the United States where they greatly strengthened the Reform cause.

The great leader of Reform Judaism in America was Isaac M. Wise (1819–1900) who arrived in the United States in 1846. He served as rabbi of a small congregation in Albany until 1854, and then spent the rest of his career in Cincinnati. His great concerns were to effect a national organization to give a degree of unity to the independent Jewish congregations, and to establish a college to train rabbis. Primarily through his efforts the Union of American Hebrew Congregations was formed in 1873, and the Hebrew Union College was founded in 1875. His Reform views were promoted through the pages of the *American Israelite*, a paper which he founded and edited. In the area of doctrine he discarded belief in a personal Messiah and in the resurrection of the dead. He also made a distinction between the Torah of God (the Ten Commandments) and the Torah of Moses(the rest of the Pentateuch), the latter being simply an application of divine truth to specific circumstances and becoming outdated as conditions changed. In terms of practice he insisted upon equal rights for women (family pews, for example, instead of segregation by sex), and introduced into the service the use of both English and instrumental music. The prayer book he compiled was an abbreviation and simplification of the traditional liturgy, with references to the Messiah and the resurrection being modified to conform to his views. Other reformers were much more radical than Wise, making a sharper break with the past, introducing original prayers into the service, and substituting Sunday for Sabbath worship. Wise's adjustment to the problem posed by a Saturday morning Service was to shift it to Friday evening, an innovation which had little support during the nineteenth century but which was to become the general practice of Reform, Conservative, and even some Orthodox synagogues in the middle of the twentieth century.

By 1880 Reform had become the dominant version of American Judaism, although a placid orthodoxy continued to find expression in scattered synagogues. The extent to which Reform leaders were willing to effect accommodation to American life, however, was soon to create a further division. The growing restiveness of a minority who were nominally within the Reform camp was brought to a head in 1883 by the serving of shrimp (a violation of the dietary laws) at a banquet honoring the first graduates of Hebrew Union College. This produced a deep emotional shock among some of the more conservatively inclined. Rallied by Sebato Morais (1823–97), the disaffected groups in 1886 founded the Jewish Theological Seminary in New York City, an institution which was to become the chief center of Conservative Judaism. Occupying a middle position between Reform and Orthodox Judaism, the Conservative synagogues did not prosper greatly until the atrocities of the Nazi era in Germany heightened the sense of Jewish identity and created a growing desire among Jews to re-emphasize the historic continuities of Judaism.

THE GREAT IMMIGRATION. The wave of Jewish immigrants which poured into the United States for three and one-half decades after 1880 introduced a new strain into American Judaism and completely changed the character of the whole Jewish community. It has been estimated that in 1880 there may have been as many as 250,000 Jews in the United States.[5] They were a relatively homogeneous group, largely German in background, and quite widely dispersed throughout the country. Most of them were related to the synagogue, that is to say, to a Reform Temple. By 1914 the Jewish segment of the population numbered not far from three million. This new Jewish population was markedly different in cultural background and represented a quite different type of Judaism. The recent arrivals were refugees from eastern Europe. They were poverty-stricken and heterogeneous. They came from different lands, and their common Yiddish tongue was spoken in varied dialects. A few were distinguished scholars, but some were illiterate and most were without skills. Unlike the older Jewish inhabitants, they crowded into the eastern cities.

The Jewish flight from eastern Europe was a response to harsh anti-Semitic pressures and pogroms. In 1882 the Russian government issued a series of decrees designed to make Jewish life impossible. The objective was stated with cynical frankness by the Tsar's most trusted advisor: "One-third of the Jews will emigrate, one-third will be baptized, and one-third will starve."[6] A similar policy was pursued in other countries of eastern Europe, most notably in Romania and Galicia (Austrian Poland),

[5] Interpretation of Jewish statistics is complicated by the fact that until well into the twentieth century, numbers were computed in terms of "heads of families." Nor are Jewish statistics comparable to those of most other religious bodies, for they usually refer to total Jewish population rather than to synagogue membership.

[6] Bamberger, *The Story of Judaism*, 324.

and the pressure continued with varying intensity until the outbreak of World War I.

Among the Jews of eastern Europe there had been three responses to the tragic condition in which they found themselves. The majority, without hope of securing full status as citizens through political and social assimilation in the lands of their birth, retreated into a rigid orthodoxy, finding inner security in an unquestioning piety and a strict observance of the Torah. Their cultural outlook was almost totally unaffected by cultural movements among the peoples about them. A second major group, those who had had some contact with contemporary thought, reacted in a fashion quite different from that of the Jews of Germany and America. Instead of seeking to create a Reform Judaism that would be consonant with modern culture, they tended to renounce Judaism and identify themselves with radical antireligious movements of social reform. The passion and intensity with which the religious Jews of eastern Europe clung to traditional forms of thought and practice made the prospect of altering these forms seem utterly hopeless, while the political structures were so repressive and class-oriented that only a thoroughgoing social revolution seemed to offer the possibility of emancipation. Emerging from this second group was a third faction, rather insignificant at the outset, which cast its revolutionary fervor into a nationalistic mold. Taking their cue from the liberation movements of the Poles, Czechs, Ukrainians, and other oppressed peoples of eastern Europe, these "Lovers of Zion" emphasized the national rather than the religious character of Judaism and began to think in terms of securing emancipation through the establishment of a Jewish state. Each of these groups was represented in the east European immigration.

Nathan Glazer has reported that the Jewish immigrants who came from eastern Europe were "a frightening apparition" to "the established, middle-class, Americanized German Jews of the 1880's."

> Their poverty was more desperate than German Jewish poverty, their piety more intense than German Jewish piety, their irreligion more violent than German Jewish irreligion, their radicalism more extreme than German Jewish radicalism. It is not surprising that the American Jews viewed this immigration with mixed feelings, and some even suggested the possibility of deflecting or preventing it.

333

The American Jews did not know which was the most objectionable: the strident orthodoxy of the immigrants (as distasteful to the dignified Orthodox who opposed Reform as it was to the adherents of Reform synagogues), the antireligious views of the social radicals, or the political separatism of the Jewish nationalists. By the end of the century, however, the antipathy had been pushed sufficiently to one side for the leaders of the older Jewish communities to engage in strenuous efforts to "uplift" the immigrants and ease their adjustment to American life. One specific project of considerable future significance was the injection of new life into the Jewish Theological Seminary which had been slowly dying as its original base of tradition-oriented synagogues had dwindled. Under the leadership of Cyrus Adler (1863–1940) the financial support of Reform Jews was enlisted to transform the seminary into an agency for civilizing the east Europeans by providing them with modern English-speaking rabbis. A fund of more than a half million dollars was collected for this purpose, Solomon Schechter (1847–1915) was brought from England to be the new president, and a distinguished faculty was assembled.

RECONSTRUCTIONISM AND ZIONISM. By 1920, 80 per cent or more of the Jewish population in the United States was of east European background, and the adherents of Reform Judaism were far outnumbered by members of Orthodox synagogues. Those unaffiliated with any synagogue, however, exceeded the combined total of all religious Jews, and the proportion of the unaffiliated was growing. The flight from Judaism, which had begun in the old country, was accelerated as a concomitant of the process of Americanization. Repelled by the "foreignness" of the religious observances of their parents, children of Orthodox immigrants drifted into indifference and even hostility to religion. Few exhibited any inclination to transfer their loyalties to more modern synagogues. The results of a 1935 survey in New York City, which revealed that approximately 75 per cent of Jewish young people between the ages of fifteen and twenty-five had attended no religious service during the preceding year, were not regarded as atypical.[7] Social centers, growing out of such social agencies as the settlement houses and the Young Men's and Young Women's Hebrew Associations, were more often the focal points of Jewish life than the synagogues.

A creative response to this situation was the Reconstructionist

[7] Glazer, *American Judaism*, 85.

movement led by Mordecai M. Kaplan (b. 1881) of Jewish Theological Seminary. Kaplan's views evolved out of the synagogue center movement which he initiated in 1918. Others had experimented with making the synagogue more attractive by developing "institutional" temples patterned after the institutional churches of the Protestants, but Kaplan's aim was a new type of Jewish community with its focus not religion but "Jewishness." His approach to religion was sociological and he sought to strengthen Judaism by relating it closely to all aspects of Jewish life—political, cultural, intellectual, and philanthropic. His central contention, fully elaborated in *Judaism as a Civilization* (1934), was that Judaism was not a religion but a religious civilization in which nonreligious as well as religious Jews shared. The synagogue should be the rallying center of Jewish people and Jewish culture even for those who did not feel strongly about Jewish religion. Traditional rituals and ceremonies were viewed as important for their instrumental value as cement which helped to bind the Jewish people together. Conservative Judaism, with its ambivalent stance between Reform and Orthodox Judaism, was best equipped to assimilate Kaplan's Reconstructionist emphasis upon both tradition and modernity. In general the Conservative synagogues adopted Kaplan's policy of fostering a broad, inclusive Jewishness while rejecting some of the more radical features of his philosophy.

Closely allied to Kaplan's view of Judaism as a civilization was the older Zionist view of Judaism as a nation. Zionism had east European roots among the nineteenth-century "Lovers of Zion" but was given its more definitive shape by Theodor Herzl (1860–1914), a Viennese reporter who was present in Paris at the trial of Captain Alfred Dreyfus. In 1894 Dreyfus had been falsely charged with treason and was subsequently convicted, a victim of virulent anti-Semitic feeling in the French army. In a state of high emotional excitement Herzl wrote a pamphlet entitled *The Jewish State* (1896). The only salvation for Jews, he insisted, was national rebirth. This necessitated a homeland, preferably in Palestine. Herzl was hailed by many as a prophet, and in 1897 the first World Zionist Congress was held in Basel, Switzerland.

The Zionist issue became the subject of prolonged debate. While Zionist leaders tended to be nonreligious, many Orthodox Jews embraced Zionism since it could be reconciled with the ancient expectation of the restoration of Israel. Conservative Jews had even fewer reservations and

335

tended to become ardent Zionists. Reform Jews, on the other hand, were generally hostile, viewing Judaism as a religion and advocating a policy of assimilation at other points. After Hitler's persecution of the Jews began in 1933 and thousands of German Jews emigrated to Palestine, the Zionist question became much less theoretical. By 1935 a majority of the Reform rabbis had moved into the Zionist camp, and in that year the Central Conference of American Rabbis abandoned its official policy of opposition to Zionism and adopted in its stead a position of neutrality. The subsequent holocaust, in which six million Jews were murdered by the Nazi state, further strengthened both the Zionist cause and the sense of Jewish solidarity. When the State of Israel was established in 1948, American Jews rallied to ensure its survival by raising astonishingly large sums through the United Jewish Appeal to aid the resettlement of refugees who were streaming into Israel from many parts of the world.[8]

THE JEWISH RELIGIOUS REVIVAL.   While the Hitler years heightened Jewish self-consciousness and drew many into participation in Jewish activities, there was no great return to the synagogue. The surge of growth in synagogue membership was to be a phenomenon of the post-World War II period. In 1937 the *American Jewish Year Book* estimated that the Reform congregations had 50,000 member families. The Conservative congregations, having gained recruits from the children and grandchildren of Orthodox immigrants, had passed the Reform group and numbered some 75,000 member families. The Orthodox congregations had the largest constituency, with about 200,000 families. Thus the combined synagogue membership represented between one and one and one-half million Jews, not much more than one-fourth of all the Jews in the country. By 1956 there was a marked change. Synagogue life was flourishing, with most of the gains having been made in the last decade. Member families of Reform temples numbered 255,000, a fivefold increase over 1937. The growth rate of Conservative synagogues was smaller, but their member families had almost tripled in number and stood at 200,000. While Orthodox Judaism represented a declining portion of the total Jewish religious community, it too was exhibiting signs of vigorous life, and its most notable intellectual center, Yeshiva College, had become a flourishing university.

[8] The total amount raised in 1948 was $201,000,000. In subsequent years the amount declined, but in 1955 it still exceeded $100,000,000.

Apart from numbers, there was a conspicuous increase in what may be termed the practice of piety. The proportion of the Jewish population attending religious services at least once a month increased from 18 per cent in 1947 to 31 per cent in 1955. Even among Reform Jews there was a strong tendency to re-emphasize traditional values, customs, and ceremonial observances. The Friday evening family Kiddush with its candle lighting became much more common and the holidays were more widely observed. In the mid-1950's it was observed somewhat skeptically that the modern Jew "does more" but "knows less." This verdict was scarcely supported by the available evidence. Not only had there been a vast increase in the number of children receiving a Jewish education through weekday classes, the Sunday school, and rapidly multiplying Jewish day schools, but publishers had discovered that there was a growing market among adults for books dealing with Jewish theology and religious life.

The revival of synagogue life may have been related to the changed status of the Jewish community. Whereas in the 1930's there had been a large Jewish working class and a strong Jewish element in the labor union movement, in the 1950's only a small segment of the Jewish population could be classified as belonging to the laboring class. As a result of their driving zeal for education, second- and third-generation east European Jews had been remarkably successful in imitating the earlier Jewish population by moving into business and the professions. These children and grandchildren of the newer immigrants also had shifted their place of residence from rundown quarters in the inner city to better neighborhoods, and many of them had become suburbanites. Having become once again a relatively homogeneous and prosperous community, mid-twentieth century Jews tended to conform to the churchgoing pattern of other middle class Americans.

Eastern Orthodox Christianity

The Eastern Orthodox churches also have a long history.[9] They look back to the early Christian Fathers, and to Athanasius, the Cappadocians, Pseudo-Dionysius, and "the seven ecumenical councils," as the source of their tradition. Perhaps Orthodox Christianity can best be identified in

[9] See Nicolas Zernov, *Eastern Christendom* (London, 1961); Ernst Benz, *The Eastern Orthodox Church: Its Thought and Life* (Chicago, 1963); and Timothy Ware, *The Orthodox Church* (Baltimore, 1963).

terms of the two separations which gave the Orthodox churches their geographical locus. The first separation was that of the smaller eastern churches—the Nestorians of Syria, Persia, and ultimately China, and the Monophysites (the Jacobite and Coptic churches) of Armenia, Syria, Egypt, and Ethiopia—which took place in the fifth and sixth centuries. The second separation was the product of a growing cleavage between the Greek-speaking and the Latin-speaking areas of the old Roman Empire. Although the ecclesiastical division was beginning to be apparent as early as the end of the sixth century, the final separation is commonly dated from 1054. As a result of these two separations, Eastern Orthodoxy was bounded on both its eastern and western sides, but it was able to expand to the north among the Slavonic peoples. As the Greek power of Byzantium dwindled, the newer Orthodox churches of the north increased in importance. After the fall of Constantinople in 1453, Moscow—"the third Rome"—tended to assume Byzantium's role as protector of the Orthodox world.

THE ORTHODOX CHURCHES. Distributed throughout eastern Europe, in Russia, and along the eastern coast of the Mediterannean, Orthodox Christianity is a family of self-governing churches, united by a common faith and order. Apart from areas of more recent expansion, these churches are: the ancient Patriarchates of Constantinople, Alexandria, Antioch, and Jerusalem; the national churches of Russia, Romania, Serbia (Yugoslavia), Greece, Bulgaria, Georgia (U.S.S.R.), Cyprus, Czechoslovakia, Poland, and Albania; and the Holy Monastery of Sinai. While the Patriarch of Constantinople is known as the Ecumenical or Universal Patriarch and enjoys a position of special honor, he has no power to intervene in the affairs of any church other than his own. His position is much like that of the Archbishop of Canterbury in the Anglican communion, which is also composed of self-governing churches spread throughout the world. Because the overwhelming proportion of Orthodox Christians (perhaps as many as 55 million) are behind the "iron curtain," it is difficult to estimate their total number. The four ancient Patriarchates have more than 2,500,000 adherents, and the churches of Greece and Cyprus have a combined total of almost 8 million adherents.

Although the Orthodox have much in common with Roman Catholics, there are significant differences in emphasis, practice, and even doctrine. The whole mood is much more mystical and much less legalistic. The mode of baptism is triple immersion. Communion is in both kinds, the communicant receiving both the bread and the wine. Infants are confirmed and receive communion immediately after being baptized. Statues (rounded images) are not permitted, and in their stead icons (paintings and mosaics) are used. Priests may marry prior to ordination, but bishops must be unmarried. The date of Easter is different (being reckoned by the Julian rather than the Gregorian calendar), and the liturgy is in the vernacular. The doctrines of purgatory and the immaculate conception of Mary are not generally accepted; and instead of extreme unction for the dying, the sick are anointed for the recovery of health. The most crucial difference is the authority Roman Catholicism confers upon the Roman Pontiff as the vicar of Christ and the infallible teacher and ruler of the faithful. Where Roman Catholics insist upon obedience to the Bishop of Rome, Orthodox Christians stress the role of the bishops in the government of the church and the authority of General Councils in the determination of matters of faith.

ORTHODOXY IN AMERICA. Eastern Orthodoxy had its beginnings in North America when missionary monks came to Alaska in the 1790's and were successful in converting large numbers of the natives. A seminary was established at Sitka in 1848 and a diocese was formed in 1867 when Alaska became a territory of the United States. In 1872 the seat of the diocese was transferred to San Francisco, and in 1905 to New York. In addition to the Russians, a few Greek communities had churches prior to 1900, but the major Orthodox influx came after the turn of the century. During the latter years of the great Jewish immigration, Slavic peoples (and Romanians) were also arriving from the countries of eastern Europe. Many of the non-Jewish east Europeans were Roman Catholic, but a large portion of them were Orthodox. And Orthodox strength was augmented by Uniates, Roman Catholics of an Eastern rite, who were reconciled in America to Orthodoxy (see pp. 340–41). Unlike the Jews, these other east Europeans did not crowd into the coastal cities. They had been recruited to labor in the mines and steel mills, and hence they were dispersed throughout Pennsylvania and along the periphery of the Great Lakes. The only significant exception to this pattern of Orthodox settlement was represented by non-Slavic immigrants, principally Greeks and Syrians (including Armenians), who were largely independent entrepreneurs and were widely scattered throughout the country.

From a total membership of not more than one hundred thousand in 1900, the number of Orthodox in the United States had risen to more than two million in 1960,[10] subdivided into at least fifteen national or jurisdictional groups. Before World War I all Orthodox Christians in America were united in a single organization under the jurisdiction of the Russian church, since it was the Russians who first brought Orthodox Christianity to the United States. The subsequent multiplicity of jurisdictions was a consequence of the Russian Revolution of 1917. With the Russian church becoming involved in a difficult and controversial relationship to the new Soviet regime, each of the Orthodox nationality groups formed separate organizations.

The Orthodox churches in America had a confused history in the post-World War I years as a result of the readjustments which then took place. The Greek church has been the largest (1,500,000 members in 1962) and most stable, but it was troubled by such disorders and frictions that it was not until 1930 that its life was fully regularized as the Greek Archdiocese of North and South America. The Russians had less unity. In 1919 a convention of Russian Orthodox, meeting in Pittsburgh, declared the Russian church in America to be "temporarily autonomous." Five years later, at a convention in Detroit, what was to become known as the Russian Orthodox Greek Catholic Church of America was formally constituted. This is the second largest Orthodox church, with a reported membership in 1962 of 755,000. A second Russian church, the Russian Orthodox Church Outside Russia, was formed in 1920 by Russian emigrés in Europe. With 55,000 of its members in America, it shifted its headquarters to the United States in 1950. The sole point of difference between these two groups is that the first group is willing to affirm spiritual loyalty to the patriarch of Moscow if he will recognize its administrative and legislative autonomy, while the second group insists that the Moscow Patriarchate has forfeited its right to be considered a true Orthodox church. A third Russian church, the Russian Orthodox Church in America (Patriarchal Exarchate) maintains an official tie with the Orthodox in the Soviet Union. It is the creature of the Moscow Patriarchate, and is so small as to be insignificant. The fourth Russian group, the American Carpatho–Russian Orthodox Greek Catholic Church with a membership in 1962 of 102,000, is a former Russian Uniate church which returned to Orthodoxy early in the century. The Ukrainians in America not only split

[10] According to the *Year Book of the American Churches* the total in 1960 was 2,680,633. This figure is no more than an approximation, for Orthodoxy, like Judaism, has tended to estimate its adherents in terms of total ethnic or national groups. Membership is generally reported in round numbers.

away from the Russians; they have suffered a threefold division among themselves. The two oldest groups are the Ukrainian Orthodox Church of U.S.A. (87,000 members in 1962) and the Ukrainian Orthodox Church of America (40,250 members in 1962). The latter was formerly a Uniate group in communion with Rome. The Holy Ukrainian Autocephalic Orthodox Church (5,000 members in 1962) was formed by World War II refugees in 1950. The Albanian, Bulgarian, Romanian, Serbian, and Syrian Orthodox were not fragmented, but their churches did not become fully stabilized in organization until around 1930.

Troubled by cultural and administrative divisions, the Orthodox churches in America began to gain full maturity only after World War II. Of the several theological seminaries which were established, those in New York and Boston became distinguished centers of theological scholarship. Paralleling the theological awakening was evidence of growing sentiment for greater unity among the Orthodox. In 1954 the Council of Eastern Orthodox Youth Leaders of America was formed which drew together most of the Orthodox youth organizations, and in 1960 a committee of Orthodox bishops began periodic meetings under the presidency of the Greek archbishop. The Orthodox churches also exhibited vitality in adjusting to the American environment. The use of English in worship, the introduction of mixed choirs and instrumental music, the installation of pews for the seating of the congregation, the development of parish organizations, and the adoption of church dinners as an important aspect of church life, were the kind of adaptation that other immigrant bodies had made prior to becoming fully integrated into American life. There were several attempts, mostly by former Episcopalians, to form an indigenous Orthodox church that would be at the same time both more American and more "catholic" and thus attract converts from other traditions. These met with little success and received little encouragement from Orthodox leaders, although at least four of these bodies were able to maintain a precarious existence with a handful of adherents.

"Disaffected" Protestants

One of the consequences of religious liberty is the opportunity for disaffection to find free and open expression. Many of the groups born of disaffection in the nineteenth century lived on into the twentieth century, some of them growing in strength, others declining. Among those which have been discussed in preceding chapters are Mormonism, Millerism, and Spiritualism; New Thought, Christian Science, and Unity; Theosophy, Baha'i, and the Vedanta Society. But there were other groups which were to have a surge of growth in the post-World War I years. Of these, with the exception of the Fundamentalist movement (see pp. 363–71), the Holiness and Pentecostal churches and Jehovah's Witnesses were perhaps the most significant. These latter groups, on the whole, were more traditional in orientation than those previously considered. One might refer to them as "sects" rather than "cults." [11] They may best be described as disaffected Protestants, for they claimed no new revelation and their intention was to recover past tradition.

THE HOLINESS MOVEMENT. The quest for perfect sanctification or holiness is as old as Christianity. In nineteenth-century America it had received powerful reinforcement from the generally optimistic temper of the time ("Jacksonian perfectionism"), from the hunger for holiness generated by the revivals, and more specifically from the pervasive influence of the strong Wesleyan emphasis upon the doctrine of Christian perfection. [12] Among the non-Methodists who responded to this "perfectionist" climate of opinion, Charles G. Finney and his colleagues at Oberlin were the most prominent. Beginning in 1839 the Oberlin group exhibited a growing interest in "the higher Christian life," and through their influence the concern for sanctification penetrated most of the Protestant denominations during the decades immediately preceding and following the Civil War. [13] The holiness revival, however, found its pre-

[11] As is true of many words, "cult" and "sect" have a variety of meanings. In this context, "cult" is used to denote those groups which are based on a claim to new revelation and/or the authoritative teaching of a new prophet. A cult tends to be forward-looking and is frequently eager to come to terms with what is considered to be "modern" thought. "Sect," on the other hand, is used to denote groups which make no claim to new revelation but instead seek to recover what they regard as an important but neglected aspect of past tradition. Thus they are backward-looking and usually highly resistant to "modern" thought.

[12] Wesleyan perfectionism was defined by nineteenth-century Methodists in terms of a "second blessing"—a work of grace (sanctification) subsequent to conversion (justification) which imparted perfect love of God and liberation from sin. Wesley never claimed sanctification for himself, and sometimes he seemed to imply that it was the culmination of a growth in grace rather than an instantaneous experience. For Wesley's views, see Harold Lindström, *Wesley and Sanctification*, trans. H. S. Harvey (London, 1946).

[13] For Asa Mahan's statement of the Oberlin views, see selection in Smith, Handy, Loetscher, *American Christianity*, II, 42–48. Wesleyan and Oberlin perfectionism had much in common, but the former tended to stress the instantaneous change wrought by the "second blessing" while the latter emphasized the more gradual change resulting from growth in grace. See Timothy L. Smith, *Revivalism and Social Reform* (N.Y., 1957), 108–12, and J. L. Peters, *Christian Perfectionism and American Methodism* (N.Y., 1956).

eminent expression among the Methodists, where it was sparked by the enthusiasm of a remarkable woman, Phoebe Palmer, and where it gained momentum through her evangelistic tours and through the organized promotional efforts of the National Association for the Promotion of Holiness which had been founded in 1867.

Methodism as a whole continued to be preoccupied with the quest for holiness throughout the latter half of the nineteenth century.[14] In spite of this unanimity, it was nonetheless a potentially disruptive emphasis, for it tended to cultivate an absolutist state of mind which brooked no compromise. This was illustrated by the Wesleyan Methodist defection of 1843 which was rooted in a demand for moral perfection on the slavery issue. After the Civil War the disruptive issue was the growing "worldliness" of the Methodist churches and their members.

Methodists had been a plain people—plain in dress, behavior, and worship. But as Methodism gained in numbers, wealth, and social status, signs of laxity began to appear. As early as 1856 the stringent rules prohibiting the use of specific items of ornamentation in dress were reduced in the *Discipline* to a general admonition, an admonition that was not sufficiently rigorous to deter Bishop Matthew Simpson's wife from appearing in ruffled silk, expensive lace, and fine jewelry. A similar loss of simplicity in worship occurred as costly edifices were built, and choirs, organs, and instrumental music were introduced. A correspondent of the *Christian Advocate* reported in 1868 that in the cities of the western states—in Ohio, Indiana, Michigan, Wisconsin, Illinois, and Iowa—the tendency was to erect "one hundred thousand dollar churches" where "wealth and style and fashion gather, and the poor have not the gospel preached to them." Two years earlier a writer in the same journal had noted with satisfaction that "by virtue of the habits which religion inculcates and cherishes, our church members have as a body risen in the social scale, and thus become socially removed from the great body out of which most of them were originally gathered." While he regarded this development as "natural" and "not undesirable," there were to be some among the less privileged who were to regard it as a betrayal of the

[14] The southern bishops constantly emphasized this theme, and the northern bishops were equally firm, as they declared in 1884, that "the mission of Methodism is to promote holiness." See *The History of American Methodism*, ed. E. S. Bucke (N.Y., 1964), II, 614–18.

summons to holiness.[15] By the end of the century the grievances were multiplying, with notice being taken of the "church theatricals" and "fairs" that were being held, and of the increasing number of church members who "dance, play cards, attend theaters, [and] absent themselves from revivals."[16]

A foretaste of what was to be a continuing disaffection was supplied in 1860 with the formation of the Free Methodist Church at Pekin, New York. Taking its stance on the declaration that "those who are sanctified wholly are saved from all inward sin" and "all their thoughts, words, and actions are governed by pure love," the new church proceeded to denounce the proud and aspiring, to voice opposition to all "superficial, false, and fashionable" Christians, and to demand of church members an affirmative response to the question: "Will you forever lay aside all superfluous ornaments and adorn yourself in modest apparel . . . , not with broidered hair or gold or pearls or costly array?" Organs, instrumental music, and pew rentals were also condemned.[17]

The Free Methodist revolt was restricted to three relatively small areas in western New York, Michigan, and Illinois, but in the 1880's evidence of more widespread disaffection found expression in the formation of numerous independent Holiness groups throughout much of rural America. While some of these "come-outer" groups were composed of people from various denominations, the larger portion were formed by dissident Methodists. By the 1890's the local fellowships had begun to coalesce into larger groupings. Most were to remain numerically unimportant,[18] but there were a few that were to exhibit a capacity for sustained growth during the first half of the twentieth century. One of these was the Church of God (Anderson, Indiana), founded in 1881 with a dual stress on holiness and Christian unity. From its initial base in the rural Midwest,

[15] W. C. Barclay, *History of Methodist Missions*, Vol. III (N.Y., 1957), 49. May, *Protestant Churches and Industrial America*, 62.

[16] *History of American Methodism*, ed. E. S. Bucke, II, 624.

[17] *Ibid.*, 346, 352, 356, 357n., 359.

[18] Some of these were the Hephzibah Faith Mission Association formed in Iowa in 1892, the Church of Daniel's Band formed in Michigan in 1893, the Metropolitan Church Association formed in Illinois in 1894, the Church of Christ (Holiness) formed in Alabama in 1894, the Church of God (Apostolic) formed in Kentucky in 1897, the Missionary Bands of the World formed in Indiana in 1898, the Missionary Church Association also formed in Indiana in 1898, and the Pillar of Fire Church formed in Colorado in 1901.

it gradually spread into the South and to the Pacific coast.[19] Another group that picked up momentum was the Christian and Missionary Alliance, founded by A. B. Simpson, a Presbyterian minister, in 1887. But the most successful was to be the Church of the Nazarene, established by a Methodist district superintendent at Los Angeles in 1895 and enlarged by mergers with an eastern Holiness group in 1907 and with one in the South the following year.[20] Fifteen years after its founding, the Church of the Nazarene had 10,000 members. Twenty years later, in 1930, it had over 100,000. In 1950 it had grown to 226,684 members, and in 1960 to 307,629. By this latter date the Holiness groups as a whole, including the Salvation Army, had a total membership of slightly more than 1,500,000.

THE PENTECOSTAL CHURCHES. Growing out of the Holiness movement was another group of churches whose combined membership by the middle of the twentieth century also was approximately 1,500,000. These were the "pentecostal" churches. Their distinguishing feature, in addition to the practice of faith healing, was an emphasis upon a "third blessing," the baptism of the Holy Spirit, which was manifest by speaking in an unknown tongue.

Modern pentecostalism was first known as the Latter Rain Movement, the name being derived from the "former rain" and "latter rain" of Joel 2:23, which was interpreted as a dual prophecy of the speaking in tongues on the first Pentecost (Acts 2:4) and of the descent of the Spirit which was to occur immediately prior to Christ's premillennial return. The movement originated with the preaching of R. G. Spurling and A. J. Tomlinson in Tennessee and North Carolina at the close of the nineteenth century. Their activity resulted in a bewildering array of Church of God organizations. The largest (170,261 members in 1960) is generally designated the Church of God (Cleveland, Tennessee),[21] but at least three offshoots bearing the same name have had their headquarters in that small Tennessee city. The confusion was somewhat reduced when one of the latter groups adopted the Church of God of Prophecy as its designation.

[19] See C. E. Brown, *When the Trumpet Sounded: History of the Church of God* (Anderson, Ind., 1951).
[20] See Timothy L. Smith, *Called unto Holiness: The Story of the Nazarenes* (Kansas City, Mo., 1962).
[21] See Charles W. Conn, *Like a Mighty Army Moves the Church of God* (Cleveland, Tenn., 1955).

Apart from the various Church of God groups whose strength is centered in North Carolina, Georgia, Florida, Tennessee, and Alabama, most of the other Pentecostal churches belong to the Pentecostal Fellowship of North America. The largest of these was the Assemblies of God, founded in 1914 at a convention in Hot Springs, Arkansas.[22] Again the terminology is somewhat confusing for the local units of the Assemblies of God are frequently called full gospel tabernacles or full gospel churches. The Assemblies of God differ from most other Pentecostal churches in that they regard sanctification as a gradual process rather than an instantaneous work of grace. Consequently, for them, speaking in tongues is the sign of a second rather than a third blessing. Beginning in 1914 with not more than 6,000 members, the Assemblies of God numbered 41,248 adherents in 1926; 318,478 in 1950; and 508,602 in 1960. Furthermore they had launched a bold foreign-mission program and had won notable successes in many parts of the world.

A more streamlined pentecostalism was represented by the Foursquare Gospel of Aimee Semple McPherson (1890–1944). With a magnetic personality, striking beauty, a flair for the dramatic, and an ability to turn the unfavorable publicity generated by her sensational adventures to her own advantage, Mrs. McPherson gathered a large following in Los Angeles where she erected the Angelus Temple. After its dedication on January 1, 1923, the Temple quickly became a major tourist attraction. Emphasizing sanctification, the gift of tongues, faith healing, and the imminent return of Christ, Sister Aimee soon had branch churches in various parts of the country. In 1927 these branches and the mother church were incorporated as the International Church of the Foursquare Gospel. After Mrs. McPherson's death, her son Robert continued her work. But without the vitality and excitement she had contributed, its growth lagged. In 1960 the church had 82,624 members.

MILLENNIALISM. While premillennial views were held by some of the Holiness and Pentecostal groups, there were other disaffected Protestants who seized upon the expectation of Christ's return to judge the quick and the dead as their major theme. This emphasis offered both present and future consolation to those who felt alienated and disinherited by the "fashionable" churches of the privileged classes. Part of the comfort was the satisfaction to be derived from the assurance that the established

[22] See Irwin Winehouse, *The Assemblies of God* (N.Y., 1959).

denominations were clearly apostate, and further consolation was gained from the conviction that the tables would soon be turned, with the mighty being put down and the humble exalted, the hungry being filled with good things and the rich sent empty away.

The "dispensationalism" of the Darbyites and the Scofield Bible (see pp. 282–83) had made significant inroads among members of many of the older churches during the latter years of the nineteenth century, and after 1920 it was to produce a growing number of independent Bible churches and gospel tabernacles. It also was to contribute to most of the Fundamentalist defections. An older premillennial tradition in America, stemming from the Millerite excitement of the 1840's, was represented by the Seventh-day Adventists and the smaller Advent Christian group. After maintaining an undramatic and modest witness for more than half a century, the Seventh-day Adventists, who had been chiefly known for their sanitariums and for fathering the breakfast-food empires of the Kelloggs and the Posts, experienced a surge of new life in the twentieth century.[23] From 62,211 members in 1906, they grew to 110,998 in 1926, to 237,168 in 1950, and to 317,852 in 1960. But these statistics tell less than half the story, for twice this number of Seventh-day Adventists were to be found outside the United States as a result of far-flung missionary endeavor during these same years. Quite surprising in view of their firm belief in the imminent end of the world was their heavy investment in publishing houses, hospitals, homes for the aged, and especially educational institutions. Not only did they maintain numerous academies, colleges, graduate schools, and both a theological seminary and a medical and dental school; but they also established a widespread network of elementary schools. Noting their many good works, one observer has commented that seldom, while expecting a kingdom of God from heaven, has a group worked so diligently for one on earth.[24]

Of all the Adventist or millennial groups, Jehovah's Witnesses are in many ways the most conspicuous and vigorous.[25] After the onset of the depression in 1929 the Witnesses often seemed omnipresent, selling the *Watchtower* on busy street corners, and ringing doorbells endlessly in an

[23] See M. E. Olsen, *Origin and Progress of Seventh-day Adventists* (Washington, D.C., 1932), and David Michell, *Seventh-day Adventists in Action* (N.Y., 1958).

[24] Gaustad, *Historical Atlas of Religion in America*, 115.

[25] The best account of the movement by an outsider is H. H. Stroup, *The Jehovah's Witnesses* (N.Y., 1945). See also Marley Cole, *Jehovah's Witnesses: The New World Society* (N.Y., 1955), and Royston Pike, *Jehovah's Witnesses* (N.Y., 1954).

effort to gain an opportunity to present their message of salvation. Then with the end of World War II, Kingdom Halls began to multiply. But it was their encounters with the law that gained the Witnesses most notoriety. Much of their trouble stemmed from their refusal to salute the flag, register for the draft, and permit their children to receive blood transfusions. Not only did these several refusals bring them before the courts, but they served to engender a popular hostility which found expression in attempts to harry the Witnesses by charging them with minor infractions of municipal codes—disturbing the peace, trespassing, violating Sunday "blue laws," and peddling without a permit.

The Witnesses have been known under a variety of names—Millennial Dawnists, International Bible Students, members of the Watchtower Bible and Tract Society, Russellites, and Rutherfordites. The founder was Charles Taze ("Pastor") Russell (1852–1916), a haberdasher and member of a Congregational church in Allegheny, Pennsylvania, who had been troubled by the notion of eternal damnation and by doubts as to the reliability of the Bible. "Stumbling," as he put it, upon an adventist preacher, he found help that was sufficient to re-establish his "wavering faith." By 1872 Russell was meeting with a small group of earnest Christians to examine the teaching of Scripture "relative to the coming of Christ and his kingdom." [26] Soon he had elaborated a millennial scheme of his own. In 1879 he began the publication of a magazine, and the following year he published his first book, *Food for Thinking Christians*. By 1884 he had won enough adherents to justify forming them into the Zion's Watch Tower Society. To disseminate his message, Russell traveled incessantly, trained "preachers," and issued a constant stream of publications, including several million copies of a multivolumed *Studies in the Scriptures*. Attention was focused on 1914 as the year when "the kingdoms of this world" will be brought to an end, and "the full establishment of the Kingdom of God will be accomplished." [27] When the year passed without the expected heavenly intervention, a re-examination of Scripture disclosed that it was Christ's return "in spirit" that had taken place in 1914, and that this was but a prelude to his visible return to lead the righteous into battle against the hosts of evil. This imminent Armageddon would mark the beginning of the millennium.

[26] Stroup, *Jehovah's Witnesses*, 4, 6.
[27] *Jehovah's Witnesses in the Divine Purpose* (Brooklyn, 1959), 55.

When Pastor Russell died in 1916 his following was not large, numbering not many more than 15,000, but positions of leadership in the Society were sufficiently coveted to occasion a severe struggle for power. The victor was Joseph Franklin ("Judge") Rutherford (1869–1942), legal counsel of the Society and Russell's attorney in his divorce proceedings and in his imbroglio over the sale of "miracle wheat." Judge Rutherford injected new life into the Society, substituted his writings for those of Pastor Russell, popularized the slogan "Millions now living will never die," [28] introduced the name "Jehovah's Witnesses" (1931), and equipped the Witnesses with phonographs so that they could utilize transcriptions of his talks in their house-to-house calls. As before it was a personality-centered operation, with Judge Rutherford replacing Pastor Russell as the authoritative teacher and leader. All this was changed when Rutherford died in 1942. This time there was no "palace intrigue," no struggle for control, for a collective leadership took over and the "personality cult" was eliminated. [29] A board of directors assumed control with Nathan H. Knorr (b. 1903) as president. Unsigned pronouncements replaced the writings of Judge Rutherford, and the portable phonographs disappeared. Henceforth the Witnesses were to be trained to do their own talking instead of relying on the transcribed voice of a leader. [30]

With Rutherford's death, Jehovah's Witnesses entered the period of their greatest growth. Activity was stepped up both at home and abroad. During the five years from 1942 to 1947 in the midst of World War II the worldwide membership almost doubled, increasing from 115,240 to 207,552; and the rate of growth was even greater during the next five years, with the total membership reaching 456,265 in 1952. By 1960 the number of Witnesses throughout the world was nearly one million, with the United States accounting for slightly more than one-quarter of the total. [31]

The message, elaborated successively by Pastor Russell, Judge Rutherford, and the directorate headed by Nathan Knorr, was calculated to appeal to the multiple resentments of those who are euphemistically described as the "culturally deprived." The central contention was that Satan's power is wielded through "the religious, commercial, and political

[28] This was the title of one of his early publications (1920).
[29] Marley Cole, *Jehovah's Witnesses*, 107–8.
[30] *Ibid.*, 211–12.
[31] *Ibid.*, 212. For detailed statistics, see pp. 220–28.

combine" which is united in oppressing the righteous.[32] These three elements in society are so intimately linked that each does the bidding of the others. All churches and religious organizations are "tools of Satan" and are utilized by the clergy as a means of securing cash income. The clergy both support and are supported by the proud and arrogant commercial class which dominates, subjugates, and exploits the poor. The wealthy in turn are protected by the governments of the world, all of which are equally wicked since they are ruled by Satan. The righteous, however, are not without hope, for the evils of the world are soon to be rectified at the battle of Armageddon when the forces of Jehovah led by Jesus will defeat the hosts of Satan; and Jesus, with the living Witnesses and the resurrected righteous among the dead, will reign for one thousand years.

While few of the Holiness, Pentecostal, and millenarian groups were as direct or as comprehensive in their appeal to the frustrated and the resentful as Jehovah's Witnesses, they all tended to thrive among those who for one reason or another felt either alienated or disinherited. And since this was a common feeling among many mid-twentieth-century Americans, these diverse expressions of disaffection—including the related Fundamentalist groups—represented a combined membership in 1960 of almost 8,500,000 persons.

The Negro churches

In many ways Negro religious life reflected the patterns and trends that prevailed in the general religious life of the nation. Most of the larger "white" denominations had Negro members. This was true, for example, of the American Baptist Convention, the Methodist Church, the two major Presbyterian churches, the Protestant Episcopal Church, the Roman Catholic Church, and the United Church of Christ. Some of these Negro members belonged to predominantly white congregations, but most were in separate Negro congregations.[33] These "integrated" churches, however,

[32] See Stroup, *Jehovah's Witnesses*, 155–61.

[33] On the congregational level the separation could be regarded as a natural grouping because of residential patterns, but the Methodists and Presbyterians carried the separation a step further by grouping Negro congregations in separate ecclesiastical units. In 1964, however, the United Presbyterian Church abolished the last of its Negro presbyteries, and the Methodist Church made provision for the gradual liquidation of its segregated "Central Jurisdiction."

accounted for only a small fraction of Negro church membership, for the overwhelming proportion of Negroes belonged to Negro denominations. Outwardly these denominations closely resembled the churches of the white majority. Of the eleven million members of Negro denominations in 1960 (up from three million in 1900), slightly more than 70 per cent were Baptists and 22 per cent were Methodists. But this outward resemblance was somewhat deceptive.

As the result of the social forces to which the Negro population was subjected, a separate Negro world had been created in America; and the Negro church was partly the product of this segregated society with a distinctive life of its own.[34] The worship was highly emotional, featuring a variety of liturgical innovations designed to encourage group participation. The theology was characterized by a strong otherworldly emphasis. The congregational singing was deeply moving, and both the emotional pitch of the services and their eschatological focus found expression in the "spirituals" which have been called the most original and enduring contribution of the Negro church.[35] With most avenues of social expression cut off and with the ministry one of the few professions open to the Negro, the church assumed an importance that has seldom been duplicated among other groups.[36] Since there was little opportunity elsewhere for a Negro to gain recognition and to exercise authority, there often was a scramble for leadership and a tendency for the churches to become personal fiefs of the pastor. This highly competitive situation led to numerous schisms, withdrawals, and reorganizations. Negro Methodists splintered into at least eight different denominational bodies. Baptist strength among the Negroes is explained at least in part by the ease with which an individual pastor could pursue an independent course, but the Baptists suffered a major denominational schism in 1917 when the National Baptist Conven-

[34] The most illuminating account is E. F. Frazier, *The Negro Church in America* (N.Y., 1964). See also C. G. Woodson, *The History of the Negro Church* (Washington, D.C., 1945); W. D. Weatherford, *American Churches and the Negro* (Boston, 1957); B. E. Mays and J. W. Nicholson, *The Negro's Church* (N.Y., 1933); H. V. Richardson, *Dark Glory: A picture of the Church among the Negroes of the Rural South* (N.Y., 1947); and J. R. Washington, Jr., *Black Religion: the Negro and Christianity in the United States* (Boston, 1964).

[35] See Howard Thurman, *The Negro Spiritual Speaks of Life and Death* (N.Y., 1947).

[36] The importance of the church in the Negro community was reflected in the fact that by the 1930's the proportion of Negroes who were church members was higher than that of the white population.

tion split into two rival organizations—the National Baptist Convention, Inc., and the National Baptist Convention of America. Other minor schisms resulted in the formation of the short-lived New Era Baptist Convention and the Progressive Baptist Convention.

The large-scale movement of Negro population into the major industrial centers of the nation, which began during World War I and continued thereafter at a steadily mounting tempo, introduced marked changes into Negro church life. Many of the urban churches became much more formal and restrained. The emotionalism of earlier days declined, "spirituals" were sung less frequently, the itinerant evangelist was less prominent, and preaching gave less emphasis to otherworldly aspects of the faith. Attention was increasingly devoted to advancing the interests of the Negro through practical action. The Supreme Court decision of 1954, which put an end to the "separate but equal" doctrine in public education, triggered a massive civil rights movement in which the Negro churches played a prominent role. A spectacular illustration of this was the bus boycott in Montgomery, Alabama, in 1955–56, which was led by the local Negro clergy and which made Martin Luther King, Jr., a national figure. Subsequent "freedom rides" to eliminate discrimination in interstate travel, "sit-ins" and "demonstrations" to obtain equal access to public accommodations, and voter registration drives, were usually planned and organized in the Negro churches and often led by their pastors.

The growing decorum and "worldliness" of many of the city churches produced much the same reaction among some of the new Negro urban dwellers as had occurred among segments of the white population. Tiny store-front churches, which reproduced the intimacy and informality of the rural churches, multiplied, and the Holiness and Pentecostal movements found ready recruits among those Negroes who looked back with nostalgia to the uninhibited emotionalism of their childhood religious experience. A whole cluster of new Negro denominations emerged—the Church of God in Christ, Christ's Sanctified Holy Church, Church of the Living God, House of the Lord, Apostolic Over-coming Holy Church of God, Fire-Baptized Holiness Church of God, Triumph the Church and Kingdom of God, Church of Our Lord Jesus Christ of the Apostolic Faith, Bible Way Churches of Our Lord Jesus Christ, Kodesh Church of Immanuel, and Free Christian Zion Church of Christ. Most of these groups were small, some almost miniscule in membership, but taken together they had almost 750,000 adherents in 1960. The Church of God in Christ, which accounted for more than half this total, was the only one which achieved any significant size. Founded in 1897 with a stress on entire sanctification and adding in 1906 an emphasis on the pentecostal gift of tongues, the Church of God in Christ numbered only 31,564 members by 1936. But thereafter its growth was rapid, and by 1960 its membership was 392,635.

Like urban whites who toyed with the teachings of Psychiana, the Rosicrucians, the "Mighty I Am," Yoga, Krishna, Vedanta, and a "beatnik" form of Zen Buddhism, Negroes also developed a variety of exotic cults in the urban environment.[37] The House of Prayer for All Nations of Bishop Charles "Sweet Daddy" Grace was a phenomenon of the depression of the 1930's, which garnered added income from the sale of Daddy Grace cold cream, Daddy Grace coffee, and Daddy Grace toothpaste. Although Daddy Grace had given God a vacation, the faithful were assured that they need not despair, for they could still be saved by grace—Daddy Grace. The Peace Mission of Father Divine (George Baker) was even more bizarre. Father Divine claimed to be God, and he called his followers "angels." In 1932, after being charged with maintaining a public nuisance in Sayville, Long Island, he moved to Harlem where he began feeding thousands in buildings known as "heavens." Later Philadelphia became a major center of the movement. The Peace Mission, which also was a phenomenon of the depression years, lost much of its momentum after World War II. Both Daddy Grace and Father Divine emphasized a nonracial brotherhood, but there were other movements that took an opposite tack. The "Black Jews" of W. S. Crowdy, F. S. Cherry, and W. A. Matthew, for example, stressed Negro separateness and even superiority. A similar point of view was represented by Marcus Garvey's "Black Nationalists" who appealed to "the God of Africa," and Drew Ali's "Moorish Americans" who found their inspiration in the Koran. In the 1960's the "Black Muslims" of Elijah Mohammed's Islam, which blended emphases derived from Garvey and Drew Ali, was reported to be the fastest growing movement among Negroes in America.[38] This may have been an overenthusiastic verdict, but it did call attention to the unusual ferment in the urban Negro communities.

[37] See A. H. Fauset, *Black Gods of the Metropolis* (Philadelphia, 1944).
[38] C. Eric Lincoln, *The Black Muslims in America* (Boston, 1961), 4.

The mid-twentieth-century religious profile

An accurate assessment of the balance of religious forces in the United States is difficult to make. It is clear that several shifts took place during the first half of the twentieth century, but available statistics are not always comparable. As officially reported, Protestant church membership in 1960 was approximately 64,000,000, the Roman Catholic total was 42,000,000, the number of Jews was 5,500,000, and the Eastern Orthodox total was roughly 2,650,000. But the Roman Catholic figure included baptized infants, while the Protestant statistics generally did not.[39] The Jewish and Eastern Orthodox figures, on the other hand, tended to be estimates of total ethnic or national groups rather than of specific religious affiliation.

Within Protestantism significant shifts in numerical strength took place during the post-World War I period. Methodists increased from 7,600,000 to 13,150,000 between 1916 and 1960, but were displaced as the largest Protestant grouping by the Baptists who had grown from 7,000,000 to 21,000,000. Lutherans surged forward from 2,500,000 to 8,000,000 to become the third largest Protestant group. Presbyterians and Reformed slipped to fourth place with a gain from 2,800,000 to 4,800,000. The growth of the Protestant Episcopal Church from 1,100,000 to 3,300,000 was somewhat deceptive, for the first figure was communicant membership while the second was the total number of baptized. The merger of the Congregational Christian Churches with the Evangelical and Reformed Church put the United Church of Christ in sixth place with 2,200,000 members in 1960. The related Churches of Christ (from 300,000 to 2,100,000) and Disciples of Christ (from 450,000 to

[39] Information supplied by the U.S. Census Bureau and the American Institute of Public Opinion indicates that the Protestant–Roman Catholic membership figures give at least a rather accurate picture of proportionate strength. A Census Bureau study in 1958 reported that of 119,330,000 Americans fourteen years of age and older, 66.2 per cent (78,952,000) regarded themselves as Protestant, 25.7 per cent (30,669,000) regarded themselves as Roman Catholic, 3.2 per cent (3,868,000) regarded themselves as Jewish, 1.3 per cent (1,545,000) identified themselves with other faiths, while 3.6 per cent (4,300,000) claimed no religious preference or were not reported. The Protestant predominance was reduced to a rough conformity with official membership figures when active identification, as reflected in church attendance, was taken into account. A survey by the American Institute of Public Opinion in 1958 reported that 44 per cent (34,740,000) of those who considered themselves Protestant had attended church the preceding Sunday, while 74 per cent (22,700,000) of those who considered themselves Roman Catholic had attended.

1,600,000) were followed by a group which had only a tenuous relationship to Protestantism, the Latter-day Saints, or Mormons, which had grown in number from 450,000 to 1,600,000 during the years between 1916 and 1960.[40]

While interesting and illuminating in some respects, such a traditional classification of the relative strength of various Protestant groupings serves to obscure one of the most significant shifts that was taking place in twentieth-century Protestantism. This was a shift that divided Protestantism into two or three loosely defined camps.

The traditional classification was largely based upon differences in polity and church government which had little relationship to the divisive issues of the twentieth century, for the latter were theologically and sociologically grounded in a way that by-passed the older distinctions. The traditional classification fails to give adequate weight, for example, to the 1,500,000 members of Holiness churches, the 1,500,000 members of Pentecostal bodies, and the 500,000 members of Adventist or Premillennialist groups. Moreover some of the smaller Baptist, Methodist, Presbyterian, and Reformed groups should more properly be classified as part of the 4,800,000 members of Fundamentalist denominations. And the Fundamentalist total ought to be even larger to take into account many individual churches, such as the Park Street Congregational Church in Boston and the Tenth Street Presbyterian Church in Philadelphia, which held Fundamentalist views and actively supported Fundamentalist agencies.[41] What is needed in place of the traditional grouping of Protestants into denominational families is a classification that takes into account the actual realignment within American Protestantism.

The dominant Protestant group at mid-century was composed of those mildly "liberal" or "progressive" denominations affiliated with the National Council of Churches. Frequently referred to as "cooperative Protestantism," these bodies represented a constituency of some

---

[40] The long-established smaller religious groups met with varying success in the twentieth century. The Mennonites doubled their membership in the 1916–1960 period (from 80,000 to 160,000), as did the Church of the Brethren (100,000 to 200,000). The rapid growth of Christian Science ended about 1940, after having tripled in number of churches during the preceding three decades. Quakers, Unitarians, and Universalists, on the other hand, had steadily declined during the first forty years of the century, but each of them made small but significant recoveries after World War II—with respective memberships of 125,000; 100,000; and 70,000 in 1960.

[41] Their respective pastors, Harold J. Ockenga (b. 1905) and Donald Grey Barnhouse (b. 1895), were prominent Fundamentalist leaders.

37,000,000 members. At the other extreme was what may roughly be described as the Fundamentalist-Adventist-Holiness-Pentecostal coalition with almost 8,500,000 adherents. Perhaps coalition is too strong a word for what is at best a somewhat arbitrary classification, but it does have the virtue of suggesting that these bodies represented a more important element in Protestant life than separate listings would indicate. In addition to these two groupings, there were more than 19,000,000 other Protestants—including 10,000,000 Southern Baptists and almost 5,000,000 members of the American Lutheran Church and the Lutheran Church, Missouri Synod—who can scarcely be classified as belonging to any coalition. While this threefold division does not produce neat packages, it does point to Protestantism's loss of homogeneity during the years of controversy and reassessment that followed World War I.

XIV

Protestant Reassessment and Recovery

For American Protestantism, World War I marked the end of an era. Kenneth Scott Latourette observed that "Protestant Christianity had entered the nineteenth century on a rising tide" and noted that it had come to the end of the century "on a rapidly ascending curve." [1] The momentum of almost two hundred years of vigorous advance had not yet been spent, and the first years of the new century found Protestantism at the peak of its apparent strength and influence. Churches were crowded, financial support was generous, programs were proliferating, and a host of good causes elicited eager and ardent devotion. It was a time of unusual moral idealism generated in part by a widespread determination among church members to "win the world for Christ in this generation." By the time Warren G. Harding was installed in the White House, however, much of the contagious enthusiasm exhibited by the churches in the prewar years had begun to be dissipated. By 1925 the usual indices of institutional health—church attendance, Sunday school enrollment, missionary giving—showed a downward trend that was to continue for at least a decade. Although not

[1] *A History of the Expansion of Christianity* (N.Y., 1937–45), IV, 458, VI, 5.

many at the time were aware that the forward thrust had been seriously blunted, it is clear in retrospect that by the middle 1920's an ebb tide had set in.[2]

The transitional years

The blunting of the long Protestant advance was foreshadowed by the fate of the Interchurch World Movement of 1919 and 1920. This was an ambitious enterprise, launched with a flourish of trumpets, that was designed to push to rapid completion the task of Christianizing the world, a Christianizing that was defined in terms of "the complete evangelization of all of life." The major Protestant denominations cooperated to make a detailed survey of urgent needs both at home and abroad, to chart a common strategy for meeting them, to allocate specific responsibilities to the different mission boards, and then, through a concerted campaign patterned after the great wartime drives for funds, to secure the necessary financial resources to carry out the plans.[3] Each denomination had its own financial goal and its own "movement" or campaign for funds, and these coordinated drives were to be supplemented by a general campaign which would tap the supposedly vast potential support of public-spirited citizens who could not be reached through denominational channels. At first a goal of $300 million was suggested, then $500 million, and the final figure was one billion dollars, with $335 million to be raised initially. Although large sums were raised by the participating denominations,[4] the joint cam-

[2] See Robert T. Handy's illuminating article, "The American Religious Depression, 1925–35," *Church History,* XXIX (1960), 2–16. "Depression" is perhaps too strong a word to describe the plight of the Protestant churches. "Recession" would be a better term. While church attendance, Sunday school enrollment, and missionary giving declined, the decline was not precipitate. The pace of advance had been slowed and then halted, but there was no shattering "crash." There continued to be much vigorous activity, and up to 1930 there was even an increase in the amount of money spent on new church buildings. With few exceptions, both church members and clergy remained confident and optimistic. Statistical trends, of course, become evident only in retrospect, and the onset of the depression in 1930 may even have contributed to the delayed response to the loss of momentum. The consequences of the economic depression were so overwhelming that other debilitating factors in the life of the churches tended to be obscured.

[3] For the fivefold objective of the Interchurch World Movement, see H. W. Schneider, *Religion in Twentieth Century America* (Cambridge, Mass., 1952), 95–96. The scope of the concern is suggested by the survey which sought to ascertain "all the facts about the religious, social, moral, physical, and economic environments through the world." Donald B. Meyer, *The Protestant Search for Political Realism, 1919–1941* (Berkeley, Calif., 1960), 9.

[4] The New World Movement of the Northern Baptists was the most successful on the basis of per capita giving, but only half the $100,000,000 goal was raised. The

paign was a costly and dismal failure which left the denominational mission boards saddled with debts incurred in the cooperative phases of the endeavor. But this was only half the story. Confident that the goals would be reached, the mission boards had overextended their commitments. Programs were expanded, new projects undertaken, and additional personnel employed. When the anticipated funds were not forthcoming, drastic and painful retrenchments had to be made.

The failure of the Interchurch World Movement can be attributed in part to the economic recession of 1920–22. Prospects for success may also have been blighted by the report of the Movement's commission of inquiry which surveyed the needs of the steelworkers and their families. The inquiry coincided with the 1919 strike of the steelworkers, which sought the elimination of the twelve-hour day and the seven-day week. The sympathetic tenor of the commission's report was not calculated to win the support of the wealthy public-spirited citizens, which was one of the objectives of the campaign. Furthermore, the report was issued at a time when the Boston police strike had created widespread fear of anarchy and when the anti-Red hysteria associated with the activities of A. Mitchell Palmer, Wilson's Attorney-General, was fostering intense antilabor sentiment. But there were more deep-seated reasons for the failure of the Interchurch World Movement. A marked shift in the mood of the American people was perhaps the most important. Moreover, long smoldering tensions within Protestanism broke out into open conflict at the close of the war, diverting to internecine strife energies which might have been otherwise employed. And finally, Protestanism was beginning to reap the consequences of a long period of acculturation.

THE POSTWAR GENERATION. For two decades Protestants had been engaged in a series of crusades to refashion the face of America and to reshape the life of the world (see Chap. XII). The war itself was but the greatest of these crusades, enlisting as it did the idealism generated by the churches in "a war to end war" and to "make the world safe for democracy." The United States had entered the conflict with banners flying, but it proved to be a dirty unheroic war which few participants remembered with anything but distaste. The peace proved equally disap-

---

Methodists, with five times as many members, raised the largest total amount. The much more modest $40,000,000 goal of the Methodist Centenary Movement had been set before the interdenominational effort had been fully elaborated, and it was far exceeded, with more than $100,000,000 being subscribed. But in the end the Methodists had many unpaid pledges and soured hopes.

pointing. Little idealism was apparent in the treaty negotiations at Versailles, and Woodrow Wilson was pilloried at home as a fool trapped by the wily diplomats of Europe. Harding's call for a "return to normalcy," a summons to put aside idealistic crusades and far-flung responsibilities, mirrored the mood of a tired and disenchanted people. Small wonder, in this climate of opinion, that the new crusade envisioned in the Interchurch World Movement met with so disappointing a response.

The postwar generation, however, was suffering from a more severe malady than mere weariness with crusades. Nor was the disenchantment which stemmed from the machinations of the diplomats at Versailles sufficient to account for the waning of idealism. The latter was more largely the product of a profound revolution in morals. Wars tend to be followed by a breakdown in public and private morality, and World War I was no exception. For many people the war was a liberating experience. Young men were uprooted and introduced for the first time to the amoral standards of army life. Women were drawn from their homes to engage in war work. The movement of population into the cities was accelerated. Each of these represented a break with accustomed patterns of life. But the war also imposed its own restrictive discipline. Those at home were driven to strenuous exertion by the effort to win the war, and those in the army were subjected to the unfamiliar and unpleasant regimentation of military life. From this perspective, it was the end of the war that brought a welcome release from the stern requirements of duty and evoked a heartfelt desire to relax and enjoy the satisfactions of a less disciplined existence. This mood, quite apart from the brutalizing effect of war, was normal for a postwar period. Parallels in other postwar epochs can be found for the scandals of the Harding administration and the heedless preoccupation of the business community with making "a fast buck." But these were symptoms only of a widespread moral laxity, a laxity that was mostly covert and did not represent an open flouting of accepted standards of morality. The more serious malady was quite different in character, venting itself in a candid and undisguised revolt which bluntly attacked the whole system of traditional manners and morals.

The revolution in morals of the 1920's is most frequently depicted in terms of "flaming youth" and the "jazz age," of "speakeasies" and "gang wars," of the gay antics of Jimmy Walker in New York and the crude boasts of Big Bill Thompson in Chicago. But it was much more than this. It was a revolution that affected all classes of society and tore people loose from their old moorings. Its roots are extraordinarily difficult to assess. As William E. Leuchtenburg has pointed out, historians have given the revolution almost no attention,[5] and others have naïvely attributed it almost solely to the breakdown of law enforcement occasioned by prohibition. It can be seen in part as an aftermath of war, but its fundamental rootage was much more remote. Technological advance, of course, had multiplied material satisfactions and weakened religious sanctions, and the booming prosperity of the twenties was a heady experience. The "status revolution" which undercut the authority of those who had traditionally set the moral standards—the "professional" classes (ministers, lawyers, teachers), the "rural gentry," and the "urban patricians"—was also involved. And not least in importance was the erosion of family solidarity and authority, which was one of the consequences of the increasing urbanization of American society and the growing emancipation of women. But it was the popular appropriation of insights derived from the teachings of such men as John Dewey and Sigmund Freud that contributed as much to the new hedonism as anything else. "Self-expression" and "self-fulfilment" became magic words, and anything that smacked of "repression" was regarded as a threat to the "psyche." While these tags of popular understanding distorted carefully devised philosophies, they had the effect of giving a supposedly scientific imprimatur to self-indulgence.

The major prophets of the moral revolt were literary figures—Theodore Dreiser, Sinclair Lewis, H. L. Mencken, George Jean Nathan, F. Scott Fitzgerald, and a host of other luminaries. Their rebellion was full of "sound and fury" and took the form of a frontal attack on what they called America's "puritanism"—an epithet for anything that interfered with the new freedom. Religion was dismissed as antiquated, false, and absurd—a blend of prudery, cant, and sanctimoniousness from which individuals must emancipate themselves if their spirits were not to be suffocated. To Joseph Wood Krutch, "sin" and "love" were empty words, and he insisted that "all the capital letters in the composing-room cannot make the words more than that which they have become—shadows, as essentially unreal as some of the theological dogmas which have been completely forgotten." [6] Concerned with the individual rather than with society, with private rather

[5] *The Perils of Prosperity, 1914–32* (Chicago, 1958), 290.
[6] *The Modern Temper: A Study and a Confession* (N.Y., 1929), 191–92.

than public experience, these writers had no interest in social reform. "Doing good" was either a dull business or, as Mencken insisted, "in bad taste." "The great problems of the world—social, political, economic, and theological—do not concern me in the slightest," wrote George Jean Nathan.

> If all the Armenians were to be killed tomorrow and if half of Russia were to starve to death the day after, it would not matter to me in the least. What concerns me alone is myself, and the interests of a few close friends. For all I care the rest of the world may go to hell at today's sunset.[7]

Not all were as blunt and callous as Nathan, but social nihilism was a fundamental theme of the *avant garde* novelists and poets. Even the care with which most of them avoided adjectives and sought to make do with unadorned nouns and verbs was part of a studied and self-conscious rejection of all idealistic sentiment.

While the cynical and deeply pessimistic hedonism of the novelists and poets and literary critics was not without influence, the revolution in morals found much more temperate and prosaic expression in the population as a whole. Spurred on by handbooks of popular psychology and carried forward in home and classroom, the revolution produced a less sin-ridden and more self-indulgent people. But, unlike the despair of the "intellectuals," the popular mood of "the booming twenties" was optimistic and affirmative, and the new freedom was geared to an increasingly undisciplined pursuit of more tangible forms of personal fulfillment. Whereas the intellectuals had lost faith in progress, the great mass of Americans were content to believe that the promises of the past had become the realities of the present. Here the waning of idealism had complacency, and even smugness, as its hallmark, and it manifested itself in the demise of the progressive movement. The only alarm was that directed against those who seemed to threaten the existing order.

In 1912 progressivism, with its zeal for reform, had been triumphant. In a three-cornered race, Taft had been far outdistanced by both his progressive rivals—Woodrow Wilson and Teddy Roosevelt. Moreover, Eugene Debs, the Socialist candidate, had amassed almost a million votes. Four years later Wilson and Hughes, who were almost equally progressive in outlook, had vied for the White House. But in 1920 progressivism was

[7] Quoted in Leuchtenburg, *The Perils of Prosperity*, 150.

362

buried under the Harding landslide, and only a remnant could be resurrected by the LaFollette-Wheeler banner in the 1924 campaign.

The churches were not unaffected by this shift in mood of the American people. The demise of progressivism was accompanied by the decline of the social gospel which in prewar years had given American Protestantism much of its verve and contagious enthusiasm. As a typical social gospel project, the Interchurch World Movement had been one of the first casualties of the fading idealism implicit in the new morality. It is true that interest in social Christianity survived in some circles, just as there were still progressives to be found, but it was mostly confined to clerical ranks and had ceased to be important as a powerful ferment in the life of the churches. The clergymen who continued to issue social pronouncements were generals with few troops. They were tolerated by their congregations, but their summons to action sparked little response.[8] Even among the clergy much of the social concern was diverted into a pacifist crusade. Shamed and humiliated by the role of many churchmen in propagating hatred during World War I [9] and revolted by the horrors of trench warfare, a large percentage of the clergy vowed that the church should not bless war again and that they would neither personally support nor participate in any future conflict.

THE FUNDAMENTALIST CONTROVERSY. If the Protestant advance was blunted by the shifting mood of the American people, it also was impeded by an intramural conflict which broke out in 1920 and divided Protestantism into two hostile and embattled camps. The protagonists were the "Liberals," or "Modernists," who sought to adjust the inherited faith to the new intellectual climate (see pp. 267–76), and the "Fundamentalists," who insisted that the old ways of stating the faith must be preserved unimpaired.[10]

[8] A failure to make this distinction weakens Robert M. Miller's otherwise cogent demonstration of a continuing interest in social Christianity in his *American Protestantism and Social Issues, 1919–1939* (Chapel Hill, N.C., 1958). See also Donald B. Meyer, *The Protestant Search for Political Realism, 1919–1941* (Berkeley, Calif., 1960), and Paul A. Carter, *The Decline and Revival of the Social Gospel, 1920–1940* (Ithaca, N.Y., 1954).

[9] See Ray H. Abrams, *Preachers Present Arms* (N.Y., 1933).

[10] See N. F. Furniss, *The Fundamentalist Controversy, 1918–1931* (New Haven, 1954), which replaces S. G. Cole, *The History of Fundamentalism* (N.Y., 1931), as the standard account of the controversy. The name was coined in 1920 by the editor of the *Watchman-Examiner* to designate those who were prepared to battle for the "fundamentals" of the faith. Eldred D. Vanderlaan, *Fundamentalism versus Modernism* (N.Y., 1925), is an anthology of statements by leading Fundamentalists and Modernists on the salient points in debate.

Theological tension, of course, had been developing over a long period of time, but it had subsided after the heresy trials of the latter years of the nineteenth century. A common enthusiasm for reform made it possible to subordinate theological differences and to gloss over divergent theological positions with pious ambiguities.[11] Almost every prominent professional evangelist regarded himself as being engaged, through his revivals, in a work of social reformation. A few, like B. Fay Mills, went all the way with the social gospel. Others, like Sam Jones, Milan B. Williams, Burke Culpepper, William E. Biederwolf, and Rodney "Gypsy" Smith, limited themselves to "civic reform" and occasionally stressed the "social service" motif. And some, like J. Wilbur Chapman, placed primary stress on personal morality. But whatever their emphasis, they tended to be welcomed as allies in the progressive movement for human betterment and were drawn unwittingly into its orbit.[12] And they, in turn, tended to mute their points of theological dissent.

Not everyone, to be sure, was bemused by this happy state of affairs. For the first time since Finney's day, a significant opposition to mass revivalism was beginning to develop within evangelical Protestantism. Even among conservatives doubts were arising as to the effectiveness of the old techniques. In 1899 George E. Horr (1856–1927), a Baptist editor, pointed out that Dwight L. Moody had acknowledged that the day of great "hippodrome" services was drawing to a close. The following year George F. Pentecost (1843–1920) abandoned his career as an itinerant evangelist, having become convinced that conversions should be obtained by patient pastoral work and not in "after meetings" where "indiscriminate 'workers' with a few texts of Scripture" seek to "railroad inquirers" into hasty and shallow decisions. This growing disenchantment with revivalism was bound to create tension, but it was the more ardent "dispensationalists" (see pp. 282–83) within the revivalist camp who were primarily responsible for introducing discord into the general harmony.

Unlike most of the professional evangelists, the more rigid "dispensationalists" found it difficult to adjust to the general enthusiasm for reform, since it ran counter to the basic pessimism of their premillennial

---

[11] See McLoughlin, *Modern Revivalism*, 350, 353–54, 361–63, 386–87, 393, 397, 402, 411.

[12] Biederwolf and Gypsy Smith, for example, were active in the Men and Religion Forward Movement of 1911–14, which had liberal leadership and a strong social service orientation.

views. Furthermore, they were not of a mind to compromise their convictions by glossing over theological differences. In 1905 Amzi C. Dixon (1854–1925), shortly to become minister of the Moody Church in Chicago, published a book in which he announced that there could be no reconciliation between science and religion any more than socialism and free enterprise could be reconciled. The duty of the church, he insisted, was to convert individuals, to keep out of politics, and to remember that there could be no true revival that was not led by "believers in the inspiration and infallible authority of the Word of God." [13] It was, however, in reaction to the intransigence of Reuben A. Torrey (1856–1928), superintendent of the Moody Bible Institute in Chicago, that the issue was fully joined.

On Moody's death, Torrey had laid claim to his mantle and had embarked on a worldwide series of revival campaigns. Late in 1905 Charles S. MacFarland (1866–1956), a Congregational pastor who had spent two summers investigating the impact of Torrey's evangelistic work in the British Isles, reported that representatives of every school of thought in Britain believed that on the whole Torrey's influence had been harmful. They objected particularly to Torrey's intemperate denunciations of those who differed from him theologically, to the artificial "machinery" of his campaigns, and to his excessive commercialism. Within a few months after the publication of MacFarland's report, ministers of various denominations in America were urging churches to dissociate themselves from Torrey's campaigns.

In response to this criticism, Torrey and Dixon launched a vigorous counterattack which culminated in 1909–12 with the publication of ten small volumes entitled *The Fundamentals,* which sought to reduce the Christian faith to clear essentials. These brief treatises were written by various men but were edited by Dixon and Torrey, and their distribution was financed by two wealthy residents of Los Angeles, Milton and Lyman Stewart. They were sent free of charge "to every pastor, evangelist, missionary, theological student, Sunday school superintendent, Y.M.C.A. and Y.W.C.A. secretary" whose address could be obtained, and eventually three million copies were distributed.[14] It is likely that serious strife would

---

[13] McLoughlin, *Modern Revivalism,* 348, 352–53.

[14] *Ibid.,* 352, 370. Furniss, *Fundamentalist Controversy,* 12. Most interpreters believe that the fright among some wealthy laymen occasioned by radical social gospel views accounts for some of the financial support Torrey was able to enlist for his campaigns.

have been provoked then had not the agitation been interrupted by the outbreak of World War I.

The career of Billy Sunday (1862–1935)—the professional baseball player turned evangelist, whose antics in the pulpit did more than anything else to discredit revivalism—bridged the prewar and postwar periods.[15] In many ways he was a transitional figure, whose early popularity was derived in part from the alacrity with which he jumped on the bandwagon of civic reform and moral uplift, and who then rode to fame on the crest of the wave of reaction against the social gospel. Even during the early phase of his career, his denunciations of liberal theology were frequent and coarse. He had no use for the "bastard theory of evolution" or for the "deodorized and disinfected sermons" of "hireling ministers" who gave up the old faith to please their liberal parishioners. Furthermore, he complained of those who try to "make a religion out of social service with Jesus Christ left out," noting that this was why the Men and Religion Forward Movement was "a lamentable failure." He exhibited nonetheless a marked ability to blend his "old-time religion" with the progressive emphasis on reform. He advertised his revivals as "civic clean-ups" which would make any town a better place in which to live. He appropriated many of the indictments leveled by the "muckrakers," and this led many progressives and social gospelers to believe that he was buttressing their cause. Even his vulgarity and "vaudeville stunts" were defended as necessary means of reaching the masses. One contemporary observer was confident that "it is as a reformer that Mr. Sunday has warmed the hearts of all who desire better things." His ideas of reform, however, turned out to be extremely limited and did not extend much beyond the suppression of the liquor traffic.[16]

Sunday was quick to respond to changing climates of opinion. From the beginning he had preached a masculine "muscular" Christianity which equated salvation with decency and manliness ("the man who has real, rich, red blood in his veins instead of pink tea and ice water"). Under the excitement of war this masculine Christianity was transformed into a barnstorming, tub-thumping "100 per cent Americanism" which insisted that "Christianity and patriotism are synomous terms" just as "hell and

[15] See W. G. McLoughlin, Jr., *Billy Sunday Was His Real Name* (Chicago, 1955), and *Modern Revivalism*, 400–54.

[16] McLoughlin, *Modern Revivalism*, 399, 410–12, 429, 437.

traitors are synonomous." Soon he was attributing German atrocities to the baneful influence of biblical criticism upon the German people. And when labor unrest developed at the close of hostilities, he was in full cry after all foreign-inspired, godless social radicalism.

In spite of Billy Sunday's diatribes, most prominent Protestant leaders at the end of the war believed that the struggle to win acceptance for new ways of understanding the Christian faith had been won, and they were prepared to resume the humanitarian advance of the prewar years.[17] But Billy Sunday was demonstrating how hostile sentiment could be aroused in the postwar climate. The American people were in no mood for any further tampering with the social order, and it was easy to demonstrate to the satisfaction of many that "modernism" and "communism" were but reverse sides of the same coin.

Perhaps the decisive factor in thrusting the controversy into public attention was the championship of the Fundamentalist cause by William Jennings Bryan, the "peerless leader" of the old populist element in the Democratic party. When Bryan entered the fray in 1920, he was able to claim a national audience and to use his magic voice and moving rhetoric to transform isolated protests into a more or less unified crusade. Soon every denomination was embroiled in conflict, with the initial attack being directed against the Interchurch World Movement and its denominational counterparts. This was followed by strenuous efforts to ferret out evidence of heresy in every area of church life and by insistent demands that remedial action be taken to guarantee doctrinal orthodoxy. Harry Emerson Fosdick (b. 1878), a Baptist preacher occupying the pulpit of the First Presbyterian Church of New York City, added fuel to the flames in 1922 when, dismayed by the demoralizing effects of the Fundamentalist attacks which he had observed on a visit to the mission fields of Asia, he seemed to fling down the gauntlet in a sermon entitled, "Shall the Fundamentalists Win?"

The qualifying phrase describing the Fundamentalist movement as a "more or less" unified crusade is important, for it did embrace diverse elements. Thus far the gathering disaffection has been depicted almost wholly in terms of the "dispensationalists," who adhered to the five-point declaration of the Niagara Bible Conference of 1895 (see p. 283),

---

[17] For the eager enthusiasm of church leaders, see Meyer, *Protestant Search for Political Realism*, 12–13.

with its stress on the verbal inerrancy of Scripture (including the Genesis account of creation) and the premillennial return of Christ, as the standard of orthodoxy. But this was initially a fringe position. The movement derived much of its strength at the outset from men who stood more squarely within the traditional life of the churches.[18]

Curtis Lee Laws (1868–1946), Baptist editor of the *Watchman-Examiner,* who coined the label "Fundamentalist" in 1920 to designate those who were prepared to battle for the "fundamentals" of the faith, was associated with a large body of genuine "conservatives," whose concern was to conserve and defend the integrity and continuity of the Christian faith. The key issue, as these moderate Fundamentalists saw it, was the authority of the Bible, for Protestantism historically claimed the authority of Scripture for the whole structure of its thought. While continuing to revere the Bible as a treasury of religious devotion, there had been a growing tendency in liberal circles to reject it as being in any sense normative. It was a suitable subject for historical study and useful for devotional purposes, but the canons of truth were to be found in religious experience. It was this tendency to forget that the Christian faith had any objective standard of truth which alarmed the conservatives. These men were far from obscurantist in their attitude toward modern knowledge. While they centered attention on the question of biblical authority, few of them wished to make an issue of evolution, biblical inerrancy, or premillennialism. They represented the type of reaction to the more extreme modernist tendencies that had long been present in Protestant seminaries. The views expressed by John A. Faulkner (1857–1931) at Drew Theological Seminary in *Modernism and the Christian Faith* (1921) and by Augustus Hopkins Strong (1836–1921), former president of Rochester Theological Seminary whose *Outlines of Systematic Theology* was widely used as a textbook in the more conservative seminaries, were typical of this broad current of concern.

Strong frankly accepted the doctrine of evolution and the methods of biblical criticism. "Neither evolution nor the higher criticism," he said, "has any terrors to one who regards them as parts of Christ's creating and educating process." The composite authorship of the Pentateuch and the existence of two Isaiahs did not disturb Strong. "Any honest Christian," he

[18] For this distinction, see the chapter by Norman H. Maring, "Conservative but Progressive," in *What God Hath Wrought,* ed. G. L. Guffin (Philadelphia, 1960), 17–28.

affirmed, ". . . has the right to interpret Jonah and Daniel as allegories rather than histories." The Bible, he insisted, is the record of a progressive revelation, "shaped in human molds and adapted to ordinary human intelligence." It is a "human composition," but it is also "God's Word," presenting "divine truth in human forms." The danger of historical criticism of the Bible, he declared, is not in the method itself but springs from the presuppositions of those who use it. "The 'historical method' of Scripture interpretation, as it is often employed, ends without Christ because it begins without him." It makes the mistake of "treating Scripture as it would treat any unreligious or heathen literature" and ignores the fact that properly to interpret the Bible one must adopt a frankly confessional stance. The point is "not how man made the Scripture for himself, but how God made the Scripture through the imperfect agency of man." To abandon the Bible as the authoritative testimony to Christ and thus in a derivative sense the authoritative ground of faith, Strong contended, would be to cut the "taproot" and imperil the very existence of Protestantism.[19]

The moderate Fundamentalists, however, were quickly upstaged by more radical and noisy elements, whose quarrel seemed to be with almost every facet of modern life. Viewed from this perspective, Fundamentalism can best be understood as a phase of the rural-urban conflict, drawing its strength from the tendency of many who were swept into an urban environment to cling to the securities of their childhood. While this characterization does less than justice to the moderate wing of the movement, it does point up the fact that in many ways Fundamentalism was as much the product of a cultural as a religious concern. It is significant that it arose among rural-oriented people in the cities before it penetrated the small towns and villages of the countryside. Furthermore, the mores which were emphasized as indispensable to the Christian life had, in the words of H. Richard Niebuhr, "at least as little relation to the New Testament and as much connection with social custom" as did those aspects of behavior which were condemned, while the cosmological and biological notions which were stressed as integral to the gospel were equally culturally conditioned.[20] Fundamentalist sentiment also was not unrelated to the sweeping tide of hyperpatriotism which was so conspicu-

[19] *Outlines of Systematic Theology* (Philadelphia, 1903), ix, 55–62. See also Strong's *Tour of Missions* (Philadelphia, 1918), 177, 181, 186–87, 191, 203.
[20] *Christ and Culture* (N.Y., 1951), 102.

ous a feature of the early 1920's. "One hundred per cent Americanism" tended to be regarded as the normal corollary of "old-time religion," and "Back to Christ, the Bible, and the Constitution" was a typical slogan. While Fundamentalism had no direct connection with the resurgent Ku Klux Klan of the 1920's,[21] the more extreme wing of the Fundamentalist movement was in some respects a parallel phenomenon.

The great body of Protestants was never fully committed to either side of the controversy, but when the more belligerent Fundamentalists took charge of the movement and formed themselves into a power bloc intent on seizing control of the various Protestant denominations and placing them in a rigid theological strait jacket, the effect was to push middle-of-the-roaders into a defensive alliance with the liberals. This shift in alignment was most clearly evident at Princeton Theological Seminary which long had been the citadel of Presbyterian orthodoxy and where Fundamentalism had its ablest spokesman in the person of J. Gresham Machen (1881–1937). Nowhere was the Fundamentalist case stated with more clarity and cogency than in Machen's writings,[22] but his ill-tempered dogmatism in personal relationships and his determination to dominate the life of the seminary drove even stanchly conservative colleagues to make common cause with the Auburn "Affirmationists."[23] Among the Baptists, the initiative was seized by a radical triumvirate—J. Frank Norris, William B. Riley, and T. T. Shields—who formed the Baptist Bible Union to promote their views and succeeded in placing their stamp on much of the movement within the Baptist ranks. Here too the bitter-spirited intransigence of the extremists caused some of the prominent early leaders of the movement to defect and work out a policy of coexistence with the liberals. By 1925, when a national comedy was acted out in the "monkey trial" at Dayton, Tennessee, with William Jennings Bryan and Clarence Darrow in the starring roles, the obscurantism, violent language, and "smear" tactics of the more vociferous Fundamentalists had so alienated public opinion generally that there was little prospect that the Fundamentalists would gain control of any major Protestant denomina-

[21] John Roach Straton, the most prominent Fundamentalist leader in New York City, publicly castigated the Klan. Others condemned the Klan's tactics, suggesting that its members should take off their masks and make their fight in the open.

[22] See his *Christianity and Liberalism* (N.Y., 1923).

[23] The "Auburn Affirmation" is printed in Armstrong, Loetscher, Anderson, *The Presbyterian Enterprise*, 284–88.

tion. In 1929 Princeton Seminary was reorganized, and Machen departed to found Westminster Theological Seminary and the Orthodox Presbyterian Church.

Most of the denominations continued to be troubled by controversy throughout the 1930's, and among the American (Northern) Baptists peace was not restored until after World War II. The ranks of the latter group were depleted by two additional schisms. The first occurred in 1932 when a group of dissidents withdrew to form the General Association of Regular Baptists, and the second took place fifteen years later with the formation of the Conservative Baptist Association of America. While Fundamentalism was a declining force throughout these years in the major denominations, it maintained itself in many local congregations, and expanded its influence through the formation of independent Bible churches and the capture of some of the smaller denominational bodies. A major source of its continuing strength was its ability to supply, through graduates of Bible schools or institutes strategically located throughout the nation, ministerial leadership to impoverished churches.

PROTESTANT ACCULTURATION. Despite the distractions of controversy and despite the shafts of ridicule directed by the "intellectuals" against those who made profession of religious faith, the mood of the Protestant churches in the 1920's was remarkably complacent. Curiously enough, during the very decades when Protestantism was reaching the peak of its prestige and apparent influence, the nerve which had impelled two centuries of advance was being cut. A long process of theological erosion had opened the way to a rather complete assimilation of Protestantism to the model of the world.[24] With its basic theological insights largely emasculated, Protestantism was robbed of any independently grounded vision of life and became more and more the creature of American culture rather than its creator. In this respect the culturally conditioned character of Fundamentalism was typical of Protestantism as a whole, the tension within Protestantism arising primarily out of the differing cultural orientation of the older agrarian and the newer urban society. "If the theology of the fundamentalists was archaic and anachro-

[24] For elaborations of this point, see W. S. Hudson, *The Great Tradition of the American Churches*, 157–225, and *American Protestantism*, 131–43; S. E. Mead, *The Lively Experiment*, 134–87; H. Richard Niebuhr, *The Kingdom of God in America*, 164–98, and *The Church Against the World* (N.Y., 1935).

nistic," Sidney E. Mead has observed, "that of the liberals was secularized and innocuous." [25]

While there were exceptions to this general characterization, by and large the Protestant churches had become victims of their own success. They had succeeded in creating a culture that in mood and spirit was recognizably Christian, and then during the first two decades of the twentieth century practically all the reforms that had been proposed to remedy the ills of society had been set in operation. Proud of their achievements and pleased that their mission had been so largely accomplished, the churches relaxed and made peace with the world.

From satisfaction with the culture, it was but a small step to the placing of confidence in the culture to nurture and sustain the Christian faith. Even before the end of the nineteenth century, Phillips Brooks had declared: "I do not know how a man can be an American, even if he is not a Christian, and not catch something with regard to God's purpose for this great land." How else could one explain "all the secular, all the studiously irreligious, all the even blasphemous attempts at education and the development of character?" The most impressive feature of American life, to Brooks, was the way in which men "outside the churches" were impelled by the spirit of America to do that which "the churches and Christianity" seek to do, being led to do "Christian work in the spirit of Christ" even when they "studiously" or "vehemently" disown him.[26] By thus investing the culture with intrinsic redemptive power, scant room was left for any special redemptive work of Christ. The distinction between the Church and the world, between the Christian and the non-Christian, was largely obliterated; and little independent wisdom and guidance was available to the Christian believer. The churches, as a result, became increasingly composed of adherents whose religious affiliation was determined more by accident of birth and persistence of custom than by conscious conviction.

The missionary thrust of a religion is one of the most sensitive indices of its vitality. Evidence was accumulating throughout the 1920's of a growing missionary apathy, which indicated how ill-prepared the churches were to withstand the effect of the general American retreat into isolation. Missionary giving steadily declined during this period of boom-

[25] *The Lively Experiment*, 186.
[26] *National Needs and Remedies: Discussions of the General Conference of the Evangelical Alliance* (N.Y., 1890), 301–11.

ing prosperity, and the Foreign Missions Conference reported in 1929 that, in contrast to the 2,700 students who had volunteered for foreign service in 1920, only 252 had volunteered in 1928.[27] It was this waning interest in missions that led to the Laymen's Foreign Missions Inquiry in 1930, whose report in 1932 reflected the questioning of the mission enterprise as it had been traditionally conceived.

The Laymen's Inquiry was instigated by a group of Baptist businessmen and financed by John D. Rockefeller, Jr. Its purpose was to study existing mission projects, evaluate their effectiveness, and determine what was worthy of continued support. Research specialists were sent abroad to collect factual information, and then, armed with this data, a "Commission of Appraisal" visited the mission fields before issuing their report.[28] The chairman of the commission and editor of the report was William E. Hocking (1873–1966), professor of philosophy at Harvard. While urging that missionary endeavor be continued, the report declared that there is no ground for "a renewed appeal for the support, much less for the enlargement, of these missions as a whole in their present form and on their present basis." A typical "big business" bias, which equated centralization with efficiency, was evident in the critical attitude of the report toward all operations based upon separate denominational entities. "A single administrative unit," free of all church control, it maintained, should be given "administrative direction of missionary effort in all fields." But the report went much farther than this. Not only did it question much of the work that was being done on the mission fields, it brought the whole philosophy of Christian missions under attack. Educational and philanthropic work was commended, but the report insisted that the missionaries should be freed from any responsibility for "conscious and direct evangelization." Far from making any overt presentation of the claims of Christ, the missionary must adopt a stance of openness toward other religions and "regard himself as a co-worker with the forces within each such religious system which are making for righteousness." As Christians, we must "be willing to give largely without any preaching, to co-operate wholeheartedly with non-Christian agencies for social improvement." The basic philosophy,

[27] See Handy, "The American Religious Depression," *Church History*, XXIX (1960), 4–5. The United Stewardship Council reported that per capita gifts for benevolence fell from $5.57 in 1921 to $3.43 in 1929.
[28] *Re-Thinking Missions: A Laymen's Inquiry after One Hundred Years* (N.Y., 1932). The factual material that had been assembled was published in the seven-volume *Laymen's Foreign Missions Inquiry . . . Supplementary Series* (N.Y., 1933).

which was fully explicated two years later by Archibald G. Baker in *Christian Missions and a New World Culture,* was to foster an intercultural penetration which would bring about a synthesis or reconception of all religions into one universal faith.

A similar indecision and hesitancy with regard to any forthright presentation of the Christian faith was evident at home. Home missions underwent the same metamorphosis that was recommended in the Laymen's report, with mission centers being transformed into social agencies. "A decreasing emphasis upon a specific church program and intensification of efforts to help the immigrant worker in the struggle for economic security and social recognition," a study sponsored by the Institute of Social and Religious Research concluded, "suggest themselves as the most constructive items on the future program of mission work." [29] As for the professional evangelists who had sought to maintain the tradition of mass evangelism, their day also was over. Finding it no longer possible to secure the necessary cooperation of the churches for citywide campaigns, most of them settled down, accepting pastorates or founding churches (or tabernacles) of their own.[30]

The churches were under considerable pressure during these years, quite apart from uncertainty as to their own vocation. Less and less reliance could be placed on habit and custom to maintain active participation in church life. In addition to the free and easy atmosphere generated by the revolution in morals which enabled many to ignore the Sabbath and neglect church attendance without compunction, there were other features of American life which made the task of the churches more difficult. The population was increasingly urban and mobile. By 1930 ninety-six metropolitan areas had emerged, twenty-two of them straddling two or more states. And once within the urban orbit, there were many who did not stay put long enough to develop strong ties to a church. Nor could the churches count on the family as an ally to the same extent as formerly, as was made evident by the rising divorce rate and the sharp decline in the practice of family devotions. Automobile production soared at almost a

[29] Theodore Abel, *Protestant Home Missions to Catholic Immigrants* (N.Y., 1933), 107.

[30] See McLoughlin, *Modern Revivalism,* 469. Billy Sunday, who continued to travel, was an exception, but he held his last "citywide" revival in the little town of Mount Holly, N.J., and mostly he was restricted to one-church revival services.

geometric rate, vastly extending the range of an individual's freedom, providing easy access to multiplying golf-courses and setting up the family weekend outing as a counterattraction to the church. Motion pictures and the radio joined the press as rivals of the churches in setting the tone of society.[31] Almost everything—the popular mood, the churches' own sense of uncertainty, urbanization, mobility, competing attractions, the decay of family solidarity—militated against the success of any attempt by the churches to maintain their congregations as a disciplined and fully committed people.

One response to this situation was a frenzied effort by some churches to "merchandise" religion with the huckstering methods of Madison Avenue.[32] "Early to bed and early rise, preach the gospel and advertise," ministers were admonished. "Selling Religion—that is the only business of the Church," proclaimed Lewis S. Mudge, stated clerk of the Presbyterian General Assembly, in supplying the churches with five sure-fire tips on how they might best vend their goods. "The old idea that a minister is above stooping to commercial devices must disappear if the church is to grow," the Methodist *Zion's Herald* informed its readers, for "ministers are salesmen with a wonderfully fine 'line' to sell their congregations." The use of printer's ink and brightly illuminated signs to advertise their services, churches were told, could change the cry of "S.O.S." to "S.R.O."—standing room only. Bruce Barton, an advertising executive, made his contribution to the cause by writing a biography of Jesus, *The Man Nobody Knows* (1925), which for two years headed the nonfiction list of best-selling books. Jesus was pictured as a master salesman, psychologist, and forceful young executive, who forged twelve men from the lower ranks into the best management team of all time.

Churches responded to the multiple exhortations with snappy slogans and promotional stunts. "A friendly church" became a familiar slogan which compared favorably with more flashy punch-lines such as "Be a Sport—Come to Church" or the hard-sell "Worship Increases Your

---

[31] The press provided much less support for the churches than heretofore. The circulation of religious periodicals dwindled, and there was a marked change in the attitude of the nonreligious press. One study has indicated that, whereas about 78 per cent of published views of religion in 1905 could be classified as favorable, by 1930 the situation was almost reversed with 67 per cent unfavorable. Hornell Hart, "Changing Attitudes and Interests," *Recent Social Trends* (N.Y., 1933), I, 403.

[32] See Miller, *American Protestantism and Social Issues*, 22–26.

Efficiency" and "Business Success and Religion Go Together." Catchy sermon topics—"The Irishmen of the Old Testament," "Two in a Bed," "The Mae West of My Bible"—were used as teasers to draw a crowd. Some of the promotional stunts were equally bizarre.

Churches with a more sedate and prosperous clientele sought to maintain their prestige and popularity by the more dignified expedient of constructing impressive gothic cathedrals, and even the less prosperous invested heavily in more modest gothic structures. In 1921 the total spent on new church buildings was 60 million dollars. Five years later the total had risen to 284 million. John D. Rockefeller, Jr., explained his interest in spending large sums on the construction of a new home for the Park Avenue Baptist Church on Riverside Drive by saying that he did not want the business community to look down on the churches.[33] There were also attempts to make Sunday morning worship more attractive by decorating it with liturgical innovations borrowed from other traditions. Unlike earlier forms of church architecture and liturgical practice which expressed in one way or another the common faith of the congregation, the new eclecticism betrayed little discernible relationship to any fundamental theological convictions.

These same churches also tended to specialize in "progressive" programs of religious education, geared to the immediate interests and capacities of the child. According to George A. Coe's *Social Theory of Religious Education* (1917), the aim of the new educational program was "the growth of the young toward and into mature and efficient devotion to the democracy of God, and happy self-realization therein." The basic assumption was the conviction that religious consciousness is a natural and progressive experience which emerges out of "an experimental pupil-teacher quest for growing values." [34] With this emphasis upon "growth" and a "continuous becoming," there was little point to the old Sunday school "Decision Day." Far from involving any crisis of conversion, church membership was regarded as simply a routine step in the normal unfolding of human life. Since everything revolved around the changing interests and capacities of the child at different age levels, churches were under strong pressure to replace the old "Akron style" Sunday school

[33] *Ibid.*, 25.
[34] See H. Shelton Smith, "Christian Education," in *Protestant Thought in the Twentieth Century*, ed., A. S. Nash, (N.Y., 1951), 241.

building, which featured a central assembly room for ungraded "opening exercises," with a more suitable educational "plant." Furthermore, churches were encouraged to employ full-time professional directors of religious education.

Much church life, of course, remained untouched by these newer expedients, for many congregations refused to adopt cheap appeals to attract a crowd and did not have the financial resources to embark upon a building program or to launch a full-blown program of "progressive" education. Moreover, many of them were still old-fashioned enough to believe that a "life-centered" Sunday school curriculum was no adequate substitute for specific instruction in the Bible. But whatever course individual churches pursued, nothing could obscure the fact that the churches were suffering a loss of prestige and authority. Throughout the 1920's overt manifestations of religious interest were being confined more and more to Sunday morning, as midweek and Sunday evening services were dropped in many parts of the country. Nor did religious leaders command the same respect as in former years. This decline was reflected in the relative economic status of ministers and in their participation as members of boards of trustees of universities, colleges, and other philanthropic organizations. In a sample of private institutions, an investigator reported that the number of clergymen who were members of their governing boards decreased from 39 per cent in 1860 to 7 per cent in 1930.[35] It was upon churches thus weakened that the blow of the economic depression of the 1930's fell, and the churches suffered from the crippling effect of the economic disaster along with the rest of the nation. Budgets were slashed, benevolent and missionary enterprises curtailed, and some churches were forced to close their doors.

Reconstruction and Renewal

Many people expected that the depression into which the nation was cascaded following the crash of the "great bull market" of 1929 would produce a return to religion. A people shorn of their material possessions, it was believed, would turn to God in some spectacular way. By-and-large they did not. Samuel P. Kincheloe of the Chicago Theological Seminary

[35] S. P. Hays, *The Response to Industrialism* (Chicago, 1957), 72.

explained this disappointment by stating that secularism had become so advanced in America that no general religious revival was possible.[36] Even churchgoing people looked to Washington instead of to God for help in their extremity. But there were exceptions to this. A rather significant revival did occur among the less secularized portions of the population, finding expression in the rapidly mounting membership of what Kincheloe dismissed as "minor 'fundamentalist groups.' " While Fundamentalist churches did participate in this somewhat *sub rosa* revival, the most striking gains were made by the Holiness and Pentecostal churches.

At the opposite end of the social spectrum, a quickening religious interest found expression in the "First Century Christian Fellowship" or "Oxford Group Movement" of Frank N. D. Buchman (1878–1960).[37] Since 1921 Buchman had been engaged in personal evangelism among students, both in the United States and abroad. Becoming convinced that Park Avenue needed conversion as much as the Bowery, a mission to America was launched in 1930 with headquarters in the parish house of Calvary Protestant Episcopal Church in New York City. The central focus was upon "the four absolutes" of perfect honesty, purity, unselfishness, and love, and upon "the five C's" of confidence, confession, conviction, conversion, and continuance, which were defined as the five stages of a "changed" life. The basic "houseparty" technique was supplemented by the activities of a traveling team, and sophisticated use was made of news media and propagandist literature, the latter including the periodical *Rising Tide* and books with such titles as *For Sinners Only* (1932), *I Was a Pagan* (1934), *Life Began Yesterday* (1935), and *How Do I Begin?* (1937). In 1939, after the movement had become known as Moral Re-Armament, thirty thousand people filled the Hollywood Bowl for the rally which preceded the second World Assembly, and an additional ten thousand were reported to have been turned away. Buchman's emphasis was highly individualistic and no great renewal of church life apparently was either intended or effected, but many prominent people professed to have

[36] *Research Memo on Religion in the Depression* (N.Y., 1937), 45 ff., 95. Cited by McLoughlin, *Modern Revivalism*, 463–64.
[37] See A. W. Eister, *Drawing-Room Conversion* (Durham, N.C., 1950), and W. H. Clark, *The Oxford Group: Its History and Significance* (N.Y., 1951). For an assessment of the later Moral Re-Armament phase of the movement, see *Moral Re-Armament: A Study of the Movement Prepared by the Social and Industrial Council of the Church Assembly* (London: Church [of England] Information Board, 1955).

had their lives changed and to have found guidance in the "quiet times" of the houseparties.

THEOLOGICAL RECONSTRUCTION.   As early as 1928 Episcopal Bishop Charles Fiske (1868–1942) was convinced that there was "evidence of a sad disintegration of American Protestantism," [38] a view that was shared by a Unitarian writer, William L. Sullivan. In an article on "Our Spiritual Destitution," Sullivan noted that religion had become "timorous, unimaginative, quick with comment upon the contemporaneous, but unable in the authentic manner of its great tradition to judge the contemporaneous by categories that are eternal." [39] In spite of the prescience of a few such men, the task of theological reconstruction was delayed. Although some were to be stirred by Reinhold Niebuhr's devastating polemics, *Moral Man and Immoral Society* (1932) and *Reflections on the End of an Era* (1934), as well as by other books written by theological professors,[40] it was not until after 1940 that more than a handful of ministers were ready to engage in a fundamental reconsideration of their theological position. Harry Emerson Fosdick was a significant exception, having announced in a widely publicized sermon in 1935 that "The Church Must Go Beyond Modernism."

There were several reasons for this delayed response. For one thing, in the midst of a depression, the working clergy were overwhelmed with the mere task of seeing that the bills were paid and the church doors kept open. Whatever time they had for reflection tended to be absorbed by an interest in social reforms that might serve to mitigate the economic plight of their parishioners. Additional thought and energy were siphoned off in the endeavor of the clergy to qualify themselves to deal more adequately with the personal problems of anxious and distraught people. It was no mere coincidence that Charles T. Holman's pioneering book in the field of pastoral counseling, *The Cure of Souls*, was published in 1932. Most important of all was the lingering impact of the Fundamentalist controversy. Attention had been centered on peripheral issues, and both parties

---

[38] *The Confessions of a Puzzled Parson* (N.Y., 1928), 191.

[39] *Atlantic Monthly*, CXXXXIII (Jan.–June, 1929), 378.

[40] Among the more important of these books were: Walter Lowrie, *Our Concern with the Theology of Crisis* (1932), Edwin Lewis, *Christian Manifesto* (1934), George Richards, *Beyond Fundamentalism and Modernism* (1934), and a series of three essays by H. Richard Niebuhr, Wilhelm Pauck, and Francis P. Miller, *The Church against the World* (1935).

379

had been driven to more extreme positions than they otherwise would have adopted, positions from which they found it difficult to retreat. And then, alarmed by the controversy's threat to institutional concerns, denominational leaders had taken charge and, in the interest of harmony, had been largely successful in ruling theological discussion out of bounds.

The theological revival which began in the seminaries during the 1930's is difficult to characterize, for it found expression in no single theological system or school of thought.[41] Its most prominent common feature was represented by Henry Nelson Wieman's announcement in 1932 of his intention henceforth "to promote a theocentric religion as over against the prevalent anthropocentric one." Influenced by Alfred North Whitehead's process philosophy, Wieman, Douglas C. Macintosh, Walter M. Horton, and Charles Hartshorne, moved in the direction of a theological realism which rejected the philosophical idealism of the older liberalism. Destined to be much more influential, however, were points of view derived from Europe,[42] where the shattered optimism of the immediate postwar years had produced an earlier theological reassessment. Although European-oriented theology in America was generally labeled "neo-orthodox," it too was multiform and varied, borrowing insights from such diverse sources as the Jewish thinker Martin Buber, the Russian Orthodox theologian Nicolai Berdyaev, the Spanish existentialist Miguel Unamuno, the French neo-Thomist Jacques Maritain, the Swedish Lutheran theologians Anders Nygren and Gustaf Aulén, and also from the varied points of view of P. T. Forsyth, John Oman, and William Temple in England. While recognizing this diversity, the European influence can perhaps best be summarized as an intermingling of neo-Reformation and existentialist emphases, with Karl Barth and Emil Brunner representing a primary stress on the Reformation heritage and Paul Tillich, who came to America in 1933, drawing more heavily on the "existentialism" of Søren Kierkegaard.

Karl Barth (b. 1886), the Swiss theologian, was the towering figure of the theological revival. Although fully accepting the historical criticism of the liberal era, Barth took his stand firmly on the Scriptures as

---

[41] For perceptive discussions of the new theological emphases, see John Dillenberger and Claude Welch, *Protestant Christianity* (N.Y., 1954), 255–83; D. D. Williams, *What Present-Day Theologians Are Thinking* (N.Y., 1959); and D. W. Soper, *Major Voices in American Theology* (Philadelphia, 1953).

[42] See S. E. Ahlstrom, "Continental Influence on American Christian Thought since World War I," *Church History*, XXXVII (1958), 256–73.

interpreted by the Protestant Reformers and insisted that it is through Jesus Christ alone that God's Word addresses man. Emil Brunner (b. 1889) was not quite so uncompromising in the rejection of all forms of natural theology and was at first more influential in the United States than his Swiss colleague. Americans tended to find Brunner's strong emphasis on one's apprehension of God being derived from a deeply personal "I-thou" encounter less forbidding than Barth's seemingly more harsh statement of much the same position.[43] While both Barth and Brunner had been influenced by "the melancholy Dane," Americans were directly exposed to Kierkegaard's writings through translations provided by Walter Lowrie and David Swenson. Paul Tillich (1886–1965) was to be the chief mediator of the type of existentialist thought represented by Kierkegaard, until the writings of Rudolf Bultmann (b. 1884) and Dietrich Bonhoeffer (1905–45), the German Protestant martyr, began to appear in English translations. Preoccupied with the problem of the anxious and agonized conscience (the sense of guilt, estrangement, and frustration which once had been so prominently displayed in revival meetings), these men manifested much the same personal concern and introspective analysis that had become fashionable among the *literati*. The self-acceptance they stressed, however, was grounded in the biblical message of justification by faith alone.

Although it is impossible to draw together into a single and consistent whole all the tendencies that were manifest in the theological revival, certain major themes can be identified.[44] The first of these was a reassertion of the sovereignty of God and a repudiation of the notion that man is the master of his own fate. By and large all the newer theologians, including even such a neo-naturalist as Wieman, were thinking in terms of a religion of "grace." Second, there was a decisive reaction against any optimistic evaluation of the human situation. The demonic power of sin was viewed much more radically than heretofore. Third, there was a renewed appreciation of the centrality of biblical revelation, with biblical

[43] Douglas Horton introduced Barth to America in 1928 through a translation of Barth's *The Word of God and the Word of Man,* and three years later Wilhelm Pauck presented a sensitive appraisal of his thought in *Karl Barth: Prophet of a New Christianity?* A translation of Brunner's *The Theology of Crisis* appeared in 1929, but *The Divine-Human Encounter,* which was not published in America until 1943, was to be his most influential work.

[44] Several of these themes are illustrated by selections drawn from the writings of Edwin Lewis, H. Richard Niebuhr, Reinhold Niebuhr, Robert L. Calhoun, and Paul Tillich and reprinted in Smith, Handy, Loetscher, *American Christianity,* II, 438–71.

theology becoming the focus of most theological discussion. Fourth, there was a revival of interest in Christology. Fifth, there was, among many, a deepening concern to recover a sense of fullness and wholeness in the life of the church. And lastly, there was a tendency among the leaders of the revival, while moving to the "right" theologically, to move to the "left" politically. The tone was set by Reinhold Niebuhr's opening remark in his *Reflections on the End of an Era:* "In my opinion, adequate spiritual guidance can come only through more radical political orientation and more conservative religious convictions than are [at present] comprehended in the culture of our era."

By the late 1940's the awakening of interest in Christian doctrine and biblical theology was no longer restricted to the theological seminaries. Lay groups began to participate in serious theological inquiry, and church school curricula began to be rewritten to give greater emphasis to biblical and doctrinal instruction. The Presbyterians blazed the way for this latter development with their *Christian Faith and Life Series* of church school materials, and other denominations quickly followed their example.[45]

THE RELIGIOUS REVIVAL.   By the 1950's it was evident that the United States was in the midst of a religious revival. Critical voices had become muted, and religion was riding the crest of a wave of popularity. Church attendance soared, contributions mounted, and unprecedented sums were spent on new church buildings.[46] Publishers discovered that serious religious books could find a profitable market, and the more popular "uplift" volumes dominated the best-seller lists for extended periods of time. Never had religion been held in greater public esteem. The pledge of allegiance to the American flag was amended to include the phrase "under God," prayer breakfasts were attended by the president and members of his cabinet, a prayer room was installed in the national capitol, and both the American Legion and the National Advertising Council embarked on heavily financed "Back to God" and "Go to Church" campaigns. Even the disc jockeys "got religion," and a survey in 1957 by

[45] For point of view represented by the Presbyterian series, see statement in Armstrong, Loetscher, Anderson, *Presbyterian Enterprise*, 301–03.

[46] From a base of $26,000,000 in 1945, the amount spent on new churches rose steadily: 1946—76 million; 1948—251 million; 1950—409 million; 1954—593 million; 1956—775 million; 1958—863 million; 1959—935 million; 1960—1,016 million. After 1960 a decline set in. In contrast to attendance figures and in spite of reports to the contrary, church membership was not increasing in proportion to the population. See W. S. Hudson, "Are the Churches Really Booming?" *Christian Century*, LXXII (1955), 1494-96.

the United States Census Bureau indicated that more than 96 per cent of the American people cited a specific religious affiliation in response to the question: "What is your religion?" Obviously there were many among the 96 per cent whose names did not appear on any church membership roll, but the fact that they so identified themselves is significant.

Unlike earlier religious revivals, the "return to religion" of the 1950's was formless and unstructured, manifesting itself in many different ways and reinforcing all religious faiths quite indiscriminately.[47] It cannot be understood apart from the climate of opinion flowing from the trauma of World War II and its aftermath. The depression of the 1930's had been a sobering experience, but the "immense and indomitable optimism" of the American people was not really shaken until the bombing of Hiroshima and Nagasaki in 1945 demonstrated the potential destructiveness of the unleashed powers of the atom. The uneasy and precarious peace of the "cold war" that followed, with its recurrent crises and continuing conflicts, heightened the sense of anxiety and insecurity. Religious overtones also were present in the confrontation between the Soviet bloc and the Western powers, because of the professed atheism of the Communist regimes. In this situation, it was natural that religion should be viewed by many as a weapon to be employed in the struggle.

As a result of what Robert Maynard Hutchins, president of the University of Chicago, called "the good news of damnation," the world of the secular intellectuals was prepared to listen to the theologians, most notably to Reinhold Niebuhr and Paul Tillich, in a way and to a degree that had not been true for almost a half century. The comment of *Time* magazine in 1956 that Tillich was an intellectual whom even the intellectuals regarded with awe may have been overly exuberant, but it nonetheless reflected the marked shift in attitude that had occurred. A much greater seriousness of concern was to be found among a steadily growing number of church members who had been brought into touch with the renewed theological interest and had discovered an unsuspected relevance of biblical faith to contemporary life. Small groups for study and devotion seemed to give promise of a more thoroughgoing renewal of church life. While this new theological interest and concern among intellectuals

[47] See A. Roy Eckardt, *The Surge of Piety in America* (N.Y., 1958), Martin E. Marty, *The New Shape of American Religion* (N.Y., 1959), Peter Berger, *The Noise of Solemn Assemblies* (Garden City, N.Y., 1961), and Gibson Winter, *The Suburban Captivity of the Churches* (Garden City, N.Y., 1961).

outside the churches and sensitive lay people within the churches was a concomitant of the religious revival, the revival also flowed through more popular channels.

The revival was given its most vigorous leadership by the heirs of the Fundamentalists. The way for their new surge of activity had been prepared by the National Association of Evangelicals, Youth for Christ, and a handful of scholars who were determined to develop an effective Fundamentalist apologetic. The National Association of Evangelicals was formed in 1942 to consolidate the forces of moderate Fundamentalism,[48] and under the leadership of Harold J. Ockenga it adopted a conciliatory policy designed to capitalize upon the demoralization of the "modernists" and to penetrate the life of the major denominations by persuasion from within rather than by leveling criticism from without. In pursuing this purpose they called themselves "evangelicals" to avoid the discredited Fundamentalist label and utilized the most up-to-date publicity techniques. Youth for Christ, the second organization spearheading the Fundamentalist recovery, was founded in 1943 to sponsor Saturday night rallies for young people and members of the armed forces. It quickly became both a recruiting instrument and a training ground for new "evangelical" leadership. The activity of these two agencies was strengthened and undergirded by a coterie of young Fundamentalist theologians whose goal was to provide a rational and philosophic defense of the Fundamentalist understanding of the Christian faith and who were willing to engage in the give and take of closely reasoned theological discussion.[49]

These several tendencies of the new Fundamentalism were brought into focus by Billy Graham (b. 1918) who had been recruited by Youth

[48] The radical come-outer wing of Fundamentalism was drawn together in the American Council of Churches, established by Carl McIntire in 1941. His violent polemics and racist associations kept his group from winning any numerically significant constituency.

[49] See A. W. Hearn, "Fundamentalist Renascence," *Christian Century*, LXXV (1958), 528–30. The most prominent of these younger men were Carl F. H. Henry, Edward J. Carnell, and Cornelius Van Til. Henry was the author of *The Uneasy Conscience of Modern Fundamentalism* (Grand Rapids, 1947), *The Protestant Dilemma* (Grand Rapids, 1949), and *Fifty Years of Protestant Theology* (Boston, 1950). In 1956 when *Christianity Today*, the major periodical voice of this group, was founded, Henry became its editor. Carnell's major books were *Introduction to Christian Apologetics* (Grand Rapids, 1948), *The Theology of Reinhold Niebuhr* (Grand Rapids, 1951), *Philosophy of the Christian Religion* (Grand Rapids, 1952), and *The Case for Orthodox Theology* (Philadelphia, 1959). For Van Til, see *The New Modernism* (Philadelphia, 1946), *The Defense of the Faith* (Philadelphia, 1955), *Christianity and Idealism* (Philadelphia, 1955), and *Christianity and Barthianism* (Grand Rapids, 1962).

for Christ in 1945 to serve as an itinerant evangelist at its rallies.[50] Four years later at a tent meeting in Los Angeles, Graham gained his first widespread public attention through the conversion of three minor celebrities—a local television star, a former Olympic athlete, and an alleged associate of the notorious racketeer Mickey Cohen. The Los Angeles success was followed by an eighteen-day campaign at the Park Street Church in Boston, and in 1950 by his first major citywide revival in Portland, Oregon. Presumably under the tutelage of Ockenga, Graham modified his style, moderated his sensationalism, expressed a distaste for interdenominational feuds, and deplored "fumbling Fundamentalists" who destroyed their effectiveness by intolerance, narrow-mindedness, and sectarianism. He expressed his own willingness to "fellowship with all born-again believers" and announced a decision to refuse any invitation to conduct a revival that was not tendered by a majority of the Protestant clergy of the host city.

Several factors, in addition to his dashing youthful appearance and generally irenic spirit, combined to further Graham's growing prominence and popularity which culminated in his dramatic "invasion" of England in 1954. One was the skillful use that was made of sophisticated organizational techniques and an adroit exploitation of a variety of publicity media, including his weekly "Hour of Decision" radio broadcasts, television appearances, and feature-length motion pictures. The second was the care that was taken to marshal support among all denominations. In London the "benediction" of the Archbishop of Canterbury was enlisted. But the most important factor contributing to his success, perhaps, was the mounting public anxiety which reached a peak during the Korean conflict and the Red-hunt of the McCarthy era.

Graham's gospel had a strong political flavor which had great appeal among ultraconservative segments of the population. Drawing a contrast with the Garden of Eden where there were "no union dues, no labor leaders, no snakes, no disease," Graham depicted the United States as "falling apart at the seams" as a result of "deficit spending," the "giveaway" foreign-aid programs, "immorality in high places," the influence of "big labor" and the "pinks and lavenders" in Washington, and "the infiltration of the left wing" into schools and churches. The "betrayals" at

[50] See Charles T. Cook, *The Billy Graham Story* (London, 1954), Stanley High, *Billy Graham* (N.Y., 1956), and W. G. McLoughlin, Jr., *Billy Graham: Revivalist in a Secular Age* (N.Y., 1960).

Yalta and Potsdam, the "twilight war" in Korea, the bungling United Nations ("they set the policies and we shed the blood and pay the bills"), were cited as evidence of the "deadly work" of Communist boring from within; and they were used to demonstrate that "we are living in the latter days" in order to drive home the urgency of repentance. Convinced that Communism was "masterminded by Satan," Graham told his audiences that it was a mistake to think that Satan can be defeated with "flesh and blood and guns and bullets." Only through a great revival that "would purge America of the rats and termites that are subversively endeavoring to weaken the defense of this nation from within" could the United States be saved and the battle won, for "the greatest and most effective weapon against Communism today is a born-again Christian." The altar call was simple and direct: "If you would be a true patriot, then become a Christian. If you would be a loyal American, then become a loyal Christian." [51]

The patriotic motif did not represent the full scope of Billy Graham's message. There was much traditional doctrine, and he often spoke to the more personal needs of people. Here the stress was upon the role of religion as a consolation which brings "peace of mind, peace of soul, peace of conscience." This latter emphasis points to another prominent feature of the surge of piety of the 1950's—the "cult of reassurance" of which Norman Vincent Peale (b. 1898), minister of the Marble Collegiate Church in New York City, has been called the "high priest."

Groups such as New Thought, Christian Science, and the Unity School of Christianity had long exploited the reassurance theme in religion, and in 1937 Henry C. Link, a professional psychologist, in a best-seller entitled *The Return to Religion* had given an aura of scientific authority to an emphasis upon the psychological value of religion in easing social adjustments (bridge-playing and church attendance were equally useful in this respect) and fostering healthy attitudes. But the full-blown cult of reassurance dates from the publication of Joshua L. Liebman's *Peace of Mind* in 1946, which quickly achieved a phenomenal sale. Liebman was a Jewish rabbi, and within a relatively brief time preachers of all persuasions, including Monsignor Fulton J. Sheen with his *Peace of Soul* (1949), were capitalizing upon this newly awakened religious interest.

Of all the "peace of mind" evangelists, it was Norman Vincent Peale

[51] McLoughlin, *Modern Revivalism*, 505–12.

who most fully captured the public imagination. From his base in New York City he issued a constant stream of books and other writings, including the fabulously successful *The Power of Positive Thinking* (1952). His was a simple "do-it-yourself" faith, calling for the replacement of "negative thoughts" with "positive thinking," that was strongly reminiscent of the teachings of Charles and Myrtle Fillmore. You can "make your life what you want it to be through belief in God and in yourself," he informed his readers. You must "think, believe, visualize success"—"think big," "believe big," "pray big," "act big." When "you decide that nothing can defeat you, from that instant *nothing can defeat you.*" Posing the question, How does one "practice faith"? he answered: "First thing every morning before you arise say out loud, 'I believe,' three times." [52]

Peale was referred to by some as "the rich man's Billy Graham," and it is true that they held each other in high esteem. While they differed theologically, they shared ultraconservative political and economic views. Peale was one of the sponsors of Graham's New York Crusade and, if the number of decision cards received from the Graham organization was an accurate index, his church reaped the largest harvest. Graham, in turn, regarded Peale as "a born-again Christian" in spite of his obvious self-help Pelagianism.

Other manifestations of renewed religious vitality

While Graham and Peale were the conspicuous symbols of the revival, its deeper currents flowed through the more normal channels of church life where many of the clergy, deeply critical of the pervasive "folk religion," sought to develop a more theologically literate laity. Attention also was given to the recovery of the vitality and theological integrity of public worship, and a type of "vocational evangelism," which sought to help individuals discover the relevance of the Christian faith to their daily pursuits, was given strong support. There was a growing awareness of the counseling role of the minister, and psychological insights and techniques began to be more closely correlated to fundamental Christian assumptions. Moreover, the churches continued their attempts to deal realistically, from

[52] *The Power of Positive Thinking* (N.Y., 1952), 154; *Stay Alive All Your Life* (Englewood Cliffs, N.J., 1957), 22, 104, 211, 263.

a Christian perspective, with some of the more urgent problems of national life.

One especially notable illustration of this latter concern antedated the revival. This was the careful attention which the churches gave during World War II to the problem of fashioning a "just and durable peace." The churches had learned a lesson from the uninhibited exuberance with which they had blessed World War I. The new conflict was viewed much more soberly. The halting of totalitarian aggression was accepted as a necessity and the war effort was strongly supported. It was recognized, however, that if the peace was to be made secure, the requirements for the establishment of international order must be clearly defined before the victory was won. To this end a conference, summoned by the Federal Council of Churches, met at Delaware, Ohio, in 1942 and drafted a report based on the following Six Pillars of Peace.

I. The peace must provide the political framework for a continuing collaboration of the United Nations [the powers allied in the war effort] and, in due course, of neutral and enemy nations.

II. The peace must make provision for bringing within the scope of international agreement those economic and financial acts of national governments which have widespread international repercussions.

III. The peace must make provision for an organization to adapt the treaty structure of the world to changing underlying conditions.

IV. The peace must proclaim the goal of autonomy for subject peoples, and it must establish international organization to assure and to supervise the realization of that end.

V. The peace must establish procedures for controlling military establishments everywhere.

VI. The peace must establish in principle, and seek to achieve in practice, the rights of individuals everywhere to religious and intellectual liberty.[53]

Probably no report ever received more serious consideration among church people. Numerous study guides were prepared, and few congregations failed to give it detailed attention. Key political leaders declared that the report was of decisive importance in creating the favorable climate of opinion in America that was indispensable to the subsequent organization of the United Nations.

[53] A more extended "Statement of Guiding Principles" is reprinted in Smith, Handy, Loetscher, *American Christianity*, II, 522–26.

Later in the McCarthy era of the early 1950's, the Protestant churches performed equal yeoman service in seeking to call a halt to the witchhunt of those years. Methodist Bishop G. Bromley Oxnam and John A. Mackay, president of Princeton Theological Seminary and moderator of the Presbyterian Church, U.S.A., provided the most signal leadership, but all major denominations adopted repeated resolutions expressing alarm at the threat to freedom implicit in the practice of character assassination, imputation of guilt by association, use of loyalty oaths as a means of thought control, and the curtailment of individual rights on the basis of the credence given to accusations by undisclosed informers without recourse to courts of law. Although a message to the churches by the Methodist bishops was equally uncompromising, perhaps the boldest action was taken by the Presbyterian General Council in a statement issued on October 21, 1953, to be read to each congregation. Picking up the theme of an address by President Mackay at the preceding General Assembly that "detestation of communism" was becoming "a new form of idolatry," the statement declared that anti-Communism can be as dangerous as Communism, that dissent and treason are not identical, and that true believers in God will not play fast and loose with the truth to preserve freedom.[54] The firm strictures of official church bodies played no small part in heartening the defenders of liberty during this difficult time and in encouraging the United States Senate to meet the issue without equivocation in the censure proceedings which grew out of the Army-McCarthy hearings.

Still later the racial crisis, which came to the fore after the Supreme Court decision of 1954 outlawing segregation in the public schools, elicited the strong leadership of many churchmen.[55] Two years prior to the action of the Supreme Court the National Council of Churches had adopted an official statement, *The Churches and Segregation,* which declared racial segregation to be "diametrically opposed" to the Christian faith. When the decision of the Court was announced, the National Council quickly issued "Suggestions for Action" to guide the churches in helping

[54] The Presbyterian statement is reprinted in Smith, Handy, Loetscher, *American Christianity*, II, 549–55.

[55] For discussions of the racial issue, with helpful bibliographies, see Kyle Haselden, *The Racial Problem in Christian Perspective* (N.Y., 1959), Liston Pope, *The Kingdom Beyond Caste* (N.Y., 1957), Paul Ramsey, *Christian Ethics and the Sit-In* (N.Y., 1961), Robert Root, *Progress against Prejudice: the Church Confronts the Race Problem* (N.Y., 1957), and James Sellers, *The South and Christian Ethics* (N.Y., 1962).

to speed compliance with the law. Unfortunately, instead of proceeding with "all deliberate speed" to carry out the directive of the Court, many southern states adopted a policy of "massive resistance" which served to create smoldering discontent in the Negro communities. One of the tragic aspects of the situation was the abdication of responsibility and leadership by the southern white churches. After passing a mild resolution commending the Court's decision, the Southern Baptist Convention retreated into silence. The record of other denominations was not notably better, although there were instances of firm and courageous leadership in some local congregations.

A new phase of the struggle began in 1956 when the Negroes of Montgomery, Alabama, put an end to segregated seating in the city's public transportation by a mass bus boycott. The leader of the boycott was a young Negro Baptist minister, Martin Luther King, Jr. (b. 1929), who was to become the principal architect of a drive to attack all forms of segregation through nonviolent action.[56] Other Negro clergymen and particularly Negro college students rallied to his support, as did leaders of the northern white churches. Several organizations, including the Southern Christian Leadership Conference of which King became president, were formed to push the program of nonviolent resistance. By 1962 the movement had spread to northern cities, where the focal points of concern were discrimination in housing, employment, and de facto school segregation.

With a succession of "long hot summers" of increasing tension in prospect, the National Council of Churches created an emergency Commission on Religion and Race to coordinate the activities of member denominations. Action programs, such as the Protestant Episcopal ESCRU (Episcopal Society for Cultural and Racial Unity) and the American Baptist BARB (Baptist Action for Racial Brotherhood), were set in motion. Several denominations established special funds to aid victims of economic reprisals and legal harassment. Prominent churchmen joined picket lines, street demonstrations, and "sit-ins," and the top echelon of official leadership was conspicuously present in the massive "March on Washington" on August 28, 1963. In the autumn the nation

[56] See his Stride toward Freedom: the Montgomery Story (N.Y., 1958), Strength to Love (N.Y., 1963), and "Letter from Birmingham Jail, Christian Century, LXXX (1963), 767–73, written in response to eight clergymen who had chided him for disturbing the peace of Birmingham.

390

was shocked by the tragic murder of four Negro Sunday school children in the wanton Sunday morning bombing of a Baptist church in Birmingham, Alabama. The following spring, during the lengthy Senate debate on the Civil Rights Bill of 1964, a Daily Protestant Assembly was maintained at the Lutheran Church of the Reformation on Capitol Hill. The prayer services of the Assembly were supplemented by briefings for those who had come to the nation's capital to make their views known to their legislative representatives. But it was the careful marshaling of support in local congregations, particularly in the Middle West, that was of decisive importance in bringing the debate to a successful conclusion.

The Protestant phase of the "religious revival" has often been dismissed as an expression of mere religiosity—a booming, surging culture religion, without depth and with little commitment, which was utilized to lend divine sanction to "the American way of life." But it was more than that. While there was much that was superficial, there also was earnest probing and a great hunger for faith. And in the confrontation with McCarthyism and in the struggle for the equal rights of all citizens, it was apparent that not all churchmen were ready to bow their knees to Baal.

XV

The Maturing
of Roman Catholicism

When Pius X issued the apostolic constitution *Sapienti Consilio* on June 29, 1908, he brought to an end the missionary status of the Roman Catholic Church in the United States and signalized the fact that it had come of age. Hitherto the church in the United States had been under the jurisdiction and control of the Congregatio de Propaganda Fide in Rome. Henceforth it was to be administered on a basis of equality with the older branches of the church in Europe. But it was not until after World War I that the Roman Catholic Church in America began to exhibit the full marks of maturity as an indigenous expression of the Roman Catholic faith.

The external marks of maturity

Maturity is an ambiguous word. It may refer to the external manifestations of entrance into adulthood, or it may connote an inner temper of mind and spirit that is no longer plagued by the insecurities and anxieties of adolescence. Generally in the maturing process, the outward evidence of maturity precedes the inward maturation. The initial concern of this chapter, therefore, is with the external aspects of a "full-grown" American Catholicism.

THE EFFECT OF WORLD WAR I. The outbreak of war in 1914 had the immediate effect of cutting off the massive influx of immigrants which had contributed so largely to the numerical growth of Roman Catholicism in America. And after the war restrictive legislation put an end to renewed large-scale immigration. This meant that for the first time the Roman Catholic Church had an opportunity to become more or less stabilized in the American environment. Throughout the nineteenth century it had been a church of immigrants—the heir of many different national traditions. Parishes were identified by national constituencies—Irish, Polish, German, Portuguese, Italian, French, Belgian, Slovak, Croatian, Hungarian, and Spanish-speaking. It was often difficult to think of them as constituting a single indigenous church. With the curtailment of immigration these nationality and language distinctions would normally have tended to disappear over a period of two or three generations, but actually the process was hastened by the strong Americanizing pressures that were so prominent a feature of World War I and its immediate aftermath. Immigrant languages were abandoned as quickly as possible, and there was a scramble among the immigrant groups to demonstrate that they were 100 per cent American. Almost within a single generation thereafter Roman Catholicism ceased to be thought of as an immigrant's church, and by 1955 the "melting pot" had to a great extent eliminated the identification of religion with specific national origins.[1]

A second consequence of the war was a greatly increased organizational unity that was achieved through the formation of the National Catholic Welfare Conference. The last of the plenary councils had been held in 1884, when the triumvirate of Gibbons, Ireland, and Keane was intent on limiting diocesan autonomy in the interest of a unified national policy. Since that time the papal delegate and an annual meeting of the archbishops had been the only channels through which the activities of the church could be coordinated. In practice this meant that the bishop of each diocese set his own policy. Neither the delegate nor the archbishops had the necessary administrative staff for over-all planning; and while the

---

[1] See Will Herberg, "The Triple Melting Pot," *Commentary*, XX (1955), 101–8, and "America's New Religiousness," *ibid.*, 243.

delegate could intervene in a diocese if an emergency situation developed, the authority of the archbishops was limited to the influence they could exert by persuasion and example. The war, however, created a situation in which specific and detailed centralized action was necessary if wartime needs were to be met effectively and with dispatch. For this purpose the National Catholic War Council (N.C.W.C.) was formed in 1917. So "sensible, visible, practical, efficacious" was its work that many bishops became convinced that some permanent form of peacetime organization should be continued as a coordinating agency for Catholic affairs. After some delay occasioned by a few bishops who feared that their independent powers would be jeopardized, the National Catholic Welfare Conference was fully established in 1921 and in the following year was officially approved by the Vatican.

Initially the work of the N.C.W.C. was divided into five departments—Education, Lay Activities, Press, Social Action, and Missions. Later it was reorganized into eight departments, with subsidiary bureaus and committees which embraced almost every area of Catholic interest and concern. The Conference, with its large administrative staff, had no independent authority, being controlled by the entire episcopate, directed by an Administrative Board of ten bishops, and existing solely to advise and assist the bishops. Nonetheless it gained such prestige that it became a highly effective instrument for establishing national policy, for issuing pronouncements in the name of the entire hierarchy, and for fostering a growing sense of unity and solidarity among American Catholics.

Another mark of growing maturity, for which the war was partially responsible, was the changing role of American Roman Catholics in the field of foreign missions. For almost a century American Catholics had been the recipients of continuing assistance from missionary societies abroad. At this point the war had a dual effect. It shut off this source of help, and by bringing mass immigration to an end it lessened the need for help. The Society for the Propagation of the Faith, with headquarters first in France and then in Rome, had long been a chief channel through which mission funds had been sent to the United States, but after the war much of its income began to be supplied by Americans. By 1957 about 65 per cent of its total budget was being met by gifts from the United States. Other contributions were made through scores of orders, congregations, and societies in various parts of the world. In terms of foreign-mission personnel the story was much the same. The Catholic Foreign Mission Society (Maryknoll Fathers) had been founded in 1911, but it was not until 1918 that its first missionaries were sent out. By mid-century, however, the Maryknoll Fathers were at work in Asia, Africa, Central and South America, and the islands of the Pacific. In the meantime other religious orders in the United States joined in the foreign-mission enterprise. In 1960 there were 6,782 Americans engaged in Roman Catholic mission work abroad, representing about one-ninth of the total Roman Catholic foreign-mission force.

INCREASE IN NUMBERS AND WEALTH. The growing homogeneity of the church, increasing unification, and vanishing dependence upon aid from abroad were not the only signs of maturity. In terms of numbers the Roman Catholic Church had become something far more than a lusty infant. By 1920 the *Official Catholic Directory* reported a total of 17,885,000 baptized members.

Many of the more thoughtful leaders were deeply disturbed by the overwhelming concentration of Catholic population in the urban centers of the nation. This concentration had made it possible to keep in touch with newly arrived immigrants, but there was a widespread feeling that greater stability would be achieved and future prospects brightened if Roman Catholicism could become firmly entrenched in rural America. The rural peasantry had always been the bastion of the faith in Europe, and the absence of any rootage in the soil was worrisome. The National Catholic Rural Life Conference was organized in 1922 by Edwin V. O'Hara, later bishop of Kansas City, in an effort to rectify the regional imbalance of the Catholic population by fostering an appreciation of farm life and encouraging Catholics to turn to the land. While some successes were achieved, the effort was largely frustrated by the general movement of population in the opposite direction.

With the flow of recruits through immigration having been reduced to a trickle, some hope began to be expressed of strengthening the church by the winning of converts. The number of conversions did increase, many being the result of mixed marriages. This, of course, was a two-way street. Some spot checks seemed to indicate that four or five Roman Catholics became Protestant for each Protestant who became a Roman Catholic. A Gallup Poll survey, on the other hand, provided evidence that the movement in both directions was roughly in balance.[2]

There were other defections stemming from the natural tendency of many people to shirk their religious obligations, but Roman Catholicism was remarkably successful in holding its own during these years. The officially reported membership was 20,203,702 in 1930; 21,284,455 in 1940; 28,634,878 in 1950; and 42,104,900 in 1960.[3] The latter figures reflect the triple effect of a swelling birth rate, the influx of refugees following World War II, and the "religious revival." By 1964 the Roman Catholic Church in the United States numbered almost forty-five million adherents. In terms of any realistic standards of membership, it had become the largest national grouping of Roman Catholics in the world.

In addition to numerical size, the Roman Catholic community in the United States was distinguished by its success in developing the largest private educational system in the world. By 1964 there were 10,902 Catholic elementary schools with slightly more than four and one-half million pupils; 2,458 high schools of various types with a student enrollment of 1,068,424; 295 colleges and universities with more than 350,000 students; and 596 seminaries in which 48,750 seminarians were engaged in preparation for the priesthood. All this was accomplished with little or no direct aid from public taxation, and at the same time a vast system of hospitals, orphanages, and homes for the aged was being maintained.

A third statistical indication that American Roman Catholicism has moved far beyond its period of infancy is the fact that it has become the wealthiest national church in the Roman Catholic world. By 1920 it had achieved its financial independence and rapidly became a chief contributor of funds for the support of foreign mission work. Moreover, as early as 1937 it was estimated that half of Rome's current income was being supplied by American Catholics.[4] Since that time the Communist take-

---

[2] For the spot-check citations, see K. S. Latourette, *Christianity in a Revolutionary Age*, Vol. V (N.Y., 1962), 17. The Gallup figures are given in "Conversion Poll Ends in a Dead Heat," *Christian Century*, LXXII (1955), 411. Also consult G. J. Schnepp, *Leakage from a Catholic Parish* (Washington, 1942), and *American Apostolate*, ed., L. R. Ward, (Westminster, Md., 1952), 8–10.

[3] There is some evidence to indicate that inadequate collection of data resulted in a marked underreporting of membership at least through 1940. Statistical procedures were gradually improved thereafter. See G. A. Kelly and Thomas Coogan, "What Is Our Real Catholic Population:" *American Ecclesiastical Review*, CX (1944), 377.

[4] See William Teeling, *Pope Pius XI and World Affairs* (N.Y., 1937), 133, 158–60.

overs in Poland, Czechoslovakia, Hungary, and Yugoslavia have undoubtedly increased the reliance of the Vatican on American support.

Representation in the College of Cardinals is often an index of the importance that Rome attaches to a particular segment of the church. Until 1921 there was never more than one prince of the church in the United States, but thereafter the number was gradually increased. Since 1959 there have been six American cardinals, a number approximating Spanish representation and exceeded only by that of France and, of course, Italy. The larger number of American priests who have been appointed to offices in the Roman Curia and in the diplomatic service of the Holy See also reflects the enhanced importance of American Catholicism in the eyes of Rome.

THE CHANGING STATUS OF CATHOLICS IN AMERICAN LIFE. Throughout the first half of the twentieth century, attention constantly was called to the marked contrast between the number of Roman Catholics and their feeble representation in positions of national leadership. The failure of Roman Catholics to attain prominence in proportion to their numerical strength was commonly alleged to be the result of a conscious discrimination designed to keep them out of posts of leadership in politics, business, and education. Although no one would contend that there were no instances of such discrimination, as an explanation of the general status of Roman Catholics in American life it is much too facile.

First of all, such an explanation fails to take into account the source of a large portion of the Roman Catholic strength. It was composed of recent immigrants drawn from the underprivileged classes of Europe. They arrived without financial resources. Many were illiterate; and of those who were not, many were isolated from the general culture by language barriers until after World War I. It normally takes at least a generation for children of the underprivileged to secure the necessary education to qualify for professional positions. More often it is not until the third generation that this type of leadership begins to emerge. Furthermore, the financial resources which usually are a prerequisite for moving ahead in the business community are only slowly accumulated by unskilled labor. And if there is any desire to provide one's children with an opportunity for higher education, these resources are quickly depleted.

Second, much of the isolation of Roman Catholics was self-imposed. To hold the immigrants true to the faith, tightly guarded enclaves were often created. Language barriers were perpetuated, and children were separated in parochial schools from other children in the community. The Knights of Columbus, the Catholic Youth Organization, the Newman Clubs, the Catholic War Veterans, and in some localities even a Catholic Junior League, served to retard assimilation into the general community and thus made it more difficult for Catholics to gain positions of community leadership.

Third, the Roman Catholic Church often projected a negative image. It seemed to be most successful in conveying an impression of what it was against—birth control, divorce, euthanasia, therapeutic abortion. The Legion of Decency, founded in 1934 to encourage higher moral standards in the production of motion pictures, is a case in point. It became much better known for the films it blacklisted than for those it approved. There were several points, including issues relating to public education and American policy toward Franco Spain, at which Catholic opinion was sharply at variance with that of many of their fellow citizens. Quite appart from any religious prejudice, there were occasions when Catholic aspirants for public office were defeated simply because they did not represent the views of the voters.

Studies based on information gathered in 1939–40 and in 1948 indicate that Roman Catholics moved up the economic ladder much faster than had generally been assumed.[5] By the latter date differences in class affiliation were rapidly disappearing. No appreciable distinctions in class, occupation, and education were found between Roman Catholics, Baptists, Lutherans, and the smaller Protestant groups; and the disparity between Roman Catholics and Methodists was not great enough to be particularly significant.

Roman Catholics gained political prominence at an even earlier date. As was to be expected, the urban centers where their strength was concentrated provided the arenas where Roman Catholics first emerged in roles of political leadership. Later they moved in increasing numbers into positions of consequence in the state capitals. If Roman Catholics were underrepresented in some state governments, it was presumably not because of their religion but because the state legislatures were apportioned to give undue predominance to rural rather than urban interests.

The nomination of Alfred E. Smith in 1928 as the Democratic

<hr>

[5] See the appendix to Schneider, *Religion in Twentieth Century America*, 225–38.

candidate for president was an event which signaled that Roman Catholics had come of age politically on the national scene. Smith was faced with a hopeless prospect. He was the candidate of a minority party, seeking office in a period of booming prosperity and having as his opponent a man with a towering reputation as a great humanitarian who, as secretary of commerce, had guided the nation into such economic affluence that men could speak of the approaching millennium when there would be two chickens in every pot and two cars in every garage. Later it was contended that Smith's religion had cost him votes.

Unquestionably there were anti-Catholic votes cast in the election. Protestants were urged to "vote as you pray," and in the South, where Methodist Bishop James M. Cannon, Jr. (1864–1944) spearheaded the campaign, the Democrats suffered major defections. But prohibition was as decisive an issue as Smith's religious faith in this defection, and all "wet" candidates were opposed with equal ardor. Actually Smith's Catholicism may have gained him more votes than he lost, for there were few other factors that would account for his astonishing achievement in lifting the Democratic percentage of the total vote from 34.12 per cent in 1920 and 28.82 per cent in 1924 to 40.7 per cent in 1928.[6] It is likely that a Protestant candidate would have fared much worse. In terms of actual votes Smith lifted the Democratic total from 8,386,000 to 15,016,000, and he did better in relationship to the Democratic vote for congressmen than any other Democratic presidential candidate in the twentieth century with the exception of Franklin D. Roosevelt. After the election of 1932, Catholic participation in political life at the national level became commonplace, and the election of John F. Kennedy in 1960 finally put to rest the myth that a Roman Catholic could not be elected President of the United States.

Expressions of new vitality

European Roman Catholics have often referred to the "activism" of the Catholic community in the United States. With rapidly proliferating parishes to staff and administer, churches to be built and schools to be

---

[6] R. C. Silva, *Rum, Religion, and Votes: 1928 Re-examined* (University Park, Pa., 1962), 4. See also Edmund A. Moore, *A Catholic Runs for President: the Campaign of 1928* (N.Y., 1956), and K. K. Bailey, *Southern White Protestantism in the Twentieth Century*, 92–110.

established, money to be raised and ecclesiastical supervision to be maintained, there was ample cause for energetic busyness. This preoccupation with immediate tasks may explain the absence of any native-born citizen in the ranks of the saints. Mother Cabrini (1850–1917), of course, was elevated to sainthood in 1946, but she was of Italian birth and rearing. It is also true that Elizabeth Bayley Seton (1774–1821), founder of the first native community of women, was beatified in 1963. But on the whole American Catholics have been distinguished for virtues other than those calling for veneration by the faithful. It is not inappropriate, therefore, to begin a consideration of the currents of thought and concern that have characterized Roman Catholicism in America by centering attention on its "social program."

THE SOCIAL PROGRAM OF THE CHURCH. For a full decade and a half after its founding, the National Catholic Welfare Conference was regarded in public esteem as almost synonomous with its Social Action Department, headed by John A. Ryan (1869–1945), professor of moral theology and industrial ethics at Catholic University.[7] Ryan was the author of a pamphlet, *Social Reconstruction: A General Review of the Problems and Survey of the Remedies* (1919), which was adopted by the administrative committee of the National Catholic War Council and became known as the "Bishops' Program of Social Reconstruction."[8] The document pointed to the need for minimum wage legislation, regulation of child labor, protection of the right of labor to organize, public housing, a national employment service, and unemployment, industrial accident, and old-age insurance. Except for a suggestion that labor be permitted to participate in industrial management, most of the recommendations of the Ryan document of 1919 were enacted into law as part of the New Deal legislation of the early Roosevelt years.

Meanwhile other Catholics were active in forwarding the cause of economic justice. The Catholic League for Social Justice was established in 1932. A year later Dorothy Day (b. 1898) helped found the Catholic Worker movement, whose monthly periodical *Catholic Worker* had a circulation in excess of 100,000 copies. In 1937 the Association of Catholic Trade Unionists was formed. Numerous "labor schools" were established to train union members and to help them combat both racke-

[7] See F. L. Broderick, *Right Reverend New Dealer: John A. Ryan* (N.Y., 1963).
[8] Reprinted in Smith, Handy, Loetscher, *American Christianity*, II, 407–14. See also A. I. Abell, *American Catholicism and Social Action* (Garden City, N.Y., 1960).

teering elements in the unions and Communist infiltration. Moreover, Charles E. Coughlin (b. 1891), the "radio priest" of the Shrine of the Little Flower in Royal Oak, Michigan, won a large following in the 1930's as a conspicuous spokesman for social justice. When his weekly broadcasts became tinged with anti-Semitic sentiment, however, his ecclesiastical superiors gradually inhibited him from further political activity.

Although the "Bishops' Program of Social Reconstruction" was explicitly based on the authoritative teaching of the papal encyclical *Rerum Novarum* (1891),[9] the stance of the church was not entirely unambiguous. Some bishops were lukewarm in their support, and many of the laity were recalcitrant. This cooling of social ardor was especially noticeable after World War II when much of the Catholic press became openly scornful of "do-gooders" and "bleeding hearts." Noting the growing disposition to give only nominal acceptance to the "social encyclicals," Bishop William Mulloy declared in 1952 that this indifferentism had "tended to paralyze the force of the teaching Church in modern American society." [10]

Roman Catholic policy was much more firm during the 1950's in the area of racial justice. Ever since the Civil War work among Negroes had followed a segregated pattern, but in the 1920's a protest movement developed which led to a series of conferences on the problems of the Negro. In 1934 the Catholic Interracial Council was organized by a Jesuit priest, John La Farge, who led the campaign against segregation in Catholic institutions. The movement began to bear fruit when the Archbishop of St. Louis in 1947 put an end to segregation in the schools of his archdiocese. The following year the Archbishop of Washington followed his example, and in 1953 the Bishop of Raleigh, North Carolina, defied the public opposition of Catholics in his diocese and opened the churches, schools, and hospitals that were under his jurisdiction to people of every race. After the 1954 Supreme Court decision which declared public school segregation to be unconstitutional, the unequivocal stand taken by Archbishop Robert E. Lucey of San Antonio and Archbishop Joseph F. Rummel of New Orleans was one of the heartening features of the situation in the South.

The tenor of Catholic political thought contrasted sharply with the

[9] The teaching was further elaborated by Pius XI in *Quadragesimo Anno* (1931) and by John XXIII in *Mater et Magistra* (1961).

[10] Cross, *Emergence of Liberal Catholicism*, 218–19.

progressive character of other aspects of the church's social program. Earlier tendencies toward an accommodation of Catholic tradition to the basic assumptions of American democracy had been arrested by Leo XIII's condemnation of "Americanism" in 1899. The alternative, in terms of any official teaching, seemed to be to look back to the Middle Ages for normative political models, and this alternative appeared to have been given authoritative sanction in 1885 by Leo XIII's encyclical *Immortale Dei* ("The Christian Constitution of States"), which rejected the doctrines of popular sovereignty and government by the consent of the governed, as well as the pernicious notions of freedom of religion, freedom of speech, freedom of assembly, and freedom of the press.[11] The encyclical conceded that, due to particular circumstances in any given nation, a full Christian organization of society may not always be either possible or practical. Under certain conditions, therefore, the church will not judge it "blameworthy" for "the people to have a share, greater or less, in the government." Indeed, at certain times and under certain conditions, "such participation . . . may even be of obligation." This concession was the "out" seized upon by those American Catholics who were familiar with the papal teaching to effect a practical adjustment to the necessities of American political life. The whole theory was explicated by John A. Ryan and Moorhouse F. X. Millar in the widely used textbook, *The State and the Church* (1922).[12] In the area of political thought, since he was forced to acknowledge that Catholic teaching involved "hard sayings" that smacked of intolerance, Ryan was cast in the role of a reactionary.

Whatever Ryan's intention may have been, the views expounded in his textbook made it possible for many Catholics in the 1950's to defend Senator Joseph McCarthy's activities on the assumption that they were based on "Catholic" teaching. By the late 1940's, however, Roman Catholic theologians had begun to challenge sharply Ryan's conclusions. John Courtney Murray (b. 1904) and Gustave Weigel (1906–64) of the Jesuit seminary at Woodstock, Maryland, were among those who took a more dynamic view of Catholic political theory, placing it in historical context, and demonstrating that political democracy could be firmly

[11] The encyclical is reprinted in W. S. Hudson, *Understanding Roman Catholicism*, 62–90.

[12] Later revised and republished by Ryan and Francis J. Boland under a new title, *Catholic Principles of Politics* (N.Y., 1940).

grounded on Catholic principles.[13] Within a decade their views were clearly in the ascendancy.

INTELLECTUAL LIFE. As early as 1928, in *The Catholic Spirit in America*, George N. Shuster was voicing the complaint that American Catholicism was intellectually asleep and exhibited "a terrible contempt for thought." Twelve years later he renewed the charge, stating that the church had "virtually no use for intellectuals." The absence of a strong intellectual tradition may be attributed to several causes. For one thing, American Catholics had been too engrossed in what have been called "brick-and-mortar" enterprises—constructing churches, schools, and other institutions—to allow much energy and imagination to be devoted to intellectual pursuits. Moreover, the average immigrant family, as has been noted, lacked both the educational background and the financial resources to foster intellectual interests. Symptomatic of this situation was the fact that in the late 1940's not a single member of the hierarchy was the son of college-educated parents. Furthermore, while great strides had been made in the development of a Catholic educational system, too many of the parochial and diocesan schools, as well as some institutions of higher learning, tended to emphasize "safeness" at the expense of "excellence" and creative inquiry. But the major reason perhaps was the inhibiting effect of the successive condemnations of "Americanism" and "Modernism."

The retreat into "separatism" from American culture which had followed Leo XIII's letter of 1899 to Cardinal Gibbons was strongly reinforced by Pius X's comprehensive attack in 1907 on the "modernist" heresies flowing from the historical researches of certain European Catholic scholars. Bishops were instructed to exercise minute supervision of both teachers and students. Three years later a decree was issued requiring all Catholics in positions of responsibility to take a detailed antimodernist oath. Although there were few in America who held the condemned opinions, the effect of the condemnation was to heighten timidity and to give full reign to an unquestioning orthodoxy. The spirit that was inculcated was reflected in the counsel given a young Paulist who was perplexed

[13] See the collection of Murray's essays, *We Hold These Truths* (N.Y., 1960), and Gustave Weigel, "The Church and the Democratic State," *Thought*, XXVII (1952), 165–75.

by some current intellectual problems. He was advised to "preach the moral law and let dogmas alone." [14]

It was not until after World War II that the situation began to change. The mingling, especially of priests, with non-Catholics in the armed forces had ended the isolation which had so largely prevailed. Also the educational level of the Catholic population was rising, thrusting to the fore questions hitherto regarded as "too hot to handle." And an awareness began to seep into academic cloisters of new theological trends in Europe. But the most decisive factor may have been such verdicts as that expressed by an English observer of the American scene that "the Catholic church in America has counted for astonishingly little in the formation of the American intellectual climate." [15] In 1955 John Tracy Ellis of Catholic University created a minor sensation with an indictment of American Catholics for their abdication of intellectual responsibility, and three years later Thomas F. O'Dea contributed an even more detailed analysis of the problem.[16]

In the meantime a vigorous controversy had developed between those who were convinced that the general culture was important to Catholics and necessitated their active involvement in it and those who insisted that a strongly guarded defensive posture was indispensable since Catholicism and modern cultural tendencies were diametrically opposed. The first position commanded massive Jesuit support, with John Courtney Murray and Gustave Weigel as the outstanding protagonists. Stressing the obligation of the church to the pursuit of truth and drawing heavily upon the new biblical and theological studies in Europe, they tended to share the belief, enunciated by Walter Elliott in the 1890's, that one who turned aside from the apologetic opportunities involved in friendly contact with non-Catholic scholars was "only a half-Catholic." The conservative citadel was the faculty of theology at Catholic University, where Joseph C. Fenton (b. 1908) and Francis J. Connell (b. 1888) took the lead in viewing the "openness" of the Jesuits as verging on indifferentism. "Polemics" rather

---

[14] W. L. Sullivan, *Under Orders* (N.Y., 1944), 111. T. T. McAvoy speaks of the "theological silence" which descended on the church. See *The Great Crisis in American Catholic History*, 344.

[15] D. W. Brogan, *U.S.A.: An Outline of the Country, Its People and Institutions* (London, 1941), 65.

[16] Ellis, *American Catholics and the Intellectual Life* (Chicago, 1956), originally published in *Thought*, XXX (1955), 351–88. O'Dea, *American Catholic Dilemma: An Inquiry into the Intellectual Life* (N.Y., 1958).

than "irenics" was emphasized as the proper approach to error, for any minimizing of the hard sayings of dogma in order to avoid offense to outsiders was to trifle with the salvation of the faithful.[17] In the 1960's, partly as the result of the "fresh air" introduced into the church by John XXIII, the conservatives were pushed into a defensive position even within the church. The ranks of the "liberals" had been swelled by recruits from non-Jesuit orders, diocesan seminaries were displaying a new openness, new scholarly journals were being published, and a growing number of Catholic colleges and universities were beginning to be distinguished by the quality of their scholarly contributions and the vigor of their intellectual life.

THE RELIGIOUS REVIVAL. Fulton J. Sheen (b. 1895) and Thomas Merton (b. 1905) were two major symbols of the post-World War II religious revival among Roman Catholics. In public esteem Sheen was often ranked with Billy Graham and Norman Vincent Peale as the preeminent spokesmen of religion during these years. A teacher of philosophy at Catholic University with a gift of speaking intelligibly and convincingly to a mass audience, Sheen gained fame as a radio and television preacher and then as the author of several widely read books. In 1950 he was made national director of the Society for the Propagation of the Faith, and in 1951 he was appointed auxiliary bishop of New York. Since much of his speaking and writing was devoted to an exposition of the Christian faith without excessive attention to distinctively Roman Catholic doctrine, he gained a wide hearing among Protestants as well as among his coreligionists. Merton was a disillusioned sophisticate who had sought peace in many places, including Greenwich Village, and finally found it in the silence of a Trappist monastery in Kentucky. His autobiography, *The Seven Story Mountain* (1948), was on the list of best-sellers for months, and his subsequent volumes—*Seeds of Contemplation* (1949), *The Sign of Jonas* (1953), and *The Secular Journal of Thomas Merton* (1959)—also aroused widespread interest.

Merton's pilgrimage was part of a striking movement to which his autobiography gave added impetus. Although a Trappist monastery had

[17] See Fenton, "The Direction of Catholic Polemic," *American Ecclesiastical Review*, CXXII (1950), 48–55, "The Church and God's Promises," *ibid.*, CXXIII (1950), 295–308, "The Lesson of *Humani Generis*," *ibid.*, 359–78, and "Catholic Polemic and Doctrinal Accuracy," *ibid.*, CXXXII (1955), 107–17. Also see Connell, "If the Trumpet Give an Uncertain Sound," *American Ecclesiastical Review*, CXVIII (1948), 23–30, and "Theological Content of *Humani Generis*," *ibid.*, CXXIII (1950), 321–30.

been established in America early in the nineteenth century, contemplative monasticism, with its vows of perpetual silence and rigorous austerity, failed to prosper in the American environment. At the end of World War II, however, a startling change occurred when hundreds of young men began to forsake the world and give themselves fully to a life of prayer and contemplation. The ranks of the Trappists (Reformed Cistercians) swelled, the number of their monasteries multiplied, and for the first time a house of the Carthusians, the strictest of all the religious orders, was established in the United States.

The surge of interest in the contemplative life, of course, was restricted to a spiritual elite. A more typical expression of the religious revival was the mounting lay participation in the life of the church, much of it associated with the burgeoning parishes of the suburbs. The lay movement was the product of the wedding of traditional American activism with postwar religious enthusiasm and the increased stress of Pius XII on the importance of the lay apostolate. So marked was the development that one clerical observer could speak with confidence of "The Coming Era of the Catholic Layman."[18]

The lay movement took many forms. The Christopher Movement, begun in 1945 by James G. Keller, enlisted those skilled in mass communications in an effort to restore Christian ideals in education, government, business life, labor organizations, and the home. Family life was the direct concern of the Cana Conference Movement, which drew couples together for instruction and discussion in both premarital and postwedding conferences, and of the Christian Family Movement, which fostered neighborhood groups for the discussion of family problems. The Confraternity of Christian Doctrine utilized lay personnel to supplement the work of the parish priest in instructing the ignorant, counseling the doubtful, comforting the sorrowing, and serving as "fishers of men." The most useful contribution of the Confraternity was in providing religious instruction for children who were not enrolled in parochial schools. Several organizations, such as the Legion of Mary, the Grail Movement, and the Convert Makers of America, had as their purpose the reclaiming of the lapsed and the

[18] This was the title of an article by W. R. Fleege in the *Homiletical and Pastoral Review*, LIV (1953), 134–39. For discussions of the lay movement, see Leo R. Ward, *The American Apostolate* (Westminster, Md., 1952), and *Catholic Life, U.S.A.: Contemporary Lay Movements* (N.Y., 1959), and several chapters in L. J. Putz, *The Catholic Church, U.S.A.* (Chicago, 1956).

winning of new converts. In addition there were many professional, vocational, and fraternal associations, adoration societies and sodalities, groups devoted to charitable activities, and a proliferation of youth organizations. Two periodicals sponsored and edited by laymen, *Commonweal* and *Cross-Currents*, fulfilled an apostolate to the intellectual community with verve and vitality. Undergirding much of this activity was the "retreat" movement which had as its goal providing laymen with spiritual instruction and linking religious contemplation with social consciousness.

Closely related to the lay movement was a developing liturgical interest, which sought to revitalize corporate worship. The religious revival had expressed itself initially among Roman Catholics in the growing popularity of many special nonliturgical devotions—the Forty Hours Adoration of the Blessed Sacrament; novenas to Our Lady of Perpetual Help, Our Lady of Sorrows, Our Lady of Fatima, Our Lady of the Miraculous Medal; and devotions to favorite saints such as St. Ann, St. Jude, St. Anthony, St. Rita, and St. Thérèse of Lisieux. But attendance at Mass was often little more than fulfillment of solemn obligation. Worshipers frequently had little understanding of the service and sat as mere spectators or performed their own private devotions by reciting the rosary. This was scarcely an adequate expression of their role as a Christian people or of their lay priesthood, nor did such routine attendance readily relate itself to their apostolate in the world. It was out of a concern to renew the life of the church through truly corporate worship that the liturgical movement was born.

The liturgical revival of the 1950's had its antecedents in nineteenth-century Europe, and even in America it had long been in process of germination.[19] The main center of the movement in America was the Benedictine Abbey at Collegeville, Minnesota, where Virgil Michel (1890–1938) was the outstanding pioneer. Through his initiative the periodical *Orate Fratres* (later known as *Worship*) was founded to promote liturgical renewal. In 1940 annual Liturgical Weeks, conferences where those interested in liturgical renewal could meet and exchange

---

[19] See E. B. Koenker, *The Liturgical Renaissance in the Roman Catholic Church* (Chicago, 1954), P. B. Marx, *Virgil Michel and the Liturgical Movement* (Collegeville, Minn., 1957), and A. H. Reinhold, *The American Parish and the Roman Liturgy* (N.Y., 1958). For a brief account, see Putz, *The Catholic Church, U.S.A.*, 301–14; and for an account of some practical applications, see Ward, *Catholic Life, U.S.A.*, 20–31.

ideas, began to be held. In addition to seeking to instruct the faithful in the meaning of the liturgy and providing them with missals so that they could follow the service, two of the chief goals of the movement were the use of the vernacular instead of Latin and the adoption of the dialogue Mass in which the people recite the prayers with the priest. Other aims included the restoration of the Holy Week Liturgy, the encouragement of daily attendance at Mass, and the use of "people's altars" placed in the midst of the worshiping congregation. By 1960 the cause of liturgical renewal was receiving widespread support, many innovations had been introduced, and the movement had deeply influenced the architecture of new church buildings. Three years later the remaining goals of the movement were largely fulfilled when Paul VI, on December 4, 1963, promulgated the "Constitution on the Liturgy" which had been approved at the second session of the Second Vatican Council.

The several tendencies of growing inner maturity within American Roman Catholicism—a deepened sense of responsibility to society and culture, a heightened emphasis upon biblical and theological study, a greater stress on the role of the laity, and an intensified concern for liturgical renewal—had been brought into focus and reinforced by John XXIII and the Second Vatican Council which he had summoned to meet for its initial session on October 11, 1962. But this remarkable pontiff, who had been expected to serve only a caretaker role, and the council he had convened made a further contribution to the Roman Catholic Church in the United States. By the new openness to the "world" that was displayed in Rome, American Catholics were enabled to shed the last vestiges of the immigrant mentality which had imposed upon them a formal apartness from the general life of the nation and had inhibited full participation in the give and take of the American dialogue. This change in mood was perhaps the most significant feature of Roman Catholicism's years of maturity.

XVI

Unity and Diversity
In American Religious Life

Throughout the history of the nation, religious life in the United States has been fluid, changing, and diverse. Experimentation and novelty have never been absent. New infusions of population from without have broadened the religious spectrum and altered the balance of religious forces, while changing circumstance and new religious vitalities within have contributed to a further shuffling and reshuffling in the relative numerical strength of specific groups. While proliferation has been constant, there has been an equally strong tendency toward assimilation and a submerging of differences in an overarching unity—a unity of spirit, mood, temper, and emphasis that has tended to give all religious groups in the United States a distinctively American character (see pp. 5–7, 14f.). In the twentieth century the diversity has also been countered by a growing trend toward institutional consolidation, additional cooperative activities, and more irenic fraternal relationships.[1]

[1] Two sociological studies of unusual insight are H. Richard Niebuhr, *The Social Sources of Denominationalism* (N.Y., 1929), and Robert Lee, *The Social Sources of Church Unity: An Interpretation of Unitive Movements in American Protestantism* (N.Y., 1960).

Trends toward unity

Within the four major groups there have been notable gains in institutional consolidation. Among Jews the traditional lines of division between Reform, Conservative, and Orthodox Judaism have been weakened, and the bonds uniting them have been immeasurably strengthened through such agencies as the American Jewish Congress and the American Jewish Committee. The Eastern Orthodox churches were somewhat tardy in establishing institutional ties, but by 1960 a council of Orthodox bishops had begun periodic meetings and most of the Orthodox youth had been linked in a common organization. The Roman Catholic Church, of course, was an organic unity, but it was pulled in several directions by cohesive nationality groups and was troubled at the national level by a lack of effective coordination of the independent powers of the bishops. The establishment of the National Catholic Welfare Conference had served to remedy the latter deficiency, and by mid-century nationality distinctions had ceased to be a divisive factor in the life of the church. Protestantism, in contrast to the other three faiths, presented a much more difficult problem, for its divisions were more numerous and more deeply rooted. Consequently any account of the twentieth-century trend toward unity, in contrast to the development of more friendly interfaith relationships, is basically the story of the determined effort to promote the unification and coordination of the work of the Protestant churches.

THE SHIFTING PATTERN OF PROTESTANT COOPERATION. Throughout the nineteenth century Protestant churchmen had been accustomed to working together. Most of them had believed that "there were plenty of targets to hit without firing at each other." The typical instruments of this cooperative activity were voluntary societies of individuals, such as the Evangelical Alliance, the Bible and tract societies, the Sunday school associations, the Y.M.C.A., the Y.W.C.A., the W.C.T.U., Christian Endeavor, and the Student Volunteer Movement.[2] These joint activities of individuals across denominational lines established habits of cooperation and developed even further the spirit of unity among Protestants. In the twentieth century, however, this relatively spontaneous form of cooperative endeavor was to be given a more formal structure.

[2] See Donald H. Yoder, "Christian Unity in Nineteenth Century America," in *A History of the Ecumenical Movement, 1517–1948* (Phila., 1954) ed. Ruth Rouse and S. C. Neill.

By 1900 most of the denominations had begun to assume direct responsibility for many of the activities previously carried on by the voluntary societies. Sunday school work, for example, began to be channeled through denominational boards of Christian education, Christian Endeavor societies were replaced with denominational youth "fellowships," and the Student Volunteer Movement played a less conspicuous role in the recruitment of missionary personnel. In similar fashion, the denominations began to implement their social concerns through official boards of "social service" instead of relying on an array of independent societies each dedicated to a single objective. In this situation, what was needed was a means of coordinating these "official" activities.

The first of the new interdenominational agencies to be formed was the Foreign Missions Conference of North America organized in 1893. Fifteen years later the Home Missions Council and the Federal Council of Churches came into being. In 1910 the Sunday School Council of the Evangelical Denominations (the name was later changed to the International Council of Religious Education) was established, and in 1920 the United Stewardship Council was founded. The distinguishing feature of these bodies was their official character, being created and controlled by the participating denominations.[3] Although the Federal Council had the fostering of a unified program of evangelism as one of its major objectives, this was viewed within the context of its general purpose, which was "to secure a larger combined influence for the churches of Christ in all matters affecting the moral and social condition of the people, so as to promote the application of the law of Christ in every relation to human life." The basic concern of the Federal Council was illustrated by one of its first acts, which was the adoption of a Social Creed of the Churches. Taken together, these several agencies provided a means of coordinating almost every aspect of the life of the churches—foreign missions, home missions, Sunday school work, stewardship, and social outreach.

The final step in the consolidation of Protestant cooperative activity at the national level was taken in 1950 when the specialized coordinating agencies were brought together to form the National Council of Churches, with divisions of Christian Education, Home Missions, Foreign Missions, and Christian Life and Work, and departments of Evangelism, Broadcast-

[3] For an account which pulls together many of the tendencies of this period, see J. A. Hutchison, *We Are Not Divided: A Critical and Historical Study of the Federal Council of Churches* (N.Y., 1941).

ing and Films, Church World Service, United Church Men, and United Church Women.[4] In the meantime, membership in the Council expanded to include seven Eastern Orthodox bodies, the Polish National Catholic Church, and the Armenian Church, Diocese of America. Thus the National Council ceased to be an exclusively Protestant body.

The national co-ordinating structure was paralleled at the state and local level by state and city councils of churches. Here, in addition to many of the concerns of the National Council, the activities included joint programs of weekday religious education, teacher-training institutes, union services, youth programs, comity arrangements, representation before municipal and state legislative bodies, provision for hospital chaplaincies, and the employment of personnel to work with probation officers. There was only a tenuous tie between the city, state, and national councils, since the official relationship at each level was with city, state, or national denominational bodies.

In rural areas a "grass-roots" unity movement developed in response to the problem created by a declining rural population. As the population became progressively depleted, many congregations faced a difficult situation, which they sought to meet by forming larger parishes, community churches, or federated churches. The larger parish was an adaptation of the Methodist circuit idea, with one minister serving several churches, frequently of different denominations. This proved to be only a stop-gap measure. The second expedient was to form several dwindling congregations into a community church, which divorced itself from all denominational connections and attempted to find a broad enough base of support by seeking to embrace the total Protestant population. Such churches soon encountered the problems posed by their isolation from any larger community and discovered that they seldom possessed the resources of leadership and vision within themselves which were necessary to maintain the vigor and continuity of church life. As a result some of the community churches sought out denominational affiliation, while others linked themselves together in what was in effect a new denomination. The most common procedure, however, was for churches with declining constituencies to federate. These federated churches maintained their former denomina-

4 See *Christian Faith in Action. The Founding of the National Council of the Churches of Christ* (N.Y., 1951).

tional affiliations, but some of them made the mistake of seeking to perpetuate separate denominational rosters of members and officers, combining only for purposes of pastoral service, worship, and educational program. This "house-divided" technique usually produced the expected results of dissension and division. The more successful procedure was to form a "united" church, with a single membership roll and a single set of officers and boards. Thus the whole church, not just a part, participated in the life of the denominations represented in the local union or federation.

Not all Protestants participated in these several manifestations of what is usually termed "cooperative Protestantism." The Southern Baptists and approximately two-thirds of the Lutherans held aloof, as did many of the smaller groups of the Fundamentalist-Holiness-Pentecostal wing of Protestantism. Several of the small and extremely conservative bodies of the latter group in 1941 formed the American Council of Christian Churches under the leadership of Carl McIntire (b. 1906). McIntire was a dissident Presbyterian minister, who joined with J. Gresham Machen in founding the Orthodox Presbyterian Church and then broke away to establish the Bible Presbyterian Church. Much of his time was spent in denouncing what he called the "soul-destroying modernism" and Communistic tendencies of the National Council of Churches. In 1942 the more moderate Fundamentalists formed the National Association of Evangelicals to "represent all evangelical believers in all denominations and groups." [5] It included in its membership local churches, conferences, some denominations, and almost a hundred educational institutions, and it also was vigorous in its criticism of the National Council.

In spite of these dissident voices, H. Richard Niebuhr was undoubtedly correct when he commented that to a dispassionate observer "the increasing unity of American Protestantism" was "more striking than its apparent diversity." Niebuhr had been making a study of theological education and he had discovered that "in their concern for the education of ministers," it was evident that the denominations thought of themselves as "branches or members of a single community" with "assignments to be carried out in partnership with other branches of one society." What was

---

[5] See James DeForest Murch, *Cooperation without Compromise: A History of the National Association of Evangelicals* (Grand Rapids, 1956).

413

true in theological education was no less true in other areas of concern, for "the idea of *Una Sancta*, of One Holy Church, is very pervasive despite relatively rare expression." [6]

DENOMINATIONAL MERGERS. The typical Protestant pattern in America has been to unite in service while preserving diversity and independence in polity and worship, but the vision of organic unity has had recurrent spokesmen. In 1838 Samuel S. Schmucker, the Lutheran leader, issued his *Fraternal Appeal to the American Churches: With a Plan for Catholic Union on Apostolic Principles*. In 1870 William R. Huntington (1838–1918), an Episcopal clergyman, published *The Church Idea: An Essay toward Unity* in which he proposed a fourfold platform of essentials as a basis for unity. His suggestion was revised and adopted by the Protestant Episcopal Church at the 1886 General Convention in Chicago, and then by a world conference of Anglican bishops at Lambeth in 1888. This "Chicago-Lambeth Quadrilateral" names as the essential bases for unity: the Holy Scriptures as the rule and ultimate standard of faith, the Apostles' and Nicene Creeds as sufficient statements of faith, the two sacraments ordained by Christ, and the historic episcopate. Still later at the World's Parliament of Religions in 1893, Philip Schaff delivered an inspiring address on "The Reunion of Christendom."

In the twentieth century at least three proposals for a broadscale union have attracted more than passing attention. In the 1940's E. Stanley Jones (b. 1884), Methodist missionary statesman and evangelist, held mass meetings throughout the country to promote what he called "a Federal Union of the Churches." In 1949 a conference at Greenwich, Connecticut, drafted a "Plan for a United Church" which would leave each congregation free to determine its own mode of worship and use of the sacraments. But the suggestion which won the most serious consideration was the Blake-Pike proposal of 1960. Speaking in Grace Episcopal Cathedral in San Francisco at the invitation of Bishop James A. Pike (b. 1913), Eugene Carson Blake (b. 1906), stated clerk of the United Presbyterian Church, proposed that the Methodists, the United Church of Christ, and other interested denominations join the Episcopalians and United Presbyterians in drafting a plan of union that would be "both catholic and reformed." The four denominations, plus the Disciples of Christ and the Evangelical United Brethern, responded to the proposal by sending

[6] *The Purpose of the Church and Its Ministry* (N.Y., 1956), 16–17.

representatives to an initial consultation in 1962. A further consultation two years later at Princeton provided evidence that considerable progress had been made in adjusting points of tension. But a Methodist General Conference report that was issued on the eve of the Princeton sessions, which stressed that any merger must take into account Methodist opposition to apostolic succession, closed communion, congregational polity, use of alcohol as a beverage, and gambling, made it apparent that there was still a long road to be traveled before all differences were reconciled.

Denominational "reunions" have been more successful than the proposals for broadly based mergers. The Methodist Episcopal Church, the Methodist Episcopal Church South, and the Methodist Protestant Church came together in 1939 to form the Methodist Church; and it is likely that Methodist negotiations with the Evangelical United Brethren Church, which was the product of the merger of two German Methodist bodies in 1946, will be successfully consummated in 1972. Presbyterians have been involved in a series of reunions dating back to the 1860's and 1870's. In the twentieth century the Cumberland Presbyterians united with the Presbyterian Church, U.S.A., in 1905, and their example was followed by the Welsh Calvinistic Methodists (an essentially Presbyterian body in spite of its name) in 1920. The United Presbyterian Church joined with the Presbyterian Church, U.S.A., in 1958 to form the United Presbyterian Church in the U.S.A., and negotiations were renewed with the southern Presbyterians in 1964. In 1961 the Unitarian and Universalist churches united in the Unitarian Universalist Association.

Meanwhile the Lutherans also had been sharing in the tide of reunion activity. The Lutherans had been something of a "sleeper" in the American scene, being largely isolated and making little impact on Protestant life as a whole. The most obvious reason they should have contributed so little to the general character of American Protestantism was that the language barrier was assiduously perpetuated as a means of preserving their European heritage by making the process of assimilation more difficult. Moreover, they were so preoccupied with the task of establishing congregations for newly arrived immigrants that they had little time or energy to move beyond their immediate parochial concerns. But the major reason perhaps was the fact that they were so badly fragmented. In 1900 there were no fewer than twenty-four different Lutheran groups each representing differing national backgrounds, differing tides of immigra-

415

tion, or differing areas of settlement, and a few representing differences of theological conviction.

After World War I this situation began to change. Large-scale immigration came to an end and the existing churches were no longer so overwhelmed by the task of supplying a ministry for newly arrived immigrants. The language barrier became increasingly difficult to maintain, and the emotions aroused by the war hastened the abandonment of efforts to maintain it. The formation of a National Lutheran Commission in 1917 to minister to Lutherans in the armed services did much to foster a *rapprochement* among the scattered Lutheran groups, as did the publication in the same year of a *Common Service Book* and hymnal. The process of consolidation was steady and sustained. In 1917 three Norwegian groups formed what was later called the Evangelical Lutheran Church; in 1918 three German bodies united to form the United Lutheran Church; in 1919 three other German groups came together in the Evangelical Lutheran Joint Synod of Wisconsin and Other States; and in 1930 the Synods of Buffalo, Ohio, and Iowa united to form the American Lutheran Church. Still others were linked in a Synodical Conference. In 1960 seven Lutheran groups voted to participate in two further mergers, with the result that almost all Lutherans (96 per cent) belonged to one of three major bodies—the Lutheran Church in America with approximately three million members; the Lutheran Church—Missouri Synod with almost two and one-half million members; and The American Lutheran Church (the definite article "The" being the difference in name from the American Lutheran Church) with more than two and one-quarter million members. By this time, partly as a result of its phenomenal growth since 1920 (almost trebling in membership between 1920 and 1960) and partly as a result of its emergence from isolation, Lutheranism had become a powerful force in American Protestantism and was contributing influential theological and ecclesiastical leadership in many joint enterprises.

The formation of the United Church of Christ in 1957 was the sole merger which bridged the lines of division that separated Protestants into denominational families, and it was accomplished in single steps rather than by a multilateral union. The participating parties were both products of previous mergers. The Congregational Christian Churches had come into being in 1931 when the churches of the Christian Connection united with the Congregationalists, while the Evangelical and Reformed Church

416

had been formed in 1934 by a union of the Reformed Church in the United States (the German Reformed Church) and the Evangelical Synod which was the American counterpart of the blending of the Lutheran and Reformed traditions in the Prussian Union of 1817. It was the hope of those who brought the United Church of Christ into being that the blending of diverse traditions in the new denomination would accentuate the strengths represented by each of them, and that the transcending of inherited cultural differences would enable them to pursue more vigorously the endeavor to be a more faithful church than had been possible heretofore.

THE ECUMENICAL MOVEMENT. Closely related to movements of Christian cooperation and unity in America was the growing concern for ecumenical or worldwide unity, which found expression in the formation of the World Council of Churches in 1948 at Amsterdam.[7] Few movements have exerted a greater influence on the American churches, most notably in the stimulation it has provided for serious theological reflection and inquiry.

Several currents of interest combined to produce the World Council of Churches. The first stemmed directly from the foreign-mission fields where divisions imported from the West seriously impaired the task of evangelism and unnecessarily weakened the small Christian communities that were struggling to maintain themselves in non-Christian societies. Although William Carey (1761–1834), as early as 1805, had suggested that an interdenominational missionary conference be held at Capetown, South Africa, to chart a common strategy, the first such conference was not held until fifty years later. These conferences were held periodically thereafter, and culminated in the great Edinburgh Conference of 1910.

The Edinburgh Conference of 1910 was of great significance for several reasons. It was the first conference composed of officially accredited delegates from the various mission societies, and, under the leadership of John R. Mott, it laid the foundation for the first of the great ecumenical bodies—the International Missionary Council. It was also at Edinburgh in 1910 that another American, Bishop Charles H. Brent (1862–1929), caught the inspiration that led to the founding of the Faith and Order Movement. He believed that churches should engage in theological discus-

[7] For the historical antecedents of this concern in Protestantism, see John T. McNeill, *Unitive Protestantism* (Richmond, 1964), and Rouse and Neill, *A History of the Ecumenical Movement.*

sion so that they might discover the extent to which they actually had a common faith and practice, and might learn from one another. As a result of his urging, the Protestant Episcopal Church in the United States issued at Geneva in 1920 a call to churches throughout the world to join in a conference "for the consideration of all questions pertaining to the Faith and Order of the Church of Christ." During the same years still another American, Charles S. MacFarland, was seeking to bring the churches together to deal jointly with the social tasks confronting them. He was certain that differences of belief were no bar to common action. The initial conference at Constance was interrupted on its first day by the outbreak of war in 1914. Some of the delegates adjourned to London to form an organization—the World Alliance for Friendship through the Churches—to deal with the most urgent of the social issues. The movement sponsored by Bishop Brent had suffered similar interruption, and it was not until after World War I that both the Faith and Order Movement and the Life and Work Movement were officially established.

Leaders in these various ecumenical bodies had become accustomed to working together in the World's Student Christian Federation which John R. Mott had organized in 1895. It was natural, therefore, for them to urge that the several movements for Christian unity on a world scale be combined in a World Council of Churches. The Universal Christian Conference on Life and Work, and the World Conference on Faith and Order, were scheduled to meet in sequence in 1937 at Oxford and Edinburgh to bring this plan to fruition. The necessary approval having been secured, a provisional constitution for the World Council of Churches was drafted at Utrecht in 1938. World War II then intervened, and it was not until 1948 that the constitution was formally adopted and the Council officially constituted. Its purpose was to foster the growth of an ecumenical consciousness among members of all churches, to promote cooperative theological inquiry, to call world conferences on specific subjects as occasion required, and to offer counsel and provide opportunities for united action in matters of common interest. Within a relatively brief time the World Council had begun to discharge these tasks, to exert an influence, and to achieve a status far exceeding the hopes of those who labored to bring it into being. "Our century has its sad features," Ernest Barker, a distinguished historian of Cambridge University, commented, "but there is one feature in its history which is not sad. That is the

418

gathering tide of Christian union." And this gathering tide was reflected in the growing success of the World Council in enlisting non-Protestant churches within its membership. By the late 1950's even the Roman Catholic Church was participating through unofficial observers in some of the conferences of the World Council.

Interfaith relationships

The middle decades of the twentieth century were marked by increasingly friendly interfaith relationships. One of the major instruments for promoting sympathetic understanding between adherents of the different faiths was the National Conference of Christians and Jews (N.C.C.J.).[8] Founded in 1928, mainly through the leadership of Everett R. Clinchy (b. 1896), a Presbyterian clergyman and a secretary of the Federal Council of Churches, the N.C.C.J. was especially vigorous in the 1930's and it established committees in many local communities to combat prejudice, ill-feeling, and strained relationships. From the beginning the National conference enlisted broad Protestant and Jewish support, but Catholic participation was mostly limited to small groups of laymen. Francis J. Connell represented conservative Catholic opinion in 1940 when he insisted in the *American Ecclesiastical Review* that such interfaith contacts seldom resulted in conversions to Catholicism which was the only potential benefit that would compensate for the risk of infecting unsuspecting Catholics with the poison of indifferentism. "Ordinarily," he declared, "the association of Catholics with non-Catholics in such organizations and meetings is a grave menace to the faith of our people."[9] Most bishops restricted clerical participation to avoid any semblance of official sanction, and as late as 1955 any Catholic participation was forbidden in 22 per cent of the dioceses.

POINTS OF TENSION. As the Catholic attitude toward the National Conference of Christians and Jews indicated, the major problem of interfaith relationships was posed by the Roman Catholic Church. Apart from the anti-Semitism of certain fringe groups, the relationship of Protestants and Jews was warm, friendly, and even cordial. And the Eastern Orthodox churches, while maintaining their doctrinal integrity,

[8] For the general spirit of the N.C.C.J., see E. R. Clinchy, *All in the Name of God* (N.Y., 1934).

[9] Cross, *Emergence of Liberal Catholicism*, 212.

felt sufficiently secure to accept membership in both the National and World Councils of Churches. The Catholic problem was complicated by several points of tension where the policy of the church seemed to run counter to established American practice, and also by an unresolved difference of opinion within the church as to the proper strategy to be pursued in a religiously pluralistic society.

Among the points of tension were those created by the refusal of the Roman Catholic Church to countenance divorce, "unnatural" methods of birth control, and therapeutic abortion. As a result of their unyielding opposition to divorce, Roman Catholics often seemed to be exercising a veto over efforts to remedy the scandalous situation in many states created by faked evidence of adultery, the securing of an "annulment" instead of a divorce decree, and the resort to out-of-state proceedings. Further compounding the scandal was the fact that these "dodges" seldom offered any protection for the children and made no provision for effecting a possible reconciliation. Catholic resistance to legalizing the dissemination of birth-control information also exacerbated public feeling, as did its insistence that concern for an unborn child must take precedence over any effort to save the life of the mother. Differences of opinion over censorship of films and magazines were also productive of friction.

But the major tension was in the area of church-state relations. As Roman Catholics became more numerous in the United States, many non-Catholics became concerned about the possible effect of the growing strength of Roman Catholicism on government. Because of Roman Catholicism's long history as a state religion in Europe, its identification with antidemocratic regimes, and its own autocratic structure, there were fears that Catholic influence in America might lead to an undermining of the constitutional provision for the separation of church and state. These fears increased in 1939 when President Roosevelt announced the appointment of Myron C. Taylor as his "personal representative with the rank of ambassador" to the Vatican. Since Taylor was a "personal" representative, the appointment did not require the approval of the Senate and there was no way of blocking it. The issue was raised again in 1951 when President Truman sought to renew representation at the Vatican with the nomination of Mark W. Clark as ambassador. This brought the matter before the Senate. When a storm of protest made it apparent that the Senate was unlikely to give its consent, Clark asked that his name be withdrawn. The issue, of course, was the preferential status accorded the

Roman Catholic Church by the establishment of diplomatic relations with the papal court.

A source of even greater tension was the effort of the Roman Catholic Church to secure tax support for its parochial schools. The question of an ambassador to the Vatican was somewhat remote, but the demand of financial aid for Catholic schools raised the church-state issue in local school districts and created sharp divisions within local communities. To Roman Catholics such financial assistance seemed eminently reasonable and just as a recognition of the contribution they made to the education of the nation's youth. To non-Catholics, apart from the constitutional issue, it raised the fearsome prospect of maintaining multiple school systems if each religious group were to be treated equally. The controversy reached its climax in 1949 when Cardinal Francis J. Spellman (b. 1889) of New York declared that sentiments expressed by Mrs. Franklin D. Roosevelt in opposition to the use of public funds for Catholic schools were "unworthy" of an American mother. In an effort to mitigate the shock of indignation his words had aroused, the cardinal made a courtesy visit to Mrs. Roosevelt, after which he announced that he had no intention of seeking general public support for parochial schools. What was desired was simply such auxiliary services as transportation of children to and from school, free lunches, purchase of nonreligious textbooks, and health care. For a number of years the debate centered on the issue of such assistance, but by 1961 the demand was being voiced for much more inclusive assistance, including federal subsidies for the erection of school buildings. By this time a way out of the impasse was being developed by Bishop John J. Wright (b. 1909) of Pittsburgh and the Pittsburgh Board of Education. This was a program of "shared time" whereby pupils in diocesan high schools attended public schools for instruction in scientific subjects and physical education.

RISE OF ROMAN CATHOLIC ECUMENISM. One of the great problems in the reduction of tension was the inhibiting of friendly discussion by a wall of separation maintained by the Roman Catholic Church. As the ecumenical movement gained momentum in the 1920's and 1930's there had been considerable hope that Roman Catholics might participate, but the dogmatic position that unity already exists in the Roman Catholic Church made this difficult. In 1928 Pius XI issued an encyclical on "Fostering True Religious Unity" (*Mortalium Animos*) in which he declared that "the Apostolic See can by no means take part in these assemblies, nor is it in any way lawful for Catholics to give to such enterprises their encouragement or support. If they did so, they would be giving countenance to a false Christianity quite alien to the one Church of Christ." The only way in which unity could be fostered was "by furthering the return to the one true Church of Christ of those who are separated from it," and this would involve belief in "the infallibility of the Roman Pontiff" with the same faith accorded "the incarnation of Our Lord." Throughout the 1940's, however, there was a growing restiveness at this blanket prohibition.

A sign of this restiveness was the controversy in the late 1940's which swirled around Father Leonard Feeney of St. Benedict's Center in Cambridge, Massachusetts. Feeney insisted on a rigorous interpretation of the dogma "no salvation outside the Church." The "invincibly ignorant," of course, could be saved through a "baptism of desire," but Feeney maintained that this "desire" to belong to the Church must be explicit. Theologians at Boston College suggested that this was an unduly harsh interpretation, whereupon Feeney accused them of heresy. When Archbishop Richard Cushing attempted to quell the controversy, Feeney refused to remain quiet and was excommunicated for disobedience to ecclesiastical authority. The condemnation of Feeney did not deal with the issue that had been raised, but the vocal opposition to his rigid views reflected a growing sentiment for a greater degree of "openness" toward non-Catholic Christians.

In retrospect it is clear that a basis for "ecumenical" conversations was being prepared in the 1930's by the revival of biblical studies within European Roman Catholicism. In 1943 two important encyclicals were issued. *Divino Afflante Spiritu* gave official encouragement to biblical study, and *Mystici Corpus Christi* gave official recognition to the emphasis of the biblical scholars upon the Pauline concept of the Church as the Body of Christ. The latter concept made it possible to "distinguish the Body of Christ, which is a society whose head and ruler is Christ, from his physical body, which born of the Virgin Mother of God now sits at the right hand of the Father and rests hidden under the Eucharistic veil." Two consequences flowed from these encyclicals. Biblical scholarship provided common ground for an interchange among scholars, and the dual understanding of the church opened the door to the possibility of regarding Protestants as "separated brethren" and "brothers in Christ." The latter possibility was carried a step farther in 1964 when Paul VI, in his encyclical on "the

Church in the modern world," referred to "the venerable Christian communities" of non-Catholic Christians as "separated churches."

The first tentative step toward establishing a relationship with other Christian groups was taken in 1949 when an "Instruction on the Ecumenical Movement" was issued in Rome by the Sacred Congregation of the Holy Office,[10] which defined the carefully circumscribed conditions under which a few highly qualified priests might participate as unofficial observers in interchurch discussions. While the Catholic Church could take "no actual part in 'ecumenical' conventions," diocesan bishops were given permission to appoint "suitable priests" to give "close attention" to these affairs and to be present when they seemed to "offer a desirable occasion for spreading a knowledge of Catholic doctrine." In authorizing such informal contacts, however, bishops were directed to take scrupulous precautions lest "a dangerous indifferentism" be fostered by "stressing things on which we agree rather than those on which we disagree," or, "what is worse still," the impression be conveyed that in matters of dogma the Roman Catholic Church is not "already in possession of the fullness of Christ and hence others are still in a position of contributing toward its perfection."

Although Roman Catholic "observers" were present at the Faith and Order Conference at Lund, Sweden, in 1952, the Archbishop of Chicago refused to allow similar representation at the Evanston sessions of the World Council of Churches in 1954. It was not until the North American Faith and Order Conference was held at Oberlin in 1957 that "unofficial" representatives attended an ecumenical gathering in the United States. By this time a growing number of Roman Catholics were beginning to recognize the necessity of breaching the wall of ignorance which separated Catholics and Protestants in America. In 1957 John A. Hardon of the Society of Jesus published a book entitled *The Protestant Churches of the United States,* in the preface of which he noted that Catholics "often have only the vaguest notion of what Protestants believe, how they worship, and what their religion means to them." [11] Nor was Hardon the sole representative of this concern. In 1955 J. J. Kane had sought to foster

[10] The text of the "Instruction" is in Smith, Handy, Loetscher, *American Christianity,* II, 579–85.

[11] Two years later Jaroslav Pelikan, a Protestant, made a similar admission in the Introduction to his book, *The Riddle of Roman Catholicism,* where he stated that many Protestants "know more about the batting averages of the Yankees or the marriages and divorces of Hollywood than they do about the life and workings" of the Roman Catholic Church.

sympathetic understanding with his *Catholic-Protestant Conflicts in America,* as did George H. Tavard in *The Catholic Approach to Protestantism,* and in 1957 Gustave Weigel published *A Catholic Primer on the Ecumenical Movement.*

The elevation of Angelo Giuseppe Roncalli to the chair of Peter as John XXIII late in 1958 inaugurated a new era in the ecumenical relationships of the Roman Catholic Church. On January 25, 1959, he announced his intention to summon a General Council of the Roman Catholic Church to bring the church up-to-date (*aggiornamento*) through purification and renewal, thus making it more effective in dealing with the problems of the twentieth century and providing a basis for the furtherance of Christian unity. To implement the latter concern a Secretariat for Promoting Christian Unity was established six months later, and invitations were sent to non-Roman communions to be represented by "official observers" at the forthcoming council. When the first session of the Second Vatican Council convened on October 11, 1962, seventeen non-Roman bodies had responded to the invitation to send "official observers," and the impact that was made by their mere presence was felt throughout the whole Roman Catholic Church.[12]

In the United States John XXIII's initiatives led to a dramatic shift in the atmosphere of interfaith relationships. Even in terms of pressing social problems there had been little interfaith cooperation, but within a month after the close of the first session of the Second Vatican Council, Protestants, Roman Catholics, and Jews came together at Chicago in a national meeting to chart a common strategy for dealing with the racial crisis. "The bishops were holding back from these meetings out of fear—fear of Rome," one theologian explained. "Now Pope John has given the Church a freedom from fear." [13] Even more important was the spate of new books dealing with ecumenical issues, which were the result of the fresh air introduced by John XXIII. Many were by Europeans, but important contributions were made by Gustave Weigel, *Faith and Understanding in America* (1959), George H. Tavard, *Two Centuries of*

---

[12] For a journalistic account of the first two sessions, see Xavier Rynne, pseud., *Letters from Vatican City* (N.Y., 1963) and *The Second Session* (N.Y., 1964). See also R. B. Kaiser, *Pope, Council, and World* (N.Y., 1963), Bernard Häring, *The Johannine Council* (N.Y., 1963); Robert McAfee Brown, *Observer in Rome* (Garden City, N.Y., 1964); and two books by Hans Küng, *The Council, Reform, and Reunion* (N.Y., 1961) and *Structures of the Church* (N.Y., 1964).

[13] Kaiser, *Pope, Council, and World,* 254.

Ecumenism (1960), and Bernard Leeming, *The Churches and the Church: A Study of Ecumenism* (1960). Moreover, interfaith conversations began to take place within the covers of a single volume, as in Robert McAfee Brown and Gustave Weigel, *An American Dialogue* (1960), T. T. McAvoy, ed., *Roman Catholicism and the American Way of Life* (1960), Wayne H. Cowan, ed., *Facing Protestant-Roman Catholic Tensions* (1960), and Daniel J. Callahan, H. O. Oberman, and D. J. O'Hanlon, *Christianity Divided: Protestant and Roman Catholic Theological Issues* (1961).[14]

The most impressive consequence of the new spirit infused into the Roman Catholic Church by John XXIII was the flowering of interfaith discussion in city after city throughout the United States. Reserve and reticence gave way to openness and friendliness, and the Catholic clergy for the first time with ease of mind could talk freely with representatives of other faiths about points of difference and tension. Equally impressive was the warmth of the response by the clergy of other faiths to the possibility of a frank exchange of views. No surrender of doctrinal positions was intended or expected, but sympathetic understanding was no longer foreclosed by estrangement. The Faith and Order conference of the World Council of Churches at Montreal in the summer of 1964 provided a notable illustration of the new spirit. Not only was the Eastern Orthodox delegation of unprecedented size, but the number of Roman Catholic "observers" and their active participation in the conference were of historic significance.

By the mid-1960's acrimonious exchanges in religious debate were becoming less and less prominent in the United States. Americans of all faiths, in the presence of diversity, were learning to live together in a way that was mutually enriching rather than impoverishing. This was one of the most hopeful features of an era that had its full share of dismaying problems to face.

---

[14] The "dialogue" had actually been initiated in restricted fashion under the "neutral" auspices of the Fund for the Republic at a seminar in May, 1958. Several documents emanated from the discussions brought into focus by this seminar—*Religion in America*, ed. John Cogley (1958), William L. Miller *et al.*, *Religion and the Free Society* (1958), Robert Gordis *et al.*, *Religion and the Schools* (1959), Robert Lekachman *et al.*, *The Churches and the Public* (1960), and William Clancy *et al.*, *Religion and American Society* (1961).

INDEX

Abbott, Francis E., 285

Abbott, Lyman, 267, 307; *Reminiscences*, 273n.; *Theology of an Evolutionist*, 267n.

Abel, Theodore, 374n.

Abell, A. I., 246; *American Catholicism and Social Action*, 303n., 400n.; *Urban Impact on American Protestantism*, 247n.

Abrams, R. H., 363n.

Accommodation Plan, 113, 165

Adams, John, 91f., 94, 101, 105; *Works*, 92n.

Addams, Jane, 312

Adler, Cyrus, 334

Adler, Felix, 285f.

Adventism, 194–96, 328, 346f., 355f.; Advent Christian Church, 196; Seventh-day Adventist Church, 196, 347

African Methodist Episcopal Church, 223–25

African Methodist Episcopal Zion Church, 223, 225

Age of Reason, 93

Ahlstrom, S. E., "Continental Influence," 380n.; "Theology in America," 168n., 274n.

Ainslee, Peter, 277n.

Alaska, 262, 339

Albright, Jacob, 125

Alcott, Bronson, 174, 188

Alcott, Louisa May, 188

Alexander, Archibald, 159

Alexander, James W., 179

Ali, Drew, 353

Allen, Ethan, 131

Altham, John, 48

Amana Society, 183

America: church membership, 7, 129f., 327f., 355f., 382n., 396; destiny of, 20f., 109–11, 152, 192, 209f., 318–22; influence of environment, 12–22; part of European society, 3–5; possibility for reform, 16–18; post-Civil War, 207ff., 263ff., 302f., 307ff.; post-World War I mood, 359–63; post-World War II mood, 383; religious character, 16, 21f.; religious configuration, 7, 327, 354ff.; sense of expectancy, 18–22

American Antislavery Society, 153

American Baptist Home Mission Society, 220

American Bible Society, 151, 153

American Board of Commissioners for Foreign Missions, 156f.

American Christian Commission, 295–98

American Colonization Society, 153

American Council of Churches, 384n., 413

American Education Society, 153, 165

American Home Missionary Society, 153, 154, 165

American Institute of Public Opinion, sample of church attendance, 354n.

American Institute of Sacred Literature, 277

American Legion, 382

American Lutheran Church, 356

American Missionary Association, 220f.

American Peace Society, 153

American Protective Association, 240–42

American Revolution, 41; attitude of denominations, 94ff.; effect upon churches, 110ff., 131f.; natural religion, 92–95; role of Anglican pretensions, 87–92; role of clergy, 96ff.; slogan, 101f., 105

427

American Sunday School Union, 153, 234

American Temperance Society, 153

American Tract Society, 153

American Unitarian Association, 161, 173

Ames, Edward Scribner, 275, 277n.

Amsterdam, Classis of, 57

Anabaptists, 52

Anderson, Courtney, 157n.

Andover Review, 271

Andover Theological Seminary, 114, 148, 156, 160, 162f., 186, 271f., 278; creed, 163, 271

Andrews, E. D., 183n.

Anglican communion, 338

Anglicans, *see* Church of England and Episcopalians

Anglo-Saxon, 320f.

Anti-Catholic sentiment, 240ff., 399

Anti-mission feeling, 149–50

Anti-Saloon League, 317

Antislavery movement, 199, 200ff.

Arizona, 226, 227

Arminianism, 65, 79, 162, 179; variant of Calvinism, 32

Arminius, Jacob, 32n.

Armenian Church, 412

Armour, P. D., 294, 306

Armstrong, M. W., *Presbyterian Enterprise*, 43n.

Asbury, Francis, 120f., 125

Aspinwell, William, 29

Assemblies of God, 346

"Associated Ministers of Hampshire," 88f.

Atkins, G. G., 323; *Religion in Our Times*, 300n.

Atlanta University, 221

Aubrey, E. E., "Religious Bearings of Modern Scientific Movement," 275

"Auburn Affirmation," 370

Auburn Theological Seminary, 165, 280

Auchmuty, Samuel, 34

Aulén, Gustaf, 380

Austin, Ann, 46

Bach, Marcus, 289n.

Backus, Isaac, 96n.

Bacon, Leonard W., 178; *History of American Christianity*, 119n.

Baha'i, 287

Baha'-u'llah, 287

Bailey, K. K., 216n.; *Southern White Protestantism*, 281n.

Bainton, R. H., 178n.

Baird, Robert, 132, 144, 179; *Religion in America*, 129n.

Baker, Archibald G., 374

Ballou, Adin, 188n., 189

Ballou, Hosea, 162

Baltimore, Lord, 11, 26f., 48

Bamberger, B. J., 328n.

Bancroft, Richard, 86

Bangor Theological Seminary, 114

Bangs, Nathan, 278

Baptist Action for Racial Brotherhood, 390

Baptist Bible Union, 370

Baptist Free Mission Society, 202

Baptist Temple, Philadelphia, 301

Baptists, 27, 29f., 43ff., 114, 121, 124, 135, 139, 201, 236, 268, 273f., 275ff., 297, 373; affinities with Congregationalists and Presbyterians, 9n., 43f.; American Revolution, 96; anti-mission, 167; beginnings, 43f.; Brown University, 44, 77; character of, 9, 43; circuit riders, 148; education, 155; in England and America, 7; foreign missions, 157; Free Will, 162, 179; Fundamentalist controversy, 370f.; General, 43; Great Awakening, 73ff.; heresy trials, 278; high church, 173; immigrants, 246; Landmarkists, 173; missions, 145f., 148, 157; National Baptists, 351f.; Negro Baptists, 221, 223ff., 350ff.; Old School division, 166f.; Philadelphia Association, 44, 75, 116; Primitive, 167, 224; post-Civil War, 217, 227ff.; post-Revolution, 111, 115ff.; religious liberty, 103, 105; revivalism, 144; "Separate" Congregationalists, 73ff.; slavery issue, 202f.; social gospel, 313; Southern Baptists, 203, 217, 281, 356; strength, 7, 23, 44f., 73f., 75, 115, 354; Virginia, 25

Barbarism, 133, 154f.

Barclay, W. C., 227n.

Barker, Ernest, 418f.

Barnes, Albert, 144, 151, 153f., 164, 179, 228, 240; *Sermons on Revivals*, 154n.

Barnes, Gilbert H., *Anti-Slavery Impulse*, 152n.; *Letters of Weld*, 198n.

Barnett, M. J., 289

Barnhouse, Donald G., 355n.

Barrett's Chapel, 120

Barry, C. J., 241n.

Barth, Karl, 168, 380f.

Barton, Bruce, 375

Bates, E. S., 287n.

Baxter, George A., 139

Bayley, James R., 309

Beard, A. F., 220n.

Beard, Charles A., 238

Beecher, Henry Ward, 266ff., 269f., 294, 299, 305

Beecher, Lyman, 136, 151n., 152f., 162, 179, 210, 228, 240, 266; *Plea for the West*, 133n.; trial, 164

Beecher, Thomas K., 301

Bellamy, Joseph, 79, 114

Benevolent empire, 153

Benz, Ernst, 337n.

Berdyaev, Nicolai, 380

Berger, Peter, 383n.

Besant, Annie, 286

Beveridge, Albert J., 318f.

Bible Conferences, 282

Bible Presbyterian Church, 413

"Bible Schools," 282f., 371

Biblical criticism, 208, 264f., 268f., 277ff., 281ff., 422

Biederwolf, W. E., 364

Bill for Establishing Religious Freedom, 104

Billington, R. A., 241n.

Binney, J. G., 221

"Birthright membership," 47

"Black Jews," 353

Blaine, James G., 265n., 318

Blair, James, 34

Blair, Samuel, 64

Blake, Eugene Carson, 414; Blake-Pike proposal for church unity, 414

Blavatsky, Helena P., 286

Bliss, Sylvester, 194n.

Bliss, W. D. P., 312

Bodo, John R., *Protestant Clergy and Public Issues*, 52n., 150n.

Boehm, John P., 57

Boehm, Martin, 126

Boland, F. J., 402n.

Bonhoeffer, Dietrich, 381

Booth, Ballington, 300

Booth, William, 299f.

Bost, G. H., *Samuel Davies*, 74n.

Boston, 7, 40, 46, 134, 159–61, 173

Boston College, 422

Boston University, 273, 278

Bowne, Borden P., 273, 278

Boyle, James, 144n.

Braden, C. S., *Spirits in Rebellion*, 288n.; *These Also Believe*, 289n.

Brainerd, David, 78

Braisted, R. W., 322n.

Brattle, William, 40

Brattle Street Church, 40

Bray, Thomas, 34f.

Brent, Charles H., 417f.

Brethren, Church of, *see* Dunkers

Bridenbaugh, Carl, *Mitre and Sceptre*, 34n., 87n.

Briggs, Charles A., 279f.

Brinton, Howard, 125; *Friends for 300 Years*, 45n.

Broderick, F. L., 400n.

Brodie, Fawn, 190n.

Brogan, D. W., 404n.

Brook Farm, 129, 188f.

Brooks, Charles A., 245

Brooks, Phillips, 270, 294, 305, 372

Brown, C. E., 345n.

Brown, J. A., 167n.

Brown, M. C., 234n.

Brown, Robert McAfee, 424n., 425

Brown, William Adams, 273, 274n.

Brown University, 44, 77

Browne, Robert, 36n.

Brownson, Orestes A., 129, 150, 174

Brunner, Emil, 380f.

Bryan, William Jennings, 307, 319, 367, 370

Bryce, James, 8, 9

Brydon, G. M., 33n.

Buber, Martin, 380

Bucer, Martin, 32, 49

Buchman, Frank N. D., 378

Bucke, E. S., ed., *History of American Methodism*, 343n.

Buckham, J. W., 269n., 274n.

Buckley, J. M., 120n.

Bucknell University, 268

Buddhism, 236, 259, 286

Bullinger, Henry, 9n., 32, 49
Bultmann, Rudolf, 381
Burchard, Jedidiah, 144n.
Burke, Edmund, *On Conciliation with America*, 7, 83
Burma, 157
Burned-over district, 190
Burr, Aaron, 64
Bushnell, Horace, 159, 175ff., 212f., 214, 234, 240, 270ff.; *Barbarism, the First Danger*, 133n.; *Christ and Theology*, 176n.; *Christian Nurture*, 177n.; *God and Christ*, 176n.; *Nature and the Supernatural*, 177n.

Cabrini, Mother, 400
Cahensly, Peter Paul, 251
Calamandrei, Mauro, 29n.
Calhoun, Robert L., 381n.
California, theological mood, 281
Callahan, D. J., 425
Calvert Papers, 26n.
Calvin, John, 9n., 32, 41, 49, 85f.
Calvinism, 9, 32, 49, 78, 160f., 162, 179, 278
Calvinists, Consistent (Strict) Calvinists, 79, 114, 163f.; Old Calvinists, 79f., 114, 135; political thought, 84f., 94, 96
Cambridge Platform, 38f.
Cameron, R. M., 222n.
Camp meetings, 137–41, 144f.
Campbell, Alexander, 124, 149, 191, 193
Campbell, Thomas, 123f.; *Declaration and Address*, 124
Cane Ridge Revival, 138
Canon, James M., Jr., 399
Canterbury, Archbishop of, 13, 35, 338, 385
Carey, William, 156, 417
Carlyle, Thomas, 181
Carnegie, Andrew, 304f., 319
Carnell, Edward J., 384n.
Carroll, Charles, 95, 126
Carroll, John, 126, 252
Carter, Hodding, 224n.
Carter, Paul A., 363n.
Cartwright, Peter, 137, 149
Carwardine, William, 311
Catholic University, 240, 250, 254–57, 310, 400, 404f.

Cauthen, Kenneth, 274n.
Chalmers, Thomas, 310
Chapman, J. Wilbur, 282, 364
Chandler, Thomas B., 173
Channing, William Ellery, 160f., 189, 198
Channing, William Henry, 174
Charles I, 11, 27, 92, 102
Charles II, 11, 27, 46
Chase, Philander, 119
Chauncy, Charles, 40, 68, 70, 72
Chautauqua, 141, 235
Cherry, F. S., 353
Chicago Evangelization Society, 298n.
Chicago Theological Seminary, 247, 299, 377
Chicago, University of, 275ff., 313, 383
Chicago World's Fair, *see* Columbian Exposition
Chorley, E. C., 171n.
Christian and Missionary Alliance, 345
Christian Association of Washington, Pa., 123f.
Christian Connection, General Convention, 124, 416
Christian Endeavor societies, 411
Christian movement, 122ff., 126, 140
Christian Reformed Church, 167, 260f.
Christian Science, 287f., 355n., 386
Christian Socialists, Society of, 312
Christian Workers, Convention of, 298f.
Christianity Today, 384n.
Christians, *see* Disciples of Christ
"Christmas Conference," 121
Church attendance, 129f., 293, 354n., 358n.
Church extension, 226ff.
Church membership, shifting pattern of, 327f., 354ff.
Church membership statistics, significance and reliability of, 129f., 354n., 382n., 396n.
Church of England, 7, 14, 24, 32ff., 37; American Revolution, 87–92, 95f.; Calvinism, 9; character of, 9; clergy, 33–36; Commissaries, 34; establishment, 24–27, 31, 88, 103–05; Great Awakening, 74ff.; "Low Church," 32; Massachusetts, 29; Maryland,

26, 34; Methodists, 75f.; New England, 35f.; New York, 30f.; ordination, 33; parish system, 14f., 25, 33; parties, 9, 32; religious liberty, 103–05; South Carolina, 26, 34; southern colonies, 24–27; strength 7, 23; vestries, 33f.; Virginia, 24. *See* Episcopalians

Church of God (Anderson, Ind.), 344f.

Church of God (Cleveland, Tenn.), 345

Church of God, General Eldership, 126, 179

Church of God in Christ, 353

Church of God of Prophecy, 345

Church of Jesus Christ of Latter-day Saints, *see* Mormons

Church of Scotland, 42

Church of the Divine Unity, 288

Church of the Nazarene, 345

Church Peace Union, 319

Church Progress of St. Louis, 242

Church, "spirituality" of, 218f.

Churches, estimating influence of, 129f.

Churches of Christ, 277n.

Churches, prosperity of, 294f.

Cities, concern for, 199, 227–34, 262, 292–302; importance of, 153f.

City church techniques, 295–302

City mission societies, 297f.

Civil rights, 352, 390

Civil War, 203, 209ff., 212f., 219f., 295

Clancy, William, 425n.

Clark, Mark W., 420

Clark, W. H., 378n.

Clarke, James Freeman, 161, 174; *Ten Great Religions*, 264n.

Clarke, John, 30, 44

Clarke, William Newton, 273f.

Clay, Henry, 192

Clebsch, W. A., 212n., 214n.

Cleveland, Grover, 318

Clinchy, Everett R., 419

Coddington, William, 30

Coe, George A., 275, 376

Coggeshall, John, 29

Cogley, John, 425n.

Cohen, Mickey, 385

Coke, Thomas, 121

Cole, C. C., Jr., *Social Ideas of Northern Evangelists*, 150n.

Cole, Marley, 347n.

Cole, Stewart G., 363n.

Coleridge, Samuel, 169, 174ff.

Colgate, Samuel, 294

Colgate Theological Seminary, 246, 273, 278

Colleges, 155f.

Collins, John C., 298

Colonies, religious characteristics, 24–32

Colton, Calvin, 136; *History of Revivals*, 158n.

Columbia Theological Seminary, 281

Columbia University (King's College), 36, 78, 89

Columbian Exposition, 254f., 264, 286

Colver, Nathaniel, 221

Colwell, Stephen, 199, 311

Community churches, 412

Comte, Auguste, 208, 284

Confessionalism, 163–68

Congregation de Propaganda Fide, 249, 392

Congregational Christian Churches, union with Evangelical and Reformed Church, 416

Congregationalists, 27–30, 36–41, 89, 163, 165, 201, 261n., 266, 277, 280, 297, 416; affinities with Presbyterians and Baptists, 9, 37, 39, 41; American Revolution, 95f.; *Cambridge Platform*, 39; Connecticut, 41; disestablished, 115; education, 155; in England and America, 7; established, 16, 102ff., 114f.; foreign missions, 157; freedmen, 221; halfway covenant, 16, 39f., 47, 73; heresy trials, 278; immigrants, 246f.; ministers, 38; missions, 145–48; Old Lights and New Lights, 72f.; post-Civil War activity in West, 227; post-Revolution, 111, 113f.; *Savoy Declaration*, 44; *Saybrook Platform*, 41; Second Awakening, 135; "Separates," 73ff., 114; "Separatists," 27, 36f.; slavery, 203; strength in colonies, 7, 23; theological divisions, 72f., 78f., 114, 163f.; union with Presbyterians, 111–13, 153, 165; Unitarian controversy, 159ff., 163

Connell, Francis J., 404, 419

Connecticut, Missionary Society
of, 146
Conservative Baptist Association, 371
Conservative Judaism, 331f., 335f.
Continental Congress, 98, 119
Conwell, Russell, 294, 305
Cook, C. T., 385n.
Cooke, Jay, 294, 306
Corey, Charles H., 221
Corporation Act, 90n.
Corrigan, Michael A., 249, 255f.,
259, 309
Cotton, John, 17, 85n., 86f.
Coughlin, Charles E., 401
Councils of churches, state
and city, 412
Cowan, W. H., 425
Cowdery, Oliver, 192
Cox, Lawanda and J. H., 215n.
Cragg, G. R., Church and Age of
Reason, 93n.
Crapsey, Algernon, 278
Cromwell, Oliver, 43, 45
Cross, A. L., 87n.
Cross, Barbara M., Bushnell, 175n.
Cross, Robert D., Emergence of
Liberal Catholicism, 241n.
Cross, Whitney R., Burned-over
District, 61n., 141n.
Crozer, John P., 306
Crozer Theological Seminary, 268
Culpepper, Burke, 364
Cumberland Presbyterians, 179,
224, 415
Cuningham, C. E., 135n.
Cushing, Richard, 422
Cutler, Timothy, 35f., 63

Dabney, R. L., 211n.
Dakin, E. F., 287n.
Danforth, Samuel, 20
Darby, J. N., 282, 347
Darrow, Clarence, 370
Dartmouth College, 78, 263
Darwin, Charles, 208, 263f.
Davenport, James, 71f.
Davidson, Elizabeth, 13n.
Davies, Samuel, 25, 74, 81, 122
Day, Dorothy, 400
Dayton, Tenn., 370
Deaconesses, 297
Debs, Eugene, 362

Deism, 92ff., 110, 131f.
Deland, Margaret, 280
Denison University, 221
Denominational concept of the
church, 81f.
Denominational mergers, 414–17
Dew, Thomas R., 201
Dewey, John, 275, 361
Dexter, Henry M., 310
Dickinson, Jonathan, 43n., 64
Dickinson College, 77
Dillenberger, John, 380n.
Disciples of Christ, 114, 124, 179, 275,
277, 354; church extension, 228;
education, 155n.; Mormonism, 191f.,
193; slavery, 203
Dispensationalism, 282f., 364ff., 367
Dissent, English, 7, 89f.
Dissenting Brethren, 81; Dissenting
Deputies, 91
Divine, Father, 353
Divine Science, 288
Dixon, A. C., 282, 365
Dombrowski, James, 310n.
Donne, John, 5
Dorchester, Daniel, 283f.
Dow, Lorenzo, 162
Draper, J. W., 265
Dreiser, Theodore, 361
Dresser, Julius A., 288
Dresser, H. W., 288n.
Drew, Daniel, 306
Drew Theological Seminary, 368
Drexel, A. J., 295
Dreyfus, Alfred, 335
Drummond, A. L., 81n.
Drummond, Henry, 234, 268
DuBois, John, 128
Dumond, D. L., Crusade for Freedom,
200n.; Letters of Weld, 198n.
Dunkers (Church of the Brethren),
32, 52f., 124, 355n.
Dunlavy, John, 185
Dunster, Henry, 44
Dury, Clifford M., 227n.
Dutch Reformed (Reformed Church in
America), 23, 30f., 49–51, 78, 125,
260, 327; American Revolution, 95;
Christian Reformed, 167; education,
155f.; Great Awakening, 61–63;
missions, 146
Dwight, Timothy, 135f.

Eastern Orthodox Churches, 6f., 236, 261, 337–41, 419f., 425; centers of strength, 339; distinctive emphases, 338f.; European background, 337f.; Greek, 262, 339–41; growth, 327; National Council of Churches, 412; Russian, 262, 339–41; statistics, 339–41, 354; theological seminaries, 339, 341; Ukrainians, 340f.; Uniates, 339; unity, 410

Eastern religions, 286

Eckardt, A. R., *Surge of Piety in America*, 383n.

Ecumenical movement, 417–19

Ecumenical spirit, 80–82, 151, 158, 167, 171, 235

Eddy, Mary Baker, 287f.

Eddy, Richard, 162n.

Eddy, Sherwood, 234

Edict of Nantes, 49

Edinburgh Conference of 1910, 323, 417

Education, concern for, 38, 77f., 154–56; colleges, 155f.; ministers, 38, 114, 116; Negroes, 220–23; theological seminaries, 156, 413f.

Edwards, Jonathan, 16, 21, 60, 64–69, 73, 77–79, 88f., 114, 136, 162f., 178, 180

Edwards, Jonathan, Jr., 270

Edwardseans, 79f.

Eliot, Andrew, 38

Elliott, Stephen, 214

Elliott, Walter, *Life of Father Hecker*, 258, 404n.

Ellis, John Tracy, 404; *American Catholicism*, 48n., 247n.; *Documents of American Catholic History*, 127n.; *Perspectives in American Catholicism*, 253n.

Elsbree, O. W., 146n.

Embury, Philip, 75

Emerson, Ralph Waldo, 174, 181, 187f., 192, 284

Emmons, Nathaniel, 162

Emory University, 215

England, John, 133, 211n.

England: constitutional struggle, 84f., 94; influence of, 5–12, 19f., 83f., 169, 173ff., 183, 194, 200, 229, 264, 282f., 299, 310, 312, 380; working classes, 294

Enlightenment, 93

Episcopal Society for Cultural and Racial Unity, 390

Episcopalians, 34f., 173, 280, 306, 341; Chicago-Lambeth Quadrilateral, deaconesses, 297; education, 155; Faith and Order initiative, 418; heresy trials, 278; "high church" sentiment, 171–73; missions, 147; Negroes, 224; ordination, 118f.; post-Revolution, 111, 117–19; Protestant Episcopal Church formed, 119; reunion after Civil War, 216–17; slavery, 203; strength, 354; western states, 228. *See also* Church of England

Episcopate agitation, 34

Esoteric faiths, 286f.

Ethical Culture Society, 285f.

European influence, 3–5, 166, 169, 176, 264, 271, 380f.

Evangelical Alliance, 296f.

Evangelical and Reformed Church, union with Congregational Christian Churches, 416f. *See also* Evangelical Synod and German Reformed

Evangelical Association, 125, 179

Evangelical catholicism, 168

Evangelical liberalism, 269–74

Evangelical revival in Britain, 59

Evangelical Synod, 261, 327, 417

Evangelical United Brethren Church, 126n., 415

Evangelicalism, 9, 78, 80, 92, 167, 178–80; Scottish, 123

Evans, W. F., 288

Evolution, 208, 263–65, 267f., 370

Faith and Order conferences, 417f., 423, 425

Falckner, Daniel and Justus, 56

Farmers, economic plight, 307ff.

Farris, H. D., 218n.

Faulkner, H. U., 292

Faulkner, John A., 368

Fauset, A. H., 353n.

Faust, C. H., 66n.

Federal Council of Churches, 275, 314, 319, 411; Conference on Just and Durable Peace, 388

Federated churches, 412f.

Feehan, Patrick A., 254

Feeney, Leonard, 422
Fenton, Joseph C., 404
Fergusson, E. M., 234n.
Ferm, Vergilius, 167n.
Fichter, Joseph H., 241
Field, Marshall, 230, 294
Filler, Louis, 200n.
Fillmore, Charles and Myrtle, 289f., 387
Finney, Charles G., 141–44, 162, 167, 179f., 185, 198, 228, 230, 232, 342; conversion, 142; *Lectures on Revivals*, 158; Methodist emphases, 179; new measures, 143f.
Fisher, Mary, 46
Fisk University, 221
Fiske, Charles, 379
Fiske, John, 267
Fitzgerald, F. Scott, 361
Fordham University, 250
Foreign Missions Conference of N. A., 323, 373, 411
Foreign-born, 207f., 237f.
Forrest, Nathan B., 215
Forsyth, P. T., 277, 380
Fosdick, Harry Emerson, 32n., 367, 379
Foster, C. I., 150n.
Foster, Frank Hugh, 269n.
Foster, George B., 275
Fourier, Charles, 189
Foursquare Gospel, 346
Fox, Emmet, 289
Fox, George, 45f.
Fox sisters, 196f.
Foxe, John, "Book of Martyrs," 19f.
Francke, August H., 53n.
Franckean Synod, 203
Franklin, Benjamin, 68, 92, 105
Franklin, John Hope, 215n.
Frazier, E. F., 223n., 351n.
Free Methodist Church, 344
Free Religious Association, 284ff.
Freedmen's Bureau, 220
Freeman, James, 160
Freeman, J. D., 289n.
Frelinghuysen, T. J., 61–63, 67
French Reformed, 49ff.
French Revolution, 93, 132
Freud, Sigmund, 361
Friends, *see* Quakers
Frontier, 61, 132ff.
Frothingham, O. B., 175n., 284f.

Fruitlands, 188
Fuller, Margaret, 174
Fuller, Thomas, *iii*
Fundamentalism, 328, 347, 384f., 413; churches, 355f., 378; controversy, 363–71, 379f.
Fund for the Republic, 425
Furniss, N. F., 363n.

Gabriel, Ralph H., 152n.
Gaebelein, F. E., 282n.
Gale, George W., 142
Gallup Poll, 396
Garfield, James A., 318
Garvey, Marcus, 353
Gaustad, E. S., 134, 347n.; *Great Awakening*, 66n.; *Historical Atlas*, 115n.
General Association of Regular Baptists, 371
George, Henry, 254
Georgetown Academy, 48
Georgetown University, 250
Georgia, 15, 25f., 88
Germans, 25ff., 32, 48, 51–58, 208, 238, 260
German Reformed (Reformed Church in U.S.), 55, 57f., 126, 169ff., 260, 297, 327, 417; American Revolution, 95; education, 155; Mercersburg theology, 168–71; post-Revolution, 125
Gettysburg, 209
Gettysburg Theological Seminary, 151, 168
Gibbons, James, 245, 249, 252–59, 309f.
Gladden, Washington, 270, 294, 308n., 309, 311f., 314
Gladstone, William, 306
Glazer, Nathan, 328n., 333
Glorious Revolution of 1688, 30, 34, 86f.
Glover, Willis B., 268n.
Godbold, A., 156n.
Goen, C. C., 71n., 73n.
Gooch, G. P., 84n.
Goodwin, Thomas, 85n.
Goodykoontz, C. B., 146n.
Gordis, Robert, 425n.
Gordon, A. J., 282, 322
Gordon, George A., 270, 273, 294

Gorton, Samuel, 28n., 30
Gospel of Wealth, 303–07
Gould, Ezra P., 278
Gould, Jay, 294
Grace, Charles "Daddy," 353
Graham, Billy, 384–87
Grant, Ulysses S., 209, 214, 295
Graves, J. R., 173
Gray, James M., 282
Great Awakening, 21, 43, 58, 59–82, 159, 209; causes of, 60f.; ecumenical spirit, 80–82; education, 77f.; effect of, 59f., 76–82; national consciousness, 76f., 99f.; opposition to, 69–72; theological temper, 78–82
Greek Orthodox, see Eastern Orthodox Churches
Greeley, Horace, 197
Green, Ashbel, 159, 164f.
Griffin, C. S., 150n.
Grinnell College, 312
Griswold, Alexander V., 119
Grose, H. B., 245n.
Guilday, Peter, 248n.
Gunsaulus, F. W., 294
Gurney, J. J., 144

Halfway covenant, 16, 39f., 47, 73
Hall, Gordon, 157
Halle, 56f.
Haller, William, Elect Nation, 19n.; "John Foxe and Puritan Revolution," 19n.; Rise of Puritanism, 7n.
Hampden-Sydney College, 77, 135
Hampton Court Conference, 86, 91
Hampton Institute, 221
Handy, Robert T., American Christianity, 17n.; "American Religious Depression," 358n.
Hanna, Mark, 315
Haraszti, Z., 188n.
Harding, Warren G., 357, 360, 362
Hardon, John A., 423
Harford, C. E., 283n.
Häring, Bernard, 424n.
Haroutunian, Joseph, 79n.
Harper, William Rainey, 275ff.
Harrison, Benjamin, 318
Hart, Hornell, 375n.
Hartford Theological Seminary, 114, 163, 178
Hartshorne, Charles, 380

Harvard College, 33, 38, 40f., 44, 68, 71f., 89, 114, 160; Divinity School, 271
Hawaii, 259, 318
Hawks, F. E., 118n.
Hawthorne, Nathaniel, 189
Hay, John, 211
Hayes, C. J. H., 3n.
Haygood, Atticus G., 215
Haymarket riot, 308
Hays, S. P., 315n.
Hazelden, Kyle, 389n.
Hearn, A. W., 384n.
Hebrew Union College, 331f.
Hecker, Isaac T., 129, 252; biography, 258
Hedge, Frederic H., 174
Hegel, G. W. F., 169, 208
Henderson, Charles R., 310n., 312
Henke, Anthony J., 56
Henry, Carl F. H., 384n.
Henry, Stuart C., 68n.
Herberg, Will, 393n.
Heresy trials, 277–81
Herron, George D., 312
Hertzberg, Arthur, 328n.
Herzl, Theodor, 335
Higginson, Francis, 18, 37
High, Stanley, 385n.
"High Church" sentiment, 168–73
Higher criticism, 208, 264f., 268f.
Hill, J. A., 197n.
Hill, James J., 294
Himes, Joshua V., 195
Hinduism, 286f.
Hiroshima, 383
Hoar, George F., 319
Hobart, John H., 119, 159, 171ff.
Hocking, William E., 373
Hodge, A. A., 282
Hodge, Charles, 165f., 170, 179f., 267, 277, 282
Hodges, William, 137
Hofstadter, Richard, 263n.
Holiness churches, 328, 342–45, 355f., 378
Holiness movement, 180, 201f., 342–45
Holiness, National Association for the Promotion of, 343
Hollis, Thomas, 38
Holman, Charles T., 379

Holmes, Obadiah, 44
Holmes, Oliver Wendell, 161
Home Missions Council, 411
Homestead strike, 308
Hooker, Richard, 14
Hooker, Thomas, 29
Hopedale, 189
Hopkins, C. Howard, *History of Y.M.C.A.*, 229*n.*; *Rise of Social Gospel*, 270*n.*
Hopkins, Mark, 152, 267
Hopkins, Samuel, 79, 114, 152, 163
Horr, George E., 364
Horton, Douglas, 381*n.*
Horton, Walter M., 380
House of Prayer for All Nations, 353
Howard Mission, 298
Hudson, W. S., *American Protestantism*, 81*n.*; *Baptist Concepts of Church*, 43*n.*; *Great Tradition of American Churches*, 61*n.*; "John Locke and American Revolution," 94*n.*
Hughes, Charles Evans, 362
Hughes, John, 128, 242
Huguenots, 49, 51
Hull House, 312
Humanitarian impulse, 197–200
Humanity, Religion of, 284*ff.*
Hungarian Reformed Church, 261
Hunter, Robert, 308*n.*
Huntington, William R., 414
Hus, John, 54
Hutchins, Robert M., 383
Hutchinson, Anne, 28*n.*, 29, 46
Hutchison, J. A., *We Are Not Divided*, 411*n.*
Hutchison, W. R., *Transcendentalist Ministers*, 174*n.*

Immigration, 207*f.*, 236, 237–40, 260*f.*, 332*ff.*
Imperialism, 317–23
Indian missions, 78, 146
Industrial development, 291–93, 302*f.*, 307–09, 324
Infidelity, French, 132, 135
Ingersoll, Robert G., 265
Inglis, K. S., 294*n.*
Institutional churches, 300*ff.*, 335
Intellectual climate, post-Civil War, 208, 262, 263–66

Interchurch World Movement, 358*f.*, 360, 363, 367
Interfaith relationships, 419–25
International Missionary Council, 323, 417
International Sunday School Association, 234
Iowa, State University of, 221
Ireland, John, 228, 241*f.*, 245, 249, 252–59, 305*f.*, 310, 317*n.*

Jackson, Andrew, 143, 154
Jacobs, B. F., 234*f.*
James I, 24, 36, 86
James II, 27, 86*f.*
James, S. V., 45*n.*
James, William, 264
Jamison, A. L., *Shaping of American Religion*, 87*n.*; "Religions on Christian Perimeter," 182*n.*
Janson, Eric, 183
Jarratt, Devereux, 75*f.*
Jefferson, Thomas, 15, 86, 92, 104*f.*, 192, 208
Jehovah's Witnesses, 347–50
Jenkins, W. S., 201*n.*
Jewish Theological Seminary, 332, 334*f.*
Jews, *see* Judaism
John XXIII, 401*n.*, 405, 408, 424*f.*
Johnson, C. A., *Frontier Camp Meeting*, 137*n.*
Johnson, Edward, 20
Johnson, Samuel, 36
Johnson, T. H., *Jonathan Edwards*, 66*n.*; *Puritans*, 18*n.*
Jones, Abner, 123
Jones, E. Stanley, 414
Jones, Rufus M., 25*n.*
Jones, Sam, 364
Judaism, *iv*, 6, 38, 236, 261*f.*, 265*f.*, 327, 328–37, 339; alienation from synagogue, 334; American Jewish Committee, 410; American Jewish Congress, 410; American Revolution, 95; Ashkenazim, 329*f.*; Central Conference of American Rabbis, 336; Conservative, 331*f.*, 335*f.*; east European immigration and influence, 261, 333; Frankfort declaration, 330*f.*; German influence, 330*f.*; growth, 332*f.*; growing unity, 410;

Hebrew Union College, 331*f.*; institutional temples, 335; Jewish Theological Seminary, 332, 334*f.*; "Lovers of Zion," 333, 335; Orthodox, 331*f.*, 334*ff.*; persecution, 332*f.*, 336; proportionate strength, 354; Reform, 329–32, 333*f.*, 335*ff.*; Reconstructionism, 334*f.*; religious revival, 336*f.*, 386; Sephardim, 329*f.*; statistics, 332*n.*, 336; synagogue center movement, 335; Union of American Hebrew Congregations, 331; United Jewish Appeal, 336; World Zionist Congress, 335; Zionism, 335*f.*; Yeshiva College, 336

Judson, Adoniram, 117*n.*, 157
Judson, Edward, 300, 302

Kähler, Martin, 277
Kaiser, R. B., 424*n.*
Kane, J. J., 423*f.*
Kaplan, Mordecai, 335
Keane, John J., 245, 249, 252–59, 310, 317*n.*
Keble, John, 173*n.*
Keil, William, 183
Keller, C. R., 136*n.*
Keller, James G., 406
Kennedy, Gail, 304*n.*
Kennedy, John F., 399
Kent, Charles Foster, 234
Kentucky revival, 137*ff.*, 185
Kerr, H. T., 170*n.*
Keswick conferences, 283
Kierkegaard, Søren, 381
Kincheloe, Samuel P., 377*f.*
King, Martin Luther, Jr., 352, 390
King's Chapel, 159
Kingsley, Charles, 310
Kinne, Aaron, 149
Kinzer, D. L., 241*n.*
Kirk, Edward Norris, 199
Kirkland, E. C., 304*n.*
Kirkland, Samuel, 78
Klein, Felix, 258*n.*
Knapp, Jacob, 144*n.*
Knights of Labor, 254, 309*f.*
Knorr, Nathan H., 349
"Know Nothing" Party, 240*f.*
Knox, John, 41, 84
Koch, G. A., 94*n.*
Koenker, E. B., 407*n.*

Kraft, Johann V., 56
Kraus, C. N., 282*n.*
Krauth, Charles Philip, 168
Krauth, Charles Porterfield, 168
Krutch, Joseph Wood, 361
Ku Klux Klan, 215, 370
Kuhn, A. B., 286*n.*
Küng, Hans, 424*n.*

La Farge, John, 401
La Follette, Robert, 263
Laity, importance of, 12*ff.*, 34, 127
Lally, Francis J., 239, 243*n.*, 303*n.*; *Catholic Church*, 239*n.*
Lane, Charles, 188
Lane Theological Seminary, 164, 200, 280
Landis, B. Y., 313*n.*
Langton, E., 54*n.*
Larger parish churches, 412
Latitudinarian sentiment, 92*f.*
Latter Rain Movement, 345
Latourette, K. S., 157, 357; *History of Expansion of Christianity*, 157*n.*
Laud, William, 9, 92; "Laud's Liturgy," 42
Laws, Curtis Lee, 368
Laymen's Foreign Missions Inquiry, 373*f.*
Laymen's Missionary Movement, 323
Lee, Ann, 140, 183–84
Lee, Jesse, 75, 121
Lee, Robert E., 214
Lee, Robert, *Social Sources of Church Unity*, 409*n.*
Leeming, Bernard, 425
Lekachman, Robert, 425*n.*
Leo XIII, 244, 255*f.*, 258*f.*, 310, 402*f.*
Leuba, J. H., 265
Leuchtenburg, William E., 361
Leverett, William, 40
Lewis, Edwin, 379*n.*, 381*n.*
Lewis, Sinclair, 361
Liebman, Joshua L., 386
Life and Work Movement, 418
Lincoln, Abraham, 209–13, 214*f.*, 219
Lincoln, C. Eric, 353*n.*
Lindsey, Theophilus, 160*f.*
Lindström, Harold, 342*n.*
Link, Henry C., 386
Littell, F. H., 52*n.*
Livingston, William, 102

Locke, John, 79, 93*f.*, 96
Loetscher, L. A., *American Christianity*, 17*n.*; *Broadening Church*, 279*n.*; *Presbyterian Enterprise*, 43*n.*
Logan County revival, 135, 137*f.*
Longstreet, Augustus, 137
Louis XIV, 51, 55
Louisiana Purchase, 6
Lowell, John, 160
Lowrie, Walter, 379*n.*, 381
Lucey, Robert E., 401
Lumpkin, W. L., 9*n.*
Luther, Martin, 20
Lutherans, 23, 55–57, 151, 167*f.*, 201, 236, 246, 261, 327, 413; The American Lutheran Church formed, 416; American Revolution, 95; deaconesses, 297; education, 155; effect of immigration, 415*f.*; growing strength and influence, 415*f.*; heresy trials, 278*f.*; Lutheran Church in America formed, 416; Lutheran Church—Missouri Synod, 167, 356, 416; National Lutheran Commission, 416; post-Civil War growth, 260; post-Revolution, 125; "Puritan Protestant" influence, 9; reunions, 415*f.*; revivalism, 144; slavery, 202*f.*; United Lutheran Church formed, 416; western states, 228
Lyell, Charles, 208

MacAuley, Jerry, 297*f.*
McAvoy, T. T., 404*n.*, 425; *Roman Catholicism and the American Way of Life*, 241*n.*; *Great Crisis in American Catholic History* (*Americanist Heresy in Roman Catholicism*), 254*n.*
McCabe, C. C., 228
McCabe, Joseph, 197*n.*
McCarthy era, 385, 389; McCarthyism, 391
McCormick, Cyrus, 230, 294
McCormick Theological Seminary, 279, 281
McCosh, James, 267
McCune, William C., 279
MacFarland, C. S., 320*n.*, 365, 418
McFarland, J. T., 234*n.*
McGee, John, 137*f.*, 140
McGee, William, 137

McGiffert, Arthur C., 280
McGready, James, 135, 147*f.*
Machen, J. Gresham, 370*f.*, 413
McIntire, Carl, 384*n.*, 413
Macintosh, D. C., 380
Mack, Alexander, 53
Mackay, John A., 389
MacKenzie, K. M., 319*n.*
McKinley, William, 315, 318
McLane, W. W., 279
Maclear, J. F., 12*n.*
McLoughlin, W. G., Jr., 143*n.*, 233*n.*; *Billy Sunday Was His Real Name*, 366*n.*; *Billy Graham*, 385*n.*; *Modern Revivalism*, 141*n.*
McMillan, John, 135
McNeill, J. T., "Democratic Element in Calvin's Thought," 84*n.*; *Unitive Protestantism*, 417*n.*
McNemar, Richard, 185
McPherson, Aimee Semple, 346
McQuaid, Bernard, 243, 249, 256*f.*, 259
Madison, James, 104*n.*
Mahan, Asa, 342*n.*
Makemie, Francis, 42*f.*, 89
Manning, B. L., 91*n.*
Marcus, J. R., 58*n.*
Maréchal, Ambrose, 127
Maring, Norman H., "Baptists and Changing Views of the Bible," 268*n.*; "Conservative but Progressive," 368*n.*
Maritain, Jacques, 380
Marshall, Daniel, 74*f.*
Marty, Martin E., 383*n.*
Martyn, Charles, 102
Maryland, 6, 26*f.*, 34; diversity, 27; establishment, 15, 27, 88; parish system, 15; settlement, 15, 27, 88; toleration, 26*f.*
Marx, P. B., 407*n.*
Massachusetts, 10, 14, 17, 27–29, 36–41, 44, 100, 115; charter, 28; establishment, 28*f.*, 102*f.*, 104; settlement, 27*f.*; toleration, 28*f.*, 44, 46
Massachusetts Proposals, 40*f.*
Mather, Cotton, 29*n.*, 37*n.*, 100
Mather, Increase, 18, 40
Mathews, Shailer, 275*f.*, 312
Maurice, F. D., 310
May, Henry F., 302
Mayhew, Jonathan, 90

Maynard, Theodore, 247n.

Mays, Benjamin E., 351n.

Meacham, Joseph, 184f.

Mead, Sidney E., 144n., 151n., 214n., 274n., 306f., 372; "Evangelical Conception of the Ministry," 13n.; *Lively Experiment*, 18n., 99n.; *Nathaniel W. Taylor*, 136n.

Mead, George Herbert, 275

Melcher, M. F., 183n.

Membership statistics, significance of, 129f.

Men and Religion Forward Movement, 364n., 366

Mencken, H. L., 361f.

Mennonites, 17, 32, 51f., 261, 327, 355n.; American Revolution, 95; post-Revolution, 111, 124

Mental healing, 287–90

Mercersburg Theological Seminary, 8, 169

Mercersburg theology, 168–71

Merton, Thomas, 405

Mesmer, F. A., 287; Mesmerism, 197, 284, 287

Methodism, triumph of, 178ff.

Methodist Church formed, 415

Methodist Episcopal Church formed, 76, 120f.

Methodist Episcopal Church, South, 203, 224f., 281

Methodists, 75f., 114–17, 122f., 125, 129n., 135, 139, 162f., 178ff., 201, 235f., 273, 299, 415; A. M. E. Church, 223–25; A. M. E. Zion Church, 223, 225; camp meetings, 140f.; centers of strength, 120ff.; Christmas conference, 121; Church Extension Society, 227f.; circuit system, 121f., 145, 147; deaconesses, 297; education, 155; Free Methodist Church, 344; freedmen, 221; heresy trials, 278; holiness movement, 343ff.; immigrants, 245f.; lay preachers, 120; McCarthyism, 389; membership, 354; Methodist Protestant Church, 224; missions, 145, 147f.; Negro Methodists, 350f.; ordination, 120f.; post-Civil War, 215–19, 227; post-Revolution, 120ff.; Primitive Methodists, 294; reunion, 415; revivalism, 144; slavery, 203; Wesleyan Methodist Church, 202, 343; western states, 227f.

Meyer, D. B., 358n.

Michaelius, Jonas, 16f., 50

Michel, Virgil, 407

Middle West, theological mood, 281

Millar, M. F. X., 402

Millenialism, 346–50

Miller, Francis P., 379n.

Miller, Perry, *Errand*, 19n.; "From Covenant to Revival," 97n.; *Jonathan Edwards*, 66n.; *Orthodoxy in Massachusetts*, 18n.; *The Puritans*, 18n.; *Roger Williams*, 29n.; *Transcendentalists*, 174n.

Miller, Robert M., *American Protestantism and Social Issues*, 363n.

Miller, Samuel, 151

Miller, W. M., 287n.

Miller, William, 194ff.

Miller, William Lee, 425n.

Millerites, 194ff., 347

Mills, B. Fay, 364

Minuit, Peter, 49f.

Missions, city, 153f., 297–300; fading interest in, 372ff.; foreign, 156f., 318–23, 373f., 394f.; frontier, 145–50, 154; home, 154, 374; rescue, 297f.; societies, 146–50

Mississippi Valley campaign, 154

Missouri, 148, 150, 193, 226

Mitchell, David, 347n.

Mitchell, Hinkley G., 278

Mode, P. G., 24n.

Mohammed, Elijah, 353

Monroe, James, 192

Montgomery, Zachariah, 243f.

Moody, Dwight L., 228–34, 268, 283, 298n., 321, 364

Moody Bible Institute, 235, 282

Moore, Edmund A., 399n.

Moore, Richard C., 119

Morais, Sebato, 332

Moral Re-Armament, 378

Morals, revolution in, 360ff.

Moravians, 17, 32, 53f., 111, 124

Morgan, Benjamin, 201

Morgan, Edmund S., *Gentle Puritan*, 79n.; *Puritan Dilemma*, 87n.

Morgan, J. P., 294, 302

Morison, S. E., 38n.

Mormon, Book of, 191f.

Mormons, 190–94, 355
Morrison, C. C., 277*n.*
Morse, Jedediah, 160, 163
Morse, Samuel F. B., 240
Mott, John R., 234, 322, 417*f.*
Mudge, Lewis S., 375
Muhlenberg, Henry M., 13, 56
Muhlenberg, W. A., 297
Muller, Michael, 242*f.*
Mulloy, William, 401
Munger, Theodore T., 270
Murch, James DeForest, 413*n.*
Murray, John, 162
Murray, John Courtney, 402, 404
Myrick, Luther, 144*n.*

Nash, Daniel, 144*n.*
Nathan, George Jean, 361*f.*
National Association of Evangelicals, 384, 413
National Baptist Convention, 225, 351*f.*
National Catholic Welfare Conference, 393*f.*, 400, 410
National Conference of Christians and Jews, 419
National Council of Churches, 314, 355*f.*, 389*f.*, 411–13, 420
Nativist sentiment, 238–45
Natural religion, 92*ff.*
Nazarene, Church of the, 345
Neander, J. A. W., 169, 176
Negro churches, 223–25, 327, 350–53; importance of, 351; A. M. E. Church, 223–25; A. M. E. Zion Church, 223, 225; Christian (Colored) M. E. Church, 225; holiness churches, 352*f.*; National Baptist Convention, 225, 351*f.*; New Era Baptist Convention, 352; Progressive Baptist Convention, 352
Negroes, civil rights struggle, 389–91; "contrabands," 220; education, 215, 220–23; migration to cities, 352; plight of freedmen, 219*f.*
Neo-orthodoxy, 380
Nethercot, A. H., 286*n.*
Nettleton, Ashahel, 141, 162, 230
Nevin, J. W., 159, 168–71, 175*f.*
New Amsterdam, 10*f.*, 16*f.*, 49*f.*
New Brunswick Theological Seminary, 125, 156

New Divinity of Yale, *see* New Haven Theology
New England, 7–9, 13, 17*ff.*, 27–30, 96–103, 111, 115, 134; establishment, 14–16; Great Awakening, 72*f.*; influence of, 8*f.*, 149; parish system, 14*ff.*; Protestant liberalism, 281; Second Awakening, 135*f.*
New England Theology, 79
New England's First Fruits, 38
New Haven Theology, 136, 143, 152, 163*f.*
New Jersey, 31, 62*ff.*; theological mood, 281
"New measures," 136, 141*ff.*, 167, 169, 179
New Netherlands, 30, 49*f.*
New Theology, 176, 178, 270*ff.*, 273
New Thought, 289, 386
New York, 30*f.* 50*f.*, 88, 99, 102, 180, 281, 293
New York Central College, 202
New York Evangelist, 198*f.*
New York Missionary Society, 146
Newell, Samuel, 157
Newhouse, Samuel, 186
Newman, J. H., 173*n.*
Newton, Isaac, 79, 93
Newton Theological Seminary, 221, 246, 278
Niagara Bible Conference, 283, 367; five points of orthodoxy, 283
Nichol, Francis D., 194*n.*
Nichols, J. H., *Romanticism in American Theology*, 8*n.*; "John W. Nevin," 170*n.*
Nichols, R. H., 113*n.*
Niebuhr, Reinhold, 379, 381*ff.*
Niebuhr, H. Richard, 58*n.*, 94*n.*, 369, 381*n.*, 413; *Christ and Culture*, 369*n.*; *Church against the World*, 371*n.*, 379*n.*; *Kingdom of God in America*, 371*n.*; *Purpose of Church and Ministry*, 414*n.*; *Social Sources of Denominationalism*, 409*n.*
Non-Christian religions, 264
Nonseparatists, 27, 36*f.*
Norris, J. Frank, 370
Northampton, 60, 65*f.*
North Carolina, 15, 25*f.*, 88, 99
North End Mission, 298
Northfield conferences, 233*f.*, 321

Norton, Andrews, 175
Notre Dame, University of, 250, 305
Nott, Samuel, Jr., 157
Noyes, John Humphrey, 185*ff.*
Nuttall, G. F., 45*n.*
Nye, Philip, 85*n.*
Nye, R. B., 307*n.*
Nygren, Anders, 380

Oberlin College, 143, 247, 342
Oberlin perfectionism, 342
Obermann, H. O., 425
Occasional Conformity Act, 89, 90*n.*
O'Connell, Denis J., 255*f.*
Ockenga, Harold J., 355*n.*, 384*f.*
O'Dea, Thomas F., 190*n.*, 404
O'Gorman, Thomas, 247*n.*
O'Hanlon, D. J., 425
O'Hara, Edwin V., 395
O'Kelly, James, 123
Oliver, Peter, 96*f.*
Olsen, M. E., 347*n.*
Oman, John, 380
Oneida Community, 185*ff.*
Orr, J. E., 180*n.*
Otis, James, 96*f.*
Orthodox Judaism, 331–36
Orthodox Presbyterian Church,
   371, 413
Otterbein, Philip W., 125
Oxford Group Movement, *see* Moral
   Re-Armament
Oxford Movement, 173
Oxnam, G. Bromley, 389

Pacific coast, 226, 236*f.*; theological
   mood, 281
Pacific Garden Mission, 297
Pacifism, 363
Paine, Thomas, 131
Pallen, Condé, 242
Palmer, A. Mitchell, 359
Palmer, Elihu, 131
Palmer, Phoebe, 343
Parish system, 14, 61
Park, Edwards A., 271
Park Congregational Church,
   Elmira, N.Y., 301
Parker, J. W., 221
Parker, R. A., 185*n.*
Parker, Theodore, 174, 189, 284

Parliament of Religions, 254, 264,
   286, 414
Parmalee, Julius H., 220
Pascoe, C. S., 35*n.*
Patton, Francis L., 279
Pauck, Wilhelm, 379*n.*, 381*n.*
Paul VI, 408, 422
Paulist Fathers, 129, 252
Peabody, Elizabeth, 174
Peabody, George, 306
Peace, Six Pillars of, 388
Peace Mission of Father Divine, 353
Peck, John Mason, 133*n.*, 150
Peale, Norman Vincent, 386*f.*
Pelikan, Jaroslav, 423*n.*
Pendleton, James M., 173
Penn, William, 11, 17, 21, 26, 31, 51*f.*,
   55
Pennsylvania, 21, 31*f.*, 46, 51–58; theo-
   logical mood, 281
Pennsylvania, University of, 78, 89
Pentecost, George F., 364
Pentecostalism, 328, 342, 345*f.*, 355,
   378
Perfectionism, *see* holiness movement
Perry, W. S., 11*n.*, 118*n.*
Persons, Stow, *American Minds*, 150*n.*;
   Free Religion, 285*n.*
Peters, J. L., 342*n.*
Philipson, David, 330*n.*
Pierson, A. T., 282, 322
Pietism, 53*f.*, 56, 59, 62
Pike, James A., 414
Pike, Royston, 347*n.*
Pittsburgh Theological Seminary, 282
Pius X, 249, 392, 403
Pius XI, 401*n.*, 421
Plan of Union, 113, 165
Plymouth, 7, 10, 17, 27, 29, 37
Polish National Catholic Church, 412
Ponet, John, 85*n.*
Pope, Alexander, 93
Pope, Liston, 389
Populists, 209
Posey, W. B., 154*n.*
Positivist Society, 284*n.*
Powell, Joab, 148
Powell, L. P., 287*n.*
Prayer-meeting revival, 228
Premillennialism, 282*f.*
Presbyterian Church in the U.S., 281,
   415

Presbyterians, 9, 14, 27, 32, 37, 41*ff.*, 70*n.*, 89, 123, 129, 135, 137*f.*, 201; affinities with Congregationalists and Baptists, 9*n.*, 37, 39, 41*f.*; American Revolution, 96, 112; *Christian Faith and Life Series*, 382; conservatism, 281*ff.*; education, 155; frontier schisms, 139*f.*; Fundamentalist controversy, 370; General Assembly, 112, 131, 140, 147, 165*f.*, 279*f.*, 283, 389; Great Awakening, 62–64, 70, 74; heresy trials, 279*f.*; McCarthyism, 389; missionary activity, 145–48; Negroes, 224; Old School-New School controversy, 163–66, 169, 201, 203, 217; Old Side-New Side division, 70, 112; post-Revolution, 111*f.*, 131; proportionate strength, 7, 23, 42*ff.*, 354; religious liberty, 103, 105; reunions, 415; revivalism, 144, 179*f.*; "spirituality of church," 218*f.*; slavery, 203, 211*n.*, 219; Synod of Philadelphia, 42; union with Congregationalists, 111–15, 153, 165; western states, 227

Prince, Thomas, 101

Princeton Review, 179

Princeton Theological Seminary, 165*f.*, 169, 267, 282, 370*f.*, 389

Princeton University, 25, 71, 77, 89, 159, 167, 173, 267, 321*f.*

"Progressive" movement, 315–17, 362*f.*

Progressive Orthodoxy, *see* New Theology

Prohibition, 316*f.*

Protestant Episcopal Church, *see* Episcopalians

Protestant Reformation, 20

Protestant acculturation, 371–77; concern for immigrants, 245–47; conservative, 277–84; liberalism, 266–77, 363

Protestants, disaffected, 327*f.*, 341–50; mixed marriages, 396

Protestantism in America: character of, 7–10; "cooperative Protestantism," 355*f.*; economic attitudes, 302–15; predominance, 6*f.*, 327; proportionate strength, 354*n.*; realignment, 327*f.*, 354*ff.*; shifting pattern of cooperation, 410–12; trends toward unity, 410–18

Provoost, Samuel, 119

Prussian Union of 1817, 261, 417

Psychiana, 353

Pullman strike, 308*f.*, 311

Purchas, Samuel, 21

Puritanism, 7*ff.*, 92, 98, 361; character of, 8–10; defined as "revival," 59; diversity of, 8*f.*; English, 41; influence of, 7*ff.*; political heritage, 84–87, 94, 96

Putz, L. J., 406*n.*

Quakers, 7, 9, 23, 25–27, 30–32, 45–47, 95, 111, 124*f.*, 144, 355*n.*

Quebec Act, 126

Quimby, P. P., 287*f.*

Racial crisis, 389–91

Ramsey, Paul, 389

Rankin, John, 137

Rappites, 183

Rationalism, 92–95, 104*f.*

Rauschenbusch, Walter, 313

Raymond, Miner, 278

Reassurance, cult of, 386*f.*

Reconstruction, 214–16, 263

Redford, A. H., 147*n.*

Reed, Andrew, 129*n.*

Reeder, G. A., 227

Reform Judaism, 329–37

Reformed Church in America, *see* Dutch Reformed

Reformed Church in the U.S., *see* German Reformed

Reid, Whitelaw, 263

Reinhold, A. H., 407*n.*

Religion as bond of unity, 209*ff.*, 215

"Religion of humanity," 284–86

Religions, Eastern, 286*f.*

Religious diversity, 10–12, 25*ff.*, 29*f.*, 50

Religious education, 277, 411

Religious liberty, 95–105

Religious revival, post-World War II, 382–87

Revivalism, disenchantment with, 364; respectability, 180

Rhode Island, 29*f.*, 44, 46

Rice, John Holt, 218*f.*

Rice, Luther, 157

Richards, George, 379*n.*

Richardson, H. V., 351*n.*

Rigdon, Sidney, 191*ff.*
Riley, William B., 370
Ripley, George, 174, 188
Ritschl, Albrecht, 271
Robert, Joseph T., 221
Roberts, C. E. B., 286*n.*
Robinson, John, 29, 37
Robinson, William, 74
Rochester "rappings," 196*f.*
Rochester Theological Seminary, 246, 313, 368
Rockefeller, John D., 275, 294, 302
Rockefeller, John D., Jr., 373, 376
Roemer, Theodore, 247*n.*
Roman Catholics, *iv,* 6, 16, 47*f.,* 126–29, 237–58, 261*f.,* 265*f.,* 269, 295, 302*f.,* 338*f.,* 392–408, 419–25; activism, 399*f.;* American College, 255*f.;* American Revolution, 95; "Americanism," 250–59, 402*f.;* Apostolic Delegate, 249, 255, 393*f.;* Anti-Saloon League, 317*n.;* Biblical studies, 422; "Bishops' Program of Social Reconstruction," 303*n.,* 400*f.;* Catholic Worker Movement, 400; church-state relations, 244, 420; Christopher Movement, 406; College of Cardinals, 397; colleges and universities, 250*n.,* 396; converts, 128*f.,* 395*f.;* Democratic party, 253; economic attitudes, 303*n.,* 305*f.,* 309*f.;* economic status, 398; ecumenism, 421–25; effect of World War I, 393*ff.;* effect of World War II, 404; elections of 1928 and 1960, 398*f.;* end of missionary status, 249, 392; foreign missions, 394*f.;* growth, 126*ff.,* 247–50, 327, 354*n.,* 395–97; immigration, 127*f.,* 295, 393; *Immortale Dei,* 244, 402; intellectual life, 403–05; interfaith relations, 240–45, 253, 419*f.;* labor, 254, 294*n.,* 295, 303*n.,* 400; liturgical movement, 407*f.; Longinqua Oceani,* 256; McCarthyism, 402; marks of maturity, 392, 395, 400, 408; Maryknoll Fathers, 395; Maryland, 26*f.,* 48; "Modernism," 259, 403; National Catholic Welfare Conference, 393*f.,* 400, 410; Negroes, 224; parochial schools, 243, 249*f.,* 396, 421; plenary councils, 128*f.,* 248*f.,* 393; political thought, 244*f.,* 252*f.,* 401*f.;* post-Revolution, 126–29; Prefect Apostolic, 127; public schools, 243*f.,* 245, 249; race issue, 401; religious orders, 128*f.,* 248, 250, 253, 405*f.;* religious revival, 405–08; *Rerum Novarum,* 303*n.,* 310, 401; role of laity, 14, 127*f.,* 253, 406–07; Rural Life Conference, 395; *Sapienti Consilio,* 392; school controversy, 128, 249*f.;* shifting attitudes, 424*f.;* slavery, 203, 211*n.;* social status, 397*ff.;* Society for the Propagation of the Faith, 394; Spanish-American War, 257*f.; Testem Benevolentiae,* 258; theological mood, 259; Trappists, 405*f.;* "trusteeism," 127*f.,* 250; Uniates, 339; Vicar Apostolic, 126; Vatican Council I, 250*n.,* 269; Vatican Council II, 408, 424; Vatican representative, 420*f.;* western states, 228
Roosevelt, Eleanor, 421
Roosevelt, Franklin D., 399*f.,* 420
Roosevelt, Theodore, 112, 315, 319, 362
Root, Robert, 389
Royce, Josiah, 273
Rummel, Joseph F., 401
Russell, Charles Taze, 348*f.*
Russian Orthodox, *see* Eastern Orthodox Churches
Rutgers University, 78
Rutherford, J. F., 349
Ryan, John A., 240, 400, 402
Rynne, Xavier, 424*n.*

St. Bartholomew's Episcopal Church, New York City, 302
St. George's Episcopal Church, New York City, 301
St. Louis University, 250
St. Mary's Seminary, 128
St. Raphael Society, 251
Salvation Army, 299*f.,* 345
Salzburg Lutherans, 56*f.*
Sandall, Robert, 299*n.*
Sankey, Ira D., 231*f.*
Satolli, Francesco, 255, 256
Saybrook Platform, 29, 41
Scandinavian immigration, 238, 260
Schaff, Philip, 9, 99, 132*n.,* 170, 180, 212*f.,* 214, 414; *America,* 8*n.;*

Church and State, 99n.; *Principle of Protestantism,* 8n.
Schechter, Solomon, 334
Schlatter, Michael, 58
Schleiermacher, Friedrich, 176, 271
Schlesinger, Arthur S., Sr., 262n.
Schmidt, Nathaniel, 278
Schmucker, Samuel S., 151, 167, 414
Schneider, H. W., 358n.
Schnepp, G. J., 396n.
Schroeder, Joseph, 256f., 310
Schuster, George N., 403
Schwenkfeld, Caspar, 53
Schwenkfelders, 30, 53
Scientific Modernism, 274–77
Scofield, C. I., 282; *Scofield Reference Bible,* 282, 347
Scotch-Irish, 25, 32, 42, 96
Seabury, Samuel, 118f.
Sears, Clara E., 188n., 194n.
Second Awakening, 73, 134–44, 145, 152, 156, 159, 162f., 185, 197
Sellers, James, 289
"Separates," 73ff., 114
Separatists, 10, 27, 36f.
Separatists of "Zoar," 183
Seton, Elizabeth Bayley, 128f., 400
Seventh-day Adventists, 196, 347
Shakers, 140, 183ff., 188, 196
Shaughnessy, Gerald, 128n., 247n.
Shea, J. G., 247n.
Sheen, Fulton J., 386, 405
Sheldon, Charles M., 312
Shields, T. T., 370
Siegfried, André, 7ff.
Silliman, Benjamin, 184n.
Silva, R. C., 399n.
Simons, Menno, 51
Simpson, A. B., 345
Simpson, Alan, 7n.
Simpson, Matthew, 343
Sisters of Charity, 128f.
Slavery issue, 164, 169, 199, 200–03, 219
Sleman, John B., 323
Small, Albion, 275
Smiley, Thomas, 166n.
Smith, Adam, 303
Smith, Alfred E., 398f.
Smith, C. H., 52n.
Smith, Elwyn A., 179n.
Smith, George Adam, 234
Smith, Gerald B., 274n., 275

Smith, H. Shelton, *American Christianity,* 17n.; "Christian Education," 376n.
Smith, Henry Preserved, 279f.
Smith, John Blair, 112
Smith, J. W., 87n.
Smith, Joseph, 190–93
Smith, Rodney "Gypsy," 364
Smith, Timothy L., *Called Unto Holiness,* 345n.; *Revivalism and Social Reform,* 150n., 342n.
Smith, William, Jr., of New York, 89, 102
Smith, William of Philadelphia, 102
Smyth, Egbert C., 272, 278
Smyth, Newman, 270
"Social Creed of the Churches," 314, 411
Social Gospel, 310–15; antecedents, 199; decline, 363; revivalists, 364, 366
Social settlements, 312
Society for the Propagation of Faith, 248
Society for the Propagation of the Gospel (S.P.G.), 34ff., 88ff., 118
Soper, D. W., 380n.
South, Robert, 86
South: ethos of, 218; isolation of, 216, 218; post-Civil War churches, 216–19; theological liberalism, 281
South Carolina, 15, 25f., 34, 88
Southern Baptist Convention, 203, 217f., 281, 356, 390, 413
Southern Baptist Theological Seminary, 281
Southern Christian Leadership Conference, 390
Spaeth, A., 168n.
Spahr, C. B., 308n.
Spanish-American War, 257f., 318
Sparks, Jared, 160
Spaulding, John, 305
Speer, Robert E., 234, 322
Spellman, Francis, J., 421
Spencer, Herbert, 208, 263, 303
Spener, Philipp J., 53n.
Sperry, Willard L., 48n.
Spiritualism, 196f., 286, 290
Springfield Presbytery, Last Will and Testament of, 123
Spurling, R. G., 345
Starbuck, E. D., 264, 274

Statistics of church membership, significance and reliability of, 129*f.*, 354*n.*
Stearns, Shubal, 25, 74*f.*
Steele, Samuel A., 222
Steel strike of 1919, 359
Steely, J. E., 173*n.*
Steffens, D. H., 168*n.*
Steinberg, M., 328*n.*
Stewart, Milton and Lyman, 365
Stiles, Ezra, 79, 91, 97, 101, 103, 109–14, 132; *Discourse on Christian Union*, 103*n.*
Stoddard, Solomon, 40, 60, 65*f.*
Stokes, Anson Phelps, 91*n.*
Stone, Barton W., 123, 140
Stone, Marsena, 221
Stover, John C., 56
Strachey, William, 19
Straton, John Roach, 370*n.*
Strawbridge, Robert, 75
Strong, Augustus Hopkins, 277, 368*f.*; *Outlines of Systematic Theology*, 369*n.*
Strong, Josiah, 293, 320*f.*; *Our Country*, 320*n.*
Strong, W. E., 157*n.*
Stroup, H. H., 347*n.*
Student Volunteer Movement, 322*f.*, 411
Stuyvesant, Peter, 10*f.*, 50
Sullivan, Mark, 319*n.*
Sullivan, William L., 379, 404*n.*
Sumner, William Graham, 265
Sunday, Billy, 366*f.*, 374*n.*
Sunday school movement, 153, 234*ff.*, 293
Swan, Jabez, 144*n.*
Swedenborg, Emanuel, 197
Sweet, W. W., *American Churches*, 122*n.*; *Methodism in American History*, 76*n.*; *Religion in Colonial America*, 11*n.*; *Religion on the American Frontier*, 113*n.*, 146*n.*; *Virginia Methodism*, 217*n.*
Swenson, David, 381
Swift, D. E., 144*n.*
Swift, G. A., 295
Swift, Lindsay, 188*n.*
Swing, David M., 279, 294
Syllabus of Errors, 244, 254

Taft, William Howard, 262
Talladega College, 221

Talmage, T. De Witt, 294, 298*n.*
Tappan, Lewis, 198
Tappert, William, 257
Tavard, George H., 424
Taylor, Graham, 299, 312, 314
Taylor, J. Hudson, 322
Taylor, John, 79
Taylor, Myron C., 420
Taylor, Nathaniel W., 136, 143, 152, 162*f.*, 167, 179, 270
Taylor, W. G. L., 197*n.*
Teeling, William, 396*n.*
Temperance, 198*f.*, 316*f.*
Temple, William, 380
Tennent, Gilbert, 63*f.*, 67, 69–71, 77, 81
Tennent, John, 63*f.*
Tennent, William, 63, 67*f.*, 74
Tennent, William, Jr., 63
Test Act, 89, 90*n.*
Tewksbury, D. G., 156*n.*
Thébaud, Augustine, 242
Theological revival, 379–82
Theological seminaries, 156
Theosophy, 286*f.*, 290
Thompson, "Big Bill," 360
Thompson, E. T., 219*n.*
Thompson, H. P., 34*n.*
Thompson, R. E., 164*n.*
Thoreau, Henry David, 174
Thorton, J. W., 110*n.*
Thornwell, J. H., 211*n.*
Thurman, Howard, 351*n.*
Tillich, Paul, 380*f.*, 383
Timberlake, J. H., 316*n.*
Timon, John, 128
Tindal, Matthew, 93
Toland, John, 93
Toleration, religious, 95–105; Toleration Act of 1689, 11, 25, 88
Tolles, F. B., *Quakers and the Atlantic Culture*, 45*n.*; *Meeting House and Counting House*, 47*n.*
Tomlinson, A. J., 345
Toqueville, Alexis de, 130
Torbet, Robert G., 173*n.*
Torey, Reuben A., 282, 365
Tougaloo University, 221
Toy, Crawford H., 281
Toynbee Hall, 312
Tracy, Joseph, 68*n.*
Transcendentalism, 173*ff.*, 176, 187*ff.*, 284

Trent, Council of, 47, 269
Trine, R. W., 289
Trinterud, Leonard J., 27n., 63n.
Trotsky, Leon, 284n.
Truman, Harry S., 420
Trumbull, H. Clay, 234
Tucker, William J., 271
Tupper, Henry M., 221
Turner, Frederick Jackson, 3n.
Twain, Mark, 301
Tyler, Alice Felt, 162n.
Tyler, Bennet, 163, 178
Tyng, Stephen H., 298n.

Ultraism, 199f.
Unamuno, Miguel, 380
Union churches, 201f.
Union Gospel Mission, 298
Union Theological Seminary (N.Y.), 165, 273, 279f.
Unitarian and Universalist union, 415
Unitarians, 72f., 114f., 129, 159–62, 173ff., 176, 178, 228, 269, 284n., 355n.; Affirmation of Faith, 161
United Brethren (Congregational and Presbyterian) of London, 42f.
United Brethren in Christ, 126, 179
United Church of Christ, 354, 416f.
United Nations, 388
United Presbyterian Church, 282; union with Presbyterian Church, U.S.A., 415
United Presbyterian Church in the U.S.A., formed, 415
United Society of Believers, see Shakers
United Stewardship Council, 411
U.S. Census Bureau, sample of religious preference, 354n., 382f.
U.S. Christian Commission, 221, 230, 295
U.S. Constitution, 104; Bill of Rights, 104; First Amendment, 99, 104, 106; Fourteenth Amendment, 104; Eighteenth and Nineteenth Amendments, 317
Unity School of Christianity, 289f., 386
Universalists, 129, 161f., 197, 355n.
Utopian vision, 183, 190

Vanderlaan, E. D., 363n.
Vanderbilt, Cornelius, 302

Vanderbilt, W. H., 295
Van Dyke, Henry, 280
Van Dyke, Tertius, 280n.
Van Til, Cornelius, 384n.
Vasey, Thomas, 121
Vatican Council I, 250n., 269; Vatican Council II, 408, 424
Vedanta Society, 286
Vincent, John H., 235
Virginia, 9–11, 13f., 24f., 33f., 74ff., 96; Bill for Establishing Religious Freedom, 104; Declaration of Rights, 99; establishment, 15, 24f., 99, 103ff.; parish system, 15, 33; vestries, 13f.
Visitandines, 128
Vivekananda, Swami, 286
Voluntary societies, 114, 117, 146, 150–54, 158, 410f.
Voluntaryism, 13f., 16, 61, 105, 110, 114
Volunteers of America, 300

Walburg, Anton, 242f.
Walker, Jimmy, 360
Walker, Williston, 9n.
Walther, C. F. W., 168
Wanamaker, John, 230, 232, 295
Ward, Humphrey, 280
Ward, Leo R., American Apostolate, 309n.; Catholic Life, U.S.A., 406n.
Ware, Henry, 160
Ware, Timothy, 337n.
Warfield, Benjamin, 282
Washington, George, 105
Washington, J. R., Jr., 223n.
Washington and Lee College, 77, 135
Washington and Jefferson College, 77
Water Street Mission, 297f.
Wayland, Francis, 303
Weatherford, W. D., 351n.
Weigel, Gustave, 402, 404, 424f.
Weinlich, J. R., 54n.
Weisberger, B. A., 135n.
Weiss, George M., 57
Welch, Claude, 380n.
Weld, Theodore Dwight, 198, 200
Welsh Calvinistic Methodists, 415
Wentz, A. R., 167n.
Wesley, John, 32n., 66ff., 75, 78, 80, 120ff., 230, 278, 304
Wesleyan Methodist Church, 202, 343

Wesleyan perfectionism, 342

West, post-Civil War, 226–28

Western (Presbyterian) Missionary Society, 147

Western Sanitary Commission, 295

Western Theological Seminary, 169, 282

Westminster Assembly of Divines, 39, 81

Westminster Confession of Faith, 8f., 39, 43f., 166, 282

Westminster Theological Seminary, 371

Weston, Henry G., 268

Whatcoat, Richard, 121

Whedon, Daniel D., 278

Wheelock, Eleazar, 72, 78

Wheelwright, John, 28n.

Whetmore, James, 36

White, Andrew, 48

White, Andrew D., 265

White, C. L., 227n.

White, Ellen Gould, 196

White, J. W., 279

White, William, 34, 119

Whitefield, George, 62, 66–72, 74f., 77f., 80f., 122, 136, 230

Whitehead, A. N., 380

Whitman, Walt, 285

Wieman, Henry Nelson, 380f.

Wilbur, E. M., 159n.

Wilbur, Sibyl, 287n.

Wilder, Robert P., 321f.

Wiley, Allen, 129n.

Willett, Herbert L., 277n.

William and Mary of England, 30, 87, 119

William and Mary, College of, 33, 201

Williams, Daniel D., *Andover Liberals*, 271n.; *What Present-Day Theologians Are Thinking*, 380n.

Williams, George H., 52

Williams, Milan B., 364

Williams, Robert, 75

Williams, Roger, 21, 28n., 29, 37, 44f.

Williams, Solomon, 72

Williams, William R., 320

Williams College, 148

Wilmer, Richard H., 214

Wilson, Woodrow, 315, 360, 362

Winchell, Alexander, 281

Winchester, Elhanan, 162

Winebrenner, John, 126

Winehouse, Irwin, 346n.

Winter, Gibson, 383

Winslow, O. E., *Jonathan Edwards*, 66n.; *Master Roger Williams*, 29n.

Winthrop, John, 17f., 20, 86f.

Wisbey, H. A., 299n.

Wise, Isaac M., 331

Wise, John, 41

Wishard, Luther D., 321

Witherspoon, John, 9n., 111

Wolf, W. J., 211n.

Woman's Christian Temperance Union, 316

Women's suffrage, 199, 316f.

Woodhouse, A. S. P., 84n.

Woodrow, James, 281

Woodson, C. G., 351n.

Woodward, C. V., 215n.

Woolman, John, 46

Worcester, Noah, 115f., 182

World Alliance for International Friendship, 320, 418

World Council of Churches, 417ff., 420, 423, 425

World War I and churches, 359f., 363; religious ebb-tide following, 357ff.

World War II and churches, 388; postwar mood, 383

World's Student Christian Federation, 418

Wright, Conrad, 159n.

Wright, John J., 421

Wright, Louis B., 5n.

Wright, W. E., 241n.

Yale College, 35f., 41, 63, 65, 68, 70ff., 79n., 89, 135f., 163f.; Divinity School, 148, 175, 186, 266

Yeatman, J. S., 295–98

Yeshiva College, 336

Yoder, Donald H., 410n.

Yogoda Sat-Sanga, 287

Young, Brigham, 193

Young Men's Christian Association, 180, 229ff., 295f., 319, 322

Youth for Christ, 384f.

Zernov, Nicolas, 337n.

Zinzendorf, Nicholas von, 53–56

Zionism, 335f.

Zwingli, Ulrich, 9n., 32, 49